# Immigration Reform

Recent Titles in the

# CONTEMPORARY WORLD ISSUES
Series

*Religious Freedom in America: A Reference Handbook*
Michael C. LeMay

*Endangered Species: A Reference Handbook*
Jan A. Randall

*STDs in the United States: A Reference Handbook*
David E. Newton

*Women in Sports: A Reference Handbook*
Maylon Hanold

*Robots: A Reference Handbook*
David E. Newton

*Homeland Security: A Reference Handbook*
Michael C. LeMay

*The Opioid Crisis: A Reference Handbook*
David E. Newton

*Abortion in the United States: A Reference Handbook, second edition*
Dorothy E. McBride and Jennifer L. Keys

*The Youth Unemployment Crisis: A Reference Handbook*
Christine G. Villegas

*Transgender: A Reference Handbook*
Aaron Devor and Ardel Haefele-Thomas

*Eating Disorders in America: A Reference Handbook*
David E. Newton

*Natural Disasters: A Reference Handbook*
David E. Newton

Books in the **Contemporary World Issues** series address vital issues in today's society, such as genetic engineering, pollution, and biodiversity. Written by professional writers, scholars, and nonacademic experts, these books are authoritative, clearly written, up-to-date, and objective. They provide a good starting point for research by high school and college students, scholars, and general readers as well as by legislators, businesspeople, activists, and others.

Each book, carefully organized and easy to use, contains an overview of the subject, a detailed chronology, biographical sketches, facts and data and/or documents and other primary source material, a forum of authoritative perspective essays, annotated lists of print and nonprint resources, and an index.

Readers of books in the Contemporary World Issues series will find the information they need in order to have a better understanding of the social, political, environmental, and economic issues facing the world today.

# Immigration Reform

## A REFERENCE HANDBOOK

Michael C. LeMay

ABC-CLIO™

An Imprint of ABC-CLIO, LLC
Santa Barbara, California • Denver, Colorado

Library of Congress Cataloging in Publication Control Number: 2019939311

ISBN: 978-1-4408-5407-1 (print)
　　　978-1-4408-5408-8 (ebook)

23  22  21  20  19      1  2  3  4  5

This book is also available as an eBook.

ABC-CLIO
An Imprint of ABC-CLIO, LLC

ABC-CLIO, LLC
147 Castilian Drive
Santa Barbara, California 93117
www.abc-clio.com

This book is printed on acid-free paper ∞

Manufactured in the United States of America

*Preface, xv*

1   BACKGROUND AND HISTORY, 3

Introduction, 3

Forerunners to Current U.S. Legal
Immigration Law, 4

    The Immigration and Naturalization
      Act of 1965, 4

    The 1980 Refugee Act, 10

    The Immigration Reform and Control
      Act (IRCA) of 1986, 13

    IMMACT, 1990, 15

The Terrorist Attacks of 9/11 and the American
Response, 19

    The USA Patriot Act, 20

    Creating the Department of Homeland
      Security and Dissolving the INS, 24

Reform Actions Taken by the Obama
Administration, 30

    Deferred Action, 30

    Immigration Reform, 32

    Border Control, 33

Reform Actions of the Trump Administration, 35

The Travel Ban, 37

DACA Annulment, 40

Conclusion, 42

References, 46


2    PROBLEMS, CONTROVERSIES, AND SOLUTIONS, 55

Introduction, 55

Groupthink in the Aftermath of 9/11, 59

Management Problems of Immigration Policy
Implementation, 61

Civil Liberties and Privacy versus Immigration
Control, 67

Comprehensive Immigration Reform, 72

Gerrymandering and the Immigration
Reform Deadlock, 77

Changes in Immigration Policy from the
Obama to Trump Administrations, 80

The Travel Ban Controversy, 83

Business Needs versus Security Concerns in Visa
Application Processing, 85

Adverse Economic Impact of Visa-Tightening
Procedures, 90

The Impact of Federal, State, and Local
Government Relations, 96

The Brain Drain Problem, 101

Immigration Concerns and Their Impact
on Social Security, 104

Conclusion, 107

References, 108

3   PERSPECTIVES, 117

Introduction, 117

Immigration Reform Legislation of 1987: Lessons from the Past, 117
*Berkley Bedell, with Kenneth Bedell*

Comprehensive Immigration Reform from the Conservative Perspective, 122
*Chuck Larson*

Refugee Resettlement as Seen through the Eyes of a Volunteer ESL Teacher, 126
*Marty Liddy*

True to Our Origins: The Democratic Party and Comprehensive Immigration Reform, 130
*Ryan Macoubrie*

Immigration Reform Dysfunction: Why Reform Does Not Happen, 134
*Tim Magrath*

How Communities Can Meet the Immigration Challenge, 142
*Ali Noorani*

All Souls Unitarian/Universalist Church: Why We Became a Sanctuary Church, 145
*Rev. Nori Rost*

4   PROFILES, 153

Introduction, 153

Organizations, 153
    Al Qaeda, 153

American Civil Liberties Union (ACLU), 155

American Conservative Union (ACU), 155

American Immigration Control Foundation (AICF), 156

American Immigration Law Foundation (AILF), 157

American Immigration Lawyers Association (AILA), 157

Americans for Prosperity, 157

Association of Patriotic Arab Americans in the Military (APAAM), 158

Border Policy Research Institute (BPRI), 159

Bureau of Immigration and Customs Enforcement (ICE), 159

Business Roundtable, 160

Catholic Legal Immigration Network, Inc. (CLINIC), 160

Center for American Progress (CAP), 161

Center for Immigration Studies (CIS), 161

Center for Migration Studies (CMS), 162

Center for Privacy and Technology Policy (CPTP), 162

Center for the Study of Hate Crimes and Extremism, 163

Center on Budget and Policy Priorities (CBPP), 163

Congressional Research Service (CRS), 164

Council of Graduate Schools (CGS), 164

Department of Homeland Security (DHS), 165

Department of Justice (DOJ), 165

Federation for American Immigration Reform (FAIR), 166

Free Congress Foundation (now American Opportunity Foundation), 167

Freedom Works, 167

Government Accountability Office (GAO), 167

Heritage Foundation, 168

Human Rights First, 169

MoveOn.org, 170

National Conference of State Legislatures (NCSL), 170

National Immigration Forum (NIF), 171

National Immigration Law Center, 172

National Rifle Association (NRA), 172

Office of Management and Budget (OMB), 173

Pew Hispanic Center (PHC), 173

Rand Corporation, 174

United States Customs and Border Protection (USCBP), 174

United We Dream, 175

Voto Latino, 176

People, 176

Bush, George W. (1946– ), 177

Carter, James (Jimmy) Earl, Jr. (1924), 178

Chertoff, Michael (1953– ), 178

Clinton, William Jefferson (1946– ), 179

Conyers, John (1929– ), 180

Durbin, Richard "Dick" (1944– ), 181

Ferguson, Bob (1965– ), 182

Gonzales, Alberto (1955– ), 183

Goodlatte, Bob (1952– ), 184

Graham, Lindsey (1955– ), 184

Guitierrez, Luis (1953– ), 185

Hanen, Andrew (1953– ), 186

Hatch, Orrin (1934– ), 187

Herman, Susan N. (na– ), 187

Hetfield, Mark (1967– ), 188

Jackson-Lee, Sheila (na– ), 189

Jean-Pierre, Karine (1977– ), 190

Jimenez, Cristina (na– ), 191

Johnson, Jeh (1957– ), 191

Johnson, Lyndon B. (1908–1973), 192

Kelly, John F. (1950– ), 193

Kennedy, Edward (1932–2009), 194

Kerwin, Don (na– ), 194

Koch, Charles (1935– ), 195

Koch, David (1940– ), 196

Krikorian, Mark (1961– ), 196

Kumar, Maria Teresa (1974– ), 197

Levin, Brian (na– ), 198

Lieberman, Joseph (1942– ), 199

McCain, John (1936–2018), 199

McConnell, Mitch (1942– ), 200

Napolitano, Janet (1957– ), 201

Nielsen, Kirstjen (1972– ), 202

Obama, Barack (1961– ), 203

Reagan, Ronald (1911–2004), 204

Ridge, Tom (1945– ), 205

Schumer, Charles E. (1950– ), 206

Sensenbrenner, James (1943– ), 207

Sessions, Jeff (1946– ), 207

Suro, Roberto (na– ), 208

Tanden, Neera (na– ), 209

Trautman, Laurie (na– ), 210

Trump, Donald J. (1946– ), 210

Watson, Derrick (1966– ), 212

Yates, Sally (1960– ), 213

5   DATA AND DOCUMENTS, 217

Introduction, 217

Data, 217

Table 5.1: Legal Immigration to the United States, 1964–2016, 217

Table 5.2: Total Illegal Apprehensions by Fiscal Year, 2000–2017, Compared to the Total Number of Border Patrol Agents, 219

Table 5.3: Customs and Border Protection Enforcement Actions, 2016–2017, 220

Table 5.4: Foreign-Born Population by Region of Birth, U.S. Census, 2010, 220

Table 5.5: Pew Research Center Immigration-Related Public Opinion Polling Data, 2018, 221

Figure 5.1: Total Southwest Border Apprehensions, 2000–2017, 222

Figure 5.2: Total Ice Removals, 2015–2017, 223

Figure 5.3: Unaccompanied Children Apprehended by the U.S. Border Patrol at the Southwest Border, FY 2014, 223

Figure 5.4: Refugee Admissions, 1991–2016, and the Top States with Highest Percentage of Initial Resettlement, 224

Documents, 224

The Immigration Reform and Control Act (1986), 224

The Immigrant Visa Process (2018), 233

The Homeland Security Act (2002), 235

The Border Security, Economic Opportunity, and Immigration Mobilization Act (2013), 238

Report on ICE Enforcement and Removal Operations (2017), 243

Executive Order 13780: Protecting the Nation from Foreign Terrorist Entry into the United States (March 6, 2017), 244

Syllabus of *Trump v. Hawaii* (2018), 250

**6    RESOURCES, 259**

Introduction, 259

Books, 259

Leading Scholarly Journals, 286

Films, 299

Videos, 301

**7    CHRONOLOGY, 305**

*Glossary, 323*
*Index, 331*
*About the Author, 355*

*Immigration Reform: A Reference Handbook* focuses on why it is so difficult to enact immigration reform policy. Since the international terrorist attacks of September 11, 2001, in particular, attempts to pass immigration law have been frequent but have largely involved minor reforms at the margins of current public policy. A comprehensive reform of immigration law has eluded Congress, which, as this book details, has been stalemated on the issue. Immigration reform exemplifies well the concept of a policy conundrum. What is politically popular and could be passed is, on the whole, ineffective in resolving the problems and controversies entailed in immigration reform. What is likely to be more effective policy or law remains unpopular— that is, unlikely to be enacted—in a bitterly divided Congress, in which hyperpartisan attitudes have largely stalemated any resolution of the issues involved in this highly complex policy and political battleground. Gaps, failures, and unanticipated consequences of current law are discussed in detail herein and have a major impact on the vexing problem of unauthorized immigration (more commonly known as illegal immigration). The flow of immigration to the United States is immense— involving more than one million authorized and unauthorized immigrants annually. It is complex and diverse. The size and composition of the immigration waves coming to the United States are affected by both external forces (push factors) and internal forces (pull factors). Immigration law is inherently *intermestic policy* in nature—that is, public policy that involves both international and domestic concerns. That inherent nature of immigration law, and its reform, is all the more politically complicated. Immigration reform is a perennial issue on the political agenda of the United States, impacting all levels of American government and politics.

The United States is a leading recipient country of asylum-seekers, immigrants applying for permanent residence status (legal immigrants), and refugees. More international migrants seek to come to the United States than to any other country in the world. The forces propelling tens of millions of persons to migrate from their nation of origin to another national home heighten the stakes and the struggles over immigration reform in American politics. Massive immigration affects not only immigration law and policy but also numerous related public policy areas: education, health care, prisons, welfare. These policy areas are impacted by national law and policy but are more in the purview of state and local policy and politics.

This volume is one within the Contemporary World Issues series of ABC-CLIO. As such, it is aimed at college, public, and university libraries. It follows a prescribed format. Chapter 1 discusses the historical background of immigration (both legal and unauthorized) to the United States. It examines the economic, cultural, political, and social contexts of the massive waves of immigration to the United States, showing the development of immigration law aimed at coping with those waves of immigration. It presents a synthesis of current studies of the issue, presented in a manner both comprehensive and unbiased for the reader's consumption, better enabling readers to form their own judgments on the issues.

Chapter 2 outlines the most vexing of problems associated with the issue of immigration and discusses proposed solutions to those problems. It addresses efforts taken by governments at all levels and branches of government to cope with those problems. It discusses how those proposed solutions come to be placed on the agenda of government public policymaking, particularly at the national level.

Chapter 3 is comprised of eight original essays by scholars and activists who are involved in immigration reform politics. It brings together key voices from diverse disciplinary perspectives that represent various positions on all sides of the immigration reform issue to enrich the view that the author is able to provide.

Chapter 4 describes an extensive array of key organizations and persons involved in the discourse of immigration reform policy and politics. It profiles the organizations and actors who are stakeholders in the politics of immigration reform policy who shape the policy debates and are key to adoption, or opposition, of proposed solutions to perceived immigration problems.

Chapter 5 presents data and documents gathered from the political discourse on the immigration reform issue. Examination of these key data and documents, presented in an unbiased manner, enables the reader to assess for themselves why the problems are so complex and difficult to resolve, and which proposed solutions are more preferable to the reader.

Chapter 6 is a resource chapter. It presents an annotated bibliography of print and electronic resources especially relevant to the issue of immigration reform. The primary resources are books and scholarly journals that offer original research on the topic. To bring a degree of "life" to the data, films and videos addressing immigration reform are also annotated.

A chronology of the key moments in the history of immigration reform is then presented. Finally, a glossary provides easy access to definitions of the key terms and concepts used in the immigration reform debate. It is followed by a comprehensive index.

# Immigration Reform

## Introduction

On September 5, 2017, President Donald Trump issued an executive order rescinding President Barack Obama's 2012 executive action, Deferred Action on Childhood Arrivals (DACA). His order gave the U.S. Congress until March 5, 2018, to enact a legislative solution to the matter. His executive order put squarely on the agenda of Congress action on DACA and possible comprehensive immigration reform (White House, 2017). Congress has been essentially stalemated in taking legislative action on DACA and on comprehensive immigration reform for more than a decade. Despite widespread and bipartisan agreement that the legal immigration system was broken, and despite public opinion favoring immigration reform rated at more than 80 percent in many public opinion polls, the hyperpartisan politics of the U.S. Congress prevented legislative action on the immigration issue. March 5 went with four failed attempts to pass an immigration fix, although a federal district court ruling preserved the DACA program for the time being. To better understand why reforming immigration has been so contentious, it is useful to review the background

President Lyndon B. Johnson (*left*) speaks after signing the Immigration and Naturalization Act of 1965 below the Statue of Liberty on Liberty Island on October 3, 1965. The act granted Chinese immigrants equal status to that of European immigrants and replaced the national origins quota system with a preference system. (Lyndon B. Johnson Library/Yoichi R. Okamoto)

3

and recent history of U.S. immigration policy and the politics of immigration policymaking for both legal and unauthorized immigration (Ackerman and Furman 2013; Brotherton and Kretsedemas 2008; Chomsky 2014; Golash-Boza 2012; Hernandez 2010; Ngai 2011, 2014; Orreniris and Zavodny 2010; Schrug 2010; Waters et al. 2007).

## Forerunners to Current U.S. Legal Immigration Law

### The Immigration and Naturalization Act of 1965

Just as Donald Trump's election to the presidency put comprehensive immigration policy back on the agenda of Congress in 2018, the election of President John F. Kennedy (JFK) in 1960 opened the way for the last time Congress passed comprehensive legal immigration reform. It resulted in the law that is to this day the basis of U.S. immigration policy. Any immigration law passed in the future will be an amendment to the 1965 act.

American politics in the early 1960s was convulsed with civil rights issues. While serving as U.S. senator (D-MA), John F. Kennedy wrote *A Nation of Immigrants* (1958/reissued 2008). In his immigration book, Kennedy, whose other book, titled *Profiles in Courage*, won a Pulitzer Prize in 1957, argued for ending the quota system that had determined legal immigration policy since 1921. Kennedy favored increasing legal immigration and establishing an immigration system that was less openly racially biased. In 1963, the Kennedy administration submitted a bill to Congress that would comprehensively reform legal immigration. It failed to pass either house of Congress. Upon Kennedy's assassination in November 1963, his vice president, Lyndon B. Johnson (LBJ) assumed the office. President Johnson resubmitted that proposal on January 13, 1965. It was introduced into the House chamber by Representative Emanuel Celler (D-NY), who was then chair of the House Judiciary Committee. In the U.S. Senate, the bill was introduced by Senator Philip Hart (D-MI). Among the bill's

32 official cosponsors were Senator Robert Kennedy (D-NY) and Senator Edward Kennedy (D-MA), brothers of the late president John F. Kennedy.

Often referred to as the Kennedy immigration act, its official title is the Immigration and Nationality Act of October 3, 1965 (Re: Amending the Act of June 27, 1952, 79 Stat. 911). The new immigration law passed the Senate by a vote of 76 to 18, and in the House of Representatives by a vote of 320 to 69 (Chiswick 1982: 37; LeMay 1987: 114; Waters, Ueda, and Marrow 2007). Where JFK had been unable to get his bill through Congress, LBJ, who was a better nose counter after having served for years as the Senate Majority leader, had two additional advantages over JFK in the politics of guiding the law through the complex committee system in Congress: (1) his landslide election in 1964 gave him substantially more liberal-leaning noses to count; and (2) he could, and did, argue the Congress should pass the bill as a "memorial" to the slain U.S. president. President Johnson had used the same argument to secure the passage of the Civil Rights Act of July 2, 1964 (Pub. L. No. 88-352, 78 Stat. 241). The successful enactment of the civil rights bill had taken one other contentious issue off the agenda of Congress, and the coalition in Congress that had enabled its passage was largely the same for the passage of the 1965 immigration law and much of Johnson's legislative agenda commonly known as The Great Society (History.com 2018; Library of Congress 2018).

The 1965 act replaced the national-origin quota system with a preference system that allocated immigration visas for permanent legal residency according to seven preference categories designed to achieve five general goals: (1) to preserve the family unit and reunite separated families; (2) to meet the need for highly skilled workers; (3) to help ease population problems created by emergencies such as political upheavals, Communist aggression, and natural disasters; (4) to better the understanding of people cross-nationally through exchange programs; and (5) to bar from the United States immigrants who were likely to represent adjustment problems due to their physical or mental health, criminal history, or dependency or for national security reasons (Harper 1975: 56; LeMay 1987: 111–112). These goals were addressed through seven preference categories for the issuance of visas, as follows:

1. First preference: unmarried sons and daughters of U.S. citizens

2. Second preference: spouse and unmarried sons and daughters of permanent residents

3. Third preference: members of the professions and scientists and artists of exceptional ability

4. Fourth preference: married sons and daughters of U.S. citizens

5. Fifth preference: brothers and sisters of U.S. citizens

6. Sixth preference: skilled and unskilled workers in short supply

7. Seventh preference: refugees (Harper 1975: 132–33; LeMay 1987: 111–114).

President Lyndon Johnson signed the bill into law on October 3, 1965, in front of the Statue of Liberty in New York Harbor (History.com 2018; LeMay 1987: 113). The new law had dramatic and immediate effect. It encased into law the family reunification approach that subsequent critics deride as chain migration (LeMay 2013: 6). Chain migration happens when friends and relatives of legal resident immigrants are drawn from specific locations by their compatriots already living in the United States who help and assist them in relocating to the United States (LeMay 2015: 7, 358).

Prior to the passage of the 1965 immigration act, and in part as a legislative strategy to get the immigration reform measures through Congress, pro-immigration reformers ended the Bracero Program (1942–1964). That program was first introduced after the United States entered World War II in 1941. It was negotiated between the U.S. and Mexican governments and signed on July 23, 1942. During the life of the program, roughly 4.8 million contract workers came to the United States primarily to work in agriculture and the railroads. Designed to be a temporary guest worker program where participants came for nine months of the year, it was meant to fill a wartime labor shortage. In fact, however, it proved to be so lucrative that it was extended until 1964. The Spanish word for arm is *brazo*, and it was used to refer to those who worked with their arms, which is in U.S. terminology referred to as manual labor. The Bracero Program was plagued with problems throughout its 22-year history: long work hours, wages that barely covered expenses, unauthorized deductions from the laborers' pay, meager and often poor-quality food, run-down and unsanitary housing, dangerous work conditions, disabling and sometimes fatal accidents, physical abuse, and racial discrimination (Calavita 1992; Hernandez 2010; Hines 2006). In the final years of the program, some 350,000 Mexican laborers came to the United States to work. They established chain migration patterns that strongly influenced unauthorized immigration once the Bracero Program was ended, and legal immigration from Mexico was set at 20,000 annually. That limit was woefully inadequate to the labor supply and demand pressures on both sides of the border.

An unanticipated consequence of ending of the Bracero Program and enactment of the 1965 Immigration and Nationality Act was an exponential increase in the flow of undocumented immigrants to the United States from Mexico and Central America. For example, in 1978 the U.S. Census Bureau estimated the number of illegal immigrants to be between 3.5 and 6 million persons. Those numbers included both undocumented persons coming across the borders and visa overstayers who came with visas and became unauthorized by breaking the conditions of their visas, for example, students on student visas accepting employment in the U.S. economy, which they were by law forbidden to do, or by overstaying the time limits of the visas (LeMay 1987: 123). The majority of unauthorized immigrants are Hispanics, about two-thirds of whom are Mexicans driven by poverty and unemployment across the highly porous 2,000-mile Mexican-U.S. border (TIME Magazine 1985). Numbering between 5 and 6 million in the mid-1980s, today, their numbers are estimated at about 11 million (Pew Research Center, 2013; and see also, Passel and Cohn 2012).

The increasing tide in both legal and unauthorized immigration raised several perplexing political questions: how many and at what rate could the nation absorb a huge wave of new immigrants; how many unskilled laborers were needed in an increasingly high-tech economy; do unauthorized immigrants drain the economy or do they actually enrich it; do the newcomers gain their foothold in American society at the expense of poor and black citizens; how possible or desirable is it to assimilate such large numbers from such diverse racial, language, and cultural backgrounds; and will the advantages of such diversity outweigh the dangers of separation and group conflict (LeMay 1987: 123)?

The 1965 comprehensive immigration act not only abolished the national-origin quota system, but it also emphasized legal terms other than immigrants and nonimmigrants, quota immigrants, and non-quota immigrants. Each sending country had an annual ceiling of 20,000 visas for permanent, legal residency to be issued by a U.S. embassy or consular office in the country of origin on a first-come, first-served basis. Immigrants did not meet any preference category, met one of the preference system categories, or were not subject to new country limits because they were immediate relatives of U.S. citizens or were special immigrants, including persons born in the Western Hemisphere, former U.S. citizens seeking to resume their citizenship, religious ministers, and former or current employees of the U.S. government abroad. Persons seeking admission under the third or sixth employment preferences are required to meet more stringent labor certification rules. The law comprised nearly 300 pages in the U.S. Code of Statutes (Pub. L. No. 88-352, 78 Stat. 241; for a summary of the law, see LeMay and Barkan, 1999: 257–261).

In the decade after the enactment of the 1965 law, immigration increased by nearly 60 percent. Immigrants from countries whose national-origin quotas were miniscule saw dramatic increases in immigration over the previous quota base. Greek immigration rose by 162 percent; Portuguese by 382 percent, and overall Asian immigration by 663 percent. Indeed, several countries showed remarkable increases: Korea by 1,328 percent, India by more than 3,000 percent, Pakistan by 1,600 percent, the Philippines by nearly 1,200 percent, Thailand by over 1,700 percent, and Vietnam by more than 1,900 percent. Immigration from European countries, which had much larger quota bases under the quota system that was specifically designed to favor immigrants from northern and western European nations, declined overall by 38 percent: Austria by 76 percent, Ireland by 77 percent, Norway by 85 percent, and the UK by nearly 120 percent (Chiswick 1982: 39; LeMay 1987: 114).

The third preference category for professionals was especially helpful for opening up immigration from Asia. Korean and Filipino health professionals entered in large numbers and thereafter used the family preference categories to bring in their family members (one form of chain migration). By 1980, more than 70,000 medical doctors alone had immigrated. By 1980 there were more Filipino physicians in the United States than there were native-born black doctors. Nurses from Ireland used the category in significant numbers. Although doing the same work as they had performed in their native countries, such health professionals could typically earn salaries that were three to four times as much in the United States as they could earn in their home countries (LeMay 1987: 114).

Although at the time of its enactment the 1965 law seemed quite generous regarding refugee admissions, allowing for 10,200 per year, that provision was soon outmoded. Events in

Cuba, Vietnam, and Haiti soon outstripped the ability to even begin to cope with the demand for entrance to the United States on the basis of refugee status. For example, from 1960 to 1980 some 800,000 refugees came from Cuba alone, and from 1975 to 1980, more than 200,000 Vietnamese came to the United States. In total, from 1975 to 1980, more than 500,000 refugees from Southeast Asia arrived, and from 1970 to 1980, another 70,000 Soviet Jews fled the Soviet Union for America. Other large waves of refugees included 110,000 from Kampuchea (formerly known as Cambodia); 30,000 from Yugoslavia; 25,000 from China and Taiwan; nearly 20,000 each from Rumania and Poland; and about 10,000 each from Czechoslovakia, Spain, and Hungary (LeMay 1987: 114–115, 123).

Congress passed the Act of November 2, 1966, to adjust to immigrant status of Cuban refugees to that of lawful permanent residents (80 Stat. 1161; summarized in LeMay and Barkan 1999: 263–264). In 1968, President Lyndon Johnson issued a proclamation whereby the United States accepted the UN Protocol and Convention relating to the status of refugees. His proclamation accepted as U.S. law the much more generous and expansive UN's definition of refugee, which did not have the geographical/regional definitions nor the ideological proscriptions—that is, fleeing from communism—of prior U.S. law (LeMay and Barkan 1999: 276–269). These actions set the stage for Congress to formally amend U.S. immigration law in the final weeks of the 1976 session.

### The 1980 Refugee Act

Congress amended the Kennedy Act by modifying the preference system to include migration from the Western Hemisphere, allowing for 20,000 from each country (Act of October 20, 1976: To Amend the Immigration and Nationality Act of 1965, HR 14535; summarized in LeMay and Barkan 1999: 270–272). Congress addressed the inadequacy of the refugee provision in the 1965 Act by allocating funds to programs that assist parolees and adjust their status, such as the Indochinese Refugee Resettlement Program. Even more significantly, Congress acted on the refugee problem by passing the Act of March 17, 1980: The Refugee Act (92 Stat. 102; see excerpts in LeMay and Barkan 1999: 272–275). The 1980 Act systematized refugee policy. It incorporated the UN definition of the refugee as a person having a "well-founded fear of persecution" based on race, religion, nationality, or membership in a social group or political movement. It allowed annually 50,000 persons to enter with refugee status and authorized the president to increase that number by notifying Congress if the president determined that events warranted an increase. After fiscal year 1984, for example, President Ronald Reagan authorized 72,000 more, of which 67,750 refugees actually arrived and another 11,600 were granted asylum (LeMay 1987: 123).

An unanticipated consequence of the Refugee Act of 1980 was a significant change in the size of the pool of refugees. Professor Arnold Leibowitz argues that in adopting the UN's definition of refugee, the 1980 Act increased the number of persons eligible for refugee status from 3 million to 13 million (Leibowitz 1983: 167; see also McClellan 1981).

California governor Ronald Reagan was elected president in 1980. By then, apprehensions of undocumented immigrants attempting to enter the country at the southern border with Mexico had spiked to between one-half million and three-quarters of a million per year. There was increasing consensus that the immigration system was broken and needed extensive reform and that the country was no longer able to control its borders (LeMay 2015: 19; Morris 1985). A special commission to study the immigration system established by the Carter administration, known as the Select Commission on Immigration and Refugee Policy (SCIRP), had recommended many changes to deal with the unauthorized immigration flow (LeMay 2015: 15; Select Commission on

Immigration and Refugee Policy 1981: 104; its recommendations are excerpted in LeMay and Barkan 1999: 278–279).
The Reagan administration responded to the SCRIP report
by establishing its own Task Force on Immigration and Refugee Policy. Reagan's attorney general, William French Smith,
headed the task force, and it made several recommendations
to the new president:

1. *Amnesty.* It recommended unauthorized immigrants living
   in the United States since January 1, 1980, be permitted to
   remain, being made eligible for resident alien status after
   having been in the country for 10 years, at which time
   they could seek naturalization—in today's jargon, a path to
   citizenship. The estimated number of such immigrants was
   5 million.

2. *Guest Worker Program.* The task force recommended that
   50,000 Mexicans be allowed to enter annually to work
   temporarily. Over the course of several years, that number
   gradually increased to hundreds of thousands.

3. *Employer sanctions.* It recommended that employers who
   knowingly hired more than four undocumented immigrants be fined up to $1,000 per violation.

4. *Enforcement.* It recommended a 50 percent increase in the
   INS budget and the addition of 1,500 new border patrol
   agents to enhance the enforcement of immigration and
   labor laws—in today's terminology, hardening of border
   control.

5. *Boat People.* In response to a wave of refugees arriving often
   in unseaworthy boats from Haiti and deemed to be unauthorized "economic refugees," the task force recommended
   that the boats be intercepted and that detention camps be
   set up to hold as many as 6,000 people pending their deportation hearings.

6. *Legal immigration limits.* The task force recommended increasing the annual limit of legal immigration to 610,000,

with special preference to those from Canada and Mexico (LeMay 2015: 15–16; excerpted in LeMay and Barkan 1999: 278–279).

## The Immigration Reform and Control Act (IRCA) of 1986

In the fall of 1981, the House and Senate Judiciary Committees took up the matter of immigration reform and the recommendations of SCIRP and of President Reagan's task force in its subcommittee on immigration, chaired, respectively, by Representative Romano Mazzoli (D-KY) and Senator Alan Simpson (R-WY). They led a bipartisan effort to enact comprehensive immigration reform. Their proposed bills took a long and tortuous path through Congress. Several bills passed one or the other of the two chambers, after hearings and consideration by multiple committees in each chamber, only to be killed in the other chamber, or dying in conference committee (Chomsky 2014; Crewdson 1983; LeMay 2015; Ngai 2014; O'Leary 2014; Schrug 2010). In part, these measures were blocked by partisan stalemates during the elections of 1982, 1984, and 1986, which had the effect of stalling compromises because of partisan bickering in both chambers and by the stands taken against compromise—seen as "surrender"—by their associated interest groups. Reforming immigration had become a public policy conundrum.

After the 1986 mid-term elections were over, and sensing a growing conservative political mood, opponents of the measure finally concluded that continued resistance might lead to an even more restrictive bill in 1987, and several caucuses (informal groups of members of Congress in the House or the Senate who shared a mutual interest and met to discuss and take positions on legislative proposals to address those interests) that had opposed prior measures were divided over the bill. The Hispanic Caucus split on the bill and voted five for and six against passage. The split among Hispanic Caucus members enabled the Congressional Black Caucus, which had been voting lockstep with the Hispanic Caucus members on the issue, likewise to split on the measure, voting ten for and eight against passage. The Border Caucus members split nine for to six against. Likewise, state delegations from states that had large foreign-born populations and large estimated unauthorized immigrant populations split as well (LeMay 1994: 58–61).

The House of Representatives passed the compromise conference bill (IRCA) by a vote of 238 to 172, on October 15, 1986. The Senate approved it 63 to 24 on October 17, 1986. President Ronald Reagan signed the measure into law on November 6, 1986 (100 Stat. 3360; LeMay 2015: 18; see an excerpt of the law in LeMay and Barkan 1999: 282–288). The law aimed at closing the back door (i.e., illegal immigration) by trying to "demagnify" the pull of the U.S. economy to unauthorized immigrants by enacting a control device known as "employer sanctions." This provision of IRCA made it illegal to knowingly hire an undocumented immigrant worker. Another IRCA provision offset employer sanctions with an appeal to the more liberal members of Congress—an amnesty program to provide legalization to estimated 3 million persons resident in the country without legal authorization to be so.

However, the employer sanctions provision failed to accomplish its goal, perhaps because IRCA allowed for 14 documents to be accepted as valid proof of a person's eligibility to work. This fact simply fueled a phony-document industry, enabling unauthorized immigrants to continue coming and employers to continue hiring them without fear of legal penalty for "knowingly" hiring unauthorized workers. Enforcement problems by the notoriously inefficient Immigration and Naturalization Service (INS), coupled with the massive use of counterfeit documents, resulted in a temporary decline in undocumented immigrants successfully crossing the border. Within a year of passage, unauthorized, undocumented immigration was back up to pre-IRCA levels (LeMay 2015: 19).

Although IRCA authorized a 50 percent increase in border patrol staff, actual increases fell far short due to difficulties in recruiting new agents and to expanding training staff and facilities. Another implementation problem with IRCA was that the border patrol's duties increased along with its staffing. After 1986, the interdiction of illicit drug traffic across the border became a prime focus in response to the 1986 Omnibus Anti-Drug Abuse Law (Pub. L. No. 99–570). Border patrol agents shifted their emphasis from unauthorized immigrant apprehension and smuggling to work with the Drug Enforcement Agency (DEA) on what was called "Operation Alliance." The border patrol also reallocated the number of staff being used to guard refugee camps and to identify, prosecute, and deport criminal unauthorized immigrants—the legal process of expulsion (Bean, Vernez, and Keely 1989: 44; LeMay 2015: 19). Net immigration during the 1970 to 1980 decade was the highest level for any single decade in the twentieth century (LeMay 1994: 22–23).

## IMMACT, 1990

In 1990 Congress moved to enact reforms of the legal immigration law and process, modifying and clarifying certain provisions within IRCA. Known as IMMACT, the Act of November 29, 1990: The Immigration Act of 1990 (104 Stat. 4981; excerpted in LeMay and Barkan 1999: 288–295) set new ceilings for a worldwide level of immigration, especially as related to the reunification of immediate family members. It redefined the preference system with respect to family reunification, and for employment, and made permanent a new category of preference called "diversity immigrants." The diversity immigrant provision had been introduced as a temporary measure in IRCA. IMMACT also established a Commission on Legal Immigration Reform and provided for a temporary stay of deportation for certain unauthorized immigrants for reasons of family unity and temporary protected status.

Despite IRCA and IMMACT, laws intended to curb illegal immigration, the size and scope of the unauthorized flow, seemed unabated. This led to political pressure to do something more in the 1990s. States that received large numbers of both legal and unauthorized immigrants, such as California, Florida, and Texas, sued the federal government in their respective federal district courts—ultimately to no avail—for the estimated billions of dollars the states contended they were required to bear for costs related to unauthorized immigrants and their children. The states argued that since the federal government failed to control the borders, they should be reimbursed for the resulting costs. Going much further than the failed lawsuits, in 1994, California attempted to legislatively reduce the draw of its economy and services and to "send a message to Congress." California passed an initiative known as the "Save Our State" Initiative, more commonly referred to as Proposition 187. The final provision of Proposition 187, the Severability clause, stated that "in the event that any portion of this act or the application thereof to any person or circumstances is held invalid, that invalidity shall not affect any other provision or application of the act, which can be given effect without the invalid provision or application, and to that end the provisions of this act are severable" (LeMay and Barkan 1999: 299; see *LULAC et al. v. Wilson et al.* 908 F. Supp. 755 [C.D. Cal. 1995]: 787–91).

The severability clause anticipated a federal court challenge regarding the constitutionality of Proposition 187. And in fact the California law was immediately brought to the federal district court by the League of United Latin American Citizens (LULAC) (see a summary of the decision in LeMay and Barkan 1999: 100–101). As anticipated, the federal district court found most of the initiative to be unconstitutional. In the 1994 election, then California governor Pete Wilson had campaigned for reelection and worked strenuously for the initiative. He won his office and the initiative was approved by 59 percent of California voters. Although the California law was for the most part overturned by the *LULAC* decision, its passage by such a wide margin did in fact succeed in sending a message to Congress.

Governor Wilson's reelection, however, was a pyrrhic victory. While his anti-immigrant stand appealed to enough voters to achieve electoral victory in the short run, his stand and that of the Republican Party so alienated voters of minority group backgrounds, and especially the children of immigrants of color, that the long-term demographic shift in the state's population resulted within a decade in turning California from a highly competitive, two-party state into a solidly blue Democratic state. By the 2016 election, California was arguably the most solidly Democratic-voting state in the nation, the bluest of blue states (*Wall Street Journal* 2016).

However, concern over unauthorized immigration, referred to as illegal immigration in both public opinion and congressional politics, rose steadily after the enactment of IRCA. As noted, the number of unauthorized immigrants crossing the border and residing in the United States dipped slightly after the passage of IRCA but soon climbed again to reach pre-IRCA levels. In 1986, the number of unauthorized immigrants was estimated at 3.2 million. That number rose to 9.3 million by 2002. A 1986 Congressional Research Service study found that among the 3.2 million unauthorized residents, 69 percent were from Mexico; 23 percent were from Canada and South America, most of whom were undocumented migrants; 6 percent were from Asia; 2 percent were from Europe, most of whom were overstayers; and another 5 percent were from all other sources (LeMay 2015: 21).

The Pew Hispanic Research Center estimated that between 2000 and 2004, another 3.1 million arrived. Another researcher put their number in 2004 at 10.3 million (Camarota 2005). Not only did their numbers grow exponentially, their population dispersed beyond the six "Gateway States." In 1990, 88 percent of unauthorized immigrants resided in six states: California, with 45 percent of the total; New York, with

15 percent; Texas, with 11 percent; Florida, with 9 percent; Illinois, with 4 percent; and New Jersey, with 4 percent. The remaining 12 percent resided in the other 44 states and the District of Columbia. In just over a decade, by 2004, 62 percent of the estimated 10.3 million unauthorized immigrants resided in the six gateway states: California with 24 percent, New York at 7 percent, Texas at 14 percent, Florida at 9 percent, and Illinois and New Jersey each with 4 percent. Thirty-nine percent of unauthorized residents lived in non-gateway states. A 2014 study by the Pew Hispanic Center found that for the first time in the historical record more non-Mexicans than Mexicans were apprehended at U.S. borders by the border patrol, and unauthorized immigrants from Mexico were crossing less often than they did before the Great Recession of 2008–2009. Moreover, the percent of unauthorized immigrants who were undocumented as opposed to visa overstayers shifted markedly, from an estimated 60–40 percent split to a 50–50 split (Krogstad and Passel 2014, cited in LeMay 2015: 22).

In 1996, Congress passed and President William Jefferson Clinton signed into law two measures that essentially enacted the major provisions of Proposition 187. Congress passed a welfare reform bill that contained several immigrant-related provisions concerning both legal and unauthorized immigrants being banned from receiving welfare benefits that were very similar to the welfare provisions in Proposition 187. That law was titled The Personal Responsibility and Work Opportunity Act of August 22, 1996. About a month later, Congress enacted the Illegal Immigration Reform and Immigrant Responsibility Act (IIRIRA) of September 30, 1996 (both acts are summarized in LeMay and Barkan 1999: 301–310).

In June 2000, Congress passed the Immigration and Naturalization Service Data Management Improvement Act (Pub. L. No. 206–215). It amended IIRIRA. The 2000 Act required the INS to develop an electronic system to integrate and provide access to the data on all arrivals and departures at American airports and seaports. The INS was charged to use such data to identify lawfully admitted nonimmigrants who might have overstayed their visits (LeMay 2015: 22–23). Events, however, overtook the INS's ability to implement the 2000 Act.

## The Terrorist Attacks of 9/11 and the American Response

On September 11, 2001, international terrorists attacked the World Trade Center in New York City (downing the Center's twin towers) and the Pentagon in Washington, D.C., sending the greatest shock to the American political system since the 1941 attack on Pearl Harbor. The attacks precipitated sweeping changes in the law aimed at combating international and domestic terrorism that had significant implications for reforming U.S. immigration policy. Laws passed in 2001 and 2002 initiated what has been called elsewhere the "storm-door era" of U.S. immigration policy and signaling the erection of Fortress America (LeMay 2015: 23; LeMay 2018: 233).

The 9/11 attacks made starkly apparent the disarray at the INS. Then Attorney General John Ashcroft ordered the INS to strictly enforce the rule requiring foreign visitors to file change-of-address forms supposedly being used by the INS and the Department of State to keep track of visitors. The nation was shocked to learn that the INS had a backlog of some 2 million paper documents, since it had not yet upgraded its record keeping to electronic data form. The paper records were stored in boxes in a Kansas City warehouse. Ashcroft's directive resulted in the INS receiving some 30,000 change-of-address forms per day, and the backlog quickly surged to 4 million. The INS reported an estimated 4 million foreigners were in the United States with expired visas. Adding to its reputation for utter ineptitude, the media soon learned that the INS had sent letters to a Florida flight school approving the student visas of two of the 9/11 attackers six months after they had perished flying the planes in the devastating attack. Not surprising, a 2002 Federal Performance Report ranked the U.S. Coast Guard an A but gave the INS a D. Border patrol agents were leaving the agency faster than they could be replaced. The performance report found that INS investigators were undertrained, overworked, and overstressed, and it assessed the INS information management system as abysmal. Congress concluded that a drastic restructuring was needed. Both Congress and the president soon acted (LeMay 2015: 23–24).

President George W. Bush acted first. On October 8, 2001, he issued Executive Order 13228. It established within the Executive Office of the President the Office of Homeland Security (Relyea 2003). President Bush appointed former Pennsylvania governor Tom Ridge as the director of Homeland Security (LeMay 2015: 24).

In Congress, Senator Joseph Lieberman (D-CT) introduced a bill (S. 1534) to establish a cabinet-level Department of Homeland Security. Then in May, he and Representative Mac Thornberry (R-TX) introduced more elaborate versions (S. 2452 and H.R. 4660). Their proposals spurred President Bush to respond. He ordered an administrative team to draft an alternative bill. Mitchell Daniels Jr., director of the Office of Management and Budget; Tom Ridge, director of the Office of Homeland Security; Andrew Card Jr., the White House Chief of Staff; and Alberto Gonzales, the White House counsel met and drafted the president's plan in late April. It was introduced in the House of Representatives as H.R. 5005 on June 24, 2002 (Relyea 2003: 617).

### The USA Patriot Act

But even before creating the Department of Homeland Security (DHS), Congress passed another law, the USA Patriot Act, that together with the DHS law best characterizes the storm-door era and best symbolizes Fortress America. Within weeks of the 9/11 attacks, a nervous Congress was virtually exiled from their offices by an anthrax contamination incident and confronted with dire warnings of more attacks to come, including bioterrorism (LeMay 2016: 92). Congress responded to President Bush's demands for a new arsenal of antiterrorism measures. Many in Congress, the administration, and indeed the general public feared that undocumented migration was an avenue through which international terrorist cells could infiltrate into the United States. For nearly a month, from the initial outbreak on October 4, 2001, coming so soon after the September attacks, Congress and the public were unable to obtain clear information about the anthrax attack from the Centers for Disease Control and Prevention (CDC). To this day, the perpetrator(s) of the anthrax incident have not been identified, caught, or brought to justice.

Despite dire warnings from civil liberty organizations arrayed on both sides of the political spectrum, Congress overwhelmingly approved the USA Patriot Act. It is an acronym for Uniting and Strengthening America by Providing Appropriate Tools Required to Intercept and Obstruct Terrorism Act. The law passed by a vote of 356 to 66 in the House of Representatives, and by 98 to 1 in the Senate. It was a hastily drafted, complex, and far-reaching law that spans 342 pages in the U.S. Code of Statutes, yet it was passed with virtually no public hearings or debate and was accompanied by neither a conference committee nor a committee report. It was signed into law by President Bush on October 26, 2001 (42 U.S.C. 5195 c (e), and LeMay 2015: 24–25; Torr 2004: 43).

The USA Patriot Act gives sweeping powers to the attorney general and the Department of Justice (DOJ). Those powers limit the civil liberties of U.S. citizens, broaden the terrorism-related definitions in the Immigration and Naturalization Act of 1965, and expand the grounds of inadmissibility to include persons who publicly endorsed terrorist activity. To its critics, the law legalizes guilt by association. It gives the national government broad powers to monitor students and resident unauthorized immigrants and to detain and expedite the expulsion of noncitizens whom the government even simply suspects of having links to terrorist organizations. The attorney general merely has to certify them as being threats to national security on whatever grounds. Critics charge that the law legalizes racial profiling of Middle Easterners (Ackerman and Furman 2013; Brotherton and Kretsedemas 2008; Chomsky 2014; Golash-Boza 2012; LeMay 2013: 91–103; Malek 2011).

Those who advocated enactment of the law (and its renewal in 2006) argued that it was an essential law enforcement tool in the government's tool bag to catch terrorists and to deter further acts of terrorism, especially by what has come to be termed the "lone-wolf" terrorist. Led by then vice president Dick Cheney, proponents of the Patriot Act I, and later its renewal by Patriot Act II in 2006, argued its coercive interrogation of a suspected terrorist allowed law enforcement officials to find and control enemy cells in the nation's midst and that its sweeping new powers were necessary to penetrate Al Qaeda. The law's antiterrorist provisions included expanded surveillance, the use of informants, revisions to search and seizure procedures (making them easier to use), the use of secret (i.e., without warrants) wiretaps, and arrests and detention of suspected terrorists, all uninhibited by the prior web of laws, judicial precedents, and administrative rules and procedures that its proponents argued had hamstrung law enforcement officials in dealing with the new terrorist threat. Within months of its enactment, DOJ officials announced that they had broken up terrorist cells in Portland, Oregon; Detroit, Michigan; and Buffalo, New York. DOJ charged 17 individuals with terrorist-related activities and targeted terrorist financing (Torr 2004: 29).

Critics of the law argue that it goes too far and is a dangerous intrusion on civil liberty protections. They consider the law a threat to constitutional checks and balances, and ultimately a threat to American democracy, which is greater than the threat posed by terrorists (Torr 2004: 16). Critics hold that the Patriot Act evades the Fourth Amendment's search and arrest warrants provision: "The right of the people to be secure in their persons, houses, papers, and effects, against unreasonable searches and seizures, shall not be violated, and no Warrants shall issue, but upon probable cause, supported by Oath or affirmation, and particularly describing the place to be searched, and the persons or things to be seized" (Amendment IV). Of course, the legal dispute hinges on what constitutes an "unreasonable" search and seizure. Patriot Act I, and II, allows officials to conduct "sneak and peek" searches, covert searches of a person's home or office, all conducted without notice to the persons thus under surveillance.

These acts modified previous provisions for the need to obtain a warrant from the Foreign Intelligence Surveillance Act (FISA) Court established by the Foreign Intelligence Surveillance Act in 1978 (50 U.S.C. 1801–1885c). Most of the FISA Court's work is conducted ex parte as required by the statute. Ex parte communication means any material, oral or written communication, relevant to the merits of an adjudicatory proceeding that was neither on the record nor on reasonable prior notice to all parties (U.S. Foreign Intelligence Surveillance Court 2018).

Mass arrests in secrecy and without judicial oversight outraged civil libertarians on the political left and right. The exercise of unilateral authority of the executive branch (DOJ, and later DHS), the use of secret tribunals, and the breaching of attorney-client communications without a specific court order are, in the eyes of the law's critics, a threat to patriotic dissent and a threat to liberty and equality of treatment before the law (LeMay 2015: 26).

And in point of fact, nonterrorists affected by the Patriot Act have been mostly Middle-Eastern immigrants and Muslims. In but a few months after 9/11, approximately 1,200 persons were rounded up by police and INS agents across the nation. They were held for months without access to lawyers, or even without charges being brought against them before an immigration judge. Some were summarily deported for even minor visa violations, of which many were in fact the fault of the notoriously inefficient processing of INS paperwork. Few were ever charged with any crime, and most were subsequently released as totally innocent, swept up in the postattack hysteria and xenophobic reaction.

The Patriot Acts make immigrants deportable—expelled—for wholly innocent association with a terrorist organization. It does so by defining a terrorist organization in such broad terms that any group that used or threatened to use violence could be so construed. The proscription on political association potentially encompasses every organization that had been involved in a civil war or a crime of violence, from a prolife group that threatened and sometimes killed abortion-clinic workers, to the African National Congress, to the Irish Republican Army, or the Northern Alliance in Afghanistan (the U.S. ally against the Taliban in Afghanistan and Pakistan). An estimated 1,500 to 2,000 persons were apprehended under Patriot Act I, their identities still held secret. Indeed, even the number can only be estimated since after November 30, 2001, the government stopped issuing daily number counts, which at that time totaled 1,182. No person of those detained was ever charged with any involvement in the 9/11 attacks. Most were cleared by the FBI of any involvement in terrorism (Etzioni and March 2003: 37–38; LeMay 2015, 26–27).

## Creating the Department of Homeland Security and Dissolving the INS

Perhaps even more impactful a development on U.S. immigration than the Patriot Act was the law passed by Congress on November 19, 2002, the Homeland Security Act, which dissolved the INS and established the Department of Homeland Security (DHS) as a cabinet-level department of the national government (Pub. L. 107–296, Stat. 2155, excerpted in LeMay 2015: 247–250). The law enacted the most extensive reorganization of the federal executive branch since the creation of the Department of Defense (DoD) in 1949 (10 U.S. Code 113). Besides abolishing the INS, the DHS Act merged 22 agencies into a huge department, now employing 240,000, making it the third-largest department of the federal government (after DoD and the Department of Veterans Affairs). The DHS Act changed dramatically many of the ways in which immigration policy are implemented (LeMay 2004: 27–28).

The DHS launched the National Security Entry-Exit Registration System (NSEERS), designed to tackle the problem of visa overstayers, who by 2002 comprised an estimated 40 percent of all unauthorized immigrants. NSEERS had three basic elements: point-of-entry registration, special registration, and exit or departure controls. It was clearly designed to prevent a future 9/11-type attack. The special registration component established a national registry for nonimmigrants (i.e., for temporary foreign visitors), such as tourists and international students attending colleges and universities in the United States, who came to the country from 25 designated nations of origin that were listed by the attorney general as countries that supported and exported international terrorism, and other persons who met a combination of intelligence-based criteria that identified them as potential security risks.

NSEERS addressed several security-related deficiencies in immigration policy and procedures made apparent by the 9/11 attacks and detailed in the commission report on the attacks and the intelligence failures that contributed to the terrorists being able to conduct the attacks. Beginning in 2003, all commercial passenger carriers by air or sea are required to submit a detailed passenger list filed electronically before an aircraft or vessel arrived in or departed from an airport or seaport of the United States. A few of its provisions were suspended in December 2003, such as the need for unauthorized immigrants residing in the United States to register annually with the DHS (as we have seen, the national government had upward of 4 million such forms backlogged and stored in warehouses in Kansas and simply could not keep up with the paperwork). Other provisions of NSEERS remained in place, such as requiring foreign nationals from Iran, Iraq, Libya, Syria, and Sudan to go through special registrations at ports of entry and to report to immigration officials (at the DHS's Immigration Control and Enforcement-ICE) before departing the United States. Other foreign nationals were also registered in NSEERS if Customs and Border Protection officers (a new bureau within the DHS) warranted it necessary based on questioning upon that person's arrival in the United States. By January 2005 persons from 160 countries were registered in NSEERS. The program provides detailed information about the background and purpose of the person's visit to the United States, as well as confirming his or her departure (Information Plus 2006: 75).

In April 2002, the Department of Justice issued a report on visa overstays that substantiated that between 40 and 50 percent of unauthorized immigrants were not undocumented, that is, persons who had crossed U.S. borders without documentation, but rather were *visa absconders*, that is, people who had arrived with proper documents as temporary visitors and who had then failed to depart the country when required to do so by the time limitations of their temporary visas (U.S. Department of Justice 2002).

The report noted that while ICE is responsible for collecting documents from incoming passengers, airline and shipping lines are responsible for collecting departure forms for outgoing travelers and then sending such forms to ICE. Problems arise if the departure forms were unrecorded because they were not collected or were collected but not sent to ICE, or the forms were sent to ICE but were not correctly recorded there. These problems make accurate assessment of the number of overstays difficult. A 2004 Government Accountability Office (GAO) report set the estimated number of overstays at 2.3 million per year as of 2000. It further noted those data did not include an unknown number of short- and long-term overstays from Mexico and Canada since Canadian visitors can be admitted for up to 6 months and Mexican citizens with border-crossing cards entering the border in the Southwest for a stay of less than 72 hours are exempt from the visa admissions tracking procedures. The GAO report faulted the tracking system identifying those entering the country but not accurately tracking when, or even if, those visitors actually left the United States by the time they were required to do so (Government Accountability Office 2004). The tracking of visa overstayers remains a vexing one to this day, despite DHS efforts to improve its IT capabilities.

Such problems should not be surprising given that the DHS tracks more than 45 million visitors per year. In a 2016 report on fiscal year 2015, the most recent available as of this writing, the DHS heralded great improvement in the tacking system data, finding that 99 percent of the 45 million visitors were confirmed having departed. The percentage of confirmed departures was up from 85 percent in 2006 (Information Plus 2006: 76). But it should be noted that 1 percent of the 45 million annual visitors means that 450,000 visitors were not confirmed to have departed and thus were likely overstayers. Indeed the 2015 report listed 527,127 nonimmigrant visitors as overstays (Department of Homeland Security 2017). It is understandable how quickly such numbers can mount up and why the DHS now estimates that 50 percent of the estimated unauthorized immigrants in the United States are overstays rather than undocumented border crossers (U.S. Department of Homeland Security 2017).

On May 11, 2003, President Bush signed a measure passed by the U.S. Congress known as the Real ID Act of 2003 (Pub. L. No. 1, 109–13, Stat. 302). The bill passed by a vote of 308 to 58 in the House of Representatives and by 100–0 in the Senate. The law set national standards for the authentication and issuance procedures for state licenses and identification cards. It covered such related issues as applications for asylum and for deportation based upon participation in terrorist activities. The law included provisions that waived laws that might otherwise interfere with the construction of physical barriers on the borders (i.e., a border fence). It mandated that states comply with its provisions. By 2014, however, the

Real ID Act was essentially moribund because about half the state legislatures passed resolutions or bills objecting to the Real ID Act as an unfunded mandate and barring their states from complying with the law (Harper 2014). The act remains controversial and legislation has been introduced to amend it (LeMay 2013: 16, 68). The Real ID Act prompted state and local actions that exemplify an approach to national-state-local relations commonly known as "cooperative federalism." States opt to cooperate with harsher federal enforcement of immigration policy or they try to mitigate federal immigration policy by working to integrate a system of policymaking rather than claiming exclusive prerogatives (Rodriquez 2014; Illinois.gov 2005; Suro 2015). As of 2011, 16 states have acted to mitigate the harsher aspects of IIRIRA (National Conference of State Legislatures 2011).

In 2004, Congress passed the Intelligence Reform and Terrorism Prevention Act (Pub. L. No. 108–458, 118 Stat. 3638). In the House of Representatives, it was approved by a vote of 336–75, and in the Senate by a vote of 96–2. President Bush signed it on December 17, 2004. The law creates a Director of National Intelligence (DNI) and approved the addition of 2000 Border patrol agents to the DHS annually for five years. It expands the federal government's authority to surveille noncitizens, including the so-called lone-wolf terrorist inspired by but not affiliated with terrorist groups like Al Qaeda or the Islamic State of Iraq and Syria (ISIS) (LeMay 2015: 31).

On October 26, 2006, President Bush signed the Secure Fence Act (Pub. L. No. 109–367), which had passed by a vote of 283–138 in the House and 90–18 in the Senate, in the main on partisan voting, with the Republicans supporting the measure and Democrats opposing it. The act approved $1.2 billion to construct a 700-mile fence on the southern border. It was estimated to take an additional $4.8 billion to construct a fence along the remaining 1,254 or so miles along the border with Mexico yet to be built as of 2016. No suggestion was made to build the fence along the even longer northern border with Canada. Some critics of the fence (and of President Trump's later-proposed border wall), including former border patrol agents, argue that the terrain is such that no such barrier is needed for about 850 miles of the remaining 1,200 miles (*Guardian* 2016).

Also in 2006, Congress renewed the Patriot Act (commonly referred to as Patriot Act II). It eased a few of the most controversial civil liberties concerns of the original act but made it easier to expel unauthorized immigrants. Undocumented immigration declined during the 2008–2009 Great Recession and has declined since 2009. According to a Pew report, unauthorized Mexicans in the United States no longer account for the most numbers of unauthorized immigrants, now being under 50 percent, and as of 2016 were at 5.6 million, down from 6.4 million in 2009 (Krogstad, Passel, and Cohn 2017).

There have been bipartisan proposals introduced into Congress to enact a Dream Act bill nearly annually since 2001 to resolve the legal dilemma of the "Dreamer" children. That designation comes from the title of several of the proposed Dream Act measures: Development, Relief, and Education of Alien Minors. Dream Act proposals have been introduced in 2001, 2006, 2007, 2009, 2010, 2011, 2012, and 2013. The first bill (S.1291) was introduced by Senator Dick Durbin (D-IL) and Senator Orrin Hatch (R-UT) on August 1, 2001.

The 2011 Dream Act proposal was analyzed and "scored" by the nonpartisan Congressional Budget Office (CBO). It estimated the act would reduce deficits by $1.4 billion over 2011–2020 and would increase government revenues by more than $2.3 billion over a decade. A University of California Los Angeles (UCLA) study estimated a Dream Act would generate between $1.4 trillion and $3.6 trillion in taxable income over a 40-year period (LeMay 2013: 15–16). The "Dreamers" organized nationally into United We Dream, the largest youth-led network, which, as of 2018, claimed more than 400,000 members among the estimated 800,000 to 1.3 million such youth (United We Dream 2018).

## Reform Actions Taken by the Obama Administration

Congressional failure to act on any immigration reform during his first term, despite numerous bills introduced, drove President Barack Obama to issue executive actions on the matter in 2012 and 2015. Although his Republican critics charged that President Obama's actions were unconstitutional and an imperial abuse of presidential powers, in fact, executive actions have been used by every president since George Washington and have been used more often by Republican presidents since Abraham Lincoln than have been used by Democratic presidents. And while President Obama used executive actions on average 33.6 times per year over his two terms as president, Donald Trump far exceeded Barack Obama by using them 55 times during his first year in office (American Presidency Project 2018).

### Deferred Action

Deferred action is an administrative relief from deportation that has been around for a long time. The think tank Center for Immigration Studies (CIS) defines it as follows:

> Deferred action is a more formal way of exercising prosecutorial discretion that is available to USCIS, ICE and CBP. There is no statutory basis for this form of relief, but it is well established as a matter of policy. . . . Deferred action enables the government to make a formal determination not to pursue removal of an unqualified or unlawfully present individual for a specific period of time, usually for extraordinary humanitarian or law enforcement purposes. For example, some foreign students affected by Hurricane Katrina were granted deferred action, as were Haitians who fled to the United States on nonimmigrant visas following the earthquake in 2010. As with other forms of relief, beneficiaries can receive a work permit. (Vaughan 2012)

President Obama authorized the DHS to allow certain non-citizens to remain in the United States temporarily, issued on a case-by-case basis (LeMay 2018: 252). In 2012, Obama issued the Deferred Action for Childhood Arrivals (DACA). DACA applicants were granted temporary, conditional legal residency if they complied with the conditions contained in the Dream Act proposals (Preston 2014: 18). Under the 2012 DACA program, applicants were required to meet the following conditions: (1) they must have been brought to the United States by their unauthorized parents before they were age 16; (2) have lived in the United States continuously since January 1, 2010; (3) have been present in the United States on June 15, 2012 (the date of the executive action), and every day since; (4) have graduated from a U.S. high school or obtained a GED certificate, or be in school on the date the person submitted an application; and (5) pay an application fee of $465, comprised of a $380 fee for employment authorization and an $85 fee for fingerprints. DACA and DAPA (Deferred Action for Parental Accountability) affected an estimated 4.4 million persons. And in 2015, President Obama granted temporary protected status to 5,000 Unaccompanied by Adult Children (UAC) for whom it was deemed too unsafe to return to their country of origin (LeMay 2018: 252).

In February 2015, President Obama issued a new set of executive actions—one broadening slightly the DACA program, and one creating the DAPA program, for parents of U.S. citizens and legal permanent resident unauthorized immigrants (LeMay 2015: 33). The expanded DACA program had no age cap, granted DACA recipients three-year work authorization rather than two years as in the original DACA executive action, and offered certification that the individual DACA beneficiary posed no security or public safety threat (NBC News 2015). However, a U.S. district judge for southern Texas, Andrew Hanen, issued an injunction order on the administration's implementation of DAPA and on expanding DACA (Adler 2015).

To date, the closest the U.S. Congress has come to passing a Dream Act was contained within a proposal for comprehensive immigration reform on June 27, 2013, when the Senate passed S. 744, by a vote of 68–32, with some bipartisan support. Introduced by Senator Chuck Schumer (D-NY), the measure had been crafted by what became known as the "Gang of Eight"—four Democrats and four Republicans: Michael Bennett (D-CO), Dick Durbin (D-IL), Robert Menendez (D-NJ), and Charles Schumer (D-NY); Jeff Flake (R-AZ), Lindsey Graham (R-SC), John McCain (R-AZ), and Marco Rubio (R-FL). In the House of Representatives, where the measure failed to pass because then Speaker of the House John Boehner (R-OH) would not bring the measure to the House floor for a vote, the bill was sponsored by a House "Gang of Eight": Xavier Becerra (D-TX), Luis Gutierrez (D-IL), Zoe Lofgren (D-CA), and John Yarmouth (D-KY); Mario Díaz-Balart (R-FL), John Carter (R-TX), Sam Johnson (R-TX), and Raul Labrador (R-Idaho) (LeMay 2018: 254; American Immigration Council 2013; Sherman and Kim 2013).

## Immigration Reform

The major provisions of the comprehensive immigration reform bill that passed the Senate in 2013 (S. 744) included the following: (1) a 13-year path to citizenship, (2) a fine, (3) a requirement that all legalizing immigrants must pay back taxes owed (which the Democrats labeled "earned legalization"), (4) stronger border control provisions that included increasing the number of border patrol agents, (5) a computerized system to oversee temporary visas and expedited deportation of visa overstayers, and (6) an expanded guest worker (H-2) program.

The Senate bill was passed by members of the Senate Judiciary Committee and reported out to the floor. Senate Republicans insisted that all major bills needed a "cloture vote," that is, approval of at least 60 votes, to pass the Senate's final vote. All 54 Senate Democrats voted for cloture, and in what was then a notable bipartisan effort, 14 Republicans voted for cloture: Lamar Alexander (TN), Kelly Ayotte (NH), John Chiese (NJ), Susan Collins (ME), Bob Corker (TN), Jeff Flake (AZ), Lindsey Graham (SC), Orin Hatch (UT), Dean Heller (NV), John Hoeven (ND), Mark Kirk (IL), John McCain (AZ), Lisa Murkowski (Alaska), and Marco Rubio (FL) (LeMay 2018: 254).

The House version of the measure died in committee. It had some differences with the Senate-passed version. Had Speaker Boehner allowed the bill to be brought to the floor for a vote, and if passed as drafted in the House Judiciary Committee, it would have sent the House and Senate versions to a joint conference committee. The House version contained the following major provisions: (1) a 15-year path to citizenship, (2) unauthorized immigrants approved for the program would be given a work authorization card good only for 10 years, (3) strengthened border control measures even tougher than those passed in the Senate version, (4) an expanded border fence authorization and increased funding for electronic surveillance, (5) a program for visa oversight and overstayer control with a timetable requiring even faster development and implementation than those passed in the Senate version, and (6) a less-expansive (H-2) guest worker program than the version passed by the Senate (LeMay 2018: 254).

### Border Control

Republicans continued to push measures best described as an approach of "hard-line on border control," sponsoring several notable measures. In 2013, Senator David Vitter (R-LA) and Representative Steve King (R-IA) introduced a bill to end birthright citizenship to persons born in the United States of parents with illegal status. Many legal scholars maintain that such a law, if passed, would be immediately challenged in federal court and ruled unconstitutional. They contend it would take a constitutional amendment to end birthright citizenship no matter the legal status of their parents.

Senator John Cornyn (R-TX) and Representative Henry Cuellar (D-TX) introduced the "Humane Act," a bill designed to amend section 235 of the Trafficking Victims Protection Reauthorization Act (TVPRA) of 2013 (H.R. 898, 113th Congress, 2013–2014). If enacted, the measure would have eased the deportation of women who were victims of human trafficking.

Another 2014 measure, the Expedited Family Reunification Act, allowed all Unaccompanied Alien Children (UAC) to be treated equally under TVPRA by removing any legal distinction between contiguous and noncontiguous nations. Many Republicans in Congress were alarmed that the number of UAC rose from 19,000 in 2009 to more than 67,000 in 2014 (U.S. Customs and Border Protection 2014). The UAC measure was sponsored by Matt Salmon (R-AZ). It allowed all UAC from Central American countries (i.e., El Salvador, Guatemala, and Honduras) to be processed as are Mexican children and be subject to immediate voluntary return (LeMay 2018: 255).

In July 2014, Senators Jeff Flake and John McCain introduced the Children Returning on an Expedited and Safe Timeline Act (Crest Act). It requires mandatory detention, the use of asylum judges, and increases in the number of refugee visas to 5,000 each for El Salvador, Honduras, and Guatemala. It further authorizes the addition of 100 temporary immigration judges to promptly hear asylum cases and reduce the backlog of such hearings. In the House of Representatives, John Carter (R-TX) sponsored the Protection of Children Act, which would likewise treat all UAC equally under TVPRA. The measure was cosponsored in the Senate by Senators Kelly Ayotte (R-NH), Lindsey Graham (R-SC), and Jim Inhofe (R-OK) (Walton 2014).

A similar bill was introduced into the House of Representatives in 2015, and then again in 2017, by Bob Goodlatte

(R-VA) and Jason Chaffetz (R-VT). They sponsored the Asylum Reform and Border Protection Act (H.R. 391). Like the Senate measures, it placed all UAC under expanded expedited removal.

Senator Mike Johanns (R-NE) and Representative Steve King (R-IA) introduced into their respective chambers the UAC State Notification Act. The measure called for all states on the southern border to deploy their state's National Guard troops to secure the border. Critics decried it as racially biased and as a militarization of the U.S. border and noted that the measure was blatantly anti-Hispanic in that only the southern border with Mexico was targeted by the measure. No such measure was even proposed for the Canadian border, despite several incidents of attempted incursion of terrorists across the northern border (LeMay 2018: 255).

In 2015, House Republicans on the Homeland Security Committee introduced a bill titled the "Secure Our Borders First Act" (H.R. 399). It is a measure using the "crack down" approach to border control favored by Republicans and staunchly opposed by Democrats in the House of Representatives.

In an attempt to break the stalemate over comprehensive immigration reform versus strict border control measures, a piecemeal approach to immigration reform, House Republicans maneuvered to block funding the DHS for several months unless a provision to defund President Obama's DACA and DAPA was included. A "clean bill" to fund the DHS was finally passed by approving a Senate-passed version. The House did so by a comfortable margin of 257 to 167, with all Democrats and some Republicans voting for the "clean" DHS funding bill (LeMay 2018: 255).

## Reform Actions of the Trump Administration

In a surprising 2016 presidential election victory that no pre-election public opinion polling had predicted, Republican Party nominee Donald J. Trump won the electoral college vote

(ECV), defeating Democrat Hillary Clinton. Polls had predicted a Clinton win of 2–3 percent margin in the popular vote, and just more than 300 ECVs. In fact, however, the Trump/Pence ticket won 306 ECVs, although the Clinton/Keane ticket did indeed win the popular vote by nearly 3 million votes. Clinton/Keane won 65,788,583 votes, or 48.3 percent, of the popular vote to the Trump/Pence Republican ticket's 62,955,366 votes, or 46.2 percent. The Trump/Pence ticket won in a few key states that determined their ECV margin: Michigan, where Trump/Pence won 47.6 percent to Clinton/Keane's 47.3 percent; Ohio, where Trump/Pence won 52.1 percent to Clinton/Keane's 43.5 percent; Florida, where Trump/Pence won 49.1 percent to Clinton/Keane's 47.8 percent; Pennsylvania, where Trump/Pence won 48.5 percent to Clinton/Keane's 47.6 percent, and Wisconsin, where Trump/Pence won 47.8 percent to Clinton/Keane's 47.6 percent (CNN 2016).

Donald Trump had campaigned on a decidedly "outsider" image that carried the election despite—or perhaps better said, because of—his unconventional style and strategy. He was openly anti-immigrant in his rhetoric, labeling Mexican immigrants criminals and rapists, and proposing to ban all Muslim immigrants and all refugees from several Middle East countries. He promised to build a wall on the Mexico border and to make Mexico pay for it. His populist-nationalist policy positions amounted to a hostile takeover of the Republican Party from its establishment wing and a 180-degree pivot from virtually all of the policies of President Barack Obama. Trump's policy prescriptions frequently differed sharply from traditional Republican long-standing views of several policy matters. His antitrade agreement positions and promises to bring back the jobs of industries shipped overseas, like coal and steel, appealed to enough voters in the key-swing states that he won the ECV despite losing the popular vote.

Immediately upon taking office, President Trump made a 180-degree shift in immigration policy from that of his predecessor, Barack Obama. Ironically, President Trump, who had criticized President Obama of an unconstitutional abuse of his office by an imperial use of executive actions, did so by his own use of executive orders. Where President Obama had used executive orders on average 33 times per year during his eight years in office, President Trump did so 55 times in his first year as president. Among his 55 executive orders, all of which were clearly designed to reverse President Obama's policies, three were related directly to immigration policy and demonstrate his intentional and nearly unprecedented rate in the use of executive orders to rewrite American policy and to undo the Obama legacy as much as possible.

## The Travel Ban

The first executive order concerned the pursuit of undocumented immigrants; it was issued on January 25, 2017, and was titled "Border Security and Immigration Enhancement Enforcement Improvements" (Executive Order 13767, 82 FR 8793). It ordered the building of a wall on the U.S.-Mexico border. Since he needed congressional action to build and fund a wall along the hundreds miles of the border, costing an estimated 3–6 billions of dollars, and since there was no funding for that in the budget he was inheriting from the Obama administration, the Trump administration, via the executive order, was merely for a "pilot project," and was modestly funded by shifting a few million dollars in the existing budget resources within the DHS budget mainly to build several "proto-type" or model sections of a wall as opposed to a fence.

On the same day, President Trump signed another order, titled "Enhancing the Public Safety in the Interior of the United States" (Executive Order 13768, 82 FR 8799). Among other things, it cut funding for what the administration labeled very broadly "sanctuary cities." The city of San Francisco immediately filed a suit in federal court claiming the order is unconstitutional. In May, President Trump's DHS established, again by executive order, an agency called the Victims of Immigration

Crime Enforcement (VOICE) Office. In June, the administration, particularly the DOJ, struggled with language to legally define what exactly constitutes a "sanctuary city" that would thereby be denied federal funds.

On January 27, 2017, President Trump issued the first immigration travel ban that called for extensively reevaluating visa and refugee programs (and rescinded March 6, after it was blocked by federal courts). The travel ban targeted seven Muslim-majority countries: Iran, Iraq, Libya, Somalia, Sudan, Syria, and Yemen. The ban blocked entry of Syrian refugees to the United States and temporarily suspended entry of other refugees and citizens from those nations for admission to the United States for a period of 90 days. The ban was justified as necessary in order to provide the new administration sufficient time to develop what it called new "extreme vetting" of immigrants from those seven countries (Executive Order 13769, 82 FR 8977).

On January 31, President Trump fired acting attorney general Sally Yates for refusing to defend in federal court his immigration travel ban order. AAG Yates had argued that the ban was unconstitutional and refused to implement the ban. On February 3, U.S. district judge James Robart of the 9th Circuit Court of Appeals in Seattle, Washington, an appointee of President George W. Bush, ruled that the ban was unconstitutional and halted enforcement of the ban by the Trump administration, immediately affecting hundreds of refugees seeking entrance into the United States and already cleared to do so by prior refugee vetting criteria (Brunner, Lee, and Gutman 2017).

The district court ruling prompted President Trump to issue a second immigration travel ban by executive order on March 6, 2017. The second order banned immigrants from six Muslim countries (dropping Iraq from the EO1 list) and suspended all refugees for 120 days. The revised travel ban order cut the number of refugees that would be accepted in 2017 by more than half—from 110,000 to 50,000. Refugees were no longer banned indefinitely. The new travel ban dropped language that favored religious minorities, which

President Trump had stated in the first travel ban would apply to persecuted Christians from the Middle East.

On March 15, U.S. district judge Derrick Watson, of Hawaii, put an emergency hold on the revised ban. Hours later, in a separate judicial case, U.S. district judge Theodore Chuang, of Maryland, issued a nation-wide preliminary injunction prohibiting the revised ban from taking effect. The March 6 travel ban order stipulated guidance for agencies to implement the new ban. With the judicial ruling placing an injunction on the ban, President Trump and AG Sessions appealed the district court decision to the U.S. Supreme Court (Gonzales, Rose, and Kennedy 2017).

On June 26, 2017, the Supreme Court partially upheld the second executive travel ban order and announced it would hold full oral arguments on the ban during its fall session. The ruling, however, exempted from the ban persons with previously approved visas and persons with a "bona fide" connection (e.g., close family member) to a U.S. citizen or permanent resident alien (i.e., a green-card holder) (*Trump v. International Refugee Assistance Project* 2017).

Immediately after the Supreme Court ruling, the DOJ issued guidelines as to what constituted "close family ties," which excluded grandparents and other extended family relatives. In July, a Hawaii judge ruled that grandparents could not be excluded. On July 15, 2017, district judge Derrick Watson stated the following: "Common sense, for instance, dictates that close family members may be defined to include grandparents. Indeed, grandparents are the epitome of close family members." Counselor officials of the State Department had earlier revised their guidelines that had excluded fiancés, now allowing them to obtain visas. AG Sessions stated that the DOJ would reluctantly return again to the Supreme Court and filed a notice of appeal (Zapotosky 2017). The administration won a partial victory in the Supreme Court, on a per curiam case, *Donald J. Trump, President of the United States, et al. v. International Refugee Assistance Project, et al.*, 582 U.S. _____ (2017), in which the Court granted a stay of application of the appellate court's decision. The Court, however, only upheld part of the travel ban's provisions. The decision allowed for the entrance of many immigrants from the six banned countries if they had a previously approved visa or were close family members.

Then, on June 26, 2018, in a 5–4 decision, the Supreme Court upheld the third revised travel ban as a constitutional use of the presidential executive order powers and as not discriminatory on religious grounds. This iteration of the ban, from September 2017, added two non-Muslim dominant countries to the list: North Korea and Venezuela, and the conservative majority on the court chose to ignore President Trump's tweets about a "Muslim ban." The majority held that the policy has "a legitimate grounding in national security concerns" and has several moderating features, such as a waiver program (Colorado Springs *Gazette* 2018).

### DACA Annulment

In the final week of January 2018, President Trump pushed the DACA/DAPA issue to a crisis level. Declaring that the programs were unlawful without legislative action to approve them, President Trump annulled the DACA programs, giving Congress until March 5 to "fix the problem." In a staged White House meeting with the leadership of both parties and from both chambers, President Trump declared that if the Congress came up with a bipartisan deal, he would sign it. Democrats tried to include a Dreamer provision in a continuing resolution on the budget to avoid a government shutdown, but two days later, President Trump suddenly announced several demands he would insist upon in the measure, after publicly stating earlier that he would not insist on conditions, and a seemingly bipartisan deal broke down. The Democrats refused to vote for the continuing resolution, forcing a government shutdown that lasted only a weekend. Although the Democrats had vowed a willingness to pass the budget resolution including funding for the border wall, President Trump announced that he would veto any measure that did not include a provision to end "lottery/diversity visas," a reduction in the level of legal immigration by one-half, and rather severe cuts in family reunification visas, which he referred to as chain migration measures. Democratic leaders insisted that the president was the major hindrance to a broader deal. His suddenly insisted-upon provisions were too much for the Democrats to support, and the government shutdown ensued. President Trump seemed to be winning the public relations battle over the weekend, and the Senate Democratic leadership caved on the shutdown, agreeing to vote for the budget resolution without a Dreamer provision on the promise from the Senate Majority leader, Mitch McConnell (R-KY), that within three weeks, and before the Trump-imposed March 6 deadline, he would hold open Senate floor debates on a stand-alone Dreamer bill.

However, without consistent presidential leadership on the issue, a permanent "fix" on the Dreamer issue remained elusive and seemingly impossible to achieve. Four different approaches to a Dreamer measure were taken up and debated in the Senate in mid-February. The Senate rejected all four bills, leaving the Dreamers in legal limbo. Both parties' most fervent supporters refused to budge and compromise, even when a bill was offered with bipartisan sponsorship. The Senate floor's "open and fair" debate showed how intractable a problem it was for Congress. For three presidents, bipartisan negotiations failed to garner significant changes to legal immigration, how to provide a legalization program for the Dreamers, or how to protect the Southern border. Senator Charles Grassley (R-IA) and six GOP senators had offered a bill that called for legalization of 1.8 million Dreamers, but including all of President Trump's stipulated provisions regarding lottery visas, chain migration, and spending $25 billion to build a border wall and harden the southern border. Charles Schumer (D-NY), the Democratic minority leader, opposed the Grassley approach. Senator Jeff Flake (D-AZ) offered a watered-down version of the GOP proposal that failed to win support from either party. Senators Lindsey Graham (R-SC), John McCain (R-AZ), and Chris Coons (D-DE) proposed a measure that included a path to citizenship for 1.8 million Dreamers (700,000 had come forward and officially enrolled in the DACA program). Senator Susan Collins (R-ME) offered another proposal including a path to citizenship for 1.8 million, providing $25 billion for border security, and preventing DACA recipients from sponsoring their parents for legal status. President Trump again threatened a veto and the bill failed by six votes, with only 8 Republicans voting "yes" on the measure. The Senate recessed, having yet again done nothing to solve the DACA crisis.

Despite having failed to act by the March 6, 2018, deadline, however, the annulment of the program announced by President Trump is at least temporarily a moot issue. On January 10, 2018, a federal judge of the Northern District of California, Judge William Alsup, ordered the Trump administration to partially resurrect the DACA program, which he had annulled and set the March 6, 2018, deadline for Congress to enact a permanent fix (Lind 2018). The court order directed the Trump administration to make it possible for persons who have or who have had DACA to apply for renewal again, which would grant them two more years of deferred action and prevent the administration from deporting them. It is an open question as to how quickly the U.S. Citizenship and Immigration Services (USCIS) would move to implement the court order. Likewise, it is unclear how long the court order would stand and remain in effect before being overturned by a higher court. However, given the appeals court ruling on the travel ban, it remains possible that an appeals court would affirm the district court judge's ruling partially reinstating DACA.

## Conclusion

The near future of comprehensive immigration reform in the storm-door era portends federal court action to resolve conflicts between the national and state levels of government, and between the executive and legislative branches of government at both levels. No comprehensive immigration reform is likely at the national level until after the 2018 mid-term elections. President Trump's proposed ban on immigration from mostly Muslim countries, his administration's increased level of deportations of unauthorized immigrants, his executive orders and political pressure to fund the building of a southern border wall, and similar "border control" provisions and approaches echo the rhetoric and the policy positions of the highly restrictive era when the quota system was the legal immigration law.

There is ample evidence that the "border control alone approach" will not substantially change the push pressures that annually send hundreds of thousands of Mexican and Central American, Asian, and other immigrants to attempt entry to the United States, both legal and unauthorized. It is clear that the demographic shifts resulting from immigration will have profound impacts on the culture, economy, and politics of the United States for decades to come. Those trends are likely to further impact the national electoral fortunes of the Democratic and Republican parties.

Despite the effort to crack down and increase restrictions, unauthorized immigration, complex refugee issues, and the continued pressure for high levels of legal immigration to the United States make immigration policymaking more complex and less predictable. Total Hispanic population in the United States continues to surge, as has legal immigration. The current high levels of both authorized and unauthorized immigration, which have risen exponentially since 1980, are resulting in demographic shifts that are truly remarkable. In 1900, for example, the population of the United States was 76 million, among which were slightly more than one-half million Hispanics. The United States Census Bureau estimates that by the year 2050, 25 percent of the projected population of 438 million will be of Hispanic origin, a demographic shift fueled by immigration from Mexico, Central America, and South America, and by their high birth rates when compared to that of the general population. The Census Bureau estimates that roughly 82 percent of the increase in population between 2010 and 2050 will be from immigration. The Census Bureau estimates that the Hispanic population will rise to 47 percent of the total U.S. population by 2050. Asian American population is projected to triple by 2050.

The economic impact of immigration continues to be controversial, with very different assessments depending upon how costs and benefits are measured. Proponents for comprehensive immigration reform advocate for a large-scale temporary guest worker program and for increased funding and staffing of ICE and the DHS, coupled with increased expedited removal and better technology to track and control immigrants and nonimmigrant visitors.

As with the economic impact, the social impact of immigration is also highly controversial and debated. Nearly every new wave of immigrants has aroused xenophobic fear that they could not or should not be incorporated into U.S. society and that they are adversely affecting American society and culture. That remains the case today. Since 9/11, suspicions about immigrants from the Middle East, especially Muslims, have risen dramatically. Mexican Americans are perceived to be incorporating more slowly and acquiring English fluency more slowly than do non-Mexican immigrants. The politics of immigration policymaking is complicated by the increasing spread of immigrants to more urban areas, approaching 10 percent or more of the population in 30 states. As of the 2010 census, the foreign-born population comprises 12.9 percent of the U.S. population. The shift in the nation of origin of immigrants since 2000 is having a profound effect on a host of related public policy areas (Barone 2013; Daniels 2005; LeMay 2013; Motomura 2006; Navarro 2005; Zuniga and Hernandez-Leon 2005).

There remains great political controversy about the health and welfare costs of continued high levels of immigration, particularly that of undocumented immigration. Federal sanctions against employers who hire unauthorized immigrants are at best poorly enforced. Expectations among persons in Mexico and Central America that some sort of asylum, amnesty, or earned legalization will be granted influence the migration decisions of some 150,000 to perhaps 200,000 Mexicans arriving annually. Tighter border controls since 9/11 have done little to staunch the flow of migrants driven more by push factors than by pull factors. Immigration, both legal and unauthorized, declined more because of the Great Recession of 2008–2009 than from any U.S. government immigration policy or construction of a border fence.

The dissolving of the INS and creation of the DHS after 9/11 interweaves issues of immigration with national security policymaking. Immigration control measures continue to remain on the agenda of Congress. Political stalemate and partisan gridlock continue to stymie efforts to enact comprehensive immigration reform. Republican efforts at piecemeal reform, stressing only the border control approach, are blocked by Democrats insisting on a comprehensive approach, with some sort of earned legalization and a path to citizenship for the Dreamers, and perhaps for many of the unauthorized immigrants already in the United States. Few serious analysts expect the United States can realistically deport 10 to 11 million unauthorized immigrants living here. Democratic efforts to enact reform are stymied by Republican insistence that no amnesty program be enacted. High levels of concern, sometimes to the point of hysteria, over international terrorism and of terrorist cells infiltrating the United States smuggled in among the undocumented flow have propelled efforts to enact a Fortress America approach to current immigration policymaking.

Executive branch frustration with congressional inaction on immigration reform of a system so obviously broken and out of control has propelled both presidents Obama and Trump to use executive action authority over immigration policy implementation to change immigration policy at the margins.

Executive actions have pitted the executive branch against the legislative branch and have resulted in federal courts becoming increasingly involved in the issue. Federal courts have held unconstitutional several such executive actions, as well as several state actions driven by frustration with the perceived failure of the federal government to control the borders, particularly in states most affected by the unauthorized immigration problem. Federalism in immigration policymaking shows a dynamism and variety of state actions both pro- and con-immigrants and immigrant rights (Suro 2015).

The shift in the composition of preference immigrants established by the 1965 Immigration and Naturalization Act has been both the results of and the cause for a series of changes in immigration law and policy since its enactment. Congressional laws, executive actions, and federal court decisions have all shaped immigration policymaking, and each has had some unanticipated consequences. The one thing that is clear is that immigration policy will continue to impact the American culture, economy, and society, its politics, and a variety of related public policy issues for decades to come (LeMay 2018; Simon 1989).

## References

Ackerman, Alissa, and Rick Furman. 2013. *The Criminalization of Immigration: Contexts and Consequences.* Durham, NC: Carolina Academic Press.

Adler, Jonathan H. 2015. "Court Issues Injunction against Administration's Immigration Policies." *Washington Post,* February 17, 2015. https://www.washingtonpost.com/news/volokh-conspiracy/wp/2015/02/17/court-issues-injunction-against-administrations-immigration-policies/?utm_term=.be4a0ebacb08.

American Immigration Council. 2013. *Cracking the Safe Act.* Washington, D.C.: American Immigration Council, Immigration Policy Center, August 27, 2013.

American Presidency Project. 2018. "Executive Orders: J.Q. Adams—Trump." http://www.presidency.ucsb.edu/executive_orders.php.

Barone, Michael. 2013. *Shaping Our Nation: How Surges in Migration Transformed America and Its Politics.* New York: Crown Forum/Random House.

Bean, Frank D., George Vernez, and Charles B. Keely. 1989. *Opening and Closing the Doors.* Santa Monica, CA: Rand Corporation.

Brotherton, David, and Philip Kretsedemas, eds. 2008. *Keeping Out the Others.* New York: Columbia University Press.

Brunner, Jim, Jessica Lee, and David Gutman. 2017. "Judge in Seattle Halts Trump's Immigration Order Nationwide; White House Vows Fight." *Seattle Time,* February 3, 2017. https://www.seattletimes.com/seattle-news/politics/federal-judge-in-seattle-halts-trumps-immigration-order/.

Calavita, Kitty. 1992. *Inside the State: The Bracero Program, Immigration and the INS.* New York: Routledge.

Camarota, Steven A. 2005. *Economy Slowed, but Immigration Didn't: The Foreign-Born Population, 2000–2004.* Washington, D.C.: Center for Immigration Studies.

Chiswick, Barry R., ed. 1982. *The Gateway: U.S. Immigration Issues and Policies.* Washington, D.C.: American Enterprise Institute.

Chomsky, Aviva. 2014. *Undocumented: How Immigration Became Illegal.* Boston: Beacon Press.

CNN. 2016. "2016 Election Results." https://www.cnn.com/election/2016/results.

Colorado Springs *Gazette,* 2018. "Travel Ban Upheld; Ruling Exacerbates U.S. Divisions," *Wednesday,* June 27, 2018, A-11.

Crewdson, John. 1983. *The Tarnished Door.* New York: Times Books.

Daniels, Roger. 2005. *Guarding the Golden Door: American Immigration Policy and Immigration since 1882.* New York: Hill and Wang.

Etzioni, Amitai, and Jason H. Marsh, eds. 2003. *Rights v. Public Safety after 9/11: America in an Age of Terrorism.* Lanham, MD: Rowman and Littlefield.

General Accounting Office. 2004. *Overstay Tracking: A Key Component of Homeland Security and a Layered Defense.* GAO-04–82. Washington, D.C.: Government Printing Office.

Golash-Boza, Tanya Maria. 2012. *Immigration Nation: Raids, Detentions and Deportations in Post 9/11 America.* Fort Collins, CO: Paradigm Books/Routledge.

Gonzales, Richard, Joel Rose, and Merrit Kennedy. 2017. "Trump Travel Ban Blocked Nationwide by Federal Judges in Hawaii, Maryland." *NPR*, March 15, 2017. https://www.npr.org/sections/thetwo-way/2017/03/15/520171478/trump-travel-ban-faces-court-hearings-by-challengers-today.

*Guardian.* 2016. "Unfinished US-Mexico Border Wall Is a Costly Logistical Nightmare in Texas." January 1, 2016. https://www.theguardian.com/us-news/2016/jan/01/unfinished-us-mexico-border-wall-texas-secure-fence-act.

Harper, Elizabeth J. 1975. *Immigration Laws of the United States.* 3rd ed. Indianapolis: Bobbs-Merrill.

Harper, Jim. 2014. "REAL ID: A State-by-State Update." *Cato Institute*, May 12, 2004. https://www.cato.org/publications/policy-analysis/real-id-state-state-update.

Hernandez, Kelly L. 2010. *Migra! A History of the U.S. Border Patrol.* Berkeley: University of California Press.

Hines, Sarah. 2006. "The Bracero Program: 1942–1964," *Counterpunch.* www.counterpunch.org/2006/04/21/the-bracero-program.

History.com. 2018. "This Day in History: July 2." https://www.history.com/this-day-in-history/johnson-signs-civil-rights-act.

Illinois.gov. 2005. *Gov. Blagojevich Announces Landmark Immigration Policy.* Springfield, IL: State of Illinois, Office of the Governor.

Information Plus. 2006. *Immigration and Illegal Aliens: Burden or Blessing?* Farmington Hills, MI: Thomson/Gale.

Kennedy, John F. 1958 (reissued edition 2008). *A Nation of Immigrants.* New York: Harper Perennial.

Krogstad, Jens Manuel, and Jeffrey S. Passel. 2014. "U.S. Border Apprehensions of Mexicans Fall to Historic Lows." Pew Research Center, December 30. http://www.pewresearch.org/fact-tank/2014/12/30/u-s-border-apprehensions-of-mexicans-fall-to-historic-lows/.

Krogstad, Jens Manuel, Jeffrey S. Passel, and D'Vera Cohn. 2017. "5 Facts about Illegal Immigration in the U.S." Pew Research Center, April 27. http://www.pewresearch.org/fact-tank/2017/04/27/5-facts-about-illegal-immigration-in-the-u-s/.

Leibowitz, Arnold. 1983. "The Refugee Act of 1980: Problems and Congressional Concerns." *Annals of the American Academy of Political and Social Science,* 467, no. 1 (May): 163–171.

LeMay, Michael C. 1987. *From Open Door to Dutch Door: An Analysis of U.S. Immigration Policy since 1820.* New York: Praeger Press.

LeMay, Michael C. 1994. *Anatomy of a Public Policy: The Reform of Contemporary American Immigration Law.* Westport, CT: Praeger Press.

LeMay, Michael C. 2004. *U.S. Immigration: A Reference Handbook.* Santa Barbara, CA: ABC-CLIO.

LeMay, Michael C., ed. 2013 *Transforming America: Perspectives on U.S. Immigration.* Vol. 3. Santa Barbara, CA: ABC-CLIO.

LeMay, Michael C. 2015. *Illegal Immigration: A Reference Handbook.* 2nd ed. Santa Barbara, CA: ABC-CLIO.

LeMay, Michael C. 2016. *Global Pandemic Threats: A Reference Handbook.* Santa Barbara, CA: ABC-CLIO.

LeMay, Michael C. 2018. *U.S. Immigration Policy, Ethnicity, and Religion in American History.* Santa Barbara, CA: Praeger Press.

LeMay, Michael C., and Elliott Barkan. 1999. *U.S. Immigration and Naturalization Laws and Issues: A Documentary History.* Westport, CT: Greenwood Press.

Library of Congress. 2018. "The Civil Rights Act of 1964: A Long Struggle for Freedom." https://www.loc.gov/exhibits/civil-rights-act/civil-rights-act-of-1964.html.

Lind, Dara. 2018. "A Federal Judge Just Ordered the Trump Administration to Partially Restart the DACA Program." *Vox,* January 10, 2018. https://www.vox.com/2018/1/10/16872766/daca-trump-court-ruling-renew.

Malek, Alia. 2011. *Patriot Acts: Voices of Witnesses.* San Francisco, CA: McSweeneys.

McClellan, Grant S., ed. 1981. *Immigrants, Refugees, and U.S. Policy.* New York: H.W. Wilson.

Morris, Milton D. 1985. *Immigration: The Beleaguered Bureaucracy.* Washington, D.C.: The Brookings Institution.

Motomura, Hiroshi. 2006. *Americans in Waiting: The Lost Story of Immigration and Citizenship in the United States.* New York: Oxford University Press.

National Conference of State Legislatures. 2011. *Undocumented Student Tuition: Federal Action.* Denver, CO: National Conference of State Legislatures.

Navarro, Armando. 2005. *Mexican Political Experience in Occupied Aztlan.* Lanham, MD: Altamura Press.

NBC News. 2015. "Obama Administration to Start Taking DACA Requests Feb. 18." https://www.nbcnews.com/news/latino/obama-administration-start-taking-daca-requests-feb-18-n296766.

Ngai, Mae. 2011. *Major Problems in American Immigration History: Documents and Essays.* 2nd ed. Boston: Wadsworth/Cengage.

Ngai, Mae. 2014. *Impossible Subjects: Illegal Aliens and the Making of Modern America.* Princeton: Princeton University Press.

O'Leary, Anna Ochoa, ed. 2014. *Undocumented Immigrants in the United States: An Encyclopedia of Their Experience.* 2 vols. Santa Barbara, CA: Greenwood Press.

Orreniris, Pia, and Madelaine Zavodny. 2010. *Beside the Golden Door: U.S. Immigration Reform in a New Era of Globalization.* Washington, D.C.: American Enterprise Institute Press.

Passel, Jeffry S., and D'Vera Cohn. 2012. *Unauthorized Immigrant Population: National and State Trends, 2010.* Washington, D.C.: Pew Hispanic Center, February.

Pew Research Center. 2013. "A Nation of Immigrants." January 29, 2013. http://www.pewhispanic.org/2013/01/29/a-nation-of-immigrants/.

Preston, Julia. 2014. "Ailing Cities Extend Hand to Immigrants: National Desk." *New York Times,* October 7, A-18.

Relyea, Harold. 2003. "Organizing for Homeland Security," *Presidential Studies Quarterly,* 33, no. 3 (September): 602–624.

Rodriquez, Cristina. 2014. "Negotiating Conflict through Federalism: Institutional and Popular Perspectives." *Yale Law Journal* 123 (6): 2094.

Schrug, Peter. 2010. *Not Fit for Our Society: Nativism and Immigration.* Berkeley: University of California Press.

Select Commission on Immigration and Refugee Policy. 1981. *Final Report.* Washington, D.C.: U.S. Government Printing Office.

Sherman, Jake, and Seung Min Kim. 2013. "House Group Has Deal on Immigration." *Politico*, May 16, 2013. https://www.politico.com/story/2013/05/house-immigration-bill-091499.

Simon, Julian. 1989. *The Economic Consequences of Immigration into the United States.* New York: Blackwell Publishers.

Suro, Roberto. 2015. "California Dreaming: The New Dynamism in Immigration Federalism and Opportunities for Inclusion on a Variegated Landscape." *Journal of Migration and Human Security* 3 (1): 1–25.

*TIME Magazine.* 1985. "Trying to Stem the Illegal Tide." July 8, 1985, 27.

Torr, James D. 2004. *Homeland Security.* San Diego: Greenhaven.

*Trump v. International Refugee Assistance Project*, 582 U.S. 2017. https://www.supremecourt.gov/opinions/16pdf/16-1436_l6hc.pdf.

United We Dream. 2018. "About UWD." https://unitedwedream.org/about/.

U.S. Customs and Border Protection. 2014. "Southwest Border Unaccompanied Alien Children FYI 2014." https://www.cbp.gov/newsroom/stats/southwest-border-unaccompanied-children/fy-2014.

U.S. Department of Homeland Security. 2017. "DHS Tracking of Visa Overstays Is Hindered by Insufficient Technology." Report Number OIG-17–56, May 1, 2017. https://www.oig.dhs.gov/reports/2017/dhs-tracking-visa-overstays-hindered-insufficient-technology/oig-17-56-may17.

U.S. Department of Justice. 2002. *Follow-up Report on INS Efforts to Improve the Control of Immigrant Overstays.* Report No. 1–2003–006. Washington, D.C.: U.S. Government Printing Office.

U.S. Foreign Intelligence Surveillance Court. 2018. "About the Foreign Intelligence Surveillance Court." http://www.fisc .uscourts.gov/about-foreign-intelligence-surveillance-court.

Vaughan, Jessica M. 2012. "What Is Deferred Action?" Center for Immigration Studies, June 15, 2012. https://cis. org/Vaughan/What-Deferred-Action.

*Wall Street Journal.* 2016. "Election Results 2016." http://graphics .wsj.com/elections/2016/results/.

Walton, Elizabeth. 2014. "U.S. Senators from AZ Introduce CREST ACT Addressing Border Crisis." *Tucson News Now,* July 17, 2014. http://www.tucsonnewsnow.com/ story/26045339/us-senators-from-az-introduce-crest-act-addressing-border-crisis.

Waters, Mary C., Reed Ueda, and Helen B. Marrow, eds. 2007. *The New Americans: A Guide to Immigration since 1965.* New York: Russell Sage/Harvard University Press.

White House. 2017. "President Donald J. Trump Restores Responsibility and the Rule of Law to Immigration." September 5, 2017. https://www.whitehouse.gov/ briefings-statements/president-donald-j-trump-restores-responsibility-rule-law-immigration/.

Zapotosky, Matt. 2017. "Judge Rejects Hawaii Bid to Exempt Grandparents from Trump's Travel Ban." *Washington Post,* July 6, 2017. https://www.washingtonpost.com/world/ national-security/judge-rejects-hawaii-bid-to-exempt-grandparents-from-trumps-travel-ban/2017/07/06/ 8e3a3252-625d-11e7-8adc-fea80e32bf47_story.html.

Zuniga, Victor, and Ruben Hernandez-Leon. 2005. *New Destinations: Mexican Immigration in the United States.* New York: Russell Sage.

HOMELAND SE
ADVISORY SY
SEVERE
Severe Risk of
Terrorist Attack
HIGH
High Risk of
Terrorist Attack
ELEVATED
Significant Risk o
Terrorist Attack
GUARDED
LOW
Low Risk of
Terrorist Attack

## Introduction

This chapter focuses on some of the major problems and controversies that developed since the Immigration and Naturalization Act of 1965, its various amendments, and the unintended consequences of the act and its various amendments as the U.S. Congress continues to grapple with efforts to control the borders and cope with both legal and unauthorized immigration, which have risen markedly since 1965.

It addresses management problems of coping with immigration reform, especially since the Department of Homeland Security (DHS) was established and problems arose in large measure from the mission complexity and the behemoth nature of DHS. The chapter focuses on problems of balancing civil liberties and privacy rights of citizens with the need to protect the nation from external attacks by international terrorist organizations and from internal threats posed by the "lone-wolf" terrorist radicalized and inspired by them. It discusses problems of technology development and the slow progress in developing IT and related electronic security measures to help control the highly porous northern and southern

Homeland Security Director Tom Ridge unveils a color-coded system that ranks the severity of terrorist threats in Washington, D.C., on March 12, 2002. The system was designed to prepare local police and the public for attacks, but its vagueness about how they were to prepare was much derided. (Mark Wilson/Getty Images)

borders of the nation. It examines the need for comprehensive immigration reform and how the stalemate in Congress over legislative action to enact such reform negatively impacts efforts to control the borders and to manage the massive numbers of nonimmigrant visitors and the legal permanent resident immigrants.

It examines the political and judicial controversies engendered by President Trump's two executive orders to impose a travel ban and federal court challenges of those travel bans.

Problems associated with business needs and with efficient and timely issuing of visa are discussed. These are examined in the context of how the tightening of student and visitor visas applications and the efforts to find and control visa overstayers have had negative impacts in implementing those applications and have caused economic problems for the United States.

The United States is a federal system. Complex relations between the national level of government with state and local governments affect immigration concerns. How active should state and local communities and bureaucracies be in assisting the national government in immigration enforcement, exemplified by the Secure Communities initiative? And in sharp contrast, why do many local governments choose to embrace the sanctuary movement? Do sanctuary cities and churches pose a security threat? Do attempts by the Department of Justice (DOJ) and the DHS to identify and financially punish sanctuary cities help security or are they dangerous threats to the nation's federal system of government and its checks and balances? DOJ seems unable to develop a legally applicable definition of what is a sanctuary city. A federal sanctuary law clashes with various sanctuary laws enacted at the city and state level. It is a legal problem that will undoubtedly concern the federal court system in the foreseeable future (Colorado Springs *Gazette* 2018a).

Federalism, coupled with the political stalemate in Congress, keeps "the Dreamer problem" from being effectively addressed. Enacting a legislative fix as opposed to temporary executive actions to confront the problem of what to do with the estimated 1.8 million Dreamer population seems to be an intractable concern and a public policy crisis.

The design, building, and financing of a border wall continues to plague Congress. Critics see the wall as a 12th-century solution to a 21st-century problem (Navarrette 2018). President Trump and his political base see the wall as a promise that must be kept. The estimated cost of a border wall means the issue will be on the agenda of a Congress that funds the federal government using a seemingly endless parade of continuing resolutions instead of approved budgets. That makes the wall and immigration reform policy for that matter perennial issues that are repeatedly delayed until later, with no realistic and politically acceptable solution in sight. Immigration reform is among a host of public policy issues that seem to defy solution.

For decades, the country benefited from a "brain drain" flow, in which gifted and entrepreneurial talented persons migrated from developing nations to the United States. That brain drain has been negatively affected by the crackdown on legal immigration as a result of reforms enacted since 9/11/2001.

The United States has an increasingly aging population and natural population growth that is near zero. Future population growth, especially of working-age individuals, is almost entirely dependent upon immigration. Proposed or enacted changes in legal immigration have, in turn, negatively affected the solvency of the Social Security system.

Legislative and executive branches often differ in their perspectives of exactly what is "the immigration problem" and the need for, and the approach to take toward, immigration reform. Those differing views of immigration have been exacerbated by the change from the Obama to the Trump administration. Even the governance style of the two presidents—from the no-drama Obama to the all-trauma Trump—has impacted the possibility of immigration reform and the likelihood, or not, of achieving comprehensive immigration reform. Both presidents have used executive actions to pursue their vision of immigration reform when they have been politically frustrated by a legislative stalemate to enact any laws to cope with various immigration-related problems. Perceived solutions are known but seem to be politically impossible to enact and implement. Solutions that might be good policy make for bad politics. Solutions that make good politics—often expressed on car bumper stickers as slogans such as "Build the Wall!"—tend to be ineffective policy.

For each of these problems, issues, and controversies, the chapter identifies key stakeholders both within and without government. It looks at each problem area and describes how a balance must be achieved between immigration policy reform and the political will and capability to achieve policy reform in light of a hyper-partisan atmosphere that makes any reform politically problematic—the immigration policy conundrum. It discusses the problem of gerrymandering and how that affects the partisan divide and stalemate in legislating immigration reform.

The chapter discusses DHS's lack of a comprehensive biometric exit system at U.S. air and sea ports of departure within the department's IT system. The DHS has conducted several pilot programs to upgrade its ability to monitor the 11 million or so visas issued annually, among whom more than one-half million are visa overstayers. The Customs and Border Patrol has conducted four pilot programs to develop and implement a biometric exit system. Currently, there are 17 different systems used to conduct investigations of an overstay status across three agencies: Customs and Border Patrol (CBP), the U.S. Citizenship and Immigration Services (USCIS), and Immigration and Customs Enforcement (ICE) (Office of the Inspector General, 2017).

The problems and issues associated with immigration reform inherently entail the need and effort to achieve a balance in public policy addressing them. Solutions to those problems can only be reached through the political process that underlies all public policy making.

## Groupthink in the Aftermath of 9/11

The policymaking process involved in immigration reform exhibits a number of problems identified by groupthink theory (LeMay 2006: 216–219). "Groupthink" is the term used for a theory extensively developed and popularized by Irving Janis (1982). It describes faulty decision making that occurs in groups as a result of forces of group cohesion. What Janis describes as typical group decision-making problems of groupthink appear to be present in immigration reform lawmaking and implementation. Janis describes several such groupthink problems that seem evident in immigration reform:

1. A failure to consider all alternatives in order to maintain political unanimity.

2. An inadequate examination of decision objectives.

3. A failure to properly evaluate the risks of the chosen solution alternative.

4. Insufficient or biased information searches.

5. The desire for group conformity and unanimity essentially overriding the need to decide effectively. (Janis 1982)

Janis notes two precursors to groupthink behavior and decision making:

1. Organizational faults such as directive leadership, lack of formal procedures, or lack of social diversity in the decision team; and

2. A challenging decision environment that includes external threats, time pressures, and/or moral dilemmas.

In the post-9/11 hysteria, conformity among the administration teams developing and proposing immigration reforms in response to the terrorist attacks and the unusual conformity in congressional lawmaking in response to the perceived security crisis short-circuited more deliberative decision making. Normally congressional policy making involves several to many committees considering proposed bills, which take months and quite often years when the proposed revision to a law is complex and far-reaching. Public hearings are typically held, allowing many voices on all sides of an issue to be heard. The two political parties typically weigh in on the proposal. Many stakeholders from government agencies most affected by the proposed law weigh in, as do lobbyists from a host of nongovernment stakeholders.

The legislative process is typically slow, often excruciatingly complex, and one which gives opponents of change the political advantage over those advocating change. Inertia is inherent in routine lawmaking. It seems especially so with regard to immigration policy reform, where for decades reform has fallen victim to the forces of inertia and stalemate. But that very complexity of the normal legislative process results in compromises in positions, a deeper examination of all the issues and concerns, and a "check and balance" of competing views on the legislation. Such a policy process tends to lessen unanticipated consequences.

Those constraints are absent when lawmaking is in the "crisis" mode of decision making, such as was evidently the case in the establishment of the Department of Homeland Security (Kowert 2002; Roots, 2003; Yehiv 2003). As noted in Chapter 1, the vote to establish DHS was 90 to 9 in the Senate and 299 to 121 in the House of Representatives. Republicans voted 212 in favor to only 6 opposed. There was virtually no debate about dissolving the INS. What comparatively little debate that did take place concerned unionization and civil service protection, and whether or not the Coast Guard should be moved to the DHS. There was almost no debate about civil liberty and privacy concerns, two aspects that are often involved in immigration reform (LeMay 2006: 218–219).

With respect to groupthink decision making and immigration reform, the only observations about "solutions" concern actions designed to prevent groupthink behavior in an organization's decision making. Those include the following:

1. Having a structured decision-making process that, when used routinely, helps prevent the shortcuts that come from groupthink.

2. Creating a decision stream that has a broad diversity of thought—particularly across the ideological and partisan divide.

3. Increasing the personal responsibility for decision participants to counter the pressure toward conformity.

4. Encouraging an initial leadership choice with respect to the level of collaboration appropriate to the decision being made. For immigration reform, this would involve having key players from affected executive branch departments and agencies, key legislative leaders from the formal committees, and the informal caucuses that have a stake in immigration policy making.

5. Using outside experts who likely have less compelling motivation to conform.

6. Insisting on bi-partisan participation in the deliberative and voting processes and using "regular order" to achieve and vote on a bill seen as a solution.

## Management Problems of Immigration Policy Implementation

The 2002 decisions on immigration reform resulted in merging 22 agencies into one huge department now comprised of and responsible for 240,000 employees. Each agency merged into DHS had its own prior "bureaucratic culture," several of which were hardly compatible with one another. That simple fact posed several management problems (LeMay 2006: 219–228). The INS and the Coast Guard, for example, had vastly different cultures; personnel management styles; bureaucratic jargon;

and data collection, storage, and analysis capabilities. When DHS was established, critics noted merging them into one department with new mission and goals would not be easy. As one critic stated:

> the behemoth known as the DHS is less than what it seems. Guided by advisors from the Defense and Justice departments and the CIA, the [Bush] administration ensured that the DHS has quite limited authority. So now, while the DHS oversees a number of areas—everything from federal airline safety to federal responses to hurricanes and floods—it has no authority to oversee the . . . activity and priorities of other agencies. These include the Defense Department, the Justice Department, and the CIA, the very agencies that are crucial to homeland defense. Instead of streamlining our domestic preparedness strategy, the DHS has simply become another agency added to the mix, equal but not primary. (Kayyem 2003: 46)

Opponents of establishing such a huge bureaucracy predicted management problems, and such problems soon surfaced. U.S. Customs and Border Protection, the border patrol, and ICE have all been criticized for mismanagement. In several reports, the Government Accountability Office (GAO) has been sharply critical of the DHS with respect to immigration reform, border control, and immigration policy implementation (Government Accountability Office 2002, 2003, 2006).

The DHS's four directorates carry out varied missions. The Border and Transportation Directorate is the most visible of the four. This directorate's budget is the largest within the department. It houses the Transportation Security Administration (TSA) and two border agencies—Immigration and Customs Enforcement (ICE), and Customs and Border Protection (CBP). Roughly half of all DHS employees work in this directorate.

The merger of so many disparate agencies into such a huge department created challenges to a federal government that is more responsive, effective, and efficient—the very values underlying the reason to create the DHS. Elishia Krauss details four management problems from the reorganization that add additional obstacles to achieving those values:

1. **Mission Complexity.** DHS has to do too much of too disparate missions with too inadequate resources. After the merger, the immigration-related agencies within the department, most in need of reform and an update in their IT capabilities, were the very agencies within the department that received the least funding for discretionary accounts.

2. **Cultural incompatibility.** Major problems arose while trying to combine disparate organizational cultures, competing technologies used in day-to-day operations, such as integrating different infrastructure platforms, software applications, applications for e-mail databases, and networking. Maintaining good communication is complicated by having to do so internally and externally between a host of federal agencies, and vertically with state and local governments that have a stake in immigration policy and its reform, and with the general public. DHS merged agencies like the Coast Guard and FEMA, which had relatively high ratings in overall management (A and B respectively), with immigration agencies noted for their notoriously poor performance management and abysmal IT technology and electronic data management (D ratings).

3. **Task obfuscation.** In its early years of operation, DHS seemed more concerned with its image than with improving its quality of operation and immigration service. The behemoth nature of DHS increases levels of overhead and administrative costs.

4. **Symbolic versus real performance results.** Creating the DHS fostered a false sense that something was being done

to really reform immigration and to effectively cope with the unauthorized immigration flow. A perfect example was the notorious and oft-derided "color-coded alert system" (Haynes 2004; Krauss 2003: 51–58; LeMay 2006: 221–222; Light 2002).

As critic Wendy Haynes notes:

> Each of the twenty-two agencies brings its own array of existing management challenges and program risks to the new mega-department. The US Comptroller General reported that many of the major components merging into the new Department already face considerable problems such as: strategic human capital risks, information technology management challenges, and financial management vulnerabilities (Government Accountability Office 2002). Add to the mix the role complexities . . . a bewildering array of congressional oversight and appropriations committees, the challenge of meeting a grueling implementation schedule, and the absence of a culture of cooperation with [the agencies], and a daunting homeland security agenda, and it begins to look more like an impossible and potential catastrophic dream. We will be witness to a mind-boggling demonstration of the complexity of joint action. (Haynes 2004: 369)

One logical solution to problems and controversies arising from the behemoth nature of DHS is to restructure the department. While that solution is logical, it is unlikely. With each year that the department exists and operates, it becomes less likely that it will be restructured in any significant way. The political pressure to do so eased as management problems eased since the department's establishment. The lessening of the management problems, the inertia of policy making, and the political support accrued over the years and vested into

DHS make restructuring unlikely. Spinning off a few agencies might be possible and would lessen the massive size of DHS. Given the Trump administration's emphasis on stopping illegal immigration and reducing legal immigration, there might be some political and congressional willingness to create a cabinet-level department of immigration, removing those functions from DHS. Such structural reform would offer the opportunity to streamline immigration bureaucracies (Wucker 2006: 222–226). In debate over immigration and DACA during the rush to meet the March 5, 2018, deadline pronounced by President Trump, Senator Grassley proposed amendments that President Trump said he would sign. It may be possible to combine some of the amendments offered by Senators Grassley and Collins into a bill that restructured DHS and established a Department of Immigration. The expanded 1.8 million DACA recipients could be legalized with the proviso that they could not sponsor their parents to be legalized under a family reunification preference. Cutting legal immigration by more than half was a bridge too far for Democratic senators to cross, but perhaps maintaining the number of total immigration while transferring numbers from the fourth and fifth preference categories for family reunification to the third and sixth employment-based categories, coupled with a legislative fix for DACA, ending the lottery visa program, and authorizing some increase in border control by, for example, expanding the border fence, building a somewhat token wall where the terrain justified its use, and enhancing electronic monitoring along the border, might win over enough Democratic votes to pass such a compromise bill.

Having a cabinet-level department of immigration might enhance programs designed to foster "patriotic assimilation." John Fonte of the Hudson Institute describes the concept: "Patriotic assimilation does not mean giving up one's ethnic traditions, customs, cuisine, and birth language. It has nothing to do with the food one eats, the religion one practices, the affection one has for the land of one's birth, or the languages one speaks. Patriotic assimilation occurs when a newcomer essentially adopts American civic values and the American heritage as his or her own" (cited in Wucker 2006: 227). Another way scholars describe such assimilation is referred to as segmented or political incorporation (Browning, Marshall, and Tabb, 2003; DeSipio 2006: 447–478; Gerstle and Mollenkopf 2001). Transferring immigration policy to a new Department of Immigration would potentially enable more resources to be used for civic and English-language education. Such English-language programs for second-language learners now meet only 5 percent of the demand. USCIS has a waiting list of 9,000 people per each adult education provider. The Houston office has the capacity to instruct about 35,000 people in English each year, yet nearly one million persons could use such classes. A new department of immigration is more likely to upgrade and revise tests for citizenship. The current test uses questions that are often redundant, technical, and all too often merely trivial. They do not emphasize concepts and values like freedom, equality, rights, and responsibilities, the very values fostered by patriotic assimilation and political incorporation (Wucker 2006: 229–230).

Separating immigration management would reduce DHS's mission complexity, as previously discussed. A major goal of the USCIS is to encourage the assimilation of permanent resident immigrants, that is, to the aforementioned political incorporation. The political incorporation model holds that for a minority community to witness an effective response to its needs, minority leaders must come to occupy positions of government authority (Browning, Marshall, and Tabb 2003; Gerstle and Mollenkopf 2001). DHS practices that target Muslim Americans and the implementation of a (Muslim) travel ban permanently color the way in which many immigrants perceive the DHS and its current immigration functions. Separating immigration from DHS might, over time, improve the reputation and perception of the immigration bureaucracy among legal immigrants. For example, the Cato Institute, a conservative think tank, noted the following:

> Even if the government's Terrorist Information Awareness program were 95 percent accurate, a search focused on the U.S. Muslim population would turn up 299,750 false positive IDs—with only 1.5 percent probability of finding a real terrorist. In other words, the government was wasting time and money and alienating the groups whose help was needed—all for precious little benefit to American security. (Wucker 2006: 147–148)

## Civil Liberties and Privacy versus Immigration Control

There is an inherent value conflict at issue in immigration security policy and civil rights and liberties policy. Striking a balance between those values in the ways such policy is pursued while safeguarding traditional privacy and civil liberties protections is an ongoing problem and concern (LeMay 2006: 261–264). The fight against international terrorist cells entering the United States within the undocumented migration flow focuses on granting the federal government powers that, in their sweeping nature, inevitably conflict with civil rights and civil liberties. Trying to achieve a balance between enhanced security and civil liberties protection has led to strange political bedfellows: that is, to an unlikely coalition of liberal civil rights groups and conservative libertarians, to gun-rights advocates and medical privacy advocates. An example of such an unlikely coalition is Patriots to Restore Checks and Balances. It joined conservative groups, like the American Conservative Union, the Center for Privacy and Technology Policy, and Free Congress, with such liberal groups as the American Civil Liberties Union and the American Librarians Association. A nationwide grassroots coalition claims that 383 communities and 7 states have enacted anti-Patriot Act laws, called "civil liberties safe zones," or what the coalition terms sanctuary cities. The coalition lobbies Congress to scale back three provisions of Patriot Act II: one that allows federal agents to conduct "sneak and peek" searches without notification, one that demands records from such institutions as libraries and medical offices, and one that uses a sweepingly broad definition of terrorism in pursuing suspects (LeMay 2006: 261).

Civil rights activists claim that DHS policies and procedures endanger the rights and freedoms of law-abiding citizens by blurring the lines between foreign and domestic spying. They certainly have proven to endanger the human civil liberty rights of noncitizens (legal and unauthorized immigrants). Although enacted to track down terrorists, information can be collected on any dissenter, citizen or not, violent or not. The classification within Department of Defense (DoD) and Federal Emergency Management Agency (FEMA) documents of peace marches and protests as "terrorist events" in 2003 is but one example of the dangerous potential of civil liberties abuses by DHS (Project Censored 2003).

Critics of the Patriot Act and the DHS Act argue that these laws allow the government increased and nearly unprecedented access to the lives of citizens and results in an unrestrained imposition on civil liberties. Wiretaps, previously confined to one telephone, can now follow a person from place to place at the behest of government agents. People can and have been detained on vague suspicion that they might be a terrorist, as seen when directed at Arab and Muslim immigrants in the aftermath of the 9/11 attacks. Detainees can be and have been denied the right to legal counsel (Wucker 2006: 141–142). Patriot Act II places the entire federal government under the jurisdiction of DOJ, DHS, and FEMA/NORTHCOM (Northern Command). Critics note there is a lack of checks and balances to protect anyone who is tagged in error, even unintentionally. The American Civil Liberties Union (ACLU) charges that post-9/11, the federal government engaged in systematic policies of torture (such as walling and water boarding at Gitmo), indefinite detention, mass and warrantless surveillance, and religious discrimination through racial and religious profiling of Arab and Muslim Americans. They argue the Patriot Act and the DHS, in enforcing many of its policies and practices, have eroded some of America's most cherished values and, in the process, made the nation less free and less safe (ACLU 2018).

As David Cole notes:

> Three principles in particular should guide our response to the threat of terrorism. First, we should not overreact in a time of fear, a mistake we made all too often in the past. Second, we should not sacrifice the bedrock foundations of our constitutional democracy—political freedom and equal treatment—absent a compelling showing of need and adoption of narrowly tailored means. And third, balancing liberty and security, we should not succumb to the temptation to trade a vulnerable minority's liberties, namely the liberties of immigrants in general, or Arab and Muslim immigrants in particular, for the security for the rest of us. The USA Patriot Act violates all three of those principles. (cited in Etzioni and Marsch 2003: 35)

Proponents of national security, by contrast, argue that *foreign citizens* in our midst have no entitlement to enter or to remain in the country, and that prudence dictates measures that change the terms under which they are allowed to remain in the United States. Mark Krikorian, director of the Center for Immigration Studies, articulates that perspective:

> It would be unfortunate, if, in our effort to prevent another 3,000 American deaths—or 30,000 or 300,000—we were inadvertently to deport some foreign citizens who pose no threat to us. But their presence here is a privilege we grant, not a right they have exercised, and we may withdraw that privilege for any reason. (cited in Etzioni and Marsch 2003: 33–34)

Sometimes groups inadvertently got caught up in the post-9/11 hysteria. An October 2004 raid by the FBI on the offices of a small charity known as the Islamic-American Relief Agency effectively resulted in the charity having to shut down due to its funds drying up. The Patriot Act expanded the International Emergency Economic Powers Act that allowed the government to seize assets of organizations while investigating it for links to terrorism. In the end, the FBI found no evidence of such links, but the damage had been done and the charity ended its operations. The raid was likely the result of confusing the Islamic-American Relief Agency with the Sudan-based charity called the Islamic-African Relief Agency, which the U.S. government claims does have links to terrorists (LeMay 2006: 263).

Critics of DHS and the Patriot Acts charge the federal government with racial profiling. They look skeptically at programs like the Total Information Awareness (TIA) program, which focuses on people who speak certain languages: Afghan languages, Arabic, Farsi, Korean, and Mandarin (Torr 2004: 61).

The Intelligence Authorization Act of 2004, which funds all intelligence activities of the United States, changed the definition of "financial institution." Prior to 2004, that referred to banks. The new definition includes stockbrokers, car dealerships, casinos, credit card companies, insurance agencies, jewelers, airlines, and any other business "whose cash transactions have a high degree of usefulness in criminal, tax, regulatory" and now possible terrorist-related matters (Martin, 2003).

DHS greatly expanded its use of expedited removals, especially for persons ordered out of the country from countries known to harbor terrorists despite the small numbers who may be threats. A 2003 staff report of the September 11 Commission found only 5,000 of the 400,000 immigrants ordered out of the United States as overstayers came from countries known to have ties to al Qaeda. Of 1,100 persons from that group of 5,000 captured in the first year, moreover, none were ever charged with terrorism-related offenses (LeMay 2006: 264).

An intended solution to those myriad problems and concerns regarding matters of privacy and civil liberties versus security was the establishment, within the DHS, of the Office for Civil Rights and Civil Liberties (CRCL). It was designed to integrate civil rights and civil liberties into all 22 of the agencies of DHS by doing the following:

1. Promoting respect for civil rights and civil liberties in policy creation and implementation, and providing advice and support for incorporation of civil rights and civil liberties protections into the department's immigration-related activities and policies;

2. Communicating with individuals and communities whose civil rights and civil liberties may be affected by department activities, and informing them of policies and avenues of redress;

3. Investigating and resolving civil rights and civil liberties complaints filed by the public regarding department policies or activities;

4. Leading the department's equal employment opportunity programs and promoting workforce diversity and its efforts to implement proactive and effective programs for promoting diversity; and

5. Ensuring that the department complies with constitutional, statutory, regulatory, and other requirements relating to civil rights and civil liberties. CRCL attempts to do so by assessing the impact of DHS policies and activities, training DHS personnel, and engaging with diverse communities (Office of Civil Rights and Liberties 2018).

In an attempted solution to those civil rights and civil liberties concerns, the CRCL office has trained privacy officials of more than 1,000 DHS staff since 2009. The CRCL office has incorporated standards into the agency's cyber security programs and initiatives and has provided specific training on the protection of privacy and civil liberties as they relate to computer network security activities provided to DHS personnel. To do so, DHS completed an overhaul of its civil rights investigations processes by creating a new complaint database system, by developing an easy-to-use online complaint submission form, by increasing access to comprehensive language services, by increasing transparency for complainants, and by improving coordination with components to track response to and implementation of its recommendations.

While applauding the creation of the Office of Civil Rights and Civil Liberties within DHS, the ACLU is less impressed with its accomplishments. ACLU's suggested solution to cope with problems of civil rights and liberties, and with privacy rights associated with the implementation of Patriot Act II, and with DHS itself, was to establish its own National Security Project. The project aims to: educate the public about abuses; shape law so that courts, Congress, and U.S. citizens can serve as an enduring check on abuse; and seeks to have the federal government renounce policies and practices that disregard due process, enshrine discrimination, and turn everyone into a suspect (ACLU 2018).

## Comprehensive Immigration Reform

Without question, many problems arise from the flow of unauthorized immigration and the political issues that migration engenders. But unauthorized immigration is a problem exacerbated by the breakdown in legal immigration law and policy. Simply put, America's immigration system is broken. As Michael Bloomberg notes, "reforming a broken immigration system is the single most important step the federal government could take to bolster the economy" (cited in Bush and Bolick 2013: 101). No realistic or lasting resolution of the unauthorized immigration problem can be achieved without a comprehensive reform of immigration law and policy. However, as previously noted, enacting comprehensive immigration reform is a public policy conundrum.

Congress has periodically attempted to reform immigration in a comprehensive way ever since the Immigration and Naturalization Act of 1965, only to amend the act at the margins. Especially since 2001, comprehensive immigration reform has become a toxic political issue.

Since 2007, the Republican Party has reached a near schism on the issue between the more business-oriented, establishment-wing of the party and the Tea Party Activist and Libertarian-leaning wing, as well as the grassroots of the party that today might best be called the Trump wing of the party. Senators John McCain (R-AZ) and Lindsey Graham (R-SC), who, in 2007, were among a Senate "Gang of Eight," co-sponsored bills with Democrats to comprehensively reform immigration policy. Since 2012, however, they have backed off that position. The Tea Party/Libertarian/Trump base of the party has labeled as amnesty what McCain and Graham called "earned legalization," which now most Republicans adamantly oppose. In short, on all immigration matters, the Republican Party has become the party of Trump. For a Republican member of congress to deviate from President Trump's position is to invite a primary challenge and is seen by most if not all Republican members as political suicide.

On the other hand, the progressive wing of the Democratic Party, including particularly the Hispanic Caucus, the Black Caucus, the Border States Caucus, and stalwarts of the liberal wing of the Democratic Party, exemplified by Senator Bernie Sanders (D-ME) and Elizabeth Warren (D-MA), have an entrenched position insisting that earned legalization and enactment of a Dream Act be included in any reform before they will support any immigration reform measure. The extreme partisan divide results in a stalemate on the issue.

What is most popular among Republicans today—a crackdown on illegal immigration through border control measures such as license laws and building the fence or a Southwestern border wall, as proposed by President Trump—makes for ineffective and inefficient policy, manifestly having cost billions of dollars with little or no impact on the rate of unauthorized immigration since 2001. Border control policy addresses "pull" factors influencing the unauthorized immigration flow. But the failed economies of Mexico and Central American countries like El Salvador, Honduras, and Guatemala and drug cartel-instigated violence in those countries underpin "push" factors. They are demonstrably more powerful influences on the migration flow than are any U.S. laws on the issue.

Events like the Arab Spring, the civil war in Syria, and the rise of ISIS in Iran and Iraq give rise to mass refugee movements, adding further pressure to the immigration issue. Foreign civil wars and domestic strife, often racially, ethnically, or religiously inspired, renew mass refugee movements compelling hundreds of thousands to millions to flee their nations of origin to migrate elsewhere. Such conditions affect both legal and unauthorized immigration flows, changing them in their overall size, composition, and origin (LeMay 2013: 70).

Other lobbying groups, like the "No More Deaths" organization, offer food, water, and medical aid to undocumented immigrants crossing the desert areas along the Mexican border on humanitarian grounds. They aim to reduce the number of deaths along the border that annually number several hundred. The Irish Lobby for Immigration Reform pushes for provisions that would benefit Irish immigrants (both legal immigrants and visa overstayers). Hispanic groups, like LULAC and LaRaza, push for an amnesty provision.

The "immigration problem" is acute in several states. In Florida, for example, the 2010 census found that among Miami's 2.6 million residents, 51 percent were foreign-born. The 2010 census estimates that among the total population, 42 million—just over 13 percent—were foreign-born residents (Bush and Bolick 2013: 139; LeMay 2013: 37; U.S. Census Bureau 2017). In June of 2002, Florida was the first state to get the 287 (g) Cross-Designation Program. It allowed state and local law enforcement to act on behalf of the federal law enforcement officials (ICE) (Bush and Bolick 2013: xi–xiii).

An attempt to pass comprehensive reform nearly succeeded in 2007, when then president George W. Bush advocated a comprehensive immigration reform bill sponsored by Senators John McCain and Ted Kennedy (D-MA). The legalization provision in the McCain-Kennedy bill, however, aroused such opposition among Republicans that President Bush was forced to stop pushing the legislation. Even Senator McCain, in an attempt to save his 2008 bid for the Republican presidential nomination, was likewise forced to withdraw his sponsorship. Although many business groups favored the plan, groups like the Minutemen opposed it, even forming vigilante groups along the Mexican border to stop illegal immigrants (*Denver Post* 2005). The National Conference of State Legislatures and the National Governors' Conference oppose any measure that does not include funding for state and local governments. They oppose what they maintain are unfunded mandates on states and localities (LeMay 2013: 70–71).

Senate Democrats introduced the Comprehensive Immigration Reform Act of 2011 (S. 1251), but Senate Republicans insisted on a filibuster-proof vote of 60, killing the bill, as it did a Dream Act measure.

A Republican-favored approach to more piecemeal immigration reform, using a crackdown approach to illegal immigration instead of a comprehensive approach, is well-exemplified by the Secure Communities program established by ICE in 2008. ICE prioritized the removal of public safety and homeland security threats, those who violated the nation's immigration laws (including those who failed to comply with a final order of removal), and those who engaged in fraud/willful misrepresentation with official government matters (i.e., used counterfeit fraudulent documents). The program uses a federal information-sharing partnership between DHS, the FBI, and state and local law enforcement to help identify in-custody unauthorized immigrants. Under the program, the

FBI automatically sends to DHS the fingerprints of individuals arrested and/or booked into custody by any state or local law enforcement agency to see if they have outstanding warrants so that the DHS can check those against its immigration databases. If such checks reveal that an individual in custody is unlawfully present in the United States or is otherwise removable, ICE takes enforcement action against violent or serious criminals, as well as those who have violated the nation's immigration laws (U.S. Immigration and Customs Enforcement 2018). In April 2018, President Trump issued an executive order that announced a "zero-tolerance" policy. President Trump, Attorney General Jeff Sessions, and the DOJ determined that even misdemeanor immigration-related infractions will be treated as "criminal actions" the same as are felonies. A consequence of that "zero-tolerance" policy, for nearly a month, resulted in the separation of an estimated 2,500 children from their parents if they entered the United States illegally, even those seeking asylum. The resulting political outcry over the policy, widely seen as immoral and an affront to basic American values, caused such political opposition, even among congressional Republicans, that President Trump was forced to initiate another executive order to keep and detain (for an indefinite period) such family members together until they have had an immigration asylum hearing. That second executive order, however, is unlikely to stand against federal court rulings on the issue without congressional authorization. Despite a hue and cry against family separation among members of Congress, it is unlikely that Congress will enact legislation on the matter.

ICE completed full implementation of Secure Communities to all 3,181 jurisdictions within the 50 states, D.C., and five U.S. territories on January 22, 2013. From its inception to its suspension, the Secure Communities program led to the removal of 315,200 criminal unauthorized immigrants. It was suspended during President Obama's second administration by order of Secretary of DHS, Jeh Johnson, on November 20, 2014.

The suspension lasted until January 25, 2017 (U.S. Immigration and Customs Enforcement 2018; Johnson 2014).

Secretary Johnson suspended the program in reaction to general hostility to it among governors, mayors, and state and local law enforcement officials around the country who had refused to cooperate with the program, and due to a number of federal court decisions that rejected the authority of state and local law enforcement agencies to detain immigrants pursuant to federal detainment orders issued by DHS. The suspension was also in response to recommendations of the Homeland Security Advisory Council Task Force. Secretary Johnson directed ICE to put in its place a program that relied on fingerprint-based biometrics, but ICE would only seek to transfer an unauthorized immigrant in the custody of state and local law enforcement when the unauthorized immigrant has been convicted of offenses listed under two priority lists, or when, in the judgment of an ICE field office director, they posed a threat to national security. In other words, unless an unauthorized immigrant posed a demonstrable homeland security risk, enforcement actions would only be taken against those who are convicted of the enumerated crimes. In response to a number of federal court decisions that held that detainee-based detention by state and local law enforcement agencies violates the Fourth Amendment, Secretary Johnson ordered ICE to replace requests for detention with requests for notification.

## Gerrymandering and the Immigration Reform Deadlock

The hyper-partisanship in Congress contributes to the decades-long deadlock of legislative action for immigration control. The degree of extreme partisanship is partially the result of gerrymandering. State legislatures draw lines to establish electoral districts, including congressional districts. They typically favor a major party to the detriment of the other major party and all minor-party candidates (Libertarian, Green Party, and so on). Gerrymandering serves to enhance the power and electoral advantage of incumbents. It is used today to dilute the votes of blacks and Hispanic voters or to concentrate power to benefit one political party.

The process is named after Elbridge Gerry, governor of Massachusetts in 1810, who drew a district in the shape of which reminded Boston journalists of a salamander. They put his name and the word "salamander" together to dub the district a gerrymander. The name stuck and now applies to any such oddly shaped district drawn to give an ethnic, racial, religious, partisan, or similar demographic advantage to one party or candidate. The practice is older than its name, however; for example, Patrick Henry designed Virginia's electoral districts in an unsuccessful attempt to foil the election of James Madison in 1788.

The present congressional districts were drawn after the 2010 election using data from the 2010 Census; the Republican Party came to power in a host of state legislatures. They drew lines to ensure that Republicans will remain in power in Congress until at least 2020 (when the next census occurs), unless courts act to invalidate district lines as they did in 2018 in Pennsylvania or unless there is a virtual revolution by voters (Stroupe 2009).

Scholars and federal courts have disputed how badly demographically skewed a district must be in order to be legally declared an unconstitutionally drawn gerrymandered district. Political parties in majority power in state legislatures continue to use the gerrymander effect, pushing the limits to pass muster with the Supreme Court or with challenges in federal district courts (Politics & Policy 2013).

The chance to gerrymander arises out of the once-a-decade reapportionment (to roughly achieve a "one-man, one-vote" balance) among districts. That rule of law was required by two watershed Supreme Court decisions. In *Baker v. Carr*

(369 U.S. 196, 82 S. Ct. 691, 1962), the Court decided that Tennessee's congressional districts were unconstitutionally apportioned after the state had failed to reapportion after several censuses. The ruling required state legislatures to redraw district lines every 10 years. In 1964, in *Reynolds v. Sims* (377 U.S. 533) the Supreme Court ruled that districts must be drawn close enough in population size to be as close as possible to "one-man, one vote." In drawing such lines, however, the legislators can dilute the opposition party's votes by cracking its voters into several districts, thereby making it more difficult to obtain a majority in any district, and packing its voters into unnecessarily safe districts and reducing the targeted party by reducing its ability to compete in the remaining districts (LeMay 2017: 105–108).

The Voting Rights Act of 1965 added racial considerations to political party registration into the mix. States began to manipulate concentrations of certain minorities (chiefly blacks, Hispanics, and, more recently and relevantly in some states, Asians), thereby changing the political landscape. Texas, for example, has used and still uses gerrymandering to dilute the votes of minorities (blacks and Hispanics especially), giving them less sway on immigration-related matters. On several occasions the Supreme Court has ruled unconstitutional such racially biased gerrymandering. The Republican-controlled legislature in Texas redistricted in 2003, instead of 2001, and drew districts that disproportionately diluted Hispanic and black votes. In 2006 the Supreme Court ruled the dilution to be in violation of the 1965 Voting Rights Act (LeMay 2017: 107). Because Texas has been racially gerrymandered for decades, the state has been a deeply "red" state, whose congressional delegation has been particularly opposed to immigration reform and is especially notably "anti-amnesty" in its voting on immigration legislation.

The states of Maryland and North Carolina are tied for the (dis)honor of being the most gerrymandered states. Using a gerrymandering rating system, they scored 88 out of a possible

100 average gerrymandering score. Republicans drew the congressional district boundaries in 6 out of the 10 most gerrymandered states, in part because of the wave election of 2010. The party's "Freedom Caucus" members have been especially anti-immigrant in their voting and do so on the basis of exceedingly "safe" districts. They are able to use the threat of running candidates in the Republican primary election against any incumbent member who fails to vote the party-line (Ingraham 2014).

Republicans have drawn a maximum number of "safe" seats for their party's congressional delegations. A 2012 study found that the Democrats were underrepresented by 18 seats in House of Representatives relative to their share of the 2012 congressional elections (Ingraham 2014).

Some states have attempted to deal with the gerrymandering problem by establishing nonpartisan special commissions to redraw district lines after every census year. Other states have given their state's courts (typically the state supreme court) the power to reapportion districts. But the practice is still done in many states to give incumbents safe seats, to advantage one party versus another, or to dilute the voters of third-party candidates. The currently disproportionately gerrymandered congressional district lines will not likely change until after the 2020 census, especially if it is another wave election (LeMay 2017: 108).

## Changes in Immigration Policy from the Obama to Trump Administrations

On taking office in 2016, President Trump immediately reversed President Obama's executive orders on immigration. He used his executive order powers to end the DACA and DAPA policies and ordered DOJ and DHS to crack down on illegal immigrants. He added presidential impetus to the Republican Party's desire to "control the borders." Trump issued Executive Order 13768, *Enhancing Public Safety in the Interior of the United States,* on January 25, 2017, which ordered his secretary of Homeland Security, John Kelly, to reinstate the Secure Communities program. From that date until the second quarter of FY 2017, 10,290 criminal unauthorized immigrants were removed via the Secure Communities program (U.S. Immigration and Customs Enforcement 2018).

Deportation hearings had backlogged during the Obama administration, which responded to the problem by suspending the Secure Communities program. With the Trump administration's renewal of the Secure Communities program, backlogs in deportation hearings rose again. President Trump's administration responded by shifting 100 immigration judges from elsewhere in DHS to hold deportation hearings at the Mexican border. Recently, the DOJ has requested the DOD to send Jag judges to the southern border to hold backlogged immigration and asylum hearing cases.

A number of solutions have been suggested to better cope with the problems discussed above. As Jeb Bush and Clint Bolick (2013) noted:

> Two thirds of Americans support a process by which illegal immigrants can obtain lawful status so long as they learn to speak English, pass background checks, and pay restitution. (Bush and Bolick 2013: 9)

They propose a provision within a comprehensive immigration reform act that they call "earned residency" (as opposed to the Democrats' "earned legalization"). Earned residency would provide a path to legal resident status as long as the unauthorized immigrants pay taxes, learn English, and have committed no substantial crimes (i.e., felonies). The legalizing unauthorized immigrants would have legal resident status, but it would not be amnesty nor would it be a short-cut path to citizenship (Bush and Bolick 2013: 40–47). Given Jeb Bush's lack of success in obtaining the Republican Party's nomination for president in 2016, losing to Donald Trump, one can reasonably assume his "earned residency" solution is not favorably received by the party's base voters.

Another often-used solution to the "control the border" problem has been to increase the size of the border patrol and to assign more agents to the Mexican border. The border patrol has been steadily increasing its number of agents, especially under DHS. In 2006 there were 11,000 agents. By 2009 there were 17,000. By 2016 the national total of border patrol agents stood at 19,828. Of those, 17,026 are assigned to the Southwest Border Sector, with only 2,059 to the Northern Border Sector (with Canada), and only 211 to the Coastal Border Sector (U.S. Customs and Border Patrol 2017). However, as seen in the previous chapter, such increases in Border Patrol agents have not resulted in commensurate reductions in unauthorized immigration.

Rather than building a wall, which they consider too costly and ineffective, Bush and Bolick recommend a combination of real and "virtual" fencing, aerial surveillance, increased border security staffing, and extending DHS authority to take security actions in the 50 national parks located within 100 miles of U.S. borders. They favor biometric identification, including use of DNA, iris scans, facial recognition, and voice imprints (Bush and Bolick 2013: 52). They also argue that enforcement-only, or secure-the-border first policy, is self-defeating. They note as DHS has cracked down, more undocumented unauthorized immigrants in the country are staying rather than returning to Mexico (Bush and Bolick 2013: 114).

Another "piecemeal" approach to better border control that has been tried, viewed as a stop-gap measure until more border agents could be approved, funded, hired, and trained, was to assign National Guard units to the Southwest Border Sector to assist the border patrol/DHS. The first such program was called "Operation Jump Start," in which 6,000 National Guard troops were ordered to the Mexican border by President George W. Bush and served there from 2006 to 2008. That approach was continued and expanded upon by President

Obama, in "Operation Phalanx," which in July 2010, began a six-month mission. It assigned 1,210 Army National Guard (ARNG) troops along the 1,933-mile southwest border to support the CBP. Their tasks included ground surveillance, criminal investigative analysis, command-and-control, mobile communications, transportation, logistics, and training support. Operation Phalanx used 12 National Guard helicopters and several fixed-wing aircraft to provide aerial operations to Operation River Watch II, which covered 200 miles of border from Laredo, Texas, to the Gulf Coast. They were credited with assisting in the apprehension of 17,900 undocumented immigrants from July 2010 to June 2011. However, the U.S. Government Accountability Office (GAO) warned that the use of National Guard troops at the border would hinder the guard's recruitment efforts and would fuel perception that the border is militarized, as well as hinder binational agreements between Mexico and the United States (King-Sweigart 2015; U.S. Army 2011; U.S. Customs and Border Patrol 2011).

## The Travel Ban Controversy

President Trump issued two executive orders imposing a travel ban that, given his campaign rhetoric and continued tweets, were widely viewed as "Muslim bans." The first ban stipulated a 90-day ban on immigration from seven Muslim-majority countries, blocked entry of Syrian refugees to the United States, and suspended for 120 days all entry through the Refugee Admissions Program. It favored admission of religious (i.e., Christian) minorities. Trump tweeted that Christians from the Middle East would be exempted from the ban. The order was immediately challenged in several federal courts. When acting attorney general Sally Yates refused to defend the order after determining that it was unconstitutional, President Trump summarily fired her. In mid-February, a judge of the Ninth Circuit Court of Appeals in Seattle, Washington, ruled that the ban was unconstitutional and halted its enforcement (Gonzales, Rose, and Kennedy 2017; Brunner, Lee, and Gutman 2017).

President Trump then issued a second travel ban that barred immigrants, including refugees, from six Muslim countries, dropping the language that favored religious minorities. Federal courts and judges in Hawaii and Maryland put an emergency hold on the second ban and issued a nationwide preliminary injunction of the travel ban. The DOJ appealed the decision to the U.S. Supreme Court, where DOJ lawyers argued that the executive order falls squarely within the president's lawful authority in seeking to protect national security. The Supreme Court partially upheld the second travel ban and exempted from the ban persons with previously approved visas, and persons with a bona fide connection, such as individuals who were "close family members," to a U.S. citizen or permanent resident alien (Powell 2017). The Supreme Court ruling included a long list of exemptions to the ban: green-card holders, those with approved visas for H-1B workers, F-1 students, J-1 exchange visitors, K-1 fiancés, L-1 intra-company executive managers, specialized transferees, O-1 extraordinary ability persons, P-1 performers, R-1 religious workers, and E-2 investors.

DOJ complicated matters further when it issued guidelines as to what constituted "close family ties," which excluded grandparents and other extended-family relatives. On July 15, Judge Derrick Watson issued a ruling interpreting the Supreme Court's June 21 decision. Judge Watson stated that common sense dictated that grandparents were the epitome of close family members. Attorneys for Hawaii offered the case of Ismail Elshikh, the imam of a Honolulu mosque, to demonstrate the "harm" the travel ban imposed on Hawaii citizens since the ban applied to his mother-in-law. Along with Hawaii, courts in Maryland and the state of Washington heard challenges to the new revised travel ban (Zapotosky 2017; Gonzales, Rose, and Kennedy 2017; Kendall and Meckler 2017).

In September 2017, the Trump administration issued a third version of the travel ban, adding two non-Muslim countries to the list of banned nations: North Korea and Venezuela. In April 2018 the administration removed a Muslim-dominant country from the list—Chad—after Chad improved "its identity-management and information sharing practices." On June 26, 2018, a solution to the travel ban controversy was reached when the Supreme Court, in a 5–4 opinion written by Chief Justice John Roberts, upheld the travel ban executive order as constitutional and within the president's broad executive powers to control entrance into the United States, based on the precedent set by the 1952 McCarren-Walter (LeMay 2018: 169). In the Court's decision, the five conservative justices determined that it did not constitute religious discrimination. It bans most people from Iran, Libya, Somalia, Syria, and Yemen (Colorado Springs *Gazette* 2018d).

## Business Needs versus Security Concerns in Visa Application Processing

Since 9/11 America has been turning its back on openness. . . . The result was that while the administration talked about balancing security and openness, almost all of its resources and effort went into time-consuming background checks on foreigners, new controls at the borders, and aggressive enforcement against anyone caught committing even the most minor infraction of the labyrinthine immigration regulations. (Alden 2008: 5, 9)

Business mogul and Microsoft founder Bill Gates observed that before 9/11 the United States was remarkably open to immigration. He noted that the visa application process, particularly for immigrants coming from our Western allied nations and for business purposes, was streamlined to attract "the best and the brightest" from abroad to infuse the American economy. He characterized America as an IQ magnet. The success of the United States in attracting the greatest talent helped the country to become a global innovation leader, enriching the culture and creating economic opportunity for all Americans (cited in Alden 2008: 49). As Alden so pointedly notes, "In an effort to keep out anyone who might again inflict such grievous harm, the United States is building a system of border controls that could rob it of much of what has made it such an impressive and successful country" (Alden 2008: 20). Amy Chua, in her book *Day of Empire*, asserts that "to pull away from its rivals on a global scale, a society must pull into itself and motivate the world's best and the brightest, regardless of ethnicity, religion, or background" (cited in Alden 2008: 21).

Prior to 9/11/2001, annually more than 10 million visa applications were processed by 843 consular officers in 230 visa-granting U.S. embassies and consulates around the world, averaging more than 1,000 visa interviews per day. After 9/11, such a pace became impossible. Applicants had to undergo a personal interview and security clearance, and security-related interviews doubled from 1.5 percent of applicants to 3 percent. Fareed Zakarian, editor of *Newsweek International*, notes that "every visa officer today lives in fear that he will let in the next Mohammad Atta. As a result, he is probably keeping out the next Bill Gates" (cited in Wucker 2006: 155).

From 1993 to 2001, non-immigrant visa applications (many for business-related travel) adjudicated by consular officers rose from 7 million per year to more than 10 million. U.S. State Department's consular affairs used a "visa express" program for Saudi Arabia. By 2006, the United States, the European Union, and the United Kingdom had negotiated problems with visa processing. It foiled a nascent plot by homegrown UK terrorists to detonate bombs on several transatlantic flights (Alden 2008: 238).

After 9/11, and the State Department and DHS clashed over the visa application program. The economic cost of strict immigration enforcement is still being measured. By 2006, one million people were waiting for the department to process their applications for permanent residency and created many problems for U.S. business, particularly technology companies.

In 2007, 53 of the State Department's consulates reported long waiting for visas to come to the United States (Alden 2008: 278–282). A new visa application program, dubbed "Visa Condor," slowed visa approval by months, and visa denials rose sharply, affecting short-term business travel. "Visa Mantis," a technology alert list, increased the volume of required security checks from 1,000 per year in 2000 to 20,000 in 2003. Business applications for temporary visas fell from over 6 million in FY2000 to 2.7 million in FY2003 (Wucker 2006: 156–157). It yet remains to be seen how the Trump administration's zero-tolerance immigration policy will impact business-related visa applications.

In the 1990s, one-third of Silicon Valley's scientific and engineering workforce were foreign-born immigrants, as were 40 percent of physical and life scientists in the U.S. educational and health services, and 25 percent of physical scientists in manufacturing (Alden 2008: 50). A 2016 report on Silicon Valley found that 71 percent of such employees were foreign-born, compared with around 50 percent in the San Francisco-Oakland-Hayward region. Silicon Valley remains the center of the tech universe. Many immigrant tech workers are employed under the controversial H-1B visa program—intended for specialty occupations—which has become a flashpoint in the fight over immigration. Opponents claim it allows foreigners to steal American jobs. In Seattle, Washington's tech industry, 63 percent are foreign-born (Colorado Springs *Gazette* 2018b).

The rush to get biometric requirements into use in an unrealistically short time created unnecessary friction when caution took precedence over common sense. This was a blow to entrepreneurial spirit in the United States and cost millions of dollars in lost business conferences, science meetings, and sporting competitions (Wucker 2006: 177–178). The demand for high-skilled workers soon outpaced the supply in the United States, as many of those "best and brightest" went, instead, to Australia, Canada, Ireland, New Zealand, and the United Kingdom.

A host of U.S. businesses report having trouble finding workers with the skills that they need. This trend resulted in another related problem—the stagnation of the flow of ideas (Bush and Bolick 2013: 71).

> America's problem is not immigration itself, but how immigration occurs—that is, whether people come desperately across the border or give up in disgust at the failure of our bureaucracy and laws, or whether they can reasonably expect that the United States will make it feasible for the workers we need to comply with its immigration laws and to welcome them into our society as they work hard to participate in the civic life of their adopted communities. (Wucker 2006: 231)

Business-related immigration, spurred by an entrepreneurial spirit, has a major impact on business start-ups, creating jobs for native-born citizens. Between 1996 and 2011, start-ups by the native-born *decreased* by 53 percent, but those by foreign-born *increased* by 50 percent (Bush and Bolick 2013: 83). Business-related immigration is especially linked to high-tech industries located in what Enrico Moretti describes as the "brain hubs" phenomenon (Moretti 2012). Every high-tech job in a metropolitan area produces 5 service jobs in the local economy, compared to 1.6 jobs created by every job in the traditional manufacturing sector (Bush and Bolick 2013: 91–92; Colorado Springs *Gazette* 2018c).

Solutions to the business-related immigration problem and controversy are essentially policies that redress the balance between the need for security and the needs of business and the U.S. economy. More than a dozen solutions have been suggested in the literature:

1. Create a National Border Administration to be comprised of the Coast Guard, Customs and Border Protection, Immigration and Citizenship Enforcement from the DHS,

and the inspection arm of the Department of Agriculture (Alden 2008: 141; Bush and Bolick 2013: 15; Wucker 2006: 227).

2. Recognize that creating a "zero-defects visa system," currently a goal of the philosophy of the Department of State's visa and consular affairs bureaucracy, is unrealistic. The United States lacks the technology to do it. The sheer size of the applicant pool makes it unlikely if not impossible. There are inadequate resources to achieve it (Alden 2008: 218–219).

3. Expand the guest-worker program linked to market demand (Bush and Bolick 2013: 27–28; Wucker 2006: 225).

4. Recognize that the risk of terrorism can only be managed, not eliminated. Sometimes the consequences to eliminate all risks are worse than learning how to live with them (Alden 2008: 291).

5. Establish a Western Hemisphere Travel Initiative (Alden 2008: 279). The United States has to get serious about once again encouraging good people to come to the United States (Alden 2008: 292).

6. Reverse the "brain drain" (Bush and Bolick 2013: 88–102).

7. Instead of focusing on what we are not, articulate what brings us together: a shared sense of faith and can-do optimism (Wucker 2006: 222).

8. Dream big again; stop blaming others for our problems and instead rely on our strengths (Wucker 2006: 223).

9. Eliminate congressional micromanagement. Allow immigration agencies to revise regulations on their own rather than legislating such changes (Wucker 2006: 226).

10. Reduce family reunification preference visas, such as adult sibling allotment, and increase preference numbers allotted to business-related immigration tied to the changing needs of the U.S. economy/job market. Family reunification

preferences now account for 63 percent of legal immigration (Wucker 2006: 227).

This solution would conform to President Trump's proposal in March 2018.

11. Enact major comprehensive immigration reform that works for our country instead of acting as a drag on the economy (Wucker 2006: 232).

12. Encourage "brain circulation" and the creation of industries that will provide jobs in immigrant-sending countries and create markets for U.S.-produced goods (Wucker 2006: 237).

13. Business needs to legally bring in the workers they need; but policy needs to establish and enforce significant financial penalties on those employers who circumvent immigration and labor laws (Wucker 2006: 232–234).

14. "Staple green-cards to the back of every diploma our universities issue to a foreign-born student" (Wucker 2006: 237).

## Adverse Economic Impact of Visa-Tightening Procedures

The fact that all of the terrorists involved in the 9/11 attacks had gotten nonimmigrant visas and entered the United States legally (i.e., as documented nonimmigrants) led to calls to reform and revise the visa system. Ambassador Mary Ryan, the Department of State's assistant secretary of state for Consular Affairs, which oversaw and implemented the visa application process, became a scapegoat for the failure to prevent the attacks (Alden 2008: 151–160).

A nonimmigrant seeks temporary entry into the United States for a specific purpose, and such individuals include the following: foreign government officials, visitors for business, visitors for pleasure (tourist), unauthorized immigrants in transit through the United States, treaty traders and investors, students, international representatives, temporary workers and trainees, representatives of foreign information media, exchange visitors, fiancé(e)s of U.S. citizens, intracompany transferees, NATO officials, religious workers, and some others. Most nonimmigrants can be accompanied or joined by spouses and unmarried minor (or dependent) children (U.S. Citizenship and Immigration Services 2018).

Immigrant visas are issued to persons seeking permanent resident immigrant status, which may or may not be subject to numerical limitations. Visas subject to numerical limitations are granted to persons qualifying for family-sponsored, employment-related, or diversity immigrant visas. Four categories of family-sponsored visa preferences include: unmarried sons and daughters and their children, spouses, and unmarried sons and daughters of legal permanent residents; then married sons and daughters of U.S. citizens and their spouses and children; then brothers and sisters of U.S. citizens ages 21 and over. There are five categories of employment-sponsored preferences: priority workers, professionals with advanced degrees or unauthorized immigrants of exceptional ability; skilled workers; professionals (without advanced degrees) and needed unskilled workers; special immigrants (ministers, religious workers, employees of the U.S. government abroad); and employment creation immigrants or "investors" (FindLaw 2018).

These visas may be issued to persons living abroad from a consular office of the Department of State; with the visa they may enter the United States and become legal immigrants when they pass through the port of entry (airport or seaport). The other path is for noncitizens already living in the country, including certain undocumented immigrants, temporary workers, foreign students, and refugees who file an application for adjustment of status—to legal permanent residence (LPR)—with the Bureau of Citizenship and Immigration Service (USCIS). They can also, at that time, file for work permits. New legal immigrants are automatically granted work permits (alien registration cards, or so-called green cards, which are now white) after becoming legal permanent residents (FindLaw 2018).

Problems and concerns developed with the visa application and processing as a result of the 9/11 attacks and the legislation induced by the attacks, such as the Patriot Acts, the creation of DHS, the Border Protection, Anti-Terrorism, and Illegal Immigration Act of 2005 (also known as the REAL ID Act) (LeMay 2015: 348–349). A number of programs with visa-complicating features were used to implement these laws, three of which are highlighted here: NSEERS, US-VISIT, and the Office of Biometric Identity Management. All of them resulted in visa application and processing backlogs, especially for nonimmigrant visas, that had a negative impact on the U.S. economy.

The National Security Entry-Exit Registration System (NSEERS) was a port-of-entry registration and departure registration requirement. It was the first of these visa control programs established after the 9/11 attacks (Alden 2008: 222–223; Wucker 2006: 144). It was applied to certain nonimmigrant visitors from Iran, Iraq, Sudan, Syria, Pakistan, Saudi Arabia, and Yemen. It further requires registration for nonimmigrants coming from any country (not just the seven specified Muslim-majority countries) if they are determined to meet criteria established by the secretary of DHS, if those individuals are referred to the DHS by State Department consular officers, or if the inspecting officer (at the port of entry) believes the unauthorized immigrants should be registered in the interest of law enforcement or national security. NSEERS-registered unauthorized immigrants were required to register their departure at a designated port (Immigration.com 2009). It was applied to temporary foreign visitors (nonimmigrants) from 25 countries listed by the attorney general as supporters and exporters of international terrorism and others who met a combination of intelligence-based criteria that identified them as potential security risks. By January 2005, individuals from 160 countries were registered on NSEERS (Alden 2008: 294; LeMay 2015: 27–28; Wucker 2006: 155–156).

US-VISIT replaced NSEERS and applied the procedures, including collection of some biometric data such as finger-printing, more generally to all nonimmigrants regardless of country of origin, beginning at the end of September 2004, when it expanded entry-exit procedures to include all visitors traveling to the United States under the Visa Waiver Program (VWP) who arrive at airports and seaports (U.S. Department of Homeland Security 2004; Alden 2008: 248–254, 294; Wucker 2006: 177).

US-VISIT was established in compliance with several laws requiring that DHS create an integrated, automated entry-exit system that records the arrival and departure of unauthor-ized immigrants (to address the problem of visa overstayers), deploys equipment (e.g., 10-point fingerprint readers) at all ports of entry to verify identities and authenticate their travel documents through comparison with biometric identifiers, and utilizes an entry-exit system that records unauthorized immigrant arrival and departure information from those bio-metrically authenticated documents. It is based on four acts of Congress: (1) the Illegal Immigration and Reform Act of 1996, (2) the Immigration and Naturalization Service Data Management Improvement Act of 2000, (3) the USA PA-TRIOT Act of 2001, and (4) the Enhanced Border Security and Visa Entry Reform Act of 2001 (U.S. Department of Homeland Security 2004).

In March 2013, DHS established the Office of Biometric Identity Management (OBIM), within its National Protec-tion and Programs Directorate. OBIM supports the DHS's responsibility to protect the nation by providing biometric identification that helps federal, state, and local governments to accurately identify persons they encounter to determine whether or not such persons pose a risk to the United States. OBIM operates and maintains IDENT—an automated bio-metric identification system that is used to match, store, analyze, and share biometric data. It is used by USCIS, U.S. Coast Guard, USCBP, ICE, TSA, and the intelligence community, DOJ, DOS, DOD, state and local law enforcement, and various international partners.

Developments with each of these programs and procedures between 2002 and 2013 have improved the biometric data used and the technology to catch, store, match, and analyze that data, as they were introduced and implemented. Each of the programs caused delays and backlogs in visa processing for both those seeking permanent residency status (legal immigrants) and especially for nonimmigrants (temporary visas of various types). Those delays and an increased number of disapprovals resulted in millions of dollars lost to the U.S. economy. Waiting time to get interviews for visa applications can take months for those coming from some countries, and security background checks for green cards and citizenship applications are measured in years rather than months (Alden 2008: 11–14; Bush and Bolick 2013: 91–101; Wucker 2006: 177–178).

There are no easy solutions to the problems and costs to the U.S. economy caused by the tightening of the visa process for security purposes. The sheer volume of visa applications for permanent immigration and especially for nonimmigrant visas inevitably causes backlogs resulting from increased security concerns. The problem is being eased somewhat as biometric technology is improved and implemented. Three additional "solutions" that have been proposed are highlighted here: the Smart Border Partnership Action Plan, the Start Up Visa Act, and a guest worker program geared to market demand wherein the guest workers would be prescreened in their country of origin.

The Smart Border Action Plan has been in negotiation with Mexico and Canada since 2002 and has entailed 22 to 30 points in an agreement between the country sending immigrants (Mexico or Canada) and the United States. (Alden 2008: 132; U.S. Department of State 2002). A number of points pertain to increased infrastructure security: (1) developing long-term planning to secure coordinated physical and technological infrastructure with growing cross-border traffic; (2) relief for bottlenecks; (3) infrastructure protection—conducting vulnerability assessment of transborder communication and transportation networks in need of protective measures; (4) harmonizing port-of-entry traffic flow on both sides of the border; (5) demonstration proposals—establish "prototype" smart port-of-entry operations; (6) increased cross-border cooperation and mechanisms between local, state, and federal levels with a focus on operations at border crossing points; and (7) financing projects at the border by exploring joint financing mechanisms to meet development and infrastructure needs.

Several points pertain to the secure flow of people: (1) pre-cleared travelers by expanding the Secure Electronic Network for Rapid Inspection (SENTRI) of dedicated commuter lanes at high-volume ports between borders; (2) establishing joint advanced passenger information on relevant flights; (3) NAFTA travel—exploring methods to facilitate the movement of NAFTA travelers, including dedicated lanes at high-volume airports; (4) safe borders and deterrence of unauthorized immigrant smuggling—reaffirm mutual commitment to the Border Safety Initiative and develop cooperation to enhance authorities and specialized institutions to assist, save, and advise migrants as well as those specialized on curbing the smuggling of people by expanding the Alien Smuggling and Trafficking Taskforce; (5) visa policy consultations—increasing frequency of consultations on visa policies and visa-screening procedures and share information from relevant consular databases; (6) joint training in the areas of investigation and document analysis to enhance ability to detect fraudulent documents and break up smuggling rings; (7) developing a system of compatible databases to share intelligence; and (8) enhancing efforts to detect, screen, and take appropriate measures to deal with potential dangerous third-country nationals and taking into consideration the threats they represent to security (Alden 2008: 132; U.S. Department of State 2002).

The Start Up Visa Act of 2011 (S.565, 112th Congress) was a bill to establish an employment-based visa for unauthorized immigrant entrepreneurs who have received significant capital from investors to establish a business in the United States. Then senator John Kerry (D-MA) sponsored the bill, which, among other provisions, has an amendment that directs DHS to terminate the status of sponsored entrepreneurs (and their spouses and children, if any) if, after three years, they fail to meet investment requirements or fail to meet job creation, capital investment, or revenue requirements (Bush and Bolick 2013: 27).

Finally, a guest worker program has been proposed that is geared to market demand and which would have the guest workers be prescreened in the country of origin (Bush and Bolick 2013: 27; Wucker 2006: 224–234). The 2018 Omnibus budget bill of March 23, 2018, provides for adding as many as 63,000 additional H-2B workers above the 2017 statutory cap of 66,000. H-2B workers are temporary, unskilled nonagriculture workers, mainly used in landscaping, grounds keeping workers, and maids and housekeeping cleaners. In FY 2016 there were 119,232 H-2B workers certified and who earned on average $12.31 per hour. In 2017 there were 133,985 H-2B workers certified, and they earned an hourly wage on average of $13.08 (Huennekens and Griffith 2018).

## The Impact of Federal, State, and Local Government Relations

Immigration policy making and implementation is complicated by the fact that the United States has a federal system of government. Immigration policy making is one of many policy areas that illustrate the problems and concerns that emerge from the devolution of policy implementation. Devolution is the transfer or delegation of powers to a lower level, for example, by a central government to local or regional administration (Udani 2013: 151–172). The devolution of policy to state and local governments impacts the inclusion of immigrants and immigrant groups. Inclusion has been defined as an individual's or group's engagement with the processes or organizations that recognize the individual or group by conferring membership or by providing resources such as entitlements or protections. It provides a sense of security, stability, and predictability, understood primarily as an ability to plan for the future (Cook 2013).

With respect to immigration policy, a considerable degree of devolution has taken place since the establishment of the DHS: 49 states, 4 territories and 6 tribal areas have established their own state departments or offices of homeland security (Homeland Security Digital Library 2018).

This section briefly discusses two concerns that illuminate the relationship between the national level of government (and particularly the DHS) and state and local governments: the Secure Communities program and the sanctuary movement (U.S. Immigration and Customs Enforcement 2018; Huennekens and Griffith 2018).

State and local governments vary considerably in their willingness to cooperate with federal law enforcement since some policing powers were devolved in 1996, with the enactment of the Illegal Immigration Reform and Immigrant Responsibility Act (IIRIA) signed into law by President Clinton on September 30 (Pub. L. No. 104–208). Based on a provision in the 1996 law, the Secure Communities program was launched in 2008. It identified unauthorized immigrants for removal by checking the fingerprints of the persons arrested or booked in custody by local authorities (Suro 2015: 117). Secure Communities ran from 2008 to 2014, when it was canceled by President Obama. It was reactivated on January 25, 2017, by executive order of President Trump. The program assists ICE's enforcement priorities for those unauthorized immigrants detained in the custody of another law enforcement agency. It employs an information-sharing partnership between DHS and the FBI that helps identify in-custody unauthorized immigrants without imposing new or additional requirements on state and local enforcement. Under Secure Communities, the FBI automatically sends the fingerprints to DHS to be checked against its immigration database. If the checks reveal that an individual is unlawfully present or is otherwise removable, ICE takes enforcement action. It prioritizes the removal of individuals who are deemed the most significant threats to public safety, determined by the severity of their crime, their criminal history, their risk to public safety, and those who have previously violated immigration laws (U.S. Immigration and Customs Enforcement 2018). ICE enforcement of the Secure Communities program is likely to be impacted (enhanced) by the DOJ's "zero-tolerance" policy, which would also apply to any and all immigrants who have committed any illegal action, even misdemeanor or minor infractions of immigration laws rather than prioritizing violent or felony acts.

ICE completed full implementation of the Secure Communities program to all jurisdictions within the 50 states, the District of Columbia, and the five U.S. territories by January 2013. As stated, the program was suspended by the DHS under Secretary Jeh Johnson, by an executive order in November 2014. President Obama's order stated that DHS should focus on deportation of "felons, not families" (Suro 2015: 118). Secretary Johnson promulgated new priorities by Memorandum to the acting director of ICE, the director of the Office of Civil Rights and Civil Liberties within DHS, and to the assistant secretary for Intergovernmental Affairs.

A number of state and local governments had already taken actions to neutralize federal regulations under the Secure Communities program. For example, in October 2014, the Catholic Legal Immigration Network noted that 3 states, 26 cities (which they called sanctuary cities), 233 counties, and the District of Columbia had restricted their cooperation (CLINIC 2014; Suro 2015: 118).

The suspension of Secure Communities under the Obama administration lasted until January 15, 2017, when President

Trump, by Executive Order 13768, *Enhancing Public Safety in the Interior of the United States*, directed the new secretary of Homeland Security, John Kelly, to reinstitute the program. DHS rescinded all of the Obama Executive Order procedures and within six months had removed more than 10,000 convicted criminal unauthorized immigrants under the newly reinstated Secure Communities program. Under all its years of operation (2008–2017), Secure Communities removed more than 315,000 criminal unauthorized immigrants (U.S. Immigration and Customs Enforcement 2018).

"Sanctuary city" is a name given to any city in the United States that follows certain procedures that shelter unauthorized immigrants. These procedures can be by law (de jure) or by action (de facto). The designation of sanctuary city has no legal meaning. The term is commonly used for cities that do not permit municipal funds or resources (e.g., police officers) to be applied in furtherance of enforcement of federal immigration laws, viewed by the municipality as an unfunded mandate. They do not allow police or municipal employees to inquire about one's immigration status (Griffith and Vaughan 2017).

Sanctuary cities are part of a broader sanctuary movement that goes back to the 1980s, when churches sheltered unauthorized immigrants from Central America (El Salvador, Honduras, and Guatemala) who were seeking asylum in the United States (Coutin 1993; Lippert 2005). The concept of sanctuary cities is deeply embedded in Western tradition, going back to biblical times. The 1980s' sanctuary movement put church and state in conflict over the fate of Central Americans fleeing civil wars, drug and gang-related violence, and who were thereby pleading for asylum. The Reagan administration, like the Trump administration today, was reluctant to grant asylum to Central Americans (and today especially Mexicans), claiming they were economic refugees, not political refugees with legitimate "fear of persecution" in their homelands. Few were granted asylum. For example, in 1984, less than 3 percent of Central Americans were given asylum, as opposed to Poles fleeing communism, who were 10 times more likely to find asylum in the United States. Iranians fleeing the Ayatollah regime were 20 times more likely to be granted asylum than were Central American applicants. An estimated 2,000 refuge seekers were aided by churches in the sanctuary movement during the 1980s (Haberman 2017).

The movement has revived and spread since the inauguration of President Donald Trump and his appointment of Jeff Sessions as attorney general. AG Sessions led DOJ's campaign against sanctuary cities by threatening to cut off federal funding. He announced on July 26, 2017, that cities and states would lose millions of dollars in federal grants unless they began cooperating with immigration agents (Yee and Ruiz 2017).

Cities have fought back in U.S. courts. Judge William Orrick of the U.S. district court in San Francisco temporarily blocked the Trump administration from withholding funding over sanctuary policies. The city attorney for San Francisco sued the administration, arguing that the policy of withholding funding violated the Constitution. AG Sessions ruled that to receive grants for local law enforcement, local governments had to agree to allow federal immigration agents access to their jails and to provide 48 hours' notice before releasing immigrants who DOJ or DHS authorities wanted to be detained for immigration violations. Depending upon how one defines a sanctuary city, there are hundreds of cities, counties, and states that are at least informally associated with the movement (Griffith and Vaughan 2017).

Many local officials oppose the announced policy, arguing that separating local law enforcement from federal immigration authorities is good policy both from a legal standpoint and from a public safety standpoint. That separation of local law enforcement departments from federal agencies like DOJ and DHS means that immigrants are more likely to come forward to report crimes and to serve as witnesses. New York's commissioner of immigration affairs holds that the concept of withholding federal funding that promotes public safety is counterproductive (Yee and Ruiz 2017).

The solution to these problems may likewise be twofold. On the one hand, the federal government could induce more participation in the revived Secure Communities program by offering greater financial support and by offering more training to local governments who agree to participate (i.e., addressing the unfunded mandate concern). On the other hand, federal courts may resolve the sanctuary city issue by ruling at the appeals level, or even at the Supreme Court level—less likely, however, given its current makeup—on the constitutionality of DOJ's policy to withhold funding to sanctuary cities. At the very least, the federal courts may clarify the legal definition of what constitutes a sanctuary city.

## The Brain Drain Problem

"Brain drain" is a term that refers to a significant emigration of talented individuals from lesser developed to developed countries. Emigration may be "pushed" by turmoil within a country or may be "pulled" by better professional opportunities in other countries, drawing those seeking a better standard of living. Brain drain causes countries, industries, and organizations to lose valuable professionals: doctors, scientists, engineers, computer scientists, and financial professionals. Such emigration affects the nation of origin in two ways: expertise is lost, diminishing the supply of professionals, and the country's economy is harmed as each professional represents surplus spending units. They earn larger salaries, so their departure removes significant consumer spending from the country of origin. According to a World Bank study, in the last decade, the largest numbers of highly educated migrants are from Europe, Southern and Eastern Asia, and Central America. In terms of a proportion of the potential educated labor force, the highest brain drain rates are in the Caribbean, Central America, and Western and Eastern Africa (Gibson and McKenzie 2011).

The United States has a long tradition of benefiting from the brain drain phenomenon. Foreign students studying in the United States rose from 50,000 in 1980 to 600,000 by the year 2000, when nearly 40 percent of the doctorates in science and engineering and 30 percent of master's degree were held by foreign-born students. In mathematics, computer science, and physical and life sciences, 60 percent of postdoctoral students doing research were foreign-born. One-third of America's Nobel Prize winners were foreign-born, and between 1990 and 2001, 50 percent of the Nobel Prize winners in the United States were foreign-born (Alden 2008: 50, 188–189).

The openness of the United States to immigration, and how much the nation benefited from the brain drain flow, changed after 9/11 and the enactment of the USA PATRIOT Act. DHS initiated the Student and Exchange Visitor Information System (SEVIS). SEVIS had been approved in 1996 but was not implemented until after the attacks (for a summary of the 1996 law, see LeMay and Barkan 1999: 304–310). SEVIS requires regular reporting by educational institutions on the enrollment status of their international students (Alden 2008: 200–202; LeMay 2013: 84; Middelstadt et al. 2011). The electronic monitoring system was rushed to implementation, and bugs in the system led to backlogs and protracted delays in correcting the data for months at a time. SEVIS produced 1,000 alerts each week, and between 2003 and 2005, 81,000 students were tagged as potential violators of the SEVIS program (Wucker 2006: 160–161). The Institute of International Education reported foreign student enrollment declined by 46 percent in 2002–2003, whereas it rose by 23 percent in the United Kingdom, by 15 percent in Canada, and by 10 percent in Australia. Between 2001 and 2004, Chinese students attending U.S. graduate schools dropped by 45 percent, and those coming from the Middle East dropped by 50 percent. America's loss was other countries' gain: especially Australia, Canada, Ireland, New Zealand, and the United Kingdom (Alden 2008: 212–213). A National Science Foundation study noted that foreign doctoral students from China, India, and Taiwan dropped dramatically (Wucker 2006: 161–164). The United States is experiencing much greater competition from

Canada, China, the European Union, Japan, and South Korea for highly talented immigrants. Europe and Asia, as of 2010, now produce more science and engineering PhDs than does the United States. By 2020, the United Kingdom is expected to triple its international student enrollment. India, Singapore, and Hong Kong are "knowledge centers" in information technology (IT). In 1975, the United States held 75 percent of all global science and engineering degrees. That number soon fell to 15 percent (Wucker 2006: 189–191).

"Visa Mantis," a technology alert list, increased dramatically the volume of required security checks from 1,000 per year in 2000 to 20,000 such checks in 2003 (Wucker 2006: 156). The United States must now seriously compete with other countries for highly talented immigrants and the needed skills they bring (Bush and Bolick 2013: 71; Wucker 2006: 195). For the first time in its modern history, the United States began to experience a negative brain drain flow.

The negative brain drain flow accelerated after the election of President Trump, whose nationalist-populist animosity toward immigration created unintended consequences. Tech workers who would have otherwise sought opportunities in Silicon Valley are starting to seek such opportunities in Mexico, China, and elsewhere overseas. President Trump signed an executive order for a government review of H-1B visas for foreign workers, which makes it harder for U.S. companies to get tech talent. Even workers already in the United States are being wooed by countries such as Canada, hoping to capitalize on the H-1B visa mess. Canada launched a new visa program called Global Skills Strategy, which makes it easier to recruit highly skilled foreign workers. Whereas in the United States, approval waits are for months, in Canada, they are approved for a visa in just two weeks. Canada launched another tech recruitment program, Go North, in 2016. It is aimed at Canadian ex-pats who had settled in Seattle and San Francisco's Bay Area. Canada has 71,000 tech companies, which comprise 5.6 percent of their total employment. President Trump complained that three-quarters of engineers in Silicon Valley are not Americans. Canada and China have jumped to attract them. After President Trump announced U.S. withdrawal from the Paris climate accord in June 2017, French president Emmanuel Macron called on U.S. climate scientists, engineers, and other innovates to seek refuge in France. Macron launched a Web site, "Make Our Planet Great Again," encouraging them to emigrate. India IT companies plan to double their operations in Mexico as the United States makes it more difficult for Indians to get H-1B visas (Kosoff 2017).

Solutions to this growing negative brain drain from the U.S. economy have been proposed. The Start Up Visa Act, previously discussed, is one such response. Another action would be making student visas plentiful and readily accessible again, as would a guest worker program for highly skilled workers geared to market demand. In STEM fields (science, technology, engineering, and mathematics), foreign students should be entitled to work-based visas for jobs in those fields (Bush and Bolick 2013: 26–28).

Another suggested solution is to develop and enact a carefully designed guest worker program that balanced promoting integration into the U.S. economy and society with a program of "brain circulation" of those skilled workers back to their homelands, providing jobs in migrant-sending countries and increasing markets for U.S. goods. Michelle Wucker suggests that the United States "staple green cards to the back of every diploma our universities issue to a foreign-born student" (Wucker 2006: 237).

## Immigration Concerns and Their Impact on Social Security

There has been ongoing controversy as to the costs versus the benefits of immigration, particularly unauthorized immigration, and especially when those costs versus benefits are projected into the future. What the analyst finds depends very much upon the assumptions used in the study or for the projections. There is less such controversy, however, in measuring the impact of immigration on the Social Security system. Analysis by the Social Security administration, by the Labor Department, by the Congressional Budget Office, by the Center on Budget and Policy Priorities, and by the Rand Corporation have all found that the impact of both legal and unauthorized immigration on the Social Security system and its Trust Fund to be positive overall, even projecting the effect out to 75 years (Van De Water 2008; Clift 2014; Dewan 2013).

Opponents of immigration reform argue that unauthorized immigrants do not contribute their fair share in taxes and drain government benefits. However, government economists with the Congressional Budget Office and Social Security actuaries, as well as think-tank analysis, like that of the Center on Budget and Policy Priorities, find that undocumented workers help to keep the Social Security trust fund in the black because they are paying into the system, typically with false Social Security numbers, which means they will never collect benefits. Their contributions, collected over many years by their employers, help keep the system solvent and benefits flowing for aging baby boomers (Van De Water 2008; Clift 2014). When the U.S. Senate passed a comprehensive immigration bill in 2013, the Social Security administration studied the likely effect of the proposed law's legalization program. The study concluded that if passed and implemented, it would add $276 billion in revenue over 10 years, while adding only $33 billion in costs. Its chief actuary projected that even 75 years out, there would be a net gain from immigrants because their withdrawals will be offset by their children's contributions. High-skilled workers pay in more than they get out, and in recent years, high-skilled workers have comprised a larger percentage of all immigrants, legal and unauthorized (particularly considering visa overstayers). Economists specializing in labor market economics agree that more immigration is better in terms of its effect on Social Security. In projecting immigrant impact into the future, two pools must be considered: those who are already here as unauthorized immigrants, about a third of who pay Social Security taxes, and the additional legal immigrants who will come. The Center for American Progress, a supporter of immigration reform, estimates that if 70 percent of illegal immigrants are legalized, they will contribute a net $500 billion in 36 years, the period that baby boomers will put a strain on the system (Dewan 2013).

Labor Department economists who studied the effect of comprehensive immigration reform projected that the benefits are even greater when looked at on a longer horizon. The Social Security administration estimated that in 2010 illegal immigrants paid a net contribution of $12 billion. If such immigrants gained legal status, they would contribute on balance even more, according to the director of the National Immigration Law Center. In general, researchers conclude that increases in immigration will improve the financial status of Social Security and that decreases in immigration will worsen it (Van De Water 2008).

To the extent that these economists' estimates are accurate, the current crackdown on immigration, both legal and unauthorized, as advocated by the Trump administration will adversely affect the Social Security Trust Fund. That adverse impact on both the U.S. economy and the Social Security system will be greater if, as happened over the past decade, a greater number of high-skilled workers who are already here opt to leave or if such immigrants not yet here decide to immigrate elsewhere, as previously discussed in the brain drain section.

Another notable impact of immigration on the economy is the fact that immigrants have a higher percentage of participation in the labor market than do native-born citizens. This reflects demographic aspects of the immigrant population. They come during their prime working ages. They tend to have more children than do the native-born. The effect of increased birth rates and higher labor market participation have a positive effect on the financial status of Social Security, resulting from an increase in payroll tax collections and more years of contributing to the fund before withdrawing benefits (Van De Water 2008).

Enacting comprehensive immigration reform is an obvious solution to the concern with the negative impact on the Social Security system because of decreased immigration. Although an obvious solution, it is not a politically likely solution, particularly given the policy priorities of the Trump administration.

## Conclusion

The problems, controversies, and possible solutions discussed here may enable planning for better immigration policy making and implementation in the future. Groupthink aspects in the rush to establish the DHS under a decidedly "crisis" atmosphere led to a number of unanticipated consequences. The behemoth size of DHS entailed management problems that have plagued the department for more than a decade, impacting all of its operations, but as we have seen, especially those related to immigration. The mission complexity associated with merging 22 agencies continues to make effective and efficient policy implementation a goal difficult to achieve. There is an ongoing tension between the perceived needs for security with traditional values of civil liberties and privacy rights. Comprehensive immigration reform presents a policy conundrum that exacerbates problems associated with a broken immigration system. The travel ban controversy of the Trump administration embroils the government in ongoing conflict between the administration and the federal court system. Analysts suggest, moreover, that the ban will not really do anything to increase security. Post-9/11 concerns have resulted in visa-processing changes that have negatively affected businesses and adversely impacted the U.S. economy, as has the tightening of visitors' visas. The U.S. federal system of government is a structural arrangement which limits the power of government, especially that of the federal government. It complicates the relationship between the national government and its bureaucracies with those of the state and local levels of government, as illustrated by the Secure Communities program and by the conflicts and controversies associated with the sanctuary movement. Until the 9/11 attacks, the United States greatly benefited from a brain drain flow. That flow has shifted markedly since 2001. Immigration policy concerns about how the national government administers policy to enhance national security contributed to a growing competition from other advanced-nation economies for highly talented migrants. Finally, the chapter examined the impact of immigration on the Social Security system and how immigration policy concerns have impacted the immigration flow that portends a long-term negative impact on the financial stability of the Social Security system and on the U.S. economy.

## References

ACLU. 2018. "National Security." https://www.aclu.org/issues/national-security.

Alden, Edward. 2008. *The Closing of the American Border.* New York: Harper Collins.

Browning, Rufus P., Dale Rogers Marshall, and David H. Tabb. 2003. *Protest Is Not Enough*. 3rd ed. London/New York: Pearson Press.

Brunner, Jim, Jessica Lee, and David Gutman. 2017. "Judge in Seattle Halts Trump's Immigration Order Nationwide; White House Vows Fight." *Seattle Times*, February 3, 2017. https://www.seattletimes.com/seattle-news/politics/federal-judge-in-seattle-halts-trumps-immigration-order/.

Bush, Jeb, and Clint Bolick. 2013. *Immigration Wars: Forging an American Solution.* New York: Simon and Schuster.

Clift, Eleanor. 2014. "How Immigrants Will Save Social Security." *Daily Beast*, November 29, 2014. https://www.thedailybeast.com/how-immigrants-will-save-social-security.

CLINIC. 2014. "State and Localities that Limit Compliance with ICE Detainer Requests." *State and Local Immigration Project.* Washington, D.C.: Catholic Legal Immigration Network, Inc.

Colorado Springs *Gazette.* 2018a. "Sanctuary Law Raises Some Issues." March 15, 2018, A-10.

Colorado Springs *Gazette.* 2018b. "Immigrants Bulk of Tech Workforce, Report Says." January 22, 2018, B-5.

Colorado Springs *Gazette.* 2018c. "Curbing Immigration Could Hurt U.S." February 27, 2018, B1–B3.

Colorado Springs *Gazette.* 2018d. "Travel Ban Upheld; Ruling Exacerbates U.S. Divisions." June 27, 2018, A-11.

Cook, Maria Lorena. 2013. "Incorporation of Unauthorized Immigrants Possible? Inclusion and Contingency for Nonstatus Migrants and Legal Immigrants." In *Outsiders No More? Models of Immigrant Political Incorporation,* edited by Hochschild, Jennifer, Jacquiline Chattpahdyay, Claudine Gay, and Michael Jones-Correa, 43–64. Oxford: Oxford University Press.

Coutin, Susan Bibler. 1993. *The Culture of Protest: Religious Activism and the U.S. Sanctuary Movement.* Boulder: Westview Press.

*Denver Post.* 2005. "1,000 Activists to Patrol Border for Migrants." March 1, 2005, A-6.

DeSipio, Louis. 2006. "Latino Civic and Political Participation." In *Hispanics and the Future of America,* edited by Maria Tienda and Faith Mitchell, 447–479. Washington, D.C.: National Research Council.

Dewan, Shaila. 2013. "Immigration and Social Security." *New York Times,* July 2, 2013. https://economix.blogs.nytimes.com/2013/07/02/immigration-and-social-security.

Etzioni, Amitai, and Jason H. Marsch, eds. 2003. *Rights vs. Public Safety after 9/11: America in the Age of Terrorism.* Lanham, MD: Rowman and Littlefield.

FindLaw. 2018. "Immigrant and Non-Immigrant Visa Types." https://immigration.findlaw.com/visas/immigrant-and-non-immigrant-visa-types.html.

Gerstle, Gary, and John Mollenkopf, eds. 2001. *E Puribus Unum? Contemporary and Historical Perspectives on Immigrant Political Incorporation.* New York: Russell Sage.

Gibson, John, and David J. McKenzie. 2011. "Eight Questions about Brain Drain World Bank Policy Research Working Paper No. 5668." *SSRN.* https://ssrn.com/abstract=1852081.

Gonzales, Richard, Rose, Joel, and Kennedy, Merit. 2017. "Trump Travel Ban Blocked Nationwide by Federal Judges in Hawaii, Maryland." *NPR*, March 15, 2017. https://www.npr.org/sections/thetwo-way/2017/03/15/520171478/trump-travel-ban-faces-court-hearings-by-challengers-today.

Government Accountability Office. 2002. *Alien Smuggling: Management and Operational Improvements Needed to Address Growing Problem.* Washington, D.C.: U.S. Government Printing Office.

Government Accountability Office. 2003. *Homeland Security: DHS Is Taking Steps to Enhance Security at Chemical Facilities, but Additional Authority Is Needed.* GAO-06–150. Washington, D.C.: U.S. Government Printing Office.

Government Accountability Office. 2006. *Overstay Tracking: A Key Component of Homeland Security and a Layered Defense.* GAO-04–82. Washington, D.C.: Government Printing Office.

Griffith, Bryan, and Jessica M. Vaughan. 2017. "Maps: Sanctuary Cities, Counties, and States." Center for Immigration Studies, July 27, 2017. https://cis.org/Map-Sanctuary-Cities-Counties-and-States.

Haberman, Clyde. 2017. "Trump and the Battle Over Sanctuary in America." *New York Times*, March 5, 2017.

https://www.nytimes.com/2017/03/05/us/sanctuary-cities-movement-1980s-political-asylum.html.

Haynes, Wendy. 2004. "Seeing Around Corners: Crafting the New Department of Homeland Security." *The Review of Policy Research* 21, no. 3 (May): 369–396.

Homeland Security Digital Library. 2018. "Government Homeland Security Offices." http://www.hsdl.org/?collection&id=1176.

Huennekens, Preston, and Bryan Griffith. 2018. "Maps: Impact of H-2B Guest Workers in 2017." Center for Immigration Studies, April 2, 2018. https://cis.org/Report/Maps-Impact-H2B-Guest-Workers-2017.

Immigration.com. 2009. "National Security Entry-Exit Registration System (NSEERS)." October 26, 2009. https://www.immigration.com/visa/general-nonimmigrant-visa/national-security-entry-exit-registration-system-nseers.

Ingraham, Christopher. 2014. "America's Most Gerrymandered Congressional Districts." *Washington Post*, May 15, 2014. https://www.washingtonpost.com/news/wonk/wp/2014/05/15/americas-most-gerrymandered-congressional-districts/?utm_term=.827d22db9b5b.

Janis, Irving. 1982. *Groupthink: Psychological Studies of Policy Decisions and Fiascoes.* 2nd ed. Boston: Houghton-Mifflin.

Johnson, Jeh. 2014. "Policies for the Apprehension, Detention, and Removal of Undocumented Immigrants." *Memorandum. U.S. Department of Homeland Security,* November 20, 2014. https://www.dhs.gov/publication/policies-apprehension-detention-and-removal-undocumented-immigrants.

Kayyem, Juliette N. 2003. "The Homeland Security Muddle." *The American Prospect* 14, no. 10 (November): 46–49.

Kendall, Brent, and Laura Meckler. 2017. "Trump Appeals Latest Travel-Ban Ruling." *Wall Street Journal,* July 14,

2017. https://www.wsj.com/articles/trump-appeals-latest-travel-ban-ruling-1500072777.

King-Sweigart, Angela. 2015. "Pennsylvania Guard Soldiers Depart for Southwest Border Support Mission." *U.S. Army*, January 6, 2015. https://www.army.mil/article/140752/pennsylvania_guard_soldiers_depart_for_southwest_border_support_mission.

Kosoff, Maya. 2017. "Silicon Valley's Trump Brain Drain Continues." *Vanity Fair*, July 5, 2017. https://www.vanityfair.com/news/2017/07/silicon-valleys-trump-brain-drain-continues.

Kowert, Paul. 2002. *Groupthink or Deadlock: When Do Leaders Learn from Their Advisors?* Albany, NY: SUNY Press.

Krauss, Elishia. 2003. "Building a Bigger Bureaucracy: What the Department of Homeland Security Won't Do." *The Public Manager* 32, no. 1 (Spring): 57–59.

LeMay, Michael. 2006. *Guarding the Gates: Immigration and National Security.* Westport, CT: Praeger.

LeMay, Michael. 2013. *Transforming America: Perspectives on U.S. Immigration.* Vol. 3. *Immigration and Superpower Status, 1845 to the Present.* Santa Barbara: Praeger.

LeMay, Michael. 2015. *Illegal Immigration: A Reference Handbook.* 2nd ed. Santa Barbara: ABC-CLIO.

LeMay, Michael. 2017. *The American Political Party System.* Santa Barbara: ABC-CLIO.

LeMay, Michael. 2018. *U.S. Immigration Policy, Ethnicity, and Religion in American History.* Santa Barbara: Praeger Press.

LeMay, Michael, and Elliott Barkan, eds. 1999. *U.S. Immigration and Naturalization and Naturalization Laws and Issues.* Westport, CT: Greenwood Press.

Light, Paul C. 2002. *Homeland Security Will Be Hard to Manage.* Washington, D.C.: Brookings Institution's Center for Public Service.

Lippert, Randy K. 2005. *Sanctuary, Sovereignty, Sacrifice: Canadian Sanctuary Incidents, Power, and Law*. Vancouver, BC: University of British Columbia Press.

Martin, David. 2003. "With a Whisper, Not a Bang: Bush Signs Parts of Patriot Act II into Law—Stealthily." *San Antonio Current*, December 24, 2003. https://www .sacurrent.com/sanantonio/with-a-whisper-not-a-bang/ Content?oid=2269175.

Mittelstadt, Michelle, Bureke Speaker, Doris Meissner, and Muzaffer A. Chishti. 2011. *Through the Prism of National Security: Major Immigration Policy and Program Changes in the Decade Since 9/11*. Washington, D.C.: Migration Policy Institute.

Moretti, Enrico. 2012. *The New Geography of Jobs*. Boston: Houghton-Mifflin Harcourt.

Navarrette, Rueben. 2018. "Big, Beautiful Wall is a 12th-Century Solution to 21st-Century Problem." Colorado Springs *Gazette*, March 18, 2018, A-11.

Office of Civil Rights and Liberties. 2018. "Mission Statement." https://www.dhs.gov/office-civil-rights-and-civil-liberties.

Office of the Inspector General. 2017. "DHS Tracking of Visa Overstays Is Hindered by Insufficient Technology." Department of Homeland Security, May 1, 2017. OIG-17–56. https://www.oig.dhs.gov/reports/2017/dhs-tracking-visa-overstays-hindered-insufficient-technology/ oig-17-56-may17.

Politics & Policy. 2013. "Gerrymandering—Proving All Politics Is Local." http://politicsandpolicy.org/article/ gerrymandering-proving-all-politics-local.

Powell, Lane. 2017. "Muslim-Country Travel Ban Upheld in Part." *JDSupra*, June 27, 2017. https://www.jdsupra .com/legalnews/muslim-country-travel-ban-upheld-in-part-70428/.

Project Censored. 2003. "Homeland Security Threatens Civil Liberty." http://projectcensored.org/2-homeland-security-threatens-civil-liberty/.

Roots, Roger. 2003. "Terrorized into Absurdity: The Creation of the Transportation Security Administration." *Independent Review* 7, no. 4 (Spring): 503–518.

Stroupe, Kenneth S. Jr. 2009. "Gerrymandering's Long History in Virginia: Will This Decade Mark The End?" *Virginia News Letter* 85, no. 1 (February). https://ceps .coopercenter.org/content/gerrymanderings-long-history-virginia-will-decade-mark-end.

Suro, Roberto. 2015. "Mitigating Federal Immigration Law: Inclusion at the Local Level." In *Illegal Immigration*. 2nd ed., edited by Michael LeMay, 116–121. Santa Barbara: ABC-CLIO.

Torr, James D., ed. 2004. *Homeland Security.* San Diego: Greenhaven Press.

Udani, Adriano. 2013. "Thwarting Federal Immigration Reform: The Politics of Welfare Devolution in the United States." In *Transforming America: Perspectives on U.S. Immigration*. Vol. 3, edited by Michael LeMay, 151–172. Santa Barbara: Praeger.

U.S. Army. 2011. "Army Releases Budget Request for Fiscal Year 2012." February 14, 2011. https://www.army.mil/article/51818/army_releases_budget_request_for_fiscal_year_2012.

U.S. Census Bureau. 2017. "Quick Facts: United States." https://www.census.gov/quickfacts/fact/table/US/PST045217.

U.S. Citizenship and Immigration Services. 2018. "Nonimmigrant." March 22, 2018. https://www.uscis.gov/tools/glossary/nonimmigrant.

U.S. Customs and Border Patrol. 2011. "National Guard Supports Border Security Efforts." March 1, 2011.

https://www.cbp.gov/newsroom/national-media-release/
national-guard-supports-border-security-efforts.

U.S. Customs and Border Patrol. 2017. "Fiscal Year 2016
Sector Profile." January 3, 2017. https://www.cbp.gov/
document/stats/us-border-patrol-fiscal-year-2016-sector-
profile.

U.S. Department of Homeland Security. 2004. "Fact Sheet:
US-VISIT." *Homeland Security Digital Library*. https://
www.hsdi.gov/.

U.S. Department of State. 2002. "U.S.–Canada Smart
Border/30 Point Action Plan Update." https://2001-2009.
state.gov/p/wha/rls/fs/18128.htm.

U.S. Immigration and Customs Enforcement. 2018. "Secure
Communities." www.ice.gov/secure-communities.

Van De Water, Paul N. 2008. "Immigration and Social
Security." Center on Budget and Policy Priorities,
November 20, 2008. https://www.cbpp.org/research/
immigration-and-social-security/.

Wucker, Michele. 2006. *Lockout.* New York: Public Affairs/
Perseus Books.

Yee, Vivian, and Rebecca R. Ruiz. 2017. "Sessions Once Again
Threatens Sanctuary Cities." *New York Times*, July 26, 2017.
https://www.nytimes.com/2017/07/26/us/politics/sessions-
sanctuary-cities.html.

Yehiv, Steve A. 2003. "Groupthink and the Gulf Crisis."
*British Journal of Political Science* 33, no. 3 (July): 419–443.

Zapotosky, Matt. 2017. "Judge Rejects Hawaii Bid to Exempt
Grandparents from Trump's Travel Ban." *Washington Post*,
July 6, 2017. https://www.washingtonpost.com/world/
national-security/judge-rejects-hawaii-bid-to-exempt-
grandparents-from-trumps-travel-ban/2017/07/06/
8e3a3252-625d-11e7-8adc-fea80e32bf47_story.html.

## Introduction

This chapter presents seven original essays on the topic of immigration reform written by activists, a former congressman, established scholars and scholars just beginning their professional careers, and stakeholders working on the frontline of politics and policy making related to immigration reform. The essays collectively provide insights and a perspective beyond and different from the expertise of the author. The essays are presented in alphabetical order of the contributors' surnames.

## Immigration Reform Legislation of 1987:
## Lessons from the Past
*Berkley Bedell, with Kenneth Bedell*

I was elected to Congress in 1974 from Iowa's sixth district. Gerald Ford was president. The speaker of the House was Carl Albert. Albert organized the work of the House of Representatives so that both Democrats and Republicans participated in writing and passing legislation. I retired 1987 after being elected six times to two-year terms.

---

Iman Akroum (*right*), a Syrian refugee living in Fresno, has a light moment with her English language teacher, Ani Chamichian, during a lesson in Akroum's home in 2017. The 1965 Immigration Act resulted in a significant increase in immigrants from the Middle East and set the stage for the Refugee Act of 1980. (John Walker/Fresno Bee/TNS via Getty Images)

There were 48 other Democrats elected with me for the first time in 1974. Although I had just arrived in Congress and my only previous elected position was serving on the Spirit Lake, Iowa, school board, I quickly became active in the work of Congress. As the session was being organized, the new members demanded that we have an opportunity to interview all the committee chairs before we voted on them. This was a bold move, but it became clear to me and others that three of the committee chairs were not the leaders the country needed. Previously, the committee chairs were named and then elected because they had served on the committee for the longest time. We were successful in replacing the chairmen of the Agriculture, Banking, and the Armed Forces Committees.

In the years between 1987, when I left congress, and 2018 many things have changed in the way that Congress works. I never spent more than $100,000 in an election to hold on to a seat as a Democrat in a district where a majority of the voters were registered as Republicans. In 2018, winning a congressional race requires raising millions of dollars. I spent very little time raising money and I didn't have a fundraising committee. I worked hard to earn the trust of my constituents rather than raising money.

When I participated in the work of the Congress, I was there to represent the interests of my district and what was best for the whole country. The committee system made that possible. Any member could introduce legislation or suggest amendments. Proposals from both Democrats and Republicans were reviewed by subcommittees and one of the standing committees. The committees made recommendations to the full House of Representatives, where final votes were taken. The subcommittees and committees invited experts to meet with them so that they could understand the implications of proposed legislation and work on developing the best legislation possible. Both Democrats and Republicans worked together on this process. It was hard work, but this is the way we spent our time rather than in fund raising.

During my last term in Congress, in 1986, we took up the issue of immigration. This was the first time that Congress had seriously addressed the issue in decades. We were able to deal with extremely complex issues because of the committee system. Sections of the bill were assigned to eight different committees. This included the Agriculture Committee that I was a member of. Looking back, it is possible to see that there were immigration issues that we did not fully understand, but I believe we did the best we could. I am proud of my "Yea" vote to support the final version of the bill that passed the House by only 55 percent. I was one of 161 Democrats and 77 Republicans who supported sending the bill on to President Reagan for his signature.

Immigration was not an important issue for my constituents in northwest Iowa. One way I gaged interest was by the number of letters I received about an issue. I only received three letters regarding immigration. Yet, as with all issues, I took my responsibility seriously to help Congress pass the best immigration law possible. This happened through the subcommittee and committee process.

As the immigration bill was being considered for a final vote on the House floor, there were still very controversial issues to be resolved. On some items there was broad consensus. By a margin of two to one, an amendment was defeated to make the penalty for hiring an illegal alien a civil rather than a criminal offence. On other issues my vote made a difference. An amendment was defeated by only two votes that attempted to remove protection for Salvadorans and Nicaraguans from deportation. I cast one of those two votes.

I voted for the amendment to prohibit INS officials from entering a farm or agricultural operation without a search warrant or permission from the owner in order to question a person believed to be an illegal alien. In this I was joined by 136 Democrats and 85 Republicans. There were 91 Democrats and 78 Republicans who voted against the amendment. Forty-one members did not vote on the amendment.

While the law was not perfect, I still believe that we were moving the country in the right direction. Then as now, our goal needs to formalize the immigration process so that immigration is controlled by clear and fair rules which are enforced. Secondly, as the bill attempted to do, we need to incentivize support for controlled immigration. We hoped we could accomplish that by placing more responsibility on those who hire immigrants. We reasoned that if people living outside of the United States knew that they would not be hired for any job unless they followed the established procedures, they would decide not to enter the country illegally. This has not worked as we had hoped because of lax enforcement and the unwillingness of Americans to cooperate in eliminating employment opportunities for undocumented workers. Third, the bill attempted to protect American workers from having their jobs taken away by immigrants. Finally, the 1986 law recognized that people who have been living and working in America for at least four years have joined our country and we provided a path for them to become legal residents and eventually citizens. The result of the law was that about 2.7 million people obtained legal status.

My colleagues in Congress and I did not foresee emerging immigration issues. We did not anticipate the increasing demand for foreign workers. The dilemma of the Dreamers, children who were brought here by undocumented parents, is another example of an issue that has emerged since 1986. Also, we did not plan for a global refugee crisis or the spiraling violence in some Latin American countries, creating large numbers of people fleeing violence rather than looking for work. And we did not provide sufficient funds to ensure the law was fully implemented. The 1986 law was a good start. The problem is that since that time insufficient attention has been given to making sure that our immigration laws and policies are changed to meet the ever-changing domestic and international realities. And, I would add, to fix those things that we didn't get quite right in the 1986 law.

The tragedy is that there are millions of people who have been victimized by our political system that has devolved into an ineffective structure to make laws that are fair, just, and in the best interest of all people who live within our borders. In 1986 laws were written by a committee process that ensured ideas from both Democrats and Republicans were given thoughtful consideration. This meant that very complicated issues like immigration policy could be carefully considered with input from experts who met with subcommittees and committees. Sadly, in just 30 years the process has been completely subverted.

The result is the tragic treatment of agricultural, construction, and other laborers who contribute to the American economy but are taken advantage of by employers because they do not have legal status. Equally shameful is our treatment of the Dreamers, who are constantly threatened with deportation. And America is not responding adequately to the global crisis of displaced persons and refugees.

There are two steps that could be taken very quickly which would make it possible for America to return to a process of making laws, including fair immigration laws, that would be in the best interest of America and demonstrate compassion for the plight of displaced persons. The first step is to remove money from the political process. All elections to national office should be publicly financed from tax dollars. This would free members of Congress from the time-consuming work of raising money, give them time to work with their constituents, and free time to participate in a committee legislative process. Also, they would think about what is in the best interest of their constituents and country rather than worry about what their contributors want them to do.

Second, the partisan structure of organizing legislative work needs to be returned to a committee structure. The partisan structure makes laws by demanding party loyalty for members of Congress. When the Republicans have a majority, the leadership writes proposed laws and then demands that all Republican members of Congress vote for those laws. When Democrats are in the majority, the partisan structure works the same way. The partisan structure removes individual responsibility. Only party loyalty matters. The committee structure benefits from the insights of all members of Congress.

I believe that if we take money out of politics and return to a committee structure of making laws, we can enact immigration laws that are fair to foreign workers and people who want to become Americans and will also promote an equitable and prosperous America.

*Berkley Bedell is a former congressman who served in the U.S. House of Representatives for six terms, from 1974 to 1987. His son, Kenneth Bedell, is the author of* Realizing the Civil Rights Dream *(Praeger, 2017).*

## Comprehensive Immigration Reform from the Conservative Perspective
### *Chuck Larson*

Sometimes not running for public office and having lived on this planet for almost 70 years allows a person to see things a little differently than do others. I remember the Immigration Reform and Control Act of 1986. Passed by Congress during the Reagan administration, this law gave amnesty to persons who entered the United States illegally before January 1, 1982. The law also had provisions to restrict knowingly hiring a person illegally residing in the United States. Another relevant law is the Illegal Immigration Reform and Immigrant Responsibility Act of 1996. This law was enacted during the Clinton administration. This law focused on stronger enforcement efforts, including a wall or border fence. Many more bills were presented in Congress during 2005–2007, for example, a bill introduced to enact the Comprehensive Immigration Reform Act of 2007. Like other measures during those years, it never was brought to a floor vote even after much debate and amendments being offered.

*Democratic President Clinton for the Wall? Republican President Reagan for amnesty? Say it ain't so.*

What I want to point out is that the issue of immigration reform and border security has been around a long while, and both political parties have taken stands on both sides of this issue. It has been kicked back and forth like a political football, with both parties hoping to gain votes in the next election.

I feel there are five major points to consider when discussing or working on U.S. immigration reform policy:

1. *Border Security.* This is the need for the wall, border patrols, surveillance devises, and other means to control border crossings, not only for illegal persons but also for drugs and contraband.

2. *Merit Immigration.* This provision allows persons to immigrate to this country legally by application. It employs a points system already used by many other countries. It would allow the United States to grant entrance to persons who are needed here, based on work skills and education.

3. *VISA Lottery.* This provision in current law needs to be eliminated. This is the exact opposite of merit immigration, in that it allows persons to enter the country simply by having their name pulled from a hat, allowing them to then be lightly vetted. It uses visas unused under the regular preference visa system.

4. *DACA Deferred Action for Childhood Arrivals.* This again is an issue being used to garner votes. It covers persons who are in this country illegally but were brought here by their parents or others at a young age, and commonly referred to as Dreamers. Most of them know of no other life or country. They are really Americans in need of documentation.

Most citizens and politicians agree that they should be given legal status and a pathway to citizenship.

5. *Chain Migration.* This allows family and relatives to enter the United States simply because of their relationship to someone who is already here. Much like lottery visa immigrants, Republicans contend that they are not well vetted, and sometimes are less than desirable as U.S. residents.

When speaking of comprehensive immigration reform, I feel that all of the elements must be considered, and Congress needs to be looking forward to more than just the next election.

There are also many elements of contention that must be considered in a reform bill, one of which is what to do with the illegal population already here? Depending on the day and to whom you are listening, there are somewhere between 10 and 20 million unauthorized persons already living in the United States. They are resident in every state and most cities. The vast majority are doing manual labor jobs that some claim Americans won't do. Simple logic will tell you that it would be almost impossible to round them all up and deport them. I don't think it would even be prudent to do so. There are, however, a number of bad hombres who do need to be deported and kept out of this country. The question then becomes, do we give them a pathway to citizenship, or just give them legal status? Another question is when do we give them the right to vote? Should they be allowed to participate in Social Security, Medicare, Medicaid, or other social programs once they are nationalized?

A sizable number of our citizens believe we should allow everyone to come here for a better life. While I would have to agree that would be wonderful, it simply is not feasible. I feel that a better way would be to help them to improve conditions in their own countries. The United States was built by people wanting to come here for a better life. They were willing to give up the old country and assimilate into the ways of this country. Most of them had the skills, or were willing to train and learn the skills, needed to succeed here. I feel that the majority of those seeking to come here in this day and age only want to be taken care of by their rich Uncle Sam. This is where merit immigration comes to the forefront. We should once again allow only those willing and able to benefit this nation, as well as themselves, to enter the United States as permanent resident immigrants.

Looking back on the bills passed in the 1980s and 1990s, they were too limited in scope and served to add to our immigration problems, rather than solving them. Such bills concentrated on illegals already here and did little to stop the migration of illegals across our borders. We will not be able to come to a bipartisan consensus until both sides can come to the table without making this a political issue. We must secure our borders first and foremost, and then we can work on the other elements.

We must also clean up our wording when referring to illegal or undocumented persons. They are not immigrants until we recognize them with a legal status. This may seem hard-hearted, but I believe it is totally necessary to get everyone involved on the same page as to what we have to deal with. The Liberals need to stop looking at these people as cheap votes for themselves, and the Republicans need to stop thinking of them as cheap labor. Yes, I used the word "cheap" in both cases because I feel this is a connotation used by both sides when looking at our illegal population. It is unfortunate that these folks get caught up in this situation only because our elected officials are unwilling to stand up for what is right and needs to be done because they are thinking only of their next election and staying in office. Reform must be done by Congress and Congress alone. The various state governments can't pass differing laws. Federal courts can't legislate from the bench. And presidential use of executive orders will not suffice.

When will we see the enactment of comprehensive immigration reform? I don't think it will be in my lifetime. But then as I said in my first paragraph, I am old, and maybe you will see it in your life.

*Chuck Larson is a retired financial advisor and a Republican Party activist residing in Colorado Springs.*

## Refugee Resettlement as Seen through the Eyes of a Volunteer ESL Teacher
*Marty Liddy*

The ad in the church bulletin read, "Make new friends. Be a volunteer ESL teacher for refugees at Catholic Charities." This caught my attention, as late in 2013 I was planning to retire soon, and knew that I would need some activities to fill in my time.

When I arrived the first day, the receptionist said, "Go upstairs. They are waiting for you in the classroom." The supervisor left a note saying what to do today. I went up and opened the classroom door. Inside were 20 adults seated facing the front. They looked like refugees, as the clothes they were wearing were a mismatch of camouflage jungle fatigues, and brightly colored hand sewn bags suspended from their shoulders carrying personal belongings or obviously donated sweatshirts with logos like Wauwatosa Swim team or Milwaukee Admirals. Two wore dark glasses, indicating blindness, and one was missing an arm. Later I learned that they were Karen refugees from Myanmar, the new name for Burma, who had been living in refugee camps over the border in Thailand for several years.

Teaching refugees was done at a very basic level and the classes contained students with varying degrees of English ability. In some respects, it was like a one-room school house. Some had no knowledge of the English alphabet. Some knew the alphabet and a few words but could not put together a sentence.

A few were "intermediates," who could read English and help me as an interpreter. This type of teaching used a lot of flash-cards with pictures. If we were teaching vegetables, there might be pictures of lettuce, tomatoes, and green beans with the name for the vegetable written below the picture of the vegetable. We would use games like Bingo with squares with pictures of the words and call out the names of the words. The winner got to be the next caller. It was a tough job getting a student to say a sentence like "It is a tomato." After several lessons a test was given individually and scored.

Refugees were also given classes in cultural orientation, which gives them some familiarity with the basic concepts of American culture. Lessons would be on topics like handling emergencies such as injuries and accidents and use of 9-1-1 and 2-1-1 telephone systems. Another might be on family safety, including home and traffic safety, and other topics would be law and the role of police, education, communication, finding work, and diet and nutrition. Coming from rural, undeveloped countries, refugees were often unfamiliar with such modern conveniences as refrigerators, supermarkets, bus transportation, inside toilets, and hospitals. At times the list seemed endless. I was naively asked if I had my students fully assimilated in six months. Assimilation is mostly not achieved until the second generation. We had horror stories. For example, one young woman got on a bus without her ID, didn't know where to get off, got scared, and stayed on the bus for 23 hours until the driver called the police. How the police located her home was the part of the story I was never told. The husband of one of my students was murdered by a robber who posed as a worker employed by the landlord. His little boy let him in the door after he was given this explanation. The funeral was the saddest event I ever experienced. A man who had sought refuge from war and persecution for his family was murdered in Milwaukee. The funeral was held on July 4.

The task before a refugee family in Milwaukee is daunting. Try putting yourself in their shoes. Fly to China carrying only a change of clothes and three months of rent money. Learn the language, find a job, get the kids in school, and, oh yes, put some money aside to pay back the air fare to the Chinese government for the trip from the United States.

A major problem in refugee teaching was class turnover. Each refugee had a caseworker who helped them with housing, obtaining medical care, enrolling children in school, and, most important, finding a job. Employment was a major objective for new arrivals and, once achieved, the refugee was not required to attend ESL classes. Thankfully, Milwaukee Area Technical College offers ESL classes at night for a small fee. Sometimes refugees left to be united with other family members in another state, or jobs disappeared in another area of the country, and they were transferred to Milwaukee. I recall a student who first arrived in the mountains near Whitefish, Montana, to work a seasonal job at a ski lodge and was then sent to Milwaukee. Another came after his employer, a casino in Atlantic City, closed. Apparently, he was the only speaker of his native language, Chin, in Atlantic City.

Another challenge was refugee children. Day care is not provided and some mothers were still nursing infants in class. Even with a volunteer sitter there was the occasional child running up to the front of class or screaming at the top of his lungs! The ability to keep your cool was a necessary trait for an ESL teacher.

Refugees face a hard life in America. In a sense they live for the future of the next generation. Learning English may be a lesser problem than adapting to changes in diet. Employment chances are excellent today, but who knows the future? Recessions eventually come. Automation will take a toll in the near future. Presently Cargill, Inc., a meatpacking company, is the largest employer of refugees in the Midwest. Many refugees work as home care aides.

The United States selects refugees using the United National High Commission on Refugees' (UNHCR), the UN refugee organization, definition of a refugee. UNHCR defines a refugee as someone who is being persecuted for reasons of religion or ethnicity. Note that this definition does not include victims of war, extreme poverty, or famine. The UNHCR definition would exclude most of the migrants making their way to Europe from Syria and Africa. The number of refugees admitted to the United States is determined by the president, with a maximum of 110,000 per year. The Obama administration met the quota, but the Trump administration has reduced the cap to 45,000. Steve Miller, Trump's advisor, is recommending a further reduction to 20,000 for the next fiscal year and favors instead giving aid to countries supporting refugee camps.

I've taught refugees from several ethnic groups of Myanmar; Karens, Chin, Chan, and Rohingya. When asked what country they are from, Rohingyas will almost always tell you Malaysia. That is where the small boats landed after they fled Myanmar several years ago. Why say Myanmar if they took your citizenship away? I've also had Congolese, Somalis, Sudanese, Bhutanese, Nepalese, Eritreans, Pakistani, Afghans, and Cubans in my classes.

The American public and government seem indifferent to the plight of refugees and migrants. I wrote to several senators, congressmen, and state department officials asking them for their position on the refugee cap. I received only one reply. It came from Wisconsin Congressman, Jim Sensenbrenner, a conservative Republican, who said that he favored the programs but felt that increased vetting was needed. A retired American Federation of Teachers union official caustically advised me that one should expect a reply only if you were a donor in excess of $10,000. Perhaps a brief acknowledgment might be sent, if your letter was part of a mailing campaign on a hot issue favored by the official.

The United States is trying to sort out our immigration policies, and how we handle refugees is part of this great question. Giving asylum and aid to people who fled intolerable situations in their homeland seems to be at the core of a democracy. We have always been a leader in this area. Interestingly, only about 20 other developed countries take in refugees, not including Japan, which steadfastly maintains that their country is only for the Japanese people. I expect the number of people who will live out their lives in camps will continue to grow, and our ESL class sizes in the United States to diminish. I am doubtful that I will ever meet a Rohingyian who fled to the camps in Bangladesh in 2017. Questions of cost and national security are at the heart of the issue. A janitor at a south side class location inquired, "Who pays for all this." Annoyed, I replied, "I do."

Refugees start businesses, hold down jobs, and it is claimed that the program pays for itself after about nine years in taxes paid back to the U.S. government. The average income for Vietnamese-Americans is now slightly more than that of the average American. Ultimately refugee resettlement is a humanitarian issue. Is America willing to contribute to and help the outcasts of the world, or is it up to Canada and Western Europe to assume this moral position? The number of refugees now coming to Milwaukee has been cut dramatically, and its ESL classes have been cancelled, as have many such programs elsewhere. Today, Canada accepts more than the United States.

*Marty Liddy is an ESL volunteer teacher in Milwaukee, Wisconsin. He is a retired librarian from the Milwaukee Area Technical College who has a BA from Marian University and a masters in library and information science.*

## True to Our Origins: The Democratic Party and Comprehensive Immigration Reform
### Ryan Macoubrie

The Democratic Party, from its earliest days (when first founded by Thomas Jefferson and James Madison as the

Democratic-Republican Party), has supported a liberal, welcoming immigration policy.

When, in 1798, the conservative Federalist Party passed a new Naturalization Act, which denied citizenship to immigrants until at least five years after they first asked for it and required that immigrants must have lived in the United States for at least 14 years before they could become citizens (up from the five years residency requirement of previous Naturalization Acts), the Republicans (as we were then called) opposed such strict restrictions.

And in 1801, when Thomas Jefferson became president and sent to the now Republican-controlled Congress his first Annual Message, Jefferson recommended:

> a revisal of the laws on the subject of naturalization. Considering the ordinary chances of human life, a denial of citizenship under a residence of fourteen years is a denial to a great proportion of those who ask it. . . . And shall we refuse the unhappy fugitive from distress that hospitality which the savages of the wilderness extended to our fathers arriving in this land? Shall oppressed humanity find no asylum on this globe?

Apart from that "savages of the wilderness" slur, Jefferson's ideas about immigration have largely remained our own. The first official platform of the renamed Democratic Party, adopted in 1840, ended with this plank:

> 9. *Resolved,* That the liberal principles embodied by Jefferson in the Declaration of Independence, and sanctioned in the Constitution, which makes ours the land of liberty, and the asylum of the oppressed of every nation, have ever been cardinal principles in the Democratic faith; and every attempt to abridge the present privilege of becoming citizens, and the owners of soil among us, ought

to be resisted with the same spirit which swept the Alien and Sedition laws from our statute-books.

And even our latest Democratic Party platforms, updated every four years, affirm our support for immigration, naturalization, and citizenship. Democrats support comprehensive immigration reform.

Contrary to what conservatives would have you believe, we Democrats do support securing America's borders and deterring illegal immigration. Security matters. Yet walls alone are not enough. People will always find ways to defeat whatever border security measures we develop, though; but that doesn't mean we should have unsecured open borders. No.

And we've got to decide what to do with all the people who have already crossed our borders without permission. Forcefully deporting every undocumented immigrant out of America would be inhuman, un-American, and economically disastrous.

That is why we Democrats support prioritizing deportations to focus on removing dangerous criminals, rather than those good people whose only offense is living here without permission. We support keeping families together, not tearing them apart.

We Democrats also support offering a path to citizenship for the estimated 10 million undocumented immigrants already living here. We support brining these people out of the shadows of our society and into the shining light of freedom.

We Democrats support President Obama's Deferred Action for Childhood Arrivals (DACA) program, which lets undocumented immigrant children petition to become Legal Permanent Residents (LPRs) without the fear of deportation hanging over them while they go through the immigration system. We support DACA being enacted into law by Congress, and thus not subject to presidential rescission.

And we Democrats support holding immigration courts to basic judicial standards: such as putting the burden of proof on the prosecution and providing defendants with legal counsel. Children who have not yet learned how to spell or even count should not be forced to defend themselves in court without a lawyer—as they must do now

To help reduce illegal immigration, we Democrats support raising the preference limits of how many immigrants can legally come into America each year. If more immigrants can enter the country legally, then fewer will enter illegally. Raising these preference limits will also help reduce the massive backlog of pending visa approvals, which keeps immigrants waiting years (sometimes even decades!) before they can finally move to America.

Conservatives would reduce this backlog by abolishing America's family-sponsored immigration system, which lets U.S. citizens and LPRs to bring their direct family members (parents, siblings, spouse, and minor children) into America. Conservatives decry this as "chain migration" and a threat to national security. It is not. Republicans want to replace this family-sponsored immigration system with a merit-based system of points.

We Democrats would support a merit-based system of points being added to the current family-sponsored system (not in replacement of it) because we believe America is great enough to be able to do two things at once, side-by-side.

And we Democrats support expanding the definition of who qualifies for asylum to include people fleeing from deadly gang violence, so no one seeking a better life here is turned away.

Two recent pieces of legislation included most of these reforms and were supported by most of the Democrats who were able to vote on the bills.

The Comprehensive Immigration Reform Act of 2006 (S. 2611) passed the Senate (62–36–2), with most Democrats voting for it and most Republicans voting against it. But the bill was never brought up for a vote or even any debate in the Republican-controlled House of Representatives, and it died there.

The more popular Border Security, Economic Opportunity, and Immigration Modernization Act of 2013 (S. 744) passed the Senate (68–32), with all 52 Democrats voting for it and even 14 Republicans also supporting it (and both independent senators). But again, even with all of this extra support, the speaker of the House, John Boehner, refused to bring it to the floor for a vote or even any debate in the Republican-controlled House of Representatives, and it, too, died there.

As President Trump would Tweet, "Sad!"

Despite these setbacks, however, we Democrats will continue to propose and support comprehensive immigration reform, creating a more liberal, welcoming immigration system for America, because it's what we believe in and because it's the right thing to do.

## Further Reading

Kennedy, John F. *A Nation of Immigrants*. 1964. Revised and Enlarged Edition. New York: Harper Perennial, 2008.

Schlesinger, Arthur M., Jr., Fred L. Israel, and William P. Hansen, eds. *History of American Presidential Elections: 1789–1984*. 10 Vols. New York: Chelsea House Publishers, 1986.

*Ryan Macoubrie is a Democratic activist in Colorado Springs and the chair of the El Paso County Young Democrats.*

## Immigration Reform Dysfunction: Why Reform Does Not Happen
### Tim Magrath

The last major immigration reform bill was passed in 1986 and signed into law by President Ronald Reagan. This bipartisan bill was aptly named after its main sponsors, Representative Romano Mazzoli (D-KY) and Senator Alan Simpson (R-WY). I watched this bill pass through the legislative process, as I worked on Capitol Hill from 1982 through 1995; I continued my congressional career working for a U.S. senator in western Maryland until 2007, and I am now a political science instructor at Frostburg State University. I watch with interest the dysfunction that characterizes Capitol Hill today. This essay sets forth competing ideas on why reform in our nation's immigration policy remains in legislative gridlock today, while considering how it succeeded the last time comprehensive immigration reform was signed into law.

When I first started working on Capitol Hill in 1974 as a Page, and full time in the early 1980s, there was a keen sense of comity between parties that does not exist today. The political parties were far less homogeneous than they are today. Major legislation, including Reagan's signature legislative achievement, the Kemp-Roth tax legislation, could only pass with major Democratic support, mainly from "boll weevils," Democrats from the South who normally aligned themselves with conservative Republicans. Political parties were far more heterogeneous than they are today. Left-leaning Republicans and conservative Democrats were commonplace in the 1980s. They are virtually nonexistent today. The causes for this purge of diversity from political parties are discussed throughout this essay. Overall the relationship between parties was better as the leadership of the parties exemplified by President Reagan's relations with Speaker Tip O'Neil demonstrated the cordial respect between differing political viewpoints. Battles on the House floor were forgotten in the evening as Republican Minority Leader Bob Michaels joined Tip, Representative Dan Rostenkowski (D Illinois), and others for a weekly poker game. Many members shared housing in D.C. regardless of their political affiliation. Respectful language was a norm, and even in the most vociferous floor battle, members would not impugn the motives of individual members. Both parties understood that the diverse caucuses of each party required cordial relations and bipartisan solutions to complex public policy issues. The relative gentle relationships fostered meaningful debate for the Simpson-Mazzoli bill. The issue of immigration reform was a bipartisan effort. Many Democrats supported this bill to give a pathway for many undocumented workers toward legal status, and frankly to curry the favor of the growing Hispanic demography in the U.S. labor unions. Unions are a key Democratic constituency who supported the bill. Most unions were at the vanguard of improving the lives and the working conditions of all workers and saw immigrant laborers as future union members. On the other hand, Republicans supported the legislation to placate an important part of their political base, business owners, including agricultural interest, dependent on workers willing to do the many difficult jobs that U.S. citizens were unwilling to do. These jobs include tending to crops and fruit trees and ultimately harvesting the crops. Other businesses needed workers in the construction trades, service workers in hotels and restaurants; from "picking" crabs in Maryland, to cutting sugarcane and planting tomatoes in south Florida. The business interests had a large stake in formulating policy to ensure a steady and reliable labor force. Both parties had important constituencies to satisfy. The essence of the Simpson-Mazzoli legislation was to provide a pathway toward citizenships for millions of undocumented workers who could demonstrate that they had been in the country for at least five years and to punish employers with fines and possible jail time for those who hired "new" undocumented workers. Critics of this legislation immediately coined this pathway toward citizenship "amnesty" for lawbreakers, and this term by sheer repetition and determination of Republican members and right-wing news outlets has now become the battle cry for those critical of additional reform efforts. Other critics pointed out that the Simpson-Mazzoli law did nothing to stop businesses from hiring newly arrived undocumented workers, as an entire industry developed to create counterfeit documents, including Social Security cards and authentic-looking driver's licenses.

Today comprehensive immigration reform is mired in partisan politics with little hope of dealing with the millions of undocumented workers living in the United States. Much of the divisive politics that is apparent today was germinated and can be placed at the feet of Newt Gingrich (R-GA), who had help from Representative Bob Walker (R-PA). The two spent countless hours in the mid-1980s through the early 1990s using a little-known legislative time period called "special orders" to lambast the Democratic Party in its entirety, and impugning the integrity of individual Democratic leaders in a deliberate and caustic fashion. Special Orders is a time set aside after the normal legislative session has concluded, "to revise and extend" debate. Members of the House can speak on whatever issues they would like, normally to an empty chamber with little notice or attention, but broadcast nationally on C-Span. Gingrich and Walker teamed up daily and for years spent countless hours, day after day, tormenting the House Democratic leadership, and accusing the collective membership of the party of everything up to and including treason. Language matters, and these two members dropped every aspect of collegiality and blew up the norms of the legislative body. They used language and surreptitious techniques to paint the Democratic Party and its collective membership of corruption and deceit, while exploding the decorum, respect, and civility that is the cornerstone of our democratic civil society. One of these techniques included addressing accusations to an empty chamber and with a fixed camera angle not allowing the viewers at home to understand that the chamber was empty, leaving the viewer believing that Democratic members accepted their accusations and had no response to the endless charges. Democratic Party leaders were negligent in not responding quickly to this pony show, and for years, Gingrich and Walker got away with their subterfuge. With exacting science, these two left many in the C-Span audience convinced that the Democratic Party was filled with corrupt members intent on destroying America from within. When Speaker Tip O'Neil finally responded by ordering that C-Span cameras pan the empty chamber, the damage had been done, and the comity between party members was frayed and wrecked on the shores of deceitful language. Concurrent with this was the rise of right-wing shock-jocks led by Rush Limbaugh, who filled the AM radio echo chamber with language that fundamentally putrefied civil discourse in a pluralistic society. Now it was okay and seemingly normal to question the integrity of those who might disagree with you. Moreover, Gingrich rose in popularity within the rank and file of the Republican House membership. They were frustrated by being relegated to minority status for over 40 years. Gingrich was elected Minority Whip in 1989 over the more collegial Ed Madigan (R-IL). While Gingrich continued to ferment revolution within his party, Minority leader Bob Michel could read the tea leaves and announced his retirement from Congress in 1994.

Gingrich actively worked for a majority by creating a Political Action Committee (PAC) called GOPAC, recruited candidates, and worked with pollster Frank Luntz. They distributed campaign kits, which included a piece entitled "Language, a Key Mechanism of Control," to would-be candidates. It taught candidates to "talk like Newt" and use language like sick, corrupt, traitors to describe Democratic opponents and the party. With much fanfare, Gingrich also created a "Contract with America." It outlined what a Republican majority would do, including 10 legislative proposals, if the electorate gave Republicans a majority. Mid-term elections historically run against the president's party and 1994 was no exception. With Gingrich's active support of Republican candidates, the first Republican majority in the House since 1955 emerged, propelling him into the speakership. Seemingly, language did matter, and the Republican Party was successful and elevated to majority status by condemning the opposition party with caustic discourse that led to a near complete breakdown in cooperation between parties in achieving legislative policy in Congress. Henceforth, nearly every legislative accomplishment, with few exceptions, was done with partisan majorities.

FOX News, created by conservative Rupert Murdoch, turned this news outlet into a partisan weapon and parroted the language of Gingrich. Its media personalities, like Sean Hannity and Glenn Beck, turned liberals and Democrats into four-letter words.

Language matters and so does leadership. Like a buffalo herd, Republicans all ran in the same direction and were disciplined communicators, while Democrats followed their more traditional disorganization in communicating to the American public. Will Rogers famously said, "I am not a member of any organized party, I am a Democrat." The party did little to confront the discipline and the well-organized message machine of the Republicans. Republicans cleaved from the herd any member who wandered from their beliefs and unified message, through primary challenges and active party support for candidates who would fight for their iconoclastic dogma. Grove Norquist, leading the Club for Growth, further instilled discipline with 98 percent of Republican candidates signing his pledge that under no circumstances would they ever raise taxes, and if they did, they would face a well-funded primary challenge.

When I first got to Capitol Hill in the 1980s, personal computers were at their infancy; today we all walk around with them in our pockets. In addition to the explosion in partisan news outlets, a computer revolution occurred simultaneously. The use of gerrymandering, the art of designing a district for partisan advantage, also exploded. Drawing a new district once took weeks or months. Today, with the right software and data, it can take seconds. The sophistication of gerrymandering has also had dire consequences for the comity between parties. Noncompetitive, "safe-districts" can now be created with exacting science to ensure that there is little competition between parties in most congressional districts. In the few states that allow "independent" commissions to design districts without partisan input, that is, California and Iowa, the elections continue to ensure a sliver of competition between parties.

The sophistication of computerized gerrymandering has reduced competition between parties in most legislative races. More than 90 percent of members of Congress face little risk of losing their seat in the general election and face only a risk in the primary. Most states have closed primaries allowing only registered party members to participate. As fewer voters turn out for the primary, the electorates that decide the make-up of Congress are typically dominated by the party faithful either extremely liberal or conservative. Moderates and independent voters—the clear majority of voters—are poorly represented in Congress and have very little impact on elections. Moreover, any member from a "safe" district who reaches out to the other side in co-authoring bills will face opposition from someone more extreme to placate the party ideologues who label compromise heretical.

Immigration reform today is caught in this ideological gridlock where members are punished for compromise and reaching for bipartisan agreements, and where extremism is rewarded with continued service in Congress. We could see this at work in the Republican primary, where Donald Trump's immigration position continued to get more extreme, as Ted Cruz tried to outflank him on the right. The end result was overt racism that pillared Mexican immigrants as rapist and murderers. Senator Marco Rubio was chastised in the primary for trying to find a solution to the immigration impasse by working in the "gang of eight," four Democrats and four Republican working for a bipartisan solution to immigration in 2013. Rubio later repudiated his effort. Republican Majority Leader Eric Cantor lost his primary reelection bid in 2014 in Virginia, to Tea Party favorite David Brat, even after he outspent his opponent massively, largely by Brat accusing Cantor of being for amnesty for illegals and for working for a solution to immigration. The fact that Cantor was punished for even trying to find a solution was not lost on other Republicans. Now Trump has raised the stakes further for Republicans by not providing any leadership on the matter and by encouraging White Nationalism. That racist creed rejects any immigration, particularly from any majority-Muslim nations. This message resonates within the Republican ranks, with large majorities, 8 percent% and more, of Republicans approving of Trump's performance in office. The few remaining in the party who would like to represent the business interests within their district and would support compromise legislation to bring undocumented workers in from the shadows are wary that they will lose Trump supporters who seem to be driving the party today.

Any hope for immigration reform today will have to wait for Democratic majorities in the House and Senate and a president focused on building a popular majority for election or reelection. Public opinion polls show that most Americans support some immigration reform, or at least a solution for the DACA residents brought to the U.S. as children. Perceptions matter in politics. Although undocumented workers are from more countries than Mexico and Central America, Latinos—the fastest-growing demographic in the United States—-perceive the animosity and hatred that seems to ooze out of the Republican Party and its leaders today. Politically savvy Republicans, determined to maintain majorities into the future, understand the shortsighted nature of the current politics and understand their party may be relegated to minority status for the foreseeable future, unless their party welcomes others into their ranks besides older white males. Many states, solid red in the past, such as Texas and Arizona, are moving the way of California. It changed from a competitive battleground state to solid blue after Latino voters shifted strongly toward the Democrats, after Proposition 187 was enacted, led by Republican Pete Wilson in 1994. Proposition 187 was perceived as anti-Latino and shifted the political dynamics of the state from competitive to the most solidly blue state in the nation. Democrats' strategy appears to be to give Republicans enough rope so they can hang themselves on the tree of xenophobia and racism. Can Republicans hold on to their majorities by exiting their base and by restricting voting through obstacles like Voter ID laws and making it difficult to vote through limiting early voting, purging registration lists, and creating long lines in minority and urban districts? Maybe so, but my guess is that the demographic blue wave will sink Republican Party progress until saner, more rational minds prevail.

*Tim Magrath is an instructor in political science at Frostburg State University in western Maryland. He served in Congress as a staffer in various capacities for 25 years, 1982 to 2007.*

## How Communities Can Meet the Immigration Challenge
### Ali Noorani

In May 2018, sitting among 10 fellow residents of her Southern California community, a woman of deep faith paused. Tearing up, she quietly remarked that her father and brother resent the change taking place around them: "They're driven out of absolute fear that they are going to lose their sense of security or identity."

This is our reality. The immigration debate has created a deep divide that we must reconcile.

This woman participated in one of 27 living-room conversations the National Immigration Forum organized over the course of spring 2018, mostly in conservative-leaning suburban and rural communities across the nation. We wanted to sit down and listen to people's views on immigration in their communities. We met with police officers, religious leaders, veterans, small business owners, immigrants, and refugees.

Through these conversations, we heard about the profound cultural and demographic transformation happening in many of these communities. These changes can prompt fear, anxiety, and hatred, paving the way for a political environment that's toxic in nature and tribal in practice.

When it comes to immigration, we have been led to believe we have a binary choice: Are we a nation of laws or a nation of grace? As the son of Pakistani immigrants who achieved the fullness of the American Dream, I say that we can be both.

So how do we achieve that balance? First and foremost, we need to understand the fears that Americans have when it comes to immigration. By understanding fears, we can develop solutions.

For many Americans, the immigration debate triggers fears in three areas: the economy, security, and culture.

When it comes to the economy, are immigrants and refugees givers or takers?

The data make a clear case that immigrants are coming to the United States to work, contribute, and make sure their children can thrive. While immigrants represent only 13 percent of the U.S. population, they represent 16 percent of the overall workforce and 73 percent of the agriculture labor force. In April 2018, for the first time, the U.S. Bureau of Labor Statistics reported that there were more job openings than people out of work—6.7 million open jobs and 6.4 million people searching for jobs. That trend continued through at least July.

Projections are that the economy will add 9.8 million jobs between 2014 and 2024, while the labor force will grow by only 7.9 million workers. No matter where you stand on the issue, one thing is certain: without the contribution of immigrants and immigration, the United States is going to fall behind.

In security terms, are immigrants and refugees threats or protectors?

Over the last five years we have worked with law enforcement across the country to better understand the intersection between local law enforcement and immigration. I have concluded that we need to bring a different perspective to the public-safety conversation, one that steers away from the lightning-rod term "sanctuary city" and focuses on the ability of the officer on the corner to serve and protect the entire community. For that to happen, the officer must be perceived as a trusted official, not an Immigration and Customs Enforcement (ICE) agent. Once law enforcement officials build trust within the community, immigrants will trust them enough to report crime.

Of course, we need a strong, secure border that keeps us safe. That means we need smart border policy based on real risks, not great slogans. I don't think a border wall is a smart investment of taxpayer dollars and would rather we spend U.S. resources at ports of entry—where most drugs, guns, and money are smuggled.

Also, we need to remember that it is perfectly legal for an adult or a child to present himself or herself to a U.S. Border Patrol agent and ask for asylum. If there is a "significant possibility" the applicant has been persecuted or has a well-founded fear of persecution or harm in their home country, he or she has the right to go through the asylum process.

Turning away asylum applicants, in the name of "zero tolerance," before applying this credible fear test does nothing to keep us safe. When America denies such applicants, the world sees a nation that has lost its moral compass.

Regarding culture, I've learned from pastors across the country and believe that the church and the great diversity of our nation's religions can bring us to a place of reconciliation when it comes to immigration.

There were signs of this in Salt Lake City in the spring of 2016. At the Church of Jesus Christ of Latter-Day Saints' biannual general conference, the theme was migration, specifically the church's role in welcoming and resettling refugees.

Elder Patrick Kearon spoke and began with scripture. He couched his call to action in the community's understanding of their own history. His closing words speak to all Americans today. He said:

> Being a refugee may be a defining moment in the lives of those who are refugees, but being a refugee does not define

them. Like countless thousands before them, this will be a period—we hope a short period—in their lives. Some of them will go on to be Nobel laureates, public servants, physicians, scientists, musicians, artists, religious leaders, and contributors in other fields. Indeed, many of them were these things before they lost everything.

This moment does not define them, but our response will help define us.

We need to make the case to our neighbors, our families, our colleagues that immigrants and immigration benefit American workers and their families. Immigrants are protecting our nation, giving back to America, and, ultimately, becoming Americans.

To do so, we need to work together, across age, race, faith, gender, and, yes, politics, to provide a new choice to Americans. Together, we can move toward an America that is a nation of laws and a nation of grace.

*Ali Noorani is the executive director of the National Immigration Forum. Prior to that position, he was the executive director of the Massachusetts Immigrant and Refugee Advocacy Coalition. He is the author of the 2017 Prometheus book:* There Goes the Neighborhood: How Communities Overcome Prejudice and Meet the Challenge of American Immigration.

## All Souls Unitarian/Universalist Church: Why We Became a Sanctuary Church
*Rev. Nori Rost*

In some regard, the decision to ask my congregation to become a host sanctuary congregation was a no-brainer. As Unitarian Universalists, we don't follow a common creed, nor do we share a common belief. In my congregation there are humanists, atheists, Buddhists, pagans, theists, and more. What binds us together as a faith community is our attempts to embody seven guiding principles. These are:

Belief in the inherent worth and dignity of every human;

Justice, equity, and compassion in human relations;

Acceptance of one another and encouragement to spiritual growth;

A free and responsible search for truth and meaning;

The right of conscience and the use of the democratic principles in our Congregations and society at large;

The goal of a world community with peace, liberty, and justice for all; and

Respect for the independent web of all existence, of which we are a part.

Unitarian Universalist churches don't seek to give you a road map for how to navigate this life (or make it to any future destinations, afterlife!); rather, we use these seven principles to provide a compass by which folks can steer by their own north star. As such, we also draw on the wisdom of many sources of inspiration to guide us; sacred texts of all religions, humanist understandings of how we evolve as a species, the prophetic voice of leaders in the cause of justice, and more.

So again, it was a no-brainer to ask my congregation to become a Sanctuary congregation. In fact, it was an idea that I have been toying with for the past few years, ever since hearing that our sister congregation, First Unitarian Society of Denver, Colorado, had made that leap.

Several years ago, they had joined a coalition of faith communities in the metro Denver area and had offered Sanctuary to two guests in the ensuing years; both of their guests were able to work out a deal with Immigration Control and Enforcement (ICE) to stay in the United States longer, as their cases were being reviewed.

So I have been thinking of taking such a leap, myself, but hadn't made it a priority to do so until after the 2016 presidential election, which put into power a man who was very vocal about not only further intimidating and attacking immigrants but who also used racist metaphors to fan the flames of bigotry and ignorance of the immigrant communities in our midst.

The justification for our Unitarian Universalist church taking on this challenge was easily found. In fact, it's not surprising to learn that virtually every religion exhorts believers to show hospitality to strangers.

Judaism teaches: "When a stranger lives with you in your land, do not mistreat him. The stranger living with you must be treated as one of your native-born. Love him as yourself, for you were strangers in Egypt. I am the LORD your God" (Leviticus 19:34).

In Islam, the Quran states: "Do good unto your parents, and near of kin, and unto orphans, and the needy, and the neighbor from among your own people, and the neighbor who is a stranger, and the friend by your side; and the wayfarer, and those whom you rightfully possess. Verily, God does not love any of those who, full of self-conceit, act in a boastful manner" (Surah 4:36).

According to the Christian scriptures, Jesus tells his followers, in the Gospel of Matthew 25: 25: 31–46, that those who will inherit the realm of God are those who have clothed and fed, and cared for him. "Then the righteous will answer him, 'Lord, when did we see you hungry and feed you, or thirsty and give you something to drink: When did we see you a stranger and invite you in, or needing clothes and clothe you? When did we see you sick or in prison and go to visit you?' 'The King will reply, 'Truly I tell you, whatever you did for one of the least of these of those brothers and sisters of mine, you did for me.'"

Other faith traditions hold equally strong teachings: Hinduism, Ba'Hai, Sikhism, Native American teachings. This makes sense to me. In every age, people of every stripe have experienced the brutality of famine, wars, disease, and other conditions that have made of them refugees and social outcasts, struggling to find a new home and a new hope for survival.

Each learned from this to feel compassion, empathy for others who might find themselves in similar straits. It is sacred work that aligns us with the holy: the ability to put ourselves in the shoes of another who is suffering is at the core of the great religions.

And so, in May 2017, All Souls Unitarian Universalist Church voted overwhelmingly to become a host Sanctuary congregation. Over 90 percent of the members present said a resounding yes to being the first (and so far, only) such congregation in Colorado Springs, Colorado. We, too, are lucky, in that as we were considering making this move as a congregation, a Sanctuary Coalition was being formed in our city. From the moment we said yes, we were part of a larger community of folks from different faith traditions, including the members of the First United Church of Christ and the Colorado Springs Quakers, both congregations who wholeheartedly came aboard the Sanctuary movement, even though they did not have the space to house an immigrant guest family, as well as a sprinkling of individuals from other faith traditions whose churches had not or would not make the decision to join the coalition.

We were not alone. Still this wasn't a decision made rashly by members of All Souls. There were many valid concerns raised during the forums held in advance of the vote. What about safety issues? What if the church were vandalized? What if an immigrant guest had an accident or was injured? Would I, as the minister, be open to arrest? What about the board of trustees?

I answered those questions as best I could, trying to assuage any fears, but the reality is, I told them, we don't know what will happen; we can't be prepared for every contingency. We must step out in faith that, regardless of what may happen, this is the right decision to make.

And of course, nothing went in the linear fashion we had hoped. In July 2017, our church basement flooded after a series of torrential rains. This meant our children's religious education department had to be moved temporarily; that was the space we were preparing for an immigrant guest. In August, well before any repairs could even be started, we had a request for Sanctuary referred to us by the Metro Denver Sanctuary Coalition. I have to be honest; I was very resistant. Not only was our basement flooded, we hadn't even begun construction on a shower project that would provide a place for any guests to get clean! It was clear that All Souls wasn't ready, and I expected the rest of the Coalition to see that. Instead, an immigrant woman said, "I would live in a closet with no running water if it meant I was able to stay with my family."

With that perspective, I changed course. At the end of August we welcomed our first guest, Elmer, and his three-year-old son, David. Elmer's wife and two other children remained in the Denver suburb, where they owned a house, but David, a U.S. citizen himself, came with his father, because they couldn't afford childcare. They moved into my office—the only space available, and I moved into the Small Hall, a fellowship area where we serve coffee and treats on Sunday following our worship service.

Currently, it has been over two months since Elmer and David have taken up residence at All Souls. David has become a great "coworker," bringing his race tracks and cars out in the Small Hall to play. Elmer is a cheerful, easygoing man who waits to hear from his lawyer what his next move will be.

I don't know what will happen; I don't know if Elmer's case is compelling enough to be granted a stay of deportation with an opportunity to present why he should be allowed to stay. As for me, it's a clear choice: Elmer and his wife both work full time, pay taxes, own a home, and are active members of their communities. They present no threat to any individuals or to the well-being of our nation. They are, in fact, assets to our nation, with so many gifts to share. It saddens me to think their family may fall prey to racist, xenophobic policies.

"Who is my neighbor," asked the expert in legalities in the parable of the Good Samaritan, found in Luke 10: 26–37.

Jesus had told him to love his neighbor as much as he loved himself, but he was looking for permission to continue to be exclusive—to name some people *neighbors* and other people *strangers*—the other, dangerous, to be avoided. Of course, most Christians know how this story ends: the neighbor is the one in need. The one in need is the one we are to love as much as we love ourselves.

And that is why it's alarming to see so many who profess to be people of faith rejecting the pleas of the immigrants and refugees in great need. With greater threats to family stability and well-being due to ICE deportation raids and the newly minted, controversial revised travel ban executive order signed by the president, we see a marked departure from the major tenets of our faiths.

I guess that's not surprising either. In tumultuous times such as these, it can be easy—comforting even—to want to define our "enemies" by race, ethnicity, religious identity. If "they" are dangerous, then the solution is clear: keep "them" out. If they're already here, drive "them" out.

But, of course, humankind is so much more complex than the good guy/bad guy name tags we want to put on people at the door of our heart. Still, I believe that, at the end of the day, we Americans will live up to the words of the poem by Emma Lazarus, inscribed on the Statue of Liberty that welcomes new arrivals to our shores.

> "Give me your tired, your poor,
> Your huddled masses yearning to breathe free,
> The wretched refuse of your teeming shore,
> Send these, the homeless, tempest-tossed, to me;
> I lift my lamp beside the golden door."

That's at the heart of what we hold dear, what our faith traditions call us to, what our humanity demands: to see our humanity in strangers and call them kin. To echo the words of another spiritual leader, Ram Dass, at the end to the day, "we're all just walking each other home."

I don't yet know what will happen with Elmer's case. I do know that I am honored to call him kin, to companion him on this journey that will hopefully lead to the home he has made for himself and his family. If not, at the very least, we have provided an opportunity for him to have more time with his family. I think Jesus, and Gandhi, and the Buddha, and Dr. King, and all the other spiritual luminaries we aspire to emulate would agree.

*Rev. Nori Rost is the settled minister of All Souls Unitarian Universalist Church in Colorado Springs, Colorado. She has an M.Div. from Iliff School of Theology, Denver, Colorado, and a D.Min. from Episcopal Divinity School in Cambridge, Massachusetts.*

## Introduction

This chapter profiles the organizations and people involved in the issue of immigration reform—whether by a comprehensive immigration reform approach or by a piecemeal approach. It begins with brief descriptions of key "stakeholder" organizations that are active in advocating for, enacting, or implementing immigration policy, to cope with immigration policy problems.

After describing and discussing the organizational actors in the arena of immigration policy making, the chapter profiles individual actors involved. These stakeholders include government officials, leaders of nongovernmental groups active in the politics of the issue, and leading scholars/analysts from major "think tanks" active on the issue. These organizational and individual profiles are presented in alphabetical order.

## Organizations

### Al Qaeda

The international radical Islamic terrorist organization has roots going back to 1979 to 1989 and the Soviet War in Afghanistan. When the Soviets invaded the country, young

---

Demonstrators chant during a rally protesting the funding of the Trump administration's immigration policies in Washington, D.C., on December 12, 2018. The protest was organized by Families Belong Together Coalition, the Center for Popular Democracy, CASA, Make the Road New York, and United We Dream. (Zach Gibson/Getty Images)

Muslims from around the world volunteered to fight a jihad, or holy war, against them. Osama bin Laden, the son of a wealthy Saudi Arabian construction magnate, volunteered, funding the movement generously and fighting actual battles.

When the Soviets departed, the leadership established a base (al Qaeda), and bin Laden became its emir and led the movement to prepare to fight anywhere in the world. He had been exiled from Saudi Arabia, and leaving Afghanistan, he moved to a sanctuary in Sudan, from where he laid the groundwork for his jihad against the West. Beginning a fatwa against the United States, al Qaeda fought the U.S. deployment in Somalia, downing two Black Hawk helicopters in 1993. They took credit for a bombing of the World Trade Center in 1993. Responding to mounting international pressure, Sudan forced bin Laden and al Qaeda to leave, and they returned to Afghanistan. He issued a new fatwa against the United States in 1998 and merged with the Egyptian Islamist Jihad, headed by Ayman al Zawahri, who became the number two leader in al Qaeda. In 2000, al Qaeda operatives attacked the U.S.S. Cole in Yemen, killing 17 sailors. On September 11, 2001, al Qaeda terrorists hijacked four U.S. passenger jet airliners and executed their devastating attack against the United States, killing nearly 3,000 civilians. The Taliban government in Afghanistan protected bin Laden and al Qaeda, and the United States launched its war to topple the Taliban government. It has since become the longest war in U.S. history. Osama bin Laden fled, decentralizing al Qaeda. Despite the United States killing Osama bin Laden and many of the leadership of al Qaeda, recent National Intelligence estimates show al Qaeda is once again gaining strength and has rebuilt itself. Today, al Qaeda and the Islamic State of Iraq and Syria (ISIS, also known as Daesh) are the leading international terrorist groups supporting and inspiring attacks on the West and on the United States in particular, and thus they are a leading threat to homeland security. They have greatly damaged the reputation of Muslims in the United

States, in part justifying the immigration restrictions of current policy and of the Trump administration's travel ban aimed at predominately Muslim countries.

### American Civil Liberties Union (ACLU)

Founded in 1920, the ACLU works nationally and through local chapters to protect the civil rights of citizens as guaranteed by the U.S. Constitution. It annually publishes many policy statements, pamphlets, studies, and reports on civil rights issues. It has frequently criticized the Department of Homeland Security (DHS) and its implementation of the Patriot Acts I and II. It publishes semiannually a newsletter, *Civil Liberties Alert*. It has been a leading partner in efforts to reform or amend the USA Patriot Act and to rectify what it determines are civil rights abuses in procedural matters designed to cope with homeland security issues, in particular, with the efforts of the DHS to remove unauthorized immigrants in an expedited manner. The ACLU has promoted a guest worker program and legalization programs more generally, and advocates for enactment of the Dream Act and for comprehensive immigration reform. It has sections for LGBT rights, Civil Liberties, and Immigration. It opposes the Trump-ordered travel ban and the "zero-tolerance" policy of the Department of Justice (DOJ) with respect to unauthorized immigrants entering the United States.

### American Conservative Union (ACU)

The American Conservative Union is the oldest and largest of the numerous conservative lobbying organizations. Its purpose is to communicate effectively and advance the goals and principles of conservatism through one multi-issue, umbrella organization. ACU supports capitalism, belief in the doctrine of original intent of the framers of the Constitution, traditional moral values, and commitment to a strong national defense. Since 1994 it has sponsored "town meet-ings" to spearhead the conservative response to support such issues as military protection and defending the homeland against international terrorists. It lobbies against liberaliza-tion of immigration policy reforms. One device it uses effec-tively is to rate the members of Congress according to their votes on issues of concern to conservatives. Those ratings are used by a host of almanac and reference guides across the political spectrum. ACU's rating system has been copied by many other organizations. It publishes many print, audio, and video materials and television documentaries to promote public opinion on its issues of concern. Since 1974 it has hosted the annual Conservative Political Action Conference, attended by thousands of conservative activists and leaders from across the country to discuss issues and controversies and has become an important factor in the Republican Party's presidential nomination process. It supports the Trump ad-ministration's travel ban.

### American Immigration Control Foundation (AICF)

Founded in 1983, the AIC Foundation is a nonprofit research and educational organization (a think tank) whose primary goal is to inform Americans about the need for a reasonable immigration policy based on the nation's interests and needs. It has published reports on what it labels America's immigra-tion crisis. It is a prominent national voice for immigration control and for educating Americans on what it views as the disastrous effects of uncontrolled immigration and, most par-ticularly, advocates for amendments of immigration law to bet-ter protect the border, address homeland security issues, and control lone-wolf terrorism. AICF conducts public education campaigns to influence public opinion on the issue, campaign-ing through direct mail, paid advertisements, opinion surveys, and public appearances by its organization's leadership on radio and television.

### American Immigration Law Foundation (AILF)

Founded in 1987 as a tax-exempt, nonprofit educational and service organization, AILF promotes understanding among the general public of immigration law and policy through education, policy analysis, and support of litigation. It has three core program areas: the Legal Action Center, the Public Education Program, and the Exchange Visitor Program. It has often been a critic of the USA Patriot Act and of the DHS's expedited removal program. It considers the current reaction to international terrorism influencing immigration policy to be a threat to civil liberties that is as great as is international terrorism itself. It opposed enactment of Patriot Act II. It is headquartered in Washington, D.C.

### American Immigration Lawyers Association (AILA)

The AILA is the national association of immigration lawyers created to promote justice and to advocate for fair and reasonable immigration law and policy. It seeks to advance the quality of immigration and nationality law and practice, and to enhance the professional development of its members who defend individuals charged with being in the United States illegally and in deportation hearings. It lobbies against what it considers to be unfair or anti-civil liberty provisions in immigration law, particularly the USA Patriot Act and the Department of Homeland Security Act. It has been an outspoken critic of and has supported litigation against the Muslim travel ban, and generally of the Trump administration's approach to homeland security, by cracking down on immigration control. It supports comprehensive immigration reform legislation. It is headquartered in Washington, D.C.

### Americans for Prosperity

This organization is a 501 (c)(4) PAC, founded in 2004, as one of the first of this type of "Superpac" organization. It is a very conservative political advocacy group lobbying on conservative issues, including a hard-line crackdown at the border immigration policy approach for DHS and Immigration and Customs Enforcement (ICE). It was founded by David Koch and Karl Rove and raises huge amounts of "dark money" to fund negative TV ads, to advocate for lower taxes, and to support government de-regulation. It is headquartered in Arlington, Virginia.

## Association of Patriotic Arab Americans in the Military (APAAM)

Created shortly after 9/11/2001, APAAM is an organization of current and former Arab Americans in the military, of whom there are about 3,500 serving in U.S. Armed Forces. It is the first organization to organize them, building a contact list of all military members, past and present. APAAM seeks to represent them with one voice. It promotes education of Americans and American Arab communities of a dual patriotism to their ancestral heritage and dedication to the United States, by emphasizing service and sacrifice as military men and women. They attempt to close the gap between bigotry, ignorance, and prejudice, on the one hand, and tolerance, on the other. They oppose the anti-Muslim bias in current immigration policy. APAAM was founded by U.S. Marine Corps Gunnery Sergeant Jamal S. Baadani, whose father was a refugee from Yemen who immigrated to the United States from Egypt. Jamal joined the Corps at age 17. He founded APAAM as a nonpolitical association to represent Arab Americans in the military, to highlight their service and sacrifice and the sacrifice of Arab Americans post 9/11. Arab Americans experienced a backlash after the attacks, including Jamal's family. They oppose the travel ban against immigrants and refugees from Iran, Libya, Somalia, Syria, and Yemen. As U.S. military members, APAAM members have sworn an oath to protect and defend the Constitution of the United States against all enemies, foreign and domestic, and are prepared to sacrifice their lives for the protection of freedom for all Americans. They are head-quartered in Ontario, California.

### Border Policy Research Institute (BPRI)

BPRI is a multidisciplinary research institute (think tank) housed at Western Washington University. It conducts research to inform policy makers on matters relating to the Canada-U.S. border that focus especially on trade and transportation, economics, immigration, and border security. Western Washington University (WWU) established BPRI to promote research, academic programs, and public forums and programs on critical policy issues affecting the Pacific Northwest region. BPRI works closely with cognate programs and departments at WWU and collaborates with many public and private entities in the Pacific Northwest region. It is directed by Professor Laurie Trautman, who leads a staff of six WWU faculty researchers and six visiting fellows.

### Bureau of Immigration and Customs Enforcement (ICE)

ICE is the bureau within the Department of Homeland Security that enforces all federal laws governing border control, customs, trade, and immigration to promote homeland security and public safety. It was established in 2003, with the creation of DHS and through the merger of the investigative and enforcement elements of the former Immigration and Naturalization Service (INS). Currently, ICE has more than 20,000 employees located in more than 400 offices in the United States and in 46 foreign countries and has an annual budget of $6 billion. ICE has three operational directorates: Homeland Security Investigations, Enforcement and Removal Operations, and the Office of the Principal Legal Advisor (OPLA). The OPLA provides the legal representation in all exclusion, deportation, and removal proceedings, against criminal aliens, terrorists, and human rights abusers in immigration courts across the country. OPLA provides critical legal support to ICE components focusing on customs, cyber security, worksite enforcement, ethics, employment law, tort claims, and administrative law issues. These directorates of ICE are supported by the Department of Homeland Security's directorate of Management and Administration. It is headquartered in Washington, D.C.

## Business Roundtable

The Business Roundtable is an association of chief executive officers of leading corporations who have a combined workforce of more than 10 million employees in the United States. It advocates public policies that foster vigorous economic growth, a dynamic global economy, and a well-trained and productive workforce essential for future competitiveness. It is selective in the issues it studies. A major criterion it uses is the impact the problem will have on the economic well-being of the nation. Working in task forces on specific issues, it directs research, supervises the preparation of position papers, recommends policy options, and lobbies Congress and the administration on selected issues. It supports establishing an expanded guest worker program, earned legalization, and comprehensive immigration reform. It opposes the travel ban and the impact of the homeland security law for causing backlogs in visa applications for foreign workers (e.g., H-1B, L-Visas). It is headquartered in Washington, D.C.

## Catholic Legal Immigration Network, Inc. (CLINIC)

CLINIC promotes the dignity and protects the rights of immigrants in partnership with a dedicated network of Catholic and community legal immigration programs, including sanctuary churches. It is headquartered in Silver Spring, Maryland. It provides research and analysis of the significant changes in immigration policy announced by the Trump administration and proposed legislation backed by the administration. It provides summary and analysis of federal court cases, such as those concerning the travel ban. It provides a three-part guide to counter hateful anti-immigrant narratives through legislative testimony, local media work, and social media outlets. It provides a webinar series for advocates in removal orders and proceedings and "practice tips" for counsels involved in enhanced enforcement of border security rules and procedures. It studies and publishes a state-by-state overview of legal mechanisms to combat the unauthorized practice of immigration law to assist noncitizen victims of that practice.

## Center for American Progress (CAP)

The Center for American Progress was founded in 2003 by John Podesta as a progressive policy research and advocacy think-tank organization. It is based in Washington, D.C. It advocates for comprehensive immigration reform, the Dream Act, and President Obama's DACA and DAPA programs and opposes the immigration "crackdown" approach of conservative organizations, the Muslim travel ban, and the civil liberties and privacy concerns arising from the USA Patriots Acts I and II and the DHS law.

## Center for Immigration Studies (CIS)

CIS is an independent, nonpartisan, nonprofit research organization founded in 1985. It is a think tank devoted exclusively to research and policy analysis of economic, social, demographic, fiscal, and other impacts of immigration on the United States. It seeks to expand knowledge and understanding of the need for an immigration policy that gives first concern to broad national interests. It describes itself as pro-immigrant but favors low immigration that seeks fewer immigrants but a warmer welcome for those admitted. Led by Mark Krikorian, it publishes *Immigration Review*. It is notably anti-illegal immigration. It is located in Washington, D.C.

## Center for Migration Studies (CMS)

Center for Migration Studies of New York was founded in 1964. It is one of the premier institutes for migration studies in the United States. It strives to facilitate the study of socio-demographic, historical, economic, political, legislative, and pastoral aspects of human migration and refugee movements. In 1969 it incorporated as an educational, nonprofit institute. It brings an independent perspective to the interdisciplinary study of international migration and refugees without the institutional constraints of government analysis and special interest groups or the profit considerations of private research firms. It claims to be the only institute in the United States devoted exclusively to understanding and educating the public on the causes and consequences of human mobility at both origin and destination countries. It generates and facilitates the dissemination of new knowledge and the fostering of effective policies. It publishes a leading scholarly journal in the field, the *International Migration Review*. For many years it held an annual conference in immigration policy in Washington, D.C., that brought together government officials, academic scholars of the issue, lawyers involved in immigration matters, and activists in immigration-related advocacy organizations, such as church-affiliated groups.

## Center for Privacy and Technology Policy (CPTP)

Center for Privacy and Technology at Georgetown Law Center is a think-tank (501)(c)(3) nonprofit focused on privacy and surveillance law and policy. It studies the impact of government surveillance and commercial data practices on vulnerable communities, such as racial and ethnic minorities, immigrants, LGBT persons, and the poor. It provides intellectual and legal foundations for reform of U.S. consumer privacy law, especially on new technologies, such as biometrics, wearables, and the Internet of Things, and cyber software and hardware. It offers technology-intensive courses for students to become leaders in privacy practice, policy making, and advocacy. It supports fellows doing research in the field. Its six faculty directors work under the founding executive director of Georgetown Law's Center on Privacy and Technology, Alvaro Bedoya. It has several research fellows and deputy technologists. Its experts work with companies and legislators to craft innovative policy and technical solutions to cyber and IT-related problems.

## Center for the Study of Hate Crimes and Extremism

A nonpartisan domestic research and policy center, it examines bigotry on both the regional and national levels, on methods used to advocate extremism, and on the use of terrorism to deny civil or human rights to people on the basis of race, ethnicity, religion (particularly against Muslim immigrants), gender, sexual orientation, disability, or other relevant status characteristics. The center sponsors public conferences, collaborates with international and national news media outlets, and maintains an Internet site with information about and in cooperation with government organizations, human relations organizations, nonprofit organizations, and law enforcement. It is housed within the Department of Criminal Justice at California State University-San Bernardino. Its director, Professor Brian Levin, was prominently interviewed by the national media after the lone-wolf terrorist attack in San Bernardino in 2015.

## Center on Budget and Policy Priorities (CBPP)

Center on Budget and Policy Priorities is a nonpartisan research and policy institute that studies federal and state policies to reduce poverty and inequality and to restore fiscal responsibility in equitable and effective ways. It was founded in 1981 to analyze federal budget priorities with a focus on how budget choices affect lower-income Americans. Currently, it responds to new developments and has entered into new areas of research. In the states, CBPP collaborates with nonprofits, including more than 40 members of the State Priorities Partnership to build their capacity for budget and policy analysis and to participate effectively in policy debates, including, most recently, immigration policy change. It is headquartered in Washington, D.C.

### Congressional Research Service (CRS)

Begun in 1914 at the insistence of Senator Robert LaFollette, Sr. (R-WI), and Representative John Nelson (R-WI), the Congressional Research Service is sometimes known as the think tank of the U.S. Congress. It publishes an annual *Congressional Research Services Review*. It works exclusively for Congress, providing policy and legal analysis to committees and to members of both the U.S. House of Representatives and the Senate, regardless of political party affiliation. It is a legislative branch agency within the Library of Congress. It has been a valued and respected resource for more than a century. Its analyses are authoritative, confidential, objective, and nonpartisan. It has recently issued research reports on national security topics, on secrecy and information policy, on intelligence, on homeland security, and on terrorism. It has a staff of 600 employees located in Washington, D.C.

### Council of Graduate Schools (CGS)

Council of Graduate Schools conducts research and coordinates programs and activities to advance graduate education and to promote U.S. competitiveness in the global economy. It has been a sharp critic of the negative impact on graduate education and graduate enrollments of the USA Patriot Acts, the SEVIS program of DHS, and of the State Department's tightening of the student visa applications programs generally. Its Best Practices Initiatives addresses common challenges to graduate education by supporting innovations and sharing effective practices with the graduate community, providing millions of dollars to support innovative projects at member institutions. It is a leading source of information and data analysis for benchmarking trends in graduate education, documenting the "brain drain" outflow since 2001. It is a national advocate lobbying for graduate education and as a resource for policy makers on issues concerning graduate education, research, and scholarship. It is an authority on global trends in graduate education. Its headquarters are located in Washington, D.C.

## Department of Homeland Security (DHS)

Created as a cabinet-level department in 2002 with the merger of 22 agencies, DHS now has a staff or more than 240,000 employees. Its tasks include aviation security, border security, emergency response, cyber security, chemical facility inspection, customs inspection, immigration control and services, guarding the nation's coasts, and protecting the president, vice president, the White House, and visiting heads of state. It combined agencies drawn from the following departments: Agriculture, Defense, Energy, Health and Human Services, Justice, Treasury, and Transportation. It merged into the DHS such notable previous agencies as the Federal Protective Service, Federal Emergency Management Agency, the Federal Computer Incident Center, the U.S. Coast Guard, and the U.S. Secret Service. It is located in Washington, D.C.

## Department of Justice (DOJ)

The Department of Justice was founded in 1870 (16 Stat. 162) to defend the interests of the United States according to the law, to ensure public safety against foreign and domestic threats, to provide leadership in preventing and controlling crime, to punish those guilty of unlawful behavior, and to ensure fair and impartial administration of justice. It is headed by the attorney general of the United States, created by the Judiciary Act of 1789. The 1870 Act established the Office of Solicitor General, who presents the U.S. cases before the Supreme Court. Its 2017 budget is $48.5 billion. Among its more notable components and programs are the Bureau of Alcohol, Tobacco and Firearms (ATF), the Civil Rights Division, Criminal Division, Drug Enforcement Agency (DEA), Office for U.S. Attorneys, the Federal Bureau of Investigation (FBI), the Federal Bureau of Prisons (BOP), INTERPOL Washington, Tax Division, U.S. Marshals Service, and U.S. Victims of Terrorism Abroad Task Force. As are all cabinet-level departments, its headquarters are in Washington, D.C. Under Attorney General Jeff Sessions, DOJ has taken a prominent role in the "crackdown" approach to unauthorized immigration, opposing amnesty and any Dream Act legislation, litigating the travel ban before federal district courts and the U.S. Supreme Court, and announcing a "zero-tolerance" policy and for some months the policy to separate children from their parents who entered the United States illegally.

### Federation for American Immigration Reform (FAIR)

Founded in 1979 by John Tanton, FAIR is a national, nonpartisan, nonprofit, public interest membership organization of conservative citizens who share a common belief that the mass immigration to the United States should be greatly reduced. It advocates a moratorium on all immigration except for the spouses and minor children of U.S. citizens. It advocates for a strict limitation on the number of refugees and supports President Trump's travel ban. It argues that the United States needs strict and reduced immigration policy to allow time to regain control of the borders, secure the nation against terrorism, and to reduce overall levels of immigration to about 300,000 a year. It advocates for a U.S. immigration policy that is nondiscriminatory while at the same time is designed to serve the social, economic, and environmental needs of the United States. It is located in Washington, D.C.

## Free Congress Foundation (now American Opportunity Foundation)

Free Congress is a politically conservative, culturally conservative think tank that is more of an advocacy organization that promotes the "culture war" and advocates returning the nation and its policies to the "traditional, Judeo-Christian, Western" cultural heritage by stopping what it labels the long slide into the moral and cultural decay of "political correctness." It was founded in 1945. It strenuously opposes illegal immigration and any program of amnesty or earned legalization or earned residency programs; favors strict enforcement of immigration laws, of an English-only policy; and rejects all forms of multiculturalism. It favored the creation of the DHS, and the USA Patriot Acts I and II. It is headquartered in Arlington, Virginia.

## Freedom Works

Founded in 1984, Freedom Works has full-time staffed offices in 10 states and claims to be a coalition of about 700,000 volunteers nationwide. It was chaired by former U.S. House of Representatives majority leader Dick Armey. It advocates lower taxes, less government, and more freedom. It strongly backs a private business-based approach to a guest worker program developed by the Krieble Foundation. It has grown into a serious force within the Republican Party and in particular in its presidential nomination process, tilting to the extreme right of the political spectrum. It advocates for strict border control and favored enactment of the USA Patriot Acts and the DHS Act. It supports enhanced interrogation and expedited deportation policies. It is a libertarian advocacy group headquartered in Washington, D.C.

## Government Accountability Office (GAO)

The GAO is an independent, nonpartisan agency that works for Congress. Often referred to as the "congressional watchdog," the GAO investigates how the federal government spends tax-payer dollars. The GAO is headed by the comptroller general of the United States, who is appointed to a 15-year term by the president from a slate of candidates proposed by the Congress through a bipartisan, bicameral commission. The current comptroller general is Gene Dodaro, who became the eighth comptroller general on December 22, 2010, when he was nominated by President Obama and confirmed by the U.S. Senate. The GAO seeks to improve the performance and accountability of the federal government by providing Congress with timely information based on objective, fact-based, non-partisan, nonideological, fair, and balanced studies. Its core values are accountability, integrity, and reliability.

Its studies and analyses are done at the behest of congressional committees or subcommittees or are mandated by public laws or committee reports. The GAO supports congressional oversight by auditing agencies and operations, investigating allegations of illegal or improper activities, reporting on the effectiveness and efficiency of policies in meeting their objectives, performing policy analyses and outlining options for congressional consideration, and issuing legal decisions and opinions. The GAO advises Congress and heads of executive agencies on ways to make government more efficient, effective, ethical, equitable, and responsive. It is consistently ranked as one of the best places to work in the federal government in the annual list of the Partnership for Public Service. It has frequently produced studies on the impact of immigration laws and critical analyses of the DHS immigration-related policies particularly related to any discriminatory impact.

### Heritage Foundation

Founded in 1973 by Joseph Coors, Paul Weyrich, and Edwin Feulner, the Heritage Foundation is a conservative think tank and lobbying organization in Washington, D.C. Its CEO is Jim DeMint. It describes itself as the leader of the conservative movement. It rose to prominence during the administration of President Ronald Reagan, when it issued its "Mandate for Leadership," which became the blueprint of the conservative agenda of the Reagan presidency. It was a leading opponent of the Obama administration's immigration policy, DACA and DAPA, and is a leading proponent of President Trump's approach to homeland security and immigration policy. It favors the travel ban, building the border wall, and expedited removal of illegal aliens as logical steps to ensure national security.

## Human Rights First

Human Rights First is an independent advocacy and action organization that is nonpartisan, nonprofit and an international human rights organization based in New York, Washington, D.C., Houston, and Los Angeles. It accepts no government funding. It challenges the United States to live up to its ideals—vigorously opposing, for example, the Trump administration's plans to restore water boarding, the travel ban, and the zero-tolerance policy, which caused the separation of unauthorized immigrant children from their parents. It promotes American leadership in the global struggle for human rights, pressing the U.S. government and private companies to respect human rights and the rule of law; demanding reform, accountability, and justice; and advocating for the rights of asylum-seekers, immigrants, and refugees. It exposes and protests injustice, advocating policy solutions to ensure consistent respect for human rights. It protects the rights of refugees, combats the use of torture, and defends persecuted minorities. It conducts campaigns to pursue specific goals so that policy makers in Washington, D.C., hear from citizen champions of human rights. For more than 35 years, it has built a bipartisan coalition of frontline activists and lawyers to tackle global challenges to human rights and to demand American leadership in protecting human rights. Human Rights First believes supporting human rights is a moral obligation but is also a vital national interest; that America is strongest when its policies and actions match its national values.

## MoveOn.org

MoveOn began in 1998 when two technology entrepreneurs, Joan Blades and Wes Boyd, created an online petition about the Clinton impeachment and e-mailed it to their friends. It went viral. Sharing a deep frustration with the partisan warfare in Washington, D.C., and what they felt was a waste of time and money on the impeachment mess, they began to circulate a petition to "Censure President Clinton and Move on to Pressing Issues." Thus began MoveOn.org as a political action committee, helping members to elect candidates who reflect the founders' progressive values and, through a variety of activities, seeking to influence the outcome of the 2000 election. Since its inception, MoveOn.org supports candidates, lobbies legislation, and advocates for cultural change, committed to an inclusive and progressive future for American society. It mobilizes its members to advocate for equality, sustainability, and justice. Organized in all 50 states, it is a large grassroots organization, seeking new opportunities for change and mobilizing to achieve them. It promotes rapid-response organizing and communication, interventions, and digital innovation. It employs rigorous data science and testing and promotes grassroots participation. It is a fierce opponent of the Trump administration's immigration policies—in particular, the travel ban, sanctuary cities policy, zero-tolerance and separation of families policy, and the expedited removal of unauthorized immigrants and asylum-seekers.

## National Conference of State Legislatures (NCSL)

The National Conference of State Legislatures was founded in 1975 to champion state legislatures by helping states to remain strong and independent, by providing information and tools to craft the best solutions to difficult problems. It has vigorously opposed the federal government's use of unfunded mandates. It opposes the use of state and local officials for federal immigration enforcement as constituting an unfunded mandate.

It advocates for state governments in federal courts to refund to state governments the costs they bear because of the failure of the federal government to adequately control U.S. borders. It annually conducts workshops for state legislators and legislative staff in every state. It seeks to improve the quality and effectiveness of state legislatures. It promotes policy innovation and communication among state legislatures and works to ensure that state legislatures have a strong, cohesive voice in the federal system. It promotes its "The States' Agenda," a blueprint for the NCSL's advocacy work on Capitol Hill. It has nine standing committees that adopt recommended policies to fight unwarranted federal preemption of state laws, unfunded mandates, and federal legislation that threaten state authority and autonomy. It has headquarters in Denver, Colorado, and in Washington, D.C.

## National Immigration Forum (NIF)

Founded in 1982, National Immigration Forum advocates to embrace and uphold America's tradition as a nation of immigrants and to build public support for public policies that welcome immigrants and refugees that are fair and supportive to newcomers. As such it opposes President Trump's travel ban. NIF works to unite families torn apart by what it considers unreasonable and arbitrary restrictions. It advocates for fair treatment of refugees who have fled persecution and for legalization of unauthorized immigrants and promotes a pathway to full political incorporation and equitable access to social protections. It advocates for fundamental constitutional rights, no matter the legal status of immigrants. It advocates for policies that strengthen the U.S. economy by working with a diverse coalition of allies—immigrant, ethnic, religious, civil rights, labor union, business groups, and state and local governments—to forge a new vision of immigration policy consistent with global realities. It fosters economic growth, attracting needed workers to the United States, and protects the rights of workers and their families. It helps newcomers to settle into their communities and helps them to improve their socio-economic status. It seeks to help localities to weave immigrants into the fabric of community life by building bonds of mutual understanding between residents and newcomers. It supported President Obama's executive orders of DACA and DAPA. It opposes President Trump's travel ban and the DOJ's zero-tolerance policy that separates children from their unauthorized parents. Its headquarters are located in Washington, D.C.

### National Immigration Law Center

The National Immigration Law Center is a national support center dedicated to protect and promote the rights and opportunities of low-income immigrants and their families. It specializes in immigration law and immigrant welfare. It conducts policy analysis and impact litigation and provides publications, technical services, and training to a broad constituency of legal aid agencies, community groups, and pro bono attorneys. It has offices in Los Angeles, Oakland, and Washington, D.C. It lobbies and works in coalition with other organizations favoring legalization and similar approaches to the illegal immigration problem. It opposes what it considers the civil liberties and privacy abuses of the Patriot Act and the DHS.

### National Rifle Association (NRA)

Founded in 1871, NRA is one of the most powerful lobbies in national politics and exemplifies the 501 (c)(4) organizations. It was founded by George Wood Wingate and William Conant Church. In the past it was largely nonpartisan or bipartisan and emphasized gun-safety training. Since 1975 it advocates strenuously for gun rights and has directly lobbied for pro-gun legislation at the state and national levels. It advocates for strict enforcement of immigration laws and the crackdown on illegal immigration and enhanced border control. Some of its members have joined "vigilante groups," like the Minutemen, who patrol the border areas to deter illegal immigration. Claiming more than 5 million members, it is headquartered in Fairfax, Virginia, and its CEO is Wayne LaPierre. They have been very prominent supporters of President Trump, contributing millions to his election campaign, and have lobbied Congress in support of his travel ban, zero-tolerance policy, and expedited removal of unauthorized immigrants.

## Office of Management and Budget (OMB)

Office of Management and Budget is a major office within the Executive Office of the President. It serves the president in overseeing the implementation of his agenda across the entire Executive Branch. Its mission is to assist the president in meeting his policy, budget and management, and regulatory objectives, and to fulfill its statutory responsibilities. These include: 1) Budget development and execution; 2) Management, including oversight of agency performance, human capital, federal procurement, financial management, and information technology; 3) Regulatory policy coordination; 4) Legislative clearance and coordination; and 5) Executive Orders and Presidential Memoranda. The Director of the OMB has regularly been involved in immigration reform policy initiatives, projecting the budgetary impact of various proposed reform bills, "scoring" legislation regarding immigration reform bills, and providing oversight of the DHS' immigration agencies, such as ICE, Customs and Border Control, and USCIS. In past administrations, the Director of the OMB has been involved in drafting immigration reform proposals for the administration.

## Pew Hispanic Center (PHC)

Founded in 2001, the Pew Hispanic Center is a nonpartisan research organization supported by the Pew Charitable Trust. It strives to improve understanding of the U.S. Hispanic population and to chronicle Latino's growing impact on the United States. Timeliness, relevance, and scientific rigor are characteristics of its work. A classic example of a think tank, it does not advocate for or take positions on policy issues. Demography, immigration, and remittances are its major research foci on unauthorized immigration matters. The Pew Forum, Hispanic Center, and Research Center are located in the headquarters in Washington, D.C. Their data and studies are regularly reported on by the mass media, thereby influencing public opinion with respect to immigration reform issues, concerns, and proposals.

### Rand Corporation

Rand is a contraction of the terms "research and development." It was the first organization to be called a think tank. Established in 1946 by the U.S. Air Force, today RAND is a nonprofit institution that helps improve the policy and decision making of government through research and analysis whose areas of expertise include child policy, civil and criminal justice, community and U.S. regional studies, drug policy, education, health, homeland security, immigration, infrastructure, international policy, methodology, national security, population and aging, science and technology, and terrorism. On occasion its findings are considered so compelling that it advances specific policy recommendations. It serves the public interest by widely disseminating its research findings. The Rand Corporation headquarters are located in Santa Monica, California.

### United States Customs and Border Protection (USCBP)

USCBP is one of the world's largest law enforcement organizations, with more than 60,000 employees. It was established with the creation of the DHS in 2002. It is charged with keeping terrorists and their weapons out of the United States while facilitating lawful international travel and trade. As the nation's unified border entity, CBP takes a comprehensive approach to border management and control, combining customs, immigration, border security, and agricultural protection into one coordinated and supportive activity. CBP is responsible for enforcing hundreds of U.S. laws and regulations, screening nearly a million visitors per day, as well as more than 67,000 cargo containers. It arrests more than 1,100 persons at the borders daily and seizes nearly 6 tons of illegal drugs. Annually, it facilitates more than $3 trillion in legitimate trade, while enforcing U.S. trade laws. The CBP's mission is to safeguard the borders by protecting the public from dangerous people and materials, yet enhancing the global economic competitiveness of the United States by enabling legitimate trade and travel. Its stated ethos says:

> We are the guardians of the nation's borders; we are America's frontline; we safeguard the homeland at and beyond the borders; we protect the American people against terrorists and instruments of terror; we enforce the law of the United States fostering the nation's economic security through lawful international trade and travel; and we serve the American people with vigilance, integrity, and professionalism.

### United We Dream

United We Dream is the nation's foremost organization of the Dreamer youth. It conducts campaigns powered by immigrants, people of color, and their allies determined to reject and oppose President Trump's immigration policies and to honor and celebrate immigrant and refugee resilience by defiance and by creating undocumented-friendly classrooms and educators. It promotes schools and campuses as sanctuary, demanding and supporting a local campaign for sanctuary cities. The organization defines sanctuary as a place promoting freedom of expression through dialogue and activism and as a place where the dignity and integrity of every individual as a human being is respected and preserved. It organizes sanctuaries to protect individuals from deportation, preventing ICE from "infecting" local law enforcement; protecting Muslims from a religious registry, surveillance, and harassment; uniting a coalition of sanctuary places against police brutality; and opposing *stop* and frisk. Its various chapters and affiliated organizations are united against misogyny and to promote woman's rights. It is a major organization that has won the hearts and minds of Latino voters. It continues to push for a permanent (i.e., congressional legislative) solution to the Dreamer problem that provides a path to citizenship by ending enforcement policies that have broken up so many families. It focuses on action at the state level, such as the granting of licenses and benefits from in-state tuition at state universities.

## Voto Latino

Voto Latino is a pioneering civic media organization seeking to transform America by organizing and recognizing Latinos' innate leadership. It uses innovative digital campaigns, pop culture, and grassroots voices to engage, educate, and empower Latinos as agents of change to build a stronger and more inclusive American democracy. It was cofounded in 2004 by Maria Teresa Kumar and Rosario Dawson. In its early days its core work was around voter registration. It expanded into civic engagement and leadership development. It claims to have registered 250,000 voters, innovated voter registration through text messaging, and help count Latinos in the 2010 census. It cofounded National Voter Registration Day. Voto Latino started a LV Power Summit Conference to bring together young people with key leaders. It has contributed one-half million dollars to young Latino innovators. It estimates there are 27 million potential Hispanic voters in the United States.

## People

*The following section presents short biographical sketches of individuals active in the arena of immigration policy making and implementation. Some are elected officials (presidents, congressmen), some are appointed officials (bureaucratic leaders, judges), some are political activists (lobbyists) on the immigration reform issue, and some are scholars/analysts heading major think-tank organizations that study and advocate on the issue from a more bipartisan or nonpartisan perspective. Their profiles are presented in alphabetical order.*

### Bush, George W. (1946– )

George W. Bush served as the 43rd president (2001–2009), a wartime president after the terrorist attacks on 9/11/2001. He was born in New Haven, Connecticut, and was enrolled at Phillips Academy in Andover, Massachusetts, in 1961. He worked in his father's Senate bid in 1964. The family moved to Midland, Texas. Bush graduated from Yale University in 1968 and then enlisted in the Texas Air National Guard. In 1973 he entered the Harvard Business School and earned an MBA business degree from Harvard in 1975, and then returned to Midland and also entered the oil business, founding an oil and gas exploration company. He married Laura Welch and they have twin daughters. His first foray into elective office politics was an unsuccessful run for the House of Representatives in 1978. In 1978 he also worked on his father's campaign for the presidency. He later joined a group of investors buying the Texas Rangers baseball team in 1989. He ran for and was elected governor of Texas, serving as its 46th governor from 1995 to 2000. He was elected president in 2000, after a closely contested race against Al Gore, who won the popular vote but lost the White House when the U.S. Supreme Court, in *Bush v. Gore* (2000), awarded the electoral college votes of Florida to Bush (Bush-Cheney won 271 ECV to 266 for Gore-Lieberman). After the attacks of September 11, 2001, President Bush declared a "war on terrorism," and his administration authored and Congress passed the USA Patriot Act, granting the executive branch sweeping powers to deal with terrorism. Congress also passed the administration-backed law to create the new cabinet-level Department of Homeland Security. He appointed former Pennsylvania governor Tom Ridge as the first secretary of Homeland Security, and later Michael Chertoff as his second secretary of DHS. The administration was noted for its crackdown on illegal immigrants and efforts to enforce expedited removal. He appointed the first director of National Intelligence in an effort to control international terrorism. He pushed, unsuccessfully, for comprehensive immigration reform and a bill that would have established a guest worker program.

### Carter, James (Jimmy) Earl, Jr. (1924)

Jimmy Carter was born in Hope, George. In 1941 he entered the Georgia Institute of Technology, and in 1943 he entered the Naval Academy in Annapolis, Maryland, from which he graduated in 1946. In 1962 he was elected to the Georgia state senate. In 1970, he was elected governor of Georgia. He was elected president in 1976. He deregulated the oil industry in 1978, pushed the Panama Canal treaty through the Senate, and he signed the Camp David Accords. His most significant contribution to the immigration reform policy area was his establishment of the Select Commission on Immigration Reform and Refugee Policy (SCIRP), whose recommendations led to the Immigration Reform and Control Act of 1986. The commission's Final Report informed the debate of immigration reform for a decade. In 1980, the hostage crisis in Iran and the failure of the INS to track Iranian students in the United States contributed to his failed reelection bid. His humanitarian work since leaving the presidency, particularly his involvement regarding the Haitian crisis, and he has worked with the United Nations on refugee problems. He was awarded the Nobel Peace Prize in 2002.

### Chertoff, Michael (1953– )

Michael Chertoff was born in New Jersey in 1953. He graduated magna cum laude from Harvard College in 1973 and magna cum laude from Harvard Law School in 1978. He was clerk to Supreme Court Justice William Brennan, 1979–1980. Chertoff was a federal prosecutor for more than a decade, investigating political corruption (he was appointed special counsel for the Senate Whitewater Committee investigating possible impeachment of President William Clinton), organized crime, corporate fraud (the Enron Case), and terrorism, He was one of the investigators of the 9/11 terrorist attacks. He was U.S. attorney for the District of New Jersey, 1990–1994. He served as a federal judge on the U.S. Court of Appeals for the Third Circuit. He was nominated for secretary of the Department of Homeland Security in 2005 by President George W. Bush, confirmed by the Senate by a vote of 88–1, and he served until January 2009. As secretary of DHS he strengthened the borders, adding many border patrol agents. While he was secretary, the DHS cracked down on sanctuary cities and illegal immigration and began construction of the border fence. He stressed intelligence analysis and infrastructure protection and pushed for development of full body scanners to be used by the TSA. After the Hurricane Katrina disaster, secretary Chertoff worked to improve FEMA into an effective organization. After his term as secretary of DHS, he cofounded The Chertoff Group, of which he is chairman, focusing on risk identification, analysis, and mitigation, and crisis management, and providing strategic counsel on global security solutions. He is a senior counsel at Covington and Burling, OOP, and is a member of that firm's White Collar Defense and Investigations group. His spouse is Meryl Justin, with whom he has two children. He cochairs the Bipartisan Policy Center's Immigration Task Force.

### Clinton, William Jefferson (1946– )

William Jefferson Clinton was the 42nd U.S. President, serving from 1993 to 2001. He was the first president of the boomer generation. He was born in Hope, Arkansas. He graduated from

Georgetown University, taking a degree in Foreign Service in 1968. He was class president in 1964–1965. He was a congressional intern with Senator William Fulbright (D-Ark) from 1964 to 1967 and was a Rhodes Scholar at University College, United Kingdom, studying philosophy, politics, and economics.

He earned his JD degree from Yale Law School in 1973, where he met his future wife, Hillary Rodham, in 1980, the year in which he ran unsuccessfully for Congress. He served as Arkansas attorney general, 1979–1981; then he ran for and won the governorship of Arkansas, serving as the 42nd governor from 1983 to 1992. While being the governor, he helped establish the Democratic Leadership Council, 1990–1991. He secured the Democratic Party nomination for the presidency in 1992 and won the White House, with Al Gore as his VP candidate, defeating incumbent president George H.W. Bush. He sent a peace-keeping force to Bosnia, was a strong proponent of expanding the North Atlantic Treaty Organization (NATO), and negotiated the world trade agreement, the North American Free Trade Agreement (NAFTA). He launched a worldwide campaign against drug trafficking. His centrist approach to budget policy helped spur an economic recovery from the "Bush recession" and oversaw the U.S. economy to its best record in decades, which lasted until he left office, with a budget surplus, the first such surplus in decades. His most notable legislations related to immigration are the two 1996 acts: the Personal Responsibility and Work Opportunity Act and the Illegal Immigration Reform and Immigrant Responsibility Act (IIRIA). He is the author of five books: *Between Hope and History* (1996), and *Clinton Foreign Policy* Reader (2000), *My Life* (2004), *Giving* (2007), and *Back to Work* (2011).

### Conyers, John (1929– )

Until 2016, John Conyers (D-MI) was the ranking member of the House Judiciary Committee, which considers all legislative bills dealing with immigration matters, such as the 1980

Refugee Act, the 1986 IRCA, the 1990 IMMACT, IIRIA in 1996, the USA Patriot Acts I and II, various Dream Act proposed bills from 2001 to 2011, the Fence Act, and the Real ID Act. Conyers served on its Subcommittee on the Constitution, Civil Rights, and Civil Liberties and was a leading critic of the privacy and civil liberties policies and procedures of the Patriot Acts and of the DHS's procedures for expedited removal of unauthorized immigrants. He is the coauthor of several books on civil rights matters: *The Politics of Cancer Revisited* (1998, with Samuel Epstein), *Warrior-King: The Case for Impeaching George W. Bush* (2003, with John Bonifaz), *Charting Your Course: Lessons Learned during the Journey toward Performance Excellence* (2003, with Robert Ewy), *What Went Wrong in Ohio: The Conyers Report on the 2004 Presidential Election* (2005), *George W. Bush versus the U.S. Constitution* (2006, with Anita Miller), and *The Constitution in Crisis* (2007, with Elizabeth Holtzman). Conyers was educated at Wayne State University. He was first elected to Congress in 1965 and is the oldest, longest-serving member of Congress—the "Dean of the House of Representatives." He has sponsored numerous bills on Crime and Law Enforcement, and on Civil Rights, Civil Liberties, and Minority Issues. He recently fought a congressional Republican-led attack on the Council on American-Islamic Relations. John Conyers is a founding member of the Congressional Black Caucus and the Congressional Progressive Caucus, both of which played critical roles in immigration reform legislative battles. He served in the National Guard and the United States Army Corps of Engineers in the Korean War. In 1957, he earned his BA, and his JD degree in 1958, at Wayne State University. He appeared in the 2011 documentary film *War on Terror*, about the George W. Bush war on terror, and in the 2004 Michael Moore documentary film *Fahrenheit 9/11*.

### Durbin, Richard "Dick" (1944– )

Dick Durbin (D-IL) is one of the Senate's "Gang of Eight" who crafted the bipartisan comprehensive immigration reform bill,

S. 744, the measure which passed the Senate in 2013. He is the 47th senator from Illinois and has served in the Senate since 1996, having been reelected in 2002, 2005, and 2014. He is a member of the Senate Judiciary Committee and of the Appropriations Committee and is ranking member on the Subcommittee on Constitution, Civil Rights, and Human Rights. He is the assistant Democratic leader in the Senate (aka the minority whip). He is a leader of the Democrats in the Senate and their chief vote counter. He is an outspoken critic of President Trump's travel ban and of the Senate Republican approach to reforming immigration policy. He supported President Obama's DACA and DAPA orders and is a cosponsor and leading advocate of the various Dream Act bills.

### Ferguson, Bob (1965– )

Bob Ferguson is Washington State's 18th attorney general, having first been elected to the office in 2012 and reelected in 2016. A former professional chess player, he is an internationally rated chess master and has twice won the Washington State Chess Championship. He began his legal career in Spokane, specializing in civil litigation after having clerked for two federal judges. He is leading the various attorneys general from 17 states in opposition to President Trump's travel ban, the zero-tolerance policy, and the policy separating children from their parents and the Trump administration's lack of a plan to reunite them with their families. He successfully blocked Trump's first travel ban from seven Muslim majority nations and has won cases he has argued before the Washington Supreme Court. His office has initiated action against human trafficking and immigration services fraud. He is a graduate of the University of Washington and New York University law school. He has won numerous awards, such as *Time Magazine's* 100 Most Influential People, the Crosscut Courage in Elected Office Award, a Victory Fund Champion for Equality, a University of Washington Political Science Department

Distinguished Alumni Award, the Council on American-Islamic Relations Ally for Justice Award, and their Defender of Liberty Award, the University of Washington's Center for Human Rights Justice Award, and Public Official of the Year (2016) Award, the SEIU (2017) Elected Official of the Year Award, among others. He is widely considered a likely candidate for Washington's Democratic Party's nomination for the office of Governor in 2020.

### Gonzales, Alberto (1955– )

Alberto Gonzales was born in San Antonio, Texas, in 1955. He served as U.S. attorney general from 2005 to 2007, succeeding John Ashcroft. As White House Counsel to President George W. Bush (2001–2005), he was instrumental in preparing legal briefs justifying enhanced interrogation techniques and was part of the administration team that prepared the DHS proposed bill. He was instrumental in drafting the Bush administration's positions on the Border Protection, Anti-Terrorism, and Illegal Immigration Control Act, and on the Real ID Act. Gonzales was educated at the U.S. Air Force Academy (1973–1975) and earned his BA degree in political science from Rice University in 1979 and his JD from Harvard Law in 1982. He and his wife, Rebecca Turner Gonzales, have three sons. Gonzales joined the law firm of Vinson and Elkins, L.L.P. in Houston, in 1982. He also taught law as an adjunct professor at the University of Houston Law Center. Gonzales was elected to the American Law Institute in 1999. He was on the board of trustees of the Texas Bar Association from 1996 to 1999, and Board of Directors of the United Way of Texas Gulf Coast from 1993 to 1994. Gonzales was Special Legal Counsel to the Houston Host Committee for the 1990 Summit of Industrialized Nations. Gonzales served as Texas' 100th secretary of state (1997–1999), where he was senior advisor to Governor George Bush and lead liaison on Mexico and border issues. He served as an associate justice of the Supreme Court of Texas from 1999 to 2001. He served as general counsel to Governor George W. Bush for three years. Since leaving the attorney general's office in 2007, he has been Dean and Distinguished Professor of Law at Belmont University College of Law in Nashville, Tennessee. He has coauthored, with David Strange, *A Conservative and Compassionate Approach to Immigration Reform* (2014) and authored *True Faith and Allegiance* (2016).

## Goodlatte, Bob (1952– )

Representative Bob Goodlatte (R-VA) obtained his BA in 1974 from Bates College and earned his JD from Washington and Lee Law School in 1977. He began his political career working for Congressman Caldwell Butler (R-VA) in 1988. He practiced law from 1970 to 1992, when he was first elected to the House of Representatives. He became chair of the House Judiciary Committee in 2017, and on its Crime, Terrorism, and Homeland Security Subcommittee as well as serving on its Select Committee on Homeland Security and its Subcommittee on Infrastructure and Border Security. He has sponsored a law imposing tougher penalties on commercial counterfeiters. He has compiled a strongly conservative voting record. He has notably sponsored the Secure Our Borders First bill, proposed by the Republican members of the Judiciary Committee in 2015. It takes a severe "crackdown approach" to immigration control. He has been a notable supporter of President Trump's travel ban, led the opposition to DACA and DAPA, and favors the building of the border wall and cutting down legal immigration, the ending of the visa lottery, and restrictions on family reunification preferences.

## Graham, Lindsey (1955– )

Senator Lindsey Graham (R-SC) was one of the Senate's "Gang of Eight." They helped pass S.744, the 2013 bill which was a bipartisan comprehensive immigration reform bill. It passed the Senate but died in the House. The bill included a

Dream Act provision, provided for increased border security funding, expansion of the fence and of electronic surveillance, but also provided for a path to citizenship for unauthorized immigrants. He is known as a military and international policy "hawk." He serves on the Senate Judiciary Committee and has been one of the very few Republicans who expressed opposition to Trump's travel ban and the zero-tolerance policy. He was one of the bipartisan groups that proposed a compromise bill for immigration reform in 2017 to end the DACA crisis before the bill was killed by President Trump's opposition. Graham is a leading Republican on the Senate Armed Services Committee.

He was born in Central, South Carolina. He graduated with a BA degree from the University of South Carolina in 1977 and obtained his JD from the South Carolina School of Law in 1981. He served in the U.S. Air Force from 1982 to 1988 and was an Air Force Reserve officer, retiring in 2015 as a colonel. He served in the House of Representatives from 1995 to 2002. He was elected to the Senate in 2002 and reelected in 2008 and 2014. He briefly sought the Republican Party's nomination for president in 2016 but was one of the first of the field of 17 to withdraw from the race. He has been a notable voice on the Judiciary Committees investigation into the Russian cyberattack to influence the 2016 presidential election.

### Guitierrez, Luis (1953– )

Luis Guitierrez (D-IL) is a key member of the House of Representative's "Gang of Eight," who sponsored the House version of the S.744 bill for comprehensive immigration reform. He has served in the House since 1992. He graduated from Northwestern Illinois University. He is a leading member of the House Hispanic Caucus and served as chairman of its Immigration Task Force. He has played an instrumental role in President Obama's decision to use executive action regarding DACA and DAPA and has sponsored the various Dream Act bills introduced in the House of Representatives. He is a leading spokesman for Latino American issues. He serves on the House Judiciary Committee and on its Subcommittee on Immigration and Border Security. He is one of the most vocal critics of the Trump administration's policies on the separation of children from their parents and its zero tolerance on illegal immigration.

### Hanen, Andrew (1953– )

Andrew Hanen is a federal judge for the U.S. District Court for the Southern District of Texas. He was appointed to the federal bench by President George W. Bush in 2002. Judge Hanen earned his undergraduate degree from Denison University, in 1975, and his JD from Baylor University School of Law in 1978. He was confirmed by the Senate in May 2002, by a vote of 97–0. In February 2015, he placed an injunction (a judicial hold) to halt implementation of key elements of the immigration initiative of President Obama's Department of Justice regarding the president's executive action known as DAPA. Judge Hanen ruled that President Obama lacked the authority to implement the new immigration program regarding the granting of a deferred status to illegal immigrants who are the parents of U.S. citizens or legal residents. The administration filed a suit challenging the ruling with the Federal Circuit Court, but in the meantime, President Trump was elected, and he issued an executive order reversing that of President Obama on both the extension of DACA and the DAPA programs. Subsequently, President Trump rescinded the initial DACA program as well, although he announced his DHS and DOJ would not act to deport any of the Dreamers for six months, during which time President Trump urged the Congress to enact a Dreamer bill. President Trump cited Judge Hanen's ruling in justification of his rescinding of the Obama executive orders and his position that Congress had to authorize any such policy to make them legal.

## Hatch, Orrin (1934– )

Senator Orrin Hatch (R-UT) is a key member and chair of the Senate Judiciary Committee and is the most senior Republican member in the Senate, having been elected in 1977. Senator Hatch is noted for his sponsorship of the Americans with Disabilities Act. He failed in his bid for the Republican Party's presidential nomination in 2000. Senator Hatch attended Brigham Young University. As the longest-serving member the Senate, he is president pro tempore of the Senate and thereby third in succession to the presidency. As chair of the Judiciary Committee, he has advocated for the Republican positions of opposing DACA and DAPA. He was one of the sponsors of a failed attempt in 2018 to pass an immigration reform bill after President Trump used his executive order powers to rescind DACA and supported Trump's demands that the bill include a significant decrease in legal immigration, an end of the lottery provision, and the building of a border wall. After the political debacle of the forced separation of immigrant children from the parents, Hatch was among a number of Senate Republicans who called for President Trump to rescind the executive order establishing the zero-tolerance policy and the family separation policy that resulted from the order.

## Herman, Susan N. (na– )

Susan N. Herman was elected president of the American Civil Liberties Union in October 2008. She leads one of the leading public advocacy organizations opposing the Trump administration's immigration policies; she leads the ACLU effort in support of numerous federal and Supreme Court challenges to the travel bans, the policies of the DHS and DOJ on expedited removal, opposition to refugees, the zero tolerance and separation of children from their families policy, among others. Prior to being elected the president of ACLU, she served on its National Board of Directors, as a member of the Executive Committee, and as general counsel. She holds a chair as centennial professor of law at Brooklyn Law School, where she teaches courses in constitutional law and criminal procedures and conducts seminars on law and literature, and terrorism and civil liberties. She writes extensively on constitutional and criminal procedural topics for various scholarly publications, ranging from law reviews and books to periodicals and on-line publications. Her recent book in its second edition, *Taking Liberties: The War on Terror and the Erosion of American Democracy* (Oxford University Press, 2011 and 2014), won the 2012 Roy C. Palmer Civil Liberties Prize. As an ACLU spokesperson, she has appeared on *NPR, PBS, CSPAN, NBC, MSNBC,* and on *Today.* In print media, she has appeared in *Newsday, TIME,* the *Huffington Post,* and the *New York Times.* She has received awards from the Japanese-American Bar Association, the United Sikhs, and the Theatre of the Oppressed NYC. She has participated in Supreme Court litigation, writing and collaborating on amicus curiae briefs for the ACLU. She earned a BA from Barnard College and a JD from New York University School of Law, and she was a law clerk for the U.S. Court of Appeals for the Second Circuit, and staff Attorney and then associate director of Prisoners' Legal Services of New York.

### Hetfield, Mark (1967– )

Since 2013, Mark Hetfield has served as president and CEO of the Hebrew Immigrant Aid Society (HIAS) and is on the forefront of activists to protect and advocate for Syrian Refugee Relief. He is an immigration lawyer, having practiced immigration law in Washington, D.C., in the prestigious law firm of Fulbright & Jaworski, LLP. He graduated cum laude with a JD degree from Georgetown University Law, from which he also received a BS in Foreign Service. He adjudicated appeals at the INS. In 1994, he was posted to the U.S. Embassy in Haiti, while the country was under the rule of the military junta. He processed in-country refugee applications, offering the equivalent of asylum while discouraging Haitians from attempting to escape in vessels that were not seaworthy. His quality assurance process increased approvals from 5 percent to 25 percent. He began his career with HIAS in 1989, serving as a caseworker in Rome assisting Jewish refugee applicants from the Soviet Union. He later joined HIAS at its Washington, D.C., office as representative and director of international operations. While at HIAS, Hetfield served as senior advisor on refugee issues at the U.S. Commission on International Religious Freedom. At HIAS he directed a congressionally authorized study on the treatment of asylum-seekers. He authored its 2005 report, still widely used and assessed as the most comprehensive study on expedited removal to date. He and his team were presented with the Arthur Helton Award for the Advancement of Human Rights, by the American Immigration Lawyers Association. Prior to his appointment as president and CEO of HIAS, he was its senior vice president of policy and programs. An expert on refugee and immigration law, policy, and programs, he transformed HIAS from an organization focused on Jewish immigrants to a global agency assisting refugees of all faiths and ethnicities. HIAS is a major implementing partner of the UN Refugee Agency and the U.S. Department of Justice. HIAS assists all who flee ethnic cleansing, violence, and other forms of persecution without regard to ethnic, racial, or religious affiliation.

### Jackson-Lee, Sheila (na– )

Congresswoman Sheila Jackson-Lee (D-TX) is an influential member of the House of Representatives who sits on three congressional committees—a senior member of the House Committee on the Judiciary, on Homeland Security, and newly appointed by the leadership as a member of the Budget Committee. She is the ranking member of the Judiciary Subcommittee on Crime, Terrorism, Homeland Security, and Investigations. She has sponsored legislation including the Sentencing Reform Act, Law Enforcement and Trust and Integrity

Act, the RAISE Act, the Fair Chance for Youth Act, Kaleif's Law, and the American Rising Act of 2015. As ranking member of the Homeland Security Subcommittee on Maritime and Border Security, she coauthored HR 1417, a bipartisan bill for comprehensive immigration reform that contains most of the provisions of the 2013 S. 744 bill and would have essentially enacted the Dream Act proposals. As past chairwoman of the Homeland Security Subcommittee on Transportation Security and Infrastructure Protection, she led to passage the Transportation Security Act of 2007, which dramatically increased funding for transportation security. She supported enhanced technology, better intelligence, increased cargo inspections, increased security for railroads, and the implementation of the 9/11 Commission Report. *Congressional Quarterly* rated her one of the 50 most effective members of Congress, and the *U.S. News and World Report* named her one of the 10 most influential members of the House. She is chair of the Congressional Black Caucus Energy Brain Trust and co-chair of the Justice Reform Task Force. She is Senior Whip of the Democratic Caucus, chairs the Texas Congressional Democratic Delegation, and is current chair of the Congressional Black Caucus Foundation Board. She earned a BA in political science from Yale University cum laude in the first graduating class that included females. She obtained a JD from the University of Virginia Law School. She is married to Dr. Elwyn Lee, also a Yale Graduate, and an administrator at the University of Houston. They have two children.

### Jean-Pierre, Karine (1977– )

Karine Jean-Pierre is a political strategist, a grassroots organizer, an advisor to local and congressional campaigns, the campaign manager for NYC's public advocate Trish James, and the deputy campaign manager for Barack Obama's and for Martin O'Malley's presidential campaigns. She was regional director for the White House Office of Political Affairs. Born in Martinique, Haiti, of Haitian immigrants, she was raised in Queens, New York. She earned an MA in Public Administration from Columbia University. She does political commentary as the national spokesperson for MoveOn.org and has articulated their opposition to all of President Trump's immigration policies on such news outlets as *Fox News*, *MSNBC*, *CNN*, *CSPAN*, and the *PBS Newshour*. She joined the Columbia University faculty in 2014.

### Jimenez, Cristina (na– )

Cristina Jimenez is cofounder and managing director of the United We Dream network. She was brought to the United States from Ecuador unauthorized by her family when she was 13 years old. She attended and graduated from high school and college as an undocumented student. She organized youth and workers for passage of pro-immigrant policies at the local and national levels for the past 20 years. She was named by *Forbes Magazine* as one of the "30 under 30 in Law and Policy" and one of "21 immigration reform power players." The *Chronicle of Philanthropy* named her one of five nonprofit leaders who will influence public policy. She cofounded the New York State Youth Leadership Council and the Dream Mentorship Program at Queens College, and served as an immigration policy analyst for the Drum Major Institute for Public Policy and an immigrant rights organizer at Make the Road New York. She holds a master's degree in public administration and public policy from the School of Public Affairs at Baruch College, CUNY, and graduated cum laude with a BA in political science and business from Queens College, CUNY.

### Johnson, Jeh (1957– )

Jeh Johnson served as the secretary of the Department of Homeland Security from 2013 to 2017. Johnson was appointed by

President Barack Obama in 2013. He succeeded Janet Napolitano. As secretary of DHS, he oversaw the implementation of all laws, policies, and procedures pertaining to homeland security and to both legal and illegal immigration. He implemented President Obama's DACA executive order. He is an American civil and criminal trial lawyer. He is a graduate of Morehouse College and earned his JD from Columbia Law School. He served as the Air Force general counsel and then, in 2009, as the general counsel in the Department of Defense. He also served as U.S. assistant state attorney in the South District of New York. Since leaving the DHS, he has been an outspoken critic of the Trump administration's policy to rescind DACA and DAPA, to establish a zero-tolerance policy on unauthorized immigration, and to forcibly separate children from their parents for entering the United States illegally.

### Johnson, Lyndon B. (1908–1973)

Born in Texas, Lyndon Johnson graduated from the Southwest Texas State Teachers College in 1927. He began teaching in Houston in 1930. He was named director of the National Youth Administration in Texas in 1935 and was elected to Congress in 1938. In 1941 he lost a campaign for the U.S. Senate and went on to serve in the U.S. Navy, serving in the Pacific theater. He was elected to the Senate in 1948, went on to serve as the Democratic whip in 1951, and became the Senate minority leader in 1953. After winning reelection to the Senate in 1954, he was elected the Senate majority leader. He directed passage of the 1957 Civil Rights Act and was elected vice president in 1960. In 1963 he assumed the presidency upon John F. Kennedy's assassination and was elected president by a landslide in 1964. His most significant contribution to immigration reform was successfully advocating for and then signing into law the Immigration and Nationality Act of 1965. He opted not to run for reelection as president in 1968 and retired to his Texas ranch, where he died on January 22, 1973.

### Kelly, John F. (1950– )

John Kelly was born in Boston, Massachusetts, in 1950. He enlisted in the Marine Corps in 1970 and was discharged as a sergeant in 1972. Following graduation from the University of Massachusetts in 1976, he was commissioned an officer of Marines, serving in a number of command, staff, and school assignments. In 1976 he married Karen Hemest and they have three children. His son, also a marine, was killed in action in Afghanistan. Kelly attended the National War College and served on Capitol Hill as the marine commandant's liaison to the U.S. Congress. He also served as special assistant to the Supreme Allied Commander, Europe, in Mons, Belgium. From 2001 to 2003, he was assistant chief of Staff G-3 and ranked as brigadier general. He then served as assistant division commander, 1st Marine Division. He was legislative assistant to the commandant from 2004 to 2007. He was promoted to major general and commanding general, 1st Marine Expeditionary Force in Iraq. He was promoted to lieutenant general and commanded Marine Forces Reserve and Marine Forces North from 2009 to 2011. He was senior military assistant to two secretaries of Defense, Bill Gates and Leon Panetta. In 2012, he received a fourth star and command of the U.S. Southern Command until his retirement in 2016. After less than a year in retirement, he was appointed secretary of Homeland Security by President Donald Trump, confirmed by a vote of 88 to 11, serving as its fifth secretary, until being appointed White House chief of staff on July 31, 2017, replacing Reince Priebus. At DHS and currently in the White House, Kelly has been a staunch advocate of the Trump administration's immigration policies, including rescinding DACA and DAPA, the travel ban, expedited removal of unauthorized immigrants, and the zero-tolerance policy. He favors reducing the legal immigration, ending the visa lottery program, reducing family reunification preference numbers, and opposing congressional enactment of a Dream Act.

### Kennedy, Edward (1932–2009)

Born in Boston, Massachusetts, to the prominent Kennedy family, Senator Edward Kennedy received his BA from Harvard in 1956, attended the Hague International Law School in 1958, and obtained his LLB from the University of Virginia Law School in 1959. He worked in his brother's presidential campaign in 1960, then as assistant district attorney for Suffolk County in 1961–1962. He was elected to the U.S. Senate in 1962. He was, without doubt, the single most influential member of Congress on immigration matters, from sponsoring and helping to navigate the Immigration and Naturalization Act of 1965 (sometimes called the Kennedy Act) through the Senate, and worked on every major immigration-related bill until his death in 2009. His most important position regarding immigration issue was his role on the Senate Judiciary Committee. He was an outspoken critic of the Bush administration on civil rights and liberties matters as they impacted debate over how to control unauthorized immigration. He cosponsored the McCain-Kennedy bill to reform immigration policy in a comprehensive manner, including provisions for "earned legalization."

### Kerwin, Don (na– )

Don Kerwin is executive director of the Center for Migration Studies (CMS) in New York, the leading progressive think tank which is a pro-immigration organization studying and advocating comprehensive immigration reform. He became its director in 2011. He is author of *Migrant Children, Uninvited Guests, and Welcoming the Stranger*, 2014. Prior to his coming to the CMS, Kerwin worked for the Catholic Legal Immigration Network, Inc. (CLINIC) from 1992 to 2008, serving as its executive director for 15 years. He coordinated CLINIC's political asylum project for Haitians. CLINIC is a subsidiary of the United States Conference of Bishops and is a public interest legal corporation supporting a national network of charitable legal programs for immigrants. Between 2008 and 2011, Kerwin served as vice president for Programs at the Migration Policy Institute, where he frequently wrote on immigration and refugee policy issues. Kerwin served as an associate fellow at the Woodstock Theological Center, where he coordinated its Theology of Migration Project, and as a member of the American Bar Association's Commission on Immigration, a member of the Council of Foreign Relations' Immigration Task Force, a board member for the Jesuit Refugee Services— USA, a board member for the Capital Area Immigrant Rights Coalition, and an advisor to the USCCB Committee on Migration, and he serves on the board of directors of the Border Network for Human Rights in El Paso, Texas.

### Koch, Charles (1935– )

Charles Koch was born in Wichita, Kansas. He is president of Koch Industries and has a personal estimated worth of more than $44 billion. Charles graduated from the Massachusetts Institute of Technology in 1959. He joined the family business and became its CEO and chairman in 1967. Like his father, Fred C. Koch, the founder of the family oil business, Charles supports ultra-conservative politics. His father was the founder of the ultra-conservative John Birch Society. Charles donates millions of dollars annually to various conservative think tanks and causes. He founded the Cato Institute in 1977 and Americans for Progress in 1984. He vigorously opposes climate change policy proposals and has financially backed the Tea Party movement. He currently supports the Freedom Caucus, which has led opposition to any comprehensive immigration reform measures. He and his brother have funded primary candidate challenges to moderate Republicans in the House and Senate in opposition to their willingness to compromise in immigration reform. He is the author of *The Science of Success: How Market-Based Management Built the World's Largest Private Company* (2007).

### Koch, David (1940– )

David Koch is the executive vice president of Koch Industries. He was born in Wichita, Kansas. He earned his BS degree from the Massachusetts Institute of Technology. He joined the family oil business in 1970, which he and his brother then built into Koch Institutes, a diversified corporation of oil pipelines, refineries, building materials, paper towels, and Dixie Cups, valued at $115 billion. In 2015, David's personal net worth was estimated at $44.2 billion. He resides in New York City. In 1984 he founded Americans for Prosperity and Citizens for a Sound Economy and supports their ultra-conservative position against comprehensive immigration reform and supports the "crackdown" on immigration and border control policies of the political far-right. In 1980, David ran for vice president on the Libertarian ticket with Ed Clark for president. He is a philanthropist, giving millions to the Johns Hopkins University School of Medicine for cancer research, $100 million over 10 years to renovate New York State Theatre in the Lincoln Center for the Performing Arts, and $10 million to renovate the fountain outside the Metropolitan Museum of Art. David and Charles spent $500 million on political activity and lobbying in 2016. According to *Forbes Magazine* David ranks ninth among billionaires, number 7 in the United States, and was ranked sixth in 2005.

### Krikorian, Mark (1961– )

Mark Krikorian obtained a BA degree from Georgetown University and earned a master's degree from the Fletcher School of Law and Diplomacy at Tufts University. He also studied for two years in Yersevian State University in the then Soviet republic of Armenia. He has held various editorial and writing positions, and in 1995, he joined the Center for Immigration Studies in Washington, D.C., and serves as its executive director. He frequently testifies before Congress and has published numerous articles in such periodicals as the *Washington Post*, the *New York Times*, the *Commentary*, and the *National Review*. He has appeared on *60 Minutes*, *Nightline*, *The News Hour with Jim Lehrer*, *CNN*, *National Public Radio*, *National Public Television*, and similar radio and television programs. He is an ardent advocate of reduced legal immigration and of strict controls to reduce or eliminate illegal immigration. He supports the Trump travel ban and the DHS's efforts to tighten border security and expedited removal of illegal aliens.

### Kumar, Maria Teresa (1974– )

Maria Teresa Kumar is the founding president and CEO of Voto Latino, one of the leading organizations empowering Latino youth and political activism. She writes her own blog and is a frequent commentator on *MSNBC*, for which she has been nominated for an Emmy Award. She was the former host for Changing America on MSNBC. She is a World Economic Forum Young Global Leader. In 2013, *Elle* named her one of the 10 most influential women in Washington, D.C., and *Washington Life Magazine* named her the Power 100 in DC. Hispanic Business named her as one of the 100 most influential Latinos in America. For her work on Voto Latino, Fast Company called her one of the top 100 Creative Minds for using technology, celebrity voice, media, and youth themselves to empower a generation of young voters. She has led Voto Latino's media campaign of resistance to the Trump administration's immigration policies, and is particularly outspoken on the zero-tolerance and family separation policy and on the various versions of the Muslim travel ban. She serves on the national boards of Planned Parenthood, Emily's List, the Latino Leaders Network, and is a Hunt Alternative Fund Prime Movers and a Council of Foreign Relations Life Member. She is a frequent guest analyst on NPR and PBS, and an opinion writer for national publications. She started her career as a legislative aide for then Democratic Caucus Chair Vic Fazio. She served on the White House Project, Imagen Foundation.

At Voto Latino, she instituted the latest in online technology. She is a graduate of Harvard's Kennedy School of Government and earned her BA in International Relations at the University of California at Davis.

### Levin, Brian (na– )

Professor Brian Levin is director of the Center for the Study of Hate and Extremism at California State University-San Bernardino (CSUSB). An attorney and criminologist, Levin studies terrorism, hate crime, and legal issues. He earned a BA, summa cum laude, in 1989 from Stanford, and in 1992, obtained a JD. from Stanford Law School. Brian Levin served as associate director-legal affairs of the Southern Poverty Law Center, and as a corporate litigator for a law firm. During the 1980s he was a New York City Police Officer working in Harlem and Washington Heights and received several citations for academics and excellent police duty. Before joining CSUSB, Brian Levin was an associate professor at New Jersey's Stockton College and an adjunct lecturer in advanced constitutional law at Seton Hall School of Law. He is author, coauthor, and editor of various books, scholarly articles, training manuals, and studies of extremism and hate crime. He has written amicus curiae briefs for U.S. Supreme Court cases, such as *Wisconsin v. Mitchell* (1993), in which he presented criminological data establishing the severity and characteristics of hate crime, and his analysis has won various awards and has been referenced in numerous social science journals and major law reviews. He has appeared in international news media on six continents and has lectured around the world. He is a court-certified expert on extremism in the United States and the United Kingdom and has testified before both houses of Congress. He has been an outspoken critic of anti-Muslim and anti-immigrant groups and policies. He opposes the racial profiling aspects of the travel ban, of the zero-tolerance policy, and the "hate rhetoric" so often articulated by the anti-immigration reform movement and groups. He has consulted for numerous state and federal agencies such as the FBI, DHS, and for universities and civil rights groups. He has appeared on national and cable network shows like *60 Minutes, Dateline NBC, The Today Show, Good Morning America*, the *O'Reilly Factor, AC 360*, and *Hardball*. He has appeared in many major American newspapers and writes front-page analysis for the *Huffington Post*.

### Lieberman, Joseph (1942– )

Former senator Joseph Lieberman (D-CT, and I-CT) earned his BA from Yale University in 1964 and received an LLB from Yale in 1967. He was a practicing attorney from 1964 to 1980. In his political career he served in the Connecticut state senate, from 1970 to 1980, including serving as its majority leader from 1974 to 1980. He was attorney general of Connecticut from 1983 to 1988, from which office he went on to be elected to the U. S. Senate, where he served until 2014. In 2000, Senator Lieberman ran as the vice-presidential candidate with Al Gore and for reelection to the U.S. Senate. He lost the vice-presidency but won reelection to the Senate. In terms of homeland security matters, he was the leading sponsor of the bill to establish the Department of Homeland Security in 2002, and for its broad restructuring of immigration and dissolving of the INS. In 2016, he was briefly considered by President Trump for nomination as the U.S. attorney general. He is ultra-pro-Israel and favored Trump's travel ban on immigrants from Muslim countries.

### McCain, John (1936–2018)

Senator John McCain (R-AZ) was born at the Coco Solo Naval Station, Panama Canal, son of Admiral John S. McCain Jr. Both his father and grandfather were four-star admirals. John McCain graduated from the Naval Academy in 1958 and the Naval Flight School in 1960. He volunteered for Vietnam, and in 1967 was shot down on his 23rd mission. He was moved to the "Hanoi Hilton" in 1969 and spent more than five years in captivity there. A true war hero, he was awarded the Silver Star, the Bronze Star, a Purple Heart, the Legion of Merit, a Distinguished Flying Cross, and a Naval Commendation Medal.

In 1981 he retired as a captain and moved to Arizona. He was elected to the House of Representatives in 1982 and reelected in 1984. Embroiled in a campaign finance scandal, he survived the controversy and went on to enact campaign finance reform, the McCain-Feingold Act of 2002. In 1987, he ran for the U.S. Senate, eventually serving four terms. He chaired the Armed Services Committee and currently and prominently serves on the Committee on Homeland Security and is an ex-officio member of the Committee on Intelligence. He co-chaired the Senate National Security Caucus. He ran unsuccessfully for the presidential nomination of the Republican Party in 2000 (losing to George W. Bush) and ran and won the nomination in 2008, but lost to then Senator Barack Obama. He was one of the "Gang of Eight" senators sponsoring the comprehensive immigration reform bill in 2013. He advocated for a congressional enactment of a Dream Act bill to allow DACA qualified youth a path to citizenship. He spoke vigorously against the Trump administration's zero-tolerance policy and on the "immorality" of separating children from their parents at the U.S. border as a political ploy to deter unauthorized immigration, asylum-seekers, and refugees from attempting to enter the United States without authorization.

## McConnell, Mitch (1942– )

Senator Mitch McConnell (R-KY) became the Senate majority leader after the 2014 Senate elections, only the second senator from Kentucky to serve as majority leader. As such, he plays the key role in all Senate legislative proceedings and led the Senate Republicans in strident opposition to comprehensive immigration reform and to the vigorous border control and other conservative policy positions of the majority on homeland security and illegal immigration matters. He previously served as

Senate minority leader in the 110th–113th congresses, and as majority whip in the 108–109th congresses. During President Obama's first term, McConnell led the Republican Conference to oppose any and all Obama legislative initiatives in an attempt to ensure that President Obama would be a one-term president. His total opposition to consideration of any immigration reform bills played a major role in compelling President Obama to use executive actions on DACA and DAPA. McConnell served as chairman of the National Republican Senatorial Committee (1998–2000). He was first elected to the U.S. Senate in 1984. He graduated cum laude from the University of Louisville College of Arts and Sciences and obtained his JD from the College of Law, University of Kentucky, where he served as president of the Student Bar Association. Prior to his election to the U.S. Senate, he served as deputy assistant attorney general to President Gerald Ford and as judge-executive of Jefferson County, Kentucky, from 1978 to 1985. He served as a senior member of the Appropriations, Agriculture, and Rules Committees in the Senate.

### Napolitano, Janet (1957– )

Janet Napolitano was born in New York City in 1957. She has never married and has no children. She won a Truman Scholarship and graduated as Santa Clara University's first female valedictorian of her class in 1979, graduating summa cum laude with a degree in political science and a member of its chapter of Phi Beta Kappa. She earned her JD degree in 1983 from the University of Virginia, School of Law. She holds honorary degrees from several universities and colleges. She served as a law clerk for Judge Mary Schroeder of the U.S. Court of Appeals for the Ninth Circuit before joining a law firm, becoming a partner in the firm in 1989. Janet Napolitano served as the U.S. attorney for the District of Arizona. As U.S. attorney, she helped lead the domestic terrorism investigation into the Oklahoma City Bombing. She served as attorney general, State of Arizona, from 1999 to 2003, where she helped write the law to break up human smuggling rings. Napolitano served as the 21st governor of Arizona, from 2003 to 2009. While governor, she implemented one of the first homeland security strategies in the country, opened the first counterterrorism center, and became a pioneer of coordinating federal, state, local, and binational homeland security efforts. She also presided over large-scale disaster relief efforts and readiness exercises. She became the first woman to chair the National Governors Association, where she was instrumental in establishing its Public Safety Task Force and the Homeland Security Advisors Council. Napolitano also chaired the Western Governors Association. She was appointed secretary of DHS by President Obama in January 2009 and served until September 2013. As secretary of DHS, Napolitano led her agency in implementation of the DACA program, but also led the Obama administration's efforts in expedited removals of unauthorized immigrants. In 2010, she was awarded the prestigious Thomas Jefferson Foundation Medal (Law), the University of Virginia's highest external honor. She was named the 20th president of the University of California on July 18, 2013, and took office on September 30, 2013, where she leads a university system of 10 campuses, 5 medical centers, 3 affiliated national laboratories, and a statewide agriculture and natural resources program. As UC president, she has been an outspoken critic of the Trump administration's immigration policies, especially on family separation and on zero tolerance.

### Nielsen, Kirstjen (1972– )

Kirstjen Nielsen is the current and sixth secretary of the DHS, sworn in on December 6, 2017, to replace John Kelly in that office when he became President Trump's White House chief of staff. She had earlier served as a former principal deputy White House chief of staff to President Trump, and as chief of staff to John Kelly during his term as secretary of Homeland Security. Ms. Nielsen grew up in Florida and earned her BS degree from Georgetown School of Foreign Service and a JD from the University of Virginia School of Law in 1999. She served as special assistant and senior director for prevention, preparedness, and response to the White House Homeland Security Council in the George W. Bush administration. Before serving in the Trump administration, Kirstjen Nielsen was a senior member of the Resilience Task Force of the Center for Cyber and Homeland Security committee at George Washington University and served on the Global Risks Report Advisory Board for the World Economic Forum. She was confirmed by a vote of 62–37 in the Senate. In January 2018 she testified before the U.S. Senate in favor of replacing the current system of immigration based on family reunification with a merit-based system. In March 2018, she led the official U.S. delegation at the opening ceremony of the 2018 Paralympic Winter Games in PyeongChang, South Korea. Since President Trump announced his zero-tolerance policy, she has been a vocal defender of the legality of the policy, including the forced separation of children from their illegal parents in an effort to "deter" illegal entry to the United States.

### Obama, Barack (1961– )

Barack Obama was the 44th president of the United States (2009–2017). He was born in Hawaii and raised by his grandparents. After working his way through college on scholarships, he moved to Chicago, where he worked with a group of churches as a community organizer to help rebuild communities devastated by high unemployment because of the closure of local steel plants. He went on to Harvard Law School, becoming the first African American president of the *Harvard Law Review*.

He returned to Chicago to lead voter registration drives, taught constitutional law at the University of Chicago, and eventually ran for the state legislature. In the Illinois State Senate, he passed the first major ethics reform law in 25 years, cut taxes for the working-class families, and expanded health care. As U.S. senator from Illinois (D-IL), Obama worked on bipartisan lobbying reform and transparency in government by putting federal spending online. He burst on to the national political scene when giving the Democratic National Convention Keynote Address in 2004. He ran for president in 2008, and after a tough primary battle with then Senator Hillary Clinton (D-NY), he was elected president and sworn into office on January 20, 2009. He was reelected in 2012. During his two terms in office, he appointed two secretaries of Homeland Security—Janet Napolitano and Jeh Johnson—and issued two executive orders impacting unauthorized immigrants—DACA and DAPA. But his administration also set a record for deporting unauthorized immigrants, by focusing on those with criminal convictions.

He and his wife, Michelle, are the parents of two daughters: Malia and Sasha. President Obama is the recipient of the Nobel Peace Prize, one of only four U.S. presidents so honored. Barack Obama is the author of three best-selling books: *Dreams of My Father* (2004), *The Audacity of Hope* (2007), and *Of Thee I Sing* (2010).

### Reagan, Ronald (1911–2004)

Ronald Reagan was born in Illinois. He graduated from Eureka College in 1932 and began a career as a sports announcer before he signed a movie contract with Warner Brothers Studio in 1939. In 1947 he was elected president of the Screen Actors Guild, and in 1954 he hosted the *General Electric Theater* television show. He campaigned for Richard Nixon for president in 1960. In 1963 he hosted the popular television program *Death Valley Days*. In 1966 he was elected governor of California and reelected to that office in 1970. He lost a bid for the presidential nomination of the Republican Party in 1976 before winning the nomination and the office in 1980. His notable contribution to immigration reform was establishment of the presidential task force on immigration that helped shape the debate of the Immigration Reform and Control Act of 1986, which he signed into law. He established the employer sanctions approach and approved its amnesty program that legalized more than 3 million immigrants. He retired from the presidency in 1989. In 1994, he announced that he suffered from Alzheimer's disease and died a much-revered former president on June 6, 2004.

### Ridge, Tom (1945– )

Tom Ridge is a Pennsylvania politician who served as the first assistant to the president as the White House Office of Homeland Security (2001–2003) and as the first secretary of the Department of Homeland Security (2003–2005). A stalwart Republican, prior to his White House and cabinet service, Ridge was a member of the House of Representatives (R-PA) from 1983 to 1995, and 43rd governor of Pennsylvania from 1995 to 2001. He was born and raised in Pennsylvania. Ridge graduated from Harvard University, cum laude, and then served in the Vietnam War as a sergeant in the U.S. Army, where he was awarded the Bronze Star for Valor. After his army service, he returned to Pennsylvania and completed his JD degree at the Dickinson School of Law, graduating in 1972, after which he entered private practice. Ridge was a district attorney in Erie and then ran for Congress. He was the first Congressman to have served as an enlisted man in the Vietnam War. He was overwhelmingly reelected five times, serving six terms. He was elected governor in 1994 and reelected in 1998. Following the September 11, 2001, attacks, President George W. Bush named him the director of the newly created Office of Homeland Security. In January 2003, the office became an official cabinet-level Department of Homeland Security, with Ridge as its first secretary.

As secretary, he oversaw the implementation of immigration policy and the merger of the former INS services into ICE,

USCIS, and USCBP. He served in that role for President Bush's first term, succeeded by Michael Chertoff. Tom Ridge then returned to the private sector. He served on several boards of directors, for the Home Depot, Hershey Company, and Exelcon Corporation, and as a senior advisor to Deloitte and Touche, PURE Bioscience, and TechRadium. He is also founder and CEO of Ridge Global LLC, a Washington, D.C.-based security consulting firm. He worked in the 2008 presidential campaign of Senator John McCain. Tom and his wife Michele have two children.

### Schumer, Charles E. (1950– )

Now the senior senator from New York and U.S. Senate minority leader, Charles Schumer was born in New York. He earned his BA from Harvard in 1971 and his JD from there in 1974. He served in the New York Assembly from 1974 to 1980 and then in the U.S. House of Representatives from 1980 to 1998. He was elected to the Senate in 1998. He was critically important in crafting compromises, making it possible to pass the Immigration Reform and Control Act of 1986, and has continued to play a critical role in virtually all immigration-related bills since then. He serves on the Senate Judiciary Committee and has replaced the late senator Edward Kennedy as the leader of the Senate Democrats when it comes to immigration reform measures. On a comprehensive immigration reform effort in 2013, which passed the Senate but failed in the House chamber, he was the leader of the Democratic members of the "Gang of Eight." In 2017 he struck a deal with President Trump for a bill which would have included money for the border wall and a legislative solution to the Dreamer issue, only for it to be pulled back by President Trump before a vote on the bill, and he failed to get DACA passed as part of a continuing resolution budget deal by threatening a government shutdown. He remains the leading voice for a DACA bill in Congress today.

### Sensenbrenner, James (1943– )

Jim Sensenbrenner (R-WI) was first elected to the House of Representatives in 1978. He was born in Chicago. He received a BA degree from Stanford University in 1965 and his JD degree from the University of Wisconsin in 1968. He practiced law from 1968 to 1969 before being elected to the Wisconsin Assembly (1968–1974). He was elected to the Wisconsin Senate in 1974, serving there until 1978. He serves as the chair of the powerful Judiciary Committee in the House and on the Select Committee on Homeland Security. He staunchly supported the use of force in Iraq and the creation of the Department of Homeland Security in 2002. He was critical of Attorney General Ashcroft's possible violation of civil liberties and calls for additional investigative powers for law enforcement. Representative Sensenbrenner insisted on strict provisions for the USA Patriot Act and Patriot Act II. He cosponsored a bill to split the INS into two separate agencies, and when they were moved to the DHS, he expressed strong concerns that internal problems in the INS would not be resolved. He has long opposed racial quotas and preferences and was vocal in his support of Milwaukee's school-choice program. He has won election and reelection by wide margins and has often been unopposed in the general election. He notably was sponsor of legislation to control illegal immigration, such as the REAL ID Act of 2005.

### Sessions, Jeff (1946– )

Jeff Sessions was nominated for attorney general by President Trump in 2016 and confirmed by the U.S. Senate in 2017. He has been an ardent supporter of President Trump's agenda related to immigration and to homeland security concerns. He strongly advocated for President Trump's travel ban executive orders. He was elected to the U.S. Senate in 1997 and chaired the Senate Judiciary's Subcommittee on Immigration and National Interest. He was reelected to the U.S. Senate in 2008.

In 2011, he was the ranking member of the Budget Committee and the Subcommittee on Banking. He is sponsor of a bill to block any funding for amnesty. He served on the Senate Armed Forces Committee and on the Environment and Public Utility Committee. He obtained his BA degree from Huntington College in 1969 and his JD from the University of Alabama, School of Law in 1973. Prior to his election to the U.S. Senate, he served as a President Reagan appointee to the U.S. attorney, Alabama southern district. While in the Senate, he was an outspoken opponent of comprehensive immigration reform and of any sort of amnesty program. He was an ardent advocate of the Patriot Act I and II and supported creation of the DHS. As attorney general he announced and has implemented the "zero-tolerance" policy and defended the use of forced separation of children from their parents if they had entered the country illegally. Critics charge he has instituted a DOJ policy to "slow-walk" asylum requests to further deter immigrants from Mexico and Central America (largely El Salvador, Guatemala, and Honduras). He cited Bible passages to justify the family separation policy, for which he has been widely criticized by various faith leaders and even threatened with excommunication from the Methodist Church for his implementation of the policy. Often at odds with President Trump because of his recusal on the Russian probe and Mueller investigation, he is nonetheless the Trump administration's most ardent proponent of anti-illegal immigration policy and procedures, opposition to DACA and DAPA, and proponent for immigration reform that would reduce family reunification preferences, increase "merit-based" economic preferences, reduce overall legal immigration, and end the visa lottery program. AG Sessions was fired from the position by President Trump in 2019.

### Suro, Roberto (na– )

Roberto Suro is the founding director of the Pew Hispanic Center, a Washington-based research and public policy organization that he founded in 2001. He was born in Washington, D.C., of Puerto Rican and Ecuadorian parents. He has written extensively about Hispanic and related issues as a journalist for some 30 years, notably for the *Washington Post*, and for *Time Magazine* and the *New York Times* as a foreign correspondent. He is author of *Strangers among Us: Latino Lives in a Changing America* (1999), and of two 20th-century fund papers on immigration matters. He is a graduate of Yale University (BA, 1973), and Columbia University (MS, 1974). He is professor at the University of Southern California and is an affiliate of the Brookings Institution as a nonresident senior fellow in metropolitan policy (since 2005), the Migration Policy Institute as a nonresident fellow (2007–2010), and on the advisory board since 2008 of E Pluribus Unum Prizes for initiatives to promote immigrant integration. He serves on the board of the Pacific Council on International Policy's Mexican Council of Foreign Relations and Bi-national Task Force on the U.S.-Mexico Border (since 2009).

### Tanden, Neera (na– )

Neera Tanden is the president and CEO of the Center for American Progress and the CEO of the Center for American Progress Action Fund. The Center for American Progress is one of the organizations that is leading the resistance to the Trump administration's immigration and refugee policies. Tanden's expertise is on U.S. economy, elections, health care, domestic politics, immigration politics, and women's issues. Her focus is on how both organizations can fulfill their missions to expand opportunity for all Americans. She served in both the Obama and Clinton administrations, as well as on their presidential campaigns. Before leading American Progress, Tanden was a senior advisor for health reform at HHS, where she worked with Congress and stakeholders on the Affordable Care Act. She was director of domestic policy for the Obama-Biden presidential campaign and worked as policy director for Hillary Clinton's 2008 presidential campaign. She served as legislative director for Hillary Clinton's 2000 Senate campaign and was an associate director for domestic policy in Bill Clinton's White House and a senior policy adviser to the first lady. She appears frequently on NBC's *Meet the Press*, ABC's *This Week*, CBS's *Face the Nation*, PBS's *Newshour with Jim Lehrer*, HBO's *Real Time with Bill Maher*, on MSNBC, CNN, and Fox. *Elle Magazine* named her to their "Women in Washington Power List." *Politico Magazine* named her to its "Politico 50," an annual list of the top thinkers, doers, and visionaries in American politics. She was included in the *National Journal*'s "Washington's Most Influential Magazine," the *Washingtonian magazine*'s "Most Powerful Women in Washington," and *Fortune magazine*'s "Most Powerful Women in Politics." She has a BS from the UCLA and a law degree from Yale Law School.

### Trautman, Laurie (na– )

In 2018 Professor Laurie Trautman was named director of the Border Policy Research Institute (BPRI) at Western Washington University (WWU). She served as its associate director from 2014 until 2018. At BPRI, she leads an important think-tank organization focusing on the U.S. northern border with Canada, a top institute and one of the best universities in the nation studying U.S.-Canada relationships. She led ongoing analysis for the NEXUS program and the proposed preclearance legislation. BPRI serves as a bridge between academic research and policy makers at the state, provincial, and federal levels. She is a graduate of Western Washington University. WWU fosters collaboration through informed policy making on both sides of the U.S.-Canada border. The Research Institute has studied border security issues after several terrorists entered the United States illegally from Canada as unauthorized immigrants.

### Trump, Donald J. (1946– )

Donald J. Trump is a billionaire real-estate mogul, former reality television star, and the 45th president of the United States.

Trump was born in Queens, New York. He was married several times to former models: Ivanka Winklmayr, from 1977 to 1992; Marla Maples, 1983 to 1999; and Melania Knauss, 2005 to present. In 1964 Trump received his degree in economics from the Wharton School of Finance, University of Pennsylvania. He took over his father's real-estate business in 1971. Much disputed, his estimated net worth is $4.5 billion. In 2004, he appeared as host of *The Apprentice*, a reality television show. In 2012, he briefly considered running for president and was embroiled in and largely led the anti-Obama "birther" movement. He strenuously opposed President Obama's DACA and DAPA executive orders, arguing they were unconstitutional and required congressional authorization to be legal. On June 15, 2015, he announced his candidacy for the Republican Party nomination for president, running in a field of 17. On July 15, 2016, he clinched the nomination and announced his choice for vice president, Governor Mike Pence of Indiana. He accepted the GOP nomination on July 21, 2016, won the electoral college vote, and was inaugurated president on January 20, 2017. He nominated John Kelly as secretary of the Department of Homeland Security and Jeff Sessions as attorney general, and they in turn issued departmental rules and regulations turning back President Obama's reform policies particularly as related to immigration reform. Despite having been a vigorous critic of President Obama's use of executive actions, President Trump issued several controversial executive orders that impacted homeland security, which greatly expanded the use of expedited removal of unauthorized immigrants. He used two such orders to issue a travel ban aimed primarily at Muslims and refugees from the Middle East. Although held unconstitutional by several district and appellate courts, the ban was ultimately ruled constitutional by the U.S. Supreme Court. He rescinded the DACA and DAPA orders of President Obama, giving the Congress a few months to pass legal authorization of the policies and pulling back from his announced willingness to sign a bipartisan bill to do so, effectively killing the effort. He ordered his attorney general, Jeff Sessions, to begin a policy of "zerotolerance" of illegal immigration, even using it against immigrants who crossed the border illegally but who had thereby only committed a misdemeanor, to charge them as criminal aliens from whom their children could be forcibly removed. It resulted in such removal of some 2,500 children before President Trump reversed himself and announced that the DOJ would no longer separate children from their parents while their immigration proceedings and asylum requests were being adjudicated, and stipulating that such detention could be indefinite rather than a court ruling specifying such detention could not be longer than 20 days. Trump tweeted his advocacy of the immediate deportation of all illegal immigrants without a judicial hearing on the matter and without due process.

Donald Trump is the author of nine ghost-written books: *Trump: The Art of the Deal* (1987), *The America We Deserve* (2000), *Trump: How to Get Rich* (2004), *Why We Want You to Be Rich* (2996), *Think Big and Kick Ass in Business* (2007), *Trump 101: The Way to Success* (2007), *Trump: Never Give Up* (2008), *Think Like a Champion* (2009), and *Time to Get Tough* (2011).

### Watson, Derrick (1966– )

Judge Derrick Kahala Watson is a U.S. district judge of the U.S. District Court of Hawaii. He was born in 1966 in Honolulu. He received his BA cum laude from Harvard College in 1988 and his JD from Harvard Law School in 1991, in the same graduating class as Barack Obama and Neil Gorsuch. He began his legal career in California as an associate in a San Francisco law firm, 1991 to 1995. He served as assistant U.S. attorney in the Northern District of California from 1995 to 2000, including serving as deputy chief of the Civil Division from 1999 to 2000. He then worked in private practice, becoming a partner in a San Francisco firm in 2003. He did pro bono work for the San Francisco Lawyers Committee for Civil

Rights and pro bono work involving human trafficking. He served as assistant U.S. attorney for the District of Hawaii from 2007 to 2013, and chief of the Civil Division from 2009 to 2013. From 1998 to 2006, Judge Watson served in the U.S. Army Reserve in the Judge Advocate General's Corps, with the rank of Captain. He was honorably discharged in 2013. In November 2012, President Barack Obama nominated Watson to serve as a U.S. district judge for the U.S. District Court for the District of Hawaii and was confirmed in the Senate by a vote of 94–0 on April 18, 2013. He is the fourth Native Hawaiian to serve on the federal bench and the only currently serving one. In March 2017, Judge Watson granted a temporary restraining order blocking President Trump's revised executive order banning entry of nationals from six majority-Muslim countries into the United States from going into effect. In June 2017, the U.S. Court of Appeals upheld the majority of the injunction, unanimously determining that President Trump had exceeded his authority under the Immigration and Nationality Act of 1965. In June, the U.S. Supreme Court partially reinstated the travel ban, setting oral arguments for October 2017.

### Yates, Sally (1960– )

Sally Yates served as a U.S. attorney and deputy attorney general and briefly acting attorney general until President Trump fired her following her refusal to defend his travel ban executive order in federal courts and the Supreme Court in 2017. She was acting attorney general from January 20, 2017, until January 30, 2017. She was preceded by Attorney General Loretta Lynch (both appointed by President Barack Obama) and was succeeded as acting attorney general by Dana Boente. She was deputy attorney general from January 10, 2015, until January 30, 2017, succeeded by Rod Rosenstein. Previous to that office, Yates was the U.S. attorney for the Northern District of Georgia, March 2010 to January 10, 2015, again appointed by President Obama, and from July 2004 to December 2004 by President George W. Bush. She was born in Atlanta, Georgia, and earned her BA in journalism from the University of Georgia in 1982, and her JD from the University of Georgia, School of Law, in 1986, graduating magna cum laude. She was executive editor of the *Georgia Law Review*. In 1989 she was hired as assistant U.S. attorney by Bob Barr for the Northern District of Georgia. In 1994, Yates became chief of the Fraud and Public Corruption Section and was the lead prosecutor in the case of Eric Rudolph, the domestic terrorist who committed the Centennial Olympic Park bombing. She rose to first assistant U.S. attorney in 2002, then acting U.S. attorney in 2004, holding leadership positions under both Republican and Democratic administrations. While a U.S. attorney, Attorney General Eric Holder appointed her to serve as vice chair of the attorney General's Advisory Committee. She was confirmed as deputy attorney general, the second-highest ranking position in the Justice Department, by the Senate by a vote of 84–12. She oversaw the day-to-day operations of the Justice Department, including its 113,000 employees. In late January, Acting Attorney General Yates warned White House Counsel that the then serving National Security Advisor, Michael Flynn, had lied about his contacts with Russia related to sanctions and that he was therefore vulnerable to blackmail by Russian intelligence. For eighteen days, nothing was done about the warning. When the *Washington Post* published her reported warning, on February 13, 2017, Flynn was forced to resign within hours. Acting Attorney General Yates ordered the DOJ not to defend Trump's executive order on travel and immigration, upholding her stated position during her Senate confirmation hearing, when questioned by then Senator Jeff Sessions, that she would disobey a president's unlawful order. Her decision not to defend in court the travel ban order as unconstitutional was essentially upheld by several federal district courts and the Appellate Court. Her action was praised by several Democratic U.S. Senators as "a profile in courage."

## Introduction

This chapter presents data on immigration-related policy, its implementation, and proposals for reform. The tables and figures present data regarding immigration flows into the United States and the actions for the implementation of immigration policy. The documents section presents excerpts of actions taken by stakeholders in the politics and policy making of immigration reform.

## Data

*Table 5.1 presents an overview of legal immigration to the United States from 1964, the year before the current law governing legal immigration to the United States was enacted, changing U.S.*

Table 5.1   Legal Immigration to the United States, 1964–2016

| Year | Number Arriving | Year | Number Arriving |
|------|-----------------|------|-----------------|
| 1964 | 292,248 | 1991 | 1,827,167 |
| 1965 | 296,697 | 1992 | 973,977 |

*(Continued)*

Construction workers erect a border wall just north of the Rio Grande River in the Rio Grande valley in southern Texas to deter undocumented immigrants from entering the United States. The effectiveness of the wall is a matter of dispute, as immigrants continue to enter illegally on a daily basis. Many miles of the 2,000-mile southern border are topographically unsuited to a wall, and immigrants can go under, over, and around a portion of the wall as well. (vichinterlang/iStockphoto.com)

Table 5.1   (Continued)

| Year | Number Arriving | Year | Number Arriving |
|------|------|------|------|
| 1966 | 323,040 | 1993 | 904,191 |
| 1967 | 361,972 | 1994 | 804,416 |
| 1968 | 454,448 | 1995 | 720,461 |
| 1969 | 358,579 | 1996 | 915,900 |
| 1970 | 373,326 | 1997 | 798,378 |
| 1971 | 370,478 | 1998 | 654,568 |
| 1972 | 384,685 | 1999 | 646,451 |
| 1973 | 400,063 | 2000 | 849,807 |
| 1974 | 394,861 | 2001 | 1,064,318 |
| 1975 | 386,194 | 2002 | 1,059,902 |
| 1976 | 502,289 | 2003 | 730,542 |
| 1977 | 426,315 | 2004 | 957,883 |
| 1978 | 601,442 | 2005 | 1,122,373 |
| 1979 | 460,348 | 2006 | 1,266,129 |
| 1980 | 530,639 | 2007 | 1,052,415 |
| 1981 | 596,600 | 2008 | 1,107,126 |
| 1982 | 594,131 | 2009 | 1,120,818 |
| 1983 | 559,763 | 2010 | 1,042,625 |
| 1984 | 543,903 | 2011 | 1.062,040 |
| 1985 | 570,009 | 2012 | 1,031,631 |
| 1986 | 601,708 | 2013 | 990,553 |
| 1987 | 601,506 | 2014 | 1,016,518 |
| 1988 | 643,025 | 2015 | 1,051,031 |
| 1989 | 1,090,924 | 2016 | 1,183,505 |
| 1990 | 1,536,483 | | |

Source: Department of Homeland Security, 2016. "Persons Obtaining Permanent Resident Status, Fiscal Years 1820–2016," in Yearbook of Immigration Statistics, 2016. Washington, D.C.: Department of Homeland Security. Online at: www.dhs.gov/immigration-statistics/yearbook/2016.

immigration from the national origins quota system to the current preference system.

Table 5.2 compares the number of illegal apprehensions by fiscal years 2000–2017 compared with the number of border patrol agents over those same years. Conventional wisdom and advocates *of immigration reform pursuing the "crackdown approach" to get tougher at the border have argued consistently that we need more border patrol agents to ensure control of the border to stop illegal immigration. The table shows, however, that there is basically an inverse relationship between apprehensions and the number of agents. As the number of border patrol agents increased from 2000 to 2017, the number of apprehensions at the Southwest Border sector in fact decreased, and did so fairly steadily. As seen in Table 5.2, in 2000 there were 1,63,679 apprehensions of illegal aliens when the border patrol had 9,212 agents. By 2017, the number of apprehensions fell to 303,916, an eight-fold decrease, but agents increased to 19,437, an increase of more than 300 percent.*

Table 5.2   Total Illegal Apprehensions by Fiscal Year, 2000–2017, Compared to the Total Number of Border Patrol Agents

| Year | Total Apprehensions | Total Number of Agents |
|------|--------------------|-----------------------|
| 2000 | 1,643,679 | 9,212 |
| 2001 | 1,235,718 | 9,821 |
| 2002 | 929,809 | 10,045 |
| 2003 | 905,065 | 10,717 |
| 2004 | 1,139,282 | 10,819 |
| 2005 | 1,171,396 | 11,264 |
| 2006 | 1,071,972 | 12,439 |
| 2007 | 858,638 | 14,923 |
| 2008 | 705,005 | 17,499 |
| 2009 | 540,085 | 20,119 |
| 2010 | 447,731 | 20,058 |
| 2011 | 327,577 | 21,444 |
| 2012 | 356,873 | 21,394 |
| 2013 | 414,397 | 21,391 |
| 2014 | 479,371 | 20,863 |
| 2015 | 331,333 | 20,273 |
| 2016 | 408,870 | 19,828 |
| 2017 | 303,916 | 19,437 |

*Source:* https://www.cbp.gov/newsroom/media-resources/stats, USBP-Southwest Border-Apps: FY 1960–2017; and BP Staffing FY 1992–2017, Border Patrol Agents by Fiscal Year.

*Table 5.3 details the enforcement actions taken by Customs and Border Protection (CBP) during fiscal years 2016–2017 against persons presenting themselves at U.S. borders seeking admission for humanitarian reasons who were detained, processed, and determined to be inadmissible, as well as total apprehensions at the borders and the interior.*

*Table 5.4 presents data from the 2010 U.S. Census detailing the foreign-born population enumerated in the census by their region of birth. Note the greatest concentration are immigrants from Mexico, Central America, and the Caribbean region, comprising more than half of all the foreign-born in the 2010 census data, reflecting the trend in immigration, both authorized and unauthorized, since 1980.*

**Table 5.3   Customs and Border Protection Enforcement Actions, 2016–2017**

| Enforcement Actions | 2016 | 2017 |
| --- | --- | --- |
| Total Inadmissibles | 274,821 | 199,844 |
| Total Apprehensions | 415,816 | 310,531 |
| Total Enforcements | 690,637 | 487,481 |

*Source:* https://www.cbp.gov/newsroom/stats/cbp-enforcement-statistics-FY-2018

**Table 5.4   Foreign-Born Population by Region of Birth, U.S. Census, 2010**

| Region of birth | Population (in 1000s) | Percent |
| --- | --- | --- |
| Total | 39,958 | 100.0 |
| Africa | 1,607 | 4.0 |
| Asia | 11,284 | 28.2 |
| Europe | 4,817 | 12.1 |
| Latin America/Caribbean | 21,224 | 53.1 |
| Mexico | 11,711 | 29.3 |
| Central America | 3,053 | 7.6 |
| South America | 2,730 | 6.8 |
| Caribbean | 3,731 | 9.3 |
| North America | 807 | 2.0 |
| Oceania | 217 | 0.5 |

*Source:* www.census.gov/acs/www/

*Public opinion polling on immigration reform matters varies among voters depending on a number of voter characteristics and on the polling source. Table 5.5 presents data from a 2018 poll by the Pew Research Center on two issues: support for a Dreamer Act and support for or opposition to building the border wall.*

Table 5.5    Pew Research Center Immigration-Related Public Opinion Polling Data, 2018

**Granting Permanent Legal Status to DACA Children (Dreamers)**

|  | Oppose (%) | Favor (%) |
| --- | --- | --- |
| Total | 21 | 74 |
| Rep/Lean R | 40 | 50 |
| Dem/Lean D | 6 | 92 |
| Men | 47 | 47 |
| Women | 33 | 54 |
| 18–49 | 34 | 57 |
| 50+ | 45 | 45 |
| College Grad | 36 | 58 |
| Non-College Grad | 42 | 48 |
| Conservative | 44 | 46 |
| Mod/Liberal | 35 | 58 |

**Building a Wall on U.S.-Mexico Border**

|  | Oppose (%) | Favor (%) |
| --- | --- | --- |
| Total | 60 | 37 |
| Rep/Lean R | 24 | 37 |
| Dem/L Dem | 85 | 13 |
| Men | 20 | 77 |
| Women | 29 | 67 |
| 18–49 | 36 | 60 |
| 50+ | 14 | 83 |
| College Grad+ | 24 | 74 |
| Non-College Grad | 24 | 72 |
| Conservative | 17 | 81 |
| Mod/Liberal | 40 | 55 |

*Source:* Pew Research Center at https://www.pewresearch.org/fact-tank/2018/01/19/public-backs-legal-status-for-immigrants-brought-to-u-s-illegally-as-children-but-not-a-bigger-border-wall/ft_18–01–19_viewimmigration-1/.

*Figure 5.1 presents a bar graph detailing total apprehensions for the month of March, annually from 2000 to 2017. It shows a steady decline in total apprehension from 2000 to 2017, with slight upticks in 2014 and 2015.*

*Figure 5.2 presents a bar graph of the total ICE removals for fiscal years 2015–2017, which shows that they are quite stable over those years.*

*Figure 5.3 presents data regarding the vexing problem of children who come across the U.S. southern border unaccompanied by an adult (UAC). In a pie chart format, it presents the number and percent of the total UAC by country of origin apprehended at the U.S. border in FY 2014. Although commonly perceived as a "Mexican migration problem," note that UAC from Mexico are actually the lowest in numbers and percentage of total UAC. The figure shows that, in fact, more such children are from the Central American countries of El Salvador, Guatemala, and Honduras. Those coming from Central America cross the border into Mexico and then*

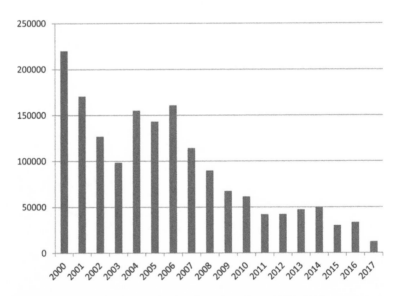

**Figure 5.1   Total Southwest Border Apprehensions, 2000–2017**

*Source:* https://www.cbp.gov/document/stats/us-border-patrol-nationwide-apprehe
nsions-citizenship-and-sector-fy-2007-fy-2017.

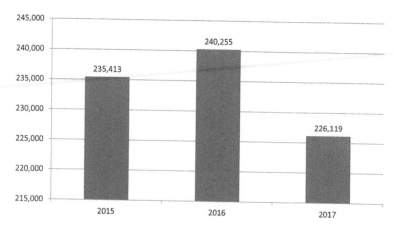

**Figure 5.2    Total Ice Removals, 2015–2017**

*Source:* https://www.ice.gov/removal-statistics/2017.

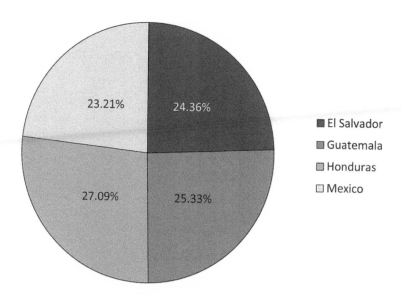

**Figure 5.3    Unaccompanied Children Apprehended by the U.S. Border Patrol at the Southwest Border, FY 2014**

*Source:* www.cbp.gov/newsroom/stats/southwest-border-unaccompanied-children.

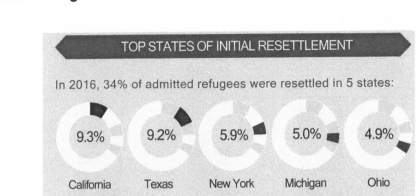

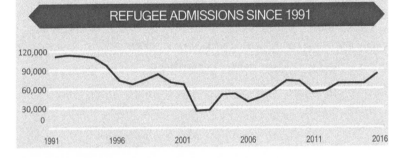

**Figure 5.4    Refugee Admissions, 1991–2016, and the Top States with Highest Percentage of Initial Resettlement**

*Source:* https://www.dhs.gov/immigration-statistics/visualization/2016.

*proceed to its border with the United States, often via "the Beast," the nickname for a freight train that travels from south to north across Mexico and on the top of which the unauthorized immigrants ride in a perilous journey to reach the border with the United States in the hope to cross, undocumented, into the United States.*

*Figure 5.4 shows a trend line of the number of admissions of refugees since 1991 and the five states that received the highest percentages of initial resettlement of refugees.*

## Documents

### The Immigration Reform and Control Act (1986)

*The Immigration Reform and Control Act (IRCA) of 1986 was the last major reform of the basis of current immigration law, the*

*Immigration and Nationality Act of 1965. The IRCA was a substantial revision because it introduced the employer sanctions approach and involved an amnesty program that legalized in excess of 3 million previously unauthorized immigrants.*

*The IRCA had a half-decade long, tangled history in its path through the U.S. Congress. In 1986, a Joint Conference Committee finally agreed on a package that could be enacted into law. Much of IRCA is still relevant, and reaction to its amnesty provisions drives Republican opposition to anything even resembling amnesty in current immigration reform proposals.*

### Title 1—Control of Illegal Immigration

SEC. 101. CONTROL OF UNLAWFUL EMPLOYMENT OF ALIENS

In general, it is unlawful for a person or other entity to hire, or to recruit or refer for a fee, the employment in the United States

(A) Any alien, knowing the alien is an unauthorized alien . . .

(B) An individual without complying with the requirements of subsection (b).

**Continuing employment**—It is unlawful for a person or other entity, after hiring an alien for employment in accordance with paragraph (1), to continue to employ the alien in the United States knowing the alien is (or has become) an unauthorized alien with respect to such employment.

**Defense**—a person or entity that establishes that it has complied in good faith with the requirements of subsection (b) with respect to the hiring, recruiting, or referral for employment of an alien in the United States has established an affirmative defense that the person or entity has not violated paragraph (1) (A) with respect to such hiring, recruiting, or referral.

**Use of Labor through Contract**—A person or other entity who uses a contract, subcontract, or exchange, entered into, renegotiated, or extended after the date of the enactment of this section, to obtain the labor of an alien in the United States, knowing that the alien is an unauthorized alien, with respect to performing such labor, shall be considered to have hired the alien for employment in the United States in violation of paragraph (1)(A).

**Use of State Employment Agency Documentation**—A person or entity shall be deemed to have complied with the requirements of subsection (b) with respect to the hiring of an individual who was referred for such employment by a State employment agency.

**Employment Verification System**—The requirements referred to [above] are, in the case of a person or other entity hiring, recruiting, or referring an individual for employment in the United States, the requirements specified in the following three paragraphs:

**(1)** Attestation after Examination of Documentation—

   (A) In General—the person or entity must attest, under penalty of perjury and on a form established by the Attorney General be regulation, that it has verified that the individual is not an unauthorized alien by examining—

   (i)  a document described in subparagraph (B), or

   (ii)  a document codified in subparagraph (C) and (D).

   (B) Documents Establishing Both Employment Authorization and Identity—A document described in this subparagraph is an individual's—

   (i)   United States passport;

   (ii)  Certificate of United States Citizenship;

   (iii) Certificate of naturalization;

   (iv) Unexpired foreign passport, if the passport has an appropriate, unexpired endorsement of the

Attorney General authorizing the individual's employment in the United States; or

(v) Resident alien card or other alien registration, if said card contains a photograph of the individual, and is evidence of authorization of employment in the United States.

(C) Documents Evidencing Employment Authorization— A document described [above] is

(i) A social security account number card;

(ii) Certificate of birth in the United States or establishing United States nationality at birth;

(iii) Other documents evidencing authorization of employment in the United States which the Attorney General finds, by regulation, to be acceptable for the purposes of this section.

(D) Documents Establishing Identity of an Individual— A document described in this subparagraph is an individual's

(i) Driver's license or similar document issued for the purpose of identification by a State, if it contains a photograph of the individual;

(ii) In the case of individuals under 16 years of age or in a State which does not provide for issuance of an identification document;

(iii) Documentation of personal identity of such type as the Attorney General finds, by regulation, provides a reliable means of identification. . . .

(3) Definition of Unauthorized Alien—the term "unauthorized alien" means with respect to the employment of an alien at a particular time, that the alien is not at the time either (A) an alien lawfully admitted for permanent residence, or (B) authorized to be so employed by this Act or by the Attorney General.

### Deferral of Enforcement with Respect to Seasonal Agricultural Services—

(A) In General—it is unlawful for a person or entity (including a farm labor contractor) or an agent of such a person or entity, to recruit an unauthorized alien (other than an alien described in clause (iii), who is outside the United States to enter the United States to perform seasonal agricultural service.

(ii) Exception—Clause (i) shall not apply to an alien who the person or entity reasonably believes to meet the requirements of section 210(a)(2) of this Act (relating to the performance of seasonal agricultural services).

### Government Accountability Office Reports—

In General—

Beginning one year after the date of enactment of this Act, and at intervals of one year thereafter for a period of three years after such date, the Comptroller General of the United States shall prepare and transmit to the Congress and to the task for established under subsection (k) a report describing the results of a review of the implementation and enforcement of this section during the preceding twelve month period, for the purpose of determining if—

(A) such provisions have be carried out satisfactorily;

(B) a pattern of discrimination has resulted against citizens or nationals of the United States or against eligible workers seeking employment; and

(C) an unnecessary regulatory burden has been created for employers hiring such workers.

REVIEW BY TASK FORCE—

(1) Establishment of Task Force—The Attorney General, jointly with the Chairman of the Commission on Civil

Rights and the Chairman of the Equal Employment Opportunity Commission, shall establish a task force to review each report of the Comptroller General.

(2) Recommendations to Congress—If the report transmitted includes a determination that the implementation of this section has resulted in a pattern of discrimination in employment (against others than unauthorized aliens) on the basis of national origin, the task force shall, taking into consideration any recommendations in the report, report to Congress recommendations for such legislation as may be appropriate to deter or remedy such discrimination.

TERMINATION DATE FOR EMPLOYER SANCTIONS—

(1) If report of widespread discrimination and Congressional Approval—the provisions of this section shall terminate 30 days after receipt of the last report required to be transmitted under subsection (j), if—

(A) The Comptroller General determines and so reports . . . that a widespread pattern of discrimination has resulted against citizens or nationals of the United States or against eligible workers seeking employment solely from the implementation of this section, and

(B) There is enacted, within such period of 30 calendar days, a joint resolution stating in substance that the Congress approves the findings of the Comptroller General contained in such report.

(2) Senate Procedures for Consideration—Any joint resolution referred to in clause (B) of paragraph (1) shall be considered in the Senate in accordance with subsection (n) . . .

**Increased Authorization of Appropriations for INS and EOIR**—In addition to any other amounts authorized to be appropriated, in order to carry out this Act, there are authorized to be appropriated to the Department of Justice—

**(1)** For the INS, for FY 1987, $12,000,000 and for FY 1988, $15,000,000 . . . to provide for an increase in the border patrol personnel . . . so that the average level of such personnel in each fiscal year 1987 and 1988 is at least 50 percent higher than such level for fiscal year 1986.

### Title II—Legalization

SEC. 201—LEGALIZATION OF STATUS

**Temporary Resident Status—**

The Attorney General shall adjust the status of an alien to that of an alien lawfully admitted for temporary residence if the alien meets the following requirements:

(1) Timely Application—

(A) During Application Period—Except as provided in subparagraph (B), the alien must apply for such adjustment during the 12 month period beginning on a date (not later than 180 days after the date of enactment of this section) designated by the Attorney General. . . .

(2) Continuous Lawful Residence Since 1982—

(A) In General—The alien must establish that he entered the United States before January 1, 1982, and that he has resided continuously in the United States in an unlawful status since such date and through the date the application is filed under this subsection.

(B) Nonimmigrants—In the case of an alien who entered the United States as a nonimmigrant before January 1, 1982, the alien must establish that the alien's period of authorized stay as a nonimmigrant expired before such date through the passage of time or the alien's unlawful status was known to the Government as of such date.

**Subsequent Adjustment to Permanent Residence and Nature of Temporary Resident Status—**

(1) Adjustment to Permanent Residence—The Attorney General shall adjust the status of any alien provided lawful temporary resident status under subsection (a) to that of an alien lawfully admitted for permanent residence if the alien meets the following requirements:

(A) Timely Application After One Year's Residence—The alien must apply for such adjustment during the one-year period beginning with the nineteenth month that begins after the date the alien was granted such temporary status.

(B) Continuous Residence—The alien must establish that he has continuously resided in the United States since the date the alien was granted such temporary resident status.

(C) Admissible as Immigrant—The alien must establish that he or she—

(i) is admissible to the United States as an immigrant . . . and

(ii) has not been convicted of any felony or three or more misdemeanors committed in the United States.

**Basic Citizenship Skills—The alien must demonstrate that he or she either—**

(1) meets the requirements of section 312 (relating to minimal understanding of ordinary English and a knowledge and understanding of the history and government of the

United States), or (2) is satisfactorily pursuing a course of study (recognized by the Attorney General) to achieve an understanding of English and such knowledge and understanding of the history and government of the United States. . . .

## Temporary Disqualification of Newly Legalized Aliens from Receiving Certain Public Welfare Assistance—

(1) In General—During the five year period beginning on the date an alien was granted lawful temporary resident status under subsection (a) except as provided in paragraph (2) and (3), the alien is not eligible for—

(I)   Any program of financial assistance furnished under Federal law;

(ii)  medical assistance under a State plan approved under Title XIX of the Social Security Act; and

(iii) assistance under the Food Stamp Act of 1977; and State or political subdivision therein may, to the extent consistent with paragraph (A) and paragraph (1) and (3), provide that an alien is not eligible for the programs of financial assistance or for medical assistance described in subparagraph (A) (ii) furnished under the law of that State or political subdivision.

### Title III—Reform of Legal Immigration Part A— Temporary Agricultural Workers
SEC. 301. H-2A AGRICULTURAL WORKERS

(a) Providing New "H-2A" Nonimmigrant Classification for Temporary Agricultural Labor—Paragraph (15) (H) of section 101 (a) (8 USC 1101 (a) is amended by striking out "to perform temporary services or labor," in clause (ii) and inserting "in lieu thereof," (a) to perform agricultural labor or services, as defined by the Secretary of Labor in regulations and including agricultural labor defined in section 3121 (g) of the Internal Revenue Code of 1954 and agriculture as defined in section 3 (f) of the Fair Labor Standards Act of 1938 . . . or a temporary or seasonal nature, or (b) to perform other temporary service or labor."

**Source:** Immigration Reform and Control Act (IRCA), Pub. L. No. 99–603, 100 Stat. 3445, enacted November 6, 1986.

### The Immigrant Visa Process (2018)

*The U.S. Department of State has laid out the steps required to immigrate legally to the United States. Those steps, and information on various types of visas available, are outlined below.*

Petition

    Submit a Petition

After Your Petition is Approved

    Begin National Visa Center (NVC) Processing

    Consular Electronic Application Center (CEAC) Processing

    Step 1: Choose an Agent

    Step 2: Pay Fees

Collect and Submit Forms and Documents to the NVC

    Step 3: Submit Visa Application Form

    Step 4: Collect Financial Documents

    Step 5: Collect Supporting Documents

    Step 6: Submit Documents to the NVC

Interview

    Prepare for the Interview

    Applicant Interview

    After the Interview

*Foreign citizens who want to live permanently in the United States must first obtain an immigrant visa. This is the first step to becoming a lawful permanent resident.*

Immigrating to the United States is an important and complex decision. In this section, you will learn about who may immigrate to the United States, the different types of immigrant visas, the required forms, and the steps in the immigrant visa process. **Because most immigrants receive visas in the family or employment based visa categories, they are a key focus of this section.** To be eligible to apply for an immigrant visa, a foreign citizen must be sponsored by a U.S. citizen relative, U.S. lawful permanent resident, or a prospective employer, with a few exceptions, explained below. The sponsor begins the immigration process by filing a petition on the foreign citizen's behalf with U.S. Citizenship and Immigration Services (USCIS).

### Immigrating Based on Family

A U.S. citizen can file an immigrant visa petition for:

- Spouse
- Son or daughter
- Parent
- Brother or sister

A U.S. lawful permanent resident (that is, a green-card holder) can file an immigrant visa petition for:

- Spouse
- Unmarried son or daughter

### Employment-Based Immigration

A U.S. employer can sponsor certain skilled workers who will be hired into permanent jobs. In some specialized fields, U.S. law allows prospective immigrants to sponsor themselves.

In addition, U.S. law provides a number of special immigrant categories, as well as an immigrant investor program.

### Number of Visas Each Year Is Limited in Some Categories

Regarding some of the immigrant visa categories, United States law limits the number of visas available each year, with certain limits by country. In these limited categories, whenever the number of qualified applicants exceeds the available immigrant visas, there will be a waiting list. In this situation, the available immigrant visas will be issued in the chronological order in which the petitions were filed. The date your petition was filed is called your priority date.

### Other Immigrant Visa Categories

Many immigrants receive visas in the family or employment based visa categories; however there are other immigrant visa categories. A U.S. citizen can also petition for the immigration of a foreign fiancé(e) to be married in the United States, or an orphan adopted abroad/to be adopted in the United States. Several immigrant visa categories that cover special types of workers or special circumstances are established by U.S. laws. The United States also conducts an annual program for Diversity Visas.

**Source:** U.S. State Department. https://travel.state.gov/con tent/travel/en/us-visas/immigrate/the-immigrant-visa-process .html

### The Homeland Security Act (2002)

*In response to the 9/11 international terrorist attacks, Congress passed, on November 19, 2002, the Department of Homeland Security (DHS) Act. It is in excess of 400 printed pages. It merged 22 federal agencies, the most extensive reorganization of the federal bureaucracy since the creation of the Department of Defense after World War II. It creates within the DHS two bureaus, each headed by an undersecretary: Border and Transportation Security and the Bureau of Citizenship and Immigration Services. This document highlights some key provisions from Title IV of the Act.*

### *Title IV—Border and Transportation Security*
SUBTITLE A—GENERAL PROVISIONS

Sec. 401. Creates the Under Secretary for Border and Transportation Security.

Sec. 401. Responsibilities—Transfers functions of the INS to the DHS.

The Secretary, acting through the Under Secretary for Border and Transportation Security, shall be responsible for the following:

(1) Preventing the entry of terrorists and the instruments of terrorism into the U.S.

(2) Securing the borders, territorial waters, ports, terminals, waterways, and air, land and sea transportation systems of the United States, including managing and coordinating those functions transferred to the Department at ports of entry.

(3) Carrying out the immigrant enforcement functions vested by statute in, or performed by, the Commissioner of Immigration and Naturalization (or any officer, employee, or component of the Immigration and Naturalization Service) immediately before the date on which the transfer of functions specified under section 441 takes effect [March 1, 2003].

(4) Establishing and administering rules, in accordance with section 428, governing the granting of visas or other forms or permissions, including parole, to enter the United States to individuals who are not a citizen or an alien lawfully admitted for permanent residence in the United States.

(5) Establishing national immigration enforcement policies and priorities.

**Subtitle B—Immigration and Nationality Functions**
CHAPTER 1—IMMIGRATION ENFORCEMENT

Sec. 411. Details the transfer of functions of the Border Patrol, INS, to the Under Secretary for Border and Transportation Security in the DHS.

Sec. 412. Establishes a Bureau of Border Security headed by a Director.

Sec. 415. Calls for a report to Congress on improving enforcement functions.

CHAPTER 2—CITIZENSHIP AND IMMIGRATION SERVICES

Subchapter A—Transfer of Functions

Sec. 421. Establishes a Bureau of Citizenship and Immigration Services headed by a Director.

Sec. 422. Establishes a Citizenship and Immigration Ombudsman office.

Sec. 425. Establishes a Citizenship and Immigration Statistics within Bureau of Justice Statistics.

Sec. 426. Concerns preservation of the Attorney General's authority.

SUBCHAPTER B—OTHER PROVISIONS

Sec. 432. Calls for elimination of backlogs.

Sec. 433. Requires a report to Congress on efforts at improving immigration services.

Sec. 435. Calls for the application of Internet-based technologies.

CHAPTER 3—GENERAL PROVISIONS

Sec. 41. Abolishes the INS as of March 1, 2003.

Sec. 45. Requires reports and implementation plans to Congress.

Sec. 46. Details immigration functions.

**Source:** H.R. 5005—the Homeland Security Act of November 19, 2002. (Public Law 107–296, 107th Congress, 116 Stat. 2135, November 25, 2002. Available online at https://www.dhs.gov/homeland-security-act-2002.

### The Border Security, Economic Opportunity, and Immigration Mobilization Act (2013)

*In 2013, the Senate passed an immigration reform bill (S.744). It exemplifies the "comprehensive immigration reform" approach. Although passed by the U.S. Senate, it died in the House of Representatives. It remains a version of what would most likely be a comprehensive approach to immigration reform that has the best chance of enactment by the Congress in 2019 or later.*

*The bill was sponsored by Senator Charles Schumer (D-NY) and passed in the Senate on June 27, 2013.*

Sec. 2. States that the primary tenet of its success depends on securing U.S. sovereignty and establishing a coherent and just system for integrating those who seek to join American society.

Sec. 3. Prohibits the Secretary of DHS from processing applications for registered provisional immigrant status (RPI) until the Secretary has submitted to Congress the notice of commencement of implementation of the Comprehensive Southern Border Security Strategy and the Southern Border Fencing Strategy.

Sec. 4. Establishes a Southern Border Security Commission.

Sec. 5. Directs the secretary of DHS to implement a comprehensive Southern Border Security Strategy for achieving and maintaining effective control between and at the ports of entry in all border sectors along the Southern Border; and a Southern Border Fencing Strategy as to where 700 miles of fencing and technology be deployed.

Sec. 6. Establishes in the Department of the Treasury the Comprehensive Immigration Reform Trust Fund.

### Title 1: Border Security

Directs the secretary to increase the number of trained full-time U.S. Border Patrol agents deployed to the Southern Border to 38,405 by September 30, 2021, and to increase the number of CBP officers by 3,500 by September 30, 2017, and increase the number of CBP Air and Marine unmanned aircraft systems, crew, marine agents, and personnel by 160; and their flight hours to 130,000 annually by September 30, 2015.

Sec. 1103. Authorizes the governor of a state, with approval as the Secretary of Defense (DoD) to order National Guard personnel to perform operations in the Southern border region.

Sec. 1104. Directs that the Secretary increase the number of crossing prosecutions in the Tucson sector to up to 210 prosecutions per day by increasing funding for additional attorneys and support staff, interpreters and U.S. marshals. It directs the Secretary to enhance border infrastructure by additional border patrol stations, upgrading and establishing additional border patrol operating bases, and establishing a grant program with DOT to construct transportation improvement at international border crossings, and authorizes FY 2014–2018 appropriations for such. It directs the president to appoint additional district judges for Arizona, California, and Texas. It increases the fee for filing a civil action in U.S. district court to $360.

Sec. 1105. Directs the USDA and Secretary of the Interior to provide CBP personnel with immediate access to federal funds in the Southwest Border region in Arizona for security activities.

Sec. 1106. Requires the CPB to deploy additional mobile, video, and portable surveillance systems, and unarmed, unmanned drone vehicles in the Southwest Border region to provide 24-hour surveillance.

Sec. 1107. Directs the Secretary of DHS to establish a two-year grant program to improve communications in the border region and authorizes appropriations for such.

Sec. 1108. Directs the Attorney General, DOJ, to reimburse state, county, tribal, and municipal governments for the costs associated with the prosecution and pre-trial detention of federally initiated criminal cases and authorizes FY2014–2018 appropriations for such.

Sec. 1110. Authorizes appropriations for the state criminal assistance program (SCAAP) through FY 2015.

Sec. 1112. Directs the secretary to provide appropriate training for CPB officers, Border Patrol officers, ICE agents, U.S. Air and Marine Division agents, agriculture specialists stationed within 100 miles of any U.S. land or marine border, or at any U.S. port of entry; and to establish CBP child custody guidelines.

Sec. 1113. Establishes a DHS Oversight Task Force and authorizes FY 2014–2017 appropriations.

Sec. 1114. Establishes an Ombudsman for Immigration Related Concerns in the DHS.

Sec. 1115. Directs the Secretary, DHS, to consider safety and family concerns in any action of repatriation of individuals apprehended for immigration violations and provides for training for CBP personnel.

Sec. 1116. Revises maximum distances in a Northern Border sector or district with DHS personnel have the authority to board and search vehicles for aliens.

Sec. 1120. Human Trafficking Reporting Act of 2013.

Sec. 1133. DHS to report to Congress every six months on removals.

Sec. 1201. Directs the Secretary to initiate certain expedited removal proceedings relating to border security.

### Title II: Immigrant Visas—Registration and Adjustment of Registered Provisional Immigrants

Sec. 2101. After certification by the Secretary DHS about national security and law enforcement clearances, to grant RPI status to certain aliens unlawfully in the U.S. (enacting provisions of the Dream Act).

Sec. 2102. Establishes a process for earned legalization of certain aliens unlawfully in the U.S. and makes those authorized RPI ineligible for any means-tested benefit. Authorizes RPIs to be issued a social security number and to enlist in the U.S. armed forces.

It prohibits an RPI alien from applying for lawful permanent status until the Secretary of State certifies that immigrant visas have become available for all approved petitions filed before the date of enactment of this Act. It states that an RPI alien may only adjust status under the merit-based system provided for by the Act.

Sec. 2013. Authorizes enactment of the DREAM ACT of 2013.

Sec. 2105. Sets a criminal penalty for up to $10,000 for a person who knowingly uses, publishes or permits the improper use of RPI application information.

Sec. 2106. Authorizes USCIS to establish a program to award grants to eligible nonprofit organizations to assist RPI applicants.

**Subtitle B: Agriculture Worker Program.** Enacts the Agriculture Worker Program Act of 2013 with all its various provisions, including make a blue card alien ineligible for any federal means-tested benefit.

Sec. 2212. Requires payment of a $400 fine, and payment of any federal tax liability.

Sec. 2232. Establishes a nonimmigrant agricultural (W-# and W-4 visa) worker program; and among its many provisions excludes W-3 and W-4 workers from any need-based federal financial assistance program.

**Subtitle C: Future Immigration.**

Sec. 2301. Establishes a merit-based point immigration administration system with 120,000 admissions per year with increases on certain specified admissions and employment conditions to a maximum cap of 250,000, allows recapture of unused visas, and allows lawful permanent resident status for such entrants.

Sec. 2303. Repeals the diversity immigrant program as of October 1, 2014.

Sec. 2304. Sets forth worldwide levels of employment and family-based immigrants.

Sec. 2305. Includes spouses or minor child of a lawful permanent alien in the definition of "immediate family."

Sec. 2306. Eliminates the per-country limit for employment-based immigrants and increases the per-country limit for family-tied immigrants.

Sec. 2307. Revises certain provisions of the family-based immigrant visa allocation system; including elimination of the visa category for brothers and sisters of U.S. citizens.

### Title IV: Reforms to Nonimmigrant Visa Programs— Subtitle A: Employment-Based Nonimmigrant Visas

Several sections revise and change the caps for H-1B to a cap of 115,000 per fiscal year; and a maximum of 115,000 visas to a maximum of 180,000 visas in subsequent years. It limits the exemption from H-1B numerical limitations to STEM occupations and increases the annual STEM allocation to 25,000.

**Subtitle B: H-1B Visa Fraud and Abuse Protection.** Several sections that revise H-1B provisions to deal with fraud and abuse.

**Subtitle C: L Visa Fraud and Abuse Protection.** Several sections address L visa fraud and abuse concerns.

**Subtitle D: Other Nonimmigrant Visas.** Establishes a Bureau of Immigration and Labor Market Research to supplement W-visa recruitment methods, conduct survey every three months on the need for W-visa cap of construction worker unemployment and report to Congress on employment-based immigrant and nonimmigrant visa programs.

**Subtitle H: Investing in New Ventures, Entrepreneurial Startups, and Technologies.**

This section contains several sections to establish a nonimmigrant X-visa for qualified entrepreneurs who invest certain amounts in U.S. businesses and which creates a certain number of jobs and generate at least $250,000 in annual revenues to the U.S., a provision of which establishes a $1,000 X-visa fee.

**Subtitle I: Student and Exchange Visitor Programs.** This subtitle contains about a dozen provisions regarding student visa integrity.

**Source:** Border Security, Economic Opportunity, and Immigration Modernization Act. S. 744 (113th). Passed U.S. Senate, June 27, 2013. Available online at https://www.govtrack.us/congress/bills/113/s744.

### Report on ICE Enforcement and Removal Operations (2017)

*ICE is a principal enforcer of immigration control. This report from fiscal year 2017 (the latest available such report at the time of this writing) illustrates the ICE Enforcement and Removal operations.*

This report summarizes U.S. Immigration and Customs Enforcement (ICE) Enforcement and Removal Operations (ERO) activities in FY 2017. ERO identifies, arrests, and removes aliens who present a danger to national security or a threat to public safety, or who otherwise undermine border control and the integrity of the U.S. immigration system. ICE shares responsibility for administering and enforcing the nation's immigration laws with U.S. Customs and Border Protection (CBP) and U.S. Citizenship and Immigration Services.

On January 25, 2017, President Donald J. Trump issued Executive Order 13768, *Enhancing Public Safety in the Interior of the United States (EO)*, which set forth the Administration's immigration enforcement and removal priorities. The DHS February 20, 2017 memorandum, *Enforcement of the Immigration Laws to Serve the National Interest*, provided direction for the implementation of the policies set forth in the EO. The EO and implementation memorandum expanded ICE's enforcement focus to include removable aliens who 1) have been convicted on any criminal offense; 2) have been charged with any criminal offense that has not been resolved; 3) have committed acts which constitute a chargeable criminal offense; 4) have engaged in fraud or willful misrepresentation in connection with any official matters before a government agency; 5) have abused any program related to the receipt of public benefits; 6) are subject to a final order of removal but have not complied with their legal obligation to depart the United States; or 7) in the judgment of an immigration officer, otherwise pose a risk to public safety or national security. The Department has directed that classes or categories of removable aliens are no longer exempted from potential enforcement.

**Impact.** In FY2017, ICE ERO conducted 143,470 overall administrative arrests, which is the highest number of administrative arrests over the past three fiscal years. Of these arrests, 92 percent had a criminal conviction, a pending criminal charge, were an ICE fugitive or were processed with a reinstated final order. In FY2017, ICE conducted 226,119 removals. While this is a slight overall decrease from the prior fiscal year, the proportion of removals resulting from ICE arrests increased from 65,332, or 27 percent of total removals in FY2016 to 81,603, or 36 percent of total removals, in FY2017. These results demonstrate profound, positive impact of the EO. The 17 percent decrease in border removals shows the deterrent effect of strong interior enforcement, while the increase in interior removals restores the integrity of our nation's immigration system and enhances the safety and security of the United States.

**Source:** https://www.ice.gov/removal-statistics/2017.

### Executive Order 13780: Protecting the Nation from Foreign Terrorist Entry into the United States (March 6, 2017)

*President Trump issued several versions of executive orders imposing a travel ban. This document excerpts Executive Order 13780, the second version of the travel ban.*

By the authority invested in me as President by the Constitution and the laws of the United States of America, including the Immigration and Nationality (INA), 8 U.S.C. 1101 *et seq*, and section 301 of title 3, United States Code, and to protect the Nation from terrorist activities by foreign nationals admitted to the United States, it is hereby ordered as follows:

*Section 1. Policy and Purpose.* (a) It is the policy of the United States to protect its citizens from terrorist attacks, including those committed by foreign nationals. The screening and vetting protocols and procedures associated with the visa-issuance process and the United States Refugee Admissions Program (USRAP) play a crucial role in detecting foreign nationals who may commit, aid, or support acts of terrorism and in preventing those individuals from entering the United States. It is therefore the policy of the United States to improve the screening and vetting protocols and procedures associated with the visa-issuance process and the USRAP.

(b) On January 27, 2017, to implement this policy, I issued Executive Order 13769 (Protecting the Nation from Foreign Terrorist Entry into the United States).

(i) Among other actions, Executive Order 13769 suspended for 90 days the entry of certain aliens from seven countries: Iran, Iraq, Libya, Somalia, Sudan, Syria, and Yemen. These are countries that had already been identified as presenting heightened concerns about terrorism and travel to the United States. Specifically, the suspension applied to countries referred to in, or designated under, section 217(a)(12) of the INA, 8 U.S.C. 1187 (a)(12), in which Congress restricted use of the Visa Waiver Program for nationals of, and aliens recently present in, (A) Iraq or Syria, (B) any country designated by the Secretary of State as a state sponsor of terrorism (currently, Iran, Syria, and Sudan), and (C) any other country designated as a country of concern by the Secretary of Homeland Security, in consultation with the Secretary of State and the Director of National Intelligence. In 2016, the Secretary of Homeland Security designated Libya, Somalia, and Yemen as additional countries of concern for travel purposes, based on consideration of three statutory factors related to terrorism and national security: "(I) whether the presence of an alien in the country or area increases the likelihood that the alien is a credible threat to the national security of the United States; (II) whether a foreign terrorist organization has a significant presence in the country or area; and (III) whether the country or area is a safe haven for terrorists." 8 U.S.C. 1187(a) (12)(D)(ii). Additionally, Members of Congress have expressed concerns about screening and vetting procedures following recent terrorist attacks in this country and in Europe.

(ii) In ordering the temporary suspension of entry in subsection (b)(i) of this section, I exercised my authority under Article II of the Constitution and under section 212(f) of the INA, which provides in relevant part: "Whenever the President finds that the entry of any aliens or of any class of aliens into the United States would be detrimental to the interests of the United States, he may by proclamation, and for such period as he shall deem necessary, suspend the entry of all aliens or any class of aliens as immigrants or nonimmigrants, or impose on the entry of aliens any restrictions he may deem to be appropriate." 8 U.S.C. 1182(f). Under these authorities, I determined that, for a brief period of 90 days, while existing screening and vetting procedures were under review, the entry into the United States of certain aliens from seven identified countries—each afflicted by terrorism in a manner that compromised the ability of the United States to rely on normal decision-making procedures about travel to the United States—would be detrimental to the interests of the United States. Nonetheless, I permitted the Secretary of State and the Secretary of Homeland Security to grant case-by-case waivers when they determined that it was in the national interest to do so.

(iii) Executive Order 13769 also suspended the USRAP for 120 days. Terrorist groups have sought to infiltrate several nations through refugee programs. Accordingly, I temporarily suspended the USRAP pending a review of our procedures for screening and vetting refugees. Nonetheless, I permitted the Secretary of State and the Secretary of Homeland Security to jointly grant case-by-case waivers when they determined that it was in the national interest to do so.

(iv) Executive Order 13769 did not provide a basis for discriminating for or against members of any religion. While that order allowed for prioritization of refugee claims from members of persecuted religious minority groups, that priority applied to refugees from every nation, including those in which Islam is a minority religion, and applied to minority sects within a religion. That order was not motivated by animus toward any religion, but was instead intended to protect the ability of religious minorities—whoever they are and wherever they reside—to avail themselves of the USRAP in light of their particular challenges and circumstances.

(v) (c) The implementation of Executive Order 13769 has been delayed by litigation. Most significantly, enforcement of critical provisions of that order has been temporarily halted by court orders that apply nationwide and extend even to foreign nationals with no prior or substantial connection to the United States. On February 9, 2017, the United States Court of Appeals of the Ninth Circuit declined to stay or narrow one such order pending the outcome of further judicial proceedings, while noting that the "political branches are far better equipped to make appropriate distinctions" about who should be covered by a suspension of entry or of refugee admissions.

(d) Nationals from the countries previous identified under section 217(a)(12) of the INA warrant additional scrutiny in connection with our immigration policies because the conditions in these countries present heightened threats. Each of these countries is a state sponsor of terrorism, has been significantly compromised by terrorist organizations, or contains active conflict zones. Any of these circumstances diminishes the foreign government's willingness or ability to share or validate important information about individuals seeking to travel to the United States. Moreover, the significant presence in each of these countries of terrorist organizations, their members, and others exposed to those organizations increases the chance that conditions will be exploited to enable terrorist operatives or sympathizers to travel to the United States. Finally, once foreign national from these countries are admitted to the United States, it is often difficult to remove them, because many of these countries typically delay issuing, or refuse to issue, travel documents. . . .

*Section 2. Temporary Suspension of Entry for Nationals of Countries of Particular Concern During Review Period.* (a) The Secretary of Homeland Security, in consultation with the Secretary of State and the Director of National Intelligence, shall conduct a worldwide review to identify whether, and if so what, additional information will be needed from each country to adjudicate an application by a national of that country for a visa, admission, or other benefit under the INA in order to determine that an individual is not a security or public-safety threat. The Secretary of Homeland Security may conclude that certain information is needed from particular countries even if it is not needed from every country. . . .

*Sec.* 3: Scope and Implementation of Suspension. (a) Scope. Subject to the exceptions set forth in subsection (b) of this section and any waiver under subsection (c) of this section, the suspension of entry pursuant to section 2 of this order shall apply only to foreign nationals of the designated countries who: (i) are outside the United States on the effective date of this order; (ii) did not have a valid visa at 5:00 P.M. eastern standard time on January 27, 2017; and (iii) do not have a valid visa on the effective date of this order. . . .

*Sec. 4. Additional Inquiries Related to Nationals of Iraq.* An application by any Iraqi national for a visa, admission, or other immigration benefit should be subjected to thorough review, including, as appropriate, consultation with a designee of the Secretary of Defense and use of the additional information has been obtained in the context of the close U.S.-Iraqi security partnership, since Executive Order 13769 was issued, concerning the individuals suspected of ties to ISIS or other terrorist organizations and individuals coming from territories controlled or formally controlled by ISIS. . . .

*Sec.*5. Implementing Uniform Screening and Vetting Standards for All Immigration Programs. . . .

*Sec.6. Realignment of the U.S. Refugee Admissions Program for Fiscal Year 2017.* (a) The Secretary of State shall suspend travel of refugees into the United States under the USRAP, and the

Secretary of Homeland Security shall suspend decisions on applications for refugee status, for 120 days after the effective date of this order, subject to waivers pursuant to subsection (c) of this section. . . .

*Sec. 7: Rescission of Exercise of Authority Relating to the Terrorism Grounds of Inadmissibility.*

*Sec. 8. Expedited Completion of the Biometric Entry-Exit Tracking System.* (a) The Secretary of Homeland Security shall expedite the completion and implementation of a biometric entry-exit system for in-scope travelers to the United States, as recommended by the National Commission on Terrorist Attacks Upon the United States. . . .

*Sec. 12. Enforcement.* (a) The Secretary of State and the Secretary of Homeland Security shall consult with appropriate domestic and international partners, including countries and organizations, to ensure efficient, effective, and appropriate implementation of the actions directed by this order. . . .

*Sec. 13. Revocation.* Executive Order 13769 of January 27, 2017, is revoked by the effective date of this order.

*Sec. 14. Effective Date.* This order is effective at 12:01 A.M., eastern daylight time on March 16, 2017.

*Sec. 17. Severability.* (a) If any provision of this order, or the application of any provisions to any person or circumstance, is held to be invalid, the remainder of this order and the application of its other provisions to any other person or circumstances shall not be affected thereby. . . .

*Sec. 16. General Provisions* . . . (c) This order is not intended to, and does not, create any right or benefit, substantive or procedural, enforceable at law or in equity by any party against the United States, its departments, agencies, or entities, its officers, employees, or agents, or any other person.

*Signed: Donald J. Trump, The White House, March 6, 2017.*

**Source:** https://www.whitehouse.gov/presidential-actions/executive-order-protecting-nation-foreign-terrorist-entry-united-states-2/

### Syllabus of *Trump v. Hawaii* (2018)

*A third version of President Trump's executive order finally was ruled constitutional by the U.S. Supreme Court in June 2018. The Supreme Court's syllabus of that ruling, in* Trump v. Hawaii, *decided on June 26, 2018, is presented here.*

TRUMP, PRESIDENT OF THE UNITED STATES, ET AL. V. HAWAII, ET AL.

CERTIORARI TO THE UNITED STATES COURT OF APPEALS FOR THE NINGTH CIRCUIT.

No. 17–965. Argued April 25, 2018—Decided June 26, 2018.

In September 2017, the President issued Proclamation No. 8645, seeking to improve vetting procedures for foreign nationals traveling to the United States by identifying ongoing deficiencies in the information needed to assess whether nationals of particular countries present a security threat. The Proclamation placed entry restrictions on the nationals of eight foreign states whose systems for managing and sharing information about their nationals the President deemed inadequate. Foreign states were selected for inclusion based on a review undertaken pursuant to one of the President's earlier Executive Orders. As part of that review, the Department of Homeland Security (DHS), in consultation with the State Department and intelligence agencies, developed an information and risk assessment "baseline." DHS then collected and evaluated data for all foreign governments, identifying those having deficient information-sharing practices and presenting national security concerns, as well as other countries "at risk" of failing to meet the baseline. After a 50-day period during which the State Department made diplomatic efforts to encourage foreign governments to improve their practices, the Acting Secretary of Homeland Security concluded that eight countries—Chad, Iran, Iraq, Libya, North Korea, Syria, Venezuela, and Yemen—remained deficient. She recommended entry restrictions for certain nationals from all those countries but Iraq, which had a close cooperative relationship with the

U.S. She also recommended including Somalia, which met the information-sharing component of the baseline standards but had other special risk factors, such as a significant terrorist presence. After consulting with multiple Cabinet members, the President adopted the recommendations and issued the Proclamation.

Invoking his authority under 8 U.S.C. 1182(f) and 1185(a), he determined that certain restrictions were necessary to "prevent the entry of those foreign nationals about whom the United States Government lacks sufficient information" and "elicit improved identity-management and information-sharing protocols and practices from foreign governments." The Proclamation imposes a range of entry restrictions that vary based on the "distinct circumstances" in each of the eight countries. It exempts lawful permanent residents and provides case-by-case waivers under certain circumstances. It also directs DHS to assess on a continuing basis whether the restrictions should be modified or continued, and to report to the President every 180 days. At the completion of the first such review period, the President determined that Chad had sufficiently improved its practices, and he accordingly lifted restrictions on its nationals.

Plaintiffs—the State of Hawaii, three individuals with foreign relatives affected by the entry suspension, and the Muslim Association of Hawaii—argue that the Proclamation violates the Immigration and Nationality Act (INA) and the Establishment Clause. The District Court granted a nationwide preliminary injunction barring enforcement of the restrictions. The Ninth Circuit Court affirmed, concluding that the Proclamation contravened two provisions of the INA: 1182(f), which authorizes the President to "suspend the entry of all aliens or any class of aliens" whenever he "finds" that their entry "would be detrimental to the interests of the United States," and 1152(a)(1) (A), which provides that "no person shall . . . be discriminated against in the issuance of an immigrant visa because of the person's race, sex, nationality, place of birth, or place of residence." The court did not reach the Establishment Clause claim.

*Held:*

1. This Court assumes without deciding that plaintiffs' statutory claims are reviewable, notwithstanding consular nonreviewability or any other statutory nonreviewability issue. . . .

2. The President has lawfully exercised the broad discretion granted to him under 1182(f) to suspend the entry of aliens into the United States. . . .

    (a) By its terms, 1182(f) exudes deference to the President in every clause. It entrusts to the President the decisions whether and when to suspend entry, whose entry to suspend, for how long, and on what conditions. It invests the President with "ample power" to impose entry restrictions in addition to those elsewhere enumerated in the INA. . . . The Proclamation falls well within this comprehensive delegation. The sole prerequisite set forth in 1182(f) is that the President "find" that the entry of the covered aliens "would be detrimental to the interests of the United States." The President has undoubtedly fulfilled that requirement here. He first ordered DHS and other agencies to conduct a comprehensive evaluation of every single country's compliance with the information and risk assessment baseline. He then issued a Proclamation with extensive findings about the deficiencies and their impact. Based on that review, he found that restricting entry of aliens who could not be vetted with adequate information was in the national interest.

        Even assuming that some form of inquiry into the persuasiveness of the President's findings is appropriate, but see *Webster v. Doe,* 486 U.S. 592, 600, plaintiffs' attacks on the sufficiency of the findings cannot be sustained. The 12-page Proclamation is more detailed than any prior order issued under 1182(f). And such a searching inquiry is inconsistent with the broad statutory text and the deference traditionally accorded to the President in this sphere. See, e.g. *Sale, 509 U.S., at 187–188.*

The Proclamation comports with the remaining textual limits in 1182(f). While the word "suspend" often connotes a temporary deferral, the President is not required to prescribe in advance a fixed end date for the entry restriction. Like its predecessors, the Proclamation makes clear that its "conditional restrictions" will remain in force only so long as necessary to "address" the identified "inadequacies and risks" within the covered nations. Finally, the Proclamation properly identifies a "class of aliens" whose entry is suspended, and the word "class" comfortably encompasses a group of people linked by nationality. . . .

(b) Plaintiffs have not identified any conflict between the Proclamation and the immigration scheme reflected in the INA that would implicitly bar the President from addressing deficiencies in the Nation's vetting system. The existing grounds of inadmissibility and the narrow Visa Waiver Program do not address the failure of certain high-risk countries to provide a minimum baseline of reliable information. Further, neither the legislative history of 1182(f) nor historical practice justifies departing from the clear text of the statute. . . .

(c) Plaintiffs' argument that the President's entry suspension violates 1182(a)(1)(A) ignores the basic distinction between admissibility determinations and visa issuance that runs throughout the INA. Section 1182 defines the universe of aliens who are admissible into the United States (and therefore eligible to receive a visa). Once 1182 sets the boundaries of admissibility, 1152(a)(1)(A) prohibits discrimination in the allocation of immigrant visas based on nationality or other traits. Had Congress intended in 11582(1)(A) to constrain the President's power to determine who may enter the country, it could have chosen language directed to that end. Common sense and historical practice confirm that 1152(a)(1)(A) does not limit the President's delegated authority under 1183(f). Presidents have repeatedly exercised their authority to suspend entry on the basis of nationality. And on plaintiffs' reading, the President would not be permitted to suspend entry from any particular foreign state in response to an epidemic, or even if the United States were on the brink of war. . . .

3. Plaintiffs have not demonstrated a likelihood of success on the merits of their claim that the Proclamation violates the Establishment Clause. . . .

(a) The individual plaintiffs have Article III standing to challenge the exclusion of their relatives under the Establishment Clause. A person's interest in being united with his relatives is sufficiently concrete and particularized to form the basis of an Article III injury in fact. Cf, e.g. *Kerry v. Din, 576 U.S.* ————.pp. 24–26.

(b) Plaintiffs allege that the primary purpose of the Proclamation was religious animus and that the President's stated concerns about vetting protocols and national security were but pretexts for discrimination against Muslims. At the heart of their case is a series of statements by the President and his advisers both during the campaign and since the President assumed office. The issue, however, is not whether to denounce the President's statements, but the significance of those statements in reviewing a Presidential directive, neutral on its face, addressing a matter within the core of executive responsibility. In doing so, the Court must consider not only the statements of a particular President, but also the authority of the Presidency itself. . . .

(c) The admission and exclusion of foreign nationals is a "fundamental sovereign attribute exercised by the Government's political departments largely immune from judicial control." *Fiallo v. Bell* 430 U.S. 787, 792. Although foreign nationals seeking admission have no constitutional right to entry, this Court has engaged in a circumscribed judicial inquiry when the denial of a visa allegedly burdens the constitutional rights of a U.S. citizen. That review is limited to whether the Executive gives a "facially legitimate and bona fide" reason for its actions, *Kleindienst v. Mandel*, 408 U.S. 754, 769, but the Court need not define the precise contours of that narrow inquiry in this case. For today's purposes, the Court assumes that it may look behind the face of the Proclamation to the extent of applying rational basis review, i.e., whether the entry policy is plausibly related to the Government's stated objective to protect the country and improve vetting processes. Plaintiffs' extrinsic evidence may be considered, but the policy will be upheld so long as it can reasonably be understood to result from a justification independent on unconstitutional ground. . . .

(d) On the few occasions where the Court has struck down a policy as illegitimate under rational basis scrutiny, a common thread has been that the laws at issue were "divorced from any factual context from which [the Court] could discern a relationship to legitimate state interests." *Romer v. Evans*, 517 U.S. 620, 635. The Proclamation does not fit that pattern. It is expressly premised on legitimate purposes and says nothing about religion. The entry restrictions on Muslim-majority nations are limited to countries that were previously designated by Congress or prior administrations as posing national security risks. Moreover, the Proclamation reflects the results of a worldwide review process, undertaken by multiple Cabinet officials and their agencies. Plaintiffs challenge the entry suspension based on their perception of its effectiveness and wisdom, but the Court cannot substitute its own assessment of the Executive's predictive judgement on such matters. . . .

Three additional features of the entry policy support the Government's claim of a legitimate national security interest. First, since the President introduced entry restrictions in January 2017, three Muslim-majority countries—Iraq, Sudan, and Chad—have been removed from the list. Second, for those countries still subject to entry restrictions, the Proclamation includes numerous exceptions for various categories of foreign nationals. Finally, the Proclamation creates a waiver program open to all covered foreign nationals seeking entry as immigrants or nonimmigrants. Under these circumstances, the Government has set forth a sufficient national security justification to survive rational basis review.

878 F. 3d 662, reversed and remanded.

Roberts, C.J., delivered the opinion of the Court, in which Kennedy, Thomas, Alito, and Gorsuch, JJ. Joined. Kennedy, J., and Thomas, J. filed concurring opinions. Breyor, J. filed a dissenting opinion, in which Kagan, J. joined. Sotomayor, J. filed a dissenting opinion, in which Ginsburg, J., joined.

**Source:** https://www.supremecourt.gov/docket/docketfiles/html/public/17-965.html

## Introduction

This chapter lists and discusses briefly some major sources of information the reader is encouraged to consult. It begins with print sources: 68 scholarly books on the subject are cited and annotated. It then lists and discusses 48 scholarly refereed journals that publish articles pertinent to the subject. Finally, it lists and discusses nonprint sources: 8 feature length films and 4 videos that give "life" and faces to the subject, illustrating the discourse and the politics of attempting to reform American immigration policy.

## Books

Ackerman, Alissa, and Rick Furman. 2013. *The Criminalization of Immigration: Contexts and Consequences.* Durham, N.C.: Carolina Academic Press.

> The authors offer a compelling narrative about immigrants, refugees, and asylum seekers and the consequences of the criminalization in the United States. Their book

---

U.S. Immigration and Customs Enforcement (ICE) officers process detained undocumented immigrants at the U.S. Federal Building in lower Manhattan, New York, on April 11, 2018. ICE detentions are especially controversial in New York, considered a "sanctuary city" for undocumented immigrants, and ICE receives little or no cooperation from local law enforcement. ICE said that officers arrested 225 people for the violation of immigration laws during the six-day operation, the largest in New York City in recent years. (John Moore/Getty Images)

explores the impact of national, state, and local laws on the psychological well-being of immigrants, how immigration became criminalized, and how the problematization of immigration becomes a political tool. It provides facts and knowledge essential for a fair and balanced debate on immigration matters.

Alden, Edward. 2008. *Closing the American Border: Terrorism, Immigration, and Security since 9/11.* New York: Harper Perennial.
Alden's book is a provocative and behind-the-scenes look at the country's efforts to secure its borders since 9/11. Based on extensive interviews with Secretary of State Collin Powell, Secretary of Homeland Security Tom Ridge, other Bush administration officials, and many innocent citizens whose lives have been upended by new security and visa policy and rules, he offers a compelling assessment of the dangers for the United States that results from the United States cutting itself off from the rest of the world.

Alden, Ewing. 2012. *Opportunity and Exclusion: A Brief History of Immigration Policy.* Washington, D.C.: Immigration Policy Center.
Alden is a senior researcher for the Immigration Policy Center, who covers U.S. immigration from colonial days to the present, showing how descendants of earlier European immigrants distrusted the "new" immigrants from South/Central/Eastern Europe and how, in turn, their descendants are now casting a dim view on those coming from Latin America, Asia, and Africa today.

Andreas, Peter, and Timothy Snyders, eds. 2000. *The Wall around the West: State Borders and Immigration Controls in North America and Europe.* Lanham, MD: Rowman and Littlefield.
A balanced but critical examination of the increasing barriers being enacted in response to increasing international

terrorism to control immigration and refugee flows into Canada, the United States, and the major immigrant-receiving nations of Europe, particularly the European Union countries.

Barone, Michael. 2013. *Shaping Our Nation: How Surges of Migration Transformed America and Its Politics.* New York: Crown Forum.
Michael Barone examines the history of U.S. immigration and how past surges in immigration have influenced American culture, society, and politics.

Bean, Frank D., George Vernez, and Charles B. Keely. 1989. *Opening and Closing the Doors.* Santa Monica, CA: The Rand Corporation.
This is an important book in a series of excellent books and monographs published by a joint Rand Corporation/Urban Institute major research project, examining in-depth immigration policy as a result of the Immigration Reform and Control Act of 1986. It is a prime example of the best of scholarly research of think tanks.

Bolich, Clint. 2011. *Death Grip: Loosening the Law's Stranglehold over Economic Liberty.* Stanford: Hoover Institution Press.
Written by the conservative Hoover Institute's research fellow and fellow of the Goldwater Institute Scharf-Norton Center for Constitutional Litigation, this volume looks at the state of economic liberty in the United States today, in the post-9/11 era of extensive regulation, explaining how the consequences of the 1873 *Slaughterhouse* cases have reverberated through the years. He examines more recent Supreme Court decisions and sees hope in the current campaign to "restore economic liberty." These reforms would, in turn, impact immigration reform, whether comprehensive or piece meal.

Brill, Stephen. 2003. *After: How America Confronted the September 12 Era.* New York: Simon and Schuster.
Brill is an award-winning journalist whose narrative reads like a thriller novel, but is real. The book focuses on how real Americans cope with the aftermath of the 9/11 attacks. He draws on 317 interviews, including a customs inspector searching cargo containers from all over the world, a young widow with three children who challenges the head of a federal victims fund, a Silicon Valley entrepreneur who makes screening devices, Attorney General John Ashcroft, and a recently hired director of the American Civil Liberties Union (ACLU), DHS secretary Tom Ridge, to paint a gritty story of coping with the post-9/11 era in America.

Brotherton, David, and Philip Kretsedemas, eds. 2008. *Keeping out the Others.* New York: Columbia University Press.
Since 2001, the United States has been making the process of legal immigration and of citizenship more difficult and contentious. These policies have sparked major protests and unrest. The authors referred here provide a history and analysis of recent immigration enforcement in the United States, showing that the current anti-immigration tendencies are not merely a knee-jerk reaction to the 9/11 attacks, but rather, they have deep historical roots.

Brown, Cynthia, ed. 2004. *Lost Liberties: Ashcroft and the Assault on Personal Freedom.* New York: The Free Press.
In this edited collection of essays, 13 leading experts confront the DOJ's assault on civil liberties. It delves into the Patriot Act's most arcane provisions. The essays catalog a long list of civil liberties important to a democratic society that the essay authors view as being sacrificed in the haste to strengthen national security after 9/11. Among the rights harmed by the law, according to the essays, are

the right to political dissent, to open government, to be from government warrantless surveillance, the right to a lawyer and a trial when charged with a crime. The essays are collected to probe the balance between rights and safety and to show that the forfeiture of civil liberties presents a greater threat than does terrorism.

Browning, Rufus, Dale Rogers Marshall, and David H. Tabb. *Racial Politics in American Cities.* 2003. 3rd ed. London: Pearson Publishing.

This book is an engaging collection of original essays by top urban scholars that focuses on the continuing struggle for minorities to gain political power in American cities, each of who has done extensive analyses of the development of urban policy to respond to minority concerns. Each essay covers a particular city's racially based electoral coalitions and leadership, examines recent political changes, their impact, and future implications. Each essay features the editors' political incorporation model which provides a framework for melding research on ethnic coalitions with mobilization strategies, and allows readers to effectively compare one city to another.

Byrne Hessick, Carissa, and Gabriel J. Chin, eds. 2014. *Strange Neighbors: The Role of States in Immigration.* New York: New York University Press.

*Strange Neighbors* is a useful, edited book on the key issues on both sides of the debate about the states' role in immigration policy, including state-by-state analyses of state and local laws passed between 2005 to 2009; data on immigration showing its ebb and flow from Latin America in response to the draw of the U.S. economy; the tensions between state and federal efforts to control immigration; efforts by states to keep illegal immigrants out of the country, and how economic and political turmoil brings out the anti-immigrant state legislation.

Bush, Jeb, and Grant Bolick. 2013. *Immigration Wars: Forging an American Solution.* New York: Threshold Edition.

Jeb Bush, former Florida governor and candidate for the Republican party nomination for president in 2016, and Grant Bolick, vice president of Litigation at the Goldwater Institute, both long-time advocates of immigration policy reform, break a bit with their past positions by arguing that there should be two penalties for illegal entry: fines/community service and ineligibility for citizenship. They argue, however, in favor of a path to citizenship for Dreamers. They advocate changing immigration policy to a demand-driven immigration system.

Cainkar, Louise. 2009. *Homeland Insecurity: The Arab American and Muslim American Experience after 9/11.* New York: Russell Sage Foundation.

Cainkar details the intense scrutiny many Arab and Muslim Americans came under post-9/11—portraying even native-born people as outsiders and focusing on immigrants from the Middle East in particular. She traces anti-Muslim attitudes that preceded the 9/11 attacks. The book combines ethnography and analysis. It draws an intimate image of what it means to be Arab or Muslim Americans today, based on hundreds of interviews.

Calavita, Kitty. 1992. *Inside the State: The Bracero Program, Immigration and the INS.* New York: Routledge.

This is simply one of the best examinations of the Bracero Program, through which the author provides insights into temporary worker programs, and the problems she persuasively argues are inevitable with that approach. It is a sobering look at guest worker programs that is insightful as the U.S. Congress again considers enacting guest worker programs as part of the current immigration reform efforts.

Castaneda, Jorge G. 2007. *ExMex: From Migrants to Immigrants.* New York: New Press.

> The former foreign minister of Mexico describes just who makes up the newest generation of Mexican immigrants and why they have chosen to live in the United States, where they work, and their hopes for achieving a better life. It breaks common stereotypes about them. It explains a century-long historical background behind the labor exchange between Mexico and the United States. Authoritative and timely, it helps make sense of the complex issue of immigration.

Chomsky, Aviva. 2014. *Undocumented: How Immigration Became Illegal.* Boston: Beacon Press.

> Chomsky's book provides a comprehensive examination of how systemic prejudice against Mexicans and other migrant workers has become woven into the fabric of American society and its immigration policies, denying them a path to citizenship long given to European immigrants. She draws parallels between laws now in place that criminalize migrants and the caste system used to oppress African Americans by Jim Crow laws.

Chua, Amy. 2007. *Day of Empire: How Hyperpowers Rise to Global Dominance—and Why They Fall.* New York: Doubleday.

> Chua provides a sweeping history of how globally dominant empires—what she labels hyperpowers—rise and why they fail. She covers empires from Persia and China to the United Kingdom and the United States. She details the reasons behind their success (an openness to outsiders and a willingness to include them in society) and the roots of their ultimate demise (by closing themselves off to outsiders). What this means for the United States is the subject of her provocative and surprising conclusion.

Clarke, Richard, and Robert K. Knake. 2010. *Cyber War: The Next Threat to National Security and What to Do about It.* New York: HarperCollins.

In this best-seller, the authors, presidential advisor, and counterterrorism expert sound the alarm about the vulnerability of the United States to a terrifying new threat—cyber war. They detail how cyber warriors on the offensive are at an advantage to those who are rushing to shore up cyber defenses. They carry the reader to the frontier of our cyber defense and expose the virulent threat to national security posed by cyber warfare.

Cole, David. 2003. *Enemy Alien: Double Standards and Constitutional Freedoms in the War on Terrorism.* New York: New Press.

Cole describes the anti-immigrant hysteria in the immediate aftermath of 9/11. He then reviews court cases that have found the Bush administration's tactic of secrecy and assumptions of guilt as unconstitutional. Cole's book offers a prescient and critical indictment of the double standards applied to the war on terror. Cole shows why it is a moral, constitutional, and practical imperative to provide every person in the United States the protection from government excess.

Coutin, Susan Bibler. 1993. *The Culture of Protest: Religious Activism and the U.S. Sanctuary Movement.* Boulder: Westview Press.

The UC-Irvine anthropology professor examines the sanctuary movement in San Francisco and Tucson that aided undocumented Central American refugees. Coutin uses analysis of academic literature on social protest with her own field work. She concludes that these grass-roots, religious-based activists have created an on-going practice of resistance rooted in daily life. She describes how the movement began and how it led its volunteers to question their own values and those of the nation, in what she terms the sanctuary movement's "inverse Orientalism." The book is prescient of today's sanctuary movement by church groups and how they have infused the local governments' "sanctuary cities" movement.

D'Appollonia, Ariane Chabel, and Simon Reich. 2008. *Immigration, Integration, and Security.* Pittsburgh: University of Pittsburgh Press.

The authors discuss the "securitization" of immigration, examining the identity discourse in Western Europe and the United States in the aftermath of 9/11. They review religious legacies and the politics of multiculturalism. They discuss European security and counterterrorism, and the changes in immigration policy in Europe and the United States, exploring what they call the "Security Myth," and the relation of national security and political asylum, focusing on security, immigration, and integration in the EU and on Muslims and the state in Western Europe, and the challenges to EU border control enforcement by looking especially at France, Britain, and Italy.

Daniels, Roger. 2004. *Guarding the Golden Door.* New York: Hill and Wang.

One of the leading authorities and immigration historians, Daniels gives a detailed analysis of U.S. immigration policy and how and why it changed over time, from 1882 to 2000.

Etzioni, Amitai, and Jason H. Marsh, eds. 2003. *Rights v. Public Safety after 9/11: America in an Age of Terrorism.* Lanham, MD: Rowman and Littlefield.

The editors present a timely scholarly debate on the complex issues of civil rights, national security, immigration, and public safety.

Gerstle, Gary, and John Mollenkopf, eds. 2001. *E Pluribus Unum? Contemporary and Historical Perspectives on Immigrant Political Incorporation.*

The editors collect original essays that explore the key issues of the incorporation of immigrants into American public life. They examine how institutional processes, civic ideas, and cultural identities shape the political aspirations of today's immigrants. The book reassesses the past and assesses what is likely to happen in the near future. Some contributors argue that the contemporary political system tends to exclude immigrants. Others remind us that immigrants in the past faced similar exclusions only to achieve power after long and difficult struggles. The book theorizes about America's civic ethos. It shows how immigrant schoolchildren are concerned with their own identities and with finding their own niche within the American system of racial and ethnic distinctions.

Gibney, Matthew J. 2004. *The Ethics and Politics of Asylum: Liberal Democracy and the Responses to Refugees.* New York: Cambridge University Press.

Gibney's book draws on political and ethical theory to examine the asylum experiences of the United States, Germany, the United Kingdom, and Australia. It explains why asylum has become such a key political issue. It provides a compelling account of how nation-states move toward implementing morally defensible response to mass refugee movements.

Givens, Terri, Gary A. Freeman, and David L. Leal, eds. 2009. *Immigration Policy and Security: U.S., European, and Commonwealth Perspectives.* New York: Routledge.

The editors bring together a collection of essays to carefully examine the terror attacks of 9/11 and subsequent events in London, Madrid, and elsewhere. It examines a broad range of issues in order to better understand them, the significant changes in the numbers of immigrants allowed to enter, and in the asylum policies of a number of nation-states. It examines how and why immigration and asylum policies have changed in response to the threat of terrorism. It presents a thorough analysis of border policies and how the intensification of immigration politics has had severe consequences for the social and economic circumstances of minorities based on immigrant origins.

Golash-Boza, Tanya Maria. 2012. *Immigration Nation: Raids, Detentions and Deportations in Post 9/11 America.* Fort Collins: Paradigm Books/Routledge.

The author critically analyzes the human rights impacts of the post-9/11 tightening of immigration law enforcement. She reveals its consequences for immigrants, citizens, and U.S. communities. She shows how families have been torn apart, reversing the long-standing value of family reunification that girds much of U.S. legal immigration policy. The book is a revealing look at the real-life immigration enforcement today and the often-devastating consequences of immigration policy and reforms in its implementation in a security-conscious world.

Gonzales, Alberto, and David Strange. 2014. *A Conservative and Compassionate Approach to Immigration Reform.* Lubbock: Texas Tech University Press.

The authors criticize what they deem the failures of immigration policy over the past 30 years, and they assert a solution to current immigration policy emphasizing border control, tougher workplace enforcement, and changes to the Immigration and Nationality Act and to the visa process. They advocate expansion of the grounds for inadmissibility. They explore nationality versus citizenship, the visa overstay problem, ways to reduce the undocumented population, and how to introduce what they term the "pathway to nationality" as opposed to a "pathway to citizenship." It offers a blue print for enhanced national security and to improve the U.S. economy. Critics will find it long on conservative but short on the compassionate approach.

Hernández, Kelly L. 2010. *Migra!: A History of the U.S. Border Patrol.* Berkeley: University of California Press.

> *Migra!* is the story of the U.S. border patrol from its inception in 1924 as a small, peripheral agency to its emergence as a large professional policy force. The author mines lost records stored in garages, closets, an abandoned factory, and in U.S. and Mexican archives. He focuses on the daily challenges of policing the borderlands, revealing how the border patrol translated the mandate for comprehensive border control into a project for policing Mexicans in the U.S.-Mexico borderlands.

Hochschild, Jennifer, Jacquiline Chattpahdyay, Claudine Gay, and Michael Jones-Correa, eds. 2013. *Outsiders No More? Models of Immigrant Political Incorporation.* New York: Oxford University Press.

> This comprehensive collection of essays provides insights for both students and scholars of the topic of incorporation within the context of Western democracies. It offers a framework to better understand incorporation and clear definitions of the terms and premises of immigrant, immigration, incorporation, diversity, and political participation.

Janis, Irving. 1982. *Groupthink.* 2nd ed. Boston: Houghton Mifflin.

> This is the second edition of Janis's groundbreaking 1972 book. Janis explains the conditions that cause the problem of group decision making that he labels "groupthink." He delineates its symptoms and a variety of indicators. He emphasizes eight symptoms: (1) an illusion of

invulnerability, (2) a collective effort to rationalize away warnings that might lead members of the group to reconsider their assumptions, (3) unquestioned belief in the group's inherent morality, (4) stereotyped views of enemy leaders, (5) direct pressure on any dissenting members to conform, (6) self-censorship of deviations from the apparent group consensus, (7) a shared illusion of unanimity, and (8) the emergence of self-appointed mindguards. It is characterized as excessive consensus-seeking and is especially apparent in "crisis decision-making" situations.

Kanstroom, Daniel. 2007. *Deportation Nation: Outsiders in American History.* Cambridge, MA: Harvard University Press.
Kanstroom examines the chilling history of how America treated outsiders as a result of communal self-idealization and self-protection. From the Alien and Sedition Acts, to the Fugitive Slave laws, to Indian removal, to the Chinese Exclusion Act, to the Palmer Raids, to the incarceration of Japanese Americans, he traces how policy sought to remove those deemed unworthy or unable to become "true" Americans. He illuminates a dark side of American history, showing that deportation has long been a legal tool to control immigrants' lives and is used with increasing crudeness in a globalized but xenophobic world, all the more heightened by the fear of terrorism.

Kowert, Paul. 2002. *Groupthink or Deadlock: When Do Leaders Learn from Their Advisors?* Albany, NY: State University of New York Press.
Groupthink is now a widely accepted explanation for policy-making fiascoes. Efforts to avoid it, however, can lead to another problem—deadlock. Kowert explores these dual decision-making problems, using the Eisenhower and Reagan administrations to demonstrate how both the leaders were capable of learning and changing their policies. He points to the need for leaders to organize their staff in a way

that fits their learning and leadership styles and allows them to negotiate a path between groupthink and deadlock.

LeMay, Michael C. 2006. *Guarding the Gates: Immigration and National Security.* Westport, CT: Praeger Security International.
This book traces how immigration policy and national security policy interwove and influenced one another over the entire history of the United States. It is the first book in the post-9/11 period to focus specifically on the role national security considerations play in determining immigration policy. It provides readers with the historical perspective necessary to assess the pros and cons of what is happening today. It analyzes the problems of moving the INS responsibilities to the Department of Homeland Security. It examines how the United States is handling the balance between homeland security and civil liberties compared to the ways in which it was done during World Wars I and II and the Cold War. It does not advocate a specific immigration policy but rather gives students and citizens tools to make up their own minds about these enduring and controversial issues.

LeMay, Michael C., ed. 2013. *Transforming America: Perspectives on U.S. Immigration.* Vol. 3. Santa Barbara: Praeger Press.
A three-volume set, with chapters by 30 authors from various disciplinary perspectives, it covers immigration to the United States from 1820 to 2012 in a thorough view of immigration in all its complexities and diverse societal impact. Volume three in the series focuses on the period of 1945 to the present.

LeMay, Michael C. 2015. *Illegal Immigration.* 2nd ed. Santa Barbara: ABC-CLIO.
This volume defines the concept and analyzes the flow of unauthorized immigration to the United States since 1970. It focuses on why immigration reform is such a

vexing problem. It demonstrates the problems and issues resulting from bad policy, the gaps, failures, and unanticipated consequences of provisions in legal immigration that contribute so significantly to the illegal immigration flow. It discusses the groups who advocate for or oppose immigration reform proposals. It emphasizes that both legal and illegal immigration policy is intermestic—involving both domestic and international concerns. It details how immigration flows wax and wane in response to push and pull factors that make the problem increasingly difficult in complexity and scope, thereby making policy responses all the more difficult. It shows how, since 9/11, a sense of "fortress America" has permeated the political debate regarding both legal and illegal immigration and how the unauthorized immigration flow has become an important element in homeland security and defense policy making.

LeMay, Michael. 2018. *U.S. Immigration Policy, Ethnicity, and Religion in American History.* Santa Barbara: Praeger Press.
This volume provides extensive data and document excerpts that illuminate the complex relationships among ethnicity, religion, and immigration to the United States over its 200-year history. It categorizes immigration to the United States into seven chapters covering U.S. immigration policy making: the Open Door Era, 1820–1880; the Door-Ajar Era, 1880–1920; the Pet Door Era, 1920–1950; the Dutch Door Era, 1950–1985; the Revolving Door Era, 1985–2001; and the Storm Door Era, 2001–2018. Each chapter analyzes trends in ethnicity and national origin and the religious affiliations of immigrant groups in relation to immigration policy during the time period covered.

LeMay, Michael C., ed. 2013. *Transforming America: Perspectives on U.S. Immigration.* Vol. 3. Santa Barbara: Praeger Press.
A three-volume set, with chapters by 30 authors from various disciplinary perspectives, it covers immigration to

the United States from 1820 to 2012 in a thorough view of immigration in all its complexities and diverse societal impact. Volume three in the series focuses on the period of 1945 to the present.

LeMay, Michael C., and Elliott Barkan. 1999. *U.S. Immigration and Naturalization Laws and Issues: A Documentary History.* Westport, CT: Greenwood Press.

This unique volume summarizes 150 documents covering all major laws and court cases concerning U.S. immigration and naturalization from colonial times to 1996.

Lippert, Randy K. 2005. *Sanctuary, Sovereignty, Sacrifice: Canadian Sanctuary Incidents, Power and Law.* Vancouver, BC: University of British Columbia Press.

Lippert closely examines 36 incidents involving 261 migrants to Canada to illuminate sanctuary policy in Canada, how the movement is localized, often isolated, frequently not primarily religious in orientation, but also remarkably successful. It shows how state authorities were kept at bay and how the migrants avoided arrest and ultimately received legal status. It is a thorough account of sanctuary practices that tackles theoretical and methodological questions. It offers insights useful to America's experience with the sanctuary movement. It is of interest to socio-legal studies, criminology, sociology, political science, social history, and religious studies. It is valuable to anyone interested in immigration and refugee law and policy.

Malek, Alia. 2011. *Patriot Acts: Voices of Witness.* San Francisco: McSweeeneys.

Malek, a former DOJ attorney, presents a groundbreaking collection of oral histories of the men and women needlessly swept up in the post-9/11 war on terror. She has them relate their harrowing stories. Some of the stories relate to discrimination at airports; still others are really shocking—like the story of the sudden and unexplained imprisonment of a sixteen-year-old. The book illuminates the human rights crisis and details the people, institutions, and organizations that tried to help victims.

Mayer, Jane. 2008. *The Dark Side: The Inside Story of How the War on Terror Turned into a War on American Ideals.* New York: Doubleday.

Mayer's book is a dramatic, riveting, and definitive narrative on the self-destructive decisions made by U.S. policymakers in pursuit of terrorists around the world. These decisions, she maintains, violated the Constitution. Ironically, they hampered the very pursuit of al Qaeda. She relates, in detail, the decisions by key players, especially Vice President Dick Cheney and his powerful, secretive advisor, David Addington, exploited 9/11 to push long-held agenda to strengthen presidential powers to an unprecedented degree. She argues they obliterated constitutional protections that define the very essence of the American experiment.

Mittelstadt, Michelle, Burke Speaker, Doris Meissner, and Muzaffare A. Chishti. 2011. *Through the Prism of National Security: Major Immigration Policy and Program Changes in the Decade since 9/11.* Washington, D.C.: Migration Policy Institute.

This technical report from the Migration Policy Institute critically examines the decade since the 9/11 attacks and how, in response, a new generation of interoperable databases and systems at the crossroads of intelligence and law enforcement has reshaped immigration enforcement at the federal, state, and local levels. It details the collection and sharing of information; a significant expansion in the use of immigrant detention; broad use of nationality-based interviewing, screening, and enforcement initiatives; and the growing state and local involvement in immigration enforcement and policy making. It shows how the security paradigm will remain the legacy of 9/11 for the foreseeable future.

Migration Policy Institute. 2003. *America's Challenge: Domestic Security, Civil Liberties, and National Unity After September 11.* Washington, D.C.: Migration Policy Institute.

This report is based on 18 months of extensive research and interviews with detainees, lawyers, senior government officials engaged in domestic security and immigration issues, and leaders of Arab- and Muslim American communities across the country. It is a comprehensive compilation and analysis of persons detained post 9/11. It concludes that the harsh measures enacted against immigrants since the attacks have had dire consequences for antiterrorism efforts, fundamental civil liberties, and national unity. The authors conclude that authorities have placed too much emphasis on immigration in its counterterrorism efforts and that immigration enforcement is of limited effectiveness. It discusses the widespread discrimination experienced by Arab- and Muslim Americans since the 9/11 attacks and explains how rampant discrimination undermines national unity.

Mirescu, Alexander. 2008. *Balancing Federal, State, and Local Priorities in Police-Immigration Relations: Lessons from Muslim, Arab, and South Asian Communities Since 9/11.* Washington, D.C.: Immigration Policy Center.

Mirescu traces changes in federal, state, and local law enforcement priorities and practices since 9/11 and details their profound impact on America's Muslims, Arabs, and South Asians. Some of those policies applied exclusively to these communities, such as special registration and selective enforcement of immigration law based on national origin or religion. It examines federal counterterrorism efforts that target these communities. It shows how a wide range of ethnic groups have been affected by the use of state and local police agencies to enforce federal immigration law. It details the use of detention and deportation authority for even minor infractions and technicalities. It criticizes the enactment and implementation of the USA

Patriot Act and its wide range of surveillance of targeted communities.

Motomura, Hiroshi. 2014. *Immigration Outside the Law.* New York: Oxford University Press.

An immigration history scholar examines the complex issue of unauthorized immigration and its myriad impacts on American politics and society.

National Conference on State Legislatures. 2011. *2011 Immigration-Related Laws, Bills, and Resolutions in the States.* Washington, D.C.: National Conference of State Legislatures.

This report by the NCSL found that in 2011 state legislatures introduced 1,607 bills and resolutions related to immigration and refugee matters. A total of 42 states and Puerto Rico enacted 197 laws and 109 resolutions. Fifteen additional bills were passed but vetoed by governors. The report compares and summarizes laws and resolutions enacted in 2011 and compares those with 2010.

National Research Council. 1997. *The New Americans: Economic, Demographic, and Fiscal Effects of Immigration.* Washington, D.C.: National Academies Press.

Continuing to contribute to the now-extensive literature examining the post-1965 wave of immigration and the degree to which new immigrants are incorporating into U.S. society socially, politically, and economically, this volume is in many ways *The Fourth Wave* circa 1997.

Ngai, Mae M. 2004. *Impossible Subjects: Illegal Aliens and the Making of Modern America.* Princeton: Princeton University Press.

This multi-award-winning book traces the origin of the illegal alien in American law and society, explaining how and why it became a central issue in American immigration policy. The author offers a close dreading of the legal regime of restriction since 1920 and shows how restriction changed and reshaped America, creating new categories of racial difference. A deeply stimulating book or impressive scholarship, it delves beneath the tip of the iceberg of formal policy and law.

Ngai, Mae M. 2011. *Major Problems in American Immigration History: Documents and Essays*, 2nd ed. Boston: Wadsworth/ Cengage.

This volume offers readings of both primary sources and analytical essays to explore themes of the political and economic forces that cause immigration, the alienation that often follows relocation, and the difficult questions of citizenship and incorporation. The volume is a careful selection of readings organized to allow readers to evaluate primary sources, test the interpretations of distinguished historians, and draw their own conclusions.

Nguyen, Tram. 2005. *We Are All Suspects Now: Untold Stories from Immigrant Communities after 9/11*. Boston: Beacon Press.

Nguyen reveals the human costs of the domestic war of terrorism and examines the impact of post-9/11 policies on people targeted because of immigration status, nationality, race, and religion. It is a compelling narrative about the families, detainees, community advocates, and others living on the frontlines of the war on terror and of people who see and experience first-hand the unjust detention and deportation of family members, friends, and neighbors. It takes the reader inside a dark world where the American Dream is transformed into a nightmare. It suggests proactive responses to the growing climate of xenophobia, intimidation, and discrimination.

Noorani, Ali. 2017. *There Goes the Neighborhood: How Communities Overcome Prejudice and Meet the Challenge of American Immigration*. Amherst, NY: Prometheus Books.

Noorani is the executive director of the National Immigration Forum and an expert in this topic. The book is aimed at the general public, and it highlights the people behind the political debates over immigration and immigration reform policies. He presents a broad picture of the policies and details the faces of those affected by them. He provides an arsenal of stories about the everyday heroes of immigration reform and of the men, women, and children who are impacted by it. He presents stories by businessmen, clergy, and law enforcement officers and others fighting on both sides of the issue, never shying away from the ugliness of the debate as he explains the barriers the nation faces for future immigration reform, showing why it has become an extremely hot-button issue. He features stories of small towns struggling with a growing immigrant population, offering a unique viewpoint from his role with various immigrant organizations and important lessons gleaned from both sides of the debate.

O'Leary, Anna Ochoa, ed. 2014. *Undocumented Immigrants in the United States: An Encyclopedia of Their Experience*, 2 vols. Santa Barbara, CA: Greenwood Press.

This two-volume set examines the lives of undocumented immigrants in the United States. The editor pulls together insights from hundreds of scholars of undocumented immigrants, providing a historical perspective for their exponential growth since 1980. The set offers a more nuanced and detailed view of them than is available in the media. The books provide timely insights about their struggle for inclusion as well as their valuable contributions to American society. The evidence-based collection promotes rational assessment of the issues involved and illuminates their struggles for assimilation and adaptation. The set details immigration and border enforcement issues that impact the daily lives of unauthorized immigrants.

Orreniris, Pia, and Madelaine Zavodny. 2010. *Beside the Golden Door: U.S. Immigration Reform in a New Era of Globalism.* Washington, D.C.: American Enterprise Institute Press.

Today's foreign-born workers comprise 16 percent of the workforce and almost half of the workforce growth from 2000 to 2010. The authors propose a radical overhaul of U.S. immigration policy to enhance economic competitiveness and long-term growth. They would largely replace family reunification with employment-based immigration, making work-based visas the rule, not the exception. They argue that the United States needs immigration policy that favors high-skilled workers while retaining some avenues for low-skilled immigration, and limiting family reunification to spouses and minor children.

Renshon, Stanley. 2005. *The 50% American: Immigration and National Identity in an Age of Terror.* Washington, D.C.: Georgetown University Press.

Renshon is a political psychologist who offers unique insight into the political and national ramifications of personal loyalties of persons holding dual citizenship. In an age of terrorism, he argues that the concept that we are all Americans is essential to national security. The book is a comprehensive examination of present immigration trends and traces the assimilation process that immigrants undergo. It deals with such volatile issues as language requirements, voting rights, and schooling. He casts a critical eye on the challenges posed over the past four decades by multiculturalism, culture conflict, and global citizenship. He offers comprehensive proposals for dual citizenship and for helping immigrants and citizens alike become more integrated into the American national community.

Rivera, Geraldo. 2008. *Hispanic: Why Americans Fear Hispanics in the United States.* New York: Celebra.

The Fox News commentator and journalist presents an account of the growth of the Hispanic population in the United States and how that growth is changing the very face of America. He examines the issue of the illegal Hispanic immigration, making Hispanics now the nation's largest minority. He exposes the racism and ignorance behind the anti-immigration movement, and the sentiments of both extremists and otherwise ordinary Americans reacting to the illegal immigration problem.

Rosenblum, Marc R. 2011. *U.S. Immigration Policy since 9/11: Understanding the Stalemate over Comprehensive Immigration Reform.* Washington, D.C.: Migration Policy Institute.

Rosenblum was deputy director of the Migration Policy Institute (MPI). This book is a report of MPI's Regional Migration Study Group. It reviews the history of immigration legislation since 9/11, focusing on the new enforcement mandates, and the unsuccessful attempts to pass comprehensive immigration reform. It finds that the history and asymmetries of the political process favor the enforcement responses and that the economic downturn stack the deck against comprehensive reform.

Rosenblum, Marc R., and Kate Brick. 2011. *U.S. Immigration Policy and Mexican/Central American Migration Flows: Then and Now.* Washington, D.C.: Migration Policy Institute.

This MPI report traces migration rates to the United States from Mexico and Central America since 1970, from less than 1 million to more than 14 million. The authors document continuities in the flow and the demographic characteristics of the migrants. The report focuses on recent dynamics shaping immigration policy and contributing to the increased anti-immigrant sentiment. The history defines and limits the policy alternatives available and highlights challenges to managing regional migration flows.

Rudolph, Christopher. 2006. *National Security and Immigration: Policy Developments in the United States and Western Europe since 1945.* Stanford: Stanford University Press.

Global terrorism has emerged as a central security issue around the world. Effective immigration and border control are now a necessary condition to maintain national security. Rudolph's book identifies the security-related implications and determinants of immigration and border policies in the United States and Western Europe since 1945. He shows how international migration presents nation-states with important choices that impact economic production, internal security, relations with other states, and national identity. He reveals how immigration and border policies are shaped by the state's desire to maximize security interests along three dimensions: defense, wealth, and stability.

Schrug, Peter. 2010. *Not Fit for Our Society: Nativism and Immigration.* Berkeley: University of California Press.

Schrug presents a view on how the immigration debate and policies have shaped America since the founding. That helps us to better understand how the immigration debates have gotten us to where we are today. He provides a sweeping review of the current immigration debates in a historical context, uncovering the dark impulses that have long undergirded nativist thought. The book is a lively and thoughtful interpretation of America's ambivalence toward immigration and its place in history.

Simon, Julian. 1989. *The Economic Consequences of Immigration into the United States.* London, New York: Blackwell Publishers.

Although Simon's book is almost 30 years old, it still offers relevant insights. It presents an objective and comprehensive inquiry into the economic consequences of U.S. immigration, and he concludes that, on the whole, immigration is beneficial to the United States. His book compares the received theory of the international movement of goods and the movement of capital. He concludes they are far less similar than is supposed. He analyzes the cost of the use of capital by immigrants and estimates the cost of the use of demographic capital.

Stana, Richard M. 2003. *Homeland Security: Challenges to Implementing the Immigration Interior Enforcement Strategy.* GAO-03-660T, Washington, D.C.: U.S. Government Printing Office.
Stana was the director of Homeland Security and Justice for the Government Accounting Office. This report to the Congress details the management challenges to effective implementation of the Immigration Interior Enforcement Strategy.

Tichenor, Daniel J. 2002. *Dividing Lines: The Politics of Immigration Control in America.* Princeton: Princeton University Press.
Tichenor's book is a study of the politics and policies of immigration from the founders' earliest efforts to shape American identity to today's revealing struggles over third-world migration, noncitizen rights, and illegal aliens. His book is a riveting story of the political battles between immigration defenders and opponents over time, and the transformative policy regimes they enacted. It is a superb narrative history of American immigration policy and reform—an important contribution to immigration history and American political development.

Tienda, Maria, and Faith Mitchell, eds. 2006. *Hispanics and the Future of America.* Washington, D.C.: National Academic Press.
This book, a companion to *Multiple Origins, Uncertain Destinies: Hispanics and the American Future*, provides detailed analyses using multiple sources to characterize a dynamic, eclectic population from multiple perspectives to evaluate whether and in what ways Hispanics are distinctive from other immigrant and minority groups.

It assesses their social integration prospects for both recent arrivals and their descendants. Collectively, the book documents how the growing Hispanic presence is being felt in schools, workplaces, at the ballot box, and in health-care systems across the United States.

Tirman, John, ed. 2004. *The Maze of Fear: Security and Migration after 9/11.* New York: New Press.

The roster of security measures enacted in the panic that followed the 9/11 attacks has in common concern about the link between migration and security. This edited volume raises vital questions about government policy and explores the many dimensions of the migration-security links, including essays about civil liberties, transnational organization, refugee populations, and politically active diasporas.

Torr, James D. 2004. *Homeland Security.* San Diego: Green-haven Press.

Torr provides a highly critical but comprehensive examination of the homeland security issue and its myriad ramifications. The author is quite skeptical of the effectiveness of the super-agency approach to the massive DHS. He focuses on the largely unanticipated consequences for managerial problems facing the huge new department.

Warner, Judith A. 2008. *Battleground: Immigration,* 2 volumes. Westport, CT: Greenwood Press.

Warner examines the political battles over legal and un-documented immigrants in the United States and the borderlands that have characterized much of American politics since 1965. She examines the most critical issues surrounding immigration, including the effects on the economy, education, and employment. She assesses the viability of the foreign-born in the United States with an emphasis on post-9/11 security and border control issues.

West, Darrell M. 2010. *Brain Gain.* Washington, D.C.: Brookings Institute Press.

West examines how gifted immigrants have led to advances in energy, information technology, international commerce, sports, arts, and culture—a "brain gain" that benefited American international competitiveness through its more open-door policy to attract unique talents from other countries. He asserts that the "vision" America has of immigration is one reason that immigration reform is so politically difficult. Public discourse emphasizes negative perceptions. Fear too often trumps reason and optimism. He describes a series of reforms to put America back on the track of a better course that enhances its long-term social and economic prosperity. He advocates "reconceptualizing" immigration as a way to enhance innovation and competitiveness to help America find its next Sergey Brin, Andrew Grove, and Albert Einstein.

Wucker, Michele. 2006. *Lockout: Why America Keeps Getting Immigration Wrong When Our Prosperity Depends on Getting It Right.* New York: Public Affairs Press.

Wucker's narrative history reviews how we shut the door to immigration after World War I, only to realize the error of doing so and reopening the door in 1965. The current record-high foreign-born population, global turbulence, and economic instability have once again pushed Americans past a tipping point about immigration and the global role of the United States. She documents the mistakes that led to our predicament today and clarifies why it would be a catastrophic error of judgment and a colossal lack of self-knowledge for America to again turn its back on the rest of the world, and in doing so, on the best of itself.

Ziegler-McPherson, Christina A. 2017. *Immigration Promotion and the Settlement of the American Continent, 1607–1914.* Santa Barbara: Praeger Press.

This book gives an in-depth look at the motivating factors behind immigration to America from 1607–1914, including what attracted people to America, who was trying to attract them, and why.

Zolberg, Aristide. 2008. *A Nation by Design: Immigration Policy in the Fashioning of America.* Cambridge, MA: Russell Sage Foundation, Harvard University Press.

The late Harvard professor explores American immigration policy from the colonial period to the present, discussing how it has been used as a tool of nation building. It covers policy at the local and state levels as well as federal immigration policy. It profiles the vacillating currents of opinion on immigration throughout American history. It examines legal, illegal, and asylum-seeking immigration.

## Leading Scholarly Journals

*Albany Law Review*

The *Albany Law Review* publishes articles that make a significant and original contribution to the law and legal scholarship, and on a limited basis, book reviews, essays, and student commentary. It is published quarterly by the university as one of three law journals. It is edited by students at the Albany School of Law. It began in 1931. It sponsors annually two symposia, one each semester, on contemporary legal topics.

*American Criminal Law Review (ACLR)*

A leading journal of criminal law, the *ACLR* provides information and ideas useful to criminal law practitioners. It is published three times per year as well as publishes an Annual Survey of White Collar Crime. Every other year, it hosts a symposium on contemporary issues in criminal law. It began in 1962 at the University of Southern California Law School but is now published independently by the Georgetown University Law Center.

## American Demographics

Published 10 times per year, this peer-reviewed journal is an outlet for multidisciplinary articles dealing with all topics related to demography, as well as occasional articles and reflective essays on migration, legal and illegal immigration, and migration's impact on homeland security. It publishes an annual resource guide helpful to any reader studying demographics.

## American Political Science Review (APSR)

The *APSR* is a quarterly peer-reviewed academic journal covering all areas of political science. It is widely considered as the leading journal of political science research and is the official journal of the American Political Science Association. It has been published continuously since 1906. Areas covered include political theory, American politics, public policy (with occasional original research articles directly examining immigration policy), public administration, comparative politics, and international relations.

## American Prospect

This monthly magazine covers politics, culture, and policy from a liberal perspective. It is based in Washington, D.C. It frequently has critical articles dealing with immigration-related issues and concerns, especially pertaining to civil rights and privacy issues.

## American Journal of Political Science (AJPS)

The *AJPS* is a peer-reviewed academic journal published by the Midwest Political Science Association. It has been published quarterly since 1973 and ranks fourth among political science journals. It publishes original research articles on all areas of political science.

### American Journal of Sociology

A scholarly, peer-reviewed quarterly journal of sociology, with frequent articles concerning immigration and integration, social trends, and policies regarding migration and both legal and illegal immigration, and occasional articles related to homeland security issues. It has useful book reviews on immigration-related topics such as the social implications of homeland security policies and how they affect social minority groups in particular.

### American Sociological Review (AS)

Founded in 1936, the *ASR* is the flagship, peer-reviewed academic journal of the American Sociological Association. It is a Sage-published journal of original works of interest to sociology, in general, and committed to advance understanding of fundamental social processes. It is published bimonthly. It is ranked second among 143 journals of sociology. It frequently has articles on minority groups and population affected by homeland security policy, the Patriot Act, and immigration policy designed to crack down on immigration enforcement and border control.

### American Studies

This is a quarterly interdisciplinary academic journal sponsored by the Mid-America American Studies Association, the University of Kansas College of Liberal Arts. It began in 1959 and has 1,000 subscribers. It offers provocative perspectives on various issues and has frequent special sections and special issues devoted to in-depth treatment of a single topic. Its book-review section keeps abreast of the latest in contemporary scholarship. It has an e-version that provides free access to all past issues.

### Brookings Review

The *Brookings Review* is a quarterly magazine focused on economic, political, and foreign policy issues. It began publication in 1982. It provides provocative articles written by professionals who know the ins-and-outs of Washington, D.C., and of the international scene. It is published by the Brookings Institute.

### California Law Review

The *California Law Review* is the preeminent legal publication of the University of California Berkeley School of Law. It is ranked among the top ten law reviews and boasts among its alumni several chief justices. It was founded in 1912. It is published six times annually and covers a variety of timely topics in legal scholarship. It is edited and published entirely by students at Berkeley Law. Each issue has a commentary and an essay section. It has a free online access e-version of past issues.

### Commentary

*Commentary* is a monthly magazine on religion, Judaism, politics, and social and cultural issues. It was founded in 1945. It has been influential on the major debates that have transformed the political and intellectual life of the United States. It is published in New York City. It regularly publishes book reviews of books written by contributors to the magazine.

### Congressional Quarterly

*Congressional Quarterly* is a division of Sage publications and publishes books, directories, periodicals, and electronic products on American government and politics and on the U.S. Congress, notably *CQ Recall* and *CQ Weekly*. It was founded in 1945. It publishes news and analysis about the U.S. Congress.

*Cornell Law Review*

The *Cornell Law Review* was founded in 1915. It is a student-run and student-edited journal publishing novel legal scholarship that has immediate and long-term impact on the legal community. It is published in six print issues annually and has articles, essays, student notes, and book reviews. It has an annual symposium issue. It recently featured an article on asylum rights. It publishes an online database of past issues.

*Corrections Today*

*Corrections Today* is the professional membership publication of the American Correctional Association. It has been published six times per year since 1938. It has an international readership, and it covers every major sector of the corrections and criminal justice fields. It has received numerous awards for publication excellence and has published award-winning feature articles. It is published in Alexandria, Virginia.

*Demography*

This peer-reviewed journal of the Population Association of America publishes scholarly research of interest to demographers from a multidisciplinary perspective, with emphasis on the social sciences, geography, history, biology, statistics, business, epidemiology, and public health, all of which are impacted by immigration problems and issues. It publishes specialized research papers and historical and comparative studies.

*Forensic Examiner*

The *Forensic Examiner* is the official peer-reviewed journal of the American College of Forensic Examiners Institute.

It has transitioned to an online, continuously published journal. It is the leading forensic magazine. It has recently published articles on asylum applications in federal immigration courts.

*Free Inquiry*

*Free Inquiry* is a magazine published six times per year for the Council for Secular Humanism. It claims to be the world's largest magazine for and about people who live value-rich lives without religion. It is published in Amherst, New York.

*Georgetown Immigration Law Journal*

This quarterly law review is the most specifically related law journal dealing with U.S. immigration law, its current developments, and reform-related matters concerning all three branches of government. It frequently focuses on illegal immigration, and occasionally on homeland security issues and concerns that impact immigration. It contains case reviews, articles, notes, and commentaries. It publishes workshop reports devoted to immigration law.

*Harvard Journal of Law and Public Policy*

The *Harvard Journal of Law and Public Policy* is published three times annually by the Harvard Society for Law and Public Policy, an organization of Harvard Law School students. It is among the most widely circulated student-edited reviews. It is a leading forum for conservative and libertarian scholarship. It began publication in 1989. They collaborate with the Harvard Federalist Society.

*Harvard Law Review*

This law review is published eight times per year. It contains original articles, case reviews, essays, commentaries, and book reviews that occasionally focus on immigration law and its reforms. It began publication in 1887. It is published by an independent group of students at Harvard Law School. It is ranked number one of 143 law journals.

### The Humanist

*The Humanist* is a bimonthly magazine of critical inquiry and social concern. It is published by the American Humanist Association (AHA), America's oldest and largest humanist membership organization headquartered in Washington, D.C. The magazine applies humanism to broad areas of social and personal concern. The AHA was founded in 1941. The magazine covers everything from science and religion to media and technology to politics and popular culture. It challenges readers with ethical critique and commentary on the central issues of today.

### Independent Review

The *Independent Review* is a journal of political economy that is a peer-reviewed periodical published quarterly since 1997. It is an interdisciplinary journal devoted to the study of political economy and the critical analysis of government policy. It is provocative, lucid, and engaging in style. Its articles range across the fields of economics, political science, law, history, philosophy, and sociology. It features in-depth examination of past, present, and future policy issues by leading scholars and experts. It has frequently featured articles on civil rights and civil liberties, and on immigration and race issues.

### International Migration Review (IMR)

The leading quarterly academic journal in the field of migration, *IMR* contains state-of-the-art research articles on migration problems and issues that affect all aspects of society. It also publishes in each issue current book reviews, document summaries, and useful bibliographies.

### Journal of Contemporary History (JCH)

The *Journal of Contemporary History* is a quarterly peer-reviewed international journal by Sage publications that features articles on 20th-century history (post 1930). It covers a broad range of historical approaches, including social, economic, political, diplomatic, intellectual, and cultural. It is a member of the Committee on Publication Ethics (COPE). *JCH* publishes book reviews. It is noted both for its intellectual rigor and its accessible style.

*Journal on Migration and Human Security*

A publication of the Center for Migration Studies of New York, it is an online, peer-reviewed public policy academic journal focusing on the broad scope of social, political, and economic dimensions of human security. It also publishes an annual, bound volume of its articles.

*Michigan Law Review*

The *Michigan Law Review* publishes eight issues annually, seven of which are comprised of articles by legal scholars and practitioners, and notes by law students. One issue in each volume is devoted to book reviews. Its online edition publishes short articles and op-ed pieces by academics, judges, practitioners, and law students, as well as timely responses to articles in the print journal. It covers important judicial decisions and legislative developments. It has been published by the University of Michigan Law School since 1902. In 2016, it was ranked as the sixth best law journal.

*Minnesota Law Review*

The *Minnesota Law Review* has been published in six issues per year since 1917 by the University of Minnesota Law School. It is an entirely student-run law review with a Board of Editors comprised of 39 editors who govern its policies and procedures. It hosts an annual symposium, such as the 2016 symposium of balancing First Amendment Rights with an Inclusive Environment on Public University Campuses and its 2009 symposium on Cyber Space and Law.

*National Journal*

The *National Journal* is based in Washington, D.C. It is a monthly magazine about current political environment that has been published since 1969. It is now part of the National Journal Group and is described as the "premier source on non-partisan insight on politics and public policy."

*National Review*

The *National Review* is a semi-monthly magazine founded by William F. Buckley, Jr., in 1965. It is a leading conservative magazine covering news, politics, and current events and culture, with analysis and commentary, and is described as the "most widely read and influential magazine for conservative news, commentary, and opinion."

*New Jersey Law Journal*

The *New Jersey Law Journal* has been published since 1878. It is a legal authority for the state with the fifth largest attorney population in the United States. It is a weekly, presenting a complete, official source for all state and federal court notices and for up-to-the-minute digest of all relevant court decisions. Its "In Practice" section features articles by contributing experts on legal developments as well as editorials by an editorial board that is a who's who of bar leaders. It is a publication of Application Lifecycle Management (ALM), an integrated media publisher headquartered in Newark, New Jersey.

*Perspectives on Politics*

*Perspectives on Politics* is a quarterly peer-reviewed academic journal established in 2003 and published by Cambridge University Press. It publishes articles for the political science profession as well as the broader society. It seeks to nurture political science as a field, publishing important scholarly topics, ideas, and innovations.

*Policy Studies Journal*

This journal of the Policy Studies Organization is produced at Iowa State University, College of Education. It
is published quarterly and contains articles related to all
issues of public policy, including immigration reform issues and policies. It also publishes occasional symposium
issues and regular book reviews.

*Political Psychology*

Published since 1980 by the International Society of Political Psychology, it is a peer-reviewed academic journal
published bimonthly. It is dedicated to the analysis of
the interrelationship between psychological and political
processes. Its contributing scholars are from the fields of
cognitive psychology, political science, economics, history, international relations, philosophy, political theory,
sociology, and social and clinical psychology. It is housed
at the European Centre for Political Psychology at Lund
University, Sweden.

*Political Science Quarterly*

*Political Science Quarterly* is a double-blind, peer-reviewed
academic journal covering government, politics, and policy. It has been published since 1886 by the Academy of
Political Science. Each issue contains six articles and up to
40 book reviews. It is a journal of public and international
affairs.

*Presidential Studies Quarterly*

*Presidential Studies Quarterly* is an interdisciplinary journal of theory and research on the American presidency by
the Center for the Study of the President and Congress. It
is published by Blackwell Publishing. Its articles, features,
review essays, and book reviews have been published since
1974 in print, and now online. It is the official journal of
the Presidential Research Section of the American Political Science Association.

*Public Interest*

*Public Interest* was a quarterly public policy journal established in 1965 by the New York intellectuals Daniel Bell and Irving Kristol. It was published until 2005. It was a leading neoconservative journal on political economy and culture aimed at journalists, scholars, and policy makers. It was based in Washington, D.C., and published 159 issues, the last few years of which had commentary on immigration policy concerns.

*The Public Manager*

The *Public Manager* is a unique monthly digital magazine about best practices at all levels of government. It focuses on the efforts of practicing public managers. It has a global audience that includes practitioners in federal, regional, state, local, and international government organizations. Its website is a useful resource for government managers at all levels. The magazine has been published since 1972 by the Society of Certified Public Managers.

*Publius: The Journal of Federalism*

*Publius* is the world's leading journal devoted to federalism. It publishes original empirical and theoretical research on federalism and intergovernmental relations. It is published for the Center for the Study of State and Local Government, Lafayette College, Eastern Pennsylvania. It is the official journal of the Section on Federalism of the American Political Science Association. It has been published since 2006. Each year, it issues an annual review of American federalism, which highlights and analyzes federalism and intergovernmental issues in the preceding year. It also publishes occasionally special issues on timely and significant trends and events.

*The Review of Policy Research*

*The Review of Policy Research* is a bimonthly peer-reviewed academic journal published by Wiley-Blackwell for the

Policy Studies Organization. It has been published since 1981. It is a political science discipline journal that focuses on the politics and policy of science, technology and environmental issues, science policy, environment resource management, information networks, cultural industries, biotechnology, security and surveillance, privacy, globalization, education, research and innovation, development, intellectual property, health, and demographics.

### Social Justice

*Social Justice* is a quarterly peer-reviewed educational journal, founded in 1974, that seeks to inform theory and practice on issues of equality and justice. It focuses on crime, police repression, social control, the penal system, human and civil rights, citizenship and immigration issues, environmental victims, health and safety concerns, welfare and education, ethnic and gender relations, and persistent global inequities. It provides social criticism as a distinctive form of knowledge and to present divergent viewpoints in a readable fashion.

### Social Science Quarterly

Published for the Southwestern Social Science Association by Blackwell, this interdisciplinary quarterly has articles of original research, review essays, book reviews, and occasional symposium issues, and contains articles dealing with U.S. immigration and illegal immigration policy, with issues related to the incorporation of immigrants and their children into majority society.

### Social Science Research

*Social Science Research* publishes papers devoted to quantitative social science research and methodology. It features articles to illustrate the use of quantitative methods to empirically test social science theory. Its research cuts across traditional disciplinary boundaries. It publishes special feature issues. They concern current pressing issues in world society, typically with a political angle in keeping with the tradition of the New School for Social Research's politically conscious history. It organizes and publishes the proceedings of a conference series. It is published by Elsevier for the New School for Social Research and has been published since 1934.

*Sociological Forum*

*Sociological Forum* is the flagship journal of the Eastern Sociological Society. It is a peer-reviewed journal that publishes innovative articles about developing topics or areas of fundamental importance to the study of society. It has been published since 1986. It is published by Wiley, in New Jersey. The journal is wide in scope, including both quantitative and qualitative empirical works that develop theory, concepts, or methodological strategies in all areas of sociology.

*Southern Economic Journal*

The *Southern Economic Journal* has been published for the Southern Economic Association (SEA) since 1933 and is the eighth oldest American scholarly journal in economics. It seeks to stimulate interest in and disseminate the results of recent research in theory and applied economics. It is published by Wiley-Blackwell. It is a quarterly peer-reviewed academic journal that is published by the SEA and the University of North Carolina, Chapel Hill.

*Stanford Law Review*

The *Stanford Law Review* is a legal journal produced independently by the Stanford Law School students. It was established in 1948. Each year it publishes one volume in six separate issues. Each issue contains materials written by its student members, other Stanford law students, and outside contributors such as law professors, judges, and practicing lawyers. It publishes cutting-edge legal scholarship. Some 2,600 libraries, attorneys, judges, law firms, government agencies, and others subscribe to the *Law Review*. It publishes short-form content online.

### White House Studies

*White House Studies* is a quarterly peer-reviewed journal of scholarship and commentary on the politics and history of the presidency and the White House. It reviews current books and publishes original and timely scholarly articles. It has a regular feature on White House history and regularly features profiling first couples. Though scholarly, its articles are generally shorter than most academic journals to be more suitable to a wide audience that includes scholars, libraries, presidential sites and institutions, and White House enthusiasts. It is published by Nova Science Journals for the University of Southern Mississippi.

### Yale Law Review

*Yale Law Review* is a student-run law review affiliated with Yale Law School. It has been published continuously since 1891 and is the most widely known of the eight law reviews published by students at Yale Law School. It is one of the most cited legal publications in the United States and generates the highest number of citations per published article. It is published eight times per year and contains articles, essays, features, and book reviews by professional legal scholars, as well as written notes and comments. It is entirely student-edited. Its online journal features op-ed pieces and responses from scholars, practitioners, and policy makers.

## Films

*The 800-Mile Wall.* 2009. 90 minutes, color.

An award-wining film by John Carlos Frey, it is a powerful, independent-produced film about the border fence and documents all the problems that would be involved in building Trump's border wall.

*Fahrenheit 9/11.* 2004. 2:02 minutes, color. Dog Eat Dog Films/IMDbPro.
This documentary film is written by, directed by, and stars filmmaker Michael Moore. He uses archival film footage and candid interviews with politicians to dramatically present his view on what happened to the United States after the 9/11 attacks.

*From the Other Side.* 2002. 99 minutes, color. Icarus Films.
Focusing on the technology developed by the U.S. military, the film views the INS attempts to stem the flow of illegal immigration into San Diego. It also looks at the desperate and dangerous flow through the deserts of Arizona. It is a multiple-award-winning documentary film by the renowned filmmaker Chantel Akerman.

*Gangs of New York.* 2002. 166 minutes, color. Miramax Films.
Director Martin Scorsese's historical look at what happened in New York in the late 1860s, based on real events and the anti-immigrant riots and focusing on the 19th-century gangs in cities like New York, New Orleans, and Chicago. It stars Leonardo DiCaprio and Cameron Diaz.

*In America.* 2002. 105 minutes, color. Hell's Kitchen Films.
This is an Irish-American-British film drama by Jim Sheridan and is the semi-autobiographical story of Sheridan and his two daughters as they struggle to start a new life in New York City, seen through the eyes of the elder daughter.

*The Kite Runner.* 2007. 128 minutes, color. Paramount Vantage.
This is the story of the devastation and the human side of the Afghanistan conflict. It is an absorbing, intelligent, and thought-provoking movie.

*Maria Full of Grace.* 2004. 101 minutes, color.
HBO Films/Fine Line Features, IMDb. A searing, compelling, and remarkable look at the plight of drug mules, women from South America who risk their lives to escape poverty by smuggling drugs into the United States in their stomachs, swallowing dozens of large, greased, watertight heroin pellets before boarding a flight to JFK.

*The Other Side of Immigration.* 2010. 55 minutes, color.
Directed by Roy Germano, this film is based on over 700 interviews in Mexican towns where about half the population left to work in the United States. It is a subtle, thought-provoking look at what happens to the communities and families left behind by the waves of undocumented Mexican migrating north in search of work.

## Videos

*Liberty and Security in an Age of Terrorism.* 2003. 23 minutes, color. Film Media Group.
This film grapples with the issues of balance between homeland security in the post-9/11 world and the basic civil liberty values central to American society. Using a hypothetical scenario, a panel of persons confront the issues and wrestle with the high-stakes questions in discussing the implications of the USA Patriot Act, surveillance of suspects, closed deportation hearings, demands for student information, and just what constitutes an unaligned combatant.

*The Patriot Act under Fire.* 2003. 23 minutes, color. Film Media Group.
For many, worrying about constitutional rights seems like an archaic luxury in the age of international terrorism. The need for tighter security made civil liberties seem less critical when the nation confronted terrorism by passing urgent measures such as the USA Patriot Act, designed

to defend the country. Two years after its passage, ABC News and anchor Ted Koppel take a hard look at the law with representatives from the Justice Department, the ACLU, and others.

*Should States Be Able to Opt Out of the Refugee Resettlement Program.* March 23, 2018. color, Center for Immigration Studies.
In this video, a Center for Immigration Studies (CIS) sponsored panel on refugees and asylum discusses the 1980 Refugee Act. It features Don Barnett, a CIS Fellow and author of a recent report on refugee resettlement and the states; Jeff Johnson, a city council member in the refugee relocation city of St. Cloud, Minnesota; and Richard Thompson, president of the Thomas More Law Center, who represents the state of Tennessee in a suit to withdraw from the program. The panel and its question-and-answer session are hosted by Mark Krikorian, CIS executive director. Available at: https://cis.org/video/Panel-Should-States-Be-Able-to-Opt-Out-of-Refugee-Resettlement-Program.

*With Us or against Us: Afghans in America.* 2002. 27 minutes, color. Filmmakers Library.
This short documentary examines the experiences of Afghan immigrants to the United States and their plight facing discrimination and hysteria after the 9/11 attacks.

Reforming immigration law and policy has been a perennial matter in American politics, for the executive, judicial, and legislative branches, and at all three levels of government in the United States. The following is a list of some of the major laws and actions taken by the United States in the past to reform immigration law and public policy.

**Laws and Actions That Set the Stage for Subsequent Immigration Reform**

**1790**   Among its first official actions, the U.S. Congress enacted a uniform rule of naturalization imposing a two-year residency requirement for aliens who were specified in the law as free-white persons of good moral character.

**1802**   Congress amends the 1790 Act by requiring a five-year residency and the taking of an oath renouncing allegiance and fidelity to foreign powers.

**1819**   Congress passes a "Manifest Law," requiring shipmasters to deliver a manifest enumerating all persons transported

Immigrant children read and play at an aid center after being released from the U.S. government detention in McAllen, TX, on November 3, 2018. U.S. Customs and Border Protection (CBP), and ICE, dealing with a surge of asylum seekers, have been releasing recently arrived families, pending immigration court dates, despite continued official "zero tolerance" immigration policies. Catholic Charities runs the Humanitarian Respite Center in McAllen to assist released immigrants before their ongoing journey. (John Moore/Getty Images)

for immigration and requiring the secretary of state to inform Congress annually of the number of immigrants admitted. For the first time, the number of immigrants who enter legally for the purpose of permanent resettlement are recorded, making the law the first official immigration act.

**1848**   The Treaty of Guadalupe Hidalgo is negotiated and signed, which guarantees citizenship to Mexicans remaining in the territory ceded to the United States by Mexico. It sets the basis for the first flow of Mexicans to the United States into which future immigrants, both legal and unauthorized, can assimilate, forging the first link to what develops as chain migration from Mexico and Central America to the United States.

**1855**   Castle Garden becomes New York City's principal port of entry for all legal immigration. Its volume of immigrants sets the stage for later developments of "visa overstayers" who are able to remain because such extensive numbers overwhelm the ability of immigration authorities to keep an accurate track of them.

**1862**   Congress passes the Homestead Act, granting acres of free land to settlers who develop the frontier land if they remain on it for five years, thereby spurring heavy levels of immigration.

**1882**   Congress enacts the first of several Chinese Exclusion Acts barring immigration of Chinese laborers, for 10 years, and denying them eligibility for naturalization. Amended in 1888, 1892, and 1904, its harsh provisions induce many Chinese immigrants to evade the law by using falsified documents, so-called "paper sons and daughters," setting the precedent for using fraudulent documents by undocumented immigrants that persists to this day.

**1885**   Congress enacts the Foran Act, making it unlawful for laborers to immigrate to the United States under contract with a U.S. employer who, in any manner, prepays passage to bring them to the country, in a way serving as a precursor to employers who hire undocumented immigrants using fake documents. The employer skirts the law by simply not verifying the accuracy of the documents even while often knowing or suspecting that they are, in fact, unauthorized immigrants.

**1886** *Yick Wo v. Hopkins* overturns a San Francisco municipal ordinance against Chinese laundry workers as discriminatory and unconstitutional on the basis of the Fourteenth Amendment, which prohibits state and local governments from depriving any person (even a noncitizen) of life, liberty, or property without due process.

**1888** Congress enacts a law commonly known as the Scott Act, which amends the Chinese Exclusion Act, rescinding re-entry permits for laborers thus ex-post-facto prohibiting their return, upheld in *Chae Chan Ping v. U.S.* (1889).

**1891** Congress expands the classes of persons excluded from admission, forbids the soliciting of immigrants, and establishes the position of superintendent of immigration.

**1892** Ellis Island is opened as the nation's leading port of entry, thus becoming the top immigrant reception station. It becomes the source of many visa overstayers from European countries.

**1894** Congress amends the Chinese Exclusion Act, extending it permanently, and further enacts a law establishing the Bureau of Immigration within the U.S. Treasury Department, the first of several home departments for immigration services.

**1897** A federal district court decides the case of *In re Rodriquez*, which affirms the citizenship rights of Mexicans based on the 1848 Treaty of Guadalupe Hidalgo, notwithstanding that such persons may not be considered "white."

**1898** The Supreme Court rules, in *Wong Kim Ark v. U.S.* that a native-born son of an Asian parent(s) is indeed a citizen despite the fact that his parents are ineligible for citizenship, affirming the constitutionality of "birthright citizenship."

**1903**    Congress passes a law making immigration the responsibility of the Department of Commerce and Labor.

**1906**    Congress passes the Basic Naturalization Law, which codifies a uniform law for naturalization of immigrants. With some amendments, it remains the law of naturalization to this day.

**1907**    Congress adds important regulations for issuing passports and the expatriation and marriage of U.S. women to foreign men, a law that stirs controversy until its repeal in 1922. President Theodore Roosevelt issues an executive order, known as the Gentlemen's Agreement, by which Japan, under extreme economic pressure, agrees to restrict emigration from Japan and Korea (then under Japanese rule). Picture brides, however, are permitted to emigrate. Congress also enacts the White-Slave Traffic Act, forbidding the importation of any woman for the purpose of prostitution or similar immoral purposes.

**1911**    The Dillingham Commission issues its report, whose recommendations become the basis for the quota system acts of the 1920s.

**1915**    The Americanization/100 Percenters campaign begins, supported by governments and private enterprises, as social movements that first attempt "forced assimilation," encouraging the adoption of English as the official U.S. language and of social customs. After World War I, its perceived failure will contribute to the disillusionment that set the stage for the quota acts of the 1920s.

**1917**    The United States enters World War I in April. Congress enacts the Literacy Act immigration bill, including a literacy test, and bars all immigrants from a specified area known as the Asiatic barred zone. The Departments of State and Labor issue a joint order requiring all aliens seeking entrance to have passports with visas issued by U.S. consulate offices in their country of origin rather than seeking permission to enter the United States only when arriving at the port of entry. Puerto Ricans are granted U.S. citizenship.

**1918**    Congress gives the president sweeping powers to disallow entrance or departure of aliens during a time of war, the first of several similar War Powers Acts by which similar presidential declarations are used in all periods of war thereafter.

**1919**    Congress passes a law granting citizenship to Native Americans honorably discharged from the U.S. military for their service in World War I. In the summer, the Red Scare, following the Bolshevik revolution in Russia, leads to the summary deportation of certain specified "radical" aliens deemed thereby to be a threat to U.S. security and serving as a precursor to the USA Patriot Act in 2001.

### Actions Taken during the Quota Era

**1921**    Congress passes the first quota act, the Emergency Quota Act, in which immigration from a particular country is set at 3 percent of the foreign- born population from that country based on the 1910 census.

**1922**    Congress enacts the Cable Act, which specifies that the right of any woman to become a citizen shall not be abridged because of her sex or because she is a married unless she is wed to an alien ineligible for citizenship. This later provision is later repealed.

**1923**    The U.S. Supreme Court rules in *U.S. v. Bhagat Singh Thind* that "white person" means those persons who appear to be and would commonly be viewed as white and are therefore ineligible for citizenship through naturalization.

**1924**    Congress passes the Immigration Act, commonly known as the Johnson-Reed Act, setting the national origin quota for a particular country at 2 percent of the foreign-born population from that country based on the 1890 census, shifting dramatically the sources of immigration from South, Central, and Eastern Europe to Northwestern Europe. It bans the admission of most Asians, who are thereby classified as "ineligible for citizenship." It also passes an act granting citizenship to Native Americans who had not previously received it by allotments under the 1887 Dawes Act or by serving in the U.S. military in World War I.

**1925**  Congress establishes the Border Patrol, charged with policing the U.S. borders against undocumented entrants and with finding and deporting unauthorized immigrants (called illegal aliens in the act) from the interior who had managed to elude apprehension at the border.

**1929**  President Herbert Hoover proclaims new and permanent quotas in which national origin quotas for European immigrants are based on a proportion of those nationalities in the total population as determined by the 1920 census and sets the total number of such legal immigrants at just more than 150,000.

**1929–1939**  U.S. immigration levels drop off dramatically in response to the Great Depression as worldwide migration drops drastically as well.

**1940**  Congress passes the Registration Act, which requires noncitizens to register their addresses every year. This process remains in effect until 1980. Millions of such forms are backlogged and lost in INS warehouses. The failure of this program contributes to the calls during the 1980s to crack down on unauthorized "visa overstayers" through enhanced capability of the INS, which is never achieved.

**1941**  President Franklin D. Roosevelt issues a proclamation to control persons entering or leaving the United States based on the first War Powers Act.

**1942**  An agreement is reached with Mexico to allow migrant farmworkers to enter as temporary labor (for nine months of the year) to satisfy wartime labor shortages in U.S. agriculture due largely to World War II. President Roosevelt issues Executive Order 9066, which leads to the evacuation, relocation, and internment of Japanese and Japanese- American citizens into concentration camps referred to as relocation camps.

**1943**    The Supreme Court decides the case of *Hirabayashi v. U.S.*, ruling that the executive orders for curfews and evacuation were constitutional based on "wartime necessity."

**1944**    The U.S. Supreme Court hands down decision in *Korematsu v. U.S.*, affirming the executive order excluding Japanese Americans from certain excluded zones along the U.S. coast is constitutional. Later in the year, in *Ex Parte Mitsuye Endo*, the court rules that the internment program was an unconstitutional violation of the habeas corpus rights of U.S. citizens—the Nisei.

**1949**    Congress passes the Agricultural Act with provisions to recruit temporary workers from Mexico, giving congressional approval to the Bracero Program.

**1952**    Congress passes the McCarran-Walter Act, the Immigration and Nationality Act of 1952. It amends the quota system somewhat and contains provisions for preferences, introducing that concept to U.S. law.

**1956**    President Eisenhower establishes a parole system for Hungarian Freedom Fighters after their failed revolution attempt, which Congress endorses in 1958, by passing an act to admit Hungarian refugees.

**1959**    Congress amends the Immigration and Nationality Act of 1952 to provide for unmarried sons and daughters of U.S. citizens to enter as "nonquota" immigrants.

**1960**    President John F. Kennedy elected.

**1964**    The Bracero Program is ended.

### Pre-2001 Actions Setting Conditions that Influence Post-9/11 Actions, Ending the Quota System and Enacting the Preference System

**1965**    Congress passes the Immigration and Nationality Act. It establishes a preference system for legal immigration that emphasizes family reunification and meets certain skill goals. It standardizes admissions procedures, setting up a system of 20,000 admissions per country on a first-come, first-served basis for Eastern Hemisphere nations, with a total of 170,000. The first ceiling on Western Hemisphere immigration is set at 120,000. Annual legal immigration to the United States is 296,697.

**1966**  Congress amends the 1965 Act to adjust the status of Cuban refugees, thereby setting up the legal distinction between refugees based on anticommunist U.S. foreign policy goals with those based on economic refugee status, like the Haitians.

**1967**  The UN Convention and Protocol on Refugees is reached and signed by 130 nations, including the United States. Refugees entering under its provisions (like the Cuban and later the Vietnamese) get resettlement assistance, but refugees coming for economic reasons (Haitians) are excluded.

**1972**  The Haitian boat people begin arriving on the East Coast, mostly in Florida. Haitian detention centers are set up in Miami, Florida, using stadium facilities as detention camps that temporarily house thousands of such refugees.

**1975**  Saigon falls after the United States pulls out of Vietnam. Vietnamese, Cambodian, and Laotian refugees flee to the United States from Southeast Asia (aka the Indochina region). They are classified as refugees from communist countries and are thereby assisted in resettlement and aided by "assimilation assistance" programs, many conducted by church-based organizations that assist immigrants. President Carter establishes and the Congress funds the Indochinese Refugee Resettlement Program. Other mass refugees come from El Salvador and include Jews fleeing the Soviet Union. Annual legal immigration to the United States is 386,194.

**1976**  Congress amends the 1965 Act, extending the per-country 20,000 limit of visa applications to Western Hemisphere nations, regulated by the preference system, and setting the conditions for the unanticipated influx of tens of thousands of undocumented immigrants from Mexico and Central America. Annual legal immigration to the United States is 502,289.

**1978**    President Jimmy Carter and the U.S. Congress set up the Select Commission on Immigration and Refugee Policy (SCIRP), which begins its work in 1979.

**1980**    Congress passes the Refugee Act to systematize refugee policy, incorporating the UN definition of refugee and setting the annual number of refugees to be accepted at 50,000 persons who have a "well-founded fear" of persecution based on race, religion, nationality, or membership in a social or political movement, and provides for the additional admission of 5,000 "asylum seekers." Annual legal immigration is 530,639. President Ronald Reagan elected.

**1981**    An economic recession begins in the first year of the Reagan administration. On March 1, SCIRP issues its final report, recommending a series of reforms that influence IRCA and other subsequent reform of immigration acts and underlie proposals even after 2001. President Reagan creates the Task Force on Immigration and Refugee Policy.

**1982**    A federal district court rules the lockup of Haitian refugees is unconstitutional, ordering the release of 1,900 detainees.

**1983**    An immigration reform bill is introduced into Congress, which begins laying the groundwork for what becomes IRCA. The U.S. Supreme Court, in *INS v. Chadha et al.*, rules that the use of a legislative veto to overturn certain INS deportation proceedings, rules, and regulations by the U.S. House of Representatives is unconstitutional.

**1984**    The immigration reform bill passes in different versions in the two chambers of Congress only to die in a Conference Committee.

**1985**    Senator Alan Simpson (R-WY) reintroduces what becomes known as the Simpson-Mazzoli-Rodino bill, which contains most of the provisions that become IRCA, including the amnesty and employer sanctions provisions.

**1986**    The U.S. Supreme Court rules in *Jean v. Nelson* on INS's denial of parole to undocumented immigrants for failure to follow due process.

Congress enacts the Immigration Reform and Control Act (IRCA), which imposes employer sanctions in a vain attempt to stop the illegal immigration of undocumented immigrants. Annual legal immigration to the United States is 601,708. IRCA's amnesty programs ultimately enable the legalization of more than 3 million previously unauthorized immigrants.

**1987** The U.S. Supreme Court, in *INS v. Cardoza-Fonesca*, rules that the government must relax certain standards used in deciding whether certain asylum seekers who insist they would be persecuted if they were deported to their homelands are eligible for asylum.

**1990** Congress passes a major reform law (known as IM-MACT) concerning legal immigration, setting new ceilings for worldwide immigration, redefining the preference system for family reunification and employment, and setting up a new category of preference called "the diversity immigrants." It enacts special provisions regarding Central American refugees, Filipino veterans, and persons seeking to leave Hong Kong. Annual legal immigration to the United States is 1,536,483.

**1993** Congress ratifies the North American Free Trade Agreement (NAFTA). Annual legal immigration to the United States is 904,193.

**1994** California passes Proposition 187, the "Save Our State" Initiative. Annual legal immigration to the United States is 804,416. Congress enacts the Violent Crime Control and Law Enforcement Act, aka the Smith Act, giving the attorney general more authority to issue S visas. Congress enacts the Violence against Women Act, granting special status through cancellation of removal and self-petitioning provisions.

**1995** Osama bin Laden issues "fatwa" versus West and the United States. Annual legal immigration to the United States is 720,461. The federal district court in California rules, in *LULAC et al. v. Wilson et al.*, that many of the provisions in Proposition 187 are unconstitutional. The GAO issues its first report on the costs of illegal immigration both to governments and to the overall U.S. economy.

**1996**    Congress passes the Personal Responsibility and Work Opportunity Act of August 22, 1996, which restricts both legal and unauthorized immigrants from many welfare benefits, thereby enacting many of the welfare restrictions of Proposition 187. Congress enacts the Illegal Immigration Reform and Immigrant Responsibility Act (IIRIRA) of September 30, 1996, with some 60 provisions of the Omnibus Spending bill, authorizing funding for 1,000 more border agents annually for five years, invoking stringent provisions against smuggling and fraudulent document production or sales, having the INS develop border-crossing cards, and setting up an employer verification system among its many provisions.

Congress passes the Anti-Terrorism and Effective Death Penalty Act. Among its many provisions, it grants to INS inspectors the authority to make "on-the-spot credible fear" determinations involving asylum. Annual legal immigration to the United States is 915,900, and the Border Patrol makes a record 1.6 million apprehensions at U.S. borders. Congress authorizes the addition of 1,000 new Border Patrol agents annually.

**1997**    The Jordan Commission on Immigration Reform, named after its chairwoman, civil rights icon Senator Barbara Jordan (D-TX), established by the 1990 IMMACT law, recommends restructuring of the INS in its final report, issued in August 1995. Its recommendations were endorsed by President William Clinton and, among others, included calling for an end to chain migration.

**1998**    Osama bin Laden signs a second "fatwa" against United States. Al Qaeda begins planning to attack the United States in what ends up as the 9/11/2001 attacks. U.S. Congress establishes the Hart-Rudman Commission on National Security. Annual immigration to the United States is 654,451.

**1999** Congress passes the Trafficking Victims Protection Act. Annual immigration is 646,568. In *INS v. Aguirre-Aguirre*, the U.S. Supreme Court unanimously rules that aliens who have committed nonpolitical crimes in their countries of origin are not eligible to seek asylum regardless of their risk of persecution when returned to their home countries.

**2000** October 12, al Qaeda operatives carry out attack on U.S.S. Cole in port of Yemen. Annual legal immigration to the United States is 849,807.

### The Post-9/11 Actions

**2001** September 11 terrorist attack on the World Trade Center Twin Towers in New York City, the Pentagon in Washington, D.C., and a hijacked plane downed in rural Pennsylvania believed to have been targeted for the U.S. Congress Capitol Buildings. Immediate calls for a crackdown on international terrorism begin. President Bush announces the "War on Terrorism." On September 18, Congress passes Authorization to Use Force against Terrorists.

October 1, 2001, the United States invades Afghanistan in "Operation Enduring Freedom." This begins the war that continues today, 16 years later and counting.

On October 8, 2001, President Bush establishes the Office of Homeland Security within the White House and the Homeland Security Council (Executive Order 13228).

On October 26, 2001, Congress enacts the USA Patriot Act, granting sweeping new powers to the attorney general, the FBI, and the DOJ, and authority to detain "enemy combatants" involved in or suspected of terrorism. The DOJ rounds up about 1,200 Muslims and arrest and detain them for days to months as being "suspected" terrorists. No one among those swept up is ever charged with terrorist activity. In November, the DOJ breaks up terrorist cells in Portland,

Oregon, Detroit, Michigan, and Buffalo, New York. The DoD begins drone attacks to kill al Qaeda leaders.

The first "Dream Act" bill is introduced. Annual legal immigration to the United States is 1,064,318.

**2002**  The INS issues notice to several of the (now dead) hijackers that they are given permission to enroll in United States-located (Florida) flight training programs. This results in immediate calls for restructuring the INS to remove the Border Patrol functions from the INS.

In November, Congress establishes the cabinet-level Department of Homeland Security. The attorney general is granted sweeping new powers for expedited removal. In March, the INS is abolished and its functions transferred to the DHS. The undersecretary for Border and Transportation Security begins oversight of Immigration Enforcement and Citizenship and Immigration Services.

The United Nations issues its Protocols on Human Trafficking and Immigrant Smuggling in Palermo, Italy, signed by 141 countries, including the United States.

National Security Entry-Exit Registration System (NSEERS) is implemented; Student and Exchange Visitor Information System (SEVIS) program is implemented. The United States opens up a detention camp at Guantanamo Bay (aka "Gitmo").

Annual legal immigration to the United States is 1,059,902.

**2003**  In January, Congress creates the Terrorist Threat Integration Center in the CIA.

Annual legal immigration to the United States is 703,542.

**2004**  The 9/11 Commission issues its final report, detailing the intelligence failures contributing to the success of the terrorist cells and their attacks.

Congress passes the Intelligence Reform and Terrorism Prevention Act. President Bush appoints John Negroponte, ambassador to Iraq, as the first Director of National Intelligence (DNI).

The National Counterterrorism Center is established, housed within the CIA.

Unauthorized immigrants within the United States reach an estimated 11 million. ICE reports 1.1 million apprehensions at the nation's borders.

Annual legal immigration to the United States is 957,883.

**2005**    The House passes the Border Protection, Anti-terrorism and Illegal Immigration Control Act, known as the REAL ID Act. Congress also passes the National Container Security Act. It enacts the Detainee Treatment Act, which forbids the use of water boarding as an enhanced interrogation technique. On February 15, Michael Chertoff is appointed as the secretary of the DHS. In August, Hurricane Katrina strikes the United States, and New Orleans, Louisiana, and Mississippi are hard hit.

Nine states pass anti-human trafficking acts, and three states pass laws mandating state and local law enforcement to enforce federal immigration laws against unauthorized immigrants. The governors of Arizona and New Mexico issue "state of emergency" declarations because of the extreme adverse effects of illegal immigration on their respective states.

Ministers of the European Union approve the use of biometric cards for immigrants to EU countries. Japan begins fingerprinting all incoming immigrants. France expels several thousand illegal immigrants. Russia imposes fines for hiring illegal immigrants. Annual legal immigration to the United States is 1,122,373.

**2006**    Congress extends the USA Patriot Act in March, officially the Uniting and Strengthening America by Providing Appropriate Tools to Intercept and Obstruct Terrorism Act.

Congress passes the Secure Fence Act, and President Bush signs it into law. The law authorizes construction of a 700-mile bollard-type fence along the southwestern border.

The Border Action Network, an advocacy group, is established.

The second "Dream Act" bill is introduced into Congress.

Annual legal immigration to the United States is 1,266,129.

Annual legal immigration to the United States is 1,052,415. A third version of a Dream Act bill is introduced.

**2007**    President Obama is elected. His administration begins a surge in the use of expedited removals to deport unauthorized immigrants. Annual legal immigration to the United States is 1,107,126. Obama appoints Janet Napolitano as secretary of DHS. She launches cyber war efforts, including establishment of the Center for Strategic and International Studies. A fourth Dream Act bill is introduced into Congress.

**2008**    President Obama uses executive action to mitigate certain aspects of IIRIRA.

Annual immigration to the United States is 1,120,818. DHS creates the Cyber Security and the Cyber Traffic systems (Einstein 1, 2, 3). The U.S. Cyber Command is established.

**2009**    Arizona passes a law mandating state and local police to demand anyone suspected of being illegal to show documents to prove his or her legal status.

In *Arizona v. United States* (132 S. Ct. 2492), the Supreme Court rules the Arizona law unconstitutional. The DHS thwarts N.Y.C. Subway system bombing attack. A fourth Dream Act bill is introduced into Congress.

Annual legal immigration to the United States is 1,042,625.

**2010**    A fifth Dream Act bill is introduced. Annual legal immigration is 1,042,625.

**2011**    Osama bin Laden killed on May 2, in a U.S. Navy Seal Team raid in Pakistan. Annual legal immigration to the United States is 1,062,040.

A sixth Dream Act bill is introduced in Congress.

**2012**    President Obama issues executive action order, DACA, granting temporary, conditional legal status to "Dreamer" children. Annual legal immigration to the United States is 1,031,631.

**2013**    Annual legal immigration to the United States is 990,553. Jeh Johnson is appointed secretary of the DHS on December 23, 2013.

**2014**  The Senate passes S. 744, a comprehensive immigration reform bill in a bipartisan vote, but the measure is blocked in the U.S. House of Representatives. Annual legal immigration is 1,016,518.

President Obama extends the DACA order.

**2015**  President Obama issues the DAPA executive action order, granting temporary, conditional legal residency to unauthorized immigrant parents of U.S. citizens and legal permanent aliens. A surge in arrivals of children unaccompanied by adults from El Salvador, Guatemala, and Honduras moves President Obama to grant "Temporary Protected Status" to 5,000 such children for whom it is deemed too unsafe to return them to their country of origin. Annual legal immigration to the United States is 1,051,031.

**2016**  February 17, U.S. District Judge, Texas, Andrew Hanen, places an injunction of the Obama administration's implementation of the DAPA order.

**2017**  President Trump is elected. In January, President Trump appoints John Kelly as secretary of DHS and Jim Mattis as secretary of the Department of Defense. On January 25, 2017, he issues an executive order to start a pilot program to build a wall on the U.S.-Mexico border.

On January 25, President Trump issues his executive order against "sanctuary cities," known as "Enhancing the Public Safety in the Interior of the United States." On January 27, he issues his (first) Muslim travel ban. On January 31, President Trump fires acting attorney general Sally Yates for refusing to defend the travel ban order in federal court. On February 3, federal district judge Robart, in Seattle, Washington, rules that the travel ban order is unconstitutional. On March 6, Trump issues a second travel ban order, which Judge Watson, a federal district judge in Hawaii, and Judge Chuang of the Maryland Federal District Court also rule as unconstitutional. On March 14, the second executive order is also blocked from implementation by court order. President Trump and the DOJ appeal to the U.S. Supreme Court.

In May, President Trump orders the DHS to establish the Victims of Immigration Crime Enforcement (VOICE) program. On June 21, 2017, the U.S. Supreme Court partially upholds the second travel ban order and schedules oral arguments on the order for fall 2017.

On July 19, the Supreme Court allowed many of the federal judge's limitations on the revised travel ban.

**2018**   In the final week of January 2018, Trump annulled the DACA and DAPA, giving Congress until March 5, 2018, to fix the problem.

Congress fails to achieve a bi-partisan deal. Democrats tried to include a Dreamer provision in a budget continuing resolution but fail, and the government closes down for a weekend.

On Friday, March 23, a $1.3 trillion budget is passed. It includes no Dreamer provision nor funding for the border wall. President Trump threatens a veto but finally does sign the budget bill into law, funding the federal government until September 2018.

On June 26, 2018, the U.S. Supreme Court, in a 5–4 decision, ruled in *Trump v. Hawaii* that the third iteration of the travel ban was constitutional.

On November 7, 2018, President Trump fires Jeff Sessions as attorney general, replacing him with an acting attorney general, a Trump loyalist Matt Whitaker.

**Absconders**   People who had been ordered deported but failed to leave.

**Adjustment to immigrant status**   A procedure whereby a nonimmigrant must apply for a change of status to lawful permanent resident if an immigrant visa is available for his or her country. The alien is an immigrant as of the date of the adjustment. It was used extensively for Cuban and Vietnamese refugees and for Hungarian Freedom Fighters.

**Advocacy**   The support given by the sanctuary movement to unauthorized immigrants involving attendance at immigration court hearings, and accompanying individuals to mandatory check-ins with the Department of Homeland Security.

**Alien**   A person who is not a citizen or national of a given nation-state.

**Amnesty**   A legal pardoning of a person who entered the United States illegally or is otherwise in nonlegal status, thereby changing his or her legal status to legal resident alien. It was used extensively by IRCA to cover more than 3 million persons.

**Apprehensions**   The physical control or temporary detainment of a person who is not lawfully in the United States, which may or may not result in an arrest.

**Biometric identification**    The use of DNA, fingerprints, iris scans, facial recognition technology, or voice imprints to screen a person as a possible terrorist and to identify unauthorized immigrants.

**Biometrics**    The use of fingerprints, facial recognition technology, and iris scans as a way of accurately identifying people in a quick and efficient manner.

**Border card**    A card that allows a person living within a certain zone of the United States border to legally cross back and forth for employment purposes without a passport or visa.

**Border patrol**    The law enforcement arm of the Department of Homeland Security.

**Brain drain**    The flow of talented migrants from lesser-developed to developed countries.

**Chain migration**    When one family member first enters the United States as a legal, permanent resident and then brings in many family members (extended, not just nuclear family members). It can also refer to immigrant groups coming who are not related but come from the same place or origin and settle in the same place in the United States, for example, drawn by ethnic or religious association in the home country.

**Conundrum**    A confusing or difficult problem or question.

**DACA**    An acronym for Deferred Action for Childhood Arrivals, which is a program of the Obama administration's DHS that protected Dreamer children from deportation as unauthorized immigrants.

**DAPA**    An acronym for Deferred Action for Parental Accountability.

**De facto**    A Latin phrase meaning "by action."

**De jure**    A Latin phrase meaning something being done "by law."

**Deportation**    A legal process by which a nation sends individuals back to their countries of origin after refusing them legal residence.

**Devolution**   The transfer or delegation of power to a lower level, especially by a central government to local or regional administration.

**Dream Act**   An acronym for Development, Relief, and Education for Alien Minors; a proposed law that would provide a path to citizenship for unauthorized immigrants brought to the United States as minor children.

**Due process of law**   The constitutional limitation on government behavior to deal with an individual according to prescribed rules and procedures.

**Earned legalization**   A proposal to allow unauthorized immigrants to change their status to that of legal permanent resident by paying fines and satisfying stipulated conditions akin to those who came as authorized permanent resident aliens.

**Earned residency**   A path to get a green card and the right to stay in the United States but not a path to citizenship. It involves paying taxes, learning English, and committing no substantial crime.

**Emigrant**   A person who voluntarily leaves his or her country of birth for permanent resettlement elsewhere.

**Employer sanctions**   A provision of the 1986 Immigration Reform and Control Act that imposed legal penalties (fines and/or prison) for knowingly hiring an illegal alien.

**Equal protection of the law**   The constitutionally guaranteed right that all persons be treated the same before the law.

**Executive orders**   Actions issued by a president, assigned numbers and published in the federal register, akin to laws passed by Congress, that direct members of the executive branch to follow a new policy or directive.

**Exempt**   An individual or a class or category of individuals to whom a certain provision of the law does not apply.

**Expedited removal**   A stipulation in law changing the procedures by which persons in the United States without legal status may be deported with fewer judicial protections to do so.

**Expulsion**    The decision of a sovereign nation to legally compel an individual to permanently leave its territory.

**Globalization**    A tide of economic, technological, and intellectual forces that integrates a global community.

**Green card**    A document issued by the DHS that certifies an individual as a legal immigrant entitled to work in the United States.

**Guest Worker Program**    A program enabling the legal importation of workers for temporary labor in specified occupations.

**H-1B Visa**    A category of temporary visa issued to a nonimmigrant, allowing employers to employ guest workers temporarily in a specialty occupation or field for a stipulated period of time.

**Illegal aliens**    Individuals who are in a territory without documentation permitting permanent residence.

**Immediate relatives**    Spouses, minor children, parents, grandparents, and brothers and sisters of a U.S. citizen or permanent resident alien.

**Immigrant**    An alien admitted to the United States as a lawful permanent resident.

**Inadmissibles**    Persons encountered at ports of entry who seek lawful admission into the United States but are determined to be inadmissible, individuals who present themselves to seek humanitarian protection under U.S. laws, and individuals who withdraw their application for admission and return to their countries of origin in a short time frame.

**Inclusion**    An individual's or group's engagement with the processes or organizations that recognize the individual or group by conferring membership or by providing resources such as entitlement or protests; it provides a sense of security, stability, and predictability understood primarily as an opportunity to plan for the future.

**Investor immigrant**    An individual permitted to immigrate based upon the promise to invest $1 million in an urban area or $500,000 in a rural area to create at least 10 jobs.

**Lone-wolf terrorist**  A person perpetrating a terrorist act or plot who is inspired by but not associated with an international terrorist group or organization, such as al Qaeda or ISIS.

**Naturalization**  The legal act of making an individual a citizen who is not born a citizen.

**Nonimmigrant**  An alien seeking temporary entry into the United States for a specific purpose other than permanent settlement—such as a foreign government official, tourist, student, temporary workers, or cultural exchange visitor.

**Overstayers**  Persons who enter the United States on a temporary visa who then stay beyond the time specified in their visa at which time they are to voluntarily depart the United States; when they overstay, their status becomes unauthorized/illegal.

**Passport**  A legal identification document issued by a sovereign nation-state attesting to the nationality of an individual for the purpose of international travel.

**Patriotic assimilation**  The adoption, by the newcomer, of American civic values and the American heritage as one's own.

**Permanent resident**  A noncitizen who is allowed to live permanently in the United States and who can travel in and out of the country without a visa and can work without restriction; the person is allowed to accumulate time toward becoming a naturalized citizen.

**Political incorporation**  A model that holds that for a minority community to witness an effective response to its needs, minority leaders must come to occupy positions of government authority.

**Prosecutorial discretion**  A privilege given to the prosecuting attorney in deciding whether to prosecute or to plea bargain, recommend parole, and so on.

**Protocol**  An international agreement governing the understanding and procedures that member states who are parties to a treaty agreed upon for a given purpose, as in the UN protocols regarding the status and treatment of refugees.

**Pull factor**   An aspect of the receiving nation that draws immigrants for resettlement.

**Push factor**   An event that compels large numbers of persons to emigrate—leave their country of origin for permanent resettlement elsewhere.

**Racial profiling**   A pattern of behavior of police officers based on racial appearance.

**Refugee**   A qualified applicant for conditional entry into the United States whose application could not be approved because of an adequate number of preference visas.

**Requests for detention**   Requests by the DHS that a local or state law enforcement agency hold an individual beyond the point at which they would otherwise be released.

**Requests for notification**   Requests that state or local law enforcement notify ICE of a pending release during the time that a person is otherwise in custody under state or local authority.

**Sabbatarian**   Religious law, norm, or customary practice as to which day, Saturday or Sunday, a religious group/denomination/cult/sect holds to be the holy day.

**Sanctuary city**   A city in the United States that follows certain procedures that shelter illegal immigrants that may be by "de jure" or "de facto" action. The designation has no legal meaning and is most commonly used for cities that do not permit municipal funds or resources to be applied in furtherance of enforcement of federal immigration laws; that is, they do not allow police or municipal employees to inquire about one's immigrant status.

**Stakeholder**   A person or an organization with an interest or concern in something, especially a business, or one who is involved or is affected by a policy or course of action.

**Unauthorized immigrants**   Those who come undocumented or break or overstay the conditions of their visas and become illegal immigrants without the status of permanent resident alien.

**Undocumented immigrants** Individuals who enter the United States without inspection or paper documentation that allows them to enter and to reside in the United States and to legally work while doing so.

**Unfunded mandates** Requirements issued by the federal government that impose a financial burden upon state and local governments without offsetting funding for their implementation.

**Visa** A legal document issued by a consular or similar state department official allowing a person to travel to the United States for either permanent or temporary reasons—such as immigrant, student, tourist, government representative, business, or cultural exchange.

**Xenophobia** An unfounded fear of foreigners.

absconders, 26, 323
Ackerman, Alissa, 259–260
Act of August 22, 1996, 18
Act of December 17, 2004,
    28, 317
Act of May 11, 2003, 11
Act of November 2, 1966,
    10
Act of October 20, 1976, 10,
    231–232
Act of October 26, 2001,
    316–317. *See also* USA
    Patriot Act of 2001
Act of October 26, 2006,
    28–29. *See also* Secure
    Fence Act of 2006
Act of September 30, 1996,
    18
adjustment to immigrant
    status, 231–232, 312
    defined, 323
advocacy, defined, 323
Afghanistan, 153–154,
    316

African National Congress,
    24
Agriculture Committee,
    118–119
al Qaeda, 22, 28, 70,
    153–154, 315–316
*Albany Law Review*, 286
Albert, Carl, 117–118
Alden, Edward, 260
Alden, Ewing, 260
alien, defined, 323
Alien Smuggling and
    Trafficking Taskforce, 95
All Souls Unitarian
    Universalist Church,
    145–151. *See also* Rost,
    Nori
American Civil Liberties
    Union (ACLU), 67–69,
    155, 187
American Conservative
    Union, 67, 155–156
*American Criminal Law
    Review*, 286–287

*American Demographics,* 287
American Immigration
    Control Foundation
    (AICF), 156
American Immigration Law
    Foundation (AILF),
    157
American Immigration
    Lawyers Association
    (AILA), 157
*American Journal of Political
    Science,* 287–288
*American Journal of Sociology,*
    288
American Librarians
    Association, 67
*American Political Science
    Review,* 287
*American Prospect,* 287
*American Sociological Review,*
    288
*American Studies,* 288–289
Americans for Prosperity,
    157–158, 195–196
amnesty, 12, 123, 323. *See
    also* earned legalization
Andreas, Peter, 260–261
anthrax incident, 21
apprehensions, 222
    defined, 323
Arab Americans, 68–69, 158
Arab immigrants, 68–69
Arab Spring, 74
*Arizona v. United States,*
    2009, 319
Ashcroft, John, 19

Association of Patriotic
    Arab Americans in the
    Military (APAAM),
    158–159
asylum, 99–100, 129–130,
    133, 144
Ayotte, Kelly, 34

*Baker v. Carr,* 1962, 78–79
Barkan, Elliott, 274
Barone, Michael, 261
Bean, Frank D., 261
Becerra, Xavier, 32
Bedell, Berkley and Kenneth,
    117–122
Bennett, Michael, 32
bin Laden, Osama, 154, 315
    killed, 319
biometric identification, 82
    defined, 324
biometric system, 324
biometrics, 324
Black Caucus, 73. *See also*
    Congressional Black
    Caucus
black voters, 78
Bloomberg, Michael, 72
boat people (Cuban, Haitian,
    Vietnamese), 12
Boehner, John, 32–33, 134
Bolick, Clint, 81–82, 261
Bolick, Grant, 264
boll weevils, 135
Border and Transportation
    Security, Directorate of,
    236

border card, defined, 324
Border Caucus, 14, 73.
    *See also* Border States
    Caucus
border control, 33–34, 43,
    73
    defined, 238–239
    sectors of, 81–82
border fence, 27–28, 45, 65,
    73–74, 122
border patrol, 15, 18–20, 82,
    223, 310
    defined, 324
Border Policy Research
    Institute (BPRI), 159,
    210
Border Protection, Anti-
    Terrorism, and Illegal
    Immigration Act of
    2005, 92. *See also* Real
    ID Act of 2003
border security, 123,
    238–240
Border Security and
    Immigration
    Enhancement
    Enforcement
    Improvements,
    Executive Order 13767,
    37
Border Security, Economic
    Opportunity,
    and Immigration
    Modernization Act of
    2013 (S. 744), 134,
    238–242

Border States Caucus, 14
border wall, 37–38, 43,
    57–58, 74, 122, 144,
    169, 217, 221
    defined, 320
Bracero Program, 6–7
    defined, 311
brain circulation, 104
    defined, 324
brain drain, 57, 89, 101–104.
    *See also* brain circulation
brain hubs, 88
Brick, Kate, 281
Brill, Stephen, 262
*Brookings Review,* 289
Brotherton, David, 262
Brown, Cynthia, 262–263
Browning, Rufus, 263
Bureau of Immigration and
    Customs Enforcement,
    159–160. *See also*
    Immigration Control
    and Enforcement (ICE)
Bush, George W., 20–21,
    27–28, 38, 75,
    177–178
Bush, Jeb, 81–82, 264
Business Roundtable,
    160

Cable Act of 1922, 309
Cainkar, Louise, 264
Calavita, Kitty, 264
California, 16–17
*California Law Review,*
    289

Canada, 29, 103–104
    border of, 35
    Go North program, 103
Capitol Hill, 134–135, 139,
    171
Card, Andrew, Jr., 20
Carter, Jimmy, 178, 313. *See
    also* Select Commission
    on Immigration and
    Refugee Policy (SCIRP)
    administration of, 11
Carter, John, 32, 34
Castaneda, Jorge G., 265
Castle Garden, 306
Catholic Legal Immigration
    Network, Inc.
    (CLINIC), 98, 160–161
Cato Institute, 67, 196
caucuses, 14
    Border States Caucus, 73
    Congressional Black
        Caucus, 14, 73
    Congressional Hispanic
        Caucus, 14
Celler, Emanuel, 4
Center for American Progress,
    106, 161, 209–210
Center for Budget and Policy
    Priorities, 105
Center for Disease Control
    and Prevention (CDC),
    21
Center for Immigration
    Studies (CIS), 30, 69,
    161, 196–197
Center for Migration Studies
    (CMS), 162, 194–195

Center for Privacy and
    Technology Policy
    (CPTP), 67, 162–163
Center for the Study of Hate
    Crimes and Extremism,
    163, 198
Center on Budget and Policy
    Priorities (CBPP),
    163–164
Central America, 34, 45,
    74, 99, 222. *See also* El
    Salvador; Guatemala;
    Honduras
Central Intelligence Agency
    (CIA), 62
*Chae Chan Ping v. U.S.*,
    1889, 307
Chaffetz, Jason, 35
chain migration, 6, 41, 124,
    133
    defined, 324
changes in immigration
    policy, 80–83
Chattpahdyay, Jacquiline,
    270
checks and balances, 22, 60
Cheney, Richard "Dick," 22
Chertoff, Michael, 178–179,
    318. *See also* Bush,
    George W.; Department
    of Homeland
    Security (DHS);
    Federal Emergency
    Management Agency
    (FEMA); Hurricane
    Katrina
Chin, Gabriel J., 263

Chinese Exclusion Act
  of 1882, 306
  of 1894, 307
Chishti, Muzaffare, 275
Chomsky, Aviva, 265
Chua, Amy, 86, 265
civil liberties, 21, 60, 67–72,
  172
civil rights, 67–72, 172
  Civil Rights Act of 1964, 5
Clarke, Richard, 266
Clinton, Hillary, 36
  Clinton/Keane ticket,
  36
Clinton, William Jefferson,
  18, 97, 122–123, 170,
  179–180. *See also*
  Illegal Immigration
  Reform and Immigrant
  Responsibility Act of
  1996 (IIRIRA); North
  American Free Trade
  Agreement (NAFTA);
  North Atlantic Treaty
  Organization (NATO)
cloture vote, 32–33
Club for Growth, 139
Cole, David, 69, 266
Collins, Susan, 42, 65,
  266–267
Colorado Springs Quakers,
  148
color-coded alert system, 55,
  64
commentary, 289
Commission on Legal
  Immigration Reform, 15

comprehensive immigration
  reform bill, 32–33,
  72–77, 75, 122–123,
  137, 206
  Act of 2006, 133
  Act of 2014, 320
Congress, 56–57, 68, 72–73,
  76, 78, 117–122, 140,
  156
  committee structure of,
  121–122
Congressional Black Caucus,
  14–15, 73
Congressional Budget Office,
  29, 105
Congressional Hispanic
  Caucus, 14–15
*Congressional Quarterly,*
  289–290
Congressional Research
  Service, 164
  Library of Congress, 164
Conservative Political Action
  Conference, 156
Contract with America,
  137–138. *See also*
  Gingrich, Newt
conundrum, 13, 58
  defined, 324
Conyers, John, 180–181. *See
  also* Dream Act; Illegal
  Immigration Reform and
  Immigrant Responsibility
  Act of 1996 (IIRIRA);
  IMMACT; Real ID Act
  of 2003; Secure Fence
  Act of 2006

Coons, Chris, 42
*Cornell Law Review,* 290
Cornyn, John, 34
*Corrections Today,* 290
Council of Graduate Schools
    (CGS), 164–165
Crest Act of 2014, 34
crisis decision making, 60
Cross-Designation Program,
    74–75
Cruz, Ted, 140
Cuellar, Henry, 34
cultural incompatibility, 63
Customs and Border
    Protection (CBP),
    26, 58, 62, 94, 173,
    174–175, 220, 305. *See
    also* border patrol

DACA, 35, 64, 123–124,
    141, 161, 169, 172,
    185, 319. *See also*
    Deferred Action for
    Childhood Arrivals
    (DACA)
annulment of, 40–42, 324
defined, 324
Daniels, Jr., Mitchell, 20
Daniels, Roger, 267
DAPA, 35, 161, 169, 172,
    185, 320. *See also*
    Deferred Action for
    Parental Accountability
    (DAPA)
annulment of, 40–42, 321
defined, 324

D'Appollonia, Ariane
    Chabel, 267
de facto (by action), defined,
    324
de jure (by law), defined,
    324
deadlock, 77–78
deferred action, 30, 31
Deferred Action for
    Childhood Arrivals
    (DACA), 3, 26, 31,
    123–124, 132–133
Deferred Action for Parental
    Accountability (DAPA),
    31, 35, 80
Democratic Party, 17, 73,
    118, 130–134, 135–142
and comprehensive
    immigration reform bill,
    130–134
platform of, 131–132
demography, 174, 290
Department of Defense
    (DoD), 24–25, 62, 68,
    81, 94
Department of Homeland
    Security (DHS), 20–21,
    23–26, 27, 35, 44,
    55–56, 60, 62, 64–72
Act of, 157, 161
directorates of, 62–63
restructuring of, 64–65,
    75–77, 80–82, 86,
    88–89, 92, 97, 100,
    107, 155, 157, 159,
    164–165, 172–173,

191, 199, 202–203,
205–206, 317
Department of Immigration,
proposal of, 66
Department of Justice
(DOJ), 21–23, 26, 39,
56, 62, 68, 76, 80–81,
84, 94, 100–101, 155,
165–166, 172, 207–208,
213–214
Department of Labor
(DOL), 105–106, 308
Department of State (DOS),
19, 86–87, 91–92, 94,
164
Department of Veteran
Affairs (DVA), 24
deportation, defined, 324
Development, Relief, and
Education of Minors,
29–30. See also Dream
Act
devolution, 96–97, 121
defined, 325
Díaz-Balart, Mario, 32
Dillingham Commission, 308
Director of National
Intelligence (DNI), 28,
317
diversity immigrants, 15
Dream Act, 29, 31–32, 73,
75, 155, 166, 241,
317–318, 325
Dreamers, 120
problems of, 56–57
proposal of, 41–42

Drug Enforcement Agency
(DEA), 15
due process of law, 313. See
also Jean v. Nelson,
1986
defined, 325
Durbin, Richard "Dick,"
32, 181–182. See also
DACA; DAPA; Dream
Act; Gang of Eight,
House, Senate; Judiciary
Committee, House,
Senate

earned legalization, 32, 73,
81
defined, 325
earned residency, 81
defined, 325
800 Mile Wall, The, 299–300
El Salvador, 34, 74, 99, 223.
See also Central America
unaccompanied children
from, 223
electoral college vote (ECV),
36
Ellis Island, 1992, 307
emigrant, defined, 325
employer sanctions, 12,
225–229
defined, 325
employment-sponsored
preferences, 313. See also
Immigration Reform
and Control Act (IRCA)
enforcement, 12

English as a second language (ESL), 66, 126–130
Enhanced Border Security and Visa Entry Reform Act of 2001, 93
Enhancing the Public Safety in the Interior of the United States (Executive Order 13768), 37, 80–81, 99. *See also* executive orders
epulsion, defined, 326
equal employment opportunity, 71
programs of, 71
equal protection of the law, defined, 325
Etzioni, Amitai, 267
executive actions, 46
Executive Order 9066 (1942), 310
Executive Order 13228, 316
Executive Order 13768, 37, 80–81. *See also* Enhancing the Public Safety in the Interior of the United States
Executive Order 13780, 244–249
executive orders, 3, 20, 56, 80–81, 150, 244–249. *See also* executive actions; Executive Order 13228
defined, 325
exempt, defined, 325

Expedited Family Reunification Act of 2014, 34
expedited removal, 70, 169
defined, 325

*Fahrenheit 9/11*, 300
family reunification preferences, 15, 89–90. *See also* Immigration and Naturalization Act of October 3, 1965
fatwa, defined, 314–315. *See also* bin Laden, Osama; terrorist attacks of September 11, 2001
Federal Bureau of Investigation (FBI), 70, 75–76
Federal Emergency Management Agency (FEMA), 63, 68. *See also* Department of Homeland Security (DHS)
federal system, 56
Federalist Party, 131
Federation for American Immigration Reform (FAIR), 166. *See also* Tanton, John
Ferguson, Bob, 182–183
First Unitarian Society of Denver, Colorado, 145–146

First United Church of
Christ, 148
Flake, Jeff, 32, 34, 41
Florida, 74–75
Foran Act of 1885, 306–307
foreign-born population, 220
Foreign Intelligence
Surveillance Act of 1978
(FISA), 23
*Forensic Examiner*, 290–291
Fortress America, 20, 45
Fourth Amendment, 22–23,
77
Free Congress Foundation,
67, 167
*Free Inquiry*, 291
Freedom Caucus, 80
Freedom Works, 167
Freeman, Gary A., 268–269
*From the Other Side*, 300
Furman, Rick, 259–260

Gang of Eight, House,
Senate, 32, 73, 140,
200, 206
*Gangs of New York*, 300
Gates, Bill, 85–86
Gateway States, 17–18
Gay, Claudine, 270
Gentlemen's Agreement,
1907, 308
*Georgetown Immigration Law
Journal*, 291
Georgetown Law Center, 162
Gerry, Elbridge, 78
gerrymandering, 77, 80, 140

Gerstle, Gary, 268
Gibney, Matthew, 268
Gingrich, Newt, 137–139
Givens, Terri, 268–269
globalization, defined, 326
Golash-Boza, Tanya M., 269
Gonzales, Alberto, 20,
183–184, 269–270.
*See also* Ashcroft,
John; Bush, George
W.; Department of
Homeland Security
(DHS)
Goodlatte, Bob, 34–35,
184. *See also* border
wall; DACA; DAPA;
family reunification
preferences; Judiciary
Committee, House,
Senate; visa lottery
Gospel of Matthew, 147
Government Accountability
Office (GAO), 26–27,
62, 83, 167–168
reports of, 228–229
Graham, Lindsey, 32, 34, 42,
73, 184–185. *See also*
Dream Act; Gang of
Eight, House, Senate;
Judiciary Committee,
House, Senate
Grassley, Charles, 41, 65
Great Depression, 310
Great Recession, 18, 29, 45
Great Society, 5, 192. *See also*
Johnson, Lyndon B.

green cards, 90–92, 94, 104, 234
defined, 326
groupthink, 59–61. *See also* Janis, Irving
precursors of, 59
problems of, 59
solutions to, 61
Guatemala, 74, 99, 223. *See also* Central America
unaccompanied children from, 223
guest-worker program, 12, 32, 89, 94, 96
defined, 326
Guitierrez, Luis, 32, 185–186. *See also* DACA; DAPA; Gang of Eight, House, Senate; Hispanic Caucus; Judiciary Committee, House, Senate

Hanen, Andrew, 31, 186, 320. *See also* DACA; DAPA
Hart, Philip, 4. *See also* Immigration and Naturalization Act of October 3, 1965
*Harvard Journal of Law and Public Policy*, 291
*Harvard Law Review*, 291–292

Hatch, Orrin, 29, 187. *See also* border wall; DACA; DAPA
Haynes, Wendy, 64
Hebrew Immigrant Aid Society, 188–189
Henry, Patrick, 78
Heritage Foundation, 168–169
Herman, Susan N., 187–188. *See also* American Civil Liberties Union (ACLU); zero-tolerance policy
Hernandez, Kelly L., 270
Hessick, Byrne, 263
Hetfield, Mark, 188–189. *See also* Hebrew Immigrant Aid Society
*Hirabayashi v. United States*, 1943, 311
Hispanic Caucus, 14. *See also* Congressional Hispanic Caucus
Hispanics, 44, 74
voters of, 78
Hochschild, Jennifer, 270
Homeland Security Act, 2002, 235–237. *See also* Bush, George W.
Homeland Security Advisory Council Task Force, 77. *See also* Obama, Barack

Homestead Act of 1862, 306
Honduras, 74, 99, 223. *See
  also* Central America
  unaccompanied children
  from, 223
H-1B visas, 84, 87, 103, 326
Human Rights First, 169
*Humanist, The,* 292
Hurricane Katrina, 30.
  *See also* Department
  of Homeland
  Security (DHS);
  Federal Emergency
  Management Agency
  (FEMA)
hyper-partisanship, 58,
  77–78

ICE, 26, 44. *See also*
  Immigration and
  Customs Enforcement
identity cards, 90–92. *See also*
  green cards
illegal aliens, 125
  defined, 326
illegal apprehensions, 219.
  *See also* border control
illegal immigration, 133
Illegal Immigration Reform
  and Immigrant
  Responsibility Act of
  1996 (IIRIRA), 18,
  28, 93, 97, 122, 314.
  *See also* border control;
  deportation, defined

IMMACT, 15–18, 314–315.
  *See also* Immigration Act
  of 1990
immediate relatives, 234. *See
  also* travel ban(s)
  defined, 328
immigrant, 142–145
  defined, 328
  and economy, 143–144
immigrant and
  nonimmigrant visas,
  233–234, 240–242
Immigration Act of 1990,
  15–18, 314–315
Immigration and Customs
  Enforcement. *See
  also* Department of
  Homeland Security
  (DHS)
Immigration Act of 1966,
  231–232
Immigration and
  Naturalization Act of
  October 3, 1965, 3–5,
  7, 9, 21, 46, 55, 73,
  117, 192, 311–312. *See
  also* Johnson, Lyndon
  B.; Kennedy, John F.
Immigration and
  Naturalization Service
  (INS), 14, 18–20, 23,
  60–61
  dissolved, 24, 45, 60
Immigration and
  Naturalization Service

Data Management
Improvement Act of
2000, 18, 118–119
Immigration Control and
Enforcement (ICE), 26,
58, 62, 67, 75, 77, 94,
98, 144, 146, 150, 158,
173, 223, 243–244, 259
immigration policy making,
58, 96–97
Immigration Reform and
Control Act (IRCA),
13–15, 17, 120–122,
205. *See also* employer
sanctions; guest-worker
program
synopsis of, 224–235,
313–314
*In America,* 300
inadmissibles, defined, 326
inclusion, defined, 326
IDENT (OBIM), 93–94
*Independent Review,* 292
Indochinese Refugees
Resettlement Program,
11, 312
Inhofe, Jim, 34
*INS v. Aguirre-Aguirre,* 1999,
316
*INS v. Cardoza-Fonesca,*
1987, 314
*INS v. Chadha et al.,* 1982,
313
INS. *See* Immigration and
Naturalization Service
(INS)

Intelligence Authorization
Act of 2004, 70
Intelligence Reform and
Terrorism Prevention
Act of 2004. *See
also* Intelligence
Authorization Act of
2004
International Energy
Economic Powers Act,
70
*International Migration
Review,* 162, 292
international terrorist cells,
67
investor immigrant, 91
defined, 326
Iran, 85, 92, 158
Iraq, 92
IRCA. *See* Immigration
Reform and Control Act
(IRCA)
Irish Lobby for Immigration
Reform, 74
Irish Republican Army, 24.
*See also* USA Patriot
Acts I and II
Islam, 147
Islamic African Relief
Agency, 70
Islamic American Relief
Agency, 70
Islamic State of Iraq and
Syria (ISIS), 28, 74,
154
IT systems, 58, 63

Jackson-Lee, Sheila,
189–190. *See also*
Congressional Black
Caucus; Dream Act;
Judiciary Committee,
House, Senate
Janis, Irving, 59, 270–271.
*See also* groupthink
*Jean v. Nelson,* 1986, 313
Jean-Pierre, Karine, 190–191.
*See also* MoveOn.org;
Obama, Barack
Jefferson, Thomas, 130–131
Jiminez, Cristina, 191. *See
also* United We Dream
Johnson, Jeh, 76–77,
191–192, 319. *See
also* DACA; DAPA;
Department of
Homeland Security
(DHS); Obama,
Barack
Johnson, Lyndon B., 10,
36, 192. *See also* Great
Society; Immigration
and Naturalization Act
of October 3, 1965;
Kennedy, John F.
Johnson, Sam, 32
Jordon Commission on
Immigration Reform,
1997, 315
*Journal of Contemporary
History,* 292–293
*Journal of Migration and
Human Security,* 293

Judiciary Act of 1789,
165–166
Judiciary Committee, House,
Senate, 32–33

Kanstroom, Daniel, 271
Keane, Tom, 36. *See also*
Clinton, Hillary
Kearon, Patrick, Elder,
144–145
Keely, Charles B., 261
Kelly, John, 81, 193, 99,
320. *See also* DACA;
DAPA; Department
of Homeland Security
(DHS); Dream Act;
Trump administration
Kemp-Roth bill, 135
Kennedy, Edward, 5, 75, 194.
*See also* Immigration
and Naturalization Act
of October 3, 1965;
Judiciary Committee,
House, Senate; Kennedy,
John F.; Kennedy-
Simpson bill; McCain-
Kennedy bill
Kennedy, John F., 4–5. *See
also* Immigration and
Naturalization Act of
October 3, 1965
Kennedy, Robert, 5. *See
also* Immigration and
Naturalization Act
of October 3, 1965;
Kennedy, John F.

Kerry, John, 96
Kerwin, Don, 194–195.
　　*See also* Catholic Legal
　　Immigration Network,
　　Inc. (CLINIC); Center
　　for Migration Studies
　　(CMS)
King, Steven, 35
*Kite Runner, The*, 300
Knake, Robert K., 266
Koch, Charles, 195. *See
　　also* Americans for
　　Prosperity; Cato
　　Institute; Freedom
　　Caucus
Koch, David, 158, 196.
　　*See also* Americans for
　　Prosperity
*Korematsu v. U.S.*, 1944, 311
Kowert, Paul, 271–272
Krauss, Elishia, 63
Kretsedemas, Philip, 262
Krikorian, Mark, 69, 161,
　　196–197. *See also*
　　Center for Immigration
　　Studies (CIS)
Kumar, Maria Teresa, 176,
　　197–198. *See also* travel
　　ban(s); Voto Latino

Labrador, Raul, 32
LaRaza, 74
Larson, Charles "Chuck,"
　　122–126
Lazarus, Emma, 150–151.
　　*See also* Statue of Liberty

League of Latin American
　　Citizens (LULAC),
　　16–17, 74. *See also*
　　Proposition 187
Leal, David, 268–269
legal immigration, 4, 12,
　　55, 57, 65, 67–68,
　　217–218
　　limits of, 12
legal permanent residence
　　(LPR), 91, 132
legalization of status, 230–232.
　　*See also* amnesty; earned
　　legalization
legislative process, 60
LeMay, Michael C.,
　　272–274
Levin, Brian, 163, 198–199.
　　*See also* Center for the
　　Study of Hate Crimes
　　and Extremism
libertarians, 73
*Liberty and Security in an Age
　　of Terrorism*, 301
Libya, 85, 158
Liddy, Marty, 125–130
Lieberman, Joseph, 20, 199.
　　*See also* Department
　　of Homeland Security
　　(DHS)
Limbaugh, Rush, 138
Lincoln, Abraham, 30
Lippert, Randy K., 274
Literacy Act of 1917,
　　308
Lofgren, Zoe, 32

lone-wolf terrorist, 28, 55,
163. *See also* terrorist
attacks of September 11,
2001; USA Patriot Act
of 2001
defined, 327
*LULAC et al. v. Wilson
et al.* (1995), 16–17,
314–315

Macoubrie, Ryan, 130–134
Macron, Emmanuel, 104
Madison, James, 78, 130
Magrath, Tim, 134–142
Malek, Alia, 274–275
management problems,
61–67. *See also*
Department of
Homeland Security
(DHS)
Manifest Law of 1819,
305–306
*Maria Full of Grace,* 301
Marsh, Jason, 267
Marshall, Dale Rogers, 263
Mayer, Jane, 275
Mazzoli, Romano, 13,
134–135, 313.
*See also* Immigration
Reform and Control
Act (IRCA); Simpson-
Mazzoli bill
McCain, John, 32, 34, 42,
73, 75, 199–200. *See
also* comprehensive
immigration reform bill;

Dream Act; Gang of
Eight, House, Senate;
McCain-Feingold bill;
McCain-Kennedy bill
McCain-Kennedy bill, 75
McCarran-Walter Act of
1952, 311
McConnell, Mitch, 41,
200–201. *See also*
DACA; DAPA; Obama
administration
Meissner, Doris, 275.
*See also* Immigration
and Naturalization
Service (INS)
Menendez, Robert, 32
merit immigration, 123,
133
Metro Denver Sanctuary
Coalition, 149
Mexico, 8, 11, 45, 74, 223.
*See also* border card,
defined
Mexican-US border, 8, 18,
35, 82, 221
unaccompanied children
from, 223
Michaels, Bob, 135,
138
*Michigan Law Review,*
293
Middle Easteners, 23
Migration Policy Institute,
276
Milwaukee, Wisconsin,
126–130

*Minnesota Law Review*, 293
Minutemen, 75, 172–173
Mirescu, Alexander,
    276–277
mission complexity, 63, 66,
    107
Mittelstadt, Michelle, 275
Mollenkopf, John, 268
Moretti, Enrico, 88. *See also*
    brain drain; brain hubs
Motomura, Hiroshi, 277
MoveOn.org, 170, 191
Muslim Americans, 66, 69
Muslim travel ban, 66, 83,
    161. *See also* Trump,
    Donald; *Trump v. Hawaii*
Muslims, 23, 44, 62–68,
    154–155
    immigrants of, 69
Myanmar (Karen refugees),
    126–127

Napolitano, Janet, 201–202,
    319. *See also* Department
    of Homeland Security
    (DHS)
North Atlantic Treaty
    Organization (NATO),
    91, 180
National Border
    Administration,
    proposal for, 88–89
National Conference of State
    Legislatures (NCSL),
    75, 170–171, 277
National Governors'
    Conference, 75

National Guard, 82–83
National Immigration
    Forum (NIF), 142, 145,
    171–172
National Immigration Law
    Center (NILC), 166,
    172
*National Journal*, 294
national origins quota
    system, 3, 5–6
National Research Council,
    277
*National Review*, 294
National Rifle Association
    (NRA), 172–173
National Security Entry-Exit
    Registration System
    (NSEERS), 25–26,
    92–93, 317
National Security Project, 72.
    *See also* American Civil
    Liberties Union (ACLU)
naturalization, 3–5
    defined, 327
Naturalization Act of 1798,
    131, 305
*New Jersey Law Journal*,
    294
Ngai, Mae M., 277–278
Nguyen, Tram, 278
Nicaraguans, 119. *See also*
    Central America
Nielsen, Kirstjen, 202–203.
    *See also* Department
    of Homeland Security
    (DHS)
No More Deaths, 74

nonimmigrant, defined, 327
Noorani, Ali, 142–145,
    278–279
North American Free Trade
    Agreement (NAFTA),
    91, 95, 314. *See also*
    Clinton, William J.
Northern Alliance in
    Afghanistan, 24. *See also*
    USA Patriot Act
NorthCom (Northern
    Command), 68

Obama, Barack, 3, 30–31,
    35, 37, 45, 80, 161,
    203–204, 319. *See
    also* DACA; DAPA;
    Department of
    Homeland Security
    (DHS)
Obama administration,
    30–35, 57, 76, 81,
    98–99, 129. *See also*
    DACA; DAPA
Office of Biometric Identity
    Management (OBIM),
    92–93
Office of Civil Rights and
    Civil Liberties (CRCL),
    71
Office of Homeland Security,
    20. *See also* Ridge, Tom
Office of Management and
    Budget, 173
Office of Principal Legal
    Advisor, 159–160.
    *See also* Immigration

Control and
    Enforcement (ICE)
O'Leary, Anna O., 279
Omnibus Anti-Drug Abuse
    Law (1986), 15
O'Neil, Tip, 135, 137–138
one-man, one-vote principle,
    79. See also *Reynolds v.
    Sims* (1964)
Operation Alliance, 15
Operation Enduring
    Freedom, 316
Operation Jump Start,
    82–83. *See also* border
    control; Obama, Barack
Operation Phalanx, 83. *See
    also* border control
Operation River Watch, 83.
    *See also* border control
Orreniris, Pia, 280
Orrick, William, 100. *See also*
    travel ban(s)
*Other Side of Immigration,
    The*, 301
overstayers, 26, 32, 56
    defined, 327

Pakistan, 92
passport, defined, 327
path to citizenship, 132
Patriot Act II, 22–24, 29, 68,
    72, 92. *See* USA Patriot
    Act
    anti-Patriot Act laws,
    67–68
*Patriot Act under Fire, The*,
    301–302

patriotic assimilation, 65–66
  defined, 327
patriots to foster checks and
  balances, 67
peacemaking process, 39
Pearl Harbor, 19
permanent resident, defined,
  327
Personal Responsibility and
  Work Opportunity Act
  of 1996, 315. *See also*
  Clinton, William J.
*Perspectives on Politics,* 294
Pew Hispanic Research
  Center, 17–18, 173–174,
  208–209
Pew Research Center polling
  data, 18, 174, 221
*Policy Studies Journal,* 295
political incorporation, 66
  defined, 327
*Political Psychology,* 295
*Political Science Quarterly,*
  295
preference system, 5–6
  categories of, 9
*Presidential Studies Quarterly,*
  295
prioritized deportations, 132
privacy concerns, 67–72. *See
  also* USA Patriot Acts
Proposition 187, 16, 141,
  314. *See also* Save Our
  State Initiative, 1994
prosecutorial discretion,
  defined, 327

protocol, defined, 327
*Public Interest,* 296
*Public Manager, The,* 296
public policymaking, 58
*Publius: The Journal of
  Federalism,* 296
pull factors, 74
  defined, 328
push factors, 74
  defined 328

Quota Act
  of 1921, 309
  of 1924, 309
  of 1929, 310
quota system, 4
Quran, 147. *See also* Islam

racial profiling, defined, 328
Rand Corporation, 105, 174
Reagan, Ronald, 11, 123,
  134, 169, 204–205.
  *See also* Immigration
  Reform and Control
  Act (IRCA); Republican
  Party
Reagan administration, 12,
  99
Real ID Act of 2003, 27–28,
  92, 207, 318
refugee, 10, 83, 126–127,
  143–144, 150
  defined, 328
Refugee Act of 1980, 10–11
refugee admissions, 9–10,
  224

Refugee Admissions Program, 9–10, 83, 224
refugee resettlement, 10, 150, 224, 312
Reich, Simon, 267
Renshon, Stanley, 280
Republican Party, 17, 73, 78, 80–81, 118, 124, 135–142, 156
anti-immigration reform, 122–126
request for detention, defined, 328
request for notification, defined, 328
rescinding DACA and DAPA. *See* Trump Executive Order, January 2018
*Review of Policy Research, The*, 296–297
*Reynolds v. Sims* (1964), 79
Ridge, Tom, 20, 55, 205–206. *See also* Bush, George W.; Department of Homeland Security (DHS)
Rivera, Geraldo, 280–281
Roberts, John, 85
Rohingya refugees, 129–130
Rosenblum, Marc, 281
Rost, Nori, 145–151. *See also* All Souls Unitarian Universalist Church; sanctuary church
Rostenkowski, Dan, 135

Rove, Karl, 158
Rubio, Marco, 32, 140
Rudolph, Christopher, 282
Ryan, Mary, 90. *See also* Department of State (DOS)

Salvadorans, 119. *See also* Central America; El Salvador
sanctuary cities, 37–38, 56, 68, 99, 144, 145–151. *See also* Secure Communities program
defined, 328
sanctuary coalition, 148
Sanders, Bernie, 73
Saudi Arabia, 92
Save Our Border First Act bill, H.R. 399, 2015, 35
Save Our State Initiative, 1994, 16, 314. *See also* Proposition 187
Schrug, Peter, 282
Schumer, Charles E., "Chuck," 32, 41, 206. *See also* comprehensive immigration reform bill; DACA; DAPA; Gang of Eight, House, Senate; Judiciary Committee, House, Senate
Scott Act of 1888, 307
Secure Communities program, 56, 75–76, 81, 97–99, 101, 108

Secure Electronic Network for Rapid Inspection (SENTRI), 95

Secure Fence Act of 2006, 28–29, 318

Select Commission on Immigration and Refugee Policy (SCIRP), 10–13, 178, 313. *See also* Carter, Jimmy; Immigration Reform and Control Act (IRCA)

Senate bill S. 744, 2014, 320. *See also* comprehensive immigration reform bill

Sensenbrenner, James, 207. *See also* Department of Homeland Security (DHS); Judiciary Committee, House, Senate; Real ID Act of 2003; USA Patriot Acts I and II

September 11 Commission, 70. *See also* terrorist attacks of September 11, 2001

Sessions, Jeff, 76, 100, 166, 207–208. *See also* Department of Justice (DOJ)

fired, 321

*Should State Be Able to Opt Out of the Refugee Resettlement Program?*, 302

Silicon Valley, 87, 103–104

Simon, Julian, 282–283

Simpson, Alan, 13, 134, 313. *See also* Simpson-Mazzoli bill

Simpson-Mazzoli bill, 13–14, 134–136, 313

Smart Border Action Plan, 94–95

Smith, William French, 12

Snyders, Timothy, 260–261

*Social Justice*, 297

*Social Science Quarterly*, 297

*Social Science Research*, 297–298

Social Security system, 57, 104–107

cards, 136

trust system of, 105

*Sociological Forum*, 298

Somalia, 85, 158

*Southern Economic Journal*, 298

southwest border apprehensions, 82

Speaker, Burke, 275

stakeholders, 58, 60

defined, 328

Stana, Richard M., 283

*Stanford Law Review*, 298–299

Start Up Visa Act, 94, 96, 104

Statue of Liberty, 3, 6, 150. *See also* Lazarus, Emma

STEM (Science, Technology, Engineering, and Mathematics), 104, 242

Strange, David, 269–270

Student and Exchange Visitor Information System (SEVIS), 102–103, 317

Sudan, 70. *See also* Muslim travel ban

Super Pac, 158

Suro, Roberto, 208–209. *See also* Pew Hispanic Research Center

symbolic performance results, 63–64

Syria, 74, 85, 158
  refugees from, 83, 117
  war in, 74

Tabb, David, 263

Taliban, 154

Tanden, Neera, 209–210. *See also* Center for American Progress; Clinton, Hillary

Tanton, John, 166. *See also* Federation for American Immigration Reform (FAIR)

Task Force on Immigration and Refugee Policy (1981), 12

task obfuscation, 63

Tea Party, 73, 140

temporary agricultural workers, 232–233. *See also* guest-worker program

terrorist attacks of September 11, 2001, 19–20, 59, 70, 86, 92, 316
  hysteria of, 70

Terrorist Information Awareness Program, 64

Terrorist Threat Integration Center, 317

Thornberry, Mac, 20

Tichenor, Daniel J., 283

Tienda, Maria, 283–284

Tirman, John, 284

Torr, James D., 284

Total Information Awareness Program (TIA), 70

Trafficking Victims Protection Reauthorizaton Act, 2013 (TVPRA), 34, 316

Transportation Security Administration (TSA), 62, 94. *See also* Department of Homeland Security (DHS)

Trautman, Laurie, 159, 210. *See also* Border Policy Research Institute (BPRI)

travel ban(s), 37–40, 43, 56, 66, 83–85, 107, 150,

155, 161, 169, 171, 320. *See also* Muslim travel ban

Treaty of Guadalupe Hidalgo, 306–307

Trump, David, 3, 30, 35–37, 39, 45, 56, 73–74, 76, 81, 83–84, 90, 97, 99, 100, 103, 134, 140–141, 169, 171–172, 175, 210–211

Trump administration, 35–37, 50, 65, 84–85, 87, 99, 106–107, 129, 155–157, 160–161, 169, 170

*Trump v. Hawaii,* 213, 250, 321

*Trump v. International Refugee Assistance Project* (June 26, 2017), 39

UN Protocol and Convention on the Status of Refugees, 312
Protocols on Human Trafficking and Immigrant Smuggling, 317

Unaccompanied by an Adult Children (UAC), 31, 34
apprehended, 223

unanticipated consequences, 11

unauthorized immigrants, 4, 7–8, 43, 55, 68, 72, 74, 76, 77, 81, 90–91
defined, 227, 318, 328

undocumented immigrants, 67, 125, 313, 329. See also *Jean v. Nelson,* 1986

unfunded mandates, 75
defined, 329

Unitarian/Universalist Church, 145–151
Colorado Springs, 146
Denver, 146

United Nations, Office of the High Commissioners for Refugees (UNHCR), 128–129

United States, 101–102, 120, 124–125

United We Dream, 29, 153, 175–176, 191

Uniting and Strengthening America by Providing Appropriate Tools to Intercept and Obstruct Terrorism Act. *See* USA Patriot Act I

U.S. Census Bureau, 7, 43–44

U.S. Citizenship and Immigration Services (UCIS), 42, 58, 66, 88–89, 91, 94, 173

U.S. Coast Guard, 19–20, 60–61, 63, 88–89, 94

U.S. Code of Statutes, 9, 21
U.S.-Mexico border, 37–38.
    *See also* border fence;
    border wall
U.S.S. Cole, 154, 316
U.S. Supreme Court, 78–79,
    83–84, 166
US VISIT, 92–93. *See also*
    National Security Entry-
    Exit Registration System
    (NSEERS)
USA Patriot Act of 2001,
    20–21, 69, 93, 102,
    155, 157, 161, 164,
    167, 172
    Patriot Act I, 317–318
    Patriot Act II of 2006, 318

Vernez, George, 261
Victims of Immigration
    Crime Enforcement
    (VOICE) Office, 38,
    321
visa absconders, 26
    applications and
        processing, 85–90
    defined, 329
    tightening of, 90–96
    Visa Condor, 87
    Visa Express, 86
    Visa Mantis, 87, 103
    Visa Waiver Program
        (VWP), 93
visa lottery, 65, 123
visa overstayers, 7

Voting Rights Act of 1965,
    79
Voto Latino, 176, 197. *See
    also* Kumar, Maria
    Teresa

Walker, Bob, 137
War Powers Act
    of 1918, 309
    of 1941, 310
Warner, Judith, 284
Warren, Elizabeth, 73
Washington, George, 30
Watson, Derrick, 39, 84,
    212–213. See also
    *Trump v. Hawaii*
West, Darrell M., 285
Western Hemisphere, 8, 89
    1976 Act, 312
    travel initiative of, 89
*White House Studies,* 299
Wilson, Pete, 17, 141.
    *See also* Proposition
    187; Save Our State
    Initiative
wiretaps, 68
*With Us or Against Us?,* 302
*Wong Kim Ark v. U.S.,* 1898,
    307
World Trade Center, NYC,
    154
World War II, 7
Wucker, Michelle, 285

xenophobia, defined, 329

*Yale Law Review,* 299
Yarmouth, John, 32
Yates, Sally, 38, 83, 213–214.
    *See also* Department of
    Justice (DOJ)
Yemen, 85, 92, 158, 316. *See
    also* travel ban(s)
*Yick Wo v. Hopkins,* 1886,
    307

Zakarian, Fareed, 86
Zavodny, Madelaine, 280

Zawahri, Ayman al, 154.
    *See also* fatwa, defined
zero-defects visa system,
    89
zero-tolerance policy, 76,
    87, 98, 144, 166, 173.
    *See also* Sessions, Jeff;
    Trump, Donald; Trump
    administration
Ziegler-McPherson,
    Christina A., 285–286
Zolberg, Aristide, 286

## About the Author

**Michael C. LeMay,** PhD, is professor emeritus from California State University-San Bernardino, where he served as director of the National Security Studies Program, an interdisciplinary master's degree program, and as chair of the Department of Political Science and assistant dean for student affairs for the College of Social and Behavioral Sciences. He has frequently written and presented papers at professional conferences on the topic of immigration. He has also written numerous journal articles, book chapters, published essays, and book reviews. He has published in the *International Migration Review, In Defense of the Alien, Journal of American Ethnic History, Southwestern Political Science Review, Teaching Political Science,* and the *National Civic Review.* He is the author of 30 academic books, more than a dozen of which are academic volumes dealing with immigration history and policy. His prior books on the subject are: *Homeland Security* (ABC-CLIO, 2018), *Religious Freedom in America* (ABC-CLIO, 2018), *U.S. Immigration Policy, Ethnicity, and Religion in American History* (Praeger, 2018), *Illegal Immigration: A Reference Handbook,* 2nd ed. (ABC-CLIO, 2015), *Doctors at the Borders: Immigration and the Rise of Public Health* (Praeger, 2015); series editor and contributing author of the three-volume series *Transforming America: Perspectives on Immigration* (ABC-CLIO, 2013), *Illegal Immigration,* 1st ed. (ABC-CLIO, 2007), *Guarding the Gates: Immigration and National Security* (Praeger Security International, 2006), *U.S. Immigration and Naturalization Laws and Issues: A Documentary History,* ed., with Elliott Barkan

(Greenwood, 1999), *Anatomy of a Public Policy: The Reform of Contemporary Immigration Law* (Praeger, 1994), *The Gatekeeper: Comparative Immigration Policy* (Praeger, 1989), *From Open Door to Dutch Door: An Analysis of U.S. Immigration Policy since 1820* (Praeger, 1987), and *The Struggle for Influence* (1985). Professor LeMay has written two textbooks that have considerable material related to these topics: *Public Administration: Clashing Values in the Administration of Public Policy*, 2nd ed. (2006) and *The Perennial Struggle*, 3rd ed. (2009). He frequently lectures on topics related to immigration history and policy. He loves to travel and has lectured around the world and has visited more than 100 cities in 40 countries. He has two works forthcoming: *The American Congress* (with Sara Hagedorn) (ABC-CLIO, 2019) and *The Immigration and Nationality Act of 1965: A Reference Guide* (Greenwood, 2020).

# ENGAGING WITH CONTEMPORARY CULTURE

*I commend Martyn Percy's new book to Anglican and Catholic laity, pastors, theologians, and bishops. All, with his sprightly prose drawing them in, will find themselves joining his search for authentic paths for Christian faith. All will also find something to disagree with. Percy's well-researched work is not a polite chat about how we can all get along better. His practical theology examines lived faith and ordinary life, where Christianity and culture meet.*
  Thomas Hughson, SJ, Marquette University, Milwaukee, USA

*Martyn Percy has provided an insightful and fresh approach to the dialogue between theology, church and world. He achieves this through a series of penetrating theological sketches touching the everyday life of churches and western culture. The accent is on engagement, the theology is practical and grounded. The result is an intellectually robust, accessible and provocative public theology. He shows himself to be a theologian at the cutting edge of contemporary Christian Theology. A joy to read and plenty of food for further engagement.*
  Stephen Pickard, School of Theology, Charles Sturt University, Australia

Theology and the churches are often considered to be at the margins of contemporary culture, frequently struggling for identity and attention. In this important new book Martyn Percy argues that a rich form of practical theological engagement is needed if the churches are to comprehend their situation in the modern world, thereby enabling them to engage more confidently with society. Drawing on a range of perspectives in the religion–culture debate, and from case studies in the USA and Europe, the book explores the myriad of ways in which culture is now shaping contemporary Christianity, and how vital an appreciation of this dynamic is for the self-understanding of churches and theology.

This book explores the crucial and continuing contribution that theology can make to public life, in an era that is often perceived to be dominated by consumerism and secularity. It will especially appeal to scholars of contemporary religion, practical theologians, and all those who are engaged in ministerial formation.

# Explorations in Practical, Pastoral and Empirical Theology

Series Editors: Leslie J. Francis, University of Wales, Bangor, UK and Jeff Astley, University of Durham and Director of the North of England Institute for Christian Education, UK

Theological reflection on the church's practice is now recognized as a significant element in theological studies in the academy and seminary. Ashgate's new series in practical, pastoral and empirical theology seeks to foster this resurgence of interest and encourage new developments in practical and applied aspects of theology worldwide. This timely series draws together a wide range of disciplinary approaches and empirical studies to embrace contemporary developments including: the expansion of research in empirical theology, psychological theology, ministry studies, public theology, Christian education and faith development; key issues of contemporary society such as health, ethics and the environment; and more traditional areas of concern such as pastoral care and counselling.

Other titles published in this series:

*A Reader on Preaching*
*Making Connections*
Edited by David Day, Jeff Astley and Leslie J. Francis

*Congregational Studies in the UK*
*Christianity in a Post-Christian Context*
Edited by Mathew Guest, Karin Tusting and Linda Woodhead

*Women's Faith Development*
*Patterns and Processes*
Nicola Slee

*Divine Revelation and Human Learning*
*A Christian Theory of Knowledge*
David Heywood

# Engaging with Contemporary Culture

## Christianity, Theology and the Concrete Church

MARTYN PERCY

ASHGATE

Published by
Ashgate Publishing Limited
Gower House
Croft Road
Aldershot
Hants GU11 3HR
England

Ashgate Publishing Company
Suite 420
101 Cherry Street
Burlington
VT 05401-4405
USA

Ashgate website: http://www.ashgate.com

**British Library Cataloguing in Publication Data**
Percy, Martyn
Engaging with contemporary culture : Christianity, theology and the concrete
   church. – (Explorations in practical, pastoral and empirical theology)
   1. Christianity and culture 2. Theology, Practical 3. Secularization (Theology)
   I. Title
   261

**Library of Congress Cataloging-in-Publication Data**
Percy, Martyn.
   Engaging with contemporary culture : Christianity, theology, and the concrete
church / Martyn Percy.—1st ed.
       p. cm.—(Explorations in practical, pastoral, and empirical theology)
   Includes bibliographical references and index.
   ISBN 0-7546-3259-8 (alk. paper) 1. Christianity and culture. 2. Theology,
Doctrinal. I. Title. II. Series.

   BR115.C8P37 2005
   261—dc22

2004013983

ISBN 0 7546 3259 8

Typeset by Tradespools, Frome, Somerset
Printed and bound in Great Britain by Antony Rowe Ltd, Chippenham

For Stewart, Nick and Tim

# Contents

*Acknowledgements*                                                          xi

**Introduction: Christianity, Theology and Contemporary Culture**            1
    Practical theology: the background                    7
    Practical theology as methodology                    10
    Practical theology: further reflections              12

**PART I  THEOLOGY, CHURCH AND CONTEMPORARY
       CULTURE**

**1  Church, Authority and the Culture of Credibility**                     19
    Roman Catholicism in North America: four writers in dialogue   19
    Teaching authority                                   29
    Authenticity and authority                          32
    Authority and discipleship                          37

**2  Christianity and Consumerism**                                         41
    Preamble: Going to church in Atlanta                41
    Religious studies, culture and contemporary Christianity   43
    Choice, consumerism and Christianity                46
    Christmas, Christianity and culture                  54
    Christianity in a secular society                   59

**3  Theology and Cultural Challenge**                                      63
    Introduction                                        63
    The deductive possibility: John Milbank and Radical
      Orthodoxy                                66
    The reductive possibility: Lieven Boeve and reflexive theology   70
    The inductive possibility: David Martin and socio-theology   74
    Reflexive religion and contemporary culture         78
    Theological engagement                              83

**PART II  ORDINARY THEOLOGY**

**4  Acuity, Clarity and Practical Wisdom**                                 89
    Introduction                                        89
    Practical theology, ecclesiology and formation      96

Describing faith: some perspectives                        99
What is theological knowledge?                             102
World-views                                                106
Summary                                                    109

**5   Mother Church**                                      **111**
Introduction                                               111
Mother church                                              114
Metaphor and metamorphosis                                 118
The nature of theology                                     122
The nature of the church                                   125
The nature of theological education                        129
Conclusion                                                 132

**6   Formation, Transformation and Liberation**          **133**
Introduction                                               133
Transformation                                             136
Liberation                                                 139
Wisdom                                                     143
Education and vocation                                     147
Understanding                                              149
Conclusion                                                 153

**PART III   THEOLOGICAL CULTURE AND THE
              CONCRETE CHURCH**

**7   Adventure and Atrophy in a Charismatic Movement**   **157**
Introduction                                               157
Interpreting Toronto: a methodological sketch             160
Immersed in the river of revival: returning to Toronto    166
Adventure and atrophy                                      172
Conclusion                                                 176

**8   A Blessed Rage for Order**                          **181**
The origin and anatomy of reform                          182
Reform: an ethnographic sketch                            187
An interpretative horizon                                 189
Money, sex and power                                       194
Reading Reform differently                                198
Conclusion                                                 203

**9   Comic Turns**                                       **207**
Introduction                                               207
Anglicanism as irony and comedy                           209

Anglicanism: comic and ironic 212
Excursion: Continuing Anglican Churches as alternative comedy 217
Further reflections 220
The cultural nature of Anglican Communion 223
Comic endings: what is the future for the Anglican
  Communion? 227
Concluding and unscientific postscript: quadripolar
  Anglicanism 228

**Conclusion: Authentic Engagement** **231**

*Bibliography* 237
*Index* 251

# Acknowledgements

I am grateful to a number of individuals and institutions in the writing of this book. To Hartford Seminary for graciously giving me the time and space to continue my research during the summer of 2002, and for the ongoing privilege of serving there as an Adjunct Professor for their estimable theology and ministry programmes. To the American Academy of Religion for providing me with a grant to undertake more fieldwork in Toronto in November of 2002. And, once again, to the Trustees of the Lincoln Theological Institute for their support and encouragement.

I would also like to acknowledge the following publications, and thank them for permission to redevelop material that has been previously published: *Reviews in Religions and Theology/Conversations* (Blackwell) in Chapter 1; *Creative Christian Leadership* (edited by John Nelson), SCM-Canterbury Press, 2004 in Chapter 4. Earlier versions of the essays contained in Part III (Chapters 7, 8 and 9) of the book have been published in the *Journal of Contemporary Religion*, the *Journal of Anglican Studies* and *Ecclesiology* respectively.

I would also like to thank the following societies and institutions for the opportunity to develop materials that were originally delivered as lectures: the World Council of Churches (parts of Chapters 1 and 4); the American Association of the Sociology of Religion (for papers given in Atlanta in 2003 and San Francisco in 2004 – Chapters 3 and 9 respectively); the contextual theology seminar at the University of Manchester (Chapter 2); and the American Academy of Religion (Chapter 7).

Lastly, I once again thank my family for their forbearance during the writing of this book. Their love and support is, as always, beyond price.

Martyn Percy

# Introduction

# Christianity, Theology and Contemporary Culture

One of the most pressing challenges faced by theology and the churches is how to engage with contemporary culture. For many, engagement, it seems, is a contested and risky affair. Some theological and ecclesiological traditions feel so threatened by the prospect of being overwhelmed or consumed by the task of engagement that they retreat before they have advanced; standing apart from key issues and debates in culture is seen to be the only way of protecting the integrity and identity of the Christian tradition. Others prefer a different strategy – namely one of deep engagement – but, in so doing, can find themselves so transformed that they become alienated from their roots. In either form of engagement, a degree of cultural bewilderment seems inevitable. A Venetian proverb sums up the dilemma: 'The artist swims in the sea, but the critic stands on the shore.'

It is my contention that theology and the churches do not have the luxury of such a choice. To engage with contemporary culture, theology and ecclesiology needs to be both critical and artistic. It needs to be at home in the sea and on the shore. It needs to be able to immerse itself in the turbulence of the waves of the sea, and yet stand apart, retaining a critical distance from the vantage-point of the shore. I further hold that the discipline of practical theology offers the possibility of such reflexivity, and this book is therefore an attempt to sketch some possibilities for the discipline in its engagement with contemporary culture. Such engagements require theology to be open to the insights of cultural studies and alert to the ways in which contemporary culture is shaping religion.

Whilst the term 'cultural studies' is often used very broadly, insofar as it pertains to all aspects of the study of culture, it can also be used more precisely to refer to a particular range of issues and disciplines. Classically, the disciplines of cultural studies have tended to include ethnography, literary criticism and socio-biology; in turn, these disciplines have touched feminism, Marxism, semiotics, aesthetics; and in turn, the field has then extended to include areas of inquiry such as consumption, production, race, class, gender and even religion.

One problem with defining cultural studies lies with the different meanings of 'culture', which vary across contexts. That said, the concept, at least when used academically, is proximate to the notion of culture used in social or cultural anthropology. Instead of being absorbed by 'high' theories of culture, or indeed with sociological meta-theories that are concerned with society, it concentrates on the world in which humanity both lives and creates. In this

respect, the study of culture recognizes that human beings exceed that natural world which is their context. Thus, 'agriculture' and 'horticulture' recognize that humanity does something to its environment; it builds and creates, and it also uses a language to describe itself and its activity. This opens up the possibility of studying communication, power relations, values, aesthetics and meaning. Culture is, put simply, the study of what is overlaid, built or imposed on the natural environment. It is therefore concerned with 'artificiality' and the meanings that are given to such 'things' (see Highmore, 2002; Strinati, 1995; Williams, 1986, amongst others).

A project that sets out to engage theologically with culture is therefore immediately faced with some dynamics that it needs to recognize from the outset. First, theology does not precede culture; theology is itself a discrete kind of culture – a system of language, meaning and power relations that attempts to theorize about the knowledge and place of God in the world. Second, churches and other religious institutions are themselves 'cultures', so a discipline such as ecclesiology, can learn much from cultural studies. Third, there is a need to bring theology into some kind of engagement with culture and cultural studies. Moreover, this cannot simply be about 'high' theories of theology engaging with 'high' forms of cultural studies. Granted, such dialogues and synergies will have their uses, but the simpler (and arguably more urgent) task of engaging with everyday life should not be overlooked (cf. Astley, 2002).

Several factors have prompted the writing of this book. At the outset, I wanted to continue developing the agenda begun in *Salt of the Earth; Religious Resilience in a Secular Age* (2001), which had argued for a range of theological and ecclesiological engagements with contemporary culture. In this volume, however, readers will be aware that the use of anthropology (especially Geertz; see also Davies, 2002), congregational studies (especially Hopewell), ethnography (Highmore, 2002; Bender, 2003), and practical theology (Browning, 1991; Farley, 2003) is much more focused. There is also a more concerted attempt to engage with everyday life, especially ecclesial life (see Part III). In this respect, the volume as a whole has a much more explicit ecclesiological focus.

I have also been fortunate to find that *Salt of the Earth* has prompted others to write on Christianity and contemporary culture, and am especially grateful for Ian Markham's critique and modification of my work in his *A Theology of Engagement* (2003). Furthermore, there is now evidence for a burgeoning volume of theological reflection that addresses contemporary culture. Recent work by Kathryn Tanner (*Theories of Culture: A New Agenda for Theology*, 1997) and Delwin Brown, Sheila Davaney and Kathryn Tanner (*Converging on Culture*, 2001), along with a host of others, are now establishing this field as both normative and critical for theologians. There are also fresh and innovative approaches to theology (for example, Jeff Astley's fine *Ordinary Theology*, 2002), and new initiatives evident in the field of ecclesiology, pioneered by scholars such as Nicholas Healy (*Church, World and Christian Life: Practical–Prophetic Ecclesiology*, 2000) and Lewis Mudge (*Rethinking the Beloved Community: Ecclesiology, Hermeneutics and Social Theory*, 2001). This

volume simply seeks to continue and extend the engagements and dialogues that others have begun, and enlarge the possibilities for studying theology, Christianity and contemporary culture.

One of the reasons for pursuing the academic agenda (theology, ecclesiology, Christianity and contemporary culture), and why it is so crucial, is that it continues to be, to a large extent, countercultural. Since the early 1960s both the academy and the popular public imagination have been in the grip of secularization theories, namely the simple assertion that as society progressively becomes more modern so it will lose its religious heritage and interests. But in the last ten years, a significant amount of revisionism has been taking place. Most scholars have realized that modernization merely heightens the role of religion on the public stage. That said, no one can survey contemporary cultural life, at least in Western Europe, and conclude that religion is as strong as it once was. But neither is it evaporating in the way that sociologists of religion once predicted. In truth, the socio-cultural changes are more complex than any single or simple theory of secularization can normally enunciate. But what, then, are the factors that have prompted cultural and religious change? Several brief points need to be made here.

First, the rise of religious pluralism has had a marked impact on religion over the past three centuries. However, this pluralism plays out differently across the continents. In Britain, the passing of the 1689 Toleration Act seriously undermined the grounds for enforcing uniform religious practice on the population. 'Dissenting traditions' steadily gained in number and influence, and this weakened the grip of 'state' religion (cf. McCleod and Ustorf, 2003).

Second, the impact of religious pluralism in America had a quite different effect. The absence of officially sanctioned religion for the populace led to a flourishing culture of religious competition that still thrives today. Religion is part of the overall commodification of American life, and choices, as in so many spheres of ordinary life, closely identify individuals and communities (see P. Ward, 2002 and Cronin, 2000). At least 50 per cent of the population go to church, and many more than this identify with a denomination or place of worship.

Third, Western Europe witnessed a gradual, but persistent, loosening of ties between church and state. This led to the gradual decrease in the power of the churches in prominent spheres of public life. In turn, this led to a decline in religious practice, which was only occasionally halted by popular revivals and other movements. (However, Europe is the exception, globally, not the rule. For the rest of the world, religious revival and growth is comparatively normal, even with the growth of modernization and consumerism.)

Fourth, there has been a general agenda of social 'liberalizing' throughout the past century. Laws on abortion, obscenity, marriage, divorce and homosexuality have all correlated with a set of cultural, political and social trends that has seen religion pushed from the public sphere to that of the private. Increasingly, performing religious tasks, duties and rituals is seen as something 'private' that is undertaken in leisure time. Fewer and fewer Roman Catholics attend confession on a regular basis; holy days of obligation, unless they fall on Sundays, are unlikely to be keenly observed.

Fifth, the decline of associations in general has had a deleterious impact upon religious institutions. Although scholars such as Grace Davie have suggested that religion has fared better than, say, trade unions, it remains the case that modern Western society (including America) is entering a 'post-associational' state (Putnam, 2000). Individuals in society are increasingly disconnected from one another, as 'soft' social structures such as the Masons, Odd Fellows and the Women's Institute have rapidly disintegrated. What has replaced these social ties is consumerism and the 'negative social capital' of television and other forms of media, which have become the new electronic public sphere.

Sixth, there is an increasing fluidity about how religious, moral and political beliefs are held within modernity (Bauman, 2000). Consumerism infects not only practice and adherence, but also alters the landscape of belief. Few Christians in the West, even those committed to various forms of conservative belief, will subscribe to literal interpretations of biblical stories or to historic understandings of doctrines, such as hell. In what Bauman calls our 'liquid modernity', more fluid forms of association and belief have sprung up, which, whilst still allowing for the possibility of meta-narratives, nonetheless relate to them differently in the twenty-first century.

Seventh, and finally, the rise of spirituality, in its various 'alternative', 'vernacular', 'folk' and other forms, continues to question the dominance of secularization theories on the landscape of the academy and the public imagination. France, a country where secularity is apparently deep and pervasive, can still boast 40 000 fortune-tellers. Most British newspapers (not just the tabloids) will have a daily or weekly horoscope, fronted by a renowned astrologer. Spirituality is a more fluid (modern?) and pervasive expression of the religious sentiments that continue to shape everyday life in a myriad ways. Theological engagements with culture, then, need to take a serious account of the grounded reality of religion in its typical contexts and situations, and not simply engage with religion conceptually, or as a 'high' and overdefined culture.

So, this book sets out to address the Christianity and culture 'problem', as well as the interrogating of appropriate theological sources and methods for ecclesiology, by exploring and testing a variety of approaches in three separate sections. Part I examines the engagement of theology, religious studies, missiology and ecclesiology with contemporary culture. Part II explores the nature of practical theology and examines the nature of theological education as it relates to churches, Christianity and culture. It also attempts to outline a different vision for theology from that of Radical Orthodoxy, which is briefly critiqued in Chapter 3. Part III, using ethnographies, the work of James Hopewell and Clifford Geertz, takes a more ecclesial turn, and explores (successively) church congregations, movements and denominations as forms of culture. (To the best of my knowledge, this is the first time Hopewellian analytical frameworks have been used to extend our knowledge of ecclesiology beyond congregations, and explore movements within the church and also examine the life and character of a denomination.)

The conclusion argues that, although Christianity is bound to paradox (that is, seemingly contradictory positions or statements) in its theological

engagement with culture, this is in itself a sacramental paradigm, rooted in the revelation of God – who is revealed through the ordinary and in agents whose 'nature' (whether ordinary or transformed) are contestable. The paradoxical nature of forms of theological engagement with culture are therefore best resolved in faithfully conceived reflexive theology and ecclesiology, dialogue and further theological reflection. Methodologically, the argument turns towards arguing for a richer form of practical theology that takes 'ordinary Christianity' more seriously and, in so doing, restores some sense of public theology as a critical and yet affirming discourse that is engaged with contemporary culture.

Readers may naturally wonder why this range of issues and particular essays are addressed, and not others. I am more than aware that the Christianity and culture debate is one of the larger and more perplexing fields for theology to engage in. For myself, I have naturally had to write as a male Caucasian Western writer, who sees the subject he addresses from within inside his own ecclesiological and theological traditions. Therefore, I can only point to, following Ricoeur, the 'authorial intention' of the work and recognize that these essays will set off different trains of thought for the reader, which cannot be known (let alone controlled). Ultimately, one can only hope to provide a series of insights, confessionally shaped illuminations and methodological slants that can help guide the reader through the myriad questions and subjects. To be comprehensive is not possible. However, each chapter is an essay in its own right and is an attempt to get at the meanings of ecclesiology and the Christianity and culture debate from various vantage-points (cf. Mudge, 2001, p. 12). Some of the work will require readers to dig more deeply; other parts of the book will simply provide a critically reflective resonance.

That said, some may still want to question why the emphasis is on the here and now; on the social situation of the churches; on what they actually *do* or might think about doing. Leaving aside my concern to address ecclesial concreteness (rather than hypothetical theological correlative theories of what the church could or should be like), there are at least three reasons that justify the ecclesial focus for tackling the theology–Christianity–culture debate.

First, I am clear that churches are cultures themselves, and therefore both form and are formed in relation to their contexts. This has an impact on public theology, ecclesial shape and wider social life. Second, much contemporary Christian faith and practice now bypasses traditional or formal ecclesiology. The situation is, to quote Mudge, one of 'post-denominational Christianity' (2001, p. 3), where many existing denominations find themselves increasingly disabled and new experimental countercultural and pro-cultural Christian communities are on the rise (ibid., p. 64). Third, new cultural shapes for expressing and embodying Christianity make the Christianity and culture debate a key area of engagement both for theology and for churches.

To give one example that encapsulates what I have expressed in the three previous points, I can point to a local Anglican–Baptist ecumenical church partnership, with an Evangelical and Charismatic identity which nestles in one of the more prosperous suburbs of my native Sheffield. The church of St Thomas Crookes has an interesting history with experimentation. It was here

that the postmodern 'Nine O'clock Service' (NOS) was born out of the 'Nine O'clock Community', a fusion of Matthew Fox's creation spirituality, various types of theology, hi-tech worship and other elements fused together to create a regular 'planetary mass' for the worshippers. However, the experiment ended in acrimony, and the church literally imploded, when the leader of the church, the Revd Chris Brain, was found to have been engaged in a level of sexual impropriety.

Nonetheless, this same church has continued its tradition of cutting-edge experimentation. It has risen, phoenix-like, from the warm ashes of the scandal that threatened to consume it. Under its new leader, the Revd Mike Breen, it has recently begun its own religious order, with the vicar becoming the Superior. The Order of Mission is Protestant, Charismatic and Evangelical, but has developed a system of tertiary association, as well as encouraging full members of the Order who are committed to a daily cycle of prayer and living in community. The church has bought and developed a new complex – Philadelphia – to enable the evangelization of inner cities throughout northern England. Members of the new Order describe the Philadelphia complex as a 'monastery in an urban setting, for the express purpose of mission'. Meanwhile, the new Superior – embodying the synthesis of globalization and commitment to the local (that is, 'glocal') – now divides his time between a new project in Phoenix, Arizona, and helping to establish new cells of the Order across the largely un-Christianized landscape of England's northern cities and urban connurbations.

The Philadelphia project and the Order of Mission mark a new development in ecclesiological patterning. The Order constitutes a new self-conscious fusion of Charismatic, Evangelical, Catholic and postmodern spiritualities. The order, organization and worship that characterizes the meetings seems to be perfectly in tune with the needs and desires of Christians drawn from the – it has to be said – mostly articulate and professional middle class of a postindustrial city at the turn of the third millennium. But it is exactly this kind of mutation that is taking place in religious life within contemporary culture that makes the task of hospitable and interdisciplinary methods in ecclesiology more urgent than ever, both for the academy and for the church as a whole. It will no longer suffice to speak of churches, in their embodiment of Christ, being 'for' or 'against' culture. The cultural map of the third millennium needs a more complex system of signs and symbols to represent the grounded reality of Christianity.

With these observations in mind, it is worth attempting to say something, finally, about the situation of the churches (and theology) within the context of the twenty-first century. The renewal of interest in religion in the postmodern situation is not without its price and irony. In contemporary postmodern culture, fluidity has replaced the concrete, and certainties have given way to subjectivity and ambiguity. As Lyotard reminds us, '... postmodernism is "incredulity at metanarratives"' (1984, viii). And as Huston Smith suggests, postmodernism is 'ambiguity elevated to apotheosis' (1990, p. 661). Postmodernism is, of course, not a systematic philosophical system; it is more of a mood and a socio-cultural force (cf. Rengger, 1995). In that sense, the challenge of postmodernism to religion lies in the very nature of the culture in

which it now finds itself embedded. This is a culture that accepts its own fragmentation and its lack of obvious moral or cultural coherence.

In such a context, religion undoubtedly lives – but no longer as a meta-narrative. It is, rather, one of the many ideologies and activities that competes for time and interest in an increasingly ephemeral public sphere. Under such conditions, churches and theology have at least three tasks: first, to be able to 'higgle' – the old English (agricultural) word that describes the process of continuing to affect things by degrees; second, to be able to 'thole' – an old Irish word that describes the process of survival under adverse conditions (for example, 'tholing' through bad times at work, or perhaps through a difficult relationship); and third, to be engaged in renewal. Now, renewal can be read in two senses here. It can mean a process of recovery and restoration, but it can also mean replacement. Here I want to suggest that both senses are implied for the churches and theology. The Christian tradition must face the present and the future, but it cannot neglect its past. Correspondingly, for churches and theologians alike, the possibilities and potential for practical theology are especially rich, since the discipline is committed to conversation (with other, non-theological disciplines and with the grounded reality of ordinary situations), as well as bearing faithful spiritual and hermeneutical witness to the Christian tradition. In the essays and sketches that follow, practical theological reasoning has been deployed, in a variety of arenas, in order to test and clarify the forms of theological and ecclesial engagement with contemporary culture that exist at the beginning of the third millennium.

## Practical Theology: The Background

The most typical kinds of theological engagement with contemporary culture are confessionally rooted and 'applied'. In other words, they are concerned to defend an existing tradition, and set about doing so by applying biblical particularities or theological priorities to perceived problems that require their attention. Roman Catholic, Evangelical and liberal traditions are all capable of engagement at this level, and an abundance of theological literature exists that either affirms or critiques culture from such standpoints. That said, a much more rarely encountered strategy is one whereby the theological or ecclesial tradition recognizes itself to be part of a discrete culture and then sets itself the task of undertaking several types of dialogue with other cultures. This encounter-based approach is far riskier, since it virtually anticipates change on the side of the inquirer. To *truly* listen will mean being open to the possibility of change (cf. Markham, 2003, p. 48ff). Moreover, I hold that it is precisely this kind of challenge that should, and could, help shape the discipline and practice of ecclesiology.

Having said that, some aspects of theological engagements with culture are less about reception and more to do with change and conversion. Just as there is a balance to be struck in religious resilience between resistance and adaptation, or assimilation and confrontation (Percy, 2001; Markham, 2003), so in engagement there is an equilibrium to be sought between passivity and

activity, and receiving and responding. I mention this, since it can sometimes be assumed that any methodology which is crafted for the purposes of inquiry and engagement must somehow be 'neutral'; and where neutrality cannot be located, some kind of confessional bias can be assumed. This is unfortunate, since most scholars in the social sciences would readily admit that there is an inherent partiality in any methodology. Sociology assumes that religion is social; anthropology assumes that it is cultural; and theology assumes that it is 'real', and irreducible. I accept these shortcomings in theories that might guide any method of inquiry. However, it is important to state from the outset that here, in this book, the methodologies are already acknowledged as being in some sense prejudicial. As Bauman notes:

> There is no choice between 'engaged' and 'neutral' ways of doing sociology. A non-committal sociology is an impossibility. Seeking a morally neutral stance among the many brands of sociology practised today...would be a vain effort.... (Bauman, 2000, p. 216)

As readers will discover, the subtext of many of the chapters in this book is that 'ecclesiology itself is a kind of social theory' (Mudge, 2001, p. 12). Contrary to Radical Orthodoxy, the use of, and dialogue with, the social sciences herein is intended to make a richer kind of theology that *engages with this world*. I do not hold, as Milbank does, that social sciences (including political theory) simply consume or nullify theology whenever any kind of fusion takes place. Ecclesiology, based on (or understood as) social theory can read and interpret the stories of the people of God, who are themselves reading the story of God through their tradition, even as they are 'performed' by it. Some understanding of concrete social and ecclesial existence is therefore vital if the churches are to truly engage with the cultures which are their contexts. Correspondingly, I hold (along with Healy and Mudge) that ecclesiology must make full use of non-theological methods and insights, which will help the church to think of itself as an organization, as well as a 'text' that is read and expressed. Thus, the underlying thread of the argument in this book is for a sociologically informed theology (which is, per se, an ecclesiology), and for a cultural–linguistic understanding of Christianity (following Lindbeck) that pays attention to the grounded reality of the church and the cultures that congregations inhabit.

It is for this reason that practical theology is the preferred methodological mode of inquiry that is adopted in the explorations that follow. To be sure, there are many types of practical theology, and it is not my purpose here to rehearse the various schools of thought that ultimately comprises a rich methodological field of inquiry. Fundamentally, practical theology is rooted in a determined form of research that often begins by learning to *listen deeply* and *well* – giving a subject or issue some serious and respectful non-directive attention in the first instance, whilst not foreclosing on the possibility of critiques and the development of a critical practical theology. The listening is undertaken in order to: provide some systematic ordering of complex and contrary materials; to reach some intelligible discernment about their shape and scope; to offer some critical reflection on relevant issues, ideas and

theories; and, finally, to discover fresh theological insight. Some of the basic tools for the above would comprise ethnography, fieldwork, interviews, textual analysis and the like.

Of course, no research takes place in a vacuum. In the arts, humanities and social sciences it is very often situated between: theories and practices; ideal situations and ideas; real situations and thoughts; blueprints for the world and concrete reality; modernity and postmodernity. We might also say that research in religion is often caught between the general and the particular; between the local and the macro. Nonetheless, research is normally about making more sense of situations than those people who are in them can normally manage; it is about genuine and free inquiry. Thus, research can be defined as re-searching – retelling or renarrating and reconstructing – either the theories that failed to deliver a sound analysis, or the 'facts' themselves. Re-searching, retelling and reconstructing are critical, related yet distinct stages within the overall penumbra of research. Their sequencing within a study – either linear, which can either be a matter of progression, or a spiral of interaction – requires the researcher to separate out and yet connect description (a range of perspectives), interpretation (a range of options) and analysis (a range of critical perspectives), leading finally to the redescription of the original issue or topic under investigation.

Since practical theology is a listening and reflective discipline, it does not seek to be dogmatic in its engagements:

> Practical theology is a critical and constructive reflection within a living community about human experience and interaction, involving a correlation of the Christian story and other perspectives, leading to an interpretation of meaning and value, and resulting in everyday guidelines and skills for the formation of persons and communities. (Poling and Miller, 1985, p. 62)

There are, of course, several other ways of describing the discipline and its focus. For Woodward and Pattison practical theology is 'a place where religious belief, tradition and practice meets contemporary experiences, questions and actions and conducts dialogue that is mutually enriching, intellectually critical and practically transforming' (2000, p. 5). For Elaine Graham it is transforming practice – the articulation and excavation of sources and norms of Christian practice, a form of *phronesis* (practical wisdom) that helps churches to practise what they preach and preach what they practise. For Duncan Forrester, it is 'the theological discipline which is primarily concerned with the interaction of belief and behaviour' (Forrester, 2000, p. 10). And for Don Browning, practical theology is utterly fundamental:

> ...all theological thinking...is essentially practical. The social and intellectual context in which theology is brought into conversation with the vision implicit in pastoral practice itself, and with the normative interpretations of the faith handed down in the traditions of the church. Theology thus arises from practice, moves into theory, and is then put into practice again.... (Browning, 1991; cf. Woodward and Pattison, 2000, p. 6)

**Practical Theology as Methodology**

According to Van der Ven (1998), there are four functions in the work of scholarship. The first is 'discovery research'; the second is 'integrative theoretical research'; the third is 'applied research'; and the fourth is 'the scholarship of teaching'. The distinction is useful, since it closely corresponds to the matrix of functions within which practical theology both situates and describes itself. As a methodology, it is critical, empathetic and reflective, but also geared towards transformation and learning. It treats discovery, integration, theory, application and teaching – and their relationship – with utmost seriousness. Thus, in any consideration of theological research and education, there is a necessary interest in not only attending to all four of the functions that Van der Ven identifies, but also investigating the extent to which they interrelate. This is a vital task for the field of theological and religious studies.

A piece of research is, ultimately, a review, reconsideration and a return – perhaps leading to a revolution; this is comparable to the transformative agenda of practical theology at work. It is this type of approach that allows us to study apparently simple things, such as a funeral tea (cf. Clark, 1982) or to ask a basic question, such as: 'Where is the theology of this group located?' Is it in their creeds and articles of faith? Or is it in their habits, customs, rituals and stories? And if the latter, how do we best discover and study them? And once we have discovered them, how do we read and interpret them? And, finally, what are the implications of such studies for the academy, with its methodologies and present understandings? (To help me address such issues, I have leant heavily on the interpretative framework of James Hopewell (1987), and some of the possibilities for his work being applied are sketched in Part Three. Readers who are familiar with my work will also note that this has involved a more anthropological turn in my writing, which has flavoured several of the chapters.)

So to repeat, the key to successful researching in religion lies in establishing that the knowledge we have is inadequate and insufficient, or even 'wrong', despite appearances to the contrary (for example, what we think we know about a church). It lies in identifying new knowledge, or how knowledge reinterpreted, might change the way in which we look at a specific topic or field (for example, history or religion). It then rests on using an established methodology to help answer a set of research questions (which may not have been asked before) and then establishing a *critical* relationship with that methodology. Finally, it leads us into a situation where we can begin to say something entirely new about the apparently familiar.

In a comparable vein, Ziebertz argues that 'practical' theology is not the opposite of 'theoretical'. Practical theology is not like systematic theological disciplines, since it focuses on 'the practice of religion ... real-life human acting within religious practice rather than logic ...'. However, practical theology does not merely seek to describe what it sees, but also to try to come to some understanding of it. In so doing, it habitually turns to the full range of social sciences to gain a deeper understanding of the social situations that it is

engaging with (Ziebertz in Roebben and Warren, 2001, pp. 105ff). In this respect there is something essentially hospitable about practical theology. It does not stand on its own dignity; it seeks partnerships and conversations at every stage. It is a fluid methodology fully in tune with Bauman's 'liquid modernity'.

All this, it seems to me, takes the would-be practical theologian well beyond the compass of merely 'reflecting' on ecclesial and cultural situations from a theological perspective, let alone trying to be 'applied'. Practical theology, at its richest, is a form of thinking that allows a range of methods to come together, to be 'tested' by the issues they are addressing, and for some degree of critical fusion to emerge. It is for this reason that I prefer the term 'refracted' to 'reflected' or 'applied' when considering how practical theology might engage with contemporary culture. The idea that the truth and purposes of God are 'refracted' – spread like a band of colour, as it were – is particularly compelling for the issue at hand. A refractive strategy is also, analogically, a good 'fit' for the fusions and strands that make up any one 'culture'. Strictly speaking, of course, 'culture' is a contested nest of issues and categories, and it could be argued that a process of refraction is required for the purposes of separation and illumination.

So to speak of theological refraction within culture is to suggest that there is a fit between the explanatory and analytical process and its subject. Refraction – as a strategy – allows disciplines and issues to pass through one another, and through so doing 'reform themselves in such a way as to manifest their capacity to mediate the primary vitality of life and understanding – that is, to manifest their capacity to integrate that through which they have passed into *their* truth (cf. Hardy, 1996, pp. 1, 203, 323–26). Put more simply, refraction is a proper dispersal of light into its constituent bands of colour, as it passes through a glass prism. In a consideration of theology, church and contemporary culture – which is rightly concerned with sociology, theology, anthropology, cultural studies and more besides – it is vital that the whole 'issue' passes through each of these 'prisms' and that each of these then sees how its own truth is effected by the refractive process.

In theological refraction (or any other discipline), for example, theology can fulfil itself through another discipline and, in so doing, enhance its own capacity to reflect, focus and enhance its primary task. To take this a stage further, refraction is in place for the clear sight of the perceptor. Only when things are 'correctly' perceived – the whole picture taken in, as it were, and processed – can the objects of refraction be addressed, affirmed or changed. Refraction is a process which divides 'strands' and then reconfigures them into an image or an interpretation. Because culture and religion are complicated 'things' to see, and often 'blurred', it is essential that the refraction is as dense and accurate as possible.

Refraction does not just mean 'interdisciplinary'. The dispersal of light – or the sifting of elements and compounds when the term is deployed in chemistry – is about a purification and intensification of original sources. When one light is refracted, the subsequent bands of light can be dazzling. But the actual refraction is not the goal. The actual goal is to discover fuller ways of reflecting

and focusing life in this or that band of colour, and not only gaining understanding *in* it, but also *from* it. Refraction, then, is the transformation of light as it passes from one medium to another; as this is done, different images are formed and experienced, and light itself is seen in a different light.

To see the issue of religion and culture as something that requires refraction is to rescue it from 'simply' being *reflected* upon. Too much reflection takes place without proper refraction, and, although much of this may be worthy, intuitive and skilful, there can be no substitute for separating out the constituent issues and disciplines, allowing them to interpermeate (pass through one another) and, in so doing, find their own proper density. Refraction also pre-empts questions of reform or revolution. It is not that refraction is against these two futures; rather, it is more likely that any reform or transformation will be *clearer* and more specific, and then carefully directed to those areas that demand that.

### Practical Theology: Further Reflections

David Hazle further argues that two distinct paradigms of theology coexist. The first sees theology as a discipline in which practical theology is one of many subdisciplines. The second conceives of theology as essentially practical, so that all kinds of theology are ultimately interrelated within the sphere of the church as the community of practice. For the most part, the first paradigm has dominated Western theological thinking, and, from such a perspective, practical theology has been merely the 'finishing school' for ministers, equipping them for the task ahead. However, the second paradigm has enjoyed increasing pre-eminence. In particular, practical theology has mounted a challenge to the nature of theology itself, has challenged traditional methodologies for theological reflection and has developed interdisciplinary approaches, especially in conversation with the social sciences. This development has enabled practical theology to evolve into a primary form of theory which challenges both the nature and the boundaries of the discipline.

Hazle builds on the work of Farley, who divides the field of theology in a slightly different way – into four. For Farley, there is, first, theology as a 'habitus' – a way of life that includes prayer, worship and discipleship. Second, there is theology as a 'science' – the grasping and disclosure of the self-revelation of God. Third, there is theology as 'sciences' – a cluster of relatively independent studies that constitute a 'faculty' in which various subdisciplines interrelate. Fourth, there is theology as a systematic or dogmatic constitution, but this is usually one that is to be found operating at some distance from ordinary life and contemporary culture. Hazle, agreeing with Farley, laments the loss of the first kind from the academy. The clericalization and professionalization of theology have removed it from the realm of the ecclesial and the situation of worship, and have driven a (false) wedge between 'pure' and 'applied'.

But what has bequeathed this new life to 'practical theology', given the prevailing separatism that modernism and secularization has visited upon the

study of theology? The answer must lie somewhere in the realm of the rediscovery of the contextual, and in the development of 'theories of action' in relation to theology. Typically, such initiatives have emerged from the edge of ecclesial, social and theological thinking. Black, lesbian, gay, feminist and other kinds of theology have been concerned with 'doing' theology; they have understood that the divisions between 'pure' and 'applied' have invariably excluded minority groups and interests. The Caribbean theologian Kortright Davis expresses the moment of epiphany within the discipline simply enough:

> Western theologians are [now] attempting to educate themselves about the new theological surges emanating from the Third World. They have finally realized that there is no universal theology; that theological norms arise out of the context in which one is called to live out one's faith; that theology is therefore not culture free; that the foundations on which theological structures are built are actually not transferable from one context to another. Thus, although the Gospel remains the same from place to place, the means by which the Gospel is understood and articulated will differ considerably through circumstances no less valid and no less authentic.... (Davis, 1990, p. 70)

Quite so. Put another way, we might say that the lesson from Pentecost is that theology (or Christianity) is always spoken in tongues, so that each can understand in their own language. There is no Christianity that lacks a local accent; there is no one, singular 'pure' version. Theology and faith are always contextual, but that does not mean a capitulation to relativism. Indeed, almost any study of Christian 'culture' could illustrate this, but, to illustrate my point, here is an extract from an early-mid-twentieth-century English hymnal, written for children in Sunday School:

> Do you see this Penny?
> It is brought by me
> For the little children
> Far across the sea.
> Hurry, Penny, quickly
> Though you are so small;
> Help to tell the Heathen
> Jesus loves them all....

As Davis says, the Gospel is the same (as God is), but the means of expression will always be variable over space, time and culture.

Hazle concludes his reflection on the nature of practical theology by noting that the discipline is inherently praxis-centred. Because of this, the branches of theology relate both to each other and other disciplines as they encounter fresh situations and new contexts. Theology is, then, a living process of thought and action, which is not simply for the specialist. Theology is the description for the reflective or refractive activity and praxis of the Christian community. And, because it is concerned with living for the kingdom of God, it always has a broader vision than its own self-concerns (Hazle, 2003, p. 366; cf. Forrester, 2000).

To conclude, we can say that practical theology is more concerned with *phronesis* (that is, practical wisdom) immersed in concrete situations than with *theoria* (that is, abstract theoretical reasoning). However, practical theology is heavily theory-laden and, arguably, of more strategic use than other theological disciplines. Critical practical theology and strategic practical theology are therefore engaged in a dynamic spiralling, which engages practice with theory and theory with practice; it refines the purposes of thinking and the deep wisdom of reflection in given contexts (Browning, 1996, pp. 6–10). Or, as I have already suggested, we might refer to this process, analogically, as refraction. Farley, summarizing our thinking, identifies seven theses that describe the scope and trajectory of practical theology as it is being used in this book of essays (Farley, 2003, pp. 42–43):

1   Because practical theology is a dimension of theological reflection and understanding and therefore is all-pervasive in the faith community, it is not restricted to a field of clergy education.
2   Practical theology is that dimension of theology in which reflection is directed to a living situation in which the believer or corporate entity is involved.
3   When response to, and interpretation of, a situation is self-consciously responsible, it can be assisted by a hermeneutic of existing in a situation. The focus of traditional and contemporary hermeneutics by texts and traditions has suppressed and marginalized the interpretation of situations. In practical theological hermeneutics the object of interpretation is the situation itself.
4   The tasks of a hermeneutic of situations are to uncover the distinctive contents of the situation, probe its repressed past, explore its relation to other situations with which it is intertwined and confront the situation's challenge through consideration of corruption and redemption.
5   The clerical activities of the traditional version of practical theology are, as situations, valid and important candidates for practical theological interpretation as are the situations of the believer and churchly communities. A practical theology of these activities and environments will correct their traditional pedagogical isolation through a special hermeneutic of these situations.
6   Practical theology, like other dimensions of theology, can and should be taught both in the church at large and in schools for educating the clergy.
7   Practical theology, as a dimension of theology and as an educational undertaking, can have a rigorous character and should be supported when appropriate by the resources, tools and disciplines of scholarship.

Broadly, we shall be working with Farley's definition of practical theology throughout this volume. Equally, however, we shall not be following Farley's delineation of the field (or that of any practical theologian) slavishly. These essays are intended to be exploratory in nature and are a deliberate exercise in 'trying on' different kinds of theoretical and practical reasoning in relation to the life of the church, the nature of theology and the relation between

Christianity and contemporary culture. They are sketches. The expectation is that the reader will use the book to reflect on their own cultural and ecclesial situations; that they will deepen their understanding of theory and practice; and that they will enlarge their vision for the possibilities of theology within the nexus of today's complex cultural milieu.

so many sudden changes in culture. There are so vast that . The greater part that the reader will find its hard to reflect on their own culture and the consequences that the differences that are the consequences of these cultural changes and that they will challenge their understanding and helping us to understand the norms of today's evolving cultural milieu.

# PART I
# THEOLOGY, CHURCH AND CONTEMPORARY CULTURE

# Chapter 1

# Church, Authority and the Culture of Credibility

Modern ecclesiology is essentially concerned with describing and analysing the shape of the contemporary church in relation to modern life and its understandings of God. Put another way, it is the internalized social expression of its doctrinal mind; ecclesiology mirrors theology. The missiology of the church, in contrast, can be more detached from the immediate self-understanding of the church. Whilst it will undoubtedly disclose something of the inner heart and mind of any ecclesial body, it can also at once be more pragmatic and experimental: testing the Spirit at work in the world, as it were. In this chapter, the exploration of Christianity within contemporary culture proceeds in two ways. First, a comparative analysis of writers addressing ecclesiological issues in North American Roman Catholicism is offered, in order to gain some preliminary understanding of how the church is developing in response to crises of authority, reception and public perception. Second, there is a broader, ecumenical focus on the teaching authority of the church, and its relation to notions of credibility and identity. Here the discussion expands to include Anglicanism and some recent ecumenical initiatives, although the shape of the argument has implicature for other historic denominations.

## Roman Catholicism in North America: Four Writers in Dialogue

Radical blueprints for reforming the Roman Catholic Church are hardly new. Hans Kung, Karen Armitage, Hans Winjgaards, to mention but a few, have all, in their different ways, advocated radical changes in theological and ecclesiological self-understanding. Whether or not one agrees with their agenda is, for our immediate purposes, inconsequential. Rather, it is important to grasp that each such writer argues with a degree of passion, cogency and tenacity for the reform of the church. They have sought to set out a new schema for the church in which its missiological shape and ecclesiological dimensions would better 'fit' with modern times. No self-respecting writer in the realm of 'public theology', it would seem, can leave the issues alone.

Paul Lakeland's recent *The Liberation of the Laity* (2003) carefully charts the situation of the laity before Vatican II, the achievement of Yves Congar, the teaching of the Council on the laity and the new emergent situation since Vatican II. But Lakeland's book contains a second part, which is arguably far more significant. Here he argues for a 'lay spirituality of secularity', the

liberation of the laity (from overt clerical domination), the shaping of mission for the postmodern world, and changes in the way the church is governed. These proposals include greater accountability and transparency, women and married people occupying roles of leadership, as well as the eventual elimination of both ecclesiastical careerism and the College of Cardinals. But such contributions to contemporary Roman Catholic ecclesiology (from both within and without) are hardly unusual at the commencement of the twenty-first century. There is widespread debate, which reflects a range of reformist agenda and discontent, as well as a predictably concerted attempt to try to maintain the current shape of the church, despite much criticism. In order to explore this ecclesiological territory in more depth, a comparative strategy will now be deployed.

Four recent books that attempt to engage Roman Catholic thinking with the everyday challenges of contemporary life are Francis Buckley's *The Church in Dialogue: Culture and Traditions* (2000), Anthony Gittins' *Ministry at the Margins: Strategy and Spirituality for Mission* (2002), John Fuellenbach's *Church: Community for the Kingdom* (2002) and Nicholas Healy's *Church, World and Christian Life: Practical–Prophetic Ecclesiology* (2000). The authors are all North American and might, therefore, have the immediacy of their context in mind as they write. No one can dispute that such an agenda is a timely one. Roman Catholics are a diverse body of believers in the third millennium. Furthermore, the relationship between 'official' and 'operant' in American Catholic religion is under increasing academic scrutiny:

> Most observers agree that there is a great deal of diversity among American Catholics.... While there was a certain amount of diversity in the 1940s and 1950s... the beliefs and practices of American Catholics have become increasingly varied since then. Studies done during the 1950s and 1960s indicated that there was more uniformity among Catholics than among mainstream Protestant groups.... More recent research, however, suggests that American Catholics' beliefs and practices are now more diverse than they were prior to the Second Vatican Council.... (Williams and Davidson, 1996, p. 102)

But there are now additional problems to note, besides the diversification of Catholic beliefs. The Roman Catholic Church in the USA has been rocked over the past few years by a series of unfolding scandals that have undermined its authority and power. The *Boston Globe* has led the way, challenging Cardinal Bernard Law and his fellow prelates over their handling of priests who have subsequently been convicted for paedophile offences. August papers such as the *New York Times* have also joined in the fray and have exposed chronic gaps between rhetoric and reality in the life of the church.

In general, it is a widely shared perception amongst the American public that most of the bishops in the Roman Catholic Church have performed very poorly in the midst of this crisis. The bishops have been reticent about being taken to task by secular law, clearly preferring to keep priestly paedophilia as an 'internal matter'. They have resented the growing clamour of voices amongst the laity for greater openness and accountability. The newly formed

'Voice of the Faithful' movement has been quickly suppressed and labelled as seditious and divisive, despite a clear programme that pursues justice and truth. And in terms of delivering any reform in the future, the bishops already seem to have promised far more than they are ever likely to deliver. Commitments to involve the laity more and to compensate victims have already turned sour. In the media overall, the bishops have shown themselves to be flat-footed and lacking dexterity, tenacity and appeal. A number of commentators have noted that, instead of looking like fathers in God, the bishops more likely resemble a disparate collection of minor mafia uncles. Trusting no-one, and having failed their own, they nonetheless expect to rule to the end, remaining above secular law at all times, sorting out their own problems in their own way.

So four books concerned with Roman Catholicism and contemporary culture ought to be timely, refreshing and helpful. Whilst these books could not have hoped to address the ecclesial cancer that was first revealed in the archdiocese of Boston (and is now known to be very widespread), one would nevertheless anticipate that Roman Catholic theological engagements with contemporary life would be able to make some important connections. For example, at a time when attendance at mass is declining and religious observance is moving from the obligatory to *à la carte*, what is the connection between the *authentic* life of the church and its claimed *authority*? How do you catechize new generations of Roman Catholics when the (so-called) 'lapsed' have distanced themselves from many of the arcane customs and beliefs of the church? It is a fact that the majority of Roman Catholics in the USA are in favour of married priests, would not mind ordained women in their parishes and don't believe that Methodists or Muslims are necessarily bound for hell. But the official teaching of the Roman Catholic Church is not quite in step with the vernacular religion of the faithful. Increasingly, 'official' and 'operant' religion finds themselves at odds with one another. For most of the time, this is a quiet, unspoken revolution.

In England, for example, the Roman Catholic birthrate has been falling for years. But good Catholic women do not take contraceptive pills for birth control – only to regulate their periods. The ends justify the means. In the USA it is hardly very different. Even parish priests turn two blind eyes: one to the official teaching of the church, the other to what really goes on amongst their congregations. Williams and Davidson (1996), in their study of American Catholicism, offer a generational explanation for the seismic shifts of the last 50 years. The pre-Vatican II generation (born in the 1930s and 1940s) viewed the church as an important mediating force in their relationship with God. When asked why they were Catholic, many participants in the Williams and Davidson study replied that it was because 'it was the one true church'. The Vatican II generation (born in the 1950s and 1960s), however, were more circumspect about the nature of the church and its absolutist claims. Interviewees were more inclined to see their priest as representing 'official' religion which, in turn, was only one religious source that fed and nurtured their private and individual spirituality. In this sense, the Vatican II generation is pivotal, since the post-Vatican II generation (born in the 1970s and 1980s) has tended to be even more liberal and open. For this generation, mass

attendance is not a priority; being a good person is more important than being a good Catholic; faith is individualistic and private – 'what really counts is what is in your heart'. Williams and Davidson conclude their study with these words:

> One thing is certain: the hands of time cannot be turned back. Societal changes, as well as changes occurring within the church, leave no doubt that tomorrow's Catholics will be very different from previous generations. The children of post-Vatican II Catholics will receive their religious education from those who never read the *Baltimore Catechism*, and are likely to know little about the changes brought about by Vatican II. The conceptions of faith post-Vatican II Catholics are apt to pass on to the next generation will look decidedly individualistic in nature.... (Williams and Davidson, 1996, p. 37)

So what kind of hope do Healy, Gittins, Fuellenbach and Buckley offer for the future of their church? How are their approaches to faith and contemporary culture-enabling, enlightening and empowering? Each author has their own approach to the debate, and offers a distinctive take on how Roman Catholicism is attempting to come to terms with the multiple and diverse pressures of modernity. These contributions will be briefly described in a moment. But the main focus of our interest here will be to dwell not so much on what the authors say as on what they don't say. In other words, this conversation should perhaps begin where the books finish. Correspondingly, I want to draw out the possible implications of each author's approach to the subject and invite them to say a little more about what needs to be done.

Francis Buckley's *The Church in Dialogue* (2000) is a warm and thought-provoking work that aspires to 'engage in fruitful conversation with various cultures, academic disciplines and religious traditions'. The scope of the chapters covers a very broad range of topics that will be of particular interest to Catholics: Mary and catechesis, ecumenism, liturgy and enculturation, and so forth. Buckley writes with freshness and poise, and his rhetorical style assumes an easy familiarity with readers. At times, the book almost reads as though one were in a distance-learning process of spiritual formation, being mentored and coached through various stages and negotiations.

Methodologically, the book is apparently influenced by educational studies (although no specific theorists are cited), and Buckley pays considerable attention to narrativity in his treatment of themes. Thus, the chapter on Marian catechesis actively promotes a theology that listens to the inductive reasoning of worshippers (ibid., p. 46), whilst at the same time advocating a deductive approach to the teaching of Marian dogma. The open, listening approach to the insights of the laity for the professional theologian also emerge with some force later (Chapter 6), where Buckley argues for an educational strategy that learns from 'popular religiosity and sacramentality'. Yet despite these encouraging signs, I have substantial reservations about Buckley's agenda. It looks to be charitable, open, committed to encounter and dialogue, and yet the text is riddled with unchallenged hierarchical assumptions.

For example, Buckley states that: 'Christianity is an adult religion, since

adults best understand and respond to revelation ... adults teach children in the family and schools' (ibid., p. 8). What children may be able to teach adults about God, worship, the church, truth, and more besides, does not seem to occur to him. Similarly, in the chapter entitled 'Building Christian Community', Buckley has no difficulty stating that:

> ... sects tend to oppose sacramentalism and institutional structures as unwarranted compromise with the world ... [such as] Pentecostals, Adventists and Quakers .... In the small sect one feels welcomed, needed, understood, loved, and helped, with a strong sense of belonging. But many drift from sect to sect, searching for the perfect community. (Ibid., p. 140)

Buckley seems to be wholly blind to his paternalism and patronizing tone, as though there was no 'real' problem with the present order he seeks to gently reform but fully support. So what emerges from Buckley's text, finally, is a vision for a church that is more open, accommodating, politer and friendlier to all those that it does not understand or know (in other words, there are *some* good things to say about sects and their members). But the underlying assumption is that all 'aliens', including the Hispanic community, on which Buckley writes movingly, will make little difference to the authority, praxis or shape of the church. The church will continue to be guided by an elite group of males who need to adapt to a new climate of pluralism, but who nonetheless must continue to dominate the church. So, the 'popular religiosity' of the Hispanics is affirmed but, in the same breath, dammed. It has something to say to the church, but this same group are, at the same time, targeted for catechizing, clearly indicating that Buckley sees their 'popular' theology as something less than 'proper'.

For Buckley, enculturation is something that the church accepts, but ultimately expects to be able to overcome. In enculturation, the church may adapt its teachings to fit a context, but there is little sense in which the culture can help to reform the church, calling it to repentance. Perhaps this is why Bernard Law can be seen on television, sitting in court, scowling at the black female judge who is compelling him to answer questions about the practice of his church. I have no doubt that Law thinks he only need answer to a higher authority, and not to an ordinary court of law, and certainly not to a woman. And that is the problem with Buckley's book. Ultimately, I do not think that *The Church in Dialogue* is serious about *true* dialogue. By dialogue, Buckley only means learning just enough about local culture to translate the Gospel into local dialects, so you can then teach the natives the one true language of the church. There is no real commitment to *listen* to the world – especially if it means that the world might change the church.

Theologically, I find that this is highly problematic. If the Holy Spirit cannot speak to the church *from* the world, calling it to new adventures, opportunities and, yes, repentance, then the extensive revelation of God is something less than what Vatican II thought (ibid., p. 5). Now, I am conscious that this is a somewhat harsh reading of a book that tries very hard to be charitable, open and reformist. Indeed, Buckley makes many concessions that some Roman

Catholics would choke on (for example, on intercommunion). But the extraordinary interiority of the rhetoric that peppers so much of the text makes me want to suggest that, to even begin to achieve a fraction of what Buckley might hope for, the Roman Catholic Church might like to begin in a different place and consider itself as a more fallible part of God's universal church, and learn to be a listening body that is as receptive as it is communicative, and as open as it is bounded.

Comparable problems are not located in Anthony Gittins' *Ministry at the Margins* (2002). Here we encounter a sophisticated yet practical theological treatise on 'how mission should be undertaken in practice' (2002, p. ix). Indeed, it is one of the few books about Christian ministry that I think one could commend ecumenically. Gittins states that his book is:

> ...offered to boundary crossers of all kinds...intended for anyone committed to outreach and inclusion...[it] is a book about ministry...a minister is the opposite of a master; not very visible and not self-important, but nevertheless necessary... margins are minimally important in themselves, yet they mark where inside meets outside...mission often takes place at the margins.... (Ibid., p. xi)

Each chapter is an excellent exposition on its theme, and Gittins writes with an intellectual depth coupled with passion and elegance that serves to strengthen the force of his argument. For example, his chapter on 'Gift-Exchange and the Gospel' uses the work of Mauss to disclose the reciprocal nature of mission. For Gittins, mission involves a prior commitment to learn and to change (ibid., p. 119). True mission across cultures involves mutuality: the desire to give must be matched by the obligation to receive. For Gittins, there can be no sense in which cross-cultural missiological dialogue can hide the kinds of hierarchies that are consistently implied in Buckley's text:

> We may have talked to people, but actually talked down to them. We may have listened to people, but perhaps selectively. Sometimes we craved relationships, but only as givers. Sometimes we set ourselves to learn from others, but only as teachers...our listening, our relationships and our teaching have been impregnated with power, righteousness, certainty, and the control of initiatives...Gift-exchange may provide structure for our ministry and teach us the place of trust and risk-taking, vulnerability and indebtedness, and mutuality in mission.... (Gittins, 2002, p. 119)

Gittins carries forward his theology of mission by carefully sketching a missiology based on the concept of hospitality. His exploration of the value of 'strangers' examines the Christian imperative to receive the alien, to welcome the foreigner, as we too, as Christians, were once aliens. Gittins, quite apart from having a fine socio-anthropological grasp of the stranger–host relationship, is able to take his thinking into finely tuned practical theological insights. Thus, he offers perspectives on the host – that is, rights, duties, obligations and ambivalence (ibid., p. 126) – and on the stranger – that is, as receiver, resource, alien and guest (ibid., p. 131) – before bringing this analysis together in an assimilation of the insights. These include a discussion of how the church can

become a more incorporative community, sharing histories, pooling resources, generating solidarity, enriching lives and mediating in the midst of hostilities.

The final chapter from Gittins is an apt crescendo for the book: 'the missionary as stranger'. Here the author offers a rewarding account of his own missiological experiences, but coupled to rich theological reflection. What is so attractive about Gittins' work is his ability to see the familiar in a strange, new and more illuminating light. Thus, Jesus on the road to Emmaus becomes a missiological paradigm – a stranger who needs to be received, in order for the Gospel to be proclaimed. But there is also the need to set this insight, as Gittins does, alongside Jesus' own teaching in relation to welcoming the stranger. The church cannot simply cast itself in the role of 'revealed' visitor, expecting the world to receive it. There are many occasions when the church must be the host to the Christ-like visitor and be transformed by the Christophany that is manifest in the face of the hungry, the stranger, the beggar and the prisoner.

John Fuellenbach's *Church: Community for the Kingdom* (2002) is a relatively traditional if well put together treatise on the church. Fuellenbach is well aware that the Roman Catholic Church has woken up to the advent of late modernity and found itself in a different world. Noting that there are several 'megatrends' that affect the church today (2002, pp. 100ff), he writes that:

> People's needs for God are no longer met in the present structures of ministry. A whole range of new ministries is required. There are 400,000 [Catholic] priests. Of these, 68 per cent care for the 40 per cent of the Catholics who live in Europe and the United States and 32 per cent minister on behalf of the remaining 60 per cent. There are not enough to take care of the sacramental needs, never mind mentioning other pastoral necessities. The church has to develop different ministries and new styles of ministry.... (Fuellenbach, 2002, p. 102)

Fuellenbach is wise enough to know that this crisis – and others within the Roman Catholic Church – will not be set straight by achieving a new level of 'objective' talk about the church (ibid., p. xiii). He understands that the sources of theology themselves are multiple: the Bible, tradition and the magisterium; the ongoing life of the worshipping community; the life situation of the committed community; and, finally, the presence of the Holy Spirit. This allows Fuellenbach to constantly talk about the church as only part of the celebration of the kingdom of God, which is, from my point of view, an intriguing and fruitful repositioning of ecclesiology.

On balance, Fuellenbach's missiology is both richer and denser than that of Gittins or Buckley. There are times when his proposals for mission and ministry, and his description of the local church, sound close to the kinds of theology one more generally finds in Congregational Studies and Practical Theology. I mean this as a compliment. Fuellenbach has managed something that few Roman Catholic writers achieve: a compelling thesis that would engage and enlighten many Protestants who are searching for a similar vocabulary to redefine their missiological purpose. There are only a few instances where I would want to quibble with his insights. For example, his description of enculturation as 'a process by which the gospel enters into a

culture' (ibid., p. 101) suggests that there is a notion of a 'pure' and *a*cultural gospel lurking somewhere in his thinking, even though the statement is qualified by his admission that the Gospel 'takes from culture all that is already gospelled, and is enriched by it'. Fuellenbach is well aware that cultures can challenge 'the Gospel' and expose those aspects of it that are merely Western.

Fuellenbach concludes his study by calling the church to two tasks. First, the church should recognize that it is no longer in an era of linear change. Second, it should establish a renewal of faith in God and a new understanding of 'God's saving plan for all God's kingdom' (ibid., p. 221). This leads to the identification of two major issues that the church will have to face if it wants to remain faithful to the kingdom: enculturation and solidarity with the poor, both of which are 'within the process of globalization'. The way forward for the Roman Catholic Church will not merely be to anticipate, predict or respond to the future. In an engaged church, it will make the future through a radical recommitment to 'Jesus' own life principles and to his message of the kingdom' (ibid., p. 222).

Finally in this section, we come to Nicholas Healy's prescient work, *Church, World and Christian Life* (2000), which argues that the authority of the church (including what the church teaches about itself), has to pay more attention to the authentic, the concrete, the ordinary and the lived or actual experience or discipleship of its people, and not just try to live its life out of 'blueprints' based on ideology or notions of revelation. To do this, Healy describes contemporary ecclesiology as an antinomy: namely the tendency on the one hand for theologians to describe the church in 'ideal terms', whilst on the other failing to address the church and its problems or possibilities of everyday life – what Healy dubs 'concrete ecclesiology'. Healy argues that the gap between the idealist and the concrete traits tends to inhibit the church in its discipleship and witness, and, furthermore, stifles the production of a coherent prophetic ecclesiology that might arise out of contextual theologies that pay greater attention to ethnography, sociology and other cognate disciplines. Healy sets about his thesis by exposing the weaknesses of what he terms 'blueprint ecclesiologies'. He writes:

> If we generalize from the wide range of ecclesiological styles of the last century or so, it is possible to detect five key methodological elements. One is the attempt to encapsulate in a single word or phrase the most essential characteristic of the church; another is to construe the church as having a bipartite structure. These two elements are often combined, third, into a systematic and theoretical form of normative ecclesiology. A fourth element is a tendency to reflect upon the church in abstraction from its concrete identity. And one consequence of this is, fifth, a tendency to present idealized accounts of the church.... (Healy, 2000, p. 26)

The discussion proceeds from here and shows how, for example, an ecclesiologist such as Dulles, in identifying 'models' of the church such as 'herald' and 'sacrament' (five models in all), allows the models to be used in both explanatory and exploratory ways. Although this approach is initially illuminating, it follows a trend that is common to many modern theologians

who reflect on the church, namely the identification of an authoritative 'supermodel' as the pre-eminent way of conceiving of the church, and then determining its authority. Thus, for Barth it may be 'the Body of Christ' that is deemed to be denotative; for Rahner it may be 'sacrament'; for Tillard it may be 'communion'.

To this analysis, Healy brings the following insights. First, all 'models' are in some sense deficient – something Dulles also acknowledges. Second, the New Testament offers what he calls 'an irreducible plurality of ways of talking about the church'. Third, the doctrine of the Trinity itself requires us to 'keep shifting our perspective[s]', and to acknowledge that no one perspective is ever 'adequate', but, rather, each needs the 'corrective pressure' of another in order to do justice to the rich and multifaceted faith we know as 'Christianity' (ibid., p. 34). As with the Trinity, so it is with the church; we are bound to a relation of intradependent competing convictions in which no one insight or model has supremacy. This leads Healy to conclude that theologians who deduce a 'complete and normative systematic description of the church from the definitive model of the church's essence' have missed the point. That is not to say that all 'models' are pointless; it is, rather, to say that the models need to be used 'contextually' in ways that aid the exploration of the many facets of the Christian church. That said, Healy still wishes to warn against what he terms 'blueprint ecclesiologies':

> ...[they] display to some degree a tendency to concentrate their efforts upon setting forth more or less complete descriptions of what the church should ideally become...the images and concepts used to model the church are almost always terms of perfection.... (Healy, 2000, p. 36)

The danger of this is that theologians can give the impression that it is 'necessary to get our thinking about the church right first, after which we can go on to put our theory into practice'. As Healy points out, blueprint ecclesiologies therefore assume that there can be agreement on the starting point for a theology of the church – and, of course, there is no such agreement, not even in the New Testament. Blueprint ecclesiologies are problematic for other reasons, too. In using models of perfection, they fail to distinguish between the church militant and the church triumphant, and between the pilgrim church and the heavenly church. Blueprint ecclesiologies tend to foster a disjunction between normative theories and accounts of ecclesial practice, and between ideal and concrete ecclesiology, thereby 'undervaluing the theological significance of the *genuine* struggles of the church's membership to live as disciples within the less-than-perfect church within societies' (ibid., p. 38).

Healy suggests that the deficiencies identified above are best corrected by a proper contextual theology. This is not to separate the church from its context but, rather, to recognize that the concrete church performs its tasks in the world, a place of ever-shifting contexts that inevitably has an impact on shaping its performance (ibid., p. 39). Here Healy pleads for greater attention to the cultural history of the church and for ethnography and sociology to help

guide the practice of the church, in order to develop a 'practical-prophetic ecclesiology' that makes use of non-theological disciplines, but without turning away from ecclesiology's primary functions, namely 'to aid the church in its task of truthful witness within a particular ecclesiological context'. Or, as I have been hinting, it is important to move away from epic accounts of the church or blueprint ecclesiologies that 'describe the church in terms of its final perfection rather than its concrete and sinful existence', and from 'normative' accounts or models rather than 'presenting careful and critical descriptions of its activity within the confusions and complexities of a particular theological context' (ibid., p. 54)

What are the implications of this for the Roman Catholic Church in its attempts to engage in contemporary (Western) culture? Healy's work appeals for a more open encounter with 'grassroots' insights that will make the church more 'real' and authentic as a teaching community. Instead of ideologies and truths being imposed on the laity from lofty heights, Healy proposes an *engagement* with the complex reality of the world that can countermoderate traditions. In other words, praxis may have an impact on the idealized blueprint. The suggestion that emerges in the book – more implicit throughout than it is ever explicit – is that teaching must be authentic if it is to be authoritative. Since much of the teaching that the church aspires to deliver is (apparently) authoritative, yet at the same time is lacking in authenticity (that is, not grounded in genuine encounters and the like), the authority can appear to be coercive and imposing rather than engaging and liberating.

So where do these four authors take us in our reflection on the present state of the Roman Catholic Church in America? Of the four, Healy seems to have articulated the most promising theological paradigm that might enable the church to transform itself. Gittins' missiology is enchanting and practical. Buckley's work, although promising in places, is less secure in its theological outlook. Fuellenbach's well-articulated but relatively traditional ecclesiology is certainly able, but seems to be reticent when faced with sharper contextual questions. Doing more for the poor and embracing enculturation is easier said than done, and I remain unclear as to how Fuellenbach's recipe, if fully practised by local congregations, will impact the wider structures and hierarchy of the church.

Of course, it is for the authors to say a little more about how they think their theology might enable the Roman Catholic Church to regain its credibility and re-engage with both believers and public alike. I am conscious that I have approached the American agenda as an English Anglican, so certain allowances will have to be made for what may have been misconstrued. I readily acknowledge that there may be perspectives and insights that I have missed, and some that I have misunderstood. Of course, that is one of the purposes of conversation: clarification. But at the risk of repeating myself, the agenda for the American Roman Catholic looks increasingly complex and awkward, and it will take much tenacity, wisdom and humility to negotiate the hurdles ahead. In particular, three issues come to mind, and I pose these as questions.

First, how can a church have authority when it is perceived to have lost its authenticity and integrity? It is all very well continuing to insist (in a hermetically sealed theological vocabulary) that the church is still *the* authority, but such assertions sound hollow and lack credibility when weighed against public disgust at the handling of paedophile priests and other scandals. Put another way, suppose we ask this question: what if the world does not want *this* church? Suppose the world only wants the church imagined by Fuellenbach – one where solidarity with the poor and enculturation are its distinguishing features?

Second, if the church is to learn from culture, where and at what point does it judge culture, and by what criteria? This question is more complex than it sounds, since many post-Vatican II Catholics now think that 'being good' is more important than 'being a good Catholic' (Williams and Davidson, 1996). If Catholicism is now a mere resource within the wider common pool of civil values and virtues, its claim to be universal and complete begins to look suspect – an archaic way of speaking about the church that nobody really believes to be true. What can be done about this is beyond the scope of the books we have discussed but, I suspect, not beyond the imaginations of the authors. Each, in their different way, is in favour of listening to the laity, learning from congregations and having theology reshaped through such conversations: but how far will they really go?

Third, what can our four authors suggest for the renewal of the church, especially when there is an emergent generation where believing through spirituality seems to matter more than belonging to a congregation? Does the church need to radically rethink itself or, perhaps, attempt a more substantial and imaginative type of re-evangelization? As Bernard Law continues to struggle to talk to, and listen to, the world around him, one can only hope that fresh voices and more attentive ears will emerge. At least these four authors, with their missiology, pastoral and practical theology, and in their different ways, offer much promise and hope for a church that often looks as though it lives its life through its past and struggles to cope with the present. Given these remarks, we now need to consider the nature and purpose of teaching in more depth.

## Teaching Authority

Not so long ago, I was invited to an august ecumenical gathering in Europe, and invited to lecture on the following subject: 'How can we teach with authority?' The premise of the question appeared to be that what the church mainly lacked in its engagement with contemporary society was *authority*, and that, without this, the church cannot be heard, is not given its due respect and can be ignored. Of course a body – of belief or believers – that is not held in high regard by the public at large and is ignored by the masses has a dubious claim on being an authority. It can preside over and proscribe for its followers but, to outsiders, the grammar of assent simply looks like a quaint curiosity or, perhaps worse, something between a hobby with too many rules and a totalitarian regime.

So, 'how can we teach with authority'? It is a simple enough, six-word question. And yet to answer it requires some genuine honesty about the premises that fund such an inquiry. We might begin by asking, 'Who is asking the question?' Who is the 'we' of this question? (The question is explored in some depth in Visser't Hooft's *Teachers and the Teaching Authorities* (2000), where a helpful distinction is drawn between the *Magistri* and the *Magisterium*.) Is this a concern of bishops, theologians, pastors, priests and educators? And, if so, is there any evidence that the laity cry out with the same voice? (I doubt it.)

I suspect that the 'we' of the question reflected the angst of many religious *professionals*, who perceive that *their* authority has been eroded by a pottage of cultural and intellectual trends, including modernity, secularization, consumerism, postmodernity, and who knows, perhaps even ecumenism. The reality of these forces allows religious consumers to compare, contrast, choose and, yes, contest their *given* sources of authority. Or one could name any other inimical force that apparently rivals Christianity's *uni*versal claims. There is, for many believers, not one universal authority, but rather a *cosmos* of competing convictions, in which universal claims look increasingly pre-Copernican in outlook. But this observation is only to point towards the fact that, behind the question, we are probably dealing with a neuralgic response to a perceived crisis. The underlying assumption seems to be that that there was once a time when, for the church at least, teaching authoritatively was (relatively speaking) plain sailing. Correspondingly, the hope and aspiration of many is to try to reclaim this pre-eminence in social and cultural positioning, and of course within the interior landscape of ecclesial communities themselves, such that the church can *command* attention by virtue of the charism of its authority.

Now, it is not my purpose here to have a debate about the nature of secularization and its relationship to the teaching office and authority of the church. That would be a separate project in its own right. Suffice to say, the situation of late modernity or postmodernity is more complex and ambivalent than it is stark. In many European countries, religion has a significant public role, and the utterances of church leaders can have, under certain circumstances, significant moral and social impact. It is not the case that secularity (whatever that is – and it is far from clear, and often poorly defined) is squeezing the life out of the role and influence of faith communities in the public spheres. In Europe, religion mutates in modernity; it doesn't disappear as some scholars have argued. People believe, but without necessarily belonging. Faith or spirituality is there, but it is more colloquial in character than those who might aspire to the mythic utopia of Christendom (Davie, 1994, 2000; Percy, 2001). I argue, following Keith Thomas, that faithful indifference to religious authority is commonplace throughout English history and not a modern malaise.

Similarly, in the USA, where the contours of public and civic religion are rather contrary, 'private' or differentiated faith continues to enjoy substantive public adherence (Casanova, 1994). Here again, however, I am bound to say that scholars, having explored contemporary North American religion, can point to considerable spiritual pluralism in the foundation of the USA. 'One

Nation Under God' was an inclusive Deist slogan in the first instance, and not a radical reinvention of Christendom for a new postcolonial nation. Of the 54 people who signed the Declaration of Independence in 1776, only three were *not* practising Freemasons – which is not to say that they were not *also* Christian. As Robert Fuller argues in his recent book (Fuller, 2001), Americans have always been fond of religious and spiritual pluralism and syncretism. So perhaps North America is not so different from Europe? And in the developing world, as if it needed to be said, religions and faith remain utterly fundamental. Indeed, following Grace Davie, I cannot help wondering if the question 'How can we teach with authority?' is a peculiarly European question (Davie, 2000, 2002).

But, given that this is the question before us, how might we proceed? As an Anglican priest, and as a practical theologian with a strong interest in contemporary ecclesiology, the religion–culture debate and ministerial formation, I find the acuity of the question to be more than testing. But I want to set about addressing it in a somewhat atypical way. To my mind, such questions are not that well served by quoting familiar dusty answers, drawn from the shelves of past ecumenical debates. Nor do I draw much inspiration from 'agreed statements' or from mono-denominational responses that simply restate the grounds for their authority and their reasons for teaching what they do.[1] To be sure, such statements and documents have their merit, but they seem to lack imagination and public engagement; they seem to assert rather than argue; they seem to be more anodyne than authoritative. But, by and large, their purpose is one of clarity within the context of interiority, and this means that they don't engage with the *public* character of the question.

In order to address the issue, I want to explore the relationship between *authority* and *authenticity*. The reason for this is simple enough. The etymology of both words lies in the prior word 'author', meaning 'the person who originates or gives existence to anything', 'the inventor, constructor and founder', and so on. Or, put more theologically, the Creator. Generally speaking, definitions of authority flow from this: 'power or right to enforce obedience', 'moral or legal supremacy', 'the right to command', 'give an ultimate decision' and so forth. 'Authentic', in turn, proceeds from authority. The authentic is 'entitled to respect', is 'authoritative' and 'entitled to belief'. But to be authentic can also involve being 'reliable, trustworthy, first-hand, original, real, actual, genuine'; it is identified more colloquially – in other words, not with ideology but with reality.

The tension between the authentic and authority is, in my view, one of the most important (but relatively unexplored) keys to understanding the apparent crisis in contemporary ecclesial identity. Put simply, people's perception of the authentic can question the authority they are placed under, just as much as an authority can interrogate the prevailing establishment. This leads to a debate

---

[1] A recent example of this was the meeting of the 38 Anglican Primates, who at the end of their deliberations issued a statement affirming that they believed in 'a living God; an incarnate God; a triune God; a faithful God; a saving and serving God'.

about the *Author* of a particular aspect of authority – does the dogma under question come from the Creator or the created (*Opus Dei* or *Opus Hominum*)? Equally, is the authentic *given* by the Author (that is, part of the created order) or called into a new existence by the Authority that is above it? (I am well aware that this antinomy is fundamentally false, since inspiration and revelation all comes *through* the agency of created order. Nevertheless, the division between the authentic and authority will serve our purposes well here, in establishing the contours for the debate.)

## Authenticity and Authority

Let me start this section by giving two examples – one ancient, and one modern – where authority is linked to the authentic and has a direct bearing on the contours of contemporary ecclesiology. We'll take the ancient example first: in what sense is St Paul an Apostle? Paul claims to have been 'the last' to see Jesus, and partly bases his apostolic claim on being a witness to the resurrected Christ, which appears to have been a criterion for being numbered amongst the elite who quickly came to be known as 'the Apostles'. Yet the writer of the Book of Acts insists that what Paul saw on the road to Damascus was not Jesus himself, but a *vision* of Jesus or a hearing of his voice. It was not an encounter with the risen Jesus in the way the Apostles or the stragglers on the road to Emmaus had known. But Paul, to keep his mission alive, needs the *authority* of an Apostle to carry the Gospel to the gentiles, so he stretches the definition of what an Apostle is by shrewdly rewriting history. But what is the truth of the matter? Paul was still a zealous Jew when Jesus ascended, and he only turned to persecuting the church after it was formed, which was at Pentecost. So he could not have met the risen Christ, and probably never met the earthly Jesus either; the fact that he never quotes Jesus directly in his letters rather confirms this. And yet he wishes to affirm, that he, 'untimely born' was the last witness to the resurrection and that he has 'seen Jesus our Lord' (1 Cor. 15:8 and 1 Cor. 9:1). The Acts of the Apostles manages to subtly undermine the claim, yet without leaving Paul's apostolic claim twisting in the wind. In the Book of Acts, Paul is not converted until one-third of the way through the treatise of Acts (9:1ff) – we have had eight chapters of early church history, without an earthly Christ, before Paul even appears on the scene.

Here is a second, more modern example, and one to which I have alluded already. The current difficulties of the Roman Catholic Church in the USA are now well documented, and they do not need rehearsing here. There is perhaps nothing new about cardinals, cover-ups and child molestation, and it is worth pointing out that there is probably no ecclesial community that could hold its head high and say that it might have handled sexual scandals in a better or fairer way. Leaving aside the financial settlements and outstanding legal issues in the USA, there can be no doubt that the more serious issue for the Roman Catholic Church in the long term is the injury done to its *credibility*. In a legal deposition, Cardinal Law (of the archdiocese of Boston) was forced to admit that it was diocesan policy to 'avoid scandal'. (Cardinal Law has since

resigned.) Thus, a letter sent to the cardinal in 1982, detailing the molestation of seven boys by one priest, was 'hushed up'; avoiding controversy was thought to be more important than exposing a crime.

The problem is this. The church uses a language about itself which is potentially problematic: phrases such as 'indefectable', 'infallible in teaching and morals', 'unerring', 'authoritative', 'complete' and 'untainted' come to mind. The scandal of the archdiocese of Boston highlights the gap between rhetoric and reality; the chasm between the authoritative and the authentic are exposed. The authority of the church lies in tatters because it has attempted to preserve its authority by hiding or ignoring the authentic – in this case, genuine abuse.

I am more than conscious that this might appear to have spun off from my original concern: authority in contemporary ecclesial theology. However, there is method in such an atypical approach, which will become apparent as the discussion proceeds. The relationship between authority and authenticity remains a fundamental concern of mine, and it, in turn, has a direct impact on establishing a theology that articulates the nature and purpose of authority, and, therefore, of education and formation. In my recent commentary on the final ARCIC document, *The Gift of Authority*, I take issue with the assumption that reaching this kind of top-level theological consensus (that is, agreements between very senior ecclesiastical and theological persons) constitutes a proper way of setting about the business of doing theology (Percy, 2003).

I make several criticisms of the ARCIC document, although I am supportive of its findings. The first criticism is that the report pays no attention to the significant doctrinal and liturgical differences between Roman Catholics and Anglicans. In ignoring these (presumably because they are deemed to be either too contentious or peripheral), the report assumes that an agreed statement makes for an agreement. It doesn't. By ignoring the genuine differences (and social histories), the nature of the report, although clearly authoritative, lacks a dimension that would give it more authenticity.

Second, the absence of local grassroots conversations, dialogues and exchanges constitutes an impoverished kind of theology. If the Report were a more extensive kind of research, it would have listened to the genuine and lived experience of those on the ground, who are practising their faith in Anglican–Roman Catholic ecumenical projects on a day-to-day basis. The authors of the Report would have wrestled with stories: with the difficulty of impaired communion – yet similar liturgies; of invalid orders – yet mutual respect. Of historic and cultural hermeneutics of suspicion – yet much personal warmth and trust. The issue of authority must be addressed in these places and by these people, but their stories do not feature in the ARCIC report.

Third, there is an assumption that cherished cultural particularities (which inevitably have theological significance) can be swept aside by a form of ecumenism that seems to presuppose its own authority. For example, the nature and purpose of the Church of England invests something in the monarch being its supreme governor, which, in turn, partly characterizes the ambivalent and open nature of English religion. At the same time, the pope is a head of state, as well as presiding over an ecclesial system in which the nature

and practice of authority 'feels' rather more proscribed to that which might be encountered in Anglicanism. Yet the ARCIC document mentions none of these matters as an impediment to full and visible unity, as though 500 years of political history and cultural conditioning were somehow irrelevant. Again, in not dealing with authentic differences, the report's authority looks thin. If people's genuine grassroots concerns have not been taken into account, exactly *how* does the report carry weight?

Part of the problem, to my mind, lies in an impoverished notion of what constitutes learning, teaching and formation in ecclesial communities. Paulo Freire understands this better than most, and in his seminal *Pedagogy of the Oppressed* (1972) he sets out the problem:

> A careful analysis of the teacher–student relationship at any level…reveals [a] relationship between a narrating Subject (the teacher) and patient, listening objects (the students)…. The teacher talks about reality as if it were motionless, static, compartmentalized and predictable. Or else he expounds on a topic completely alien to the existential experience of the students. His task is to 'fill' the students with the contents of his narration…. (Freire, 1972, p. 45)

Granted, this is a characterization of teaching and is designed to undermine the (usually unacknowledged) authority of the teacher and the power of knowledge. Nonetheless, Freire's critique is sharp and penetrating. He sees that this approach to education turns students into 'containers – into receptacles to be filled by the teachers'. Education becomes an act of depositing; instead of communicating, the teacher issues communiqués. Students 'bank' knowledge, and in so doing, claims Freire, '[file] themselves away through [a] lack of creativity'. In the 'banking system' of education, knowledge is a gift bestowed by those who consider themselves knowledgeable upon those who are considered to be ignorant. Freire sees this as a form of oppression, negation and stifling of genuine inquiry.

Freire's anti-thesis is a libertarian approach to education, which 'drives towards reconciliation'. Rather than the 'banking system' with its endemic paternalism, he proposes a philosophy of education that is collaborative and 'problem-posing', namely the undertaking of a process in which power relations are suspended and then explored, placing the whole focus of inquiry and its objects (that is, students and teachers alike) within a reticulate intradependent educational context. Freire then argues that 'authentic liberation' (part of the purpose and goal of education – 'the truth shall set you free') is a process of humanization, which cannot be imposed, since it is not a deposit to be made *in* people but is, rather, part of the praxis of liberation. Thus, liberating education 'consists in acts of cognition, not transferrals of information' (ibid., p. 53).

The implications of Freire's work for the question of authority now begin to emerge. Teachers and students become jointly responsible for a process in which they grow and are liberated: 'In this process, arguments based on "authority" are no longer valid; in order to function, authority must be on the side of freedom' (ibid.). This leads Freire to conclude that 'banking education'

has a tendency to '[mythicize] reality, to conceal certain facts which explain the way men exist in the world...[it] resists dialogue'. On the other hand, liberating and problem-posing education stimulates creativity, reflection and critical thinking. It affirms praxis, and is characterized by 'revolutionary futurity' (ibid., p. 57).

Freire's concerns correspond more or less directly with those that I briefly sketched in my discussion of the ARCIC report, *The Gift of Authority* (see Percy, 2003). The failure of the authors to consult widely means that certain issues and realities are overlooked. I must also add a further concern. In what sense can 'authority' be truly a 'gift'? Only, it seems to me, if it is asked for, wholly offered (that is, not imposed) or appreciated for what it gives of itself. But to be a true gift, in any conventional sense, it no longer becomes the property of the donor, since it becomes part of the economy of exchange – it can be received with thanks, or rejected as unsuitable. Authority, as a 'gift', implies a covenant relationship, in which obedience cannot be commanded as of right. Of course, *The Gift of Authority* belongs to that economy of education that believes in 'banking' select portions of knowledge (and ignoring others), and the ARCIC report is, arguably, its final deposit, and a way of ordering that knowledge hierarchically. The 'gift' is not given; it is insistently imposed. Moreover, the 'gift' never becomes the property of the receiver, or something to share, since it is clear that the true owners remain the authors and definers of the range and capacity of authority.

To sum up, *The Gift of Authority*, though laudable in so many ways, *lacks* ultimate authority because of its insufficiency in grounded authenticity, and is therefore part of the problem (not the solution) to the crisis of authority in ecclesiology and ecumenism. If such reports don't deal in 'real' issues and don't consult with 'real' Christians and their churches, it will not gain the authentification of the masses of the laity that it *needs*, which will ultimately deprive it of any authority – the very thing it presupposes it has. It is simply theological double-speak to say that a document still has authority even when no-one pays attention to it, or believes in it.

For many, Freire's philosophy of education will appear to be far too risky for the status of ecclesial authority. If faith is turned from monologue to dialogue, from the credal to liberating praxis, and from the concrete to the fluid, will it be meaningful to talk of authority at all any more? Indeed, isn't this precisely the problem for churches and theological educators today? There are disagreements not only about the identity, nature and purpose of fundaments, but also about how they should be read, interpreted and applied. Again, to partly address this question, it is necessary to draw on insights from the philosophy of education. I make three brief points.

First, it must be remembered that there are various types of knowledge that constitute the Christian communities of which we are part, and which form the basis of ecclesial authority or the personal fundaments that construct the Christian lives of individuals. There is considerable plurality amongst the churches. For example, those that are liturgically or doctrinally formed (that is, through tradition), may struggle to relate to those churches where certain experiences (for example, speaking in tongues) validate membership and give

grounds for authority. For some, the authority of orders will be pre-eminent. For others, the validation of authority rests on charismata, experiences of the numinous and the ability to reify the life of the Holy Spirit within the midst of the congregation. Within this matrix, the weight of authority given to scripture, tradition, reason and culture will vary enormously. In other words, Christian 'knowledge' (and therefore authority) is a deeply contested concept.

Second, knowledge, and therefore the authority that proceeds from it, is not an inert corpus of material lying 'out there' in some ethereal world (Barnett, 1990, p. 43) but is, rather, part of the dynamic discourses that constitute communities. That is not to say, of course, that knowledge is *only* a social construction of reality (to parody Berger and Luckmann, 1971). It is, rather, to own the fact that knowledge requires *commitment* in order to assume an authority, and this must be an ongoing dynamic process which is open to constant renewal. Furthermore, knowledge has different competencies that are related to its purposes. Practical knowledge has a different authority to that of academic knowledge (Barnett, 1994, p. 160). A knowledge that ceases to have value or meaning for a community inevitably loses some of its authority. Knowledge and authority must therefore be continually rediscovered in the ordinary processes of dynamic sociality; it can never assume a right to privilege without the sacrifice of engagement and debate. (Here we speak of nothing less than 'the word made flesh': God's communication and truth is propositional and relational; eternal, yet dynamic; established and given, yet open and eschatological.)

Third, and following the previous two points, we might ask how authority functions in the church as a *learning* community. To what extent are ecclesial communities equipped with the resources to become communities of critical reflection, or exploration, and of distinctiveness? This question goes to the heart of the knowledge–authority axis and makes further demands on the assumptions about the kinds of knowledge that underpin authority. We might say that in a modernist mindset, the contours of authority are well articulated, and the purposes of knowledge attainment clear and precise. But in a more postmodern climate, there is an almost in-built sense of indecision, indeterminacy and openness (Doll, 1989, p. 250). The ends that may be perceived turn out to be only beginnings: rule books become guidebooks; the pillar of flame a beacon to guide rather than a light to follow; and the shaping of ecclesial communities becomes a process of development rather than a comparatively static correspondence to a finite body of knowledge.

Having made these points, it is important to acknowledge that considerable ecclesial and theological difficulties would be involved in inculcating them wholesale into the life of the church. At worst, an uncritical adoption of the philosophy outlined above could lead to a vapid relativity in terms of definition and distinctiveness. Churches do (and must) stand on some kind of authority that is supported by its corpus of knowledge. However, this brief excursion into contemporary educational philosophy highlights a major problem in considering authority within ecclesial communities. The problem, simply put, is one of reception rather than content. If churches are unwilling to embrace new (more collaborative and less doctrinaire) philosophies of learning and teaching, then

the authority of the church is no longer *received* in the same way. Being more imposing (even if this is for the sake of a predetermined unity) is no substitute for the liberation of enabling – even if that does lead to distinctiveness and difference.

## Authority and Discipleship

To return to the crisis in ecclesial authority, one could begin almost anywhere, but I hope you will forgive me if I confine my comments to the Church of England and the Anglican Communion, to which I belong as a priest and theologian. Like many churches these days, we seem to have no need of external critiques, as we seem to grow our very own prophets of doom. Norman (2002), for instance, argues that the Church of England has lost its authority because of its uncritical inculcation of humanism, pluralism, secularity and materialism. His views on knowledge are the antithesis of mine. Writing of the encroaching secularization within the church, he asserts that:

> The crucial switch was from confessional instruction to liberal education . . . educated opinion of the time used the word 'indoctrination' pejoratively; indoctrination, however, is what every ideology needs to practise in order to secure its survival . . . the result for the propagation of Christianity has been catastrophic. (Norman, 2002, p. 15)

Norman's attack on authority within his own Communion is therefore short on surprise. He blames the 'imprecision' of definition and 'the modern individualising of religious choice' for the crisis (is this really new?). Yet, despite identifying the 'absence of a coherent source of authority' as the modern malaise for the Church of England, Norman argues that the repository of authority is 'the People of God': '[Christ] established a means of communicating his truth . . . and committed the message not to a philosophical system, or even to written texts, but to an organic agency, a living body of people . . . ' (ibid., p. 93). So, although, to be fair, Norman acknowledges that authority and truth have always been contested within the church (even the pages of the New Testament reflect this, as we have already noted), what is to be done about this?

Norman's guarded uncertainty about what to do in the absence of clarity raises a familiar spectre in the church. If no-one can be absolutely sure about what texts and traditions guide us in our teaching and deliberations, then certainty will prove elusive. And yet this is precisely the point. We walk by faith, not by sight. The need for certainty is, as Robert Towler pointed out some decades ago, a pathology rather than a pathway (Towler, 1984). And yet it is the differences and disagreements between and within churches that raise the prospect of division, which, in turn, appears to further undermine authority. But need this be so?

In David Brown's two recent treatises (1999 and 2000), he argues that it is the very pluralism of scripture itself that can help address the contested field of authority. In *Tradition and Imagination* (1998) he is concerned to maintain a strong emphasis on revelation, but at the same time combine it with an account of tradition, which is the main medium of revelation. In other words, he sees the medium and the message as inseparable, thus allowing him to identify places where developing tradition may correct misunderstandings of truth, and where truth may continue to reform tradition. Behind this process, Brown sees the hand of God 'continuing to involve himself intimately with humanity' and a role for the community of faith in helping believers discern where the process of revelation has now reached. In *Discipleship and Imagination* the argument is taken a stage further:

> ...in the Bible and beyond more often than not truth has emerged through lively *disagreement*, and not simply by formal acceptance of an existing deposit or simple deductions from it. The ability to envisage alternative scenarios has thus always been integral to the healthy development of the tradition. Unilinear theories of development must therefore be abandoned, and the search for consensus *within* conflict be taken with much more seriousness, whether we are thinking of later church history or even the Bible itself. (Brown, 2000, p. 291, emphasis added)

Brown's point resonates with the earlier excursions into educational philosophy. But where does this leave the authority of the church? The question has been put badly and deliberately. In the (so-called) Great Commission (Matt. 28: 18–20), Jesus states that 'all authority in heaven and on earth has been given to *me*...therefore go, and make disciples of all nations'. Where is the authority of the church here? It is ultimately with Christ, which is not to say that that the church has no authority. It is, rather, to remind the church that it does not possess the truth; it is, instead, possessed by the Truth, which is not the same.

This change of emphasis places the church at the feet of Christ and reminds the disciples that they continue to be a learning, disciplined and discovering community of believers who are gathered faithfully around the Word and sacrament, and continue to be fed, nourished and transformed by the living triune God who creates, redeems and sustains. The teaching authority of the church can therefore only rest upon how the church itself allows itself to continue to be taught; how it listens, and models its conversation and education, must be as important as what it says and does in the name of the authority that it has been given.

It is sometimes tempting, when surveying the global Anglican Communion, to imagine that the church will be split asunder by its inability to agree on the ordination of women, the place of homosexuals in holy orders, or indeed any other matter that is held to be inimical to its coherence. The arguments can be bitter, with authority claimed by all who are deeply engaged in such disputes. Yet, at the same time, there is also ample evidence to suggest that conversation and negotiation leads to fresh perspectives on what it means to be a church.

In a recent article on same-sex relations and the debate in East African Anglicanism, Kevin Ward shows how 'the attempt to make definitive pronouncements on sexual ethics and human relationships cannot foreclose on the continuing struggle to establish and foster appropriate human relationships and the institutions which sustain them' (K. Ward, 2002, p. 111). Ward's work shows that, for the church to establish a definitive authority on same-sex relationships, it will have to *engage* with the authentic and complex sexualities it is attempting to rule on. Perhaps inevitably, it will not be able to indoctrinate, for the world is too complex and multifarious. But to educate, and to teach with authority, it will need to be a participant within conversations and encounters that it might not either be able to initiate or control, listening to the Spirit within, whilst also understanding that the same Holy Spirit may choose to speak to the church from the outside, and from the unexpected places.

At this point, it would be right to recognize that many will still be fearful for the fate of faith and order if the question of unity is decoupled from that of authority. But this is where the burden of this chapter starts to emerge. I am advocating more open and faithful disagreement (celebrating the diversity of discipleship) as a part of ecumenical dialogue and truth-seeking, which in turn is to be seen as a truer pathway to the churches owning a more authentic teaching authority. But how can I be sure that such a programme will be faithful to tradition? To answer this, I turn to an area of research that was my first love: Christian fundamentalism. As I argued almost ten years ago, the structure of fundamentalistic thinking is, far from being simple and clear, highly complex, differentiated, accommodating and fluid (Percy, 1996a). Exegesis, eisegesis, interpretation and exposition abound. The Bible can function almost totemically in some communities, whilst in others it provides illumination, inspiration and canonicity, but is rarely read or regarded as wholly inerrant.

There is, in short, no *precise* agreement on the nature of the Bible and what it determines of itself for fundamentalists. Some have 'high' views of inspiration, but have abandoned inerrancy. Others qualify inerrancy, insisting that the doctrine only applies to original autographs, excludes grammatical errors or misspellings and is exempted from lack of precision in certain matters, or apparent contradictions. This leads scholars to identify at least five different versions of the doctrine of inerrancy: *propositional* (absolute); *pietistic* (that is, a kind of spiritual biblicism); *nuanced* (some portions of scripture weigh more than others); *critical* (identifies non-essential errors); and *functional* (limited inerrancy or particular infallibility).

I have deliberately taken the discussion slightly 'off-piste' here to show that, even in fundamentalistic communities, there is considerable divergence on what constitutes an inerrant Bible. And bearing in mind that, for such communities, authority flows *from* the inerrancy of scripture (which is to say that ecclesial and ministerial authority is regarded as being *under* the Word), the patterns of authority and teaching in such communities will vary widely. Where there are similarities between them, they may be morphological rather than doctrinal (style, not substance). Of course, a review of the authority of the Bible in

different denominations would reveal a similarly significant range of diversity. Some treat the sacred text as a 'rule book' (instructions to be followed, carefully), others as a guidebook (a few rules, many recommendations, warnings, suggestions and so on), and most interchange between the two. (But is it not the case that the parabolic tradition of Jesus gives the church precisely this permission to act so fluidly?) We may have agreement on *what* the fundaments of tradition are, but not on how to understand them, what weight to place on different aspects of faith and order, nor how to *be* Christian in the contemporary world. (But even this is far from secure. The Salvation Army neither baptizes nor celebrates the Eucharist, but in what sense, though, can they *not* be regarded as Christian? For many in the world, they are a pre-eminent sign of the presence of God and the ministry of Christ, incarnate in some of the most demanding places.) Ecclesial communities are unavoidably hermeneutical rather than (vapidly) receptive. They are *within* the (ultimate) parable of Jesus Christ – experiencing God's story of incarnation, redemption and resurrection as it continues to unfold within them and around them, the Word made flesh (McFague, 1975).

Thus, the authority of the churches – at least in public life – is constituted in the calibre, character and depth of its discipleship. If this sounds too slippery, we would do well to remember that the New Testament offers remarkably little by way of definition as to what a Christian actually is. Christians are known by what they do (activity and vocation), some words that they say (confess), and by what they have (the Spirit of God). But the New Testament does not give the churches a credal definition of what, precisely, a Christian must (or must not) believe in order to count themselves amongst the saints. To be sure, creeds are important, if not vital, for maintaining unity and identifying authority, both internally and externally. But the authority of the church depends primarily on an authentic discipleship that manifests the love of God for the human race and for the whole of the created order. 'We' are known by our fruits, not our seeds.

The stress on discipleship as the fundamental basis for teaching authority takes us back to the start of this chapter and the insistence on the need for parity between authenticity and authority. An emphasis on discipleship also indicates why, on certain occasions, the church fails to be *received* as an authority by the world, since it lacks authenticity and characterful discipleship. Put more strongly, I would argue that the teaching authority of the church rests not on dogma, but on discipleship. And this is surely why, in the (so-called) Great Commission of Matthew 28, there is an explicit link between authority, teaching and the making of disciples. It is a reminder of some words that are usually attributed to St Francis: 'Go and make disciples of all nations. And if absolutely necessary, use words.'

# Chapter 2

# Christianity and Consumerism

## Preamble: Going to Church in Atlanta

The means and modes by which religion can reflect culture, and culture religion, are myriad and multifarious. It is never easy to say at what point culture has appropriated religion and at what point religion has consumed culture, and then begun to sacralize it. In this chapter the exploration is once again centred on the churches and Christianity, but with specific attention being paid to the contribution that religious studies can make to the analysis of the religion–culture debate. Of course, to consider a field as large as this would require more space and time than can be given in a volume such as this. Correspondingly, the foci of the chapter, for the purposes of contextualizing the discussion in the concrete life of the church and contemporary, will rest in a consideration of the impact of consumerism and choice on the shaping of religious identity and behaviour.

By way of preliminary reflection, let us consider two examples of contemporary church life, both drawn from a single day of churchgoing in Atlanta, Georgia. A visit to the Lutheran Church of the Redeemer suggests that it might be a fairly ordinary experience. The church was founded in 1903 and was the first English-speaking Lutheran congregation in the city. The building is of stone and, in its architectural aesthetics, exhibits influences from late nineteenth-century Protestantism. More modern extensions have been added to provide offices, a library and education facilities.

Arriving early for the 9.45a.m. Jazz Service, one is confronted by a gathering that reflects both the theological priorities of the church together with its adopted jazz culture. The main lobby that one first enters from the street feels spacious and airy and is carpeted much like a conference centre. In the middle of this lobby a long series of tables are laid out for a breakfast buffet, with other tables positioned in the corners and at the sides of the room serving coffee, lemonade and other refreshments. The table is a place of gathering: people arriving for the service meet with those who are leaving from the end of the 8a.m. Eucharist. In one corner, a saxophonist, pianist and percussionist lead the gathering in casual hymn singing, set to a jazz beat. Children watch, some dance lazily in the warmth, others sit in comfy chairs and just watch, whilst many adults join in the mellow preamble to the main worship service. The service has no obvious formal beginning, but the music and the beat draw attendees into the emerging spirit of the worship.

This is 'jazz religion' – orchestrated but free, ordered yet casual, easy-listening and entertaining, yet somehow worship. As the gathering thickens, the choir, acolytes and clergy join in the throng, mingling with the worshippers.

There is no formal procession to lead people into the church itself, but somehow the music reaches a level of intensity that begins to move the congregation from the lobby into the main sanctuary, where they take their places in pews and chairs. The lobby is the 'gathering place' – where worshippers meet and greet, and begin to turn to the sanctuary space.

In the service itself, formality (which included a baptism that week) is mixed with more free-flowing jazz praise. The hymns, all of which are traditional, have been set to an upbeat jazz tempo. The congregation participates in the act of worship by singing, but also by responding to the requests for prayer. A time is set aside for worshippers to write down their prayer requests, and, while this is being done, a soft and haunting jazz melody plays. The clergy then move amidst the congregation, collecting the pieces of paper in baskets. They then take them to the sanctuary steps and read a précis of these requests, which is itself shaped within the overall intercessory pattern. This moment is, arguably, the height of the service: the clergy gather the needs of the congregation and then place them before God, but in such a way that the whole congregation can share in the needs expressed. The service concludes with more jazz hymns and improvised music.

The service seems to be intensely personal, and yet also corporate. The gathering and the offering of the prayer requests at the high point of the liturgy, which is at once both casual and ordered, creates a sense of immediacy within the congregation, which the jazz worship appears to complement. The jazz shapes the sacredness of the liturgy, but the liturgy also consecrates the moods, motifs and concerns of the individuals that make up the congregation. Religion and culture are set together in a paradoxical, dynamic and rich fusion. (For further discussion of pragmatism, jazz, spirituality and religion, see Dean, 2002).

A quite different experience can be encountered within the gay subculture of the same city. The New Covenant Church of Atlanta is a gay and lesbian 'mega-church' that proudly proclaims that 'the Spirit of God is being poured out upon all people (Acts 2:17)'. The church has a core membership of several hundred, and attendance figures can easily run to a couple of thousand for certain high days and holy days. But if this seems like an example of niche ecclesial marketing, it is nothing in comparison with the work of the Gospel Girls and the (self-styled) Revd Morticia de Ville, two 'drag queen' acts that lead singing and services in the Atlanta gay bar scene. Journeying out to Burkhart's Pub, one is confronted by a normal American bar, packed out on a Sunday evening. But what marks out the venue for special attention is the entertainment, which is simultaneously secular and sacred. The singers, who clearly dress to impress, use a repertoire of jazzed-up hymns, spirituals and popular music that clearly evoke a form of vernacular spirituality, to which the audience responds.

Similarly, at the nearby Buddies Bar, the Gospel Girls are engaged in both entertainment and ministry. It is not easy to say where one begins and the other ends. The evening closes with the Gospel Girls moving amongst the audience, exchanging the peace in an extended moment of fraternal piety: the whole experience almost defies definition (c.f. Althaus-Reid, 2003).

Both these events are more obviously a cultural representation of religion, but in the very act of representation, religion is given its own (new) life within a fresh and surprising context. Just as with carol singing and other kinds of corporate sharing in 'vernacular' or 'folk' religious songs, the two 'drag gospel bars' of Atlanta show that religious materials and artefacts (that is, hymns, sentiments and so forth) are part of the cultural furniture and not simply confined to what religious institutions express, celebrate and formally reify. The division between religion and culture cannot easily be sustained and can be shown to be premature, or perhaps even false (Hall, Neitz and Battani, 2003, pp. 43–44). Religion and culture are not to be divided. As Niebuhr perceptively notes, the attempts of churches to free Christianity from culture are always doomed to failure:

> Christ claims no man as a purely natural being, but always as one who has become human in culture; who is not only in culture, but into whom culture has penetrated. Man not only speaks but thinks with the aid of the language of culture. Not only has the objective world about him been modified by human achievement; but the forms and attitudes of his mind which allow him to make sense of the objective world have been given him by culture.... (Niebuhr, 1951, p. 69)

## Religious Studies, Culture and Contemporary Christianity

Although Emile Durkheim asserted that the cardinal distinction between the sacred and profane lies at the heart of all religions ('things set apart... and forbidden'), the focus of culture within the field of religious studies clearly questions such sharp definitions and distinctions. The turn of religious studies towards cultural studies is by no means new, but the recent attention given by scholars to religion and popular culture has had a profound impact on the shaping of other debates. For example, the volume of material devoted to popular culture and religion has seriously questioned the adequacy of secularization theories, as well as their proponents. If religion can indeed be found almost everywhere and anywhere (for example, theology and film, religion in *The Simpsons*, spirituality and consumerism – see Pinsky, 2001), then any understanding of apparent religious decline in the Western hemisphere must be revised and redescribed. New explorations and evaluations of religion and contemporary culture are needed to make sense of the changes that are now taking place, such as the processes whereby religion is increasingly subject to privatization, individuation, differentiation and dissipation but, in all probability, not to secularization.

The agenda sketched here is continually raised (though not resolved) in a burgeoning range of studies that concern themselves with religion and popular culture. For example, Elaine Graham's *Representations of the Post/Human: Monsters, Aliens and Others in Popular Culture* (2002), for all its anticipated advancement in the field of practical theology, is rather overwhelmed by the fields of cultural and religious studies that it engages with. Exactly where does theology end and cultural studies begin? In this study, and many others like it,

it is not clear. It remains a fascinating but ultimately inconclusive scholarly adventure. There is plenty of attention to anthropology, cultural studies, gender studies and the like, but it is not clear whether this is a work of theology per se or, rather, a contribution to theological studies with a focus on ethics. The study, for all its sagacity and penetration, takes us to the edge of potentially rich theological engagement, but it does not enter the Promised Land.

Similarly, Mazur's and McCarthy's (2001) study of religion in popular American culture offers an impressive meta-mapping covering an almost limitless sphere of inquiry but, inevitably, can do little more than generalize about particularities and particularize on generalities. However, their approach is promising, insofar as it focuses on the concentrated context of North American religion in popular culture. The book covers a vast field: subjects range from barbeques (food and faith), holidays, commercialism, sport, TV and the like. The main methodological and interpretative approach is set within a Geertzian frame of reference:

> ... his functionalist – rather than essentialist – framework permits [the authors] to explore what religion does for its adherents rather than what religion is... religion and culture are not really things in and of themselves; they are systems of meaning that humans give to things, to the stuff of everyday life.... (Mazur and McCarthy, 2001, p. 5)

Following Geertz, religion and culture are conceived of as 'webs of significance' (ibid.) that connect human thought and behaviour. But, in turn, such connections cannot always be so easily discerned. Mazur and McCarthy warn:

> ... [these] things cannot be calibrated, measured, replicated or easily diagrammed. They are real enough – or rather, their perception is clothed with 'an aura of factuality' – and they are based on things out there (somewhere), but their significance lies in the meanings given to those things by the people who use them in whatever fashion. Using this view here, we are relieved of the burden of finding religious things, and can look more widely for the religious meanings attached, explicitly or not, to such activities as eating, dancing, and calling in to a radio talk show... (Ibid.)

The question arises: is this theology simply capitulating to cultural studies and evacuating its essentialist preoccupations for a vapid functionalism? Or is it setting out on a journey of discovery and engagement that will enlarge its own self-understanding? In the best traditions, it is (hopefully) the latter, and one of the reasons why the matrix of practical theology is such a compelling methodology within this field is precisely because it is committed to risk, engagement and interdisciplinarity: it seeks sagacity within the contemporary cultural milieu. The search for meaning is a legitimate concern for theology, and as individuals, groups and societies clearly look for and find religious meaning outside the proscribed 'formal' religious dogmas and institutions,

theology has an obligation to move beyond its more familiar frontiers and in to the hinterland of cultural studies.

Such a move will necessarily relocate theology within a larger definition of religion, which in itself will require theologians to pay attention to those scholars who are less interested in defending theological priorities and are instead more deeply engaged in the rich task of describing and understanding the religious world and its many meanings and subtleties. Here, we turn to Clifford Geertz:

> The notion that religion tunes human actions according to an envisaged cosmic order and projects images of cosmic order onto the plane of human experience is hardly novel. But it is hardly investigated either, so that we have very little idea of how, in empirical terms, this particular miracle is accomplished. We know that it is done, annually, weekly, daily, for some people almost hourly; and we have an enormous ethnographic literature to demonstrate it. But the theoretical framework which would enable us to provide an analytical account of it . . . does not exist. (Geertz, 1973, p. 90)

Thus, for Geertz, religion is:

> (1) a system of symbols which acts to (2) establish powerful, pervasive, and long-lasting moods and motivations in men by (3) formulating conceptions of a general order of existence and (4) clothing these conceptions with such an aura of factuality that (5) the moods and motivations seem uniquely realistic . . . . (Ibid.)

Geertz fully appreciates that enormous weight rests on 'symbol' in this definition. Moreover, 'symbol', like 'culture', is being used to cover a huge compass of activity. Nevertheless, the definition works at many levels, precisely because religion is also encountered in a myriad ways. As Geertz notes, for one person, a dark cloud is a sign that bad weather is on the way. For another, it is an omen of ill-fortune. For yet another, it is an answer to a prayer: God is sending rain. For another person still, the cloud is a sign from a deity that points to something beyond mere meteorology.

Geertz also sees that just as temporal symbols (such as clouds) may be ascribed meaning, so other, more material, objects 'store' meaning for individuals and groups (ibid., p. 127). Thus, a cross, rosary or a crescent will each provide an instant trigger that cascades meaning to their bearers, relating ontology and cosmology, aesthetics and ethics. Similarly, stories contribute to ideology as a cultural system (ibid., p. 193). Meaning is found not just in plain 'dogma', but also in the myths, stories and folklore that inhabit and shape religious identity:

> The culture of a people is an ensemble of texts, themselves ensembles, which the anthropologist strains to read over the shoulders to whom they properly belong . . . . But to regard such forms as 'saying something of something', and saying it to somebody, is at least to open the possibility of an analysis which attends to their substance rather than to reductive formulas professing to account for them . . . . As in the more familiar exercises of close reading, one can start anywhere in a culture's

repertoire of forms and end up anywhere else. One can stay . . . within a single, more or less bounded form, and circle steadily within it. One can move between forms in search of broader unities or informing contrasts. One can even compare forms from different cultures to define their character in reciprocal relief. But at whatever level one operates, and however intricately, the guiding principle is the same: societies, like lives, contain their own interpretations. One only has to learn how to gain access to them . . . (Geertz, 1973, pp. 452–453)

At this point, the synergy between religious and cultural studies is especially rich. However, it is important to state, for the purposes of this study, that the attention given to religion through the social sciences or cultural studies does not necessarily anticipate a reductionist reading. Although it may be true that a significant number of scholars engaged in these disciplines would assume that their interpretative methodologies were almost inherently secular, it need not be so. Religious studies can, in other words, be sufficiently self-composed to be 'related' rather than 'relative'. A comparative, social or neutral standpoint (which, as Milbank (1991) reminds us, are a form of secular violence or tyranny attempting to 'police the sublime') need not be an end in itself. Correspondingly, the kind of (French Enlightenment reductionism) sentiments expressed in Pascal Boyer's *Religion Explained* need not be representative of religious studies:

Rituals do *not* create social effects but only the *illusion* that they do. . . . Thoughts about the social effect and thoughts about the ritual sequence are combined since they are about the same event. So rituals are naturally *thought* to produce social effects. . . . (Boyer, 2002, p. 292, emphasis added)

In contrast to Boyer, I hold that it is presumptuous to assume that religious rituals merely create the impression of being affective and effective. To my mind, this is a genre of socio-cultural studies that has strayed a little too easily into territory that it need not concern itself with. Questions of meaning are not the same as those of ultimacy and ontology. Boyer's explanation for religion, although compelling, is interpretative rather than complete. Given these preliminary remarks, we now turn to the specific question of religion, choice and consumerism. The discussion is then extended by a consideration of Christmas and some of the recent scholarly work that has focused on its religious, cultural and theological significance.

## Choice, Consumerism and Christianity

In this section, we begin with another vignette that is in keeping with the Geertzian approach that flavours much of this thesis. But, this time, the story is more personal. I begin with a confession: timekeeping is not my strong point. So, as I drove purposefully down the road one wet, April evening a few years ago, I was already slightly late (as usual) to pick up my son from Cubs. But, I mused, there was no need to panic, since the ever-enthusiastic Cub leader normally overran the meetings by at least 10–15 minutes. Sure enough, I

arrived at the entrance to the church hall to discover a group of parents waiting somewhat tardily for their offspring to come out. However, as I joined the small throng preparing to show solidarity in patience, I realized that I had walked into a rather terse and tense discussion. Each parent was clutching a letter from Akela, which reminded parents and Cubs that Sunday was St George's Day, and that Cubs were expected to attend church parade (indeed, the letter stated that it was 'compulsory'). Smart kit and clean shoes were also specified.

The parents stood around, discussing the word 'compulsory'. One looked bewildered and cast around for empathy as he explained that his son played soccer on Sunday, so attendance was doubtful. Another mused that the family were all due to be away for the weekend, and that changing plans for a church parade was neither possible nor desirable. Another looked less than pleased that a 'voluntary' organization such as the Cubs which, she added, her son attended by choice, should now be using words like 'compulsory'. There was no question of obligation; attendance and belonging was a matter of preference. (Presumably the oaths which her son had taken were simply part of a traditional and quaint ceremony that had little actual meaning.)

At the beginning of the twenty-first century, a small vignette such as this is not untypical in Western Europe. Since the Second World War era, the culture of obligation has rapidly given way to one of consumerism. Duty, and the desire to participate in aspects of civic society where steadfast obligatory support was once cherished, has been rapidly eroded by choice, individualism and reflexivity (see Putnam, 2000). Granted, this is not the place to debate such a cultural turn. But its undoubted appearance on the landscape of late modernity has posed some interesting questions for voluntary organizations, chief of which might be religious establishments. Increasingly, churches find themselves with worshippers who attend less out of duty and more out of choice. There is, arguably, nothing wrong with that. But under these new cultural conditions, churches have discovered that they need to be much more savvy about how they shape and market themselves in the public sphere. There is no escaping the reality: the churches are in competition – for people's time, energy, attention, money and commitment.

But it is that last word, 'commitment', that has become such a slippery term in recent times. Few regular or frequent churchgoers now attend church twice on a Sunday, as was once normal practice. For most, once is enough. Many who do attend on a regular basis are now attending less frequently. Even allowing for holidays and other absences (say, through illness), even the most dedicated churchgoer may only be present in church for 70 per cent of the Sundays in any given year. Many clergy now remark on the decline in attendance at Days of Obligation (that is, major saints days or feast days, such as the Ascension). The committed, it seems, are also the busy. The response to this from the more liturgical churches has been to subtly and quietly adapt their practice, whilst preserving the core tradition. For example, the celebration of Epiphany may now take place on the Sunday nearest to 6 January and not on the day itself. A number of Roman Catholic churches now offer Sunday mass on Saturday evenings, so that Sunday can be left as a family day, or for

whatever other commitments or consumerist choices that might now fall on the once-hallowed day of rest. In a survey of American Christians undertaken in 1955, only 4 per cent defected from the faith of their childhood. Thirty years later, a comparable survey revealed that one-third had left their spiritual and religious roots in search of something new (Foster and Hertzog, 1994, p. 23). The culture of choice is transforming churches into market-led spiritual suppliers, especially as worshippers expect their faith and religious values to be a matter of selection rather than obligation. (On this, see P. Ward, 2002, pp. 69ff). As we saw in Chapter 1, the age of the *à la carte* Catholic has already come.

It is not my purpose here to venture into a debate about the precise nature of secularization. Whatever that process is supposed to describe, it seems to me that it can never do justice to the intrinsically inchoate nature of religious belief that characterized the Western European landscape and its peoples long before the Enlightenment, let alone the Industrial Revolution of the nineteenth century and the cultural revolutions of the twentieth century. The trouble with standard secularization theories is that they depend on exaggerating the extent and depth of Christendom. They assume a previous world of monochrome religious allegiance, which is now (of course) in tatters. But in truth, the religious world was much more plural and contested before the twentieth century ever dawned. So what, exactly, has changed? Despite my reticence to accede too much ground to proponents of secularization theses, I readily acknowledge that the twentieth century has been the most seminal and challenging period for the churches in all their history. Leaving aside their own struggles with pluralism, postcolonialism, modernity, postmodernity and wave after wave of cultural change and challenge, the biggest issue the churches have had to confront is, ironically, a simple one: choice. Increased mobility, globalization and consumerism have infected and affected the churches, just as they have touched every other aspect of social life. Duty is dead: the customer is king. It is no surprise, therefore, to discover churches adopting a consumerist mentality and competing with one another for souls, members, or entering the marketplace itself and trying to convert tired consumers into revitalized Christians.

One such initiative is the Alpha courses, begun by Nicky Gumbel from Holy Trinity Brompton, in London. The Alpha courses have attracted millions of followers worldwide and have arguably achieved the distinction of becoming the first internationally recognized global 'brand' of Christianity. In an important and timely study of Alpha courses, Stephen Hunt (2003) uses the well-established sociological framework of the spiritual marketplace (drawing on Ritzer, Lyon and others), in order to illustrate something of the impact of commodification on contemporary religion. Significantly, he demonstrates that the increasingly consumerist cultural turn adopted by the churches that advocate Alpha does not necessarily lead to an increase in the level of religiosity. Or, perhaps put more acerbically, the number of customers for the courses does not necessarily translate into a new army of dedicated converts.

Correspondingly, Alpha is more like a creature of its culture, and far less countercultural than many of its champions imagine. Its features chime almost

too perfectly with postmodern consumer culture: a stress on relationships; a definite nod to the therapeutic; dogma presented with a distinctly 'light' touch; a course to try, but not necessarily a long-term commitment. This is not a criticism, I should add: it is merely an observation. Alpha is arguably the first example of 'mass branding' for Christianity, replete with its own logo, publications, clothing, cookbooks and other non-essential, but-desirable, merchandise such as baseball caps, fleeces, t-shirts, pens and the like. (On popular religious materialism, see McDannell, 1995.) Just as Sidney Carter once lamented those churches that had made their version of Jesus or salvation 'copyright', we now have a version of Christianity that is 'patent pending': the Alpha brand enjoys legal protection, in order to distinguish itself from any pale imitator.

Besides the 'marketplace' framework that Hunt deploys in his analysis, his book is also to be welcomed for its firm grounding in ethnography. As a discipline, ethnography comes in all shapes and sizes: some is mainly quantitative, whilst other kinds can be mostly qualitative; some depend on formal questionnaires and clearly proscribed methods, whereas other kinds are more like 'participant observation' and accept the partiality of the observer/ interpreter as a given. Hunt's journey through planet Alpha (he is both a pilgrim seeking answers and a stranger entering a world he does not belong to), enables the reader to glimpse, perhaps for the first time, how a form of religion, far from challenging consumerism, has itself been consumed by it. Again, this is not a criticism so much as a commonsensical observation. Recent work by Giggie and Winston (2002) shows that modern cities (replete with their pervasive commercial cultures) and religious traditions interact in dynamic, complicated and unexpected ways, producing expressions of faith that aspire to rise above the conventional cacophony of everyday city life. Alpha is just such a product: a faith *of* the market and a faith *for* the market. As David Lyon perceptively notes:

> ...consumerism has become central to the social and cultural life of the technologically advanced societies in the later twentieth century. Meaning is sought as a 'redemptive gospel' in consumption. And cultural identities are formed through processes of selective consumption. (Lyon, 2000, p. 74)

Put more strongly, we might say the regard of humanity for Western modernity is an expression of a piety in which capitalism has itself become a global religion, at least in practice, if not always belief (Goodchild, 2002). So, is Alpha doing no more than successfully marketing a specious brand of Christianity within the wider consumerist cultural milieu, wherein the 'commodification of religion' is taking place? Laurence Moore's seminal study *Selling God* provides a partial answer. Moore argues that secularization theories should give way to an understanding of religion in the modern world, whereby it has become one of a number of 'cultured' and 'leisured' activities that individuals now purchase or subscribe to. Once, religion might have taken a somewhat 'standoffish' attitude to consumerism, and would have only entered the marketplace to censor and condemn it. But now, argues Moore,

...the work of religious leaders and moralists in the market-place of culture [is] immediately entangled in a related but distinguishable enterprise. Rather than remaining aloof, they entered their own inventive contributions into the market. Initially these were restricted to the market of reading material, but their cultural production diversified. Religious leaders...[started to compete] with the appeal of popular entertainments. By degrees religion took on the shape of a commodity.... (Moore, 1994, p. 6)

Hunt's important study is devoted to showing just how far that process of commodification has been reified in Alpha, and how religion can both consume and be consumed by the processes of free-market capitalism. But we can also add a further insight here. Alpha is also a creature of culture. Its structure is a 'fit' for contemporary culture, where the therapeutic and relational have superseded the hegemony of rules and regulations in the formation of churches and Christian life. As one trinity of sociologists note:

...the modern project destroyed religious culture based in interdiction (rules) and replaced it with therapeutic culture based in relations.... (Hall, Neitz and Battani, 2003, p. 25)

Quite so. But what does it really mean to talk about 'consumer religion'? Hall, Neitz and Battani's study of culture is riddled with references to the power of consumerism; they describe a society in which religion has to a large extent, been marginalized – pushed into the sphere of the private (ibid., pp. 130ff., 250ff). So, if the Geertzian definition of religion advanced earlier was both reasonable and fair, some description of consumerism is also necessary here. The idea that capitalism has produced a consumer society is primarily a postwar perception. Typically, the 'consumer society' nomenclature identifies a series of trends that have moved in parallel: the shift from heavy industry to new technology; service providers and entertainments as the new 'industry'; increased consumption as a focus of social activity; the gradual triumph of lifestyles and choice over discipline and obligation; and the shift from associational societies to post-associational societies (see Putnam, 2000).[1]

Of course, these remarks are mere characterizations, but they are not without foundation. Veblen's (1953) account of 'conspicuous consumption' charts the rise (in modern societies) of a new bourgeois and leisured class that is identified less by class and occupation and more by its association with lifestyles that express choice and status. In a different vein, Horkheimer and Adorno (1972), in their discussion of the culture industry, suggest that late

---

[1] 'Post-associational' refers here to First World industrialized and urbanized communities where 'soft' forms of social ordering – such as intracommunal participation through voluntary organizations, shared leisure, charitable or other pursuits – has been steadily eroded by the rise of individualism and consumerism. The impact of this can be measured through the decline in affiliation to, amongst others, local or national political organizations (for example, scouting), the Freemasons or Women's Institutes. The shift in social patterning is profound – from implicit cohesion to one of explicit adhesion.

modern and postmodern life is a distinct mode of production. Commodities are then, perhaps strangely, those materials that society produces to combat alienation. The advantage of this view is that it rescues the 'culture–consumer' debate from the crude and unsophisticated charge that consumers are merely passive pawns within a clever capitalist conspiracy. Instead, consumers are colluding with the forces of material and social production by 'purchasing' pleasure, meaning and fulfilment in what is an otherwise alienating and highly constrained mode of social existence.

The fusion of religious and cultural studies can be enriched further if one considers the central place of shopping in contemporary life (see Miller, 1995, 1998). As an activity, shopping is not only necessary but also, for many, a pleasure. The phrase 'retail therapy' has entered the vocabulary of vernacular life. In theorizing from the perspective of cultural studies, shopping is 'quasi-utopian'; it points towards a future in which there is time and leisure to enjoy the commodities that have been acquired. Their acquisition symbolizes a future with less stress and more time. The shopping mall (cathedrals of consumerism) provide a social focus that encompasses eating, entertainment and gratification, centred on an understanding of humanity that elevates the autonomy and individuality of the consumer. Consumption, then, is a major mode of social expression, and it is perhaps inevitable that it would find its way into religion. But in what ways can such influences be charted?

McDannell's (1995) work shows that Christianity's absorption with consumerist culture is longstanding, but has accelerated in the capitalist optimism of the postwar years. In her richly descriptive and analytical book she examines how the production of religion has shifted from the textual (that is, books, tracts and so on) to encompass the ephemeral (for example, baseball caps, fridge magnets and the like). Inevitably, specious Christian critiques of religious and secular consumerism – themselves, ironically, a product of consumerist culture – are never far behind. Tom Beaudoin's *Consuming Faith* (2003) argues for a spirituality that 'integrates who we are with what we buy'. Interestingly, the premise of this thesis is that what individuals buy, eat and wear says much about their deepest values. Correspondingly, this thesis calls for a deeper practical wisdom in engaging with consumerist culture (but otherwise sees no way out of it, and accepts it as a given).

A different perspective can be gleaned from Graham Ward's intriguing treatment of religion and consumption (Ward, 2003). Here, Ward argues that religion is inherently driven by consumption because it is so tied up in desire. In his illuminating discussion of Herman Melville's *Moby Dick*, he shows how some of that desire is misconceived and, equally, how it is also shaped by events and destiny, and ultimately refined. However, he also warns that:

> ... the momentous growth in consumer culture that began in the nineteenth century paralleled the new Smithsonian economics of free trade and the avaricious drive for conquest, are reflected back in the fears, fascinations and figurations of 'religion', the turns to cosmotheism, the Romantic metaphysics of the absolute spirit, the deity who dominates, and the aesthetics of the sublime. A series of related works cross and recross these various discourses: 'consume', 'consummate', 'consumer' (we might

even add the medical term 'consumption'). This Promethian will, commanding and indomitable, is driven and haunted by a lack as infinite as it is unappeasable. The obsession is death-bound and mad with an absence it can only surrender itself to . . . .
(G. Ward, 2003, p. 113)

This characteristically acerbic (but richly and densely expressed) critique is at variance with more empathetic critiques that can be harvested from that of other scholars whose work might be best expressed as a fusion of theology and cultural studies. For example, Pete Ward's exemplary *Liquid Church* (2002) suggests that shopping characterizes most of contemporary life. Drawing on the work of Bauman, Baudrillard, Bourdieu and James Twitchell, Ward notes that:

> Our competency as a shopper is challenged not so much by the choice of products, events, and experiences but by what they represent: the hopes and dreams, the aspirations and pleasures. To shop is to seek for something beyond ourselves. To reduce this to materialism is to miss the point, or more importantly it is to miss an opportunity. For this 'reaching beyond ourselves' indicates a spiritual inclination in many of the everyday activities of shopping. Rather than condemn the shopper as materialist . . . [the] church [should] take shopping seriously as a spiritual exercise . . . .
> (P. Ward, 2002, p. 59)

The turn towards ecclesiology and missiology takes us back to one of the more central concerns of this book, namely understanding and interpreting contemporary culture and its relation to religion. Ward continues his excursion into the world of the 'spiritual shopper' by reminding his readers that what consumer culture craves is not objects, but their meaning. Thus, conspicuous consumption is not rampant materialism, but is rather a means of exchange and the enjoyment of meanings. Citing the work of Twitchell again, Ward suggests that advertising culture can therefore be understood as being like religion:

> . . . [they are] part of a meaning-making process. Religion and advertising attempt to bridge a gap between ourselves and things, and they do this by offering a systematic order . . . . (Ibid., p. 60)

Consumption is therefore more about meaning than acquisition; consumerism is more about identity than materialism. Strictly speaking, then, the threat posed by consumerism to Christianity is not the material versus the spiritual. It is, rather, a competition between systems of meaning and identification. In this regard, we can suggest that advertising has a teleological and utopian dimension to it: it suggests a new order that is to come. In effect, it offers a promise of salvation within a culture that is already saturated with meanings and materialism. Advertising – pointing towards, bearing witness to and proclaiming – is a fundamentally evangelistic art-science. That which is raised up on the hoardings, reflected on our screens or placed in our hands through mailings or literature is offering ultimacy and dependency. In effect, it is a (seductive?) way out of multiple meanings and materialism through *this* offer

or *that* product. Advertising adds meaning and interpretation to the objects of desire. Advertising, as an industry and art form, recognizes that desire, not need, drives our choices and shapes our consumption. It understands that the culture of obligation and assumption has ceded the moral high ground to that of consumption. Correspondingly, authority, institutions and ideologies have to be desired and liked; they can no longer be imposed (but, for an alternative view, see hooks, 1994).

If evidence were needed that the age of the 'Worshopper' had arrived, one needs to look no further than the mega-churches of North America. These are churches that are catering for several thousand members and employing large numbers of staff in substantial sites. I have visited several over recent years, and their most striking feature remains their capacity to engage with the scope of human desires. A drive to South Barrington near Chicago will surely draw you to Willow Creek Community Church, one of the largest and most prominent mega-churches. The church – in reality a giant conference and meeting centre, with a bookshop, several restaurants, lecture theatres and a large sanctuary – can accommodate about 5000 people at any one time. As a result, the church runs four identical services over the weekend: two on Saturday evening and two on Sunday morning (see Hoover, 2000).

The church as a whole is mostly devoid of explicit religious symbolism, and the services are a fusion of uplifting folksy Christian messages, moral (but not too prescriptive) advice and some singing. The services are 'performative' set pieces that adopt a 'magazine-type' format – carefully choreographed, sensitively hosted and thought-provoking. They are stirring and compelling, but without being demanding or intrusive. However, it is the resources centre that is arguably the most striking feature of the church. The sheer range of self-help, support and encounter groups is overwhelming. There are several types of social group: bowling, soccer and other leisure pursuits for all ages. The therapeutic provision is comprehensive and engaging. There are groups for 'Moms and Daughters Hurting', 'Fathers and Sons Bonding', individuals coping with their own sexuality, or individuals who suspect that they might have problems with the sexuality of their partner. There are support groups offering counselling, help through bereavement, loss, eating disorders (obesity and anorexia) and more besides. On my visit there I counted more than 40 different kinds of self-help, therapeutic and support groups, as well as several dozen groups devoted to sport and leisure activity. The total number of people involved ran into several thousands.

The composition of Willow Creek's membership mostly reflects its context. The congregation is mainly white, affluent, college-educated and working in the city, with a large percentage aged between 30 and 50. The sermons carry an evangelistic timbre coupled to a politically (slightly) left-of-centre appropriation of ethics. In some ways, the ethos of Willow Creek could be reasonably characterized as the 'First Church of Christ the Democrat'. However, a fuller and deeper ethnography of Willow Creek would, I suspect, identify the gathering as a distinctive brand of consumer church: worship, lunch, family activities, leisure events and self-help groups fuse together in a seamless

consumerist experience. The division between secular and sacred is utterly obliterated.


## Christmas, Christianity and Culture

The absence of clear or obvious divisions between the secular and the sacred is undoubtedly puzzling for many within the Christian tradition. This, added to the ascendancy of consumerism, presents a perplexing problem for the churches at a time when they are seeking to recover their identity within an age besieged by assumptions relating to the triumph of secularization. Arguably, this is especially concentrated in the meaning and purpose of Christmas. For many within the Christian tradition, the consumerist appropriation of the festival produces an almost neuralgic response. However, such concerns are hardly particular to modernity. As Jennifer Rycenga notes:

> ...shunned by the Puritan authorities of early New England because of its connections to pagan seasonal celebrations and to sexual and alcohol excesses, the colonial Christmas was celebrated mainly by the working class as an occasion for public revelry and carnival. The eighteenth century often became riotous...the transformation of Christmas into a domestic holiday coincided with the growth of consumer culture in nineteenth century America.... (Rycenga, 2000, p. 142)

Similarly, Nissenbaum (1996) argues that Christmas was transformed in relatively recent times. True enough, the New English Puritans of Massachusetts banned the festival. They had their reasons, and argued that it simply encouraged drunkenness and riot, with poor 'wassailers' allowed to extort food and drink from the well-to-do. Nissenbaum notes how seventeenth- and early eighteenth-century diarists described the festival:

> 'highly dishonourable to the name of Christ...[The people] are consumed in...playing at cards, in revellings, in excess of wine, and mad mirth...' (Revd Increase Mather, Boston, 1687)

> 'The Feast of Christ's Nativity is spent in revelling, dicing, carding, masking and in all licentious liberty...by mad mirth, by long eating, by hard drinking, by lewd gaming...' (Revd Cotton Mather, 1712)

> '...the festival is a scandal to religion, and an encouraging of wickedness...a pretence for drunkenness, and rioting, and wantonness...it is the occasion of much uncleanness and debauchery... (Revd Henry Bourne, Newcastle, England, 1725)

According to Nissenbaum, Revd Bourne noted that Christmas carols, though sung enthusiastically, were often 'done in the midst of rioting and chambering [a common term for fornication] and wantonness...' (Nissenbaum, 1996, p. 7). Yet, by the nineteenth century, the festival had been transformed into one of domesticity and consumerism. Nissenbaum shows how this social transformation depended, to some extent, on drawing upon earlier spiritual traditions,

such as St Nicholas, Baboushka and other popular folk tales. The practice of giving gifts (especially to children) also marked a new economic and social confidence, which also coincided with significant cultural and political changes in attitudes to children. The elevation of Christmas to its present celebratory epoch also draws upon older cultural traditions: the observance of the winter solstice, a brief period of leisure and plenty in an otherwise demanding agricultural year, and so forth. Indeed, the current 'tradition' is replete with ironic overlays. The origin of the legend of St Nicholas (*c*. 300 AD), a patron saint of children, can be traced to modern-day Turkey, a predominantly Muslim country. The story was subject to many variations over several centuries. The image of Santa Claus was transformed in 1844 by Clement Cark Moore's saccharine poem ''Twas the Night Before Christmas', causing many artists to portray Santa as an elf-like figure in a green cape. But the red cape and white beard is primarily the work of another artist, Haddon Sundblom, who dressed Santa in red as a part of the commercialization of Christmas that was propagated by Coca-Cola. The result was the white-bearded, red-caped, black-booted jolly old man we now associate with the festivities (Witzel and Witzel, 2002, pp. 1001–117). But Santa's journey has been a long one: a Christian saint from a country that later became Muslim, to becoming the icon synonymous with Christmas, who owes part of his identity to a global commercial corporation.

Santa's evolution shows that it is almost impossible to draw precise lines between consumerism, culture and religion. The churches' initial collusion in eliding Christ's birth with a range of more secular or non-Christian celebratory themes has meant that their hold over Christmas has been rather tenuous. For some, it is a time of piety; but for many, it is a carnival. Christmas is, ironically, a difficult holiday to Christianize (Nissenbaum, 1996, p. 8; Marling, 2000, pp. 321–55).

However, Rycenga, amongst others, argues that even the modern consumerist-saturated Christmas represents some form of deep, nascent 'residual Christianity'. The season has the potential for the 'consecration of dense symbols' in a cluttered calendar: the giving of gifts, the family, the vulnerability of a newborn child and so forth. Thus, according to Rycenga, and using the work of Grimes, even something as 'simple' as Christmas shopping is at least a secondary act of religious ritual, for it is:

> ...performed, embodied, enacted, gestural (not merely thought or said), formalised...not ordinary, unadorned)...repetitive...collective, institutionalised...patterned...standardised...ordered...traditional...stylised...deeply felt...sentiment laden, meaningful ... symbolic, referential ... perfected, idealised ... ludic ... religious ... conscious, deliberate.... (Grimes, 1990, p. 14)

In such a reading, the shopping mall can be interpreted as a 'cathedral of consumerism': laden with altars, icons and votive opportunities, it speaks of gift, desire and fulfilment. Of course, such comparisons only take the analysis so far. But to its credit, it is the provenance of religious studies to locate and interpret the religious that is beyond the immediate or obvious bounds of faith

traditions. And, in a consumerist society, there can be little doubt that the synergy between consumer culture and religion is complex and interactive. According to David Docherty, the key to reading the relationship between religion and consumerism lies:

> ... not in the opposition between the symbols of natural and transcendent faiths, but in the analysis of the way the former appropriates the latter only to discover that it has swallowed something alien, something that at some stage will burst out and consume the social order that initially consumed it .... (Docherty, 2000, pp. 82–108)

Thus, Christmas is a place where culture and religion collide and compete for meaning. And beneath that synergy of consumerism and spirituality lies a battle for the control of Christmas. However, it cannot be obvious where, precisely, the battle-lines are to be drawn, for what some may regard as plain consumerism, will, for others, be gestures that richly and ritually symbolize gift, love and a gesture towards the transcendent. Susan Roll's fascinating (1995) exploration of the origin of Christmas goes further than most theological treatises by suggesting that the key to the debate lies in developing a theory of time. Roll's central thesis is that the great feasts of Christianity are not, by nature, historical commemorations of actual episodes in history linked to specific and verifiable dates. The feasts are, rather, linked to the explanation of religious ideas (Roll, 1995, p. 23).

Epiphany can be taken as one example of this. The actual date of the coming of the Magi is, relatively speaking, of secondary importance in the Christian tradition. Indeed, some Christians may regard the story of the 'three wise men' as a myth. But this is unlikely to impact on the celebration of Epiphany (literally, 'manifestation'). The feast, because it takes account of the flight of the holy family into Egypt and Herod's massacre of the innocents, is habitually interpreted as being concerned with journeying, exile, violence, refugees, coming and going, visions, dreams, recognition and disguise, and 'true' wisdom. The story is laden with meanings that have embellished the tradition down the centuries. It can be taken to symbolize a range of representative powers recognizing the lordship of the Christ child: gentile, occult, Eastern, non-Christian – all have scope within the brevity of the Gospel account. Other Christian traditions emphasize the aspect of pilgrimage and searching; of surprise and gift; of the vulnerability of the Christ child. But in all these forms of ritual and theological remembrance, the actual time or history of the event is secondary: it is the meaning of the events that are primary.

This leads Roll to suggest that, for several centuries, commercial time has been 'normative'. The time of the church and the time of the merchant (or farmer) are no longer the same. This change can be traced back to before the Industrial Revolution, Reformation or Renaissance. In truth, argues Roll, it is the church that has always adapted to culture and the seasons, by investing them with particular meaning. There are three reasons for this. First, humanity does not look for meaning in time; it creates meaning in time. Second, human activity searches for meaning and sustenance beyond basic needs and seeks to

enrich life. Third, money and consumerism form the basic mode of exchange and interconnectedness (Roll, 1995, p. 38).

Building on this observation, Roll argues that there are two types of time in Christian tradition and culture (ibid., p. 236ff). *Anticipative* time refers to a rhythm of time in which the build-up leads to a peak, followed by rapid decline. *Extensive* time, on the other hand, refers to a pattern in which the high point occurs at the start of the time-segment and is developed during this period. The distinction is useful in several ways. For example, we can immediately see that 'secular' Christmas time is mainly anticipative in character: it can begin when the shops first start selling and advertising wares (say, September), and ends on 1 January. On the other hand, more formal Christian Christmas time is primarily extensive in character; its time of preparation begins in Advent and the season officially concludes at Epiphany.

But the two become blurred, of course. Advent, although anticipative in one sense, is almost wholly lost on the secular world (except through Advent calendars). Churches also make significant concessions to (extensive) secular and consumerist time. Only the strictest churches will avoid carol services during Advent; many will hold Christingle services, nativity plays and other liturgical events, whereby the Christmas message intrudes into Advent. However, these observations merely strengthen Roll's thesis, since they show that in Christianity, at least in its multifarious vernacular forms, actual time (and what it signifies) is less important than the meanings that are attached to festivals.

To earth this discussion more practically, I need only consider the array of events that typically takes place in my local parish church during December. The most popular service is Christingle, which is developed from a Moravian tradition. The children are all given oranges (symbolizing the world), with a candle stuck in the middle (symbolizing the light of Christ). The oranges are made into orb-like objects by red ribbon that is wrapped around the middle (symbolizing the blood of Christ), and four sticks that hold sweets or dried fruit (symbolizing the gifts of God in creation). The high point of the service is when the lights of the church are dimmed, the candles all lit and carols are sung. This service always takes place on the Sunday evening before Christmas Day, and for many families and individuals it is their 'Christmas' service.

In contrast to this emergent and popular tradition, the celebration of Epiphany is markedly low-key. In a number of churches the festival will be celebrated on the Sunday closest to 6 January and not necessarily on the day itself. Correspondingly, in my own home, we have a ritual of inscribing C + M + B, and the date of the new year on our front door, and then processing around the house with the Wise Men from the nativity set. This is a deliberate countercultural shared activity that says something else about the nature of the season and time. However, it is a moot point as to which visitors to our house would understand the alphabetical formula that is chalked up in our porch each year.[2]

---

[2] C + M + B = Casper, Melchior and Balthasar – traditional names for the Three Wise Men.

Given the drift of the discussion so far, it might be tempting to imagine that consumerism, coupled to notions of secular anticipative time, is eclipsing religious notions of time and their meaning. Is there, indeed, a distinct loss of sacred time against normative commercial time? Superficially, it would seem so. Where there is no link with consumerism, sacred time often suffers a loss of extensive meaning. One need only think of feasts such as Ascensiontide, or Whit Monday, and see that their celebration and marking within the public sphere has deteriorated significantly in the last 25 years. Once public holidays cease to be linked to religious events, the sacred loses something of its pre-eminence. On the other hand, Christmas and Easter flourish, arguably, because of the continuing consumerist links with the festivals, and the fact that the religious events are still marked with public holidays. However, lest this sound complacent, a number of Northern European countries are ambivalent about Good Friday being a public holiday. Increasingly, this means that many who celebrate Easter may have fairly inchoate views about Holy Week. Easter Monday as a holiday, on the other hand, flourishes because of its consumerist ties, which is ironic, since Easter Monday has no significant Christian meaning.

However, there is a double irony at work here. The very fact that consumerism continues to draw upon and inhabit religious ideas and events for its own ends also means that religion continues to quietly peddle its countercultural message. As Roll points out, the sentimentalizing of the nativity story at the height of consumerist indulgence creates alternative spaces for different meanings. The lighting of candles, the deliberate elevation of memory, the effort of kinship: each nuance of the Christmas story can act against the consumerist culture that has brought it into the public domain (Roll, 1995, p. 239). Ironically, it is the commercialization and enculturation of Christmas that saves it. It acts to: give alternative meanings to consumerism; give added meaning to consumerism; and take people from the material and functional to the transcendent and mysterious (ibid., pp. 243–73).

Put another way, it is possible to see festivals such as Christmas as secular/sacred and public/private 'felt' Days of Obligation, in which many more will participate than those who actively identify with a formal religious group. Conceptually, this is an aspect of 'believing without belonging' (Grace Davie) or of the social 'structure of feeling' (Raymond Williams) that revolves round a season (ibid., p. 240). Thus, we might return to our Geertzian perspective and restate that it is useful to regard religion as a culture (Warren, 1997, p. 23). It is a signifying system, which demands allegiance. Thus, religion and culture conflict and conflate in equal measure. Religion structures feeling and mystery, orders life, and is itself ordered by life. But it is precisely because religion is a culture (based on the resources of hope and vision) that it can critique contemporary culture (ibid., p. 190). And it is at its richest when it does this in ways that chime with contemporary culture and resonate with the totality of human life and experience. The duty of theology, then, is to be both temperate and engaging, for it can never easily divide religion and culture:

> ... perhaps one way to express the task, or *a* task, of theology, is that of structuring mystery. One might go a little farther and call it even imposing structure on mystery,

but this involves crossing a boundary into an arena where humans have little power, and what we have merely tends to encourage *hubris*.... (Roll, 1995, p. 9)

## Christianity in a Secular Society

This chapter has not attempted to deal systematically with theories of secularization. This has been a deliberate choice, in order that fresh vistas of insight can be opened up on the 'Christianity and contemporary culture' debate. However, in this concluding section, it is perhaps appropriate to say something about perspectives on secularization that I have adopted and which, to some extent, condition the remainder of this monograph.

Secularization is, of course, a highly contested concept. In general, the word is used to describe the relatively recent decline of religion in the Western world. However, even with this very basic understanding, there are some immediate problems. First, religious affiliation in the USA – in theory a liberal, modern state – remains vibrant. Second, Europe seems to be the exception, rather than the rule, when it comes to a general decline in religious interests. Third, it is far from clear that religious interests necessarily decline in direct proportion to the rise of industrialization, modernity, globalization and the like. At the height of the Industrial Revolution in Victorian Britain, church attendance stood at record levels. In post-Second World War Britain new denominations and new religious movements have flourished.

Several objections can be raised against the secularization thesis. First, apparent religious decline (in terms of formal attendance at a place of worship or belonging to a religious organization) must be measured against member-ship of other voluntary organizations or associations. Granted, fewer people belong, formally, to a Christian denomination when compared to the interwar or Victorian periods. But almost all forms of association have declined steeply since those days (cf. Putnam, 2000). There are fewer Scouts and Guides, trade union membership has waned, and there are now fewer members of the Conservative Party than there are Methodists. Recreationally, there are fewer people in our cinemas and football grounds than 70 years ago.

Second, there is reason to doubt the idea that fewer and fewer people are turning to official or mainstream religion. For example, the Victorian period saw a revival of religion and religious attendance that lasted for about 40 years. Yet the trend at the beginning of the eighteenth and nineteenth centuries was the very opposite of this: church attendance was, on the whole, derisory. The evidence for church attendance during medieval times is contestable; some scholars assert that religious observance was strong and others argue that it was, at best, patchy.

Third, statistical surveys continually support the thesis that Europe is the place where the vast majority of the population continues to affirm their belief in God, but then proceeds to do little about it. As a result, church attendance figures tend to remain stubbornly low. Yet this is not a modern malaise, but is rather a typical feature of Western societies down the ages. Granted, there have been periods of revival when church attendance has peaked. But the

basic and innate disposition is one of believing without belonging – of relating to the church and valuing its presence and beliefs, yet without necessarily sharing them.

Correspondingly, scholars are divided on how to interpret contemporary society and its apparent secularity. Sociologists such as Peter Berger have effectively repented their predictions of the 1960s, and now argue that Western society, with all its capitalism and consumerism, remains religious. Historians can now show that increased church attendance may be a response to social unease and dislocation. The Industrial Revolution and the resettlement of postwar Britain both saw a rise in church attendance that may be viewed as a reaction to social upheaval.

Other scholars, such as Callum Brown, have argued that secularization is neither a product of the Industrial Revolution nor of Enlightenment thinking, but is in fact a rather more recent phenomenon. In *The Death of Christian Britain* (2000), Brown argues that the cultural revolution of the 1960s has broken the cycle of intergenerational renewal that was so essential to Christianity's survival. Arguably, the rise of popular culture has done more than any other thing to marginalize Christianity (and religious observance in general) and provide people with other arenas for absorption and entertainment.

Similarly, Robert Putnam's *Bowling Alone* (2000) shows that the rise of popular culture in the USA has had a deleterious effect on many different types of association and voluntary society. Putnam's thesis demonstrates that 'negative social capital' has built up to such an extent that religious affiliation may ultimately be affected. In a country where churchgoing is a normal activity – as many as 50 per cent of the population attend on a regular basis – Putnam's thesis may point to some interesting future trends.

That said, Danielle Hervieu-Leger's (2000) work suggests that religious memory still persists in societies that are apparently acquiring religious amnesia. Although the cycle of intergenerational renewal may be distorted by the invasiveness of popular culture, her work suggests that religion only mutates under such conditions. It may be pushed from the public sphere to the private realm, but it still appears to be able to shape society at critical points. Far from turning their backs on religion, modern societies seem to be perpetually absorbed by it – something argued more than a quarter of a century ago by David Martin (1978).

But lest this sound too complacent (on behalf of the churches), it is important to remember that there is *something* in secularization. There can be no denying that people's perception of social ordering now seldom depends on theological, religious or meta-moral constructions of reality. Society has shifted in its orientation – from a reliance on (or at least a reference towards) theological metanarratives to one that is altogether more pragmatic and contigent, where ambiguity has been raised to a level of apotheosis.

Added to this, we can also note the rising number of 'new' spiritualities, the range and volume of which have increased exponentially in the postwar era. Again, choice (rather than upbringing, location and so on) is now a major factor in determining the spiritual allegiances that individuals may develop.

Moreover, it is not easy to discern where the boundaries now lie between leisure, exercise and spirituality. As the consumerist individual asserts their autonomy and right to choose, clear divisions between religion and spirituality, sacred and secular, and church and society are more difficult to define. Thus, consumerism and choice simultaneously threatens, but also nourishes, religion and spirituality. Spiritual self-help books and other products, various kinds of yoga and meditative therapies, plus an ample range of courses and vacations, all suggest that religious affections and allegiances are being transformed, rather than being eroded, in contemporary society. 'Secular' society seems to be powerless in the face of a curiously stubborn (and growing) social appetite for inchoate religion and nascent spirituality, in all its various forms. So whilst it is true that many in Western Europe are turning from being religious assumers to religious consumers, and are moving from a culture of religious assumption to religious consumption, in which choice and competition in the spiritual marketplace thrive, there may be less cause for alarm than has been assumed.

Ultimately, religion and culture should never be divided up as subjects or objects. Their relationship is fundamental to religion and has been conceived by some as inherent to the nature of society. Cultures include hereditary values that lead to individual, social and collective views on behaviour, beliefs and attitudes. It is generally a mistake to try to define religion outside such social patterning. Religion and spirituality provide a variety of templates for the ordering of individual and collective courses of action, and for culture more generally. Often, religion gives expression to the most cherished or critical moments of social life. Moreover, most major religions have social vision: they wish to see some degree of congruence between social organization and the faith that they espouse.

Typically, the presence of religion within society is characterized by both sacred and social cultivation. Even in faiths which claim a high doctrine of revelation, the expression of the spirituality will be social and disseminated. However, the complex connectedness between religion and society can most easily be seen in national, local or state religions. For example, occasions such as Remembrance Sunday, Mothering Sunday, Harvest Festival and the celebrations of Christmas and Easter within the Western Christian tradition can be highly flavoured with cultural artefacts that have not originated from within the heart of the religious tradition. Medieval mystery plays, equally, can be nascent spiritual vehicles for pursuing a particular social agenda that is relevant to its cultural context. The popularity of carol singing at Christmas is an example of commonplace spiritual and cultural material being widely used outside the control of mainstream religion.

As etymologists of the word 'religion' have noted, the portmanteau word comes from two older Latin words meaning 'to persistently bind together'. Religion, by its very nature, is socially experienced and expressed, and is concerned with having an impact on social realms that are beyond the sacred. Correspondingly, divisions between 'religion' and 'society', although common-place, are invariably false. This is because religion exists not only in its own right, but is also public and finds that its materials, sacred truths, stories,

images and ideas are part of the wider cultural furniture. As I have hinted already, even an apparently innocent phrase such as 'Happy Christmas' bears testimony to this. Religion is so thoroughly a part of society that it cannot be separated out entirely from its context as though there is somehow a pure essence that could be studied. Equally, and to repeat, society takes such a hand in creating and ordering religion, that society itself cannot be properly understood without some reflection upon religious ideals and practices.

In conclusion, three particular issues that focus the study of religion and culture are worthy of further attention. First, globalization appears to lead to an increase in spiritual pluralism. Under such conditions, societies that have been ordered through one particular religion now find themselves having to adjust and accommodate a range of faiths within the public sphere. This can create some ambiguities and occasionally lead to tensions between competing convictions. At this point, society can appear to be less coherent and may struggle to reconcile some of its religiously-funded but implicit values with other more explicit faith claims.

Second, there seems to be little evidence that religion is becoming less of a feature within contemporary culture. For example, the interest in spirituality – religious and sacred sentiment outside the immediate control of formal religion – has been burgeoning for many years in the Western world. It would seem that, in the midst of consumerism and secularization, people are turning more than ever to texts and techniques that inspire and enchant. This appears to result in the continual (if somewhat diffuse) infusion of inchoate spirituality at every level of society, suggesting that society, no matter how atomized and incoherent, persists in its quest for sacral meaning amidst the everyday reality of mundane modernity.

Third, vernacular Christian spirituality appears to thrive in the gaps between the ideal and the real, and between formal and operant religion. At its most visible, a faith offers a means for expressing and ordering public grief, celebration and memorialization, at local, national and international levels. It is precisely at the breaking points of human existence that religion lends the strength and vision to society to reconfigure itself and imagine new beginnings. Religion, in other words, still has the marked capacity to enable society to exceed itself and, in so doing, improve upon the present and build for the future. Religion is that which 'binds' things together; spirituality is its expression. Individuals, ideas, communities and nations, set alongside their pain, grief, hopes, healing and celebration, are brought together in ways that continue to sustain and nourish societies, enabling them to see beyond the immediate and transitory and catch a glimpse of the timeless and the ultimate. Societies, it would appear, have always needed this. Religion not only provides it; it also gives meaning to the very cultures that continue to seek the something that is more than human.

# Chapter 3

# Theology and Cultural Challenge

## Introduction

During the last 50 years, and since Niebuhr's ground-breaking *Christ and Culture* (1951), a significant number of theologians have attempted theological engagements with 'culture'. Broadly speaking, there have been two major modes of engagement in relation to contemporary culture, which have to some extent bifurcated. The first tradition broadly conceives of the engagement as a form of interlocking combative encounter with contemporary culture. The second broadly sees it as a form of intrarelated binding, covenant or commitment. Both lead to the formation of their own distinctive cultures (for example, characteristic missiological and ecclesiological outlooks), which increasingly do not know how to talk to one other. Although the adoption of both strategies delivers a certain degree of poise and reflexivity, their inability to relate to one another leads to an impoverished form of public theology. In effect, both traditions could be said to be somewhat culturally dyslexic (the etymology of the word lies in a conflation, from the Greek *lexis*, 'to speak', and the Latin, *legere*, 'to read'). Thus, and of culture, it could be said that modern theologians and the churches tend neither to speak properly nor read well.

Niebuhr suggests that there are five theological responses to the complexity of a Christian faith immersed in culture. The first type stresses the opposition between Christ and culture; this is the Christ *against* culture. The second type is diametrically opposed to the first: 'there is a fundamental *agreement* between Christ and culture'. This is the Christ who is *of* or *for* culture. These two basic types represent the two primary faces of engagement that can be identified in the life of the church, and the remaining three types all flow from these two primary typologies. However, there are also four distinct types of religion–culture relationships that can be identified: religion is part of culture; culture is part of religion; culture may be 'religious'; and religion and culture can undertake a variety of serious academic dialogues. It is the last of these that we are mainly concerned with in this book, although that will enable a 'reading' of the other three types.

Given the issues already sketched and critiqued in the preceding chapters, the incompleteness of both faces of engagement may already be apparent. Rather as Troeltsch thought, the bearers of the Christian tradition long to give something to the world, but invariably do not know how (or what, perhaps?). On the one hand, Christians can provide symbolic legitimation for the prevailing society and culture, thereby generating the 'church type' of interaction that theologians such as Barth were so critical of. On the other hand, there can be protest against the prevailing powers and an attempt to set

up a counter-society, thereby generating the 'sect type' response that Tillich was so critical of.

Arguably, the resolution of this is far from easy. It may partly depend on appreciating the axis of paradox that is inherent in engagement, and seeing it as a necessary device for poise, theological commitment and discernment. However, no sooner is this contemplated than another paradox begins to emerge: God meets us 'outside' conventional forms of revelation, but then also comes to us in culture and engages with us through the ordinary, even as we attempt to delineate the tradition and experience through our own paradoxes such as the Radical Orthodox.

It could be argued that a theology of culture needs to be a *collation* of the two faces of engagement if theology is to re-inhabit public space. In so doing, it can be both a 'thick description' of reality as much as it can become a critique or affirmation of the same. As we have already hinted, such an argument may be pursued by paying some attention to specific and commonplace religious motifs and practices that have become part of the 'cultural furniture' of society, including sacramental practice, such as baptism, or the celebration of Christmas. The actualities of these beliefs and practices – Christian traditions that have deep roots within culture – *require* theologians and the churches to rethink their *pastoral* nature as part of a new theological understanding – what Nicholas Healy might call 'practical–prophetic ecclesiology' rather than 'ideologies of the church'.

So to return to Troeltsch, baptism, for example, is not administered adequately by either the 'church type' or 'sect type' orientation, since the controlling ideology normally restricts the mode and tenor of cultural engagement. Yet if the ministry of the church is to reflect God's self-gift in Jesus Christ, then there will be an element of praxis in the pastoral which will actually *shape* the gift that is defined and delimited by the ideological. Baptism (or in more vernacular lingua, 'christening') will be at once an ambiguous sacrament of welcome at the very *borders* of the church even as it proceeds from its *centre* and speaks of a specific intensity of faith. Thus, rightly conceived, the sacrament invites a church–world 'negotiation' (between 'culture' and 'religion', or 'orthodoxy' and 'vernacular religion') as a sign of God's grace and inclusivity, but without penalizing the borders of its necessary exclusivity. As one cultural commentator notes: 'religion is not effective because it is otherworldly, but because it incarnates this otherworldliness in a practical form of life...a link between absolute values and daily life' (Eagleton, 2000, p. 38).

Thus, a theology of culture that understands a social–sacramental approach to the religion–culture divide might invite us to get beyond an imagination that traces a transition from a secular reality (that is, bread, water, and so on) to a sacred state (that is, of transformed materials), and to no longer belong to the categories we thought we imagined. Rather, we would belong to a transformed community that has a wisdom that is above the inherently false secular–sacred divide. Ironically, it is in the pastoral that the paradoxes of the two faces of engagement can begin to be resolved, for they are 'lived out' in other forms of creative tension. The church can relearn the art of becoming a 'genuine

community of argument', marked by mutual respect, diverse discipleship, common engagement and respectful critique.

Such a view might lead us to explore the identity of culture as a hybrid or relational affair, and a theology that closely corresponds to that reality, yet without actually mirroring it. In other words, there is the space for the paradox to affirm and critique what is created. There can be a sense of the gap between the sign and referent, even though a social sacramental theology may 'saturate' such a space. Because Christian identity itself is both contested and relational, it hinges both on cultural engagement and being open to direction from the free grace of God. This might allow us to relate the 'core' values of religious belief to society/culture in a more reflexive manner, which in turn creates new possibilities for theology as a public discourse. Drawing inspiration from writers such as David Tracy, *conversation* can be commended as a major mode of theological engagement. Equally, *collage* can be considered as an analogical and methodological description for how theology is to be constructed in relation to culture. In so doing, theology is able to attend to whole areas of human experience and understanding that are normally neglected by faith communities. But such a move requires a risk – namely of theology ceasing to operate as an autonomous discipline ('private grammar of faith') – and to take its place as a distinctive mode of discourse that seeks to operate within wider social and academic contexts.

Ultimately, theology should not be considered as a mode of reflection that can be placed at the margins of culture; it should claim its full citizenship as a member of that culture. The particularity of theology should not be allowed to collapse into, or be confused with, privateness. Particularity and publicness are not opposed. A theology of engagement that makes a virtue out of paradox (as an axis that brings poise and reflexivity) can seek to be *empathetically participative* within culture and can make a distinct contribution to public life.

In view of these preliminary remarks, we now turn to consider and critique three different types of theological engagement with contemporary culture, each represented by a key figure. The divisions (or rather characterizations) follow the work of Peter Berger and his *The Heretical Imperative* (1980), which attempts to systematize the responses of theologians in three distinct modes. The first is the deductive possibility. Here the Word of God (or the tradition) is the starting point, and there can be no other way of knowing God. The gain of this theological outlook is certainty and mastery in the mist of cultural confusion. John Milbank and 'Radical Orthodoxy' have been chosen to represent this outlook. The second mode is the reductive possibility, where it is deemed that the tradition has to be rationalized in order to be credible for the modern age. In reductionism, the core of the tradition (ethics?) has to be rescued from the thick veneers and overlays of myth that have obscured the tradition over time. 'Faith' has to be freed from 'religion', and reflexivity is a byword for this approach. The Belgian theologian Lieven Boeve has been selected to represent this tradition. The third approach, according to Berger, is the inductive possibility. Here there is a movement from tradition to experience or, more accurately, the recovery of experience as a means of reconstituting the tradition in the modern world. The inductive possibility traces the religious

experiences that began the tradition. In that sense, it is profoundly sociological, but at the same time not reductive. David Martin has been chosen to represent this approach. In considering all three, our focus remains firmly ecclesiological. In other words, we are concerned with these authors' theology in terms of its capacity to shape the church in the task of engaging with the complexity of contemporary culture. In pursuing this line, we are drawing on the agenda outlined earlier, and in particular the challenge laid down by the work of Nicholas Healy, namely to identify models of the church that take a serious account of the actuality of ecclesial life rather than 'blueprints'.

## The Deductive Possibility: John Milbank and Radical Orthodoxy

As Gavin Hyman suggests, one of the great ironies about the end of foundationalism is that it has heralded the return of religion. As institutions and ideologies collapse and decay at the beginning of the twenty-first century, religion (that which was dormant and repressed) has reappeared. There are undoubtedly many reasons for this: making sense of life in the midst of chaos; providing consolation in the midst of alienation; offering hope in the midst of doubt. Hyman suggests that there have been two principal theological responses to the resurgence of religion. The first, ironically, has been to reassert anti-foundationalism. Typically, such theological strategies are represented by figures such as Don Cupitt and Mark C. Taylor. Although their theological projects are quite distinctive, they nonetheless 'write within the post-Nietzschean space of the death of God and the postmodern space of the end of metanarratives' (Hyman, 2001, p. 2). The second tradition is arguably broader and represents an attempt to recuperate theology, even though it will now be informed by postmodern thought. The principal 'school' that champions this move is Radical Orthodoxy, identified through writers such as John Milbank, Graham Ward, Gerard Loughlin and Catherine Pickstock. Radical Orthodoxy, as a movement – and simply expressed – is an attempt to recover premodern modes of theological thought, fusing them with postmodern thinking, in order to counter the 'apotheosis of modernity'. This gives rise to various labels for the theological school and its stratagem: 'postmodern Augustinianism', 'conservative postmodern theology', 'post-modern orthodoxy' and, finally, 'Radical Orthodoxy' (see Milbank, Ward and Pickstock, 1999).

It is important to understand that the Taylor–Cupitt and 'Radical Orthodox' stratagem, although quite different, are linked by the fact that they are both responses to modernity. The former sees modernity as inevitable and, to some extent, desirable. The latter regards it as a form of violence and oppression that has resulted in 'secular tyranny' (Hyman, 2001, p. 52). However, the rich irony of this assertion is that it is itself a form of violence. In refuting, dismissing and attacking modernity, Milbank's insistence becomes a kind of compelling form of intolerance that reasserts Christian 'mastery' over all other narratives and cultures.

It is not my purpose here to engage systematically with the entire range and depth of Milbank's work. My primary concern here is to offer an evaluative sketch that will explore the adequacy of Radical Orthodox theology as a form of engagement with contemporary culture. This immediately brings us to one of the most critical points of interest in relation to Radical Orthodoxy: the role and scope of the 'human sciences'. For a significant number of theologians (for example, Farley, Lindbeck and Martin), the use of the human or social sciences has been an important and staple complement to their theological work: 'the sociological imagination as classically deployed undercuts religious and theological pretensions' (R. Roberts, 2002, p. 191). Milbank, in contrast, sees such alliances as problematic and deadly. He asserts that such partnerships are doomed either because theology becomes an adjunct of secular reason or because theology then alienates itself by confining itself 'to intimations of a sublimity beyond representation' (Milbank, 1990, p. 1). In response, a number of theologians claim that the social sciences have been misnarrated in order to be outnarrated. As Roberts notes:

> Sociology as a discipline should not be construed *reductively* and *exclusively* in terms of the perverse metanarrative of secular reason. Sociology and the social sciences may also be classically understood as the *critical representation* and *clarification* of patterns of social organisation necessary to the sustenance of humane societies, rather than (as Milbank would have it) the partner in the promotion of an allegedly necessary and totalitarian violence of order. The tasks of theology and sociology are mutual at least inasmuch as they address the human condition in exploratory and interpretative terms, and do not subsume (in however virtuosic a fashion) *everything* under the dance of death and totalitarian logic of Western secular reason. Moreover, sociology and theology which embody concerns for the other cannot afford to neglect or express contempt for ethnography, that is the effective representation of and interpretation of what is actually happening in human lives. Both theology and the social sciences should be concerned in their distinctive ways with life and with how things are – and might be. (R. Roberts, 2002, p. 206)

Put another way, a theology that is uninformed by the social sciences may turn out to be very clever and erudite in some sense, but it may also be ultimately 'unreal'. But there are other concerns with Radical Orthodoxy as a suitable theological means of engaging with culture. First, Radical Orthodoxy is a peculiar alliance of the premodern and the postmodern. That said, it would not be fair to describe it as 'anti-modern': it isn't. But the movement is concerned, generally, with the scale of influence that modernist and Enlightenment thinking has had on theology. It regards that influence with suspicion. In this respect, Radical Orthodoxy wants to reinstate theology as a primary narrative for social, political, cultural and philosophical discourse. It critiques and demonizes social sciences as 'modernist meta-narratives' that are, in reality, the illegitimate kith of theology (although they are apparently unaware of their parentage). Radical Orthodoxy holds that there can be no neutral 'social' readings of the world or traditions that do not depend on a prior ontology of knowledge.

Second, Radical Orthodoxy, as a term, is a curious oxymoron. Postmodern and paradoxical, it shifts a little too easily between conservative and liberal positions, dogmatism and praxis. One is tempted to ask: what is the difference between Radical Orthodoxy and conservative heterodoxy? It is an ecclesial programme, often guilty of a degree of idealism and imperialism. It pays little attention to other faiths and the grounded reality of pluralism, or indeed of complex local congregations. It treats the church as a given construct – the City of God. In contrast, I take the view that there is no version of Christianity that is without a local accent. No-one can speak, or ever has spoken, of 'pure' Christianity or 'pure' theology. The dialect is always particular: Rome, Geneva, Canterbury, Atlanta – Christianity speaks in tongues that are tinged and tilthed in local contexts. In my own recent writing I point out how Radical Orthodoxy resembles the missiology of Leslie Newbigin – with its insistence on the reality and primacy of Christendom – but with Radical Orthodoxy having overdosed on metaphysics. Correspondingly, some critics describe Milbank's programme as a kind of postmodern quasi-fundamentalism.

Third, and a point that may seem odd to some, although relevant to the discussions on modern ecclesiology that follow, I note that most of the leading lights in Radical Orthodoxy are English Anglicans (with 'catholic' tastes), and I want to suggest that this has a particular bearing on the shape and identity of Radical Orthodoxy. If I am right – that Radical Orthodoxy is a marriage of the premodern and the postmodern – then what we have is an alliance (or versions) of Patristic, Scholastic and Renaissance thinking fused together with continental philosophy, with its face set squarely against modernity. But is the target not also liberal Protestantism? I think it must be. (Milbank, for example, ridicules 'the poverty of Niebuhrism' – see Lovin, 1995). But more particularly, Radical Orthodoxy could be read as a movement that tries to *renarrate* the church. I find this interesting, because Anglicanism's peculiar genius is *not* to have solved the problem of its own identity – although that looks increasingly ragged as a virtue, at present. Anglicanism is episcopal, yet synodical; Catholic, yet Protestant – the *via media*. It is no surprise, therefore, to discover that most of the leading lights in Radical Orthodoxy are of the Anglo-Catholic tradition. Indeed, there is something rather Tractarian about Radical Orthodoxy. Perhaps this is unsurprising, given that the spiritual crucible of the key figures of Radical Orthodoxy is Anglo-Catholicism, with its emphasis on aesthetics, romanticism and idealism. So the Protestants were right. If episcopacy was not extirpated, it would come to dominate the church. Ultimately, Radical Orthodoxy wants to impose a basic kind of 'solvedness' on the church and society. In Radical Orthodoxy we witness a kind of assertive intellectual episcopacy that believes it is ordained and consecrated to control. Its programme is simple: to reorder the world and church by outnarrating its existing meta-narratives. Hence, the premodern and postmodern unite to refute the modern – a classically Tractarian move, but with a postmodern twist.

Fourth, it is worth contrasting Milbank's work to Ward's. Milbank's is striking, strident and original. Ward's work, however, is original in a quite different sense: as interpretative montages and pastiches. Ward's work ranges perceptively, imaginatively and often deeply over vast fields of intellectual

inquiry. In a matter of a few pages, one can find oneself rubbing shoulders with poets, philosophers, political thinkers, theologians and novelists, with the subject matter fusing together doctrine, sexuality, psychology and sociality. It is, strangely though, a form of theology that is a product of its culture and time. Access to material makes fast, penetrating and absorbing critiques or theses possible. But there is a strange sense in Ward's work in which one feels one is watching a master-artist of bricolage or montage at work. It is postmodern reconstructionism: artful, inventive and subversive. For example, what makes Ward's (1995) treatment of Barth and Derrida an intriguing theological project is not that he has read either one correctly; most of his critics seem to agree that he hasn't. It is the fact that he has put them together at all that makes a statement, which is as once performative, dramatic and affective, even as it is ultimately unpersuasive. But such work should not be confused with other kinds of art.

So we might say that Ward's work turns out to be something akin to an elaborate Luboc montage. Or then again, perhaps a better comparison is to a (great) contemporary fashion design. It captures the spirit of the age (late 1990s and early twenty-first century), and yet pushes those boundaries of taste in a voguish and intriguing manner. The cut and styling of the theology is sharp, attracting the eye. The paradox of the theological composition is daring yet familiar – urban chic meets Oxbridge tweed? This is avant-garde theology, to be sure. But for all its novelty, it is strangely unoriginal. For Ward is primarily a designer and shaper of materials; but he does not spin his own yarn, nor weave his own cloth. Ward's theological substance is constituted in a style of fusions. Here, postmodern theology has come of age.

These points assume a greater relevance when they are set within the field of modern ecclesiology, Christianity and contemporary culture. Modern ecclesiology, as conceived by Nicholas Healy, Edward Farley and others, is concerned with the shape of the church in relation to modern life. Modern ecclesiology does not reject 'idealist' claims for the church – such that it is 'the body of Christ' – and so forth. It takes such theological claims with utmost seriousness. But it also understands the church to be a social gathering, and one that is therefore open to the kinds of interpretations and clarifications that are normally gleaned from the social sciences. Modern ecclesiology is therefore always more than a simple restatement of theological principles; it takes account of context, and understands the church to be both ascription and description, projection and revelation. It is as much about excavating the 'archaeology of the house of faith' as it is about any ontology. Radical Orthodoxy, in contrast, although advocating a kind of recovery of the past, is nonetheless an exercise in inventive imagination. It gives birth to thought, but not to action. It reconceives the church of the intellect, but not the church of the ordinary world.

Towards the end of *The Word Made Strange* (1997), Milbank offers an analogy of faith, comparing it to a giant gothic cathedral. It can never be seen as a whole, yet it is; it is always complete, yet never; it is enclosed, yet boundless. Milbank's analogy is, I think, an ironic moment of self-defeat for Radical Orthodoxy, since the analogy expresses that, no matter how much a

cathedral is a given, a sacred space and more than the sum of its parts, it is also the work of human hands.

That is why I am drawn to Nicholas Healy's *Church, World and Christian Life* (2000), where he calls upon theologians to take more notice of the 'concrete church' and of social sciences such as ethnography. He argues that too much ecclesiology is shaped by 'blueprint' or 'ideal' descriptions of the church – what the church could or should be like, but not what it is actually like. Put another way, modern ecclesiology ought to take more account of its actual shape and context than it normally does. In such an equation, theology need have nothing to fear from social sciences when it comes to understanding and interpreting the church. Modern ecclesiology will always be apples and oranges – the proverbial fruit salad. It will explicate and interpret claims to be the body of Christ against the observations and interpretations of sociologists and those others from the social sciences. It will come to see that, no matter how churches imagine themselves theologically, they can also be understood sociologically and without that being a necessarily reductive exercise. This is a vital task in theological engagements with culture, which will include recognizing the cultural determinants within any given theology. Ultimately, the debate is not whether sociology can contribute to modern ecclesiology – it clearly can. The question is in what ways, and by how much? Verily, there are many rooms in my father's house.

## The Reductive Possibility: Lieven Boeve and Reflexive Theology

Beyond the Cupitt–Taylor theological tradition, which might be understood as a capitulation to modernity, and the tradition of Radical Orthodoxy (a refutation of the same) there is a vibrant range of theological approaches to modernity that constitute a 'third way'. Writers such as Tanner, Farley and Browning make a serious attempt to engage the tradition in ways that are deep yet reflexive. Indeed, their arguments usually depend, to some extent, on understanding Christian tradition as being inherently and dynamically 'open'. Their views will be touched on later. But, from a European perspective, let us first examine Boeve's theological approach to the crisis facing Belgian churches in the twenty-first century. Boeve's diagnosis is as follows:

> ...the church is so out of touch with modern culture and society that the church is obstructed in its efforts to initiate. Only when the church is able to bring its doctrine, ethics, spirituality and organisational structures up to date will faith become a credible option once again... the diagnosis leads one to the unavoidable conclusion that an ever-increasing gulf exists between contemporary culture and the Christian faith. The days of 'traditional', cultural Christianity are numbered.... (Boeve, 2003, p. 6).

Boeve's thesis rests on a number of assumptions. He accepts that the Catholic Church (at least in his own context of Flanders) once determined the shape and scope of human sociality. However, that same church is now struggling; the

transmission of faith is flagging, and this has had a deleterious effect upon the cultural domain, which has become rapidly de-Christianized. Traditional Christianity is, in effect, worn out. Boeve argues that the church needs to accept that it is ill-equipped to face the challenges and questions posed by contemporary culture. It then needs to recontextualize its presentation and meaning and, in so doing, create a new and more respectful dialogue between Christianity and contemporary culture. Granted, the foundations for the thesis are contestable. But Boeve's response, interestingly, is not to reassert the tradition. It is, rather, to find modes and patterns of engagement that will 'rescue' the church from a kind of self-imposed private exile. This assertion is based on his sophisticated understanding of secularization, which is primarily problematized as a range of cultural moments that have pushed religion from being a public discourse and praxis into the realm of the private:

> ...secularisation emerged as the direct consequence of functional differentiation... diverse sub-systems emancipated themselves from the all-embracing religious horizon...[religion] lost its prominent role [the] all-encompassing source and point of reference for human values and convictions...religion was forced to take on the form of a sub-system, developing, among other things, its own logic, institutions and role patterns. Religion came to focus exclusively on the promotion of the religious function in society, side by side with, yet distinct from, the other institutions. In doing so, religion was forced to withdraw from public life, its relevance reduced to the organisation of the private arena and intimate relationships, side by side with the fulfilment of a comfort/consolation function.... A second consequence was the generalisation of values. Where the local community once derived its convictions with respect to truth and value entirely from its own traditions, this was now only viable (and to a lesser and lesser degree) in the private arena.... (Boeve, 2003, p. 39)

These observations resonate strongly with our earlier remarks on consumerism, religion and culture. The collapse of ideologies and meta-narratives is mirrored in the demise of institutions and forms of public and civic association. The ties that bind society are increasingly undetermined, at least by any obvious moral force. Sociality is thus rendered more fragile, and depends on collections of individuals to make up the gap that is created in a post-associational culture. Boeve, noting this cultural turn, writes:

> The root causes of individualisation are to be found in the centuries old process of modernisation...[1] increased education; [2] increased economic capital which guarantees material independence; [3] urbanisation; [4] mobility; [5] massively expanded leisure possibilities; [6] persistent rationalisation of life.... (Boeve, 2003, p. 53)

For Boeve, postmodernity can actually be defined as 'reflexive modernity'. Correspondingly, he readily accedes that the overall narrative in which Christianity is now situated is one of 'marketisation' – this is the only master narrative. In such a context, Christians operate reflexively within the reflexive society. However, there is a danger in this:

...there is evidence of the religious consumer exercising his or her right to self-determination. The result is an a la carte religious identity. Religious communities often fall in line with this process and become 'service providers'.... (Boeve, 2003, p. 55)

But Boeve argues that even in the market-driven world, stories continue to be told and faith survives. He calls on the churches to engage in open, rather than closed, narratives of tradition. What does he mean here? The open narrative is framed, but inviting. But it is not overly dominating; it is not a 'meta' in the 'over' sense, but in the 'with' sense. Jesus, rather like the parables he tells, invites us into a realm of questions and multiple interpretative possibilities. Jesus is, in some sense, 'the open narrative of God'; the incarnation is an aspect of the reflexivity of the life of the Trinity.

To speak of reflexive theology is, then, to speak of a semi-fluid but substantial mode of being. Theology is always more than just thinking about God. It is art, dance, liturgy, protest and practical. It is an *activity*. As Paul Van Buren reminds us, it is the movement of people 'struck by the biblical story, in which they undertake to revise continually the ways in which they say how things are with their present circumstances, in the light of how they read that story' (Van Buren, 1969, p. 53). Where and when the story strikes, there is power, response and religious community: the body of God, the church. Indeed, following Pierre Bourdieu, it is possible to see sociology as fieldwork in theology (Bourdieu, 1990, p. 28). Because God does not come to us 'neat', but through agents and ambiguity, it is necessary to examine how power is diluted and distorted – and perhaps even expose how we are deceived. It is not only theology that can speak about the power of God. Sociology may test the agents of power, as much as political science may examine their moral use and abuse: the 'monarche' of God is generally transferred to states, individuals and ecclesial structures. It is in these places that we find the power of God translated. In view of these remarks, three points for further reflection seem an appropriate point with which to conclude this section.

First, orientation in the culture of late modernity remains a serious issue for many who are religious and wish to defend some conceptualization of God, whether it be absolute or qualified. In part, a better orientation may be achieved if modernity and postmodernity are better understood. A clue to how this might be achieved comes, ironically, from a sociologist. Anthony Giddens prefers the term 'post-traditional' to postmodern, and suggests that society is now engaging in 'social reflexivity' (Giddens, 1991, pp. 21–43). According to Giddens, people have to filter rapidly growing amounts of information for themselves, such that they are increasingly reflexive about how they are influenced by ideas and, in turn, how their actions influence society. Social reflexivity is an individual and communal process of reflection and action that allows foundationalism or meta-narratives to have a bearing on the world without necessarily dominating. In other words, ideology participates in the world without becoming totalitarian. In Giddens' view, therefore, moral fundamentalism is a much greater danger to society than (controlled?) moral relativism.

Reflexivity is an important concept here. It is no accident that post-liberals and 'post-evangelicals' are at the forefront of constructing meaningful dialogue between traditions that were once alienated from each other (Phillips and Okholm, 1996). But there are dangers to be heeded as well. Theology and ecclesiology might be swayed by culture rather than discerning it and exercising discrimination (Williams, 1989, p. 103). It is not clear what would test 'reflexivity': the very concept itself risks engulfment (Flanagan, 1996, p. 26). Reductionism, relativism and failure most likely lie ahead if the reflexivity does not correspond to some form of revelation. As von Balthasar notes, there must be a sociality that relates to what is limitless, beautiful, radiant, revealed and transcendent: reflexivity without this is just choice and self-evaluation (von Balthasar, 1982, p. 28). The Christian traditions of immanentism and interventionism could combine to counterbalance reflexivity and, in some ways, re-inhabit the gap created by the discourses of modernity.

And yet, second, and linked to the first point, it does not follow that reflexivity with foundations leads to their compromise and eventual erosion. The suggestion being made by Giddens is that a post-foundational culture presents new opportunities for relating to fundaments. In an even more positive vein, Kieran Flanagan has suggested that power 'may reach a perfection in a theological context' that sociology and 'culture' cannot match, and that theology can enable (sociological) reflexivity and, in effect, call it to account (Flanagan, 1996, p. 207).

Third, and linked to the second point, what Middleton and Walsh call 'anti-totalizing' meta-narratives become highly desirable commodities as vehicles for the power of God in this new post-foundational[1] situation (Middleton and Walsh, 1995, p. 107). The question, already put, is how can any meta-narrative be anti-totalitarian? 'Meta', when used in conjunction with narrative, means 'above': dominant, or reigning over. But in other usage, it can mean 'with', 'by' or 'beyond', as in the case of metaphysics. Perhaps the task for narratives about the dominion of God in a postmodern world is not to be 'over' the world, but in reflexive theology to be both with it and beyond it. In other words, stories of power and domination become rewritten as stories about love and relationship. Furthermore, 'with' implies a journey, where truth is encountered in the future through teleology or eschatology. Christianity is transformed from a propositional religion into a pilgrimage, in which God goes with us, yet is beyond us. This, it seems to me, is the heart of Boeve's theology – it is deeply reflexive reductionism that seeks to engage faith with contemporary culture.

---

[1] 'Post-foundational' refers to societies that have moved beyond accepted meta-narratives and embraced a more postmodern ethos.

## The Inductive Possibility: David Martin and Socio-theology

The selection of David Martin's work to represent the Bergerian inductive theological strategy may seem puzzling to some, especially as Martin is primarily known as a sociologist of religion. However, David Martin's scholarship also extends into several types of theology. He is comfortable working within doctrinal, ecclesiological and homiletic fields; he is also equally at home operating within pastoral and practical theology. Arguably, his work is too diverse and complex to be easily categorized (although this could also be said of Boeve and Milbank). To be sure, it is not immediately obvious how Martin's theology might be identified as inductive. However, a few preliminary observations can set the scene. First, Martin's sociological foci dispose him to concentrate on the social constructions of reality that have a direct bearing on the shaping of (religious) experience. Second, his interests in ecclesial cultures (perhaps especially Pentecostalism) suggest that he is more alive than most to the possibilities of experience being recovered in order to reanimate tradition. Third, Martin is also well aware of the socio-theological dynamics of induction, whereby the cyclical movement between tradition and experience is constantly reborn in ecclesial contexts that are themselves immersed in contexts that demand a memory and resonance of the past in order to shape the present and the future. Such trajectories of thinking can be traced in *A Sociology of English Religion* (1967), a profound reflection on practices, attitudes, beliefs and opinion, to explanations and structures of belief, to the more homiletic tone of *Christian Language and Its Mutations* (2002), which examines the aesthetics, fundamentals and dynamics of belief in relation to modernity. Throughout, Martin is consistent in taking 'ordinary' Christian experience seriously, and in reflecting upon it sociologically, theologically and inductively.

So, whether it is doctrine, liturgy, Pentecostalism, Methodism or Anglicanism, Martin's work has often brought new insights to those communities, as much as his writing has illuminated other scholars. Undoubtedly there are personal reasons why this may be so. David Martin is a scholar who is critically engaged with his subjects, but also deeply aware of their own reality and integrity. But in order to consider Martin's inductive theological approach, let us first examine his distinctive approach to the sociology of religion:

> ...at the simplest level he can organise surveys based on sound principles of selection and questionnaire construction to elicit given ranges of fact ... the next level could be that of interpreting and collating survey results ... quite clearly, this level of interest includes an assessment of all these various kinds of data in historical perspective. There remains the level of what may be called institutional analysis: the relation between the social structures of the Church and the structures of society at large at the national and local level. The task here includes a long-term and intimate knowledge of 'geological' shifts in this structure.... (Martin, 1967, p. 107)

Lest this presumes too much omni-competence on the part of any sociologist, Martin is at pains to stress the limits of their discipline. He states that, whilst on the one hand, 'without such research, comment is useless', the only possible

comments after research are in fact 'cautionary': a sociologist can only 'indicate the range of possible interpretations . . . before any [one] interpretation can become persuasive'. Thus, '[he] is a man with a set of tools, a training, a group of relevant queries . . . some accumulated insights which probably bear on the problem in hand . . . [he] is not a conjuror . . . '. Then, critically, he adds that a sociologist must have, built into their intellectual armoury, 'a scepticism about conventional "images" and how the world "works", or explanations of current social phenomena' (ibid.).

Here, Martin's description of sociology contains more than a hint of rigour. He is arguing for a form of inquiry that goes beyond appearances and generally held assumptions, which in turn propels us into the original reasons and motivations for actions, structures, beliefs and organizations. In particular, Martin is critical of the extent to which the culture of well-meaning but amateurish guesswork guides so much of the church's thinking. Martin points out that the Church of England collects 'just enough statistics to know that it has a variable temperature, but supports no investigation to find out why' (ibid., p. 108). His work often criticizes the churches for their absence of a real research culture and calls upon them to reconsider their 'empirical condition' (in other words, to reflect inductively on their experience) as well as the methods of investigation and interpretation that can service their actuality.

The epicentre of Martin's agenda for the churches, arising out of his inductive stratagem is simple enough to narrate. His theology is not 'pure' in that he does not begin with metaphysical or philosophical questions. Generally speaking, Martin's theological reflection, begins with the lived experience of individuals or groups or with the professed creeds in relation to their contexts. It is, in other words, engaged. In that sense, it is proper to describe Martin's theology as classically 'practical', meaning that he is prepared to see how culture, contexts and experience shape the range and trajectory of theological discourse, on the basis that it has always done so. This, however, does not lead to reductionism. It is precisely because experience is taken so seriously in relation to tradition that Martin can be identified as a practical theologian in the inductive tradition. (Practical theology in the deductive tradition is normally called 'applied' theology, and in the reductive tradition it is termed 'contextual'.)

To press these distinctions further, the difference between proper practical theology and systematic theology can often be as stark as that between an artist and an engineer. At the risk of extending the mechanistic metaphor further, Martin is well aware that the church largely prefers to commission and collect ornaments, but it seldom builds machines. And when it attempts the latter, the design is normally a good decade or so out of date. This is a tendentious remark, granted; but it should be obvious to many sociologists that churches do not normally know how to organize or investigate themselves, are poor at gathering accurate data about their own ecclesial life, and even poorer at interpreting it. In short, they are aesthetically gifted, yet often structurally frayed and dated. Martin's practical sociology (or perhaps his understated ecclesiology) takes this dynamic seriously. He is aware that beauty (even when it is simply constituted in order, creeds or liturgy) is what shapes experience, and it is this that gives birth to tradition.

David Martin's sociology and practical theology is, correspondingly, sharp and coherent when he comes to address the English parish church. In a now famous essay, he notes that 'sociology cannot answer evaluative questions about the social role of the church; it can however clarify thinking by elucidating unacknowledged presuppositions which may be shaping current thinking' (Martin, 1988, p. 43). It is with such inductive socio-theological thinking that he can rein in some of Leslie Newbigin's theological reflection on the nature of the church, describing it as 'eloquent' but 'tenuous'.[2] Martin, as a theologian and sociologist considering the apparent increase in 'associational' patterns (that is, a more congregational–denominational approach to mission) for the church, prefers to begin with social reality rather than Newbigin's dubious biblical eisegesis. To do this, Martin narrates a picture of the situation in England as being somewhere between Northern Europe and Northern America. He is characteristically generous to the American 'associational' model, pointing out (rightly) that some churches that have 'only been put up within ten years [are] riddled with community functions...doing an extraordinary business in putting out tentacles into the wider community' (ibid., p. 46). In Scandinavia, the 'competition is *very* limited', but the service the church offers to the community is 'utterly ecumenical', by which he means socially and theologically comprehensive. This picture describes the broad sociological context. But why has the parish church declined?

Martin is not sure that it has, exactly, and as with his work on confirmation, he presses the church to look a little harder at the material it is offering and a little longer at the audience that it supposes it has lost. That said, he makes some remarks that are sociologically cautious and are in turn designed to caution the church. For example, he points out, following Hugh McLeod, that between 1880 and 1930, various social and economic factors caused the rich and powerful to lose interest in the church. Labour movements, expanding public services and consumerism all played their part: England became progressively more areligious (but note, *not* anti-religious).

Martin then sets about discussing and critiquing various strategies that attempt to address the decline in the status of the parish church. North America and Europe are discussed, but neither offers a viable model for the Church of England. 'Modernising' or reforming is put up and then pulled down; Martin does not think that 'producing a new book of liturgy...is somehow going to transform the overall situation' (ibid., p. 49). So far, he is proved right. The sudden introduction of the *Alternative Service Book* for the Church of England was certainly no panacea, but Anglicans cannot know (because they have not researched) whether modern rites have arrested decline or, in fact, caused it.

Martin's assertion that ecumenism is 'associated with weakness' is equally worthy of attention. So far as Martin is concerned, denominational collaboration is unlikely to 'make much difference'. Besides, there is no

---

[2] Newbigin's ecclesiology could be justly characterized as Evangelical, adopting a hostile and negative stance on Christianity's relationship with post-Enlightenment culture.

sociological evidence that competition between denominations impedes the overall mission of the church, even if it is theologically and ecclesiologically undesirable. Martin also rejects the 'less means more' argument: that if only the churches could lose financially draining church buildings, clergy and so on, there would be resources to do more. He cites some examples of Finnish churches, which are fantastically equipped and resourced but otherwise comparatively empty; only 4 per cent of the population attend church on average, dropping to 0.5 per cent in the inner cities. The other strategies discussed are handled in a more polemical way. Martin rejects liberalizing trends in theology, ranging from left-wing proclamations to process theology. Finally, he also dismisses the recovery of communitarian models of the church as a viable strategy, believing that it does not really cut into the problem.

The conclusion of Martin's essay is as an eloquent apologia for the parish church as one will ever read from a sociologist: a homily, if you will. Writing out of a deep sociological consciousness that is richly informed through practical theology, he notes that, despite so many social trends moving against the parish church, it nevertheless retains strengths and virtues. He points out that:

> ...many of the networks of charity, of voluntary work and of the arts, especially music, link up with the social network of the parish...then there is latent 'folk' religion which....does have some kind of focus in the parish church, notably through rites of passage...the parish church [also] offers some kind of meaning which is embodied architecturally...it [is] often the only non-utilitarian building in certain areas. It is *there*...[suggesting that] people are still in some ways located, whatever social or geographical mobility does to them...[enabling] them to retain a sense of place, a sense of origin, a sense of continuity...[this] goes back several hundred years. (Martin, 1988, p. 51)

One might accuse Martin of preaching at this point, but that would be unfair. But in terms of the theology and sociology on its own ground, Martin is again ahead of his time here, quite consciously writing a language of enchantment, imagination and nostalgia into the discipline. It is this sort of work that makes Martin's sociology and practical theology so engaging and persuasive. It is a practical theology and sociology rooted in the contextual situation of the churches, helping them to meet triumph and tragedy in social trends and statistics, to deconstruct the academic and cultural trends that impact belief, and to inculcate the wisdom of discernment.

In Martin's inductive thinking, the sociology of religion emerges as an attempt at categorization – 'establishing normative epochs' for meaning (D'Costa, 1996). It concerns itself with describing phenomena in commonsensical ways, creating categories of meaning and knowledge in order to give a 'social' account of what it sees. Thus, 'religion' tends to be treated like a 'thing' – an 'object' of scientific analysis – and deconstructed accordingly. Correspondingly, religion is broken down into its (alleged) constituent parts (for example, sacred–profane and so on) or referred to in functional terms (such as 'social legitimization', 'projection' and so on). Like many modernist

human sciences however, it often fails to see *itself* as a construction of reality –
social or otherwise. As Catherine Bell points out, 'that we construct "religion"
and "science" is not the main problem: that we forget we have constructed
them in our own image – that is a problem' (Bell, 1996, p. 188).

In saying this, Bell is suggesting that a 'pure' description of phenomena is
not possible. Any good inductive theological strategist would know this. But
scholars in both the human sciences and theology are engaged in an
interpretative task and describe what they see according to the prescribed
rules of their grammar of assent. Sociology of religion has often tended to
assume a humanist-oriented perspective which has sometimes imagined itself to
be 'neutral'. Thus, sociologists describe what they see, whilst theologians and
religious people are said to 'ascribe' meaning to the same phenomena. On the
other hand, those who have had religious experiences feel that what they
experience is 'real', and the sociological account is therefore deemed to be at
best complementary and at worst unrepresentative. Invariably, both
approaches forget that 'religion' is a complex word with no agreed or specific
definition. It is the task of the inductive theological strategist to understand the
present, seek the wisdom of the past and, in so doing, change the future.


## Reflexive Religion and Contemporary Culture

To return to contemporary culture, we are now in a position to reinstate the
normality of religious practice as primary material with which theology should
be rightly concerned. The danger of being preoccupied solely with a theological
stratagem for engaging with contemporary culture is the possibility of
assuming that the primary locus of religious activity is organized (in churches)
and easily observed. But, in reality, any post-associational (Western) society
has hundreds of different outlets and expressions of spirituality and vernacular
religion. For example, Flory and Miller's recent work draws attention to the
practice of tattooing within Evangelical youth subcultures. Despite the clear
biblical prohibitions on marking the body (Lev. 19: 28), the authors have
uncovered new attitudes to baptism that are countercultural and yet profoundly Christian (Flory and Miller, 2000, p. 15). Granted, the connection
between baptism and tattooing may not strike one as being immediately
obvious, but Flory and Miller are able to show that, just as baptism is an
invisible mark (of the cross, and usually on the forehead) so tattooing can, in
certain types of youth counterculture, be a deliberately visible and indelible
mark that signifies the promises and fruits of baptism: repentance, rebirth, and
belonging. In this way, the tattoo performs the same task as the sign of the
cross with water and oil; it is the outward sign of an inward grace. Similarly,
Grimes has recently drawn attention to the vernacular spiritual responses to
the Estonia ferry disaster of 1994, in which several hundred lives were lost
(Grimes, 2003). Once again, the shaping of religious experience in response to
traumatic events is discovered to be a delicate fusion of 'official' and 'operant'
religion, in which the culture of grief and loss is reified into a newly constituted
spiritual expression.

These two examples, though apparently slight, lead us to a provisional observation – namely that any assessment of adequate theological engagements with contemporary culture must rest on three specific tests. First is the extent to which such a theology is *reflexive* within modernity. Second is the ability of that theology to cope with *events* that are basically outside its control or obvious purview. Third is the degree to which such a theology is prepared to *engage* in empathetic dialogue with culture, listen and take account of the views of others. Each of these characteristics assumes that theology (and ecclesiology) can no longer afford to sit on its dignity. Nor can the discipline of theology judge the world or other disciplines from a position of privilege. In other words, theology should be capable of risking itself in all kinds of social, intellectual and cultural intercourse, since it depends, to a large extent, on a quality of engagement for its value as a public discipline.

To test this further, we now turn to one of the most seminal and defining global events in the twenty-first century, namely the events of 11 September 2001. Almost everyone will have their own personal recollections of this day – where they were, how they heard the news, what they did and how they reacted in the aftermath. I arrived home that day for my youngest son's fifth birthday party. I had been at a conference all day and was quite unaware of the news. When I walked into the house, at around 5.15p.m., I was prepared for the usual bunfight. But instead of the frantic celebratory atmosphere, the mood was sombre, anxious and uncertain. Nobody quite knew what was happening – only that a lot of people had died that morning, and that you had to keep watching repeats of sparse news footage to drink in the magnitude of the events.

Earlier in the day, a colleague in Connecticut, about two hours' drive from New York, had just started a seminar on Jewish–Christian–Muslim relations, hosted by Hartford Theological Seminary, a renowned research institute. By 9a.m. the seminar had stopped, and the leaders of different faiths had gathered around a TV to watch the breaking news. By noon, they had moved to the chapel to offer collective prayer, united in their disbelief and shock, and yet bound together by faith. The outcome of that day is a remarkable book called, unsurprisingly, *11 September: Religious Perspectives on the Causes and Consequences* (Markham and Abu-Rabi', 2002), in which theologians reflect on the events and their significance.

Theologians are often not the best people to reflect on events; their eyes are more usually fixed on the timeless and on those select issues that might affect the future of faith. But 11 September is one of those pivotal moments in time that prods theologians and asks them what they are doing to facilitate dialogue and understanding across the faiths, especially when one of the underlying causes of 11 September centres on contested sacred space many thousands of miles distant.

Ian Markham, one of the authors and editors of the book, identifies four major responses to (or discourses surrounding) the 11 September attacks. The first is the mainstream American interpretation that sees the assault on the World Trade Center and the Pentagon as an attack on freedom, democracy and the American way of life. The second response understands the attacks to

be an indirect assault on Israel by Arab terrorists. A third response by some Americans is to see the other side of this claim and adopt a more empathetic attitude to the plight of the Palestinians, and therefore question American foreign policy in the Middle East. Fourth, a significant number of Americans adopt a 'mainstream' Christian fundamentalist stance and understand the attacks of 11 September to be, in part, the judgement of God upon an increasingly secular and liberal America. God, in other words, has allowed this to happen in order to punish America for its national sins and immorality. Such views were faithfully recorded in a discussion between Pat Robertson and Jerry Falwell, with Falwell claiming in a live television broadcast that '[to] all of them who have tried to secularize America, I point the finger in their face and say, "You helped this happen".'

As Markham points out, there is little dialogue taking place between these groups and distinct discourses, and interreligious conversations that might foster better understanding are still relatively rare occurrences. But, if there is to be any real hope, institutions and faiths must begin to take responsibility for promoting such dialogue. This is all well and good, but I wonder whether there is room for a fifth mode of discourse at the table – that of the ordinary Americans and their responses to 11 September?

When I was next in New York myself, I caught a taxi from the public library down to the General Theological Seminary. I chatted with the driver as we dodged the traffic and asked what she had been doing on the day. She recalled her bafflement at the plumes of smoke coming from downtown Manhattan and how, when the roads had become gridlocked, a man selling newspapers ran out to her cab and told her to turn on the radio. When she realized what was happening, she set off for the Twin Towers and began ferrying people, but soon the roads became blocked completely. 'It was then', she said, 'that people started drifting past me in slow files, like a kind of well-ordered biblical exodus.'

Take a trip round Manhattan now, and the fencing surrounding the World Trade Center Church is festooned with photographs, messages, flowers and candles. Up near Bleeker Street, a shop selling ceramics has appropriated a whole street corner and covered the fencing with individual glazed tiles that carry messages of grief, hope and peace. Brightly decorated, the tiles have turned a major road into a shrine. In fact, almost everywhere you turn in downtown Manhattan, you can see a flag, a candle, a picture or a message. The vernacular religion of New Yorkers – which the British became familiar with at Hillsborough and after the death of the Princess of Wales – is everywhere to be seen. At the heart of this most secular city, religion seems to be leaking out on to the streets. But what are we to make of this?

In a recent collection of essays, Peter Grimes suggests that there are three approaches to ritual that demand theological attention. The first conceives of ritual as unchanging and being almost independent of human agency. In such a view, ritual is 'highly symbolic acting', covering the annual and transitional points of life. Exponents of this outlook include Victor Turner and Mary Douglas. A second view regards ritual as focusing on the 'changeless', with 'high rituality' now becoming immersed in everyday life, especially for those on

the margins of society. A third view places an emphasis on performance and process that then defines actors. In other words, the ritual is assessed through its capacity to help shape the social construction of reality when that reality is itself shattered or challenged. Thus, in terms of event-driven theological reflection, a reflexive form of theological engagement that takes a serious account of people's experience has more to commend it, especially in terms of its capacity to discern how and why operant religion or vernacular spirituality operates in response to traumatic events.

Grimes, noting how society responds to events such as the Estonia ferry disaster, suggests that ethnographies that explore religion and society reveal several things. First, the church continues to provide rites and other mourning tools that provide shape and meaning for society. Second, in public memory the church buildings continue to serve as sacred places. Third, priests and ministers continue to function as symbolic representatives and ritual actors in social situations. Fifth, for many individuals, lighting a candle is a symbolic action. Sixth, church bells have resonant symbolic functions in times of grief and solace. Seventh, the significance of prayers and orchestrated silence has a public value far beyond the meaning that can be intended (Grimes, 2003, p. 191). Whilst this does not amount to an especially sharp theory of religion in public life, the commonsensical nature of the observations should not be underestimated. The treatment of ritual reminds theologians that religion is public and is part of the cultural furniture; it is a resource for more than just the faithful. Correspondingly, a theology of engagement needs to be continually committed to dialogue, overhearing that is, patient and attentive listening to the conversations of the world in which the churches and theology are habitually not included, and to an encounter and event-based mode of praxis.

That said, and to return to the events of 11 September, it would not be unfair to suggest that, for most New Yorkers, the dominant mode of discourse in the wake of 9/11 continues to be one of incomprehension. On one of my earlier trips past Ground Zero in 2002, a woman who had lived in New York for 20 years turned to me and said: 'I can't believe they did that. All those people in that building. Why? I can't believe it.' Some years on, I suspect she still speaks for most Americans. And it is not difficult to see why. The sudden and violent removal of the Twin Towers has left a permanent visual scar on the New York skyline and on the collective memory of its inhabitants. They grieve not just for their people, but for their city and its wounds. They are still a people numb with shock; they cannot believe what they no longer see.

The reactions of theologians to 11 September are as diverse as they are interesting. Consider, for example, this response to the events from a Radical Orthodox perspective:

I had been attending a conference on paradise that day when I heard the news.... The shadow of the twin towers of the World Trade Center stretch across this whole work, yet I have remained silent about the events in the United States on 11 September 2001. That demands an explanation, on moral grounds. I am not certain I can ever provide such an explanation...I could not weave...11 September into my

narrative as if I understood the part it played in the unfolding logic of 'true religion'.... (G. Ward, 2003, p. 154).

Events, in other words, seem to confound the Radical Orthodox perspective. And this particular event comfortably neutralizes the 'outnarrating' agenda that lies at the heart of the theological movement. In contrast, however, Markham and Abu-Rabi''s contribution to understanding the events is located in dialogue, listening and engagement. Starting with 'events' as 'pivotal moments' that can change theology, Markham recognizes that moments outside the separate world of theology can have a profound impact on its course and weight as a discipline and field. He sees dialogue (not just talking) as an essential component in constructing a new theology that can cope with the cataclysmic events of 9/11 (Markham and Abu-Rabi', 2002, p. 206). But what makes the book all the more theologically rich is the variety of perspectives that are brought into dialogue with one another and also with the events of 11 September. Jack Ammerman's essay explores the theological priority of moving from data collection to documentation, and ensuring that ethnography is at the centre of any future theological reflection on the events. Nancy Ammerman examines the vitality of religion and social capital exhibited in the wake of the tragedy. Perspectives from Ibrahim Abu-Rabi' and Ingrid Mattson critique the role of the violent Islamic praxis.

Is there any hope of these discourses about 11 September leading to something more? As I have already hinted, I suspect the answer lies with the ordinary American people. But it also lies in being prepared to engage with others on a basis of mutuality and exchange. Furthermore, and as Ian Markham points out, such engagements may be costly and may themselves turn into transformative encounters rather than static exchanges. In 'over-hearing' the world of another, one is naturally invited to reconsider the foundations of one's own beliefs. To truly engage will be to change and to discover something of the richness and diversity in the traditions of others, as well as the depths and reflexivity of one's own (Markham, 2003, pp. 8–15). Equally, a practical theology of engagement needs to consider that there are moments when assimilation is appropriate; when resistance is essential; and when dialogue, encounter and deliberately conceived 'overhearing' are vital, if a larger understanding is to be arrived at (ibid., pp. 48–56).

If I may offer a simple illustration of this at a practical ecclesial level, I recall a visit I made in 2002 to a small city in the Mid-West to audit a college for a British university. I go every year, and our hosts, always most gracious in their hospitality, duly escorted us to their favourite restaurant. Now, it turned out that most of the staff at the restaurant were Muslim (or at least Middle Eastern), and on 13 September 2001, several large black sedans had rolled up to the premises and taken the staff away for questioning. Their families had no idea where they were taken to, and no idea when they would be back. The usual courtesy telephone call to one's attorney seems to have been set aside. The shroud of 'national security' in the wake of the attacks seemed to snuff out any talk of civil liberty. (Just recently, Congress has passed a bill allowing the government to 'monitor' all cellphone calls.) But with no staff, the business

could not run and was in danger of closing. A local church leader, hearing of the restaurant's plight, arranged for local Christian volunteers to help run the restaurant until the Muslims were released. This duly happened after several weeks, but the church, meanwhile, had kept the restaurant viable.

I offer this story because the Muslims and the Christians in this small city had had little to do with each other up until this point. It was a prime example of events causing what Markham calls 'overhearing' in engagement; this is the praxis of deeper listening. My guess is that had this taken place in Britain, most Christians would have written to their MP and protested, but the business would have closed due to lack of staff meanwhile. In other words, the contours of 'civic religion' run differently and deeply in America, and they appear to be shared across faiths: respect for your neighbour, and a belief in their future and yours, together. Granted, it is not much of a discourse, but it is a sign of hope when people of different faiths can come together over a shared and common interest, even if it is only lunch at an American diner.

**Theological Engagement**

The burden of this chapter has been to explore the potential and limits of three types of theological engagement with contemporary culture. Granted, Milbank, Boeve and Martin could each be said to exceed the category into which they have been placed. All three are, in fact, richer and more sophisticated than Berger's categorizations allow. However, as a guide to the task of engagement, Berger's work serves its purpose. We can see that Boeve's reflexivity is well motivated and does not necessarily lead to an ecclesial or theological impoverishment. Milbank's reassertion of tradition – a fusion of the premodern with the postmodern – is no less engaging, even if many will struggle to articulate what kind of church this theological agenda actually envisages. (Radical Orthodoxy is, strangely, somewhat impotent when it comes to looking at ecclesial vision and the fruit that might issue from such a daring ensemble of theological perspectives.) David Martin's strategic thinking, more sociologically informed than the work of Nicholas Healy, takes the grounded experience of the church seriously as a major component within the structuring of theology and the life of the church. It begins with engagement and consistently leads to a rich form of *phronesis*.

However, ecclesiologically and in terms of theological engagements with culture, I suspect that a fusion of reflexivity (or limited reductionism) and inductive approaches will be the principal mode of orientation for theology and the churches for the future. As I have already hinted, Martin's inductive strategy can work for the church, perhaps producing materials that complement or form practical or pastoral theology, or various boundaries for ecclesiology. This is because sociology tries to offer empiricism married to imagination – forming, exploring and critiquing social reality no less than religious tradition and theology. How strange, then, that Radical Orthodox has worked so hard to distance theology from the social sciences in order to preserve the 'purity' of theology. Milbank's book, *Theology and Social Theory*

(1990) still remains one of the key rallying posts for the Radical Orthodoxy camp. It is, in many ways, a brilliant and sharp book yet, as I have argued before, it is also a 'hermeneutic of suspicion about hermeneutics of suspicion': strangely anti-liberal and anti-modern; oddly pro-Christendom. Whilst there is undoubtedly plenty to admire from Radical Orthodoxy, its trajectory is troubling in places. Subsequent offerings from the Radical Orthodoxy camp have attacked the 'discipline' of religious studies or emphasized that all social sciences are 'descended' from theology, either as legitimate heirs or as distant bastard children. Such critiques possibly have their merits, but they lack generosity.

For example, what father or mother tells each of their children, throughout their lives, that all their achievements are really those of their parents? Or that without them, they would not exist, so, please, always acknowledge your debt and know your place? Radical Orthodoxy does not argue so much for the restoration of theology as 'queen of the sciences' as it does for the church and theology being the father of us all. Even if this is entirely true – which I doubt – what about some considered praise for other 'disciplines' that can now teach theology, inform it, civilize it, dialogue with it or even outnarrate it? Is theology so small and shy, or old and grumpy, as to be unable to acknowledge the breadth and depth of other constructions of reality, even if it still wishes to be considered as revealed? David Martin's work offers a sociology and inductive theology in the service of the church, but in a spirit of gentility and humility. It does not threaten but, as we have seen, it does challenge. Theology must take account of such voices if it wishes to be in any way public and 'practical'.

In contrast, it would hardly be unfair to characterize much of Radical Orthodoxy as profoundly docetic: a kind of disembodied rhetoric that, for all its eloquence and brilliance, lacks any real earthiness. In its dismissive attitude towards other strains of theology and the social sciences, it also sets itself apart from, and above, other potential conversational partners. It is a character-istically tough and abrasive form of theological discourse, despite its playfulness. This, I suppose, makes it a kind of pushy theological bullying accompanied by an element of self-justification. Furthermore, because it almost never starts from where people are, it fails to produce any kind of ecclesial vision or realism into which individuals and communities might wander. So where does all this lead us? Mudge, in his vision for sociology and theology fused together to form a critical ecclesiology, suggests that the problem with Radical Orthodoxy is that:

> ...[it] risks a kind of institutional docetism. I fear as well that Milbankian communities are going to be unable to communicate with Christian communities of other persuasions, but only with other Milbankian communities, a prospect which looks very like the birth of some new communion. [But] I want churches to share many of the common preoccupations of a world that human science is helping to make one. We may all find affinities between ecclesiological social science and social theories of other kinds, owing, it may be, to common origins or common aims. But whether or not this happens, we want ecclesiological social theory to hold other viewpoints in respect; to be in conversation with them. They can help keep us honest. (Mudge, 2001, pp. 6–7)

So Radical Orthodoxy is indeed a curious phenomenon in theology when one considers that there are many forms of ecclesial correlation for each of Berger's three types of theology. The deductive, reductive and inductive, in turn, have many forms of ecclesiological manifestation that express their theological priorities. But to press the question again, where would the church of Radical Orthodoxy be, and what would it look like? The mere fact that we don't know the answer to this question suggests more than just aloofness; it also points to a reticence, possibly a lack of commitment, and arguably to a deficiency in engagement. One can imagine several kinds of church that embody a deductive theological stratagem: Evangelical, conservative or even Catholic. Likewise, reductive churches that embody radical or contextual traditions are common-place, especially within the liberal Christian tradition. Ecclesiologies that embody an inductive theological stratagem are more difficult to identify, but they probably find expression in Pentecostalism, Quakerism and in other spheres where spiritual experience is a valued theological priority.

But it is simply not easy to imagine, let alone locate, the church of Radical Orthodoxy. For all the talk of 'outnarrating' modernity, Radical Orthodoxy is a curiously unengaged theological movement. Like its Tractarian ancestors, it lives in the world of aesthetics, imagination and play; it splices together the premodern and the postmodern, and opposes the modern; and it is usually above conversation and beyond comprehension. Such an end point is no place from which to begin a strategy of theological and ecclesial engagement with culture. More listening, humility and openness will be needed if the churches are to recover their poise in the public sphere as agents of social transformation and socio-spiritual renewal. It is to this exercise we now turn in Part II of this book where we attempt to sketch a vision for theology and education that genuinely engages with cultural complexity.

# PART II
# ORDINARY THEOLOGY

# Chapter 4

# Acuity, Clarity and Practical Wisdom

## Introduction

A theologian, on being approached by an earnest young student, was asked: 'What is your methodological starting point?' The theologian replied simply; 'A theologian is always beginning in the middle of things' (R. Williams, 2000, p. viii.). The wit, clarity and acuity of the reply says something important about the nature of theology and about what it is engaging with. In this chapter we now turn to considering the nature of theological formation by exploring it in relation to contemporary culture through the discipline of practical theology and paying particular attention to the shape of theological education. The study, like the discipline of practical theology itself, is critically reflective, refractive, meditative, praxis-based, searching and inquiring. It seeks to challenge and transform existing understandings of theology, theological education and contemporary culture in ways that are empathetic and constructive.

We might begin by noting that, oddly, the history of specialized theological education, at least in England, is curiously brief. When the bishop of Gloucester tested his clergy in 1551, of 311 priests only 171 could recall all ten of the commandments from the Old Testament. In 1530 William Tyndale complained that few priests could recite the Lord's Prayer or translate it into English (Percy, 2001, p. 87). But perhaps this is not so surprising, since there were no seminaries or theological colleges in which to train priests. Indeed, technically, there were no degrees in theology or divinity to be studied at Oxford or Cambridge, since what we now call 'classics' and 'philosophy' were the only subjects read. Theological colleges emerged in the nineteenth century and were a response to the increasing secularization of the universities, contemporary culture and part of the general movement within many professions to separate out specialist institutions for training within general education. As medical and law schools emerged, theological colleges were born too, shaping the identity of a 'profession' that had, hitherto, seldom relied on specialist knowledge for the practice of theology – what we now call 'professional ministry'.

This chapter is not, however, about the origin and development of theological colleges. Undoubtedly, it would be interesting to subject religious seminaries to a thorough Foucauldian analysis, but that is beyond the scope of our enquiry. However, beginning with a brief discussion of formal (professional) theological training is no accident. Many of the assumptions about the character of theology are formed, in seminaries, not by the theology itself, but by the underlying (and normally undisclosed) culture of education. Sometimes

this culture is practised unwittingly by the staff, perhaps under the guise of supporting a particular dogmatic or ecclesial position that reflects the values of the college. At other times, the college may deliberately set out to unsettle the beliefs of students, challenging them and questioning them, acting as an agent of disturbance or as a catalyst for change. Much of this can be observed almost casually in most seminaries, and yet, oddly, it is seldom reflected upon.

In this chapter I want to draw away from the conventional antinomies that characterize most debates about the nature of theology and contemporary culture, theological formation and education. Typically, these antinomies pitch liberal against conservative, traditional against progressive, dogmatic against radical, and more besides. To be sure, this kind of dialectic has its place in educational philosophy; for example, in tension, students may discover a middle path. But such assumptions can presume too much; that this method (which can be, at times, aggressive), automatically leads to the student reaching their own position of accommodation. This may happen, of course, but equally it may not. Some students may become dissatisfied with the polarity and conclude that the antinomy renders the subject itself to be highly suspect.

The genesis of this argument lies in a simple, commonplace idea within the philosophy of education: there can be no teaching without learning. Or, put another way, excellent teachers must first become learners. However, beneath the surface of this apparently obvious observation lies a penumbra of questions about the relationship between teachers and learners, amidst the art and craft of education. In the field of theological studies, and in the education and formation of the church more generally, those who hold the office of 'teacher' are seldom perceived or identified as learners. Education is, in other words, a process in which the teacher disseminates knowledge to learners. The learners seldom obtain the opportunity to instruct their teachers or to enter into any kind of serious theological dialogue. But this is, as we noted in Chapter 1, not surprising in a culture where the church can sometimes speak of itself in terms of perfection, indefectability and God-given authority, justified by a range of terms such as '*ex cathedra*', 'infallible' and 'revealed'. In an educational economy of this kind, knowledge is immutable; learning can only mean 'banking' knowledge, and adapting or applying it to specific situations. Indeed, the etymology of the term 'seminary' (that is, a place of formation and training for religious professionals, leaders and teachers) is closely linked to the more static term 'dissemination' – the 'spreading around' of seeds or knowledge.

Whilst I readily acknowledge that this is a characterization of sorts, it is hardly unfair. Many who teach in the church – leaders, educators and pastors – are trained and formed in an environment that assumes that the task of education is to implant (correct) knowledge in those contexts where they minister. The training process does not assume that a congregation or context will be able to teach the teacher. The training process does not teach people how to continue learning. Any consideration of what constitutes teaching and learning within a discipline is invariably timely. In this section, our exploration is concerned with the meaning of theological education (especially focusing on ministerial formation – the relationship between theological colleges or

seminaries and the churches that the ministers serve in) and how its definition and scope can both be broadened and deepened.

Correspondingly, the style of this chapter (continuing the strategy of pursuing a meditative critical–reflective or refractive approach) is intended to resonate with, and reach, a theological public who may already have concerns about theological training and formation. Throughout the United Kingdom, churches have had to face a series of challenges that have raised questions about their nature and purpose. Financial difficulties, secularization, critical engagement with traditionalism, lack of resources, disenchantment, consumerism and other forces have all played their part in creating a climate of uncertainty for churches. Educationally, one might say that many churches and denominations are now finding that they still possess (and cherish) the answers to questions that no-one is asking any more. It is my contention that addressing the crisis in teaching and learning (and their relationship) within the church is an important and necessary agenda. The guiding assumptions that have shaped ministerial training and formation are in serious need of urgent reform. To paraphrase Paulo Freire, the time for oscillating between naive and ironic (or shrewd) readings of the church is past, for both will maintain the status quo. Only a revolution will do.

But a revolution will depend on having some understanding of what theological education could or should be. Clearly, this type of theological education could only be a small contribution to a debate – a debate, incidentally, that is hotly contested within the churches. But the contribution is intended as a meditative–critical reflection on the possibilities for theological education, and although primarily focused on the concerns of Anglicans, the insights nonetheless may have wider implications. In advocating a strategy and philosophy of education-for-change, I offer a thesis that is intended to counter and question the prevailing assumptions about theological education in church and seminary culture, namely the expectation that theological education is there to inform, support and consolidate tradition – but not to change it.

In contrast, I hold that theology that fails to be critically reflective and transformative is not only a failure to inculcate advances in educational philosophy and practice, but an actual betrayal of the Christian tradition itself and a failure of nerve in the field of theology. In relation to this, it is important to understand that there is still, in many universities, an implicit and residual relationship between the structure and shaping of degree courses and the kind of theology that is also pursued in theological colleges. A number of older university departments in Britain can still (comfortably) accommodate trainee ministers within their degree programme (as part of their training), suggesting that 'Divinity' lives on in the academy. Newer university departments that tend to concentrate on 'religious studies' tend to have little, if any, connection with theological colleges. So there is a kind of double impoverishment at work here. Even where theological colleges and their ordinands are strongly linked to university departments of theology and religious studies, it tends to be the older, more established departments that offer 'Divinity' degrees.

The type of research offered fits in with Van der Ven's first, second and third types (1998: cf. the Introduction): discovery, theoretical–integrative research

and applied research. But, critically, it has an impact on the fourth dimension of scholarship: teaching. It is this matrix that is assessed through the methodology of practical theology. Furthermore, and mindful that my concern and subject is primarily the Anglican Church, I nonetheless want to suggest that my own use of the word 'research' in this essay means 're-search', which is only to say that I take a new and original look at a very old subject. The relationship between teaching and learning, and their actual definition, in theology and in the churches, forms the crucible of concern that governs the reflections in this chapter. It is my contention that seminary education simply misunderstands the nature of education, culture and the church itself – a primary arena of shared learning that is a 'community of practice'.

The implications, however, for epistemology, practice, transformation and development, should be far-reaching. A piece of re-search is, ultimately, a re-view, re-consideration and a re-turn – perhaps leading to a revolution; this is comparable to the transformative agenda of practical theology at work. I am conscious that to reflect on theological education is, ultimately, to offer a critique of the definition and scope of the actual discipline of theology. In other words, a critical–meditative chapter of this kind, focused on the meaning of theology and educational practice in relation to contemporary culture, is an inherently and unavoidable political critique of the term 'theology' – what it means, who does it and where it is to be found. But that last sentence is something for the reader to make a judgement upon sometime later.

To shape this sketch a little more, I want to briefly return to the recent writing of Edward Norman, an Anglican priest and scholar, former Reith lecturer and noted conservative and scourge of liberalism. In his *Secularisation* (2002), Norman attacks the church for its uncritical and wholesale embracing of modernism. His study of secularization is, by the publisher's own admission, '*not* a systematic attempt to describe and identify every feature of the fading religious landscape'. It is more of a *Tract for the Times* than a methodical appraisal of religion in the crucible of contemporary life. Norman's book will confirm the mindset of all those who are 'saddened by the decline of institutional religion in Britain', but it offers little by way of comfort to those who might want to extricate the church from the milieu of modernity.

Norman writes with clarity and candour. At times the argument is sweeping and irresistible, and yet it is always presented in the most economic prose. Norman has no time for the 'is the glass half-full or half-empty?' debate when it comes to the Church of England. For Norman, the Church of England is not so much a sacred vessel as a kitchen colander – so full of holes that it can hold nothing. Moreover, the Church of England has brought about its own downfall by its wholesale accommodation of vapid liberalism, which has inevitably had a deleterious effect on its identity, authority, teaching, truth, leadership and ministry.

Thus, Norman can confidently assert that the problem behind falling church attendances is 'the absence of a systematic teaching office' which is 'at the root of all their difficulties' (note 'theirs', not 'ours'). He continues:

...when an organism cannot identify its enemies it gets taken over by them...the body needs immunology...it has long been a feature of modern Anglicanism [that] it cannot, as an institution, resist the adoption of alien ideas and attitudes, of false doctrine, when it does not have an immune system. (Norman, 2002, p. 121)

And so Norman goes on to attack 'modern' spiritual relativism, 'decades of reductionism and scepticism' and the like. It seems that only Catholics, who adhere to an indefectible teaching office, and Evangelicals, who are 'loyal to scripture', are capable of resisting Norman's imagined invasion of cancerous liberalism and secularism.

Some will doubtless applaud this less than subtle attack on the church and feel that it rings true and hits home (hard). But a thesis of this kind is very shaky for all kinds of reasons. Here are just a few. First, it assumes that the (alleged) present crisis is a new one and a particular creature of liberalism or modernity. But, if this is so, how are we to account for miniscule church attendances in centuries that pre-dated the Enlightenment? Second, Norman misconstrues the heart of liberalism, which is to engage faith with modernity; it is a way of holding and valuing Christianity and rarely an evacuation of its content. Far from being vapid, liberalism attempts to be creatively faithful to Christ in a changing world. Third, Norman's polemic, for all its poise, represents an odd kind of *alliance* with secularization. Like a number of Catholic and Evangelical commentators, he seems to need to believe in secularization more than ever in order to reclaim the church for his own agenda. As I have remarked before, after newspaper editors, the only people who really *truly* believe in secularization are scholar-priests like Norman, who then seek to make educational, doctrinal and ecclesial capital out of opposing it (Percy, 2001). Put more sharply, the attack on secularism is really only another way of opposing liberalism, which is then turned into a crusade for the imposition of conservativism, which is held up as the guarantor of truth, teaching and authority.

In contrast to this agenda, I want to suggest that an important key to a practical and effective theology that engages with contemporary culture lies in hospitality rather than exclusivity. Or, put another way, we might say that the only way to develop a critical conversation with contemporary culture is through discerning accommodation. Henri Nouwen has suggested that (theological and spiritual) hospitality consists of:

...the creation of a free space where the stranger can enter and become a friend instead of an enemy. Hospitality is not to change people, but to offer them space where change can take place. It is not to bring men and women over to our side, but to offer freedom not disturbed by dividing lines. It is not to lead our neighbour into a corner where there are no alternatives left, but to open up a wide spectrum of options for choice and commitment. (Nouwen, 1975, p. 51)

This leads us to an early but critical point in our argument about the nature of engaging theology within contemporary culture. Can it be a discipline that listens? Can it be a place that receives the stories and experiences of strangers? Can it practise genuine hospitality? The turn towards stories and narratives at

this point is no accident. The ability to listen to, and receive, the stories of others is one of the primary ways in which the practice of reception and hospitality can be identified, since it indicates the degree of openness within the host. As Daniel Taylor suggests:

> ...story gives us a kind of knowledge that abstract reasoning cannot. One of the advantages of *story knowledge* is its concreteness and specificity. Stories give us individualised people in specific times and places doing actual things. Rationality tends to sidestep the messy particulars to deal directly with the generalised concepts behind the particulars. In doing so, it often strip-mines reality, washing away tons of seemingly useless details to get to the small golden nuggets of truth.... (Taylor, 1996, p. 30)

Of course, one of Paulo Freire's aims was to help people achieve 'deep literacy' – to become aware of the far from innocent forces that can shape lives and institutions. Freire argued that deep literacy comes through dialogue. It is in conversation and reflection that we become aware of how we are *determined* by our cultural inheritance. Moving beyond that can be achieved if we are willing to critically question what we think we know (Morisy, 1997, p. 66).

'Story knowledge' will be seen by many to be a weak substitute for the concreteness and certainty of doctrine and creedal formulae. And yet the power of stories for conveying theological material should not be underestimated. Jesus, after all, spoke in parables. Moreover, there is substantial evidence to suggest that churches are (in a memorable phrase coined by James Hopewell) 'storied dwellings'. Churches are cultures that are shaped by world-views and particular kinds of theological stories that continue to have an impact on, and resonance amongst, individuals and communities. As a result of this, a real focus on the kinds of stories that congregations both store and tell can reveal much about the church's theological priorities and its praxis.

Having made these points, it is important to acknowledge that some, at least, would have considerable ecclesial and theological concerns in inculcating such insights into the life of the church. If all churches do is receive the stories of strangers, what else are they there for? I suspect that, at worst, some would fear that an uncritical adoption of the philosophy outlined above could lead to a vapid relativity in terms of definition and distinctiveness. Churches do (and must) stand on some kind of authority that is supported by its corpus of knowledge. However, this brief excursion into one aspect of contemporary educational philosophy highlights a major problem in considering authority within ecclesial communities. The problem, simply put, is one of reception rather than content. If churches are unwilling to embrace new (more collaborative and less doctrinaire) philosophies of learning and teaching, then the authority of the church within contemporary culture itself is no longer likely to be *received* in the same way. Being more imposing (even if this is for the sake of a predetermined unity) is no substitute for the liberation of reception and enabling – even if that does lead to distinctiveness and difference.

So, is there some middle ground between Norman and Freire? Is there a philosophy of education that treats tradition and imagination with equal

seriousness? Is there a way of conceiving of theological education that respects tradition and truth whilst also acknowledging the value of doubt, criticism and openness? Part of the answer to these questions may lie in an apparently unlikely place, since the educational philosophy that I want to propose in this essay is liberal in character. Let me say at once that I do not use the term 'liberal' as an opposite to 'conservative'. Rather, I use it in the most constructive sense. I see liberalism as an 'open frame of reference', a way of regarding truth and valuing wisdom, rather than an evacuation of the content of faith or some kind of demystification. Indeed, the phrase 'frame of reference' works analogically.

As someone who was raised 'low church' in my childhood and gradually evangelicalized throughout my teens and twenties, I became very aware, even if uncritically at first, as to how many of the truths we held were controlled by prior frames of reference. For example, it is obvious that the Bible does not speak of itself at all, let alone as an infallible text. And yet 2 Timothy 3:16 would be regularly used to frame all debates about biblical reliability: 'all scripture is inspired by God . . .' was a frequently intoned mantra. But no-one ever bothered to say where the Apocrypha fitted into this, let alone mention the synoptic problem. Similarly, for debates on sexuality, where the Bible is confusing and reticent, key texts conditioned not only how we looked at the rest of the Bible, but also how we viewed the world. We were framed, and in turn we framed everything we saw.

Looking at life through a frame has its advantages; the picture remains in focus and frozen. The view never changes; only your view on the view alters. But for the curious, there are too many unanswered questions. Who made the frame? What lives and moves outside the frame? What aspects of the picture are obscured by the frame? It is at these junctures that an enquiring liberal mind and an accompanying spirituality start to take root. For myself, I soon realized that the frames of reference I was working with were too particular; to parody J.B. Phillips, 'your frame is too small'. The realization that the portrait of faith I had been staring at for most of my life actually *surrounded* me, totally (but openly, not suffocatingly) changed not only my theology, but also my spirituality. Moreover, I began to appreciate the ways in which I myself was in the picture. The frames suddenly became almost redundant; they now remain useful for capturing detail and focusing on issues, but their limits (as well as their relativity and selectivity) are recognized for what they are.

Expressed more conventionally, an authentic liberal philosophy of theological education works with boundaries, not barriers. In liberal theological education the borders of faith are open, because it is recognized that God is both outside and inside those borders. This then assumes that the only acceptable frame of reference is an open frame, which allows the viewer to look beyond the immediate and catch a glimpse of the ultimate. The missiological dimension of this is explored in writings such as Vincent Donovan's *Christianity Rediscovered* (1982) and J.V. Taylor's *The Go-Between God* (1972). Open frames of reference let God in, who is, *de facto*, not the

property of the church. Or, to paraphrase Sydney Carter, 'Jesus is *not* the copyright of the church'.

## Practical Theology, Ecclesiology and Formation

As I noted in the Introduction, the methodological approach to the question of theology's identity and of theological formation is drawn from the arena of practical theology. If practical theology begins anywhere at all, it is in the recognition that the nature of theology is both practical and public as it seeks to make some sense of the relationships between belief and practice, faith and the world, and church and society. As I noted at the beginning of this chapter, it is in the nature of practical theology to 'begin in the middle'. Practical theology is a listening and reflective discipline; it does not seek to be dogmatic in its engagements. For Killen and de Beer, the discipline is about a level of critical–reflective engagement with tradition:

> ... exploring individual and corporate experience in conversation with the wisdom of a religious heritage. The conversation is a genuine dialogue that seeks to hear from our own beliefs, actions, and perspectives, as well as those of the tradition. It respects the integrity of both. Theological reflection therefore may confirm, challenge, clarify, and expand how we understand our own experience and how we understand the religious tradition. The outcome is new truth and meaning for living .... (Killen and de Beer, 1994, p. viii)

This suggests that, in terms of education, aspects of practical theology closely correspond to certain types of educational philosophy. One thinks immediately of Brookfield's 'critically reflective teacher' (1995), or Van der Ven's distinction (following Levi-Strauss), between the engineer and bricoleur. The engineer systematically thinks, conceives and executes. The bricoleur, in contrast, builds something out of the disparate elements through doing, experiencing and reflecting (Van der Ven, 1998, p. 40). Clearly, theological education is more bricolage than engineering. Kathryn Tanner in describing the tasks of 'mainstream theology', almost accidentally articulates a type of practical theology (and the nature of theological education) that is fundamental to the identity of the discipline:

> The basic operation that theologians perform have a twofold character. First, theologians show an artisanlike inventiveness in the way they work on a variety of materials that do not dictate of themselves what theologians should do with them. Second, theologians exhibit a tactical cleverness with respect to other interpretations and organisations of such materials that are already on the ground .... The materials theologians work on are incredibly diverse ... theologians use a kind of tact requiring numerous ad hoc and situation-specific adjustments. In contrast to what the values of clarity, consistency and systematicity might suggest of themselves, even academic theologians do not simply follow logical deductions where they lead or the dictates of abstract principles when arriving at their conclusions. They do not construct their theological positions by applying generalities to particular cases, or emend them by

trying to reproduce the same clear meanings in the terms of a new day, so as to convey them across putatively accidental differences in circumstances and vocabulary. Instead, they operate by tying things together – the Latin meaning of *religare*, after all, is to bind.... (Tanner, 1997, p. 87ff)

Tanner's description of theological method is one of skilled and discerning praxis. Tanner displays a characteristic ease in describing the discipline of theology, locating its functioning in active formation. So practical theology becomes a critical and creative *art* – something that is created and shaped within each context and is appropriate to its environment. Within contemporary culture, it is aware that it is both culturally formed, as well as being an agent within culture for the express purposes of ongoing social formation. But this notion of practical theology being a discipline (like religion itself) that binds is also worth paying attention to. One might reasonably ask, 'Bind what, exactly?'. Certainly practical theologians are used to bringing together different materials and holding them in tension.[1] But perhaps what makes practical theology so appealing as a discipline within contemporary culture is its ability to pull together different strands of thinking and material into a new kind of relationship and purpose.

So what are the hallmarks of practical theology? In what ways does a practical theological approach constitute a method or discipline? Woodward and Pattison suggest 14 characteristics:

1 Practical theology is *transformational activity*...

2 ...not just concerned with the propositional...[it] finds *artistic and imaginative* ways of thinking and expressing pastoral theological insights...

3 *confessional and honest*...truthful about the world and religious experience...

4 *unsystematic*...it continuously has to re-engage with the fragmented realities and changes of the contemporary world and the issues it presents....

5 *truthful and committed*...[it tries] to discern the reality of situations...committed to helping people and situations change...

6 *contextual and situationally related*...explore and contribute to immediate contexts, situations and practices...

7 *socio-politically aware and committed*...[learns] from praxis-based liberationist theologies that apply the tools of suspicion to theology as well as to the social and political order...

8 *experiential*...takes contemporary people's experiences seriously as data for theological reflection, analysis and thought...

9 *reflectively based*...lived contemporary experience is an important starting point for engaging...

---

[1] If I might be use a mechanistic analogy at this point, there is something 'Gripple-like' about practical theology. A gripple is a device (varying in size) that brings broken or loose wires together. A gripple can be used to mend wire fences, but also to suspend lights or other objects using wires. Its function is (a) binding; (b) holding materials in tension; (c) supporting weights that are far greater than itself.

10 *interrogative*... [not] monolithic and instructional [but] more interested in asking good questions than ... trying to confine [people] within the restraints of [tradition] ...

11 *interdisciplinary* ... uses ... methods and insights ... that are not overtly theological ...

12 *analytical and constructive* ... help[s] people to construct ideas about how they might change ...

13 *dialectical and disciplined* ... critical conversation ... practical theologies hold in creative tension a number of polarities such as theory and practice, reality and ideal, what is and what ought to be, etc ...

14 *skillful and demanding* ... there is much to learn about how to work with different methods, types of material, situations, etc.... (Woodward and Pattison, 2000, pp. 15–16, adapted)

These methodological observations are the substantial criteria that explain how and why theology is being explored and evaluated, and also to what ends. Practical theology, in other words, is the vehicle for a critical–meditative reflection on the place and meaning of theology within the 'real' church, with special attention being paid to praxis and transformation. Two American writers distil Pattison and Woodward's categorizations into just eight hallmarks. For these authors, practical theology is:

[1] a distinct genre of theological discourse; [2] formally analogous to secular ideology; [3] grounded in a dialectic of theory and praxis; [4] works from a critical construction of the essence of a religious tradition; [5] creates distinct theological models of self and history; [6] with the help of other genres of public discourse it leads to social policy formation, decision and action; [7] establishes a mode of socialisation; [8] that is truth dependent. (McCann and Strain, 1985, p. 209; cf. Kinast, 2000)

I have already hinted that the notion of theological education as liberation (following the work of Freire) has been influential on my thinking. Education as the practice of freedom and theological education as transformative pedagogy have reshaped my views on what it means to be free and open, critically constructive, experiential, visionary, culturally reflexive, life-forming, constructive and interactive. This has partly come about through reconceiving theological education as 'conversation' – balancing the 'hermeneutics of retrieval' (as Ricoeur might say) with the 'hermeneutics of hospitality' – as Nouwen might affirm (see Astley *et al.*, 1996, p. 159) – or, put more colloquially, balancing the obligation to teach and speak with the need to listen and learn. Theologically, and following scholars such as Lindbeck (1984) and Schreiter (1985), we might say that it is useful to distinguish between *traditio* (that is, what is taught) and *tradita* (that is, how things are taught). Exactly how the church conveys its message may say more about its theology than it really knows; the mode of education may reveal what educationalists are often wont to call 'the hidden curriculum'. Some of these matters will be returned to later on, where questions of praxis can be more properly addressed, and where

we return once more to the discipline of practical theology. But, for now, we turn to a deeper consideration of the work of James Fowler and James Hopewell, and its implications for 'concrete ecclesiology'.

## Describing Faith: Some Perspectives

For almost any student of theological or Christian education, the standard point of departure for the voyage is James Fowler's seminal study, *Stages of Faith*. Fowler's work was written in 1981, and the book has effectively established itself as a 'classic' text for explicating the journey of faith – through the motif of stages. Fowler's work is arguably the major portal gateway into the burgeoning world of theological education, providing a reliable and incisive model of progressive understanding that appeals to educationalists and theologians alike. Fowler's work, by his own admission, is heavily influenced by the approaches of Kohlberg and Piaget and seeks to build bridges between theologians and scholars of human behaviour. Indeed, we might say that what Kohlberg and Piaget did for moral and cognitive development respectively, Fowler achieves for faith development; the subtitle of the book does not overreach itself when it states that the volume is concerned with 'the psychology of human development and the quest for meaning'. Fowler postulates that there are six stages of faith, and these need briefly describing before a foundation of critical reflection can be laid for the remainder of the chapter. It will become apparent that, whilst Fowler provides a useful starting point for reflecting on theological education, there are certain gaps in the approach, as well as particular assumptions that need to be challenged.

Fowler's first stage is the 'Intuitive-Protective': 'the fantasy-filled, imitative phase in which the child can be powerfully and permanently influenced by examples, moods, actions and stories of the visible faith . . . most typical of the child of three to seven' (Fowler, 1981, p. 133). Fowler regards this stage as being the one where the imagination is at its most explosive and productive and where logical thought does not inhibit either the visualization or actualization of belief. On the positive side, Fowler sees this faith stage as part of the birth of the imagination. More negatively, the mind of the child can be 'possessed' by the very images it produces. The key to moving on to another stage lies with the child, and is concerned with sifting fantasy from reality, and to 'know how things are'. (It is this stage, or rather the failure of a young girl to evolve from it, that is wonderfully captured in the semi-autobiographical novel of Jeanette Winterson, *Oranges Are Not The Only Fruit*, 1991.)

The second stage is the 'Mythic-Literal': 'the person begins to take on for [themselves] the stories, beliefs and observances that symbolize belonging to [their] community . . . beliefs are appropriated with literal interpretations . . . symbols are taken as one-dimensional and literal in meaning' (Fowler, 1981, p. 149). The key features of this stage are the rise of narrative and the emergence of story, drama and myth as primary vehicles of faith which, in turn, give meaning and coherence to experience. However, the stories must be 'balanced' (or fair and reciprocal, according to Fowler), such that paradox and

tragedy are, by and large, excluded from this stage. Thus, a typical reciprocal story from a school assembly is this. In hell, people have plenty of food to eat, but the knives, forks and spoons that are used are too long to get the food from plate to mouth, so everyone starves, yet all the while being surrounded by food. Heaven is identical, but different in one respect only: people have learned, with the same implements, to feed each other. The story bears a resemblance to the ancient classical legend of Tantalus, from which the English language derives the word 'tantalize', although the school assembly story 'balance' is less brutal in its resolution than its classical counterpart.

The third stage, 'Synthetic-Conventional', understandably makes some of the inroads that the second stage cannot achieve. Fowler rightly assumes that, by a certain age, the child has a social network beyond the immediate family, with many new spheres demanding attention. Correspondingly, faith 'must provide a more coherent orientation in the midst of that more complex and diverse range of involvements'. It must 'synthesize values and orientation . . . [and] provide a basis for identity and outlook' (ibid., p. 172). According to Fowler, the third stage still lacks a perspective where one can stand outside beliefs and reflect upon them systematically. Fowler suggests that this may not happen until a child begins to leave home, which suggests he has teenagers in mind. However, 'teenage' denotes a stereotypical mindset here, rather than an age band. The third stage has scope for rebellion and rejection but is, at the same time, looking for deeper patterns of integrity and may still be quite idealistic in orientation.

The fourth stage is described by Fowler as 'Individuative-Reflective faith' (ibid., p. 182) and is characterized by a number of key movements: from individuality to group commitment; from subjectivity to critical reflection on one's own strongly held beliefs; from self-fulfilment or self-actualization to social service; from absolutism to relativity. In this fourth stage a form of adulthood emerges that becomes self-aware of its own frames of reference and world-views, and their relative contingency. It is possible that a certain amount of deconstruction or demythologizing may take place. Correspondingly, the stage, as a stage of faith, may actually implode at this apparent point of maturity: confidence in conscious processes of thought and their ability to 'master' faith may lead to its rejection altogether. Thus, the rite of confirmation, normally offered in the Church of England at about the age of 14 as a rite of passage into adulthood, can be justly described by the sociologist David Martin as 'the Church's Leaving Certificate'.

The fifth stage, 'Conjunctive Faith', involves the development of those elements that were suppressed or overlooked in stage four. Citing Ricoeur, Fowler notes how this stage can constitute a 'second naivete', in which older symbolic power from earlier stages are now re-united with conceptualization at an adult level. In other words, there may be 'a new reclaiming and reworking of one's past . . . [and] an opening to the voices of one's "deeper self" . . . ' (ibid., p. 198). Fowler regards this stage as being 'unusual before mid-life', partly because the sustainability of this stage depends on the development of the ironic: 'a capacity to see and be in one's or one's group's most powerful meanings, while simultaneously recognizing that they are relative, partial and inevitably distorting apprehensions of divine reality'. In other words, this stage

can subject faith to radical doubt, but without tearing apart the very fabric of belief or losing any affinity with it. There is a paradox inherent in this stage, as one would expect. Whilst this is Fowler's ultimate stage of maturity, a retreat into original religious habits and beliefs becomes possible. Adults can regress in faith, but usually know what they are doing – at least at some conscious level – and have the ability to return to the ironic and relative at any time.

The sixth stage, Universalizing, is closely related to the fifth stage but is, in Fowler's view, 'exceedingly rare': 'the persons best described by it have generated faith compositions in which their felt sense of an ultimate environment is inclusive of all being... they become incarnators and actualizers of the spirit of an inclusive and fulfilled human community' (ibid., p. 201). To illustrate the stage, Fowler chooses representatives such as Gandhi, Martin Luther King Jr, Dietrich Bonhoeffer and Dag Hammarskjöld, individuals who, in Fowler's view, cherish particularities, but only as 'vessels of the universal'. The vision narrated here is one of mystic–social connectedness, in which divine principles transform both individual lives and socio-political situations through an appeal to human futurity and transcendence.

In describing these stages, it should be immediately recognized that Fowler himself acknowledges that journeying from one to another is not a simple matter of linear progression. The formation of faith is complex: cyclical and oscillating; the movement is more typically a dynamic spiral of transformation than a matter of simple advancement. But having said that, there are some particular problems with the motif of stages, suggesting that, whilst Fowler is a useful gateway through which to forge into the territory of theological education, his work does not provide a map or vessel which offers comprehensive navigational support. Three brief points need making here.

First, Fowler's work focuses on individuals. Whilst this undoubtedly has its strengths, I suspect that it underplays the extent to which the faith communities can form faith, and, in turn, the 'stages theory' tends to ignore the significant *demands* that religious bodies can make upon believers. Put another way, there may be a nascent schizophrenia between private beliefs and public faith, with the individual selecting or screening aspects of their apparent formation. A good example of this might be assenting to a literal belief in hell, whilst at the same time expecting to be reunited with all one's 'unsaved' loved ones.

Second, although Fowler tries to distinguish between types of knowledge, he doesn't go far enough. In fact, most of the 'knowledge' that Fowler describes seems to be fairly settled and concrete; it is only the perception of it that alters the individual. A similar charge can be levelled at Freire (1973), who in critiquing the 'banking theory of knowledge' (with its deposits), treats knowledge as a mainly static, unchanging body of information. In fact, many kinds of knowledge have a life of their own (Christian tradition even talks of 'the *lively* deposit of faith'), which can continually transform the receptor. In other words, although Fowler is primarily interested in how people process knowledge, he seems to be unaware of the power of knowledge to process people. This is not mere semantics; it is an important distinction – some types of knowledge convert their receptors altogether, and do not merely move them on a stage.

Third, in failing to attend to different types of formative knowledge, Fowler manages to ignore what behavioural psychologists call 'qualia': subjective but shared experiences and knowledge of the world, such as the smell of coffee, the taste of mango or the look of love – or, come to that, the smell of incense, the taste of bread and wine at the altar rail, or the kiss of peace[2] (see also Barnett, 1990 – 'knowledge captured in action, in performance, in practice and in sheer experience'). Granted, there may be certain types of physiological, biochemical or neurological tests that can be applied which deconstruct these 'tastes', but we are not concerned with proving their existence. My point is that many aesthetic dimensions to life are forms of knowledge that are not easily described or taught (for example, the taste of coffee). And, in my view, this is particularly true in religion, where habits, apparently informal practices, visual images, sounds, symbols and what might seem to be fairly ordinary human interaction can play a significant part in faith development and theological education (Graham, 1996).

We will return to this final point in a moment, but before leaving Fowler for the time being, we should remember that the primary burden of his work is to offer a childhood-to-adult theory of theological education. In so doing, he unavoidably commits himself to the proposition that 'adulthood' equates with 'maturity', and that stages one to four are all prone to 'break[ing] down' at some point – usually because of the individual's inability to move on to stage five. This theory is developed for a more corporate climate (that is, communities) in *Becoming Adult, Becoming Christian* (1984), where greater attention is paid to the inner landscape of adult Christian life. The agenda is also taken up with some force in the writings of John Hull (1985), amongst others. That said, Fowler still sees movement between stages as being most likely to be precipitated by crises, and his rhetoric in *Stages of Faith*, at several points, seems to imply that each stage, until stage five is reached, is ultimately unsustainable and naturally immature (or at lest deficient in maturity).

In other words, and to summarize, the framework he offers us for understanding faith development is already interpretative and laden with value-judgements. What I want to suggest in its place in the rest of this chapter, and to moderate and complement Fowler's work, is the idea that a 'world-view' also predetermines the character of theological education and formation, and that this may be a more helpful lens through which to view theological education. But before doing so, it is necessary to develop my earlier remarks on qualia.

## What is Theological Knowledge?

In theory, 'theology' is derived from two Greek words: *theos* (god) and *logos* (word or reason) – knowledge of God.[3] In practice, however, theology covers a

---

[2] For an amusing discussion of qualia, see David Lodge's novel *Thinks* (2002).

[3] See Grigg (1990, p. 1): 'it is broadly construed as any kind of talk or reasoning about the divine....'

broader range of concerns. Whilst it may primarily be concerned with metaphysics, philosophy, systematic and dogmatic theology and the primary texts that bear witness to what is deemed to be revealed, the discipline is not only 'of' God but also 'about' God. Theological knowledge deals with those traditions, texts and penumbra that mediate revelation, and is therefore rightly concerned with human history and social development. Like many disciplines within the humanities, it has a contested hierarchy of subjects and disciplines. In church history, for example, those who work in the field of Patristics are more likely to be concerned with doctrine than, say, those who work on more recent developments. Similarly, a subject like pastoral theology is invariably something of a Cinderella compared to dogmatic or systematic theology.

But where theology is more unusual amongst the humanities, and perhaps unique, is that the discipline is purveyed, practised and performed in churches and communities by millions of 'non-specialists' – at least in academic terms. In other words, there are numerous non-professional and non-academic contexts in which theology is practised 'unofficially'. Without at all wishing to be patronizing, an average church congregation is just such a context. Whilst it is likely that the minister will have professional theological training, and perhaps a degree in theology, the chances are that the vast majority of the congregation will not be conversant with academic theology. Nonetheless, theological views will be apparent at every turn; the congregation will most likely know what it is committed to, and what it is not. Furthermore, there may be a high quality of articulated faith, which suggests that faith or theology has been 'learned' in ways that are not commonly thought of as teaching. The most obvious example of this is, I suppose, liturgy, where the regular and rhythmic recitation of creeds and formulae seem to 'school' individuals and communities into their belief system and common Christian practice. Worship is a form of learning and therefore a form of teaching. No less significant is the built environment for worship. A plain whitewashed walled 'preaching box' carries an important theological message and is no less a theological treatise – a sermon in stone, if you will – than an ornate Gothic cathedral or a rambling country church (see Visser, 2001).

Two less obvious examples may also focus attention on the practice of theology. Consider, for example, the phenomenon of the funeral tea – a virtually indispensable part of a mourning ritual. After the service has taken place, the event seems to have no obvious theological value. However, if one were to read the tea as part of the response to loss, it takes on a different hue. The event can signify respect, solidarity, humanization, the need for conversation and reminiscence, and suggests reliability in the face of uncertainty. It can also be a highly ritualized event in its own right, reflecting social order and reordering in response to loss and trauma (Clark, 1982, p. 110; Nieman, 2002). In other words, the event – apparently devoid of theological meaning – can be read as an extension of the theological sentiments that are expressed in the liturgy: 'blessed are they that mourn, for they shall be comforted'. But the importance of funeral teas is never explored or taught at theological colleges; their value is something that most congregations learn and perpetuate in the midst of loss; their occurrence needs no academic or

professional prompt. At the same time, the manner of the hospitality clearly reveals something about the theological priorities of ecclesial communities.

A second example concerns dress codes. In a North American church, one of the ten elders elected by the congregation refuses to wear a suit and tie as the others do. He is also late for meetings and sometimes does not turn up at all. The nine elders petition their pastor to have the errant elder removed, claiming that the casual mode of dress signifies disrespect (to God), and is mirrored in 'sloppy attendance habits'. The pastor makes enquiries of the dissenter and discovers that he has his reasons for dressing down; he wants the church to be more relaxed and less stuffy; he thinks formal attire inhibits worship and suggests a more mellow, relaxed God, to which, of course, he is committed. So he does not miss meetings to be rude or to make an obvious point; he simply doesn't think it matters that much, *theologically*. And that, of course, is itself theologically significant.

These two examples show something of the almost casual way in which theological knowledge is held by non-specialists, and practised and purveyed by congregations. But if these examples are part of the economy of theological knowledge, it raises a question as to what actually constitutes theology. Three brief observations about the purposes of theology can be made in this respect. Following Nieman (2002), I hold that theology is, first, a matter of *identity*: an innate and self-conscious language in which the church says something about what it intends to be. To be sure, assertions about God are vital here, but no less vital are the invitations to stay behind afterwards for coffee and refreshments, or someone offering to visit in the week. Second, theology constitutes a *world-view*; it presumes and promotes a cosmology which can enable or constrain behaviour. Thus for some, raffles and lotteries are a good (and fun) way to raise money for the church; for others, it is gambling and therefore a vice. Third, theology is *critical*; it offers, discerns and transforms as it sifts material, enabling individuals and communities to regulate their roles in relation to their fundaments (Nieman, 2003, pp. 200–201).

I am conscious that this is an unusual way of describing theology, but my purpose here is a simple one, namely to challenge what is meant by and counts as theology. I want to say at the outset that I do not think that every single practice within a faith community constitutes theology. However, I do want to suggest that many apparently 'ordinary' customs and routines arise out of deeply embedded theological commitments that deserve more serious attention when considering the process of theological education within faith communities. If we are to explore the meaning of theological education, the implicit needs as much attention as the explicit; the practice as much as the theory; the vernacular faith as much as the credal beliefs that are espoused. In view of this, I concur with James Nieman, and offer this (modified) definition:

> Theology is about fundamental assertions that sustain individuals and communities, rejuvenate beliefs, support institutions, and reify power. (Nieman, 2002, pp. 202–203)

Let me briefly unpack this. Fundamental assertions are claims made by the adherents as well as those claims made upon them. Sustenance follows immediately from this, since the ultimacy of fundamental assertions must provide nourishment and be sufficiently buoyant and reflexive to carry individuals and congregations through bad times as well as the good. Rejuvenation of beliefs does not necessarily mean revision, but is instead meant to imply something about the renewing character of theology. Equally, support of institutions, involves a qualification: it is not necessarily an affirmation of the status quo in any static sense, but, rather, connotes the sense in which theology legitimizes and transforms practice. Finally, the reification of power is the production of effects or materials from ideas and results in faith communities being able to see and experience the fruit of their reflection and labour.

Stated like this, theology is found almost everywhere (that is, it is located and widespread within all ecclesial communities), and is no longer confined to the academy, seminary or solo professional working in an apparently non-theological context. It also affirms Wade Clark Roof's assertion that:

Theological doctrines are always filtered through people's social and cultural experiences. What emerges in a given situation is 'operant religion' will differ considerably from the 'formal religion' of the historic creeds, and more concern with the former is essential to understanding how belief systems function in people's daily lives. (Roof, 1985, pp. 178–79)

In short, I am promoting a theology of the qualia as a serious focus of inquiry for identifying what theology is, especially in regard to teaching and learning. Furthermore, the theology of congregations – normally implicit – will shape how gatherings are construed and practised, and will normally be able to indicate what significance can be attached to apparently unstructured practices (Graham, 1996). This means that, in studying theology (working with a broader definition), many types of knowledge can be included within the theological penumbra that would normally be excluded. Demography, geography, local history, architecture, custom, order and organization, and a study of activities, can all reveal the sorts of theological knowledge that are present within local churches.

Of course, this approach to the subject of theology opens it out considerably, but my purpose in doing this is twofold. First, if types of theological knowledge are more broadly conceived, then deeper questions about the nature and purpose of theological education can be asked. Conversely, and, second, in challenging the traditional limits that are normally set around theology, as a discipline, we may be able to interrogate the hidden curriculum that has hitherto guided many academies, seminaries and colleges. To take this argument further, I want to suggest that world-views (rather than stages of faith) present a more viable way of examining theology and theological education. In the next section, therefore, we briefly examine the work of James Hopewell (as a contrast to Fowler), before moving on to some brief closing comments in this chapter.

**World-views**

James Hopewell's distinctive approach to congregational studies has potentially rich implications for the study of theological education. James Hopewell died in 1984, but his posthumously published *Congregation* (1987) became a seminal study in contextual and practical theology. To summarize briefly, Hopewell maintained that the theology of a congregation, its values, virtues (and therefore, most probably, its discrete learning and teaching practices) were not carried in formal dogma, but were rather bound up in shared stories and complementary world-views. (This is explored and applied in more detail in Part III of this book.) Hopewell based his theory on sensitive ethnography, coupled to a rich understanding of the power of narrative for framing group and individual ecclesial identity. Using the work of Northrop Frye (*The Anatomy of Criticism*, 1957), Hopewell developed a simple 'world-view test' which was able to position congregations and individuals in terms of their theological outlook. The grid proposed by Hopewell consisted of four 'points' or genres.

First, the Canonic genre is likened to Frye's notion of tragedy. Individuals or communities that are primarily Canonic tend to rely on an authoritative interpretation of the world 'often considered [to be] God's revealed word or will, by which one identifies one's essential life' (Hopewell, 1987, p. 69). The Canonic genre, when tested, is most evident in conservative religious groups and outlooks. (Interestingly, where I have used the world-view test and adapted it for interreligious groups, Evangelicals and Muslims score heavily in this genre.) Second, the Gnostic genre relies on a more intuited process of a world that develops from 'dissipation towards unity'. Hopewell regards this genre as similar to Frye's conceptualization of comedy. (The Gnostic genre is most commonly encountered in strength in Quaker and Buddhist individuals.) Third, Hopewell suggests that the Charismatic genre requires 'reliance upon evidence of a transcendent spirit personally encountered, where supernatural irregularities are regularly witnessed'. This is linked to Frye's explicit notion of 'romance'. (Pentecostals, Revivalists and Charismatically-oriented Christians do seem to fit this third category.) Fourth, Hopewell suggests that the Empiric genre has a tendency to rely on evidence and is fond of realism. In turn, this is linked to Frye's notion of irony. (Most 'liberal-minded' religious adherents are heavily Empiric – and are also fond of irony, paradox and so on.)

The implications of Hopewell's programme for investigating the meaning of theological education may not at first be immediately obvious. However, three brief points need to be made in order to establish the superiority of the 'world-view' approach over that of Fowler. First, Hopewell links his genres to a grid, which allows individuals and congregations to be heavily oriented towards one genre, whilst also being affected by their sympathies to other points on the grid. In the world-view test, it is rare for individuals or communities to emerge with results that exclude one or more of the genres entirely. Thus, someone who is heavily Empiric may also be partly Gnostic and slightly Charismatic, but may score only one or two points for being Canonic. Equally, very few come out with four equally balanced scores. The suggestion of the world-view test is that

people's attitude to faith is preconditioned by their world-view. This may, of course, be theological in origin, but the point is that this continues to shape attitudes to learning and teaching. Put another way, Hopewell offers a lens through which it is possible to identify how people process information and what knowledge they value – as well as what is set aside.

Second, Hopewell also shows how differing types of knowledge and information material can help form religious adherence. Instead of a linear progression through stages (*à la* Fowler), Hopewell offers a pattern of reticulation in which competing convictions and tensions (the four different genres) can be used to *negotiate* the world with a more reflexive faith. Furthermore, as if to underline this theory, Hopewell compares potential church attendance to the commercial activity of house-hunting, noting how individuals and communities reflect different values (Hopewell, 1987, p. 19ff). The implications for teaching and learning are rich. Hopewell points out how some house-hunters focus on the *contextual* nature of the dwelling: 'viewed in this way, a dwelling is a texture whose weaving reveals the strands that originate in the larger context of the neighbourhood'. Alternatively, some focus on *mechanisms*, 'and how well the house does its job'. Typical features of 'mechanistic' approaches to church life and education focus on aims, outcomes, programme effectiveness and demonstrable success. Hopewell likens mechanistic approaches to church life to engineering. This approach is in stark contrast to those who value churches as *organisms*, where the interior and exterior of the house are primarily assessed on their aesthetics and the ability of the building to 'fit' with the natural biography of the house-hunters. Hopewell equates this approach to church life as architectural. The *symbolic* approach explores how the building conveys and reifies meanings, and what it communicates to its wider context. Symbolic concerns typically focus not on effectiveness, but on reception and meaning within a wider community. In each of these approaches (rather like the genres of the world-view), knowledge, learning and teaching is handled and valued in different ways by individuals and communities. Apparently trivial knowledge (for example, 'How does our church *look*?') takes on a whole new significance.

Third, in concentrating on narratives and world-views rather than stages, Hopewell avoids the trap that Fowler baits for himself by implying a linear progression from one stage to the next. Even allowing for a cyclical understanding of Fowler (in which there can be oscillation and regression as well as progression), I find Hopewell's approach to be altogether richer because of its stress on *narrative* as a primary place of learning and development (Hopewell, 1987, p. 46ff). If Hopewell is right to assert that congregations' and individuals' self-perceptions are primarily narrative in form,[4] its communication is mainly by story and that it participates in wider society thorough social narrative structures, then we can begin to see a rather different approach to theological education emerging. This would be one in which judgements are

---

[4] See also Hauerwas, 1996, p. 97ff, in which Hauerwas argues that everything the church is and does is 'religious education'.

not made on what is believed or what is taught (formally or dogmatically), but rather on what story or plot is being followed, with proper and due attention paid both to the qualia (the apparently insignificant or trivial) and the world-views that seem to play a major part in performing the type of theological education that may occur in any given situation.

The turn towards narrativity is one of the more striking features of Hopewell's work, and it resonates with our earlier observations about stories and their importance. How and what congregations *recollect* identifies their *plot* and its course or cycle. Without recollection, congregations drift; with it, they narrate their lives together in communion with God, in the midst of triumph and tragedy, opportunity and adversity, and more besides. As Charles Winquist puts it:

> Storytelling can be allied to homecoming because homecoming is more than the collection of actuality. It is more than a bare statement of facticity. Homecoming is a recollection of experience. Our remembrance is an interpretation. We tell a story about the actuality of experience to lift it into the context of meaning that speaks out of the reality of possibility as well as actuality. The *prima material* of meaning encompasses the possibilities from which the particularity of historical fact is made determinant. The re-collection of experience attends the fullness of reality. As strange as it may seem, re-collection allows us to think ahead to the original ground of experience and become conscious of the finality of meaning that coincides with the origination of the actual. (Winquist, 1978, p. 108)

So, in telling the story of the congregation, we unravel its plot:

> ...church culture is not reduced to a series of propositions that a credal checklist adequately probes. The congregation takes part in the nuance and narrative of full human discourse. It persists as a recognizable storied dwelling within the whole horizon of human interpretation. (Hopewell, 1987, p. 201)

If this last point sounds a little too far-fetched, we may do well to remember that Paulo Freire's own educational philosophy actually starts to chime quite well with Hopewell's insights.[5] Freire believes that individuals and communities reach points of understanding and gain self-consciousness by recognizing themselves sequentially in time: 'they develop their power to perceive critically the way they exist in the world with which and in which they find themselves [when] they come to see the world not as a static reality, but as reality in process, in transformation' (Freire, 1972, p. 70). Hopewell suggests that, here, Freire has perceived that, to achieve liberation, people need first to discover their own historicity: they need to discover themselves in the historical plot, not in abstract mechanistic concepts (Hopewell, 1987, p. 198). But, if anything, Freire goes further, arguing that individuals and congregations need to embrace 'conscientisation' (that is, education for critical consciousness) where

---

[5] See also Tony Harland's (1997) work on stories about small-group teaching, which uses a problem-based approach to reflect.

traditionalist approaches ('unquestionably allied to the ruling classes') are set aside in favour of an education that is an instrument of transforming action (Astley *et al.*, 1996, p. 167). Or, as Brookfield (1995) suggests, teaching needs to lose its 'innocence' if it is to avoid being blamed for failing to deliver education; only critical reflection can break the spiral for educationalists as they seek to impart knowledge that transforms.

## Summary

The primary burden of this chapter has been to establish sufficient grounds for 'faithful doubt' both in the identity of theology and in the enterprise of theological education in relation to any kind of engagement with contemporary culture. The purpose of this approach has been to show that there is no clear agreement on the nature of theology as a discipline, whilst at the same time there is no real clarity about the nature and purpose of education and formation in relation to theology, nor any measure of agreement as to what constitutes teaching and learning in theological communities. The work of James Fowler, although extremely promising in so many respects, has been described with the aim of showing (albeit briefly) its shortcomings. Indeed, other critics of Fowler have pointed to his problematic use of the term 'faith' as though it were a more or less conscious choice in which persons moved from stage to stage of their own free will (Dykstra and Panks, 1986, p. 9).

In contrast, I have tried to show how many different types of (theological) knowledge within ecclesial communities, as well as personal experiences and individual spiritualities, actually constitute part of the learning and teaching process. This is what Astley (2002) calls 'ordinary theology'. Through the more adequate lens of world-views (proposed by Hopewell), we have been able to catch a glimpse of how knowledge and learning is 'pre-framed' by outlooks which are themselves, no doubt, created by dogma, experience and other types of knowledge. By paying attention to Hopewell's richer 'narrative matrix', stories take on a more significant role in formation, but without excluding the more obviously credal or dogmatic formulations that are assumed to be the basis of catechesis. This is important, and something to which we shall return in Part III, for it constitutes a kind of research that is often given scant attention by academics, who all too easily divide research between 'pure' and 'applied'. But strictly speaking, the word 'research' needs to be understood against its Enlightenment definition and etymology (Van der Ven, 1998, p. 66). To 'research' meant to break away from the notion that knowledge was based on a given authority and, regardless of how assertive or commonplace that knowledge was, to reassess its claims in the light of new questions. Research, properly conceived, therefore always has a profound effect on tradition-bound institutions – such as universities, colleges or churches – especially within contemporary culture.

With these thoughts in mind, the argument may now advance a step further and begin to explore theology as a critical and reflective 'habit of wisdom' (Farley, 1988), whereby theological knowledge begins to become part of the

economy of practical wisdom, in which mechanistic conceptualizations of teaching and learning are set aside in favour of more holistic approaches to the discipline. This is crucial for the development of models of theological engagement within contemporary culture. In order to pursue this, I will be offering a novel treatment of theological education that owes much to feminist insights, which in turn, as has been suggested, has implications for the self-understanding and self-description of theology. As we have already noted, no consideration of theological education can avoid some inherently political reflection on the actual nature of the core discipline itself. Correspondingly, redescribing the shape of theology (as a culture) will have implications for how the discipline engages with contemporary culture and arrives at a different point of self-understanding.

# Chapter 5

# Mother Church[1]

## Introduction

Once asked to characterize the differences between the present generation of ordinands and those that were ordained in the 1960s and were now near retirement, I made a simple observation. To my mind, those who are presently being trained (through theological education) for ordained ministry seem to be influenced by an educational culture that is centred on being 'answer-based'; correspondingly, they often do not know how to ask questions. In contrast, their predecessors from 40 years ago were drawn from a 'question-based' educational culture, but they were often reticent about answers. I suspect that the difference (and, granted, it is a characterization) can be traced in other professions besides ministerial formation. And yet the observation exposes a profound cultural shift between enabling faithful doubt and belief on the one hand, and depositing information as a means to education on the other. We have already seen how various 'models' of theological education don't quite do justice to the richness of the enterprise: Fowler's stages have been critiqued; Freire's notion of 'banking' and its remedy is also deficient; and Hopewell's world-views, whilst arguably most promising, can only be preliminary.

In this chapter we move from models to metaphors (or more accurately, a single metaphor), and work with insights from feminist theology. In practice, feminist theologians have paid more attention to issues of inequality, power, leadership and hermeneutics than they have to theological education itself. However, there are some notable exceptions that are briefly worth mentioning, which in turn will inform the argument on metaphor.

Rebecca Chopp's *Saving Work – Feminist Practices of Theological Education* (1995) argues that the contours of theological education must be transformed as increasing numbers of women are enrolled into college, seminary and university theological programmes. Chopp maintains that one of the major paradigm shifts for theological education is that women have now moved away from 'merely' being subjects in the discipline to becoming practiioners. Moreover, women bring with them a collection of concerns, insights and skills that are normally excluded from male-dominated theological pro-grammes. Chopp, citing authors such as Dykstra and Panks (1986), suggests that *bodiliness* (a refusal to accept the conventional antinomy between the spiritual/intellectual and the emotional/physical) and *habitus* (not only ordered

---

[1] I am especially grateful to the Revd Emma Percy for her writing and thought in this area, which first encouraged me to take the arena seriously.

learning, but also space for the emotional, aesthetic, affectional, spiritual, spatial and empathetic) are amongst the qualities that distinguish feminist approaches to theological education (Chopp, 1995, p. 17). Building on this foundation, she presses for the practice and inculcation of narrativity in theological programmes (again resonating with our use of Hopewell), which in turn can challenge and enhance 'the practice of ekklesia' (ibid., pp. 45ff) on issues such as sin and patriarchy. The book concludes by employing the metaphor of 'quilting' to describe the practice of feminist theological education. This is suggestive, hinting at the collective, collating and colourful ways in which theological insights are brought together, besides drawing attention to the (normally underrated) aesthetic dimensions in creating theology, and the (apparently) more common reticulate habits of women in sharing their lives and work:

> ...[the] quilt is made from hundreds of scraps of material of all different sizes, textures, colours, and shapes. It is beautiful in its diversity...[and] represents the piecing together of our everyday experience in a communal act of love and the acceptance of all people and life experiences. It redefines beauty, and by redefining what beauty is beautiful, feminist theology deconstructs and reorders values, norms, and structures.... (Chopp, 1995, p. 96)

Chopp's approach to theological education is part of a rich vein in feminist theology that challenges the habitual compartmentalization and disembodiment of theology, as though the discipline were not about life itself. For example, Francis Schussler Fiorenza (1988) explores and analyses three 'typical' theological approaches to theological education. The first focuses on the nature of the subject; the second on the church (mission and identity); the third on ministry. Fiorenza argues that each approach has its limitations, and calls for a more integrated and comprehensive approach that can 'clarify both the possibilities and limits of theological reflection on theological education' (Fiorenza, 1988, p. 101).

Similarly, Mary Elizabeth Moore (1991) approaches the subject of theological education with *stories* that are designed to highlight the conventional segregational character of theology. Working within a North American context, she challenges the cherished division between the sacred realm and public space, which habitually confines religion to being a 'private' matter. In place of this dualism (which she identifies as 'destructive' of women's lives and stories), she proposes an alternative world-view in which the 'sacred and the public are held together'.

From a British perspective, Mary Grey (1989) suggests several 'feminist images of redemption' that are centred on mutuality and empowerment, which might then be applied to theological education. Grey discusses reclaiming (or recovering), self-affirmation, self-knowledge and mutual empowerment, which in turn support the underlying thesis in which human wholeness is fundamental to the teaching–learning enterprise. Again, what is distinctive about the feminist approach here is the attention to the embodied and the emotional, and

the refusal to allow physical–mental or spiritual–material dualisms to suffocate valid world-views:

> Accepting the truth of relationality as underlying existence and claiming this as power for development, means mutual empowerment in ever-deepening levels of mutuality. But as long as the...separatist model prevails in society, will mutuality seem merely a soft option, accused of lacking intellectual rigour?...Redemption in education means all these things: refusal of the victim situation, recovery of self-image, the process of coming to self-knowledge and the discovery of layers of connectedness. But it will be an ongoing story: redemption is also reclaiming, the reclaiming of those despised areas of the self, of memories and forgotten experiences of wholeness. It is also the reclaiming of stories which are yet to be told.... (Grey, 1989, p. 26)

Grey's work propels us once more into the inherently political character of reflecting on the meaning of theological education within the church. Grey is well aware that 'salvation' involves liberation-through-education, delivering women and the church from a range of materials that are explicitly or implicitly oppressive and thereby impair identity:

> [Education] will reclaim images and symbols from sexist and exploitive connotations...[reclaim] the silences beyond the boundaries of language and culture barriers...[whilst] being creative in pushing to the telling of new stories...redemption for education...focuses on the total well-being and becoming of the human person...redemption as mutuality challenges even when human brokenness and finitude prevail, and calls for just relation[s] to be established as part of an ongoing process.... (Grey, 1989, p. 27)

The connection between Freire, Hopewell and feminist insight is now emerging more clearly, and it continues to raise one of the original questions that we set out to address earlier, namely 'What is theological knowledge?'. From the writers discussed so far, it should be obvious that theological education is now beginning to be renarrated as a more extensive collection of disciplines and insights, in which life-experience and narrative can be equally and mutually formative and challenging. Culturally, within most ecclesial communities, this is an important threshold to appreciate when education and formation are issues for consideration, since some may see attention to the experiential and the narrative as too threatening and subversive for the credal and dogmatic. The pressure to marginalize the feminine is almost irresistible within some ecclesial communities. At times, it feels as though the very existence of the church depends on maintaining a dualism between thinking and *feeling*, as though what is felt, sensed and expressed would undermine the ordered hierarchies of truths and those that protect them. In what follows, therefore, I propose to reconsider a traditional metaphor within the church for teaching, learning, nourishment and formation: mothering. As we shall see, proper attention to the depth and capacity of the metaphor offers considerable scope for revisiting the nature of theology and the purposeful lives of the communities that are formed out of the discipline.

## Mother Church

An immediate foray into the (academic) territory of mothering, feminism and theological education fails to reveal very promising results. Mothering is an issue that lives on the edge of feminist praxis and thinking for obvious political and social reasons; it only becomes an issue when it prevents women from achieving their goals. Similarly, mothering is not a subject on which many theologians in 2000 years of Christian theology have had much to say. Generally, what has been said has been patronizing, paternalistic and prescriptive. Where feminist theology has made a contribution in challenging the tradition, it has more often than not focused on the oppressive 'idealization' of women (for example, virgin-mother, submissive wife, silent women, deacon[ess], martyr-saint and so on) that has continued to serve male power interests. Women achieve recognition through loyalty, self-denial, virtue and purity, not by their wisdom, courage or leadership. Alternatively, if 'idealization' fails, then women (in the Christian tradition) have often been seen as a source of ecclesial threat, impurity, sin, divisiveness and more besides. In short, it is rare to find feminist reconstructions of the Christian tradition (in relation to education, formation and leadership) that work with the fairly ordinary metaphor of 'mothering'.[2]

This is a pity, especially when one considers the breadth of primary biblical material that dwells on mothering as a metaphor for conveying something of the character of God. In Margaret Hebblethwaite's reflective essay 'Motherhood and God' (1984), she draws our attention to the variety of support that exists within the Judaeo-Christian tradition. For example, Psalm 131, verse 2 states:

> I have calmed and quieted my soul, like a weaned child at its mother's breast, like a child that is quieted is my soul . . . .

This, perhaps strangely, implies that the *weaned* child may return for comfort and nourishment, suggesting that the process of formation does not proceed in an orderly, linear way. The emerging child or adult may move freely between dependence and independence. The relational dimension of the mothering metaphor is also found in other books of the Bible:

> Can a woman forget her suckling child, that she should have no compassion on the [fruit] of her womb? Even these may forget, yet I will not forget you. (Isai. 49: 15)

> Like newborn babes, long for the pure spiritual milk, that by it you may grow up to salvation; for you have tasted the kindness of the Lord . . . (1 Peter 1: 23–2: 3)

---

[2] See, for example, Moltmann-Wendel, *The Women Around Jesus* (1982) and Joan Chittister, *Women, Ministry and the Church* (1983), who offer, respectively, a Protestant and Roman Catholic perspective on women in education and leadership. Moltmann-Wendel does discuss Jesus' attitude to mothers, but seems to be unaware of the potential of the metaphor in the wider biblical tradition. Chittister, although a Benedictine nun and Prioress (and therefore presumably *very* aware of titles such as Mother Superior, and all that this may mean), ignores the metaphor altogether.

Here, suckling is not a form of regression, nor indeed is it especially linked to an infantile stage. Rather, the metaphor is being used to make an association between the salvation and formation of persons and the loving constancy of God. Hebblethwaite extends her argument further by drawing on post-biblical Christian tradition. Augustine, for example, speaks of God feeding Christians from her breast: 'what am I but a creature suckled on your milk, the food that perishes?' (Augustine, 1961, p. 71). Both Anselm and Julian, in the more mystical tradition, work with the mothering metaphor, as does Catherine of Siena and Teresa of Avila (Hebblethwaite, 1984, p. 135). However, Hebblethwaite is most concerned to turn these metaphors into some kind of educational currency, and she ultimately argues that 'much [theological education] is *non-verbal*' (my emphasis). Furthermore, where it becomes verbal, it is first and foremost *story*, long before it becomes credal and dogmatic – or perhaps we should say 'detached'. And this simple observation takes us to an important place in developing the metaphor of mothering as a primary way of conceiving of theological education. It serves to remind us that the learning experience within the church is, initially at least, a suckling one. And that, whilst detachment, individuation and maturity may be appropriate at a later stage of development, the intradependency of weaning is not necessarily cast aside; the close relational bonding of spiritual and theological nourishment through suckling may continue.[3]

Yet there are deeper reasons – both sociological and theological – why the metaphor of mothering for theological education and formation deserves further attention. For a start, and to put it rather bluntly, 'mothering' is a very different act to that of 'fathering'. A child can be fathered in seconds, but, even leaving aside the period of gestation, the act of mothering bears a different timeframe, extending 16 years or maybe more than that. There are other differences, too. A child is dependent on a mother in a way that a father may never know; a mother must let go of a child if he or she is to mature, in a way that a father can never quite comprehend.

As we have already noted, there is a strong theological tradition that emphasizes God (and Jesus) as being mother-like, just as the Holy Spirit can also be referred to as 'she'. Yet this aspect of our analogical imagination has been repressed over time by the establishment of God as 'male' and a 'father'. It is the masculine language that is the dominant tradition in Christianity; the feminine language, most especially that of motherhood, has been largely forgotten. Yet for medieval mystics such as Bernard of Clairvaux, feeding off Christ's blood was like suckling God's breast milk; it nourished the soul. Indeed, the mystics often celebrated the maternal nature of God and Jesus as a way of stressing divine tenderness and instinctive love. Sometimes the imagery

---

[3] For a slightly different discussion see Hodgson (1999). Hodgson argues that the true pedagogue (the Greek *pais* (= child) and *aegin* (= leader)) is the 'child leader'. However, in the community of the church this makes us all children, and Hodgson correctly points out that this dynamic was not lost on early church fathers such as Clement and Origen, who understood their instructive role to be one of guide, 'helmsman' and teacher.

would be sentimental, but its purpose was to remind believers that gestation, birth and nurture were, so to speak, aspects of God's feminine or maternal side. As Caroline Walker Bynum points out in her *Jesus as Mother* (1982), St Anselm (1033–1109, and an archbishop of Canterbury) can write quite unapologetically in one of his devotional writings:

> But you Jesus, good Lord, are you not also our mother? Are you not the mother who, like a hen, collects her chickens under her wings? Truly master, you are a mother...for by your gentleness, those who are hurt are comforted; by your perfume, the despairing are reformed. Your warmth resuscitates the dead; your touch justifies sinners... you, above all, Lord God, are mother...'. (Anselm, cited in Bynum, 1982, p. 114)

A concentration on God or Jesus as mother had profound implications for the structuring of ecclesial authority and theological formation in medieval Christendom. Indeed, the irony of focusing on the mothering metaphor is that it can actually help to overturn the patriarchy that has been so inimical within Christian institutions for many hundreds of years. True, the centrality of Mary in Christian teaching has celebrated the various virtues of motherhood, but it has still tended to ascribe a subordinate, even passive, role to women through Mary's example. Yet those who once led monastic communities – including men like Bernard of Clairvaux – were keen to promote their leadership in terms of being 'mothers' of their communities, not just fathers. For Bernard and his contemporaries, the maternal imagery offered a way of ordering relationships within monastic communities. Correspondingly, terms like 'mother', 'nurse', 'breast', 'womb' and 'feed' carried a particular authority for religious leaders that transcended gender, for they were linked to education, formation and the very life of faith. Thus, to a novice whom he fears has departed the monastery for the world, Bernard of Clairvaux writes:

> I nourished you with milk, while yet a child, it was all you could take...but alas, how soon and how early you were weaned. Sadly I weep, not for my lost labour but for the unhappy state of my lost child...torn from my breast, cut from my womb.... (Bernard of Clairvaux cited in Bynum, 1982, p. 116)

But where do these reflections on the mothering metaphor take us? To what extent can the metaphor be a viable way of renarrating the theological task and the nature of theological education? Here, several observations come to mind, which subtly subvert received traditions and understandings and construct a novel form of feminist theological thinking applied to the field of theological education.

First, the metaphor of mothering is a 'cluster metaphor', which draws in several themes and ideas that are central to educational theory. Briefly, the metaphor can celebrate connectedness and also (as we noted earlier), eschew the formal and disembodied boundaries that divide the physical from the emotional. 'Mothering' is one of those metaphors that tie relationships and learning up in bundles, but not necessarily in a suffocating or restraining way.

Relationality is affirmed, but so is the ambiguity and messiness of 'coming to be' and the necessary dependency on another – in a series of acts and within a relationship, rather simply a single 'deposit'. Therefore, some paradoxical parallels begin to emerge in the process of educational formation with which the mothering metaphor 'fits'. Whilst autonomy is desirable for some, the relational remains important. Equally, it is in the act of 'letting go' that mothering is fulfilled; and yet, it is precisely at this point that a further relationship of mutuality (to quote Mary Grey again) becomes possible. There is also something deeply ordinary about mothering, which is perhaps again suggestive of the educational task that faces churches – commonplace, intimate nourishment that leads to maturity and freedom.

Second, the mothering metaphor takes us into rich areas of cultural practice and biological reflection. We might ask, 'How is mothering learned?' And the answer is, of course, seldom through training, but rather through example and instinct. To be sure, effective mothering can benefit from training and reflection, but the primary recognition in this observation is that Christianity is something that is mainly caught and not taught. In other words, and in relation to theological education, there are various kinds of theological knowledge – some of which are known at a deeper level than the creedal and dogmatic.

Third, motherhood profoundly alters theological outlooks in a myriad ways. Whilst cool, reasoned detachment may have its place in formation, the continual activity of parenting can also prioritize *passion* in the relationship. Immediacy can also be reconsidered; the deep instincts and reflexive processes that are 'natural' to mothering and not thought through before being enacted are also suggestive for theological education. Perhaps it is also true to say that pregnancy provides one of the first opportunities to truly reflect on the mystery of creation and the extent to which what is created is free, or obliged to its creator. Furthermore, mothering may be seen as a residual form of resistance to a society dominated by technology under the heel of capitalism (Rothman, 2000), which, again, has implications for educational praxis.

Fourth, the whole process of mothering is itself mysterious and ambiguous, and perforates many of the traditional barriers that pervade theoretical constructions of reality. As Bonnie Miller-McLemore (1994) notes, in the pregnant body the self and other coexist; lactation subverts the artificial boundaries between self and other, inside and outside. Mother love is, ultimately, not a 'power over', but a 'power with' – precisely what the feminist theologians discussed earlier have been saying. As Trudelle (2001) notes, becoming a mother involves becoming an educator and learner all at once; the antinomy between teaching and learning is dissolved.

Fifth, as a mother gives birth, so must she also die. There the creative and generative forces must face their own *telos*. Yet it is in giving that she receives, and it is in the very act of sacrifice that there is gain. At this point the mothering metaphor perhaps reaches its most intense meaning. Mothering is a gift, and a gift that sets free, liberates and enables adult human life to be and to flourish. At the same time, there is an irony here, since good mothering could anticipate (but not expect or demand) the return of the child – not as a child, of course, but rather as someone who has become fully 'other', yet conscious of

mutuality and intradependency. In some respects, the mothering metaphor is, at this point, a good 'fit' for a healthy development in the supervisor–postgraduate relationship. In year one, the student learns from the supervisor; in year two, they learn together; in year three, the supervisor learns from the student. In connection with Hopewell's world-views, we might also point out that mothering attends to the contextual, organic, relational and symbolic. Furthermore, 'canonic' mothering is a very different kind of nurturing to that found in the 'ironic' genre, as much as the 'romantic' and 'gnostic' will be oppositional.

The mothering metaphor remains, of course, just that: a metaphor. But it is one that I believe has promise and potential for re-imagining theological education as something that is reciprocal, generative and creative, involving passion, commitment, sacrifice and vocation. At the same time, it is ordinary, pedestrian, demanding, draining and utterly absorbing. I strongly suspect that when educational praxis is experienced as 'bad mothering' that pupils strive to quickly individuate and then to perpetuate independence and isolation in ongoing learning processes. However, when educational praxis is experienced as 'good mothering', rich possibilities of relationality and mutuality occur.

To summarize, education as mothering helps us to see that there are several layers to theological education. Some is learned behaviour; some natural; some reflexive and habitual; some biological; and some ascribed and designated (as in adoption).[4] Education-as-mothering is, in other words, a varied activity in which many participate unwittingly, a few self-consciously, but nearly all significantly. As a metaphor, it points us all towards something more inclusive: better parenting, in which nurture and nature combine to form persons, as the parents themselves are transformed in the activity of self-gift, sacrifice and the shaping of others. Furthermore, the reciprocal nature of the discipline, redescribed here, is suggestive for the patterning of theological engagement with contemporary culture. With these thoughts in mind, we now turn to some further analysis of the metaphor and its capacity for transforming the practice of theological education.

### Metaphor and Metamorphosis

One potential problem of the mothering metaphor is its innate capacity to idealize the infantile stage. In ordinary parlance the phrase 'mother knows best' is generally used to terminate further questions and imply a hidden and higher source of knowledge that is not immediately available to all. Similarly, the phrase 'father knows best' can be encountered in particular ecclesial communities – normally those of a male priest – to infer that there are questions and matters that need addressing, which are beyond the competence of the laity and are best left to the professionals. Clearly, in using the metaphor

---

[4] Of course, the whole idea of the mothering metaphor also serves to suggest that there are different ways of knowing. See Belenky *et al.* (1986).

'mother' for the church as a community, no such hierarchy is meant to be implied. However, mention of the mother–child relationship (as a metaphor) does invite further reflection on the process of nurturing and development and, in particular, on the educational process. By way of preliminary comment, several things can be said, linking to the earlier critical description of Fowler's work.

First, and linked to Fowler's proposed early stages of faith development, we can concur with Edward Farley's notion of 'the fragility of knowledge' (Farley, 1988). Because theological knowledge is relational as well as propositional, personal as well as public, and emotive–expressive as well as reasoned, there is a particular task that falls to ecclesial communities in handling questions, doubts, crises and the like. Moreover, the fragility of theological knowledge is something that is normally only understood from the vantage-point of maturity. Under such circumstances, *how* knowledge is held becomes as important as the content of faith itself. This is where the 'mothering church' can anticipate some of the pastoral and practical issues that surround theological education, and help to nurture individuals and communities through different tiers of understanding and alternative hermeneutical insights, leading to new horizons of possibility.

Second, the mothering metaphor leaves a door open to a subject that is rarely, if ever, mentioned in theological education: play. By 'play' I do not mean a leisure activity that is divorced from the serious. On the contrary, playtime and activity are amongst the most formative arenas of human development. It is here that imagination and creativity are ignited. It is in play that a sense of justice and competition can be developed. It is at play that we can also learn to work together. And, of course, play is part of the activity and space that is provided by good parenting as well as by institutions such as schools. But what would it mean to speak of play in relation to theological education? Without wishing to impose a pun, it may give permission for individuals and congregations to toy with texts and traditions in inventive ways that allow for new types of creative flourishing. The idea of play also suggests, helpfully in my view, that not everything in religion should be treated seriously and reverently all the time. A religion (and an education) without laughter is a bleak and impoverished experience. Play and laughter permit new perspectives, and may open up additional possibilities for teaching and learning (Alves, 1972).

Third, there is a relationship between the need for certainty and the fostering of faithful doubt. In Robert Towler's ground-breaking work (1984), a critique of 'conventional religion' is offered that looks at the pathological and neuralgic need for varieties of religion which refuse to mature. Although the work is a product of a particular sociological imagination, its implications for education are immediately apparent. Towler perceives 'a lust for certitude' (Towler, 1984, p. 99) that is inimical for faith development: 'Certitude is the absence of doubt. The need for certitude is the attempt to escape from doubt' (ibid., p. 107).

I could not, of course, claim that the mothering metaphor as a suggestive approach to theological education in contemporary culture immediately

overcomes this apparent problem. However, I suspect that a practical understanding and exercise of the metaphor does hint at the type of educational nurture that should be at the heart of all Christian communities. This would be one where various types of certainties, at various stages of development, are set aside or built upon until a relationship of mutuality and maturity is established. Granted, this standpoint presupposes that the nature and substance of theological material can be agreed upon – and very often it is not. What to some is a 'childish' belief is, to another, a non-negotiable fundament. So how can the stalemate be addressed?

I have already noted in my critique of Fowler that change does not necessarily come about through linear progression. Furthermore, in this treatment of the mothering metaphor, I have been careful to point out that the mothering task is a shared ecclesial vocation, and not one that lies solely in the hands of religious professionals. In Bruce Reed's remarkable study of religious change (1978), the author advances a compelling theory of 'oscillation'. For Reed, religious behaviour comprises two elements. The first is a human *process* of alternation between states of dependence and autonomous living, which Reed maintains is natural and universal in the life of the individual and is synchronized in social units such as groups, institutions and societies. The second is a *movement* which provides a rationale, in myth and theology, for the symbolic acts and objects through which the process manifests itself. Reed then goes on to identify patterns of church life which, according to the forms taken by the process, can be restrictive, functional, destructive or enabling.

The value of Reed's insights for the development of theological education are buried deep within his analysis and methodology – but they are there. For example, the oscillation theory resonates with some of my earlier remarks on good mothering. Reed recognizes that the processes of development are less linear and more cyclical-spiral. Regression may accompany transformation; dependence may lead to extradependence and finally flourish into intradependence – but there may still be some space for regression (Reed, 1978, pp. 73 and 170). The burden of Reed's work is to expose the ways in which flight, fright and fight lead to impoverished forms of dependency within ecclesial communities and therefore prevent the furtherance of theological education and increasing maturity. Thus, a retreat to 'sectarianism' or 'ecclesiasticism' (ibid., p. 79) which, on the surface, look very different, are in fact two sides of the same coin. Both represent an inability to cope with the multiple overwhelmings of modernity, and they constitute a theological stance that has terminated further theological questioning and suspended 'ceaseless wondering'.

From a more feminist perspective, Sara Ruddick (1983) proposes a theory of 'maternal thinking' that also has implications for education. Although not writing from a faith, Christian or theological perspective, Ruddick nevertheless offers reflections that complement our earlier observations. She draws attention to processes of nurturing in motherhood and suggests a triangle of virtues that are intradependent yet also mildly conflicting. On the one hand, mothering is committed to the preservation of the child. On the other hand, it is committed to the growth and individuation of the child, which requires

sacrificing preservation: children, to come in to maturity, have to be allowed to discover, take risks and experiment. The third point of the triangle is that of acceptability, whereby the adult seeks to socialize the child into the world. But this is done, mindful that skills in questioning and subverting the social order are part of the 'entry requirement' for adult life ('shaping an acceptable child'). Ruddick suggests that the mother/teacher undertakes her task with a combination of humility and hope,[5] and that maternal thinking, applied to education and formation, is more about 'holding' than (the more male) notion of acquiring.

Unsurprisingly, the agenda that emerges from Reed's and Ruddick's work is closely associated with the focused attention we have directed on to the mothering metaphor. We are left with binary paradoxes that are not there to be solved, but are there, rather, to act as guides. Thus, we can say that, whilst mothering anticipates and desires change (in the self and in the child), each stage is cherished for what it is, and a degree of relational regression (within an overall economy of increasing maturity) is permitted, if not desirable. Equally, whilst individuation is to be welcomed, and a mature autonomy encouraged, affiliation and intradependence are also nurtured for their own sake. The metaphor, in other words, is suggestive of a particular type of metamorphosis, in which the mother learns as the child grows, and the mother grows as the child learns. The church, as the 'mothering community' (in terms of theological education) is not only a source of creativity and nourishment; it is also a repository of the reciprocal and intradependent, in which teaching and learning is exchanged mutually.[6]

Another difficulty with Fowler's 'stages' is that the individual must lose his or her mother-theology at each stage in order to progress to the next. One of the attractions of Hopewell's world-views is that there is a type of theological mothering that corresponds to each of the proposed genres. In the case of the Canonic, the nurturing is strict and uncompromising, but for the sake of the child's (eternal) safety. In contrast, the Empiric is mellow and ironic, and perhaps almost too 'hands-off' and liberal. The romantic genre may be characterized as cloying, smothering and directional, with the Gnostic as semi-detached and faintly alternative or even mystic.

However, it is important to grasp that intradependency is not Reed's goal. Certainly, we have moved away from independence – the fifth stage of Fowler's spiritual development – as a goal. Instead, intradependency is the very ground of possibility for teaching and learning: it is a way of being. It is in the

---

[5] Her actual phrase, following Spinoza, is 'resilient cheerfulness' (Ruddick, 1983, p. 218).

[6] See Hodgson (1999). Hodgson draws our attention to the Socratic notion of education as midwifery: 'Socrates' mother had been a midwife, and he said that he learned from her the art of bringing forth ... the art he used was that of questioning, dialectic, by which he was able to draw the idea of the good, the true, the universal out of the experiential particularities of his interlocutors. He was the first to arrive clearly at the great insight that truth is brought forth by thinking, thus that it is discovered within our own subjectivity, and that subject and object are one' (p. 16).

realization that we are interconnected and interrelated at every level – social, emotional, personal and formative – that the intradependency can become a foundation for becoming a learning and teaching community. This is something to strive for. But it is also something that does not cast aside the stages and world-views of others.[7]

These observations are partly made in jest, but they have a deeper purpose, namely to remind us, finally in this chapter, that there are many different styles of mothering and that these styles correspond to a variety of outlooks and values. To be sure, mothering is a substantial activity. But like education itself, the 'how' can be as important as the 'what'. I am reminded of a gentle rule that was once imparted to me at a Romanian monastery, where the discipline seemed to be severe and yet everyone was cheerful. The rule was this: nothing is demanded; everything is suggested. Theological education, like good mothering, probably asks for no more than this. How it is offered will, to an extent, determine what is returned.

**The Nature of Theology**

In the Introduction and in the previous chapter, I argued that the church needed to be taken seriously as a place in which theological education is present and formative, quite apart from any explicit teaching that might be offered. Architecture, music, ambience, the structuring of social relations, the organization of ecclesial polity and other factors may all make a substantial contribution to theological or Christian education and formation. We have also noted that the *how* of education may be as significant as the actual content. But we can go a little further at this point, and say that the *how* is pregnant with theological significance and cannot easily be separated from content.

For example, in ecclesial communities where there is less stress on mechanistic effectiveness and outcomes, and more emphasis on symbol, the organic and the contextual, it is reasonable to suppose that means often matter more than ends. Indeed, even in the most ardent and devoted congregation where mechanistic priorities remain high, the underlying power of the polity of civility should not be underestimated. It can be far more important to conduct a thoughtful, appreciative, well-ordered, civilized (but ultimately inconclusive) debate than it can be to cut to the quick and reach a decision. Many congregations, and not a few of their ministers, have discovered that the imposition of directive decisions (which may be ultimately *right*) is often unwelcome if those decisions circumvent consultation, the coming together of minds and hearts, debate and mutual learning.

Theologically, and following Lindbeck (1984) and Schreiter (1985), we can reaffirm the useful distinction between *traditio* (that is, *what* is taught) and *tradita* (that is, *how* things are taught). Indeed, it is Lindbeck (1984, pp. 30–45)

---

[7] Strictly speaking, Fowler's sixth stage is the mystical intradependent stage. But in spiritualizing and idealizing it, he makes it a remote and rare possibility, not an essential social foundation.

who alerts us to the *performative* aspects of doctrine (that is, experiential–expressive and cultural–linguistic). A theological emphasis on the incarnation, for example, leads to a particular style of ministry and a particular form of missiology and church polity. Equally, a preferred form of behaviour can help select and shape the preferred theological fundaments. Exactly how the church conveys its message may in fact say more about its theology than it really knows; the mode of education may reveal the 'hidden curriculum' and the underlying theology.

So what of the nature of theology in relation to educational praxis and the church? Following Nieman and Rogers (2003), four observations come to mind. First, theology is *public*. It is the work of groups, congregations and conversations. Creeds or formulae are rarely formed in a vacuum or designed by specific individuals without reference to social questions and contextual pressures that are exterior to the life of a congregation, church or more extensive communion. Second, theology is *practical*. It explicitly sets out to discern the linkages between belief and behaviour, and addresses particular issues that concern the internal life of the ecclesial community. Third, theology is *plural*. Since congregations contain a multiplicity of theologies and world-views, competing and complementary convictions, and more besides, the *expression* of theology arises out of both unity and plurality, and its effectiveness is judged against its performative capacity to speak for more than one voice or viewpoint. Fourth, theology is *particular*. Specific to itself, theology articulates the self-conscious identity of congregations: 'we believe...'. But it is also bilingual, since a church has one language for speaking within, as it were, its own house, and quite another for the public domain, which takes us back to the first point.

Understood like this, the nature of theology can be understood as something that is essentially practical and concerned much more broadly with listening, learning and teaching. Moreover, the manners, codes and customs of ecclesial polity are often in common and ambiguous ownership. The way in which children are schooled into receiving consecrated bread and wine at the Eucharist will invariably be determined by a significant range of largely hidden theological assumptions that are present in any local congregation. In this regard, Schreiter (1985) is wise to draw our attention to the structure of local theologies, in which particular hermeneutics (local readings of sacred texts *and* meanings), certitude (what a congregation thinks is sure or fundamental knowledge) and praxis (practical wisdom) play a part in the ongoing educational formation of ecclesial communities.

The fourfold definition of the *nature* of theology, following Nieman, resonates with our earlier observations concerning the primary *purposes* of theology. First, theology articulates *identity* in which the church says something about what it intends to be. Second, theology constitutes a *world-view*; it presumes and promotes a cosmology that may enable or constrain behaviour. Third, theology is *critical*; it discerns and transforms material, enabling individuals and communities to regulate themselves in relation to their fundaments.

As we have already hinted, it is in the arena of worship that much theological education and Christian formation takes place. So it is perhaps surprising that so little attention has been focused on the grammar of assent, behaviour and symbolization that might occur in worship.[8] There are numerous theological treatises on the meaning and interpretation of worship, and, also within the discipline of theology, a significant amount of work devoted to homiletics and to liturgy (mainly from a historical or pastoral perspective). As Jeff Astley helpfully points out, part of the difficulty may be that worship 'produces' learning, even if it is not itself 'education' (Astley *et al.*, 1996, p. 244). However, this observation has to be balanced against the fact that worship does *not* in fact have an educational purpose: 'Religious people do not worship in order to do or become anything else, to teach or to learn. Worship is an end in itself' (ibid., p. 245).

Nevertheless, it is clear that worship can school, shape, teach and enculturate participants at some of the deepest levels possible. As Anton Vrame's intriguing meditation, *The Educating Icon*, (1999), shows, participation comes before explanation; experience comes before understanding. In this respect, Vrame argues that the early Christians had a distinctive philosophy of education long before they could articulate one. Vrame looks to the work of Elliot Eisner (1979, 1985) in the support of his thesis. For Vrame, catechesis is part of the 'sacrament of education' (Vrame, 1999, pp. 181–201); Christians are informed, formed and transformed in dynamic relationality; the 'hidden' curriculum is the discovery of the sacred in the gaze of the image or icon, as well as the relationship between the viewer and the object.

Similarly, Astley offers several penetrating observations about the character of worship in relation to learning. First, worship not only expresses certain religious attitudes, experiences and affections, it also *evokes* them, and they, in turn, then become part of the active learning memory. Second, learning *about* the worship of another (person, faith, community) also influences the shape of belief and what might ultimately constitute education. Third, individuals and communities learn *from* their experiences of worship. They understand that certain words, images, kinds of music, activities and aesthetics actually produce effects that further shape the contours of belief (Astley *et al.*, 1996, p. 246).

These observations prompt Astley to use a word about worship that we have already employed earlier in relation to doctrine: 'performative'. In other words, certain words, phrases, statements and sentences don't merely *mean* something, they also *do* something – they perform. It is not appropriate, at this point, to become drawn into the wider debate about speech–act theory and the technicalities of locution (a 'simple' statement), illocutionary acts (that is, making a judgement, issuing a demand) and perlocutionary acts (that is, what I

---

[8] My own analysis of charismatic worship as laying a foundation for religious experience and subsequent teaching has become a familiar landmark in the analysis of charismatic ecclesial communities. However, I have yet to see any similar applied to more mainstream/historic denominations. See Percy (1996a).

do by saying something – intimidate, warn, encourage and so on).[9] Suffice to say, worship is an activity that is far more than verbal assertion. It is an utterly transformative pursuit in which the worshipper is taught and can teach, learns and is learned, regresses and progresses.

Astley builds on these insights with the work of the Canadian philosopher Donald Evans (1979), in particular his notion of 'attitude-virtues' which he describes as 'pervasive stances for living, or modes of virtue in the world' (cited in Astley *et al.*, 1996, p. 247). Attitude-virtues, perhaps naturally enough, are in opposition to 'attitude-vices', with the virtues proclaiming 'what ought to be'. They are therefore close to the more performative aspects of doctrine and correlate closely, at least conceptually, with our definition of nature of theology and its purposes. Expressed like this, worship becomes a mode of discourse and behaviour in which learning about the way the world ought to be is regularly remembered and celebrated. Or, as we said earlier in this essay, religion is 'caught' before it is 'taught'; but in the very activity of catching, there is learning.

This brief mediation on worship as an alternative way of conceiving of the nature of theology resonates with some of our earlier observations relating to the nature of theological education. By focusing on worship, we can begin to sense that the totality of activity and experience within any given ecclesial community can constitute the teaching–learning environment. Moreover, in pulling away from narrow and static definitions of doctrine, we have also been able to gain some sense of just how plural Christian formation is – in other words, how the pedagogical activity of the church involves the whole person and not just the mind. It is in this 'totality' that doctrine is learned and taught. As John Bernstein notes:

> ...the early catechists showed in their pastoral activity that the Christian teachings demanded the life of the affections. Their concern for the latter, however, did not represent the commitment to an experiential catechesis as against, say, an instructional one. The disposition of the heart was of such importance not as surrogate for the church's teachings but precisely in virtue of the place those teachings must find in the life of the newly baptised. The fear, remorse, zeal and joy of the paschal season were marks of religious understanding...(Bernstein, 1978, p. 194)

## The Nature of the Church

Having considered the nature of theology, we now turn to the nature of the church. Here it will be necessary to build upon the earlier insights about the public, practical, plural and particular nature of theology (all of which produces doctrine which is ultimately performative) and try to identify and establish the types and styles of ecclesial polity that foster the *how* (rather than

---

[9] Astley is in debt, of course, to the work of J.L. Austin. See Austin (1962).

the *what*) of theological education. We might begin by offering a skeletal outline of the different ecclesiological approaches to instruction and education, which are themselves rooted in doctrine and ecclesial assumptions. We have already seen that the world-views offered by Hopewell can be roughly equated to ecclesial types, styles and norms (for Canonic read 'conservative', for Ironic read 'liberal' and so on). But here we are more concerned with ecclesial polity than outlook (that is, structure as an expression of value), in order to reflect more fully on the meaning of theological education within its primary environment. To achieve this I am going to work with conventional vernacular descriptors for churches – 'low', 'middle' and 'high' – briefly discussing each in turn.

In the 'low' paradigm, words and texts are presented as being pre-eminent. The basis of faith and unity will be constituted in agreed statements, and the catechesis will be didactic in character: belonging means agreeing with what has already been said and is likely to be said. Symbols, customs, aesthetics and what we have termed the 'theological qualia' of individuals and communities will, of course, be significant. But their place and interpretation will, to a large extent, be governed by a notion of teaching and learning that has already come to a mind on apparent peripherals – that is, the Oreologians will already have decided on the 'core' and 'central' issues with which theology is to be concerned and therefore, by definition, will have identified those matters that are held to be of marginal interest. An example of education/induction in 'low' ecclesiology is the Alpha course, which consists of 12 short meetings that introduce the uninitiated into the 'basics' of Christianity through didactic methods.

'High' ecclesiology is traditionally associated with an emphasis on sacraments and symbols as primary mediators of the presence of God. This does not mean that words are unimportant but, rather, that, in 'high' ecclesiologies, there is an in-built interpretative and experiential pluralism which can only be managed not by words, but by positioning power and authority in a recognized office (such as a bishop). 'High' ecclesiologies are more likely to see education as a broad form of induction into the Christian life, in which worship may feature significantly. An example of education/ induction in 'high' ecclesiology is the Roman Catholic Adult Initiate Curriculum, which lasts about two years and teaches through multifaceted exposure to the presence of the church.

The 'middle' ground, suffice to say, may combine insights from the high and the low in varying proportions. However, it is important to understand that the middle ground is not simply occupied by broad or liberal-minded souls who accept accommodation and pragmatism. For example, Pentecostal groups that combine word and experience may also belong in the middle category, since they seek not only to teach, but also to evoke experiences of the numinous as a means to furthering education. Notably, many who occupy the middle ground use a range of courses that stress such motifs such as journeying, pilgrimage and searching. In so doing, they may offer basics or fundaments as guides, but are unlikely to suggest that such things can all be known at the beginning: much is to be 'discovered'.

Of course, this outline sketch is a mere characterization of ecclesial educational praxis. Its main problem is its presumption that churches possess a settled and uniform nature that renders the adoption of different types of learning and teaching unlikely. In fact, nothing could be further from the truth, and this is what makes reflecting on the nature of the church in relation to educational theory so compelling. For example, consider the ways in which many denominations have attempted to use Alpha courses. Equally, consider the number of churches that have adopted more long-term programmes of induction that concentrate on presence, relationships, spirituality and pilgrimage.

Inevitably, questions of ecclesial praxis return us to the debate on the nature of theology. During the latter half of the twentieth century, theologians squabbled over the 'practical' nature of theology, and the relationship between orthodoxy and orthopraxis. Generally, the latter is deemed (at least by its opponents) to have confused witness or action with theology. By its proponents orthopraxis is held to be a more earthed, genuine and engaging way of *doing* theology (see McCann and Strain, 1985). The distinction is again helpful when it comes to considering the specific forms of educational habits that might embody many ecclesial communities. McCann notes that orthodoxy has been 'shunted aside like a senile but still tyrannical relative, more embarrassing than awe inspiring' (McCann, 1985, p. 39). Quoting the work of Charles Davis (1980, p. 130), who is no fan of orthopraxis himself, McCann continues the critique:

> Religion when maintained as orthodoxy claims a permanent self-identity, remaining unscathed by social and practical changes. It involves some purely theoretical center of reference to serve in an abstract speculative way as a norm of identity. There are indeed conflicting orthodoxies, but the differences are conceived as basically theoretical. Then presupposition of orthodoxy is the contemplative conception of knowledge, according to which knowledge is the result of disinterested viewing of reality by individuals. Orthodoxy is that contemplative conception applied to religious truth. (McCann and Strain, 1985, p. 39)

Once again, this critique draws our attention to the performative aspects of doctrine and ecclesiology and also raises questions about the nature of the church in relation to its wider environment. In fact, it is something of a myth to suggest that there is anything like the kind of purist doctrine that Davis attacks, any more than there is a 'pure' church. All ecclesial communities are, in their own way, socially engaged accommodations of contemporary culture, even if the nature of that response is one of self-conscious withdrawal. In other words, each form, type or style of ecclesiology (and its education) is a form of orthopraxis; there is no body that is working in a vacuum. As Edward Farley notes:

> Theology, that is, ecclesial reflective inquiry, does not itself determine or originate the realities that attend the ecclesial community. Theology does not found these realities but is founded by them. Thus, a theological failure is a failure to bring such realities to expression in the mode of understanding. (Farley, 1982, p. 183)

This is not a particularly startling observation, except perhaps for those who imagined the (or their) church to be an *a*cultural body that was shaped by revelation and tradition, and never by society. This is why Farley argues that the nature of theology is partly concerned with 'the attempt to bring pretheological apprehended realities to formulations intended as true...' (ibid., p. 183). For Farley, the nature of the church therefore has something to do with making the experience of reality more real, concrete, comprehensible and true. In other words, the nature of the church is interpretative and educational; it is a catalyst and agent through which life may be experienced more fully, deeply and clearly – 'a *depth continuity* which undergoes major or minor alterations' (ibid., p. 373).

So what does it mean to belong to the church that has a nature such as the one I have outlined? Is it reasonable to describe the church as a crucible of educational praxis? Several points can be made by way of concluding this middle section. First, we can say that Christian identity, doing theology and belonging are linked, and that these are critical markers for a consideration of theological education and Christian formation. We have already noted that Christianity itself is both a propositional and relational religion. When Jesus writes, he does so only in the sand. The 'word made flesh' is witnessed not by an autobiography, but by other writers and interpreters who construct their own narratives of significance; it is these ambivalent and multifaceted traditions that constitute what is revealed.

Second, hermeneutics – what Lucien Richard (1988) economically describes as 'getting across distances' – is part of the nature of the church; it is an interpretative community. In terms of educational praxis, the church in its teaching, worship, aesthetics and general qualia offers a rich and absorbing framework not only for interpreting life, but also for locating and discerning, for that same world, the transformative possibilities that are associated with the power and presence of God.

Third, the church (like theology) is plural, and yet not divided. The collective and shared memory of salvation, spoken and celebrated on a regular basis in worship and teaching, is also experienced and anticipated in a myriad different ways. It remains possible to speak of the church as an integrated learning community, one of praxis whereby 'people come into their own' and yet have a deepened sense of belonging: in Farley's words, 'a depth continuity'.

Finally, the church is a community of openness; even the most sectarian and communitarian are necessarily incomplete and open to new vistas of interpretation and fresh horizons of possibility. In this sense, the nature of the church is partly concerned with hospitality, which is a core value and attribute of ecclesial nature. Orthopraxis is unavoidable, and, in many respects, highly desirable. As John Cobb puts it:

> ... the more deeply we trust Christ, the more openly receptive we will be to wisdom from any source, and the more responsibly critical we will be both of our own received habits of mind and of the limitations and distortions of others ... (Cobb, 'The Religions' in Hodgson and King, 1982, p. 299)

From these observations, we now move to a deeper consideration of the nature of theological education.

## The Nature of Theological Education

Given the different types and styles of ecclesiology, there can be no surprise at the different forms of theological education. Three types were outlined in the previous section, but these were descriptions that were derived from a relatively arbitrary ecclesiological taxonomy. As I noted at the time, this was more of a characterization than an analysis. More substantial attempts to describe the field do exist, such as Jack Seymour's and Donald Miller's *Contemporary Approaches to Christian Education* (1982). In an earlier exploratory journal article (with the same title as the book), Seymour makes the case for there being at least six types of Christian education: religious instruction; socialization/enculturation (in other words, the development of particular lifestyles and ecclesial characters, habits, customs and so on); development; liberation; 'educational system' (Seymour uses this term to refer to Christian schools when church and state are separated); and interpretation. To some extent, we have already touched on each of these, and Seymour's work makes it clear that the approaches are not necessarily mutually exclusive; there can be overlaps, adaptive mixtures for particular contexts and other types of partnership. The burden of Seymour's work is to plead for an approach to theological education in which 'the educating church, the school of Christian living, must be built', such that education is not marginalized as just one aspect of the life of the church. In Seymour's and Miller's view, becoming the learning, teaching and ministering church requires the reinstatement of education as a priority at every level of its being (Seymour and Miller, 1972, p. 10).

However, this is easier said than done. We have already referred to the work of Edward Norman (2002), his attacks on secularization and liberalism within the church, and his advancement of a thesis claiming that the church no longer instructs 'the faithful in the faith'. Although we have disagreed with his dismissal of liberalism and have begun to argue that churches provide cultures of discrete learning that are not immediately obvious or didactic (that is, qualia, and so on), there can be no question that churches devote remarkably little time to reflecting on education. For Edward Farley, the church must redress this balance by conceiving of education as 'ordered learning', whilst also recognizing that the vast majority of churchgoers 'remain largely unexposed to Christian learning' (Farley, 1985, p. 158). Farley advances his argument in a number of ways.

First, he points out that 'teachers' are listed in Paul's *Letters* as one of the earliest historic offices of the church. The tradition of teaching is, in turn, linked to the more ancient Hebrew and Greek notion of *paideia*, meaning to 'nurture' and 'discipline'. Jesus himself adopted the term 'Rabbi', which again points to the centrality of the educational task in early Christian tradition. So far as Farley is concerned, education is 'a social necessity' if a movement is to

perpetuate itself. At the same time, however, Farley is aware that education in the church has a deeper purpose; it enables individuals and communities to discern truth from falsehood, deceit from wisdom, and to link faith and reality, which is done *through* theology. But this last point begs a question. If theology is a central, mediating and discerning discipline that is intrinsic to the nature of the church, why is theological education so rarely practised at grassroots levels? As Farley says:

> ... what history has done to the word 'theology' is reduce its meaning to its objective referent (a series of doctrines, beliefs) and then narrow its locus to the specific school and scholarly enterprise which deals with doctrines. Given this objectification and professionalisation of the term, theology becomes the possession of schools and a group of scholar-teachers ... these narrowings are now so stamped on the church ... that the rescue of the word is highly unlikely .... (Farley, 1985, p. 161)

Farley argues that, in the older sense of the word, 'theology' was:

> ... not just the scholar's possession, the teacher's trade, but the wisdom proper to the life of the believer ... faith was practical knowledge having the character of wisdom because it had to do with the believer's ways of existing in the world. (Farley, 1985, p. 162)

This leads to Farley arguing for the fostering and nourishment of 'practical wisdom' as a means of enabling the ordered learning that individuals and communities seek. It is this kind of programme that will assist Christians in interpreting their faithful responses to reality, which will in turn be resourced by interpretations of tradition and heritage, hermeneutics and educational stratagem.

Third, Farley critiques three areas that might prevent the establishment of a more widespread educational culture within the churches. These areas, which have already led to 'educated clergy' and 'uneducated believers', are: the professionalization of theology; the paucity of the homiletic tradition; and the generalizing of the meaning of education. At this point, Farley's critique is close to the borders of those educationalists who write within the tradition of liberation theology. Farley wants to see theology taken out of the 'private' hands of professionals and an ecclesial elite and restored to its proper place as a common language in which all can participate. This approach to the *nature* of education, then, assumes a much wider range of participants and a far more practical (rather than theoretical) discourse that is related to everyday life. It questions apparently given hierarchies and, in so doing, interrogates the very meaning and material of the subject.

If Farley is right, and theology has indeed shifted from being a general (but deep) *habitus* of wisdom to becoming a term that is more commonly associated with a system of doctrines, what else might be said about the nature of education that can help rescue the term 'theology' from the private–professional world of theologians and clergy and restore it to its proper public place within contemporary culture? Part of the answer, I suspect, lies in a recovery of a *spirituality* of education. The term is used quite deliberately, and

in using the word 'spirituality' I adopt a term that is ambiguous, 'spongy', imprecise and yet accessible, open, identifiable and substantial. Spirituality, unlike theology, is something that many may possess and articulate; it need not be 'official' or 'approved', but can function, nevertheless, as a sustaining world-view.

Spirituality also implies a more dialogical, open, empathetic and grounded approach to religion and everyday life. Furthermore, if the nature of theological education is to be primarily conceived as a form of spirituality, we can then reconnect the educational agenda with some of the sentiments expressed earlier in the chapter about mothering, individuation, maturity and intradependency. Spirituality is also suggestive for the character and vocation of teachers:

> The purpose of education is to show a person how to define [himself] authentically and spontaneously in relation to [his] world – not to impose a prefabricated definition of the world, still less an arbitrary definition of the individual himself.... (Merton, 1979, p. 3)

Margaret Guenther (1992), in her provocative book on spiritual direction, argues that both the term and the role need demystifying. In much the same way as we have been arguing for theological education, Guenther suggests that real spiritual direction is grounded in daily life, in the ordinary, in the mundane and in the ambiguities of everyday experience. But her reflections go deeper and connect with many of the threads of our previous argument.

For Guenther, spiritual direction is *hospitality*. The teacher or mentor must be able to operate as a listener/learner as well as a speaker (Guenther, 1992, p. 6ff). (We have already stated that theological education must involve a hermeneutic of hospitality.) It is from this place that the spiritual director can become a *teacher*, although Guenther reminds us that teaching is 'a dangerous activity': it stirs hearts and minds and causes us to question prevailing standards and norms. Moreover, good teaching lies not in giving answers so much as in educating people into asking questions (ibid., p. 54). Guenther concludes her tripartite model by identifying the spiritual director as a *midwife*, and expresses similar sentiments to those we touched on in Chapter 2. The midwife brings to birth, enables and assists. The midwife coaches and encourages, and draws out the strengths and new life in others. Ultimately, for Guenther, theological and spiritual teaching is a kind of reciprocal guidance. The teacher leads individuals and communities to thresholds and is present when they are encountered, at the moments of transition and engagement. Teaching, then, is an art form in itself, part of the mystery of education in which persons are drawn to new vistas of openness and expanding horizons of opportunity and reflection.

Described like this, the potential or actual nature of theological education seems a very long way away from what most people will encounter in churches: dogmatic glaciation, static truth and no sense of journey. Furthermore, churches too easily assume that people learn in the same way and therefore adopt a 'one size fits all' approach to their catechesis. Again, this suggests that

the churches have an impoverished philosophy of education that guides them in their teaching. For example, Everding *et al.* (1998), building on the work of Fowler, identify four different types of theological learner: affiliating, bargaining, conceptualizing and dialectical. All have resonance with our earlier suggestions for a theology that engages with contemporary culture. But with rare exceptions, such differences of learning perspective amongst the laity (or the clergy, for that matter) are seldom recognized. Perhaps this is why there is a perceptible rise in the number of adults who belong to various 'post-church' movements – post-evangelicals, post-liberals and more besides. People's dissatisfaction is probably not so much with the content of Christian faith as with the underlying educational philosophy that delivers it and often fails to admit to certain types of hermeneutic, particular lines of questioning, and the use of imagination and creativity in rereading the tradition. Alan Jamieson (2002) is right to suggest that the only remedy to this can be conversation between post-church groups ('leavers') and those who remain.

## Conclusion

To conclude this chapter, we need only say one thing: that there is a relationship between nature and nurture that ecclesiologists would do well to reflect on further. In the Christianity and culture debate, this is critical and vital for the shaping of theology. Whether it is the nature of theology, the church or of theological education, the actual attention to the nurturing of those who encounter these things is no less a vital task for educators. To understand the church as educational praxis is to begin to appreciate that it is in its very life, care and intellectual nurturing that its truer nature is expressed. Too often, the nature of the churches' teaching is preached as though it were an abstract, and the nurturing added as an afterthought.

In contrast, I am arguing that the nature of the church is deeply connected to educational nurturing, and that, therefore, different types of learning, experience, encounter and questioning should be treated with the utmost seriousness. As Astley notes:

> ... that the church is the fundamental context for Christian education is not in itself controversial, and it might even be argued that the life of the church simply *is* Christian education.... Ecclesiological reflection upon Christian education, however, is always in danger of a kind of abstraction and idealization which must be corrected by attention to the life of the churches, as communities with a range of functions and activities.... (Astley *et al.*, 1996, p. xvi)

It is therefore vital that orthopraxis sits closely with orthodoxy in any consideration of the church as educator or learner. It is not simply the case that 'we are *what* we teach', but also 'we are *how* we teach'.

# Chapter 6

# Formation, Transformation and Liberation

## Introduction

Central to the concern of Part II of this book has been the argument that the life of the church, with all its ambiguity and richness, constitutes a major place for, and resource of, theological education. This argument has been set against the prevailing assumption that theology is only for academic or clerical professionals and is a specialist subject requiring particular types of formation that are open to only but a few. Furthermore, in pressing for a more inclusive and accommodating philosophy of education within the church, the argument has, inevitably, challenged the nature of the discipline itself, calling into question distinctions, boundaries and identities. In this chapter I want to look more specifically at the shape of theological training for clergy, but without losing sight of the wider picture for ecclesial communities. At the same time, we will retain a focus on the church as a primary place for formation, transformation and liberation.

Perhaps unsurprisingly, there are a number of mainstream theologians who are already at the forefront of this debate, although very few of them are 'applied' in their thinking, or are developing a form of practical theology of education that might address some of our deeper concerns. But one senses that this agenda is still quite fresh for the discipline of theology, and that, despite the inevitable political difficulties we have hinted at, there is an inherent spirit of 'reception' within the subject that makes it look beyond its borders for fresh insight and wisdom. Consider, for example, these two recent contributions in the field of theology and religious studies.

First, Ursula King challenges the dominant enlightenment paradigm for studying religion, which assumes that religion could be apprehended and comprehended through 'some form of objective, scientific knowledge' (King, 2002, p. 382). Arguing that such approaches are becoming *passé*, she suggests that the new scholars of religion need to strike a balance between being generalists, comparativists and specialists. Moreover, there is also a need for the scholar to recognize that a certain amount of empathetic immersion into the field of inquiry is no bad thing, since this also constitutes part of the learning process, to which, presumably, universities and individual researchers are committed. Thus she writes:

> Our specialized findings should not remain imprisoned in an ivory tower existence but, rather, need to be integrated into meaningful knowledge related to human praxis and a viable life world...the viable transformation of religious studies will depend on whether it has sufficient flexibility to respond to different ideas, to a different

context of study, and to the need for a different purpose.... This is a tall order, but I believe passionately that religious studies can fire people's minds and hearts; it can help them to know and understand, to analyse and explain, but also to love, to grow strong and confident and to care and be compassionate. In other words, as an object of human enquiry the study of religions can communicate an empowering intellectual and emotional vision.... (King, 2002, pp. 383–84)

Such a passionate plea for (so-called) 'neutral' religious studies has an almost confessional ring to it, but it clearly strikes a note for a different kind of learning experience and intellectual formation.

Second, and similarly, David Ford argues from a theological perspective that the churches need to take their identity as 'learning communities' more seriously. A learning community is one which 'facilitates the learning of all of its members and consciously transforms itself and its context'. Thus:

> ... perhaps [the church's] main contribution is to be a good learning community itself, where there is joy in knowledge, understanding, insight and wisdom. Can it be a place where people learn to love God with all their minds and to relate everything – all fields of knowledge and all of life – to who God is and what God does? (Ford cited in Archsbishop's Council, 2001, p. 32)

Here Ford appeals to the vocational dimension of the church, arguing that intellectual hospitality is vital to the discipline of theology and to the life of the church. As we have noted before, the church can be strong on its 'teaching office' (or ministry), but it is less clear about how it is a learning organization, a listening body and a reflexive entity.

Taking such an agenda forward would, of course, require a more collaborative approach to learning. Unfortunately, with rare exceptions, such programmes are rarely found. Commenting on the fragmentation and concentration of theological training programmes in the USA, Poling and Miller note how ordinands (or seminarians) are pulled deeply into isolated and disconnected wells of expertise, such as biblical studies, church history and various types of (competing) theologies. In contrast, they argue for a process of:

> ... community formation [establishing] critical awareness of the tradition, focused community planning... reinterpreting the interplay of covenant and tradition... the [pastor/priest/minister] relates so as to stimulate the formation community... [standing] between the interpretive and political processes... as midwife to community formation.... (Poling and Miller, 1985, p. 147)

Poling and Miller are conscious that there is a deep problem in theological education and formation. First, its lack of groundedness in the real or authentic life of the church means that ordinands or seminarians quickly unlearn, forget or distrust all that they have been taught at theological college. Second, this leads to a weakening of their ties with their congregations, because what has been offered (and quickly discarded) was essentially abstract and verbal. Third, the former students learn to distrust not only their teachers, but

also the idea of teaching; they quickly lapse into 'what works', and, at best, manage a kind of orthopraxy:

> Action and reflection methodologies encourage instant theologising, quick responses to whatever is offered. The disciplines of scholarship are replaced by agility of response. (Poling and Miller, 1985, p. 149)

More likely, however, they will be slightly schizoid in theological orientation: cherished theories seldom match practice. The irony here is that the depth of theological formation has probably not gone deep enough. Interestingly, Poling and Miller suggest that the missing element from many theological programmes is any serious attention to the ways in which a sense of *community* is a major part of the process of formation.[1] Rather, as I have been arguing throughout, it is as and when the community recognizes that the environment and context itself is educative that something deeper can commence. Once students realize that the theological college or seminary itself is merely *part* of the schooling process, they can begin to understand how what they are studying relates to who and where they are, what they are about, and what they are about to become.[2]

Inevitably, we are drawn to saying that most theological education rarely reflects on itself (as a dynamic, process and so on), and is seldom able to evaluate its performance. This is extraordinary when one considers the all-pervasive nature of theological reflection across faith communities, which is by no means restricted to professional clerics or academics. Edward Farley, in one of the more influential essays in the field of theological formation, calls for a 'hermeneutic of situations' in which the taught and skilled interpreter will learn to:

> ... uncover the distinctive contents of the situation, will probe its repressed past, will explore its relation to other situations with which it is intertwined, and will also explore the 'demand' of the situation through consideration of corruption and redemption ... a practical theology of these activities and environments will correct their [that is, the clergy's] traditional pedagogical isolation through a special hermeneutics of these situations .... (Farley, 1987, p. 67)

Again, this approach challenges some of the fundamental assertions relating to the nature of theology. In Farley's thinking, the situations are themselves the crucible for learning and teaching, not something other to which theology is 'applied'. In theological education, therefore, stories, world-views and narratives take on a new significance as the *place* of engagement and interpretation. Or, put more theologically, Christian education becomes an expression of the incarnate dimensions that it ultimately bears witness to.

---

[1] Poling and Miller also criticize theological colleges for being 'in bondage to upper middle-class interest[s]' and male interests: 'the concerns of blacks, Hispanics ... native Americans, Asian and African Christians are seldom represented ...'. (1985, p. 148).

[2] For an alternative vision, see Pobee (1997) and Ferris (1990).

One final point relating to the place of evaluation needs to be made in this brief section. We have already suggested that critical self-reflection, for the church and its theology is a difficult issue. Because the church believes that it teaches 'The Truth', questions of performance and evaluation seem to imply a certain relativity to what is essentially timeless. For many Christian traditions, evaluation simply drags revelation down to the level of the world. But it need not be so. Evaluation is an opportunity to reflect critically on how effective theology might be for its tasks, including the formation of individuals and whole communities for ministry. Evaluation should be seen as a potential partner, not a secularist policing activity that has invaded the realm of the sacred. But a certain parable puts it better:

> In the beginning God created the heavens and the earth . . . and God saw everything He made. 'Behold,' said God, 'it is very good'. And the evening and the morning were the sixth day. And on the seventh day God rested from all his work. His archangel then came unto him asking: 'God, how do you know that what you have created is "very good"? What are your criteria? On what data do you base your judgment? Aren't you a little close to the situation to make a fair and unbiased evaluation?'
>
> God thought about these questions all day, and His rest was greatly disturbed.
>
> On the eighth day God said, 'Oh Lucifer, why don't you just go to hell!?'
>
> Thus was evaluation born in a blaze of glory. (Adapted from Pattison and Woodward, 2000, p. 301)

## Transformation

We have already touched on the hesitancy and fear surrounding evaluation in relation to theological education and formation. But we also maintain that evaluation is an essential component in the service of transformation. Of course, evaluation is nothing more and nothing less than judging the worth of an activity, and, as such, *informal* evaluation takes place in ecclesial communities all of the time (Pattison and Woodward, 2000, p. 302). However, the hostility to its formal inculcation is a serious problem for the churches as they seek to transform themselves and adapt to the new environment of the twenty-first century. In truth, the problem is deeper and more widespread than is at first apparent. The churches, in valuing their tradition, are not only slow to change; they are also often guilty of resisting it. Proper admiration of the past quickly becomes a dialectical mode: modernity versus the sacred, change versus tradition, and more besides. Paradoxically, transformation can be seen as a sign of weakness and a lack of depth.

Reflecting upon this dynamic more personally, two stories come to mind. First, in attempting to investigate the changing patterns of healthcare chaplaincy in England, I was able to secure a generous grant from a prestigious research body to enable the appointment of a Research Fellow. In the process of designing the research, I naturally approached the Church of England's Hospital Chaplaincy Council to see if they would contribute to or participate in the research. I was surprised to be turned down flat on the basis

that 'we know all there is to know about the field, and we can't really see what you are doing this research for' (see Orchard, 2000). The research went ahead anyway, and, unsurprisingly, the Research Fellow discovered a wide range of practices in hospitals related to the delivery of chaplaincy services. Some NHS Trusts had proper systems of accountability, and worked hard to make (state-funded) chaplaincy religiously inclusive by thoroughly involving non-Christian faiths in the shaping of the service and the profession. On the other hand, the Research Fellow also discovered hospitals where the chaplaincy service was ill-defined, poorly managed, lacking in sensitivity to non-Christian faiths and generally offering a poor service to patients and hospital alike.

One can only guess as to why the Church of England should resist research into its own performance at this level, particularly when hospital chaplaincy is mainly funded by the state. But the educational implications are, arguably, the more serious issue here. Research-led investigations into ministerial performance (evaluation) could feed directly back into the present state of theological education. One might ask: 'How are Anglican chaplains (who constitute almost 70 per cent of the state funding for hospital chaplaincy) supposed to relate to ministers of other faiths and build religiously-inclusive chaplaincy teams?' It is not as easy as it sounds when one considers that the study of non-Christian faiths (or even, for that matter, other Christian denominations) is not part of the approved curriculum for trainee ministers. Neither does the subject become an issue during continuing ministerial education. In other words, the church is deficient in research-led education to enable processes of transformation. And because of this lack, it resists change, including self-critical reflection that would lead to transformations of its own educational formation.

Second, a similar problem exists when it comes to analysing why clergy leave ordained ministry. Each year, approximately 220 clergy leave full-time ordained ministry in the Church of England.[3] The data is collected, but has never been reflected upon. The educational cost alone of this apparent 'wastage' is surely substantial, and yet researching the phenomenon – which might lead to transformations in selection, training, the management of clergy and so forth – is fiercely resisted at almost every level. Again, one can only guess as to why the Church of England would not wish to look at such an obvious area of research. But the lack of critical self-reflection continues to prevent any kind of transformation.

Now, in advocating evaluation, I am, of course, conscious of its limits, especially in relation to theology and the church. Not everything can be counted: skills are not easily measured; teaching and learning may resist certain types of commodification. Besides, theology is an art, not a science, and its appeal and argument are more usually aesthetic than systematic. This leads me to say that the deeper philosophical purpose of evaluation lies in *valuing*. Teaching people to value something or someone is one of the higher callings in

---

[3] Substantial studies do exist in the USA. The Hartford Center for Religion Research has conducted a number of surveys for different denominations that examine why clergy leave full-time ministry.

the vocation of education, so it therefore follows that the politics of evaluation must be securely located in the economy of valuing, in which worth is affirmed, but flaws can also be identified, discussed and, where possible, corrected (see Pattison and Woodward, 2000, p. 303).

The advantage of considering questions of transformation from the perspective of valuing is that it anticipates critical self-reflection in the service of improvement and broader social flourishing. In her ground-breaking *Transforming Practice* (1996), Elaine Graham uses the Aristotelian concept of *phronesis* to identify the type of 'practical wisdom' that ecclesial communities need to seek in order to adapt and transform themselves. Using the work of Don Browning (1991) as an additional foundation, Graham argues that practical theology as transforming practice can come about when it is reconceived as 'the articulation and excavation of sources and norms of Christian practice' (Pattison and Woodward, 2000, p. 104). By this phrase, Graham means much more than is immediately apparent. She is suggesting that theological education (especially pastoral studies) needs to pull away from alliances with 'soft' therapeutic sciences and clerical concerns and move towards seeing practical theology as something that is 'primarily undertaken with and by intentional communities of faith'. In other words, as I have been arguing throughout, theological education needs to take seriously ecclesial communities as a primary *place* and *focus* of theological education. But how would this become transforming practice? Five points need to be made here.

First, one understanding of practical theology is to enable churches to 'practise what they preach'. To do this, particular attention needs to be paid to the habits, customs and beliefs of churches, in order to identify what it is they value and espouse. Graham argues that this kind of inquiry requires a 'postmodern' methodology of *bricolage* (Lakeland, 1997) – one that pieces together fragments of knowledge, aware that disclosure of identity is often ambiguous and incomplete (Graham in Pattison and Woodward, 2000, p. 106). (Suffice to say, these sentiments complement the feminist perspectives offered in Chapter 4, which meditated on the quilting metaphor.)

Second, Graham argues that the postmodern is less of a successor to modernity and more of a complementary and critical corrective to it. It is through postmodern templates that the hubris of modernity can be questioned; its optimism, literalism, imperialism, objectivism and totalitarianism can be interrogated, and its limits probed. From here, the *alterity* of communities (including churches) can move from the margins into the mainstream as their voices are heard afresh.

Third, a focus on the entirety of Christian practice allows for a new opening up of the boundaries and horizons of Christian education. Once *praxis* and *context* is seen to be 'hermeneutically primary', Christian experience is properly repositioned as the *origin* of theological formulation, and not the application of 'learning' upon experience. Correspondingly, ecclesial communities are once again established as the primary ground of theological education, as a critical discipline that interrogates the norms and values that shape and guide all corporate activity, through which 'the community enacts its identity' (Graham, p. 109).

Fourth, practical wisdom, which emerges out of the first three stages, now breaks through the typical theory – practice or abstract – applied dialects and now sees all writing, speaking, theorizing and activity within churches as performative *practices* that bind communities together, enabling them to share commitments and values. Thus, the *phronesis* of an ecclesial community is both inhabited and enacted. Theological education and spiritual formation is an innate part of the *ordinary* life of the church.

Fifth and finally, Graham's attention to *alterity* (otherness) invites churches to reflect on their diversity and inclusiveness. Distinguishing between disclosure and foreclosure, Graham notes how certain groups, practices, needs, insights and agendas are often overlooked or silenced by the churches. True theological education, therefore, in order to fulfil its transformative vocation, must pay constant attention to 'the other'. This requires not only openness (in terms of boundaries and horizons of possibility), but also a hermeneutic of suspicion that will have the capacity to excavate norms and sources with a critical–reflective mind (Graham, 1996, p. 112).

To earth these observations a little more, let us return to an instance that we referred to earlier in this section: clergy leaving full-time ordained ministry. With Graham's insights to hand, we are now in a better position to understand why the agenda (in terms of research, better pastoral care and a review of selection and training methods) is so easily marginalized within the churches. To explore this area would require the registering of pain, the recognition of failure, the hurts and wounds that institutions inflict on individuals, as well as those that individuals inflict on institutions. It is a messy, complex arena to address, and one that could only begin to be approached through narrative *bricolage* (that is, a sensitivity to people's stories, an acuity for the latent oppression inherent within many practices and organizations and so on) and methodological *bricolage* (that is, ethnography, ecclesiology, pastoral studies and the like). Furthermore, it requires the church to explore its own types of marginal alerity and, in so doing, revisit its praxis in the light of its conventional norms and sources, excavating their meaning and application. So, we might ask, what does Christian tradition have to say to people who, for whatever reason, fail in Christian ministry? What do the codes and rules of the church say, and, more importantly, what do they *convey* to those who have departed or been forced to leave? How is the pain and grief of the laity who lose a minister addressed or recognized? How is the hope of redemption manifested in disciplinary procedures (occasionally trials) and other measures that are sometimes taken against a departing minister? It is in addressing the pain, here, in the body of Christ itself, that transforming practice can begin to emerge and offer the genuine possibility of the renewal of theological education.

## Liberation

Our observations take us, quite naturally, back into the field of liberation theology, a term that is loosely used to describe a variety of theologies that

makes the specific liberation of a group (marginalized or oppressed by virtue of class, race, gender, sexuality, wealth, ethnicity and so on) its primary purpose and a theological fundament. The roots of liberation theology lie principally in Latin American theology and also in the civil rights struggles within the USA. But at the very base of these roots lies a theory of education that was first developed by Paulo Freire. For Freire, two approaches to education must be rejected. The first is the traditionalist, which defends 'class interests, to which that faith is subordinated'. Here, Freire cites an example of how faith is narrated as something to be 'protected' against the potential ravages of revolution or Marxism. Second, he opposes the alternative modernizing agenda, which is deemed to offer reform so as to only 'preserve the status quo'. Freire rejects both these options in favour of a prophetic perspective on education that envisages education as 'an instrument of transforming action, as political praxis at the service of human liberation' (Freire, 1973, p. 544; Astley *et al.*, 1996, p. 167). For Freire, that will necessarily involve a further, more radical excavation of norms and sources. Thus:

> They [that is, the churches] discover through praxis that their 'innocent' period was not the least impartial ... [when others] insist on the 'neutrality' of the church ... they castrate the prophetic dimension.... (Freire, 1973, pp. 524–45)

Freire's agenda has been taken forward by a variety of scholars. For example, Thomas Groome (1980) argues (rather as I have) that Christian praxis is the normative form of theological education. This contribution, from a more mainstream (Western) theologian opens up the possibility of theology beginning with the praxis of the poor. But, at the same time, the more radical edge of liberation theology should not be lost in the milieu of praxis-centred theology, for the *desiderata* of liberation theology remains liberation, not development. There is a perpetual rawness to liberation theology that refuses to be consolidated and consoled by accommodationist strategies that do not fully embrace a radical revolutionary revision of structures and contexts.

Again, this type of assertion about the nature and purpose of theological education takes us back to one of our prior questions: the nature of theology itself. What or, perhaps, who is it for? There are several different answers to this question, but our purpose in opening up this brief section on liberation with attacks on neutrality is to show that there is no point on the theological compass that is non-directive. In other words, an inquiry into the nature of theological education is an inherently political process that challenges the shaping and ordering of the discipline itself, long before anything is ever 'taught' by anyone.

That said, liberation theology still stands within a broader tradition of theology – that of the hope of transformation. As Richard Grigg perceptively argues, religion itself can be defined as 'a means toward ultimate transformation' (Grigg, 1990, p. 8; cf. Streng *et al.*, 1973, p. 6). But although one might try and distinguish between theology and religion – theology being the 'intellectual approach to the infinite' – the distinction barely works in practice, since:

...the infinite that theology attempts to understand is just that infinite which can aid us in dealing with fundamental practical dilemmas connected to our finitude... theological reflection tends always to point to religious practice (Grigg, 1990, p. 8)

Grigg extends his theorizing to reflect on the particularity of liberation theology and what is methodologically distinctive about its programme for the field of theological education. Drawing on the work of Robert Long (1978), Grigg identifies six characteristics of liberating hermeneutics.

The first is 'a different starting point'. Instead of beginning with abstract theories, liberation theology commences with the 'experience of being marginalised or excluded'. Second, there is a different interlocutor. Liberation theology does not seek to persuade non-believers with intellectual or philosophical doubts; rather, it works with the people who are oppressed. Third, liberation theology uses different tools. It sets aside metaphysical speculation and opts for the insights of sociologists, political theorists (often Marxist) and historians. Fourth, liberation theology offers a different analysis. Instead of assuming a harmony between peoples and a degree of neutrality in methodology, it presumes that injustice is already in-built. Fifth, there is a different tone to the engagement. Instead of assuming that there will be a definitive Truth or principle to be arrived at, liberation theology maintains that the struggle for justice and truth will be ongoing and be known only in perpetual praxis. Sixth and finally, liberation theology proposes a different kind of theology. Instead of truth 'from above' (that is often then imposed on the world), liberation theology seeks to discover liberating truth in praxis, through a process of critical reflection. It is these six characteristics that, together, will begin the process of transformation that may actually and ultimately enable liberation (Grigg, 1990, pp. 75–76).

Having discussed liberation theology and education, it is important to state that the promulgation of formation, transformation and liberation as essential characteristics of theological education are by no means confined to the field of liberation theology. Postmodern writers have been quick to identify the agenda as one that is consonant with their own hermeneutics of suspicion in relation to modernity. Consider, for example, the African-American literary scholar, bell hooks:

> To educate as the practice of freedom is a way of teaching that anyone can learn. That learning process comes easiest to those of us who teach who also believe that there is an aspect to our vocation that is sacred; who believe that our work is not merely to share information but to share in the intellectual and spiritual growth of our students. To teach in a manner that respects and cares for the souls of our students is essential if we are to provide the necessary conditions where learning can most deeply and intimately begin.... (hooks, 1994, p. 13)

As Hodgson (1999, p. 4) notes, hooks sees that teaching 'touches, evokes, energises the very depths of the human, liberates peoples to realise their potential and transform the world'. He links hooks' work to that of John Dewey (1966) who maintained that teaching and education has a sacral dimension to it precisely because it is the means by which human beings

maintain themselves through renewal. But how exactly is education the 'practice of freedom'?

Peter Hodgson (1999, pp. 71–80) argues that the tradition is an ancient one, although more implicit than explicit in early theological writings. Gregory of Nyssa, for example, saw Christian *paedia* as renewal, liberation and transformation through individuals imitating Christ. It is here, claims Hodgson, that we first encounter a language of transformative pedagogy. The theme of freedom and education also emerges in the work of Herder and Hegel, with the latter showing particular concern for families and the state and the education of children. Where poor children were put to work at an early age, lack of education meant lack of freedom and a form of economic slavery. Here, the practice of freedom took priority over the consciousness of freedom: Hegel's work is unavoidably political.

Hodgson develops his thesis by suggesting three separate areas where theological education and liberation combine to make a richer theology. To some extent these areas already echo points I have made earlier, but they merit some further elucidation here, as we seek to establish the meaning of theological education. First, Hodgson agrees with Freire's assertion that liberation is not a deposit made in humans. Rather, it is a praxis: 'the action and reflection of human beings upon their world in order to transform it' (Hodgson, 1999, p. 75). As Freire notes:

> The teacher is no longer merely the-one-who-teaches, but one who is himself taught in dialogue with the students, who in turn while being taught also teach. They become jointly responsible for a process in which all grow.... (Freire, 1972, pp. 66–67)

What Freire is saying here is that the subject matter *gives* itself (especially in theology), and that teachers and students are caught up in the dynamic of this gift, which in turn creates, sustains and then transforms their relationships. To be taught, then, means not to be taught *things*, but to be taught *how* to think, which alone can then enable transformation and liberation.

Second, education as the practice of freedom is about radical democracy and social transformation. However, this transformation may not only be about resisting and challenging established social norms, it may also involve enabling society to live more peaceably with its many differences and diversities. One of the higher vocations of education is to enable 'the celebration of differ- ence...[but] persons must learn how to play the politics of difference' (Hodgson, 1999, p. 77).

Third, education as the practice of freedom is potentially conflict-midden and painful. Education presupposes transformation, and this will necessarily involve clashes with prejudices, habits and 'acceptable' forms of behaviour. In other words, it is only when truth is disputed that truth can emerge. And it is only by entering the debate that a dispute can take place. This takes us back, again, to the character and shape of theology. It is not something settled, signed, sealed and delivered. It is, rather, a way of educating: one that is forming, transforming and liberating. Freedom, then, is not easily attained.

The road to liberation (through the practice/praxis of education) is full of traffic with competing interests and travelling in different directions. The would-be traveller is not guaranteed a safe and smooth passage.

Thus far, this chapter has sought to show how theological education might be reconceived as a process of formation, transformation and liberation, culminating in the idea that it is the practice of freedom. I have offered an overview of how this might work, recognizing that the application of the essentials discussed will take on markedly different characters in various types of ecclesial communities. However, I have also sought to show how education as the praxis of freedom is a corporate, dynamic and collaborative exercise, rather than something that is done to or for individuals. Inevitably, the debate and discussion is political in character, since the excavation of the meaning of theological education takes us back to challenging the nature and purpose of the discipline itself. However, we cannot leave the debate at this point, poised as it were, for an endless number of ongoing political disputes.

Hodgson suggests that the way forward for transformative pedagogy is to recognize that it has a dual responsibility quite apart from its vocation to challenge and liberate. The first is to offer 'connected teaching'. Hodgson reverts to the Socratic midwife analogy that we noted in Chapter 2. Teachers draw out truth from their students and enable the dialogical processes of education. The creation of this 'space' also enables spiritual formation and resists the 'banking' model of education in favour of nurturing, encouragement and trust. 'Connected teaching', in other words, assumes a level of cooperation with the student; it requires grace, communion, reserve, inspiration and inclusion.

Second, learning is seen as cooperative. Hodgson asserts that teaching and learning is at its best when the role of the teacher shifts from 'expert/authority figure to facilitator/coach' – one who 'observes, monitors and answers questions'. Again, recognition of the shared nature of learning is at the heart of a transformative pedagogy, and this, in turn, questions many of the prevailing assumptions about the nature of theological education that are present in most churches. Certainly, the recipe advocated here is one fraught with risk, but it issues a simple invitation. Can churches learn to be learners again? And can its teachers learn to truly teach, rather than simply indoctrinate?

## Wisdom

In Part II of this book, I have been arguing that theology and theological education needs to be reconceived as a more holistic endeavour, rather than conceiving of theology as a discipline that is solely within the provenance of academics and professional clerics, one in which the whole church participates in the shaping and transformation of its life. Inevitably, this has raised questions about the nature of theology itself, and, in turn, has led to the inference that much of the present (confessionally-led) theological education for ministers in seminaries and theological colleges is too tied in with

clericalism and pseudo-professionalism. Of course, many clergy *are* professional in the conduct of their day-to-day ministry, and this is to be applauded
and encouraged. But full-time ministers are not 'professionals' in the ways in
which other professions (such as lawyers or doctors) understand the term.
Clergy can function professionally, but they do not possess skills and
knowledge that easily separate them from the laity. They may have specific
functions (ontological, or of representation, for example) that set them apart
from their congregations, and these may include the power to absolve, bless,
consecrate and the like, but there is not the same gap between professional and
non-professional that are encountered in other types of work.

Part of the difficulty in reflecting on theological education is in addressing
the question: 'Who is it for?' Clearly, many individuals and congregations
would assert that, within reason, it is for everyone. And as we have already
argued, the life of the church itself constitutes a kind of theological education
in its own right. Beyond this, many would assume that theological education is
the 'discipline' of the 'professionals'. But this is doubtful, since the clergy of
most denominations can, at best, only be described as 'semi-professional', on
account of the fact that pay, structures, patterns of accountability and
reviewing procedures are, at best, ad hoc. The vocational nature of the clerical
'task' ensures that clergy are free to practise their 'trade', within reason, how
they wish. The demands on their time may be many and varied, but the actual
ecclesial or sacramental obligations only constitute a small percentage of their
duties.

This observation is in no way meant to deny the clergy of their skills. On
the contrary, it is intended to draw attention to the fact that, theologically, the
wisdom of God is not 'something' that is in the possession of only a few.
Strictly speaking, it is a gift that is part of the whole church and can be
exercised and discerned by any number of individuals or groups at various
times. Moreover, the wisdom of God is not something that is necessarily
'learned' in any conventional sense, as though at school or college. It is
sometimes formed out of spiritual experience; equally, it may also come from
the qualia of the church, or from worship. It is no accident that spiritual
directors and mystics talk about 'the school of prayer' or 'spiritual lessons';
they are pointing to a different kind of knowledge and to a different aspect to
the theological formation of the church that is not concerned with curricula.[4]

Most writers in the field of theological education have an understanding of
this dynamic. Hodgson, for example, in describing education as 'paideia',
confesses that:

> ...for education to happen in its most fullest and most radical sense the paideutic
> power of God is required. This is what makes education an intrinsically religious
> endeavour.... (Hodgson, 1999, p. 87)

---

[4] For example, the classic 'spiritual fruits' that are prayed for at confirmation for each candidate
are acquired through disciplined discipleship and the free bestowal of God's graciousness. They are:
grace, wisdom, understanding, counsel, spiritual strength, knowledge and true godliness.

Hodgson looks back at the Old Testament and New Testament tradition of Sophia (the wisdom of God) and, using theologians such as John Cobb, David Kelsey and Edward Farley, identifies wisdom as a [new] way of seeing (ibid., p. 89), where reasoning, contemplation, the affections and action are brought together in a new and enhanced harmony. This leads him to reflect on the teaching of wisdom, and quite naturally, as a Christian theologian, he identifies Jesus as 'the incarnation of wisdom':

> What is distinctive about Jesus is not incarnation as such but the uniquely powerful manifestation of divine Wisdom in his teaching, which is at once his praxis of care, healing, and gathering. His teaching assumes a normative, paradigmatic quality in human history. It simply has the power in a profound way to draw people out of their daily preoccupations and petty provincialisms into an encounter with the eternal, with ultimate truth and value, with unbounded love, with a radical, transformative freedom. Jesus does not set this forth in a series of propositions, laws or theoretical statements. Rather, very much like Socrates, he engages in conversation with people, forcing them to reflect on their own traditions and to think about their deeper meaning. Rather than offering something totally new, Jesus radicalizes the shared traditions. He is the teacher who brings the Torah alive in such a remarkably powerful and direct way that its implications could not be avoided.... He teaches with an authority that is evident to all who hear him (Matt. 7: 29). He is called 'Rabbi' or 'Teacher'.... (Hodgson, 1999, p. 98)

But, of course, Jesus does something that Socrates does not do: he speaks in parables, an event in themselves, insofar as they have no fixed meaning and yet say and mean so much. Theologically, they mirror the incarnation itself in that they are relational, rather than propositional, in character. They are bounded stories, and yet they open up horizons of possibility and vision that is part of the economy of God's freedom. In parables, everyday logic is turned on its head: errant sons are welcomed back with celebration; 99 sheep are abandoned, wastefully, for fear of losing just one; workers are seldom rewarded in proportion to their effort. Parables can be read and reread, but their meaning and interpretation is never exhausted, because as agents of instruction, teaching and learning, they 'live' as stories that continue to shape and mould individuals and communities.

Hodgson concludes his meditation on wisdom in theological education by identifying the 'depth dimension or transformative power' of three basic elements in wisdom. These are: critical thinking, heightened imagination and liberating practice. What is noteworthy about these qualities is his insertion of qualifiers. No-one could really dispute that wisdom consists of thinking, imagination and practice. But the insertion of 'critical', 'heightened' and 'liberating' gives a different edge to his theology of education. To some extent, the proper place of the critical has already been touched upon in this chapter – the necessity of encouraging faithful doubt as a means to growth is a given within education, especially theological. The heightening of imagination, however, depends on the ability and courage of individuals to 'think outside the box' – to take risks with formation in the wider pursuit of transformation. A heightened (and deepened) imagination is, clearly, an appropriate quality to

encourage within any discipline, but it is, at the same time, something that confesses that the discipline is incomplete and requires new insight. Liberating practice, in turn, requires the courage to challenge, reject, overthrow, recreate and more besides, and places education once again at the service of freedom and social flourishing; the liberal spirit is connected to liberation.

In order to draw this together more, let me offer a concrete and practical example of wisdom operating within a context of 'collective vocation', namely an all-age parish weekend.[5] The theme of the weekend was studying scripture, and part of the education and formation of the church members (all ages, from 7 to 70 plus) was to consider the question of how to read the Bible. Rather than simply ask the question, several manageable groups (again mixed, all-age) were created and given large sheets of paper, crayons, glue and magazines to make collages or drawings. The exercise was introduced by the facilitor holding up a large plain leather-bound black Bible and inviting the groups to design a cover for it that reflected its contents. They were also told that 'Bible' is a word that only means 'collection of books' and asked to come up with a better title. As the groups worked, small historical stories were offered to feed their imaginations: the first English Bible; how the Bible came to be divided into chapters and verses; amusing mistakes in early printings of the Bible; early Celtic illuminated manuscripts.

The covers that were produced were remarkable, as children and adults had contributed ideas on mostly equal terms. Naturally, the inspiration behind each individual idea was what the group thought the Bible meant to them, or perhaps their idea of the most memorable or significant stories. This, in turn, quite naturally promoted a discussion about why stories or sayings were valued by some but not by others, and vice versa. Even more illuminating was the attempt to 'capture' the Bible in a new title. There were some humorous ones (*Would you Adam and Eve it?*), some dogmatic (*The Truth, the Whole Truth and Nothing but the Truth*), and some that tried to bridge dogma and humour (*God: The Autobiography*).[6]

However, the whole group – almost 100 people in all – eventually settled on a new title: *God – Some Stories By His Friends*. But the agreement was by no means unanimous. Some felt that 'his' was too gender-specific, which led to further (slightly heated) discussion. A few felt that the word 'stories' implied that what the Bible said might not be true or who, at best, fable-like. Others protested that the Bible was full of stories that were not 'true' (such as the parables), if 'truth' meant something that was 'historically verifiable'. Others said that large parts of the Old Testament were fables and shouldn't be read as history. Some people were agitated that an essentially 'fun' and collaborative exercise was now exposing some quite deep divisions in the group about the nature of scripture – a book that, in theory, unites Christians. But the discussion was well managed, and nobody lost their temper.

---

[5] This is an exercise I have used myself on several occasions, but I was first introduced to it by the Reverends Debbie and Michael Peatman, to whom I am grateful.

[6] This latter title was rejected, as participants said biblical writings were *about* and not *by* God.

As I reflect on this event, I realize that I have rarely been part of a meeting where critical thinking, heightened imagination and liberating practice came together so well, and for such a diverse range of people. Naturally, there was, in the end, no agreement about the precise nature of the Bible, but that is what the exercise taught us. You can't know a book by its cover; you can't judge a book by its title. Perhaps there was a hidden wisdom in such an economic title, and (normally) such dull or generic covers. Perhaps what we learnt was this. When we stood outside the Bible, we couldn't agree on what it was. But when we read it together, we were mysteriously united, even as we were transformed. As Auden (1955, p. 46) says:

> Truth in any serious sense
> Like Orthodoxy, is a reticence...

## Education and Vocation

In an important contribution to this debate, Nicholas Wolterstorff argues that the question of vocation not only goes to the heart of theological endeavour, but also raises profound questions in society about the nature and purpose of education. Basing his analysis on North American schools and colleges, Wolterstorff argues that amongst the primary purposes of Christian education are forming persons within a pluralistic society and 'educating for shalom' (Wolterstorff, 2002, pp. 253ff). According to Wolterstorff, this type of vocation involves risk and care, and also requires churches to resist indoctrinating people into faith. For Wolterstorff, addressing his own Evangelical constituency, such an approach to education is utterly deficient:

> It may seem true to you that a college is a place for people to soak up a tradition and not to learn to think, but do not suppose then that what you are proposing is Christian education. It may seem safer to you to advise your students to keep out of contact with opposing religious systems, but do not suppose then that the still-born, culture-abstracted system you present has much at all to do with Christian education. It may seem surer to you to demand of your students that they memorize a whole list of dogmatic propositions... but never for a moment delude yourself that you are participating in Christian education.... (Wolterstorff, 2002, p. 10)

That risk and care should emerge as themes within the consideration of vocation need not surprise us. Wolterstorff is arguing for pluralism to be taken seriously as a *co-educator*; without risking dogmatic certainties in conversation, trial and critical inquiry there can be no true education. But, of course, the character of this engagement must be shaped around the care of the student and an overall care for the process of engagement. The reason for this is that the deeper purpose of education is revealed, according to Wolterstorff, in the collective aspect of vocation: educating for shalom. And this is achieved through care in the enunciation of the tasks and invitation of education – 'teaching for gratitude' and 'teaching for justice'. Thus:

> Education is ultimately always shaped by a vision of the nature and possibility of human flourishing...the vision of human flourishing that underlies the biblical narrative and proclamation is what biblical writers call shalom. Shalom is harmony and delight in all one's relationships – with God, with other human beings, with culture, with nature, with oneself. The picture...is an essentially relational picture – and then, a multi-relational picture...Christian education is education that strives both to exhibit shalom and equip for shalom.... (Wolterstorff, 2002, p. 262)

Wolterstorff's vision is a particularly 'biblical' one that naturally arises out of his Evangelical and Bible-based hermeneutics. Although useful in a number of respects, many will struggle with his theological strategy – an inductive methodology that legitimizes praxis from a scriptural base for the purposes of establishing a definitive type of 'Christian' education. Much more promising are the essays in the collection from Jones and Paulsell, entitled *The Scope of Our Art* (2002). In this volume, the authors set out to explore the common nature of the vocational task in theological education, but from a wide representation of disciplines. The editors acknowledge that there were 'profound theological differences among us' and that 'our pedagogical practices were diverse, as were our understandings of our tasks as theological teachers' (Jones and Paulsell, 2002, p. vii). Nevertheless, a rich conversation ensues, which deepens and heightens the sense of what vocation might mean.

For example, Clark Gilpin sees the vocation of theological education as a 'vibrant attachment to public thoughts' (ibid., pp. 3ff). For Paul Griffiths it is 'particularly Christian intellectual habits' (ibid., pp. 32ff). Paul Wadell sees the task as enabling his students 'to grow captivated by God' (ibid., pp. 120ff). Susan Simonaitis argues that it is to initiate students into 'the difficult discipline of genuine conversation' (ibid., pp. 99ff). Bonnie Miller-McLemore and Rosemary Skinner Keller press their case for an understanding of vocation that includes the whole of one's life and is therefore linked to values, behaviour and discipleship. But there is a unity in the collection of essays which further supports our contention that theological education needs to be seen as more of a collective vocation:

> ...several common touchstones emerged. We had all been influenced, it seemed, by Simone Weil's work on attention, especially in relation to intellectual work. All of us were intrigued by her claim that academic study can hone our capacity for attention, making us better able to be present to God and to our suffering neighbour. We felt that cultivation of attention in our teaching and our learning, our reading and our writing, our relationships with our colleagues and our administrative work was crucial to the practice of our vocation. Mindfulness, generosity, hospitality, and discipline also emerged as common themes.... (Miller-McLemore and Keller in Jones and Paulsell, 2002, p. ix)

The essays – space does not permit a detailed, individual discussion of each – are remarkable for their identification of the costly nature of teaching. Essayists speak easily of the 'cultivation of wisdom', the need for 'generative lectures' that encourage conversation, discipline that enhances 'compassionate listening', and sharing in the 'constant struggle to understand the world of their

students'. There is, however, in the final analysis, no agreement on the nature of vocation for the theological educator, although most of the authors are drawn to an illustration from the early church father (Cappadocian) Gregory Nazianzen (329–390 CE):

> ...[our] vocation is the care of souls... the scope of our art is to provide the soul with wings.... If it abides we are to take it by the hand; if it is in danger, to restore it; if it is ruined... [to redeem it]. (Jones and Paulsell, 2002, p. 202)

In view of these remarks, we can say that vocations are better understood in terms of calling and gift, which we might say, theologically speaking, are extensions of the generosity of God. Yet, as we have already hinted, there can be no avoidance of the political and social implications of even the most spiritualized vocation, and certainly not of those vocations that are related (more generally) to the caring or formation of persons. Arguably, a key task for theology and the churches at the turn of the millennium is to underline the imperative of vocations as an essential fundament in the proper ordering of a just society. This does not necessarily return society to religion or to some kind of spirituality, whether specific, collaborative or general. Yet such a move might at least prevent the ethos and ethic of service from becoming overwhelmed by inimical market forces. The restoration of the vocational holds out some real possibilities for the reconstitution of society not only in terms of gift, offering and collaboration, but also in terms of a thorough and prophetic critique of the prevailing cultural and political powers that shape educational praxis.

## Understanding

Understanding theological education as a collective vocation – something shared out within ecclesial communities and between students and teachers – has emerged as a major key to the renewal of theological education in churches, seminaries and theological colleges. The renarration of the nature and tasks of theology, and the argument against its clericalization and professionalization, have led us to a point where we can now begin to make some tentative closing remarks. However, like all conclusions within the realm of practical theology – especially one that is concerned with theological education – the words will have to be tested, honed and implemented with a proper praxis. This is because vocational professions such as teaching are of vital interest to theology. As Jenkins suggests, proper reflection on the nature of service and vocation is part of theology's task and its contribution to public life:

> ...to revive a proper priestliness right across our society, we [need to] persuade one another widely that the time is ripe not only for the rehabilitation of the caring professions but also for a readiness to speak up in the form of a caring *confession*...quality of life is more important than consumption of goods...cher-

ishing people and sustaining the earth is more important than growth...and belonging and finding meaning and enjoyment together is more important than competition.... (Jenkins, 1990, p. 76)

Correspondingly, it is important to recall that the task of practical theology itself is not simply to provide empathy with a well-meaning and articulate theological gloss. It is, rather, more serious and costly: 'constructive statements about God's relation to human experience which leads to strategies of liberating action...[and]...the analysis of experience and culture through the use of critical [theory]' (Graham and Poling, 2000, pp. 163–66). A good practical theology of theological education will, in other words, seek the necessary transformations that might advance liberation and critical self-reflection, helping the churches, individuals and colleges come to terms with the nature and tasks of theology in fresh and relevant ways that might further enable social and human flourishing.

But where exactly does this take us? What does it mean to talk about 'faith in the church' in the same breath as 'the meaning of theological education'? The title chosen for this chapter was deliberately provocative, and I have been arguing throughout that the church, in all its plurality as a culture, place, repository of belief and customs, is the primary location for theological education and formation. It is in working in, through and with the whole church that the whole people of God encounter wisdom and gain under-standing. Although I have been arguing against specific specialization in theological education, I have, of course, recognized that some are called to that vocation. What is at issue, then, is the manner of their engagement with the community and the extent to which educators *listen* and pay proper attention to the important theological disclosures that are present in ecclesial and spiritual qualia. This leads me to make several points about the character of theological education by way of conclusion. Clearly, these points are not exhaustive, but they do resonate with the concerns expressed at the beginning of this chapter, and their adoption opens up new and rich possibilities for understanding theology as a collective vocation.

First, theological education is a dialogue or conversation. In Christian theology, there is no 'abstract' or 'pure' method of theology. It is essentially a responsive, reflective and reliable means of resolving issues in relation to problems and particular contexts. As I have argued from the outset, all theology is, essentially, *practical*: the discipline is birthed in praxis. This means that the discipline not only has to teach; it has to listen. Moreover, the discipline is concerned with educating 'listening persons into [being] active learners' (Melchert, 1998, p. 293).

Second, theological education is a kind of schooling in apprenticeship, and it steers individuals and communities through life; it is not just an abstract philosophy or part-time pursuit. The New Testament bears witness to a variety of apprenticeship models that are concerned with discipleship, some of which are quite radical (for example, Jesus' call to leave families, leave the dead unburied, and so on), and others which are perhaps more obvious (for example, Paul and Timothy). But it is important to grasp that apprenticeship is

more dialogical than hierarchical: guidance prevails over obedience. As Melchert states:

> [The apprentice] begins by watching, performing routine tasks, gradually learning to understand... often this cannot be taught, yet must be learned... [some things] cannot be transmitted in a purely verbal manner.... there are some things that only 'make sense' when they have been mastered.... (Melchert, 1998, p. 293)

Third, theological education can be playful and teasing: 'it does not command so much as it seeks to persuade' (Murphy, 1990, p. 15). I have already touched upon the parabolic pedagogy of Jesus, which is, of course, as intrinsically playful as it is unsettling. The idea of playfulness is not meant to imply that education is not serious; it clearly is. It is, rather, to discover again that play is one of those means through which we learn more than we can be taught, and that certain types of teasing can unpick new meanings and open different vistas of interpretation. (As we saw earlier, an essentially playful exercise about the nature of scripture exposed serious opinions about how the Bible was to be regarded and read).[7]

Fourth, theological education is concerned with forming persons of integrity (Melchert, 1998, p. 301). This points to some of the self-critical dynamics that we explored earlier. Biblical wisdom literature is peppered with biting satire and exposures of hypocrisy, and consistently points out the gaps (to use modern idiom) between rhetoric and reality, belief and behaviour. This is important for theological education, because integrity is closely linked to the 'integral' or 'whole', and here again we return to the theme of discipleship in relation to theological education, and the nature and purpose of theology. Good theological education, rightly conceived, can explore and address the 'gaps' in churches and Christian lives, putting together those things that have long been held apart (ibid., p. 302).

Fifth and finally, theological education is a type of death and resurrection. Just as Fowler's stages (with which we began) have to fall and die before a new stage can be born and lived, so it is with theological education. To learn in theology, one must constantly let go of cherished truths and dogma, and learn to face the possibility of death and new life together. Too often, ecclesial communities, seminaries and theological colleges, like many other institutions, invent traditions, customs or beliefs that deny death or seek to evade it. Sometimes educators, in order to avoid conflict, will collude with this. At other times, the death of an idea or school of thinking is forced too quickly and eagerly, leaving the student no time to grieve for cherished ideas that they may need to let go of. It is at this point that the vocational nature of the theological educator reaches its peak:

---

[7] See the extended discussion in Melchert (1998, pp. 295–301). Melchert argues that Socrates, Plato and other classical philosophers understood that 'serious play' was a profound catalyst and agent within the pedagogical economy. Furthermore, the wisdom literature of the Bible is full of ironic play and wise teaching that is, on the face of it, simply 'folk humour'.

[It] is both to allow the needed death of the old and then to use one's caring to sustain and support the learner in finding and shaping new truth and thus new life. There are even times when a teacher has to do the hoping for a learner, for experience has taught the teacher that there is a path on the other side of the pain.... (Melchert, 1998, p. 304)

Furthermore, as I noted in the Introduction, the study of congregations is also something that is not taught at theological colleges. This means that the qualia of the church are too often easily dismissed and that 'operant religion' is not treated as seriously as 'formal religion' (Roof, 1985). The ancestry of this absence lies in a profound imperfection in the notion of theological education, and in an extremely poor understanding of theology. James Hopewell once again draws our attention to the agenda:

...an analysis of both local congregational idiom and the way the gospel message confronts and yet is conveyed by that language would be a better starting point for efforts to assist the local church. Rather than assume that the primary task of ministry is to alter the congregation, church leaders should make a prior commitment to understand the nature of the object they propose to improve... many strategies for operating upon local churches are uninformed about the cultural constitution of the parish; many schemes are themselves exponents of the culture they seek to overcome. (Hopewell, 1987, p. 11)

Thus, the theological enterprise for which we are ultimately arguing emerges as something altogether richer and more empathetic:

To ponder seriously the finite culture of one's own church, given the promise of God's redemptive presence within it, opens up a vast hermeneutical undertaking. The congregation recedes as primarily a structure to be altered and emerges as a structure of social communication within which God's work in some ways already occurs. The hermeneutical task is not merely the mining of biblical revelation in ways meaningful to individuals. It is more basically the tuning of the complex discourse of a congregation so that the gospel sounds within the message of its many voices. (Ibid.)

This means that theological education is about finding God both in the church and in the wider culture of ordinary life, knowing and experiencing faith in its operant, as well as formal, expressions and their capacity to teach, form and transform.

I began Part II by noting that reform of theological education was a live issue for the churches. I have then tried to show how the traditional 'teaching church' (and its theological education) lacks an appropriate philosophy of education to guide the formation of its theological education. This is due to narrowly conceived definitions of theology that take little account of the multiplicity of ways in which people learn about God and acquire their own theology. All too frequently, those who want to offer theological education want to exclude certain types of knowledge and experience from the 'discipline', as though this somehow constituted a proper delimiting and concentration of the subject. So, the 'teaching church' fails to connect with authority because it dismisses authenticity and the integrity of the lives and

experiences of individuals. It also tends to concentrate its 'education' for clergy or ministers into one single period (prior to ordination or licensing) and puts few resources into ongoing educative processes that take place throughout ministerial life.[8]

In contrast I have attempted to show that theology is for everyone. I have advanced the argument through a classic type of 'practical theological approach', which takes issues and contexts seriously and allows them to shape and form the theological debate. This has allowed me to suggest that theological education is more about shared and different world-views than it is about linear progression through stages. It is more about discipleship, apprenticeship, mothering, parenting and nurturing than most will want to admit. And, if it is education at all, it should be about the transformation and liberation of individuals rather than the preservation of ideas and institutions. But to get to this point requires letting go, listening deeply and patiently, and becoming a learner yourself.

## Conclusion

After all that has been said, curricular questions necessarily come to the surface. What could or should a theological college programme look like? How would such a programme, concentrated in a seminary or theological college, flow out into the life of the church? How does the life of the church flow into the seminary? Following Van de Ven (1998) and Jones in Jones and Paulsell (2002), here are some brief but revolutionary suggestions for curricular development, which are mindful of the need for seminaries to become 'settings for formal enquiry in which people's beliefs are tested, nurtured, criticized and revised' (Jones and Paulsell, 2002, p. 202).

1  First, the teaching of critical–reflective skills should be extended across all disciplines offered at theological college, and encouraged in churches. Such skills should not be confined to pastoral or practical theology.
2  Congregational Studies should be taught as a separate discipline, enabling ministers to read and learn from their congregations. (The possibilities for this are indicated in Part III of this book.)
3  Congregations should be reconceived by 'professional' theologians or trainee ministers as 'communities of practice', in which the theological understanding, knowledge and practice of a given church can help shape theology itself. A community of practice can teach those who come with knowledge, and seek to deposit it. Congregations should also be understood as contexts of 'informal' learning and teaching, where beliefs and understandings are shaped by shared practice, rather than shared dogma.

---

[8] Inevitably, the 'deposit-banking-episodic' approach to education is replicated in parishes and congregations by the ministers themselves, leading to further impoverishment in collaborative learning and a deficiency in the idea of theology being a shared vocation.

4  Educational philosophy should be taught and developed as a distinct area within theological colleges. Given that one of the primary tasks of a minister is to fulfil the office of teaching, it is a scandal that educational theory (teaching and learning) is not addressed explicitly.

5  Correspondingly, challenges to tradition should be squarely faced with research – the continual interrogation of the basis for faith and ministry, both for the individual and the community.

6  Practical theology should be taught in more depth than it is at present. Currently, theological colleges tend to view the area as 'pastoral' or 'reflective' for ministry; it is not seen as sufficiently significant to be able to probe mainstream traditions. But as we have seen, this is not the case at all. Practical theology is, arguably, the *core* professional discipline for clergy.

7  The range and compass of subjects offered at seminaries should be expanded; at present there is little attention to cultural studies or to social sciences. This inevitably makes theological education into a discipline that either ignores the world or attempts to dominate or outnarrate it, without ever really engaging with it. The result is either ignorance or arrogance – neither of which is desirable or necessary.

8  Correspondingly, it should be recognized that any reflection on theological education is, *prima facie*, an inquiry into the nature of the discipline itself. Constant critical reflection can enable and empower the academy, churches and the public sphere to change. Education-as-transformation is a vital vocation.

9  Finally, churches should consider setting up research and development units which help shape the educative agenda for their seminaries and the formative ecclesial and missiological horizons for churches. In other words, research should lead and inform teaching. This is not only an educational strategy; of itself, it constitutes a powerful statement about the life and work of the Holy Spirit in the church and world at large. Put another way, to inspire, theology and theological education should primarily be inspired. This is both its calling and fulfilment.

# PART III
# THEOLOGICAL CULTURE
# AND THE CONCRETE
# CHURCH

# Chapter 7

# Adventure and Atrophy in a Charismatic Movement[1]

## Introduction

In Part III of this book we turn to the study of the concrete church and deploy the interpretative framework of James Hopewell (1987). Successive chapters sketch how his work, applied to various ecclesial situations, illuminates the study of the church and practical theology. This chapter explores the romanticism of a Charismatic congregation. The next chapter looks at the tragic world-view of a movement within the Church of England. The closing chapter in this Part identifies a denomination (Anglicanism) as comic–ironic in its outlook. To the best of my knowledge, this is the first time that Hopewell's interpretative framework has been used on something more than congregation, and, although one should be cautious about its applicability to movements and denominations, I suspect that there are valuable insights that gained from such an analysis.

Dating from 1994, the 'Toronto Blessing' is the name for a phenomenon that is associated with the Toronto Airport Christian Fellowship. From its very foundation, the Vineyard Christian Church in Toronto had experienced many of the things that would be typical for Christians within the fundamentalist–revivalist tradition: miracles, healings, an emphasis on deliverance, speaking in tongues, and a sense of the believers being in the vanguard of the Holy Spirit's movement as the new millennium approached. However, what marked out the Toronto Blessing for special consideration were the more unusual phenomena that occurred. A number of followers trace the initial outpouring back to Father's Day, the result being that some prefer to call the movement 'the Father's Blessing' (Chevreau, 1994).[2] There was an unusually high *reportage* of people being 'slain in the Spirit'. A number would laugh uncontrollably, writhing on the floor (the leaders of the movement dubbed this 'carpet time with God'), make animal-like noises, barking, growling or groaning as the 'Spirit fell on them'. Others reported that this particular experience of God was more highly charged than anything that had preceded it (see Hunt, 1995;

[1] I am grateful to the American Academy of Religion for the award of a research grant in 2002, which helped me to undertake some of the fieldwork reflected in this study.

[2] Ironically, and according to the late John Wimber, a founder member of the Vineyard Church, the seminal moment in the formation of Vineyard ministry, the parent movement for the Toronto Blessing, is traced to Mom's Day, 1980.

Poloma, 1996; Percy 1996a, 1996b, 1998, pp. 281–89; Richter and Porter, 1995; Smail, Walker and Wright, 1995).

Thus, the 'blessing' became known by the place where it was deemed to be most concentrated. To date, around 2 million visitors or 'pilgrims' have journeyed to Toronto to experience the blessing for themselves. Many of these pilgrims report dramatic miracles or supernatural interventions, substantial changes in their lives, and greater empowerment for Christian ministry. More unusual claims have included tooth cavities being miraculously filled with gold, and 'dustings' of gold on the hair and shoulders of believers, indicating a specific spiritual anointing. Some have even claimed that children born to believers will have supernatural resurrection bodies. A small number of other women of child-bearing age claimed to have had spiritual pseudo-psychetic experiences.

Despite the extraordinary success of the church, John Wimber (1934–97), founding pastor of the Vineyard network, excommunicated the Toronto fellowship for '(alleged) cult-like and manipulative practices'. Some Evangelical critics of the 'Toronto Blessing Movement' cited the influence of the Rhema or 'Health and Wealth' movement, through the Toronto Fellowship's own connections with Benny Hinn and Rodney Howard-Browne, as another reason for Vineyard-led secession (Hilborn, 2001, pp. 4–10). In January 1996 the Toronto Vineyard became independent. But, under the leadership of its pastor, John Arnott, it has flourished and continues to exercise an international ministry in the fundamentalist–revivalist tradition.

The Toronto Airport Christian Fellowship still meets in a converted trade centre on an industrial estate that is less than a mile away from the main city airport. Contextually, it is conveniently located in a matrix of highways that criss-cross downtown Toronto. There are no residential areas remotely near the fellowship, and members or visitors need a car to travel to meetings – but this is not unusual in North American churchgoing. Local hotels that are linked to the airport and conference economy also enjoy a good reciprocal relationship with the fellowship and its 'pilgrims'. The fellowship building is functional, comprising offices and meeting rooms, plus a large sanctuary area for celebrations. It is a spacious, adaptable building. For example, there was once a large area at the back of the church that was segregated into track lanes. This is where worshippers, at the end of a service, could stand waiting for individual ministry to take place. A minister stood in front of the worshipper, and a 'catcher' was positioned behind them. When, or if, a worshipper fell to the ground – 'slain in the Spirit' – they were caught, and the minister moved on to the next worshipper on their track, leaving the previous one on the floor to 'marinade in the Spirit'. Worship or revival meetings can last several hours, but pilgrims can also avail themselves of cafe facilities if they need physical rather than spiritual refreshment. Yet as a cultural creature of its time, the Toronto Blessing, despite its claims to represent a pre-eminent type of pneumatological power, ironically seemed to place *less* emphasis on aggressively reified spiritual power (a particular feature of John Wimber's teaching in the 1980s – for example, 'power evangelism'), and, through its distinctive grammar of worship, put more *accent* on concepts such as the 'softness' and 'gentle touch' of God

and the desirability of acquiescence in the believer. The popular worship song 'Eternity' (by Brian Doerksen, 1994, Vineyard/Mercy Publishing), sung many times over by followers and set to a soft melody, perhaps captures this best:

> I will be yours, you will be mine.
> Together in eternity
> Our hearts of love will be entwined.
> Together in eternity,
> Forever in eternity.
> No more tears of pain in our eyes;
> No more fear or shame.
> For we will be with you,
> Yes, we will be with you,
> We will worship,
> We will worship you forever.

It is through this distinctive grammar of assent that the fellowship continues to configure its life. The motto of the fellowship is 'to walk in God's love and give it away', and the life of the congregation emphasizes this in its ministerial distinctiveness. Thus, there are programmes for single parents (for example, '*Just Me and the Kids* – Building Healthy Single Parent Families: a twelve week program for single parents and their kids'), a conference entitled *Imparting the Father's Heart* ('Are you called to minister the Father Heart of God? This course will take you deeper into the Father's love... giving you the tools to give it away... topics include the need to be fathered, hindrances to receiving the Father's love, shame, Father issues, prodigal issues, orphan heart...') and various schools of ministry or programmes that centre on spiritual–therapeutic approaches to brokenness, abuse, neglect and failure.[3] There are also some social and welfare programmes that reach out to the poor and homeless.

More generally, we should also note that the Toronto Blessing was one of the first revivalist movements to be promoted through the Internet, and to a lesser extent on television networks such as CNN. (Indeed, I debated with John Arnott live on television on the BBC 2 *Newsnight* programme in 1996.) Through skilful marketing and public relations, the Toronto Blessing spread its message and testimonies quickly and easily; it rapidly developed into an 'internet-ional' movement. But, with the benefit of hindsight, the net benefit of the 'Blessing' seems to have been individual and atomized, rather than a spur for the world of revivalism. Indeed, the epiphenomena associated with the 'Toronto Blessing' succeeded in dividing many constituents within the world of Charismatic Renewal, with some declaring that the manifestations of spiritual outpouring (for example, laughter, howling and animal noises) were Satanic, whilst others proclaimed them to be a pre-eminent sign that this was the prelude to the greatest revival ever. In retrospect, neither side – promoter or detractor – could claim an interpretative victory (see Hilborn, 2001).

---

[3] All taken from leaflets on display at the Toronto Airport Fellowship.

Perhaps all that now can be said is that the experiences of those attending Toronto Blessing meetings since 1994 seem to have been primarily cathartic; one could almost describe the effect of the Blessing on worshippers as having been something like a cleansing spiritual enema. However, the influence of the Toronto Blessing has steadily waned since the late 1990s, and its position and prominence within global revivalism and the Charismatic marketplace have been quickly forgotten. The movement, after a period of intense etiolation, has been subject to some serious atrophy. There are now comparatively few visitors to the Toronto Fellowship, and the phenomenon is now rarely mentioned in revivalist circles.[4] Scholars such as Festinger (1957) might see this as a simple matter of cognitive dissonance – the process whereby a belief or expectation, having been disconfirmed, is nonetheless adhered to (and perhaps even more strongly). In this scenario, the much anticipated fruits and blessings of revival are usually deemed to have arrived as promised and predicted, but have just not been widely perceived and reified. Margaret Poloma (1996) pays some attention to this perception in her analysis of the Toronto Blessing. However, the majority of churches that were initially supportive of the Toronto Blessing seemed to have moved on quickly, redeveloping their focus as well as their interpretation of the phenomenon. For some, the promised revival is deemed to be 'manifest' in the phenomenal success and growth of Alpha courses (see Hunt, 2000). Only a few Christian fellowships and churches have continued to focus on exotic spiritual epiphenomena, such as miraculous gold fillings occurring in tooth cavities, or dustings of gold on the shoulders and the hair, indicating a special anointing. (Suffice to say and, despite the claims made for these miracles on various websites, the evidence for such miracles remains circumstantial and uncorroborated.) We should also note that a small number of Vineyard churches have become more liturgically-oriented in the wake of the Blessing: spiritual experience has led to an embracing of tradition and order.

### Interpreting Toronto: A Methodological Sketch

On my return to the Toronto Airport Christian Fellowship, I wanted to see how it was dealing with the decline in demand for its conferences, and how it was coping in a post-millennial climate in which the rhetoric of a much-anticipated global Charismatic revival had patently receded. The added grist for such a study was that, strictly speaking, for the past 25 years many scholars have only been predicting uniform growth for conservative churches, especially those with a Charismatic flavour (see, for example, Kelley, 1972; Tamney, 2002; Cox, 1994; Miller, 1997 cf. Weber 1946, pp. 295ff). Only a small minority

---

[4] Visitor figures are hard to procure. The Fellowship claimed – with some justice – that up to 2 million had visited between 1994 and 2000. The visitor figures are now harder to calculate, as the Fellowship runs so many commercial conferences that delegates are indistinguishable from pilgrims. My own estimation is that the combined numbers of delegates and pilgrims visiting annually is between 50 000 and 75 000.

of scholars have predicted the very opposite of this in relation to Charismatic Renewal and revivalism, especially in relation to the Toronto Blessing (see Walker, 1998, pp. 313–15; Hunt, Hamilton and Walter, 1997).

In this micro-study, I wanted to explore how participants now understood the movement of which they were still a part – one that had witnessed stunning but ultimately unsustainable growth, followed by 'wilting' – a process that biologists know as etiolation. Put more colloquially in the rhetoric of the 1980s and 1990s that partly constructed the language and vistas of 'power evangelism' and 'power healing' programmes, I wanted to see how adherents have lived through the 'boom and bust' years.

So how did they now interpret the apparent atrophy of revivalism? Of course, pilgrims and members tend not to construct their self-understanding in these terms, and this immediately raises some sensitive questions not only about appropriate methodological approaches within the field, but also about participant observation. Nevertheless, there can be no substitute for being there. As James Hopewell notes:

> ... the fullest and most satisfying way to study the culture of a congregation is to live within its fellowship and learn directly how it interprets its experiences and generates its behaviour ... participant observation ... as the term suggests [involves the analyst] in the activity of the group to be studied [whilst] also maintaining a degree of detachment .... (Hopewell, 1987, p. 86)

As a general guide, three distinctive, but closely related, tactical trajectories have conditioned my reading and reappraisal of the Toronto Blessing some six years after my first visit. The first is drawn broadly from anthropology, the second from ethnography and the third from 'congregational studies'. Each focus their attention upon first-hand accounts of *local* practices and beliefs, rather than solely being concerned with 'official' texts (see, for example, Geertz, 1973, 1983; Dey, 1993; Maykut and Morehouse, 1994; Hammersly and Atkinson, 1995; Atkinson, 1990; Mishler, 1991; Burgess, 1984). In this regard, the disciplines are more 'behaviourist' than 'functionalist'. The distinction is important, for it moves research away from concentrating on the primary claims of 'pure' or 'central' religion (or its analysis) towards the grounded reality of praxis. (For example, it might assess a number of Roman Catholic congregations and their practices, rather than ask the Vatican or theologians what such churches should be doing or believing.) In other words, the focus shifts from 'blueprints' about the way the church or congregation could or should be to that of 'grounded ecclesiology' – discovering how and why Christian communities are put actually together in their localized context (see Healy, 2000). It is through a matrix of conversation, interviews, observation and the savouring of representative vignettes that one can begin to piece together a more coherent picture of what it is like to belong to a group, to be a pilgrim and to believe (see Harrington-Watt, 2002; Bramadat, 2000; Dempsey, 2002).

For the purposes of this study, the work of Clifford Geertz has proved to be most illuminating. Geertz is an anthropologist of religion, and his two

principal works are *The Interpretation of Cultures* (1973) and *Local Knowledge* (1983). Both these works argue for research that consists of ethnography and theoretical approaches. In my own research, I have tended to treat religion as a complex cultural system. That is not to say that I, in any way, ignore or reject any idea of revelation, divinity or 'genuine' religious experience. Theologically, I expect such things to be treated seriously, and I expect their reality to have some sort of impact on any empirical study. But I do not think that 'religion' is only the repository for revelation. I regard it as a complex system of meaning: a mixture of description and ascription; of deduction and induction.

For Geertz, a cultural system is a collection of symbols – objects, gestures, words, events and the like – which all have meanings attached to them, exist outside of individuals and yet work inwardly to shape attitudes and guide actions. Referring to Max Weber, Geertz takes the view that man is 'an animal suspended in webs of significance he himself has spun'. Furthermore, to explain cultures, Geertz takes the view that analysts and interpreters have to engage in 'thick descriptions', not thin ones. It is important to understand what people *mean* by a word or gesture, so that we can understand its *significance*. An obvious example is two boys – one with a twitch of the eye and another who winks. A 'thin' description would say they made the same movement. A 'thick' description' unpacks the significance of the wink, what the gesture means and infers, why it is unspoken language and so forth. That said, the study of culture is not just about meanings, as though the currency of behaviour was agreed. People often do things that are countercultural. This means that anthropologists can often do little more than faithfully reconstruct what people did and meant, and then interpret this. Cultural analysis is 'guessing at meanings, assessing the guesses, and drawing explanatory conclusions...' (Geertz, 1973, p. 20). Geertz regards his interpretative anthropology as being constituted through 'ethnographic miniatures' – small studies that paint a bigger picture of society, a tribe or culture.

This means that Geertz tends not to be in favour of 'general' theories. He sees anthropology not as 'an experimental science in search of a law, but as an interpretative one in search of a meaning' (ibid., p. 5). Thus, an anthropologist, like a doctor, cannot predict what will happen – say, that a child will develop flu – but an anthropologist can *anticipate* what might happen, based on patterns they have observed, studied and interpreted. At this point, anthropologists have a variety of ideas at their disposal: ritual, structure, identity, world-view, ethos, to name but a few. Thus, Geertz is primarily interested in religion as a cultural system, or the 'cultural dimensions' of religion, because he sees culture as a pattern of meanings or ideas, carried by symbols, by which people pass on knowledge and express their attitudes to knowledge. 'Common sense' can be a system as much as any political ideology. So for Geertz, as we noted earlier, religion is:

[1] a system of symbols which acts to [2] establish powerful, pervasive, and long-lasting moods and motivations in men by [3] formulating conceptions of a general order of existence and [4] clothing these conceptions with such an aura of factuality that [5] the moods and motivations seem uniquely realistic.... (Geertz, 1973, p. 90)

Geertz expands this definition by reminding his readers that religions distinguish between world-views and ethos. A world-view is the way things could be or should be: 'blessed are the poor, for theirs is the kingdom of heaven'. And an ethos is the way things are: 'they gave alms to the poor'. In ritual and belief, ethos and world-view are often fused together; religion expresses both. The moods and motivations created within an ethos reach towards a world-view – the ways things could or should be. Of course, there are limits to what can be done with Geertz's work. Many scholars regard him as a functionalist, but this may be more of a compliment than an insult. Like many anthropologists, he is compressing complex data into a system of agreed symbols and contours – not unlike a cartographer. And, as with cartography, there is no map that is drawn to a 1:1 scale, which records what the observer sees. A good map is a *guide* to a field or an area; the chosen symbols help us to look on unfamiliar terrain with some agreement – churches with spires, a pub, a post office, an incline and a forest of deciduous trees. Insofar as it goes, Geertz offers us a reasonable, accurate and creative way of navigating through complex data and making some judgements about the shape of the subject. And as with maps, each is *specific*, but uses general ideas to help us create an accurate impression.

As a discipline, ethnography (our second tactical trajectory) comes in all shapes and sizes: some is mainly quantitative, whilst other kinds can be mostly qualitative; some depends on formal questionnaires and clearly proscribed methods; other kinds are more like 'participant observation' and accept the partiality of the observer/interpreter as a given. As Wuthnow points out, ethnography is 'a highly diverse set of techniques and practices' (1997, p. 246). It can be closely related to anthropology – the direct observation of social events, and reflections on first-hand accounts, drawn from the field. Equally, however, ethnography can also be a matter of data collection: church records, interviews and other kinds of primary data are brought together to help construct an assemblage of resemblance (Wuthnow, 1997, p. 246). But fundamentally, as Courtney Bender notes, ethnography is also always:

> ...about human relationships: it is built (or broken) through trust and through barter and exchange of various kinds. Although [we] focus on fieldwork relationships, ethnographers carry on simultaneous dialogue and exchange (and human relations) with the scholarly community and other texts as well. These concurrent dialogues make ethnographic research unique amongst investigative journeys.... (Bender, 2003, p. 148)

Bender describes the delicate balance between stepping into 'streams' of events and conversations and the need to stay just outside them. There is an ambiguity in making 'their' talk 'our' talk, in order to bridge the gap between the gaze of the ethnographer and the lives that are being lived. Inevitably, the ethnographer is not simply a passive listener, but is an active agent in conversations, and becomes a reflective partner in dialogue. This requires a degree of self-awareness in the ethnographer; they must not only be attentive to

the words and moods they study, but also be conscious of their own vocabulary and emotions in a given situation.

Bender recognizes that her ethnography does not 'reproduce' the voices of others. Those events that are recorded are inevitably shaped by the particularity of the ethnographer – what strikes them will not necessarily be what strikes another. As Foucault famously quipped of his own ethnography, 'I am not a pipe': there is no neutral conduit through which 'pure' information flows from source to receptor (this seems to me to be more of a common-sensical observation than anything particularly postmodern). This means, as Bender notes (quoting James Clifford), that dialogue occurs as ethnographers 'try on' different languages and perspectives:

> Dialogic[al] textual production goes well beyond the more or less artful presentation of 'actual' encounters. It locates cultural interpretations in many sorts of reciprocal contexts, and it obliges writers to find diverse ways of rendering negotiated realities as mini-subjective, power-laden and incongruent.... (Clifford, 1986, pp. 14–15)

Put more succinctly, the expression of dialogue in an ethnographer's text will inevitably contain more than the author could intend. Granted, the text will convey what the author wants to say, and the recorded dialogue will 'fit' their interpretative framework. But there will also be, as Bender says, enough 'surplus' to question these interpretations. This admission is important, for it alludes to the limits of explanation, but without implying a necessary equality between speakers and the ethnographer. The ethnographer is therefore free to identify those common 'stories' and 'typical' events that they deem to occur most frequently, or to be of most significance for a community. This, in turn, can allow such communities to be 'read' for 'deep meanings'. But the door is always open for others to listen to the community under investigation in quite different ways, and offer a different interpretation (Bender, 2003, p. 150). However, the keys to good ethnography remain constant: immersion in a community; many hours of patient and deep listening; conversation and rapport; not jumping to premature conclusions; not adopting interpretative matrices too early on in an investigation; faithful (or verbatim) recording of narratives and voices; shaping the material coherently; being attentive to the fact that nothing can be studied without being changed – either the material or the investigator.

As Bender quips, there are, in the end, really only two kinds of (intellectual) books: (1) the stranger who comes to town, and (2) someone who goes on a journey. In ethnography, she notes, one always finds oneself in the second category, but always with some sympathy for the first:

> [T]he ethnographer is always in some sense a pilgrim... a seeker... we go on trips to undiscovered countries or, armed with notepads and a 'critical eye', we make our own countries strange... [but] fieldwork [also] compels us to circle back on ourselves, our ideas, and our worlds, just as it also compels us to keep moving toward answers to our questions about the worlds of those around us.... (Bender, 2003, p. 151)

The third methodological trail – appropriately enough – draws upon the burgeoning field of congregational studies (see Ammerman, 1997; M. Williams, 1974; Eiesland, 1998; Dorsey, 1985), but with a special focus on the interpretative framework provided by James Hopewell (Hopewell, 1987; Ammerman *et al.*, 1998, pp. 91–104). In many ways, the discipline is a natural complement to anthropology and ethnography, since practitioners of congregational studies pay particular attention to the local or 'concrete' church rather than to the 'ideal' constructions; such studies stress the value of uncovering 'operant' rather than 'official' religion. In other words, and reflecting what I noted earlier:

> As slight and predictable as the language of a congregation might seem on casual inspection, it actually reflects a complex process of human imagination. Each is a negotiation of metaphors, a field of tales and histories and meanings that identify its life, its world, and God. Word, gesture, and artefact form local language – a system of construable signs that Clifford Geertz, following Weber, calls a 'web of significance'. Even a plain church on a pale day catches one in a deep current of narrative interpretation and representation by which people give sense and order to their lives. Most of this creative stream is unconscious and involuntary, drawing in part upon images lodged long ago in the human struggle for meaning. Thus, a congregation is held together by much more than creeds, governing structures and programs. At a deeper level, it is implicated in the symbols and signals of the world, gathering and surrounding them in the congregation's own idiom. (Hopewell, 1987, p. 11)

Hopewell, rather like certain anthropologists (he was heavily influenced by Geertz) and ethnographers in the field, takes the many and multifaceted *stories* of faith seriously. Rather than simply attending to the credal statements and articles of faith that are said to provide ecclesial coherence, ethnography and congregational studies probe deeper and listen to (and observes) the expressive narratives of belief that make up the practice of a community. It is by attending to the apparently *trivial* – testimonies, sayings, folk wisdom, stories, songs and so forth – that one can begin to understand the truer theological construction of reality under which believers shelter. But what exactly emerges from this 'narrative trawl'? As we shall see, there are many rhetorical shards that speak of heroism, romance, adventure, risk and reward, and, whilst these may lie scattered on the surface of congregational storytelling, their origin comes from deep within the movement. To repeat Wade Clark Roof's observations, the beliefs of churches cannot be construed entirely in terms of their credal statements:

> Theological doctrines are always filtered through people's social and cultural experiences. What emerges in a given situation is 'operant religion' will differ considerably from the 'formal religion' of the historic creeds, and more concern with the former is essential to understanding how belief systems function in people's daily lives. (Roof, 1985, pp. 178–79)

So, in telling the story of the congregation, we unravel its plot:

...church culture is not reduced to a series of propositions that a credal checklist adequately probes. The congregation takes part in the nuance and narrative of full human discourse. It persists as a recognizable storied dwelling within the whole horizon of human interpretation. (Hopewell, 1987, p. 201)

This observation is important, for it would be a mistake to read or judge the Toronto Blessing movement by its formal declarations of belief. (Most adherents are, in any case, unaware of these and would regard them as unimportant.) So, although the Toronto Airport Christian Fellowship does have a Statement of Faith and also adheres to certain formal credal articles, its main purpose is to position itself as a mainstream (Evangelical) ecclesial organization. To focus on these elements as constituting the core identity of the fellowship would be to entirely miss the point, however. It is the combination of divine dramaturgy (healings, miracles and the like) and the distinctive romantic grammar of assent that attracts believers by the thousand and then enriches their lives. Phrases such as 'you will be led into greater intimacy [with God] and personal renewal' are abundantly present in literature and teaching, peppering pamphlets and 'pep talks' alike. Similarly, worship songs such as 'I Can Feel the Touch of Your Presence' and 'Dancing in Daddy's Arms' are manifestly more important for the constituent contouring of belief and practice within the fellowship than any creed. The operant stress is on tactile, almost romantic–somatic encounters with God, which lead to deep cathartic spiritual moments, which then provide liberating and generative possibilities for individual spiritual renewal and further empowerment.

### Immersed in the River of Revival: Returning to Toronto

Given the context of atrophy – the pretext for this short study – it might be asked how the stories of faith within the Toronto Airport Christian Fellowship are beginning to change. Given that the much-hyped and predicted global revival has not taken place, what kinds of narratives do 'pilgrims' and members now use to describe their ongoing commitment to a fellowship whose influence and popularity has manifestly waned (cf. Festinger, 1957)? Interestingly, there is both some continuity and development to focus on here, but it is the latter which highlights a theme I had not fully developed in my earlier study. In my original research, based on my 1996 visit, I had especially registered the romantic metaphors and motifs in worship, teaching and testimony that seemed to shape the overall horizon of belief and possibility. There was a superabundance – almost an overwhelming – of appeals to the romantic nature of God and of the believer's desire for intimacy and oneness with God, and of the reciprocal desire of God, Jesus and the Holy Spirit for the believer's heart and soul. Much of this was constituted in a grammar of paternalism and passionate (or quasi-erotic) intimacy (see Percy, 1997, pp. 71–106; Heather, 2002, pp. 28–38).

Yet during my visit of 2002, I was struck by just how little the appetite for this faith-world had abated. There had been some routinization of Charisma in

the Weberian sense. There was less spontaneity and more order; there were signs that a Charismatic movement was evolving into a young church. But there were also factors that pointed to a sustained and original vibrancy. 'Pilgrims' and members were still hungry and thirsty for God; and God was, apparently, still hungry and thirsty for them too, for the rhetoric of passionate and romantic intensity remained buoyant. That said, the numbers of attendees were a fraction of what they were, and the rhetoric that anticipated (and to some extent hyped) the possibility of global Charismatic revival had all but disappeared. How then, I wondered, did members and 'pilgrims' understand the failure of God to slake their desire for global revival? Given that 'intimacy with God' had been (and still was) advocated as the path to ultimate individual spiritual empowerment, which would then pave the way for the pre-eminence of Charismatic renewal throughout the world, surely followers of the Toronto Blessing would have a theological narrative that dealt with the growing sense of dissonance?

The answer to these questions lay in paying closer attention to narratives that emphasized a spiritual theme that is closely related to the romantic world-view, but which I had underestimated in my earlier research. I speak, of course, about adventure and the idea that 'pilgrims' and members are caught up in God's own narrative of involvement in the world, which in revivalist and Charismatic world-views is often understood as a form of adventure, of which romance is but only one type. In focusing on narratives of adventure, the language and actuality of atrophy could be located and understood – read not in terms of dissonance but, rather, understood as a vindication of 'the ongoing story of struggle'.

But before reflecting further upon the theme of adventure and its relation to Charismatic atrophy, it is first necessary to describe the present situation of the Toronto Airport Christian Fellowship in a little more detail. Turning up for a regular nightly revival meeting, which begins at 7.30p.m. and normally ends about four hours later, I was greeted at the door by a smartly dressed woman who introduced herself: 'Hello – tonight will be your night for a miracle.' All revival and prayer meetings commence with intense periods of corporate worship. Participants sometimes dance to the music, but most make gestures with their hands or arms, either raising them high (and then keeping them still) and some also move them in a slow sweeping, encompassing or wiping fashion, as though polishing an invisible giant globe.

Some of the gestures seem to be more eccentric than this, at least to an observer. As I stood amongst the worshippers, a woman near me clapped her hands haphazardly around her body, as though swatting a fly, and cried out 'Ho!' or 'Hah!' (loudly) with each clap. A man in front of me raised his hands during the sermon at points where he was in intense agreement with the speaker and cried out words such as 'transformation!' and 'change!'. During praise, some women danced around freely, twirling brightly coloured flags and ribbons. A male member of the ministry team moved along rows of seats and prayed with people by blowing on them forcefully and loudly, making a wind-like sound. As he did so, the supplicant, normally already standing with arms raised, buckled and fell to the ground, where others then gathered around and prayed. As the worship continued, the songs proclaimed that believers are

'dancing on the mountain top with God'; another song announced 'God of the Breakthrough...all things are possible through you'. Still another worship song declared that:

> You are my health
> Your are my hope
> Your are my help,
> So I'm gonna lift You up....

On my return to Toronto, I had expected the distinctively romantic and mildly quasi-erotic accent of the movement that had permeated the worship to have subsided. But, if anything, the romantic genre had become even more explicit and intense than before. The structuring and grammar of worship made overt use of sexual analogies that were drawn from biblical and Christian tradition, but then intensified as they were interpreted. One worship leader explained that 'worship means "to kiss towards" – to come into His tender presence; so let Jesus *respond* to your loving...'. There was a real sense in which worship regularly progressed through three distinct phases: wooing or courting Jesus; 'mystical foreplay', often accompanied by heightened use of musical instruments, but with little singing (that is, delicately stroking or touching the chords of a guitar or keys of a piano – brushing them *so* lightly yet intensely in an erotic and suggestive sequence of notes rather than 'music'); relational consummation, which could include signing in tongues and other activity, sometimes leading to cathartic responses. But is such an interpretation fair, or merely tendentious?

The key is to recognize the way in which the encounter with Jesus is understood in specifically romantic terms. Thus, recent praise compilations (available on CD, tape and in books) offer '*Intimate Bride* – gentle worship for soaking in God's presence', '*Warrior Bride*' (with a picture of a young woman in full bridal regalia holding a large sword) and '*Passionate Bride* – songs of intimacy and passion for soaking in God's presence'. These products are illustrated with pictures of a bride embracing or encountering Jesus, the biblical analogy of 'marriage' to Jesus having been literalized and individualized. Other collections of songs include 'How Big is He?', 'I Can Feel the Touch', 'Take Me' and 'Soaking in Glory (in the River)'.

It seems that this worship continues to appeal more to women than men. At the daily morning meetings ('Wake Up Call for Revival', 10.30–12.30), close to 95 per cent of the attendees were women, with an average age of 57. These meetings are far smaller but no less intense than those I encountered six years ago and attract around 50 people. But the format remains almost identical, with the meeting opening in worship songs that suggest a unique, tactile intimacy with Jesus:

> Lord, Show me your face,
> So I can touch your brow
> Lord, show me your face
> So I can see your smile....

These prayer meetings are led by women, and are mainly for women, and the rhetoric reflects the desires and concerns of the dominant age group (50–60 plus).[5] Prayer is offered for those who suffer from anxiety or sleepless nights. Women are advised to try to create a prayer room in their homes, 'tastefully decorated in colours that help you to *relax*'. Other advice includes to 'keep a "Dream Journal", and share them with your Cell Group leader'. During ministry, the value of 'resting' was frequently stressed; resting with Jesus would combat stress, alleviate anxiety and also bring stillness and strength back into the family home. Sometimes this counsel would extend into vivid analogy: 'reach out your hand – can you sense the fragrance of the Lord here? This is a place of peace, and it feels like *velvet* . . . .' In the fellowship's bookshop and resource centre customers can buy fragrant oils for the house as well as scented candles with names such as 'Rose of Sharon', 'Myrrh', 'Frankincense' and 'Lily of the Valley'.

The morning meetings tend to contain a smattering of teaching drawn from the Bible, but are mostly distinguished by a constant resort to 'folk wisdom', stories and aphorisms that seem to engage the audience. More often than not, the talks are aimed at giving handy and homely hints for living a distinctive Christian lifestyle. Again, this thematic approach to teaching is reflected in the fellowship's resource centre. Adherents can buy books on Christian approaches to parenting, family life, marriage, health and healing, devotion, revival, leadership and ministry. There are also books on men's and women's spirituality, and books for children and teenagers. Books on doctrine or theology would be a rare find. Furthermore, there is no neglect of watery or liquid analogies to remind adherents that they are part of a 'wave' or 'river' of revival. Several letters in the fellowship's magazine, *Spread the Fire*, now include endings such as 'yours in the flow' and 'yours, in the river'. One article headline states bluntly: 'Power Conference Leaves Everyone Saturated.'

Worship in the larger revival meetings also shows no sign of being less intense than it was six years ago, although the numbers of participants are also smaller. But worship continues to be central; one leader proclaims that 'as we bless the Lord, his presence begins to fall'. If I may make an aside here, the study of the *theology* of worship is interesting at the Toronto Fellowship, because it effectively marks out the activity of intimate worship as the primary mediator between God and humanity. Worship becomes the conduit for encounter with God – an agency and catalyst that manifests the 'I–thou' relationship.[6] Performative worship is therefore elevated to a high sacramental status (that is, God is 'reified' *in* this activity, not simply inferred, described, remembered or represented). This observation is also borne out by close attention to the numerous slick aphorisms that pepper presentations. Thus,

---

[5] Although on one morning I attended, there were ten people only, and the time of fellowship consisted of watching a video of an old revival meeting on a wide videoscreen.

[6] Thus, a typical sermon from a visiting speaker argues that God appears *in* glory, and therefore the task of the worshipping community is to *produce* the glory so that God will appear. If the glory

'God is looking for a reason to come to you, not a reason to leave you', and 'God is looking for a reason to bless you, not a reason to punish you' sound fairly reasonable and, to some extent, comforting. But deeper reflection on the phraseology might suggest that these aphorisms create a sense of *distance* between God and the individual (an accidental trope), which only intimate worship can bridge. In other words, the rhetoric implies a doctrine of *conditional* grace, despite appearing to say the very opposite of this.

But some aspects of the fellowship continue to produce surprises. The novelty of a 'spiritual car wash', in which the congregation pass through a 'tunnel' of pastors who 'spray and brush' each individual with the 'anointing power of God' is a typically innovative form of ministry that combines a theology of immediate and reified divine power with a contemporary mechanistic cultural construction of reality. Equally, some worshippers bring their own musical instruments to meetings. One evening when I was present, a woman had brought a giant rams' horn with her, and the speaker, when he saw this, insisted that she blow it hard to announce the presence of the Lord in the 'Holy of Holies'. 'Let the horn proclaim Zion!' he cried, and the people joined in with whoops of delight and loud acclamations of 'Amen!' and 'Praise God' as the horn was blown loud and long.[7] On another evening, one visiting speaker from South Africa, who appeared to be at complete liberty to address the congregation, prophesied at length in rhyming couplets, albeit in a fairly rudimentary way:

> ...thus the Lord *says*,
> I am with you until the end of *days*,
> and though you may have *striven*,
> know that you shall be *forgiven*....

The slightly 'corny' or 'retro' language of revival that is spoken in meetings is perhaps a surprise, but speakers are probably doing no more than trying to link the present to the past. Inevitably, as the movement wanes, a 'tradition' is being appealed to in order to sustain momentum and provide a historical repository for memories that can recontextualize the dramaturgy. There are often allusive appeals to previous Great Revivals (and their leaders, such as Smith Wigglesworth, George Whitfield amongst others), presumably in an attempt to establish a sense of historic continuity (or rapport?) for 'pilgrims' and members. References enhance the sense of spiritual adventure for believers,

---

is *created* by the congregation, or in the heavenly realm by angels, God can appear, but it is a quality of worship that is deemed to *produce* glory, which is regarded as the necessary context for God's presence to be manifest.

[7] The Toronto Fellowship exhibits an intense interest in Israel as the fulfilment of God's purposes 'as we near the end times'. Many of the talks elide the identity of Israel with the pioneering spirit of the fellowship. In sermons, the Old Testament appears to be more of a resource than the New Testament.

underlining the requisite pioneering and 'tarrying identity'[8] that is so endemic within revivalism.

There is also plenty of audible praying in tongues, which is encouraged and orchestrated from the stage by speakers and worship leaders alike. Worship continues to be punctuated by individuals in the congregation crying out loud sporadically, groaning or moaning loudly, and letting out involuntary yelps of agreement, occasional piercing cries of ecstasy, or offering loud interjectory words of encouragement. Many people in the congregation twitch and shake, with some appearing to have their legs regularly buckle, as though being oppressed by a great weight. Many who are prayed for fall backwards, apparently 'slain in the Spirit'. But the numbered tracks and lanes that used to filter and organize believers for this ministry have now been replaced. More ambiguous thick green lines or bands which are woven into the pattern of the carpet, and which run in several areas of the sanctuary, now demarcate where believers should stand before they fall during times of 'soaking' ministry. Here again, we should note that where there was once one large area for this ministry, there is now a range of much smaller areas scattered around the sanctuary, marked out on the carpet, only a few of which are used in any one evening.

However, the types of people coming forward for healing ministry have altered little in six years: caucasian, middle-class and (late) middle-aged. The list of diseases and ailments cured is also a familiar canonical litany that reflects the needs of the congregation. Thus, there are 'suspected cancers' said to be healed on the spot, with 'depression', 'nightmares', 'back pain', 'angina', 'urinary tract infections', 'cancer of the ovaries and colon' and 'persistent headaches' all dealt with by Jesus, immediately. Naturally, each of these complaints is internal, usually unverifiable and not normally linked to any social cause such as malnutrition or poverty. But to make such an observation is simply to point to the fact that the 'healings' are part of the overall performative experience within the revivalist context. Their efficacy lies not in being 'proved', but in their power to persuade and perform within the divine dramaturgy that unfolds each day within the sanctuary.

So far, these reflections suggest that the life of the Toronto Airport Christian Fellowship remains buoyant and continues to evolve, albeit centred on fewer participants who are concentrating more intensely on some of the core themes that marked out the fellowship for attention and research in the first place. But, given that a process of atrophy is also underway, how does a Charismatic movement such as the Toronto Blessing and its parent fellowship come to understand itself? How does it reconcile its belief in a global revival with a steady decrease in its own popularity? I want to suggest that part of the answer to this question lies in repositioning the romantic genre (that dominates the

---

[8] That is, addressing the primary spiritual tasks through a variety of works, which may include 'spiritual warfare'. Here, we are dealing with a sense of the perpetual journey and struggle to bring about the kingdom of god on Earth, and also to be able to present yourself spotless at heaven's gate on the Last Day.

world-view and worship of the fellowship) and seeing romance as being derivative of a theology of adventure, which in turn can make space for atrophy.


## Adventure and Atrophy

According to Hopewell's congregational studies, based on participant observation and thematic analysis and interpretation, Charismatic Christians and revivalists configure their lives and meaning through a primarily romantic genre:

> ...the charismatic narrative is a more frightening and thrilling place...souls are eternally damned in it, yet God does not fail those who trust in him...the world in which the charismatic lives is fundamentally equivocal and dangerous, challenging the believer to seek its blessings amid the peril of evil forces and events. God's steady providence, however, accompanies the self who launches out toward God in an exciting romantic adventure.... (Hopewell, 1987, p. 76)

The romantic world-view generally eschews mundane reality in favour of witnessing supernatural signs. It deliberately ventures into a world of uncertainty; it is the world of the 'perilous journey'. But this search or spiritual quest is rewarded, for, as Hopewell points out, 'the romantic journey ends in the triumph of God's love': 'the hero becomes the home of God's Spirit' (ibid., p. 78). In a romantic world-view (that is, a congregation's perception of how things should or could be), the primary motif is adventure. Individually, the response to weakness is tarrying, and the resolution is empowerment. Corporately, conventionality is overcome by charism, which leads to transformation. Cosmically, perpetuity is usually addressed by signs and wonders, which will then lead to the coming of the Day of the Lord. In the world of adventure, authority is discovered in the evidence of God's immanence, the continuity of God's providence and the recognition of God's blessings. Critically, a romantic world-view understands that spiritual adventure is the context in which the strength of the romantic relationship with God is discovered, tested and refined. The 'heroes' of romantic stories are those who persevere through trials and tribulations, and who remain constant and faithful in the midst of adversity. In this respect, the underlying romantic theology of the Toronto Blessing movement depends, to some extent, on 'reading' Jesus' life as part of God's adventure with humanity. Just as it is an adventure following Jesus, so Jesus himself is often portrayed as the proto-adventurer, and as the 'pioneer of faith'. In talking to individuals at the Toronto Fellowship, and in listening to speakers and their talks and sermons, one is continually struck by the emphasis on *blessing* – those who receive it are those who venture beyond conventionality. Furthermore, the adventure to acquire blessing only becomes possible when one has been pre-empowered and equipped with some kind of anointing, divine charge or what some describe as being filled with 'the liquid love of God'.

In a Christian community that mainly configures its life through the romantic genre, there is a close relationship between *ethos* and *world-view*. The ethos of a place is the palpable experience and tone of a place – the very character of the culture that is encountered. A world-view, in contrast, is a philosophy of life that indicates how the world could or should be. In the romantic genre, ecclesial reality, no matter how imperfect, is normally regarded as a significant foretaste of what is to come; heaven is already partly revealed. The perceived experience of divinity within the worshipping community is regarded as an aperitif; the banquet is to follow. Correspondingly, the sense of adventure that both sources and governs the romantic genre tends to take on elements of dramaturgy and narrativity that stress exploration and pioneering. This might sound like a mundane remark, but it is in fact crucial. Adventurers not only pass over and through boundaries, they also return to the worlds from which they claim, with new stories, fresh revelations and novel perspectives from afar, which change the environment of their homecoming.

Furthermore, an adventure is not, strictly speaking, quite like a vacation, pilgrimage or ordinary journey. An adventure is something that happens *to* someone. People seldom opt to go on adventures; adventures are events, dramas and stories upon which individuals and communities are *taken* – they are event-driven, with no obvious plot. In the course of an adventure, there is no control over the beginning or end of the drama (one can only choose to see it through, or to opt out). Furthermore, because the outcomes of adventures are seldom known, there is no point at which a conclusion can be naturally reached. Necessarily, an adventure engages its subjects; it is packed with risk and reward, uncertainty and vindication, threat and promise. As Georg Simmel suggests, adventure is 'defined by its capacity to have necessity and meaning: [there] we abandon ourselves to the world with fewer defences and reserves than in any other relation'. In other words, the adventurer can be characterized as having 'daring...with which [the adventurer] continually leaves the solidities of life' (Simmel, cited in Levine, 1971, pp. 187–90).

The motif of adventure, then, allows a threefold cyclical sequence of movement for believers: leaving the present life and its conventionality; encountering the new world; returning home, and then transforming the homeland from which one has come with the tales of the new world. But critically, the motif of adventure also begins to offer some clues as to how a Charismatic movement might begin to cope with apparent atrophy.[9] In the world of adventure, the romance (with God or Jesus) may remain constant, or

---

[9] I say 'apparent atrophy', but it is, in reality, undeniable. The sanctuary area had been almost full each night when I visited in 1996. That same area has now been skilfully partitioned such that the size of the area has been reduced by about two-thirds, and this area itself is only two-thirds full each night. The area underneath the mezzanine that was used for ministry is now walled up and used for seminars and offices. A 'chill-out' zone for ministry that was available in 1996 is now fully partitioned off for children's ministry – a giant wooden 'walk-in' 'Noah's Ark'. The overall effect is to create a smaller, more intimate space – but for far fewer people. Evening meetings attract about 300–400 people, and morning meetings only about 50 – sometimes far fewer. This is a significant reduction from 1996.

even steadily intensify, but that does not prevent setbacks. When these occur, they only serve to test the quality of the adventurous romantic relationship and underline its fundamental importance to the believers. So adventure allows for the negotiation of atrophy – it is only a 'blip' or test in the longer, bigger, divine drama. The prevalence of Charismatic authority – 'resting on devotion to … exceptional heroism' (Weber, 1968, p. 24) – provides further support for the romantic world-view.

Similarly, a reappraisal of sermons at the Toronto Airport Christian Fellowship also suggests that the ideal 'model' Christian that is being promoted is the 'Pilgrim-Adventurer'. The highs and lows of Christian living are sustained by a deep, romantic, passionate and intense relationship with Jesus. But it is this foundation that creates the context for coping with apparent atrophy and setbacks. In a world where the horizons of possibility are shaped by the promise of adventure – including rewards – tarrying for revival is a duty and a joy. Correspondingly, the biblical archetypes of heroism that are most frequently appealed to in sermons tend to be Old Testament figures who are reconstructed as pioneers. Characters such as Abraham, Moses, Joshua, Noah, and even Jonah, are represented as proto-Pilgrim-Adventurers who set an example for believers today. This is intriguing, for in my original research on the Toronto Blessing in 1996, I suggested that, strictly speaking, visitors to the Toronto Airport Christian Fellowship were not really 'pilgrims' at all, because the location of the church was immaterial to receiving the Blessing. I now accept that this view needs to be modified. Visitors to Toronto are unquestionably pilgrims, but not in any conventional anthropological sense. For a believer, the pilgrimage is entirely internal – a thrilling adventure that takes place within the individual's rugged and breathtaking interior spiritual landscape, in which adversity and reward combine within the overall ecology of the broader spiritual adventure that constitutes the divine drama for each visitor or member.

To some extent, this observation can be verified when one talks to individuals about how they now understand the term 'harvest'. Six years ago, references to 'harvesting' peppered many talks and sermons. The Toronto Airport Christian Fellowship launched 'Partners in Harvest', an umbrella term for other North American and Canadian churches that wanted to belong to a network that linked revivalism to Evangelism. 'Harvest' was suggestive of produce and growth and had a clear resonance with Gospel imagery and analogy. But the term now seems to have evolved into a cipher for the spiritual fruits within the lives of individuals. The 'harvest' is now less 'out there' – whole 'fields' of potential converts, as it were – and more concerned with the growth, development and the interiority of the individuals' spiritual life. Of course, this means that the phenomenon of atrophy is much more difficult to assess, since 'growth' is still always being claimed, despite appearances to the contrary. In an interview, one member of staff explained to me that the cell meetings that produce the most growth are those for men or women only. When I gently press the question, 'Does that mean numerical growth?', the reply is modest and temperate: 'Oh, you know, growth takes many forms; like

it could be spiritual growth, or growth of another kind. It could be Evangelism, yes, I suppose. It depends.'

The cellular structure of the Toronto Airport Christian Fellowship has existed from the outset. The cells comprise small groups of people meeting in specific localities for prayer, worship and fellowship. Cell groups meet in each others' homes on a weekly basis, for perhaps an hour or two. The numbers involved in cell groups are perhaps the best indication of the present size of the Toronto Fellowship; by their own estimation there are 150 groups with perhaps 1000 members. There are cell groups for families, young adults, men, women and couples. The fellowship believes that the most popular cell groups are single-sex. The advocacy of the cell structure is not unusual in a North American church context, but its promotion at the Toronto Fellowship tells us something about its direction and development, namely that it is leaving its 'movement identity' behind and is on the way to becoming a church. Being a committed member of the fellowship is now constituted through belonging to a cell. This also helps the fellowship differentiate between members and attendees; the leadership's estimates are that there are about 2000 regularly coming to meetings, but 'core' membership is around 1000 – a noticeable reduction in numbers from the figures I collected in 1996.

Naturally, the fellowship does not see this picture in terms of atrophy or decline. The language of harvest and the 'Pilgrim-Adventurer' world-view ensures that any notion of fallowness is only read as part of an overall narrative of growth. Thus, one of the noticeable changes from six years ago is the more intense concentration on youth work. There are about 250 children in the youth programme, approximately 100 teenagers and around 50 in the 'young adult' category (20–30). Part of the main sanctuary has been partitioned to create a giant 'walk-in' Noah's Ark, in which some of the youth ministry can take place. For older youths, it is also interesting to note that the Toronto Fellowship now practises 'Christian Bar Mitzvah' with its children, in which the passage from childhood to adulthood is marked with a ceremony of blessing (by pastors and parents), which also includes walking across a makeshift bridge as part of the symbolic ritual. Here again, there is a ritual of pioneering and journeying to complement the movement to childhood to adulthood. The ritual creates a sense of freedom fused with security: a *safe* journey in life – with the Lord.

The new focus on youth and children's work indicates that the adults who have settled in the church are now raising the next generation of revivalists: routinization is settling in, and the fellowship is moving quickly away from a movement identity into an ecclesial one. Six years ago there was little youth work to speak of; now it is essential to ensure the future of the fellowship through organic growth, as it seems not to be occurring in other ways that are numerically significant (that is, through evangelism). The new rituals seem to inculcate the youth into the 'Pilgrim-Adventurer' and pioneering identity that so intensely flavours the Toronto Fellowship. It is here that they learn that the true meaning of being a pioneer – they are both travellers and settlers, doing something wholly new, yet totally familiar.

**Conclusion**

The apparent atrophy of a Charismatic movement – in this case, the Toronto Blessing – is indeed a complex phenomenon. For adherents within the movement, the decrease in numbers attending the fellowship, and the overall waning influence of the movement as a whole, means little. Thus, a conversation with an administrator at the fellowship reveals that they 'are cutting back on [staff] numbers at the moment, because we don't want to be, like, well you know, top heavy'.[10] But this is not interpreted as being indicative of decline. The Pilgrim-Adventurer travels lightly. There is no real narrative of deterioration in the romantic adventure – only temporary setbacks and the embracing of leanness, so that travel may be swifter and more reflexive. Romantics are incurably positive and optimistic about their future: in the arena of adventure, the faithful pilgrim always prevails. In such a world-view there are times of abundant harvest to look back on and cherish, and there are times to look forward to when the harvest will be plentiful again. Living between the lands of sowing and reaping (to borrow a well-worn phrase from Pentecostalism) only serves to consolidate the identity of the fellowship, and invites the faithful to cease travelling (for the time being), and begin settling. Indeed, such consolidation may turn out to be the Promised Land – the harvest of plenty that was promised.[11]

So, strictly speaking, adherents would regard any apparent routinization as merely temporary, since the culture of revivalism requires believers to be ready, at any point, to become restless pilgrims and adventurers once more. Meanwhile, the fellowship dwells within that unique hinterland of adventure and security; being neither a church nor a movement, but a *fellowship* (settled, yet reflexive), it knows that its time will come again. Adherents have no need of theories of cognitive dissonance to explain themselves (they do not, in any case, really apply here), and nor do they perceive themselves to be in decline. In the mind's eye of the faithful, God 'is doing a new thing' each day, and the temporary lull in revivalist intensity is simply regarded as a period of waiting, during which time the Toronto Airport Christian Fellowship continues to hone and intensify its distinctively passionate grammar of assent and quasi-erotic spirituality.

Further afield, we should note that the Vineyard movement as a whole (the parent church for the Toronto Fellowship) has found it difficult to sustain growth and maintain identity in the wake of the death of their founder and

---

[10] Source: interview, November 2002. Staff numbers are difficult to calculate, as some are paid, some are voluntary and some part-time in both categories. There may be as many as 150 staff spread across all areas of work, including the School of Ministry and international development.

[11] In conversations with other members of Vineyard churches and those who have left the Toronto movement altogether, but remained within Charismatic Renewal, these motifs seem to persist: a new journey is underway – a new adventure with God. There is an irony here. Those who leave the movement do not necessarily regard it as having failed. Rather, they see their identity and purpose as being continually restructured within a romantic world-view, in which all journeys and pilgrimages are ultimately ascribed some worth.

patron, John Wimber, in 1997. Under Wimber's leadership, Vineyard fellowships were bound together by a concept of 'kinship' and an understanding of their leader's charismatic and apostolic authority. This meant that the fellowships enjoyed a degree of homogeneity in their praxis; there was, in effect, a distinct 'Vineyard style' that marked out the fellowships from other types of Charismatic Renewal and contemporary revivalism. Indeed, one of Wimber's legacies to the Association of Vineyard Churches was the proscribing of ten 'vital signs' that provided a 'genetic code' for all Vineyard churches. But, in the space of five years, much of this has changed.

Privately, a number of the Vineyard leadership now acknowledge that three key divisions have emerged within the Vineyard movement. Some churches have attempted to return to the 'original recipe' that first made the reputation of Wimber and his churches, namely a concentration on 'power evangelism' and 'power healing'. A second stream have developed an ethos that is close to that of 'Seeker Churches'.[12] A third stream has seen some pastors adopting a more liturgical and sacramental tone in their fellowships or churches. Some pastors now robe for worship, and the Eucharist has become the central rite for the congregation. There are now women pastors too – something that Wimber would not have permitted. Where there was once homogeneity, there is now considerable diversity in liturgical style and theological substance: the Vineyard movement is losing its coherence, and becoming a broad-based (but small) denomination. At the same time, a degree of routinization is already apparent in those Vineyard churches that are faithful to their past. A survey of some British Vineyard fellowships reveals that worship now follows a set pattern or 'recipe': worship, offertory, weekly announcements, teaching, more worship, ministry, before ending with coffee and doughnuts.[13]

At the same time, many Evangelical churches of various denominational persuasions have adopted aspects of Vineyard praxis – in effect, giving themselves a Vineyard 'make-over' – but have nonetheless remained true to and within their denominations. This has ensured further diversity for revivalism, and also ironically blunts the impact of various Charismatic movements. In effect, mainstream churches feel free to adopt those traits and teachings that they find congenial from within the world of revivalism, but they do not actually transfer their allegiance to that world. In other words, they treat the revivalism as a collation of resources from which they can pick and

---

[12] 'Seeker Churches' exist in various forms throughout North America in a variety of denominational guises, although they are predominantly Evangelical and Charismatic in ethos. Bill Hybels, pastor of Willow Creek Church in South Barrington, Chicago, is widely regarded as their pioneer. Seeker Churches deliberately set out to remove all 'churchy' barriers that might prevent people from attending or joining churches. Thus, at the Willow Creek church itself, there are no robed ministers, no hymn books, no altar, nor obvious Christian symbolism. The church 'services', as such, resemble accessible 'magazine-style' TV chat shows – interviews, features, 'staged' discussions or seminars, and perhaps some drama. The church attracts enquirers and committed members, and aims to cultivate patterns of Christian lifestyle that resonate with contemporary culture.

[13] Source: Bristol Vineyard, UK – weekly notice sheet, October 2001.

choose, and also discard, as they seek to maintain and renew their own traditions. This means that their Jerusalem – the Golden City of Revivalism – is simply *not* being built; the contemporary revivalist movement is becoming a widely dispersed resource, rather than a concentrated settlement of believers that might rival mainline denominations. It is becoming enculturated and syncretic, reflecting its spiritual and ecclesial pragmatism, together with its theological alterity (see Hunt, 1995, pp. 257–72; Jongeneel, 1992; Hunt, Hamilton and Walter, 1997).

The implications of all this for Charismatic Renewal, the future of the Toronto Blessing movement and for Vineyard churches are by no means easy to predict. Clearly, the primary motif of the 'Pilgrim-Adventurer', although peculiarly intense in Toronto, might be said to have emerged as a major interpretative key for Charismatic Renewal more generally within this study.

Hermeneutically, we can now see that the notion of the Pilgrim-Adventurer provides a viable narrative and world-view, through which Charismatic Christians can construct and reconstruct their identity in the midst of change and decline, as much as in growth. Whilst careful limits would have to be placed upon the 'pioneering' identity, it should be clear that the principal contribution made by the Toronto Blessing movement to Charismatic Renewal is not the exotic miracles and the spiritual epiphenomena, so much as the confirmation and consolidation of the identity of Charismatic Christianity as faith for those who seek to venture beyond conventionality. Understood like this, the evolution of the Pilgrim-Adventurer in Charismatic Renewal can be read as a romantic and conservative movement that is morphologically similar to some of the radicalism that broke out of liberal Christianity in the 1960s and 1970s. Both now share a sense of purpose that stresses moving on, breaking existing paradigms and thereby renewing the tradition. But the question marks that hang over such movements remain stubbornly simple. How can the identity of a revolutionary, radical, renewing movement be maintained if it subsequently becomes mainstream? How can a 'movement' ever become 'settled' and thereby consolidate itself? I suspect, at least in this case, that it can't. Charismatic Renewal, like the Toronto Blessing itself, is destined to wander. The faith of the Pilgrim-Adventurer demands movement, not security, which is both its strength and weakness.

In my final 24 hours at the fellowship, I listened intently to a talk given in the morning by a woman who told her small congregation (numbering perhaps 40), that she thought 'Jesus really wanted us all to just rest at the moment'. 'We were battle-weary', she added, 'and Jesus was longing to just let us rest with him, soak in his presence, and be still.' We were, in effect, being offered a cipher for the temporary hibernation of revivalism. In the romantic world-view, a period of rest for the warrior bride or pilgrim adventurer is naturally only a precursor to a new quest, or perhaps even a fresh battle. As the time of ministry began (more 'carpet time', 'soaking' and 'marinading in the Spirit') several women simply stretched out on the floor and relaxed. They were resting with Jesus – being still in the presence of God.

Ultimately, this quiet hibernation of a small but influential branch of revivalism cannot be surprising; this is the reality of its organic but temporary

atrophy. As the writer of Ecclesiastes reminds us, there is a time to rest, and a time to wake and rise. And after all the feverish and intense activity of the Toronto Blessing movement at its absolute peak, worshippers were now being quietly encouraged to embrace a period of passivity, punctuated only by the stirrings of our romantic–passionate and personal relationship with Jesus. And as I tried to slip out of the main sanctuary meeting that same night, where the prayer and praise had been as exuberant as ever, lasting for more than four hours, a woman seated on the ground near the doorway beckoned me over. 'You look tired,' she said.

'I am', I replied.

'We're all tired', she added, 'and I feel the Lord is just using me to tell you that what you need to do is go home and rest. I think the Lord is telling me to tell you that. It's a word of encouragement for you. We all need rest – we all need to rest with Jesus. He'll take good care of us.'

I nodded in agreement. Every good adventure story ends with a well-deserved rest for the hero and reader alike. The Pilgrim-Adventurers were now having their respite, for the time being, at least. Perhaps it was still too early to close the story and utter the words 'The End'?

# Chapter 8

# A Blessed Rage for Order

Before theology and doctrine can ever exist, there must first be stories. They are stories of faith, of course. And before stories, there must be encounters, experiences and reflection. Churches are, moreover, as James Hopewell reminds us, primarily 'storied communities and dwellings'. Ecclesial communities and their members occupy, for the most part, that precognitive hinterland: a place where lives and norms are not so much governed by formal religious rules and dogma, as by a complex tapestry of stories and affinities that bind believers together. This is true religion – being continually bound together by shared narratives, common interests and particular practices, that turns a group of individuals into a 'congregation'.

I make no apology for beginning in this way, as I, too, want to start with a story from 15 years ago. In many ways it is a simple story. At the theological college I attended for my ordination training (1988–90), I was walking down the corridor one day, returning to my study. I ran into a fellow ordinand whom I had seen that morning in chapel. It was now afternoon, but there was something different about him. He usually wore smart jeans or corduroys, well-polished brown brogue shoes, a shirt (sometimes with a tie) and a smart-casual sports or tweed jacket. However, on this particular day I couldn't help noticing that his arm was in a sling, and he was trying to conceal his injury. I asked him if he was all right. He replied that he was fine. So I asked him how he came by the injury. He explained that he had been having a discussion that morning with a close friend, who normally shared his theological views. The discussion was about whether or not righteousness was 'imputed' or 'imparted', but it had developed into a raging argument. So much so, in fact, that the ordinand now standing in front of me had finally smashed his fist into a college noticeboard in disgust at his friend's views. The force of the impact had fractured some bones, and he had had to go to the local hospital for treatment. He didn't seem to be embarrassed by this 'accident'; the injury he sustained, he suggested, showed just how important the issue was. And with that, he left.

I recall the story for several reasons. First, because of the force, passion and aggression that colours the narrative, coupled with the incongruity of this story being spoken softly, deeply and earnestly by a young man who one would not normally have associated with violence. Second, because the display of violence did seem to reveal a hidden rage for ordering the church and policing its theology. Third, because the display of force was immediately justified: this showed 'just how important' the issue was.

I recognize at once that this story is both unusual and atypical in relation to Conservative Evangelicalism. Furthermore, the event took place in 1989, some

four years before the formation of Reform, and it is the analysis of this movement within the Church of England that we are primarily concerned with in this chapter. There can be no doubt that, had Reform existed in the late 1980s, my bandaged colleague would have been a member. He was an ardent disciple of the Revd Dick Lucas, then rector of St Helen's Bishopsgate, London, an avid proponent of *Read, Mark, Learn* (Lucas, 1986), a regular mentor to the Christian Union and a staunch opponent of women's ordination (on grounds of headship). But, at the same time, the story, with its overtones of violence and aggression, reflects a commonly held perception about Reform. Even the secular British media have dubbed Reform 'the Taliban of the Church of England'. The story, of course, chimes with such sentiments: it points towards the deep and barely controlled spiritual and theological *rage* that many regard as one of the defining hallmarks of the movement. And, paradoxically, this rage is being expressed by otherwise (normally) ultra-polite and (allegedly) upper-middle-class Christians who mostly hail from the home counties or the prosperous suburbs of larger cities throughout England. In what follows, I want to explore not only the rise of Reform in the Church of England, but also examine some of the reasons why, theologically and sociologically, a movement made up of people who really know how to *behave* (both culturally and in terms of manners) has also developed a decidedly aggressive side to its character, and how this has been done within a church and worldwide Communion (or Commonwealth) of churches that are implicitly bound together by a code of manners (Percy, 2000, pp. 114–25).

After briefly considering the history of Reform – a movement that is now more than ten years old – I will go on to look at some methodological perspectives before turning to some of the key issues that define Reform's agenda. Some further analysis will examine the prospects for denominations (Anglicanism in this case) in a postmodern world, where churches are bound together less and less by a common form of governance and more and more by a shared ethos and moral affinity. The conclusion looks at the implications of the relative strength of Reform within the context of the Anglican communion as a whole. Suffice to say, this chapter is more exploratory in nature, and as much an exercise in testing methodologies within the broad penumbra of modern ecclesiology. It is not intended to be a definitive account or interpretation of Reform: from the outset, I recognize that the movement itself merits far more attention than a single chapter in a book can possibly give it.

## The Origin and Anatomy of Reform

One of the surprising aspects of Reform is its size. It currently has approximately 1600 members. The number of churches that would categorically identify with the movement is probably less than 50, and perhaps as few as 30. It is difficult to be precise about this last statistic, as clergy who lead churches may well insist that their congregation is 'fully supportive of Reform',

but hard data to back this up simply do not exist.[1] Clergy will often assume that a congregation's support of them and their ministry amounts to their tacit agreement with his or her theological position. In fact, such concord is quite rare, even in the most apparently homogenous congregations. Congregations – even those that may be content to be identified as Conservative Evangelical – are likely to be places of doctrinal divergence rather than credal concurrence. However, statistics that seem to reveal a relatively low level of support for Reform should not be used to underestimate the scale and importance of the movement. It wields considerable national influence and also has a significant international profile through links with the diocese of Sydney (cf. Jensen, 2002), and enjoys other liaisons in North America.

As a movement, Reform was born on 22 February 1993. The text of the original leaflet, stating the aims and purposes of the movement, identifies its fundamental doctrinal core before listing its major concerns:

> ...for some years groups of mainstream Evangelicals have met to discuss issues in the church and nation. These issues include the authority of and sufficiency of Scripture; the uniqueness and finality of Christ; the priority of the local church; the complementarity of men and women... [We are] Christians first, Evangelicals second, and Anglicans third... [we have] committed ourselves to unite for action under the authority of Scripture as God's word... Historic Anglican theology is committed to continuous Reformation of the church. We are committed to the reform of ourselves, our congregations and our world by the gospel... Reform is urgently needed... [because] the gospel is not shaping and changing our church and our society: our society seems to be shaping and changing us. A biblical Christian voice is heard too little in our society. The Church of England seems to have lost confidence in the truth and power of the gospel.... To reverse these trends we are committed to change and growth. Such change will be costly.... We do not believe this change can come from the denominational centre. The local church must take back responsibility for the denomination... (Holloway, 1993)

The agenda outlined is specific and direct. The leaflet identifies a particular kind of stance as being 'orthodox' and implies that the wider denomination has lapsed in its belief, confidence and responsibility. In terms of process, this inevitably leads to a call for financial realignment and establishing the local church as the primary locus of mission and discipleship. This agenda is, in turn, driven by a broad appeal to the ongoing work of the Reformation. In effect, the leaders of Reform are doing nothing less than eliding their own identity and agenda with that of the original Reformers of the sixteenth and seventeenth centuries. Except that, this time, the enemy is not the papacy: it is modernity and liberalism, which is deemed to have betrayed the historic missiological calling of a national church.

---

[1] For example, the Revd Philip Hacking, the former chair of Reform and a former vicar of Christ Church Fulwood, Sheffield, estimates that some 60 members of his congregation joined Reform out of a possible 1200 regular attendees. But he maintains that the vast majority of attendees, whilst not being members of Reform, would be fully supportive of its agenda.

Although the precise birth date of Reform can be easily identified, the date (and process) of its conception is a little more contentious. Worth mentioning are several recent moments in postwar English Evangelical history, each of which may stake a claim to have been influential in the genesis of Reform. First, the decision of the General Synod of the Church of England to ordain women to the priesthood in November 1992 could undoubtedly be seen as the 'final straw' or 'trigger' that galvanized Evangelical leaders into action. As Ian Jones points out, those Conservative Evangelical leaders who opposed women's ordination were wholly unprepared for the measure to be approved and thereafter vowed to be more organized in order to address other key issues that they saw on the horizon (such as women bishops, the ordination of homosexuals and so on – see Jones, 2004).

Second, Reform also owes a partial debt to the (relatively successful) campaigning of the Revd Tony Higton during the 1980s. Higton, the rector of Hawkwell in Essex, launched an influential pressure group called Action for Biblical Witness to Our Nation (ABWON) which petitioned the General Synod, published several tracts and engaged in numerous high-profile public debates, most notably on sexuality and interfaith worship. Higton, himself a member of General Synod, also edited *Sexuality and the Church: The Way Forward* (1987), which was a systematic and robust Conservative Evangelical refutation of homosexuality. Higton was a kind of middle-aged *enfant terrible* within the General Synod, and his terrorizing tactics, use of the media and strident polemical voice won him many admirers. More particularly, Higton demonstrated that the 'liberal centre', which many assumed to be at the heart of the Church of England's governance, could be seriously challenged and called to account by some well-organized campaigning.

Third, the growing presence of Conservative Evangelicals within the Church of England can be traced, in part, to the seminal (Evangelical Congress) Keele Conference of 1967. Dr Martyn Lloyd-Jones had called upon Evangelicals to leave their respective denominations and form a new denomination. But within the Church of England, this move was tenaciously resisted by John Stott and Jim Packer, amongst others, who eventually won the day. But this moment in modern church history set a course for Evangelicals that would lead to other kinds of conflict. Specifically, in deciding to remain within Anglicanism and to work for 'evolution within', Conservative Evangelicals quickly organized themselves into groups and networks that could maintain their identity and promote their causes.

Fourth, and despite the numerical strength of postwar Evangelical Anglicanism, some tensions were beginning to emerge within the movement. On the issue of women's ordination, it was increasingly apparent that many Evangelicals felt that there were no longer any clear biblical reasons that should prevent women being made priests. Evangelical identity was also successively transformed and eroded by Charismatic Renewal, which seemed, at least to its Conservative Evangelical detractors, to pay far too much attention to the realm of feelings and not enough to the Bible. Furthermore, the gradual emergence of a broader and more accommodating mainstream 'Anglican-Evangelical' identity, which grew increasingly popular from the

1970s onwards, put Conservative Evangelicals much more on the defensive, even to the point of making them appear reactionary. This is perhaps best illustrated by the debacle that surrounded the publication of *Churchman* in 1984. The editor at the time, Revd Peter Williams, was dismissed from his post for publishing some articles about the authority and inspiration of scripture, which departed from the normal 'classic' Conservative Evangelical stance. To the non-Evangelical eye, the slight differences between the views of, say, Jim Packer and James Dunn would hardly seem to be significant, but the trustees of *Churchman* saw it differently. The argument led to several committee members breaking away from *Churchman* and a new journal, *Anvil* being launched. *Anvil* subsequently became the voice of those who were more inclined to call themselves Anglican-Evangelicals; *Churchman* retained the loyalty of those who preferred to call themselves Evangelical-Anglicans.[2]

Fifth, a particular kind of elite Conservative Evangelicalism has also been influential in the genesis of Reform. Bodies such as the Church Society, Inter-Varsity Fellowship (IVF), and its successor UCCF (Universities and Colleges Christian Fellowship) have naturally played a significant part in forming future leaders within Evangelicalism. In the latter case, with its distinctive Articles of Faith (a ten-point doctrinal schema), UCCF/IVP have been able to secure a degree of credal homogeneity amongst Christian Union groups that has eluded other denominational affiliations and more radical groups such as the Student Christian Movement. However, what is particularly intriguing about Reform is that some of its leaders had their Christian faith formed within a relatively small cartel of elite public schools, often followed by a university education at Oxford or Cambridge. The backbone of the student work will often have included some exposure to the Iwerne Minster Camps, which offered a very specific kind of programme under the tutelage of Nash and the Fletcher brothers.[3] (These camps would include 'lady helpers', but not women speakers.) Sociologically, these camps and meetings appeared to be promoting what some scholars now refer to as 'muscular Christianity' – particular kinds of male bonding centred on exercise and spiritual study (Money, 1997; Magdalinski and Chandler, 2001). Thus, a typical Iwerne Minster midrash of instruction (which I have often overheard), and aimed at students, runs like this (paraphrased):

> Living the Christian life can be likened to three cats walking on a wall, one named Facts, one named Faith and the other named Feelings. Now they have to walk on the wall in the right order, or they will all fall off. Facts must always lead, and then

---

[2] But Reform takes the view that whilst 'Anglican-Evangelicals' have developed 'caring, intelligent and thorough local parochial ministry', they have always been unable to challenge the dominant 'liberal-Catholic leadership' of the church.

[3] However, Reform leaders are at pains to point out that many of its council members lack this 'pedigree'. The previous chair, Philip Hacking, suggests that Reform is more of a grassroots movement. Similarly, the support enjoyed by the Jensen brothers within the diocese of Sydney is to be found more amongst the lower-middle classes and skilled blue-collar workers than amongst Sydney's elite social circles. See Jensen (2002) and Judd and Cable (1987).

followed by Faith, with Feelings coming last. If Feelings ever leads, Facts and Faith both fall off the wall . . . .

Sixth, over the last 25 years a number of other pressure groups have grown up that have directly contributed to the genesis of Reform. Several could be named, but one of the groups most closely allied to Reform has been the Proclamation Trust, founded by the Revd Dick Lucas, formerly rector of St Helen's Bishopsgate. The Proclamation Trust has enjoyed a wide ministry in the Church of England and is primarily devoted to promoting a particular kind of expository preaching and the promulgation of courses that teach 'Christian basics' (for example, *Read, Mark, Learn*). It should be noted, however, that Reform, in common with other Conservative Evangelicals, regard the Alpha course (a product of a more Charismatic–Evangelical mindset, and originating from Holy Trinity Brompton) as too liberal and quite unsound. (Indeed, prominent Conservative Evangelicals such as Philip Jensen, archbishop of Sydney, have consistently attacked the Alpha course.)

Seventh, and finally, some leaders within Reform appeal directly to the early heroes of the Reformation (such as Wycliffe) or to seventeenth-century Anglican thinkers who were themselves heavily influenced by Cromwellian Puritanism. In this regard, some Reform leaders are inclined to oppose the 'liberal-catholic drift [which] is destroying the Church of England' (Holloway, 1993, p. 3). The claim to be Reformist is therefore to be treated with the utmost seriousness within Anglicanism. Reform leaders are not simply arguing for a particular kind of moral coherence as the basis for ecclesial communion, they are also advocating a specious form of Protestantism that will exclude the excesses of Charismatic Renewal and the aesthetics of Anglo-Catholicism. In other words, Reform is promoting a kind of clear, plain, morally certain and pedagogically cerebral Christianity. Conversion is achieved through intellectual persuasion; discipleship is maintained through embodying the convictions of the mind in disciplined living. There is little scope for ambiguity or difference, for the Bible is held to be clear on all matters of importance. It is a case of 'Trust and Obey' – there is no other way.

To conclude this section, we turn to the Reform Covenant itself. Besides identifying its fundamental life through the usual credal formulae, it is important to understand the association as a movement of *resistance*. Throughout Reform's documents, the themes of correction, confrontation, reformation and reassertion are prominent:

> . . . [We affirm] . . . the divine *order* of male headship, which makes the headship of women as priests-in-charge, incumbents, dignitaries and bishops *inappropriate* . . . the *rightness* of sexual intercourse in heterosexual marriage, and the *wrongness* of such activity both outside it and in *all* its homosexual forms . . . the *urgent* need for decentralisation at national, diocesan and deanery level, and the need to *radically reform* the present shape of episcopacy and *pastoral discipline* . . . . (Holloway, 1993, p. 1, emphasis added)

Properly speaking, we might say that Reform exists because of concerns with money, sex and power. As an organization, it is more focused than the Church

Society, an older and more traditional body for Conservative Evangelicals. In particular, Reform seeks to campaign on a specific range of issues, each of which is underpinned by a concern to reaffirm the authority of scripture and the priority of the local church as the primary locus for mission and evangelism. Were it not for the anxieties of Conservative Evangelicals on these matters, Reform would probably not exist. This is an issue to which we shall return, but, before doing so, we need to explore the ethnography of the movement in more detail.

### Reform: An Ethnographic Sketch

The primary material for this study has been gathered within the context of a broad ethnographic framework. This has principally been achieved in four ways: through interviews with key leaders in Reform, and also with individuals on its periphery;[4] through searching through Reform's records and statements (accessible on its own website); by reflecting on stories, encounters and vignettes gathered over the last decade; and by collecting over 50 newspaper articles and commentaries drawn from a wide variety of sources. The written pieces collected came from secular national newspapers, church newspapers, and articles in church journals, which were all published in 2003 at the height of the Jeffrey John, Gene Robinson and New Westminster debates.

Granted, I have not conducted formal quantitative fieldwork in my research of Reform, at least in a form that might be understood by Bender, Clifford and others and was sketched in the previous chapter, (although the interviews I conducted have been a very important feature in constructing this study). Instead, I have chosen to write from the vantage-point of someone who, as an Anglican priest and theologian, is constantly caught up in the narrative streams and cross-currents that the movement creates. I have known a number of Reform's members throughout my ordained life. Indeed, Reform is now a recognizable feature of the landscape of English Anglicanism: it has become a necessary part of the ecclesiological 'cultural furniture'. Encountering Reform is unavoidable, and I have long been puzzled by the sombre effervescence of the movement, and have aspired to study its characteristics and interiority. But what would qualify me, as a more distant observer than a decidedly engaged fieldworker, to claim any knowledge of the movement at all?

First, although it is true that Reform came into being in 1993, the seeds for the movement were germinating in the soil of Conservative Evangelicalism long before that. As someone who was raised in a 'normal low Anglican Church', I lived through, first-hand, a number of the emergent tensions between Charismatic Renewal and Conservative Evangelicalism, as they were expressed in a local congregation. They fascinated me at the time, and continue

---

[4] Specifically with a former chair of Reform, a member of the Council, a leading moderate Conservative Evangelical, and a clergyperson from the Diocese of Sydney (who is not an Evangelical, and provided comment as an 'outsider').

to do so. The conflict between spiritualities that celebrated the sensate and those that embodied the cerebral, the arguments over worship, sermons, order and gifts of the Spirit: these are but a few examples. There is now, of course, some interesting literature that explores the phenomenon of the 'post-Evangelical' (see P. Ward, 1997; Tomlinson, 1995).

Second, my own exposure to the wider Anglican–Evangelical culture has been continuous. For the most part, this has been as a direct result of studying and researching Charismatic Renewal for the past 15 years, and therefore being unable to avoid the Conservative Evangelical forces that have typically opposed it. In the course of such research, I have often encountered texts and individuals who were happy to espouse a proto-Reform agenda after they had finished critiquing contemporary revivalism. This was especially true of my ordination training (1988–90) where followers of the Revd Dick Lucas, although small in number, made their presence felt and disclosed their theological schema publicly, and in fairly unambiguous terms.

Third, in my own research and writing, I have always been careful to distinguish between Conservative Evangelicalism and fundamentalism. I have been critical of James Barr for lumping the two together, even though it can sometimes *feel* that there are morphological similarities (Percy and Jones, 2002; cf. Bebbington, 1989). In my view, avoiding the 'fundamentalist' label is important. Using such a label for movements such as Reform is often no more than a lazy attempt to demonize and dismiss the movement. In fact, Reform is far too complex and specific to be included as a world within the fundamentalist universe. I mention this only to make clear that much of my information about Reform and Conservative Evangelicalism has been gleaned from the *underside* of my primary research on Charismatic Renewal, revivalism and fundamentalism (see Percy, 1996a; Percy and Jones, 2002; Harris, 1998). On the one hand, I have encountered Conservative Evangelical movements and exponents through their tussles with Charismatic Renewal, which might even include their opposition to Alpha courses. On the other hand, in my study of fundamentalism, I have inevitably had to study certain aspects of Conservative Evangelicalism, partly in order to clarify, at least in my own mind, that it is not really a form of fundamentalism.

Fourth, as a curate, university chaplain and post-ordination training tutor, I have encountered ordained and lay members of Reform at several levels. During training as a curate, clergy colleagues who were members of Reform would habitually boycott deanery and diocesan events that did not fit with their priorities. Reform curates would normally absent themselves from any kind of additional training programmes, as they were deemed to be 'unsound'. As a university chaplain in Cambridge, I would routinely discover that students were being urged to stay away from college chapel by 'Reform-type' clergy. As a post-ordination tutor, I would later listen patiently as a young Reform curate explained to me and other curates how and why they barred people from Holy Communion, and effectively excommunicated individuals for such 'offences' as divorce and remarriage.

Fifth, and to return to Bender's earlier observation, I find myself constantly caught up in the streams of events and conversations that characterize

Conservative Evangelicals and the Reform movement. Over several years, I have collected a substantial litany of vignettes that have slowly demanded systematization and interpretation – like collecting the individual pieces of a jigsaw over a long period of time. For example, I recall meeting Revd Tony Higton at NEAC in 1988 and discussing with him his principled stance to not stand and applaud the archbishop of Canterbury's address, as other delegates did. On another occasion, I puzzled over a small number of fellow ordinands who, when they did not entirely agree with the content of a sermon, would pointedly leave chapel before receiving communion, usually slamming the heavy oak door as they left. As G.K. Chesterton once famously quipped, 'a gentleman is never unintentionally rude'. If that is true, it left me, as an observer, with an uncomfortable paradox – namely that these normally well-mannered young men, mostly from upper-middle-class backgrounds, educated in elite public schools and often with an Oxbridge pedigree, *meant* to demonstrate rudeness. But over something as trivial as a sermon that they found troubling? It would seem so.

Finally, in the process of this research, and more typically within the ethnographic framework, I have conducted interviews with key individuals and engaged in correspondence with others, both formal and informal. I cannot claim that this endeavour is comprehensive; it has been limited by lack of resources and time. Whether or not what follows is reasonable and representative is for others to judge, but I hold that it is. At the same time, I readily acknowledge that I am not *reproducing* the voice of Reform in this exercise; instead, I am inviting the reader to see a relatively new Christian movement in a particular way. What follows is a critical contemplation of a Christian tradition that is proud of its zeal and tenacity, and is unashamed of its politics; my invitation is to ponder the ways in which the world of Reform is put together, both culturally, sociologically, ecclesiologically and theologically.

Briefly, my approach is primarily ethnographic insofar as I attempt to provide an in-depth account of a movement. The study also takes the cultural aspect of religion seriously and tries to make some serious sense of its complexity. Furthermore, as an ethnographic study, it also aims to describe the texture of the movement. As such, the study tries to avoid theoretical generalizations as far as possible in favour of concentrating on details. To paraphrase Durkheim's comment on religion, a study of this kind accepts that any representation it offers is necessarily metaphorical and symbolic but, in being like this, it is not inevitably unfaithful (cf. Wuthnow, 1997, p. 247). An ethnographic sketch is, in other words, just that: a sketch. Like any map or drawing, it can never reproduce reality; it can only represent it as accurately and artistically as possible.

## An Interpretative Horizon

Within the field of Congregational Studies, James Hopewell (1987) provides a promising perspective from which to gain some understanding of Reform. Hopewell contends that individual congregations and, more broadly, networks

of churches are united less by credal formulae and more by world-views, which in turn are configured through the kinds of narratives that 'construct' specific households of faith:

> ... world views reflect and give a focus to group experience, providing a map within which words and actions make sense. The setting of a congregation is the order by which its gossip, sermons, strategies and fights – the household idiom gain their reasonableness. What is expressed in *daily intercourse* about the nature of the world is idiomatic, responsive to a particular pattern of language, expressing a particular setting for narrative. Tales in a local church tend to travel in packs: one good story evokes another, one member's account of an illness, for example, is usually reciprocated in kind. In comradeship and commiseration members top each other's stories, building up the world setting that they together inhabit. (Hopewell, 1987, p. 85, emphasis added)

Although Hopewell's primary interest is in local congregations, his work offers considerable illumination in exploring and analysing Reform's world-view. Hopewell, following Northrop Frye (1957), argues that churches are essentially 'storied communities' and that these stories can be understood as corresponding to the four basic literary genres, namely irony, comedy, romance and tragedy. This means, in effect, that the principal stories configuring a church or cluster of churches will usually turn out to be primarily oriented towards one of these major genres. However, Hopewell is careful to point out that individuals, movements and congregations must be properly situated within this 'quadripolar analysis' and are therefore unlikely to be, say, entirely ironic or romantic in their world-view – there will be mixtures and variables.

The literary genre that most closely corresponds to the world-view espoused by members of Reform (and more generally to that of Conservative Evangelicalism) is the 'tragic' – what Hopewell calls the 'Canonic negotiation'. According to Hopewell, the Canonic negotiation is:

> [r]eliance upon an authoritative interpretation of a world pattern, often considered [to be] God's revealed world or will, by which one identifies one's essential life. The integrity of the pattern requires that followers reject any gnosis (i.e., knowledge) of union with the pattern but instead subordinate their selfhood to it. Characteristics of the Canonic orientation are similar to Frye's tragic genre.... (Hopewell, 1987, p. 69)

Developing this observation, Hopewell exports and converts the basic literary theory into some explicitly theological and ecclesiological conceptualizations. When comparing Hopewell's basic framework to the Reform Covenant, we can see how illuminating the reading can become. For example, Hopewell claims that the primary narrative motif of the Canonic negotiation is sacrifice and that its movement is 'union toward subordination' (ibid., p. 70). The Reform Covenant seems to reflect this: 'we who subscribe to this Covenant *bind* ourselves together in fellowship to *uphold, defend* and *spread* the gospel of Jesus Christ according to the doctrine of the Church of England ... ' (emphasis added).

Personally, socially and cosmically, there are specific theological resolutions to certain scenarios. In a personal situation of hubris, the response is generally surrender and the resolution is justification. In a social context a situation of vice is met with the response of righteousness and the resolution is judgement. Cosmically, principalities and powers are engaged with passion and the resolution is the arrival of the kingdom. Similarly, Hopewell identifies the cognitive features of this world-view. Authority is posited in God's revealed Word and will; the focus of integrity is scripture; valued behaviour is obedience. Conceptually and typically, God is Father, Jesus the saviour, and evil (or the enemy) is a personal devil. The Bible is the word of God; a minister a messenger of God; the Eucharist a memorial; the church a covenant; and the Gospel salvation.

In the Reform Covenant, the Articles of Faith seem to reflect the Canonic world-view sketched by Hopewell:

> ...specifically we lay emphasis on the universality of sin, the present justification of sinners by grace through faith in Christ alone, and their supernatural regeneration and new life through the Holy Spirit...the calling of the church and all Christian people to a life of holiness and prayer according to the Scriptures...the significance of personal present repentance and faith as determining eternal destiny...the infallibility and supreme authority of 'God's Word written' and its clarity and sufficiency for the resolving of disputes about Christian faith and life.... (Hopewell, 1987, pp. 60ff)

Hopewell, in his explication of the Canonic world-view, suggests that:

> ...in this negotiation, the controlling canon provides integrity...for Canonic Protestants the inviolable canon is God's word, the Holy Scripture. The Bible in their Canonic eyes is completely reliable and authoritative. (Hopewell, 1987, p.79)

In other types of negotiation, the self or reason might be deemed to be the arbiter in the midst of life's complexities. But in the Canonic negotiation, God's revealed Word and will is already predetermined in the canon of scripture. As Northrop Frye notes, 'whether the context is Greek, Christian or undefined, tragedy seems to lead to an epiphany of law, of that which is and must be' (Frye, 1957, p. 79). But what does an 'epiphany of law' mean here, exactly? Hopewell answers this question by describing the Canonic outlook in more detail:

> One is not free and good. One is lost and sinful, and one's story develops the costly consequences of one's depraved nature. If the self remains disobedient, refusing to recognise the sovereignty of God, then life continues to deteriorate and ends in hell. If, however, one repents and accepts the lordship of Christ, one takes on a different yoke, of suffering love and obedience. (Hopewell, 1987, p. 80)

In other words, an apotheosis of the self is an anathema to the Canonic world-view. Everything – the self, church and world – must submit to the predetermined will of God that is clearly and unambiguously revealed.

Correspondingly, this personal spiritual programme, when mapped on to a movement and brought into a church or denomination as an agent of transformation, is inevitably and radically insistent on its agenda:

> The moral fibre of the nation is decaying; families, schools, cities and [the media] are close to disaster. Only by a massive mission can this nation be saved. Churches must become obedient, 'Bible-centred, Bible-believing, Bible teaching churches'.... (Hopewell, 1987, p. 80)

Hopewell's observation can be compared with that of a mainstream exponent of Conservative Evangelicalism. The 'fit' is precise:

> It is the tragedy of much modern theology, and of whatever church life is influenced by such theology, that it has chosen to follow its culture rather than the word of God. It has accepted the negative verdict on the Bible of movements such as the Enlightenment, and has tried to substitute other revelations or other versions of revelation. These must be doomed to failure.... (Jensen, 2002, p. 274)

Although I think that Hopewell is entirely correct to emphasize these aspects of the Canonic negotiation, I am less convinced that the full features of Frye's definition of tragedy necessarily apply to Conservative Evangelicals or to movements such as Reform. In Hopewell's use of Frye, it is suggested that the Canonic negotiation anticipates failure, death and tragedy; in effect, rewards and 'ultimate happiness is deferred to an afterlife'. But whilst the Canonic Christian life is undoubtedly characterized by submission and obedience, these should be properly understood as disciplines or virtues of empowerment for this life. In other words, the sombre, sober and serious ways in which Canonic Christians approach the church and shape their own spirituality is intended to achieve some measure of triumph in the midst of tragedy. In other words, Canonic Christians believe that they operate within a tragic world and also in tragic consequences for that world. However, these consequences can normally be avoided by resolute obedience and faithfulness. If tragedy continues to afflict a believer who is faithful to this calling, the rewards (usually deferred until the afterlife) will necessarily outweigh the consequences.

The Canonic world-view, then, is a particularly tight and resilient type of Christian belief. It sees the affliction of the self or the persecution of a movement as confirmation of its value and righteousness. It sees the triumph of the self or of a movement as God's vindication of principled Christian living. Ultimately, individuals and movements shaped by the Canonic negotiation are quite *prepared* to be defeated – unlike Hopewell, I do not accept that the Canonic negotiation *expects* defeat. In my view, the Canonic negotiation could more properly be said to anticipate grinding out a gritty, disciplined and ultimately righteous victory, in which falsehood and compromise were comprehensively defeated and shown to be less than the full Gospel. Put another way, Canonic conservative Christians are not to be compared to a latter-day St Sebastian, tied to a stake of persecution and stoically awaiting the onslaught of the many arrows of modernity and liberalism to pierce their skin, as they surely await the bliss of heaven. Rather, they are more like St George

(or at least he of the popular iconography and myth), spearing the dragon of error and heresy and rescuing that fair damsel (that is, the church) from the suggestive and seductive whisperings of that great tempter, liberalism. In the fight for righteousness and truth, injury and perhaps even death may be anticipated, but the risks are nothing when compared to the eternal rewards on offer. The journey ahead may be perilous, but the valiant knights of canonic Christianity are bidden to the fight, to go forth and crusade.

In one way, Hopewell could be said to have already understood my reservation about the actual extent of his narrative theory. In his discussion of tragic tales he acknowledges that 'the self in tragedy, as in romance, is heroic'. However, tragic heroes in the Canonic genre are vindicated and saved rather than cured or freed. Only by identifying with God's revealed Word or will can salvation be obtained. So the heroes (or leaders) within the Canonic genre are not necessarily those who embody exemplary suffering. They will, instead, be those who devote themselves to a disciplined and selfless life in which sacrifice and obedience are paramount. As Linda Bamber puts it, the Canonic world is one:

> ... that is separate from us who inhabit it; it will not yield to our desires and fantasies...this means that tragedy, recognition – *anagnorisis*, the banishing of ignorance – is a major goal.... (Bamber, 1982, p. 22)

Here we have an account, developed from the Hopewellian reflections on tragedy, that partially explains why Reform concentrates so heavily on teaching, preaching and instruction to constitute its essential life and identity. It is important to note here that, from my discussions with members of Reform about the priorities of Jesus in his earthly ministry, it seems that the majority of individuals within the movement propagate the view that Jesus was primarily a teacher. Of course, although the most common title for Jesus used in the Gospels is indeed 'Rabbi' – teacher – most people I have talked to within Reform go further than this and suggest that the primary mode of Christ's teaching was preaching. This is, in itself, contestable. Moreover, even if it were true, little, if any, account is taken of the ambiguity of parabolic interaction, the multifaceted ways in which parables can be taken and interpreted, what actually constitutes teaching and learning (one suspects a very un-Freirian 'banking model' rather than anything shrewd or revolutionary), nor the other ways in which Jesus 'taught', such as through specific actions, practices or behaviour.

From the perspectives gleaned so far, the Reform world-view can be properly summarized as follows. The world is a sinful place, from which the individual must be saved. The church, in order to fulfil its missiological task as an agent of salvation, must be opposed to the world and its vices as well as to any form of accommodation of worldly standards. The tragic or Canonic outlook expects that serious, sober and disciplined discipleship to be a primary means of ensuring that the tragic nature of the world does not have tragic consequences for those caught within its snares. This is ultimately, then, an advocation of a form of separatism, which of course can lead to something

akin to sectarianism. However, within the Canonic world-view, the purpose of separatism is centred on prophetic condemnation, individual purgation and a sharing in salvation; there is no separatism for the sake of it. In other words, the Canonic world-view is a means by which participants – either individuals or movements – can imagine the reordering and cleansing of the church itself. It is a form of systematic postmodern Puritanism; saving the church from itself and the world, and thereby rescuing souls from the inevitable and tragic consequences of disobedience and unbelief. The Canonic world-view is a gnosis of certitude; the faith rests on 'received facts' that are sufficient and clear. Those who think otherwise are leading the church astray and destined for annihilation either in this life or the next.

## Money, Sex and Power

One consequence of the tragic outlook is that it inevitably tends to treat the church as an acultural entity. Because the Gospel is absolute, it must also be expressed, embodied and reified in ways that ultimately transcend culture, and perhaps even subjugate it. I do not propose to take issue with that particular missiological presupposition in this chapter. Suffice to say, such issues have been dealt with perfectly well by a number of theologians over the years, as well as by scholars within Evangelicalism, and also by some notable novelists (one only has to recall Barbara Kingsolver's recent *The Poisonwood Bible* or Herman Melville's *Omoo* and *Tipee*.) My observation is, rather, intended to question the wisdom of a world-view that does not pay proper attention to enculturation. It should perhaps be obvious that, even within a strictly biblical framework of understanding, no-one speaks or learns their Christianity *without* a distinctly local accent. The story of the outpouring of the Holy Spirit at Pentecost is a reminder – as though one were ever needed – that Christianity has always spoken in the many-and-tilthed tongues of its adherents. There is no type of Christianity that does not bear the trace of its 'accent of origin'. Even Alpha courses, despite their global appeal, feel and sound like they grew up in Knightsbridge. Roman Catholicism (that great oxymoron), retains its 'Roman' accent (a concentrated, imperial and centralized power), despite its 'Catholic' (global) claim.

These preliminary observations aside, the focus of this short section is concerned with three key themes that appear to preoccupy the public agenda of Reform: money, sex (or gender) and power. The concerns over these issues are, I want to suggest, not at the *heart* of the Reform. Rather, they are better understood as symptomatic of the deeper disquiet that accompanies the tragic world-view. It is far too easy, in my view, to narrate Reform as an ultra-Protestant schismatic body that simply wants its own way on certain issues and will go to almost any lengths to secure their purity, identity and autonomy. Witness, for example, how one commentator expresses a widely shared perception of Reform:

In effect, this is exactly the strategy pursued with such success by Reform and Forward in Faith within the Church of England. Behave as if the schism were an accomplished fact, withhold your money, treat your bishop with the distant ecumenical courtesy normally due to a neighbouring Imam, control your own appointments, and tell your congregations that everyone else is a doomed heretic or dupe of doomed heretics .... (Brown, 2003, p. 16)

In contrast, I have found that, in my interviews with Reform members and leaders, there are more measured views to be harvested. For many, if not most, the central concerns are the authority of the Bible and the priority of local mission: clashes over money, sex/gender and power are simply identified as prominent obstacles that can impede the effectiveness of the local church and undermine the authority of scripture. But the obstacles themselves do not constitute a 'cause'. Nor do ministers of Reform see themselves as 'congregationalist', turning their backs on the obligations and opportunities of parochial ministry. On the contrary, such ministers seem to be deeply engaged in parish or 'local-contextual' ministry and seek to draw in significant numbers of people that reflect the culture in which their native ministry operates. Increasingly, a number of churches in the Reform penumbra see 'church planting' in other parishes as an extension of that missiological strategy. Having perceived – correctly, to some extent – that a parish church will not appeal to all its parishioners, they do not seek to undermine the parochial framework, but instead see their activity as complementing a 'system' that no longer works as comprehensively and deeply as it once did. In that respect, they are merely demonstrating a nascent prowess: to develop an effective missiology within a consumerist, postmodern and post-institutional world. For Reform members, the demands of the Gospel and the call to repentance must supersede any 'man-made' regulations about the ordering and governance of the church. So any rigid appeal relating to 'parish boundaries' that impedes a wider mission and ministry will simply be interpreted as yet another obstacle to be overcome, for the sake of the Gospel.

Strictly speaking, the issues of money, sex/gender and power belong together in any assessment of Reform. Analysts tend to treat them as separate foci of concern, whereas in reality these issues form an interrelated nexus of problems to which Reform addresses itself in a particularly systematic manner. Moreover, as we have noted before, the issues are merely deemed to be the presenting 'symptoms' that riddle a sick body (the church). The deeper malaise is, from the perspective of the tragic world-view, disobedience to God, and a failure to honour the authority of scripture. Thus, David Holloway writes:

... [we] met in London to discuss, think and pray about financial issues in the Church of England. [We] were discussing the right way forward for 'net-givers' in responding to the ever-larger financial demands for central church funds – 'the quota'. Huge sums of money are now subsidizing work that Evangelicals often believe is frustrating the gospel.... The context is increasing theological liberalism in the church at large; and growing bureaucratic centralism especially at the Diocesan but also at the General Synod levels. As a response some mainstream larger Evangelical churches that are 'net-givers' are already capping their quotas.... The

goal of this action is not merely responsible stewardship, financial competence and long-term viability but mission. The needs of the nation are seen as more important than the comfort of the church. The conversion of England in our nation's desperate spiritual and moral condition is a priority.... (Holloway, 1993, p. 1)

In this narration, it is the wider church that is being written-up as 'deviant'. Withholding income from central funds is therefore 'responsible' and a foundation for reconstructing a more faithful form of mission that is less centred on the 'comfort' of the church and more focused on evangelism and the moral renewal of the nation. It therefore follows that Reform members see themselves as acting correctively, prophetically and creatively rather than obstructively. Thus, Holloway notes that 'many mainline Evangelical churches are no longer willing to pay for a combination of ineffectiveness and doubt at the centre' (Holloway, n.d., p. 2).

Reform's concern with sex and gender are, perhaps surprisingly, a little more difficult to access. On the matter of gender, Reform continues to assert 'the divine order of male headship' as an important article of faith. But, privately, many leaders within the movement acknowledged that there are considerable differences of opinion and varieties of practice within Conservative Evange-licalism. Some openly admitted that the issue of women priests was now 'water under the bridge'. Thus, although some Reform churches are 'Resolution A' parishes, and would therefore not welcome a female incumbent, there was little sign of real opposition to the ministry of women priests in general. Some had no real difficulty with women preaching and celebrating the Eucharist. Some went further and indicated that women bishops would not necessarily be a divisive or decisive issue for them, nor perhaps even a crisis. In that respect, Reform seems to have already anticipated that a campaign against women bishops is likely to divide Evangelicals more than it unites them.

However, the same cannot be said for sex outside marriage, and in particular, homosexual practice. Again, it is important to report that, in my interviews with Reform leaders and in conversations with other Conservative Evangelicals, all were concerned to emphasize that they were not 'obsessed' with the issue; that they were not homophobic; and that they were not seeking to make the issue into a litmus test of orthodoxy or unity. Such claims seem to be reasonable when one considers that there are far fewer publications from Reform on sex and gender when compared to the volume that address money and power. Whilst the nomination of Jeffrey John and Gene Robinson as bishops of Reading and New Hampshire respectively has pushed the 'gay issue' to the fore, Reform seems to have put relatively few resources into addressing homosexuality. The reason for this, I suspect, is that Reform needs relatively few 'formal' religious statements on the matter, given that coherent opposition is widespread within the culture of 'operant' Evangelicalism. For example, R.T. France's recent *A Slippery Slope?* (2000), a rather slight publication in many ways, seems to be characterized more by reassertion than by argument.

In some of my interviews with Conservative Evangelicals and Reform members, I pressed the question of what it would take to establish a conversation on the 'gay issue'. With more or less uniformity, interviewees

could not foresee a conversation with 'practising' gay Christians taking place at all, since they regarded homosexuality itself as sinful. Dialogue with bodies such as the Lesbian and Gay Christian Movement (LGCM) was also seen as fairly pointless as, in the words of one commentator, 'both sides seem to regard the other as intransigent, shrill fundamentalists'. But for Reform members, the foundation for any dialogue on the issue would have to respect the authority of scripture on such matters. Correspondingly, the kind of agenda laid out by Jakobsen and Pellegrini (2003) in their recent book on sexual regulation, and arguing for freedom and tolerance, is the very antithesis of a Reform-type position which would assert that such freedom and tolerance amounts to a rebellion against, and a rejection of, God's sovereignty (cf. Jensen, 2002, pp. 266ff; Higton, 1987).

But the issue of sexuality is not quite as closed as it might first seem. In one interview with a Reform member, I mused on the fact that what the dialogue needed was another Michael Vasey – an 'out' gay priest who would not let go of his mainstream Evangelical identity, but who published one of the few good hermeneutical books on the issue in recent years, *Strangers and Friends* (1997). During one interview, a Reform leader spoke regretfully about the Revd Roy Clements, a Baptist minister who had been a close mentor to, and supporter of, both Reform and the Proclamation Trust and had been a senior figure in the Evangelical Alliance. But Roy left his pastorate in Cambridge when, after 20 years of marriage, he became 'reconciled' to his homosexual nature and went to live with a male partner. He now works independently as a minister and has some involvement with LGCM. The Reform leader said that he still could 'not understand this', and that their parting was a cause of deep grief to him, but he could no longer see how they could dialogue anymore. This was a genuine 'tragic' story, and narrated by the Reform member in classically tragic terms: a stalwart of the Gospel who had lost his way. Or put in more Bunyanesque terms, the Vasey–Clements stories are akin to *Pilgrim's Regress*.

Finally in this section, we turn to power. As an issue, it is closely related to money. As we have already suggested, it is a mistake to conceive of Reform as schismatic or 'congregationalist'. Members and leaders are not against parish ministry and pro-eclectic. Neither are they necessarily intent on working against the dioceses in which they minister. They are, rather, radically attempting to reposition the local church as the primary locus of mission and evangelism within a community. In Reform's understanding of the church, the local is the catholic. Correspondingly, excessive centralization is seen as a threat to ministry, by being a drain on resources. Reform, contrary to what its critics say, does not want to withhold money. Instead, it wants to exercise some degree of choice in how it is spent and, in particular, to see that it is spent effectively. In that regard, Reform's position on money and power can be interpreted, in Hopewellian terms, as 'mechanistic' with its focus on effectiveness, evangelism and results (Hopewell, 1987, pp. 22–24). That said, there is also a sense in which the argument for the local church to define itself and self-govern has a long tradition within mission history. Evangelical missionaries such as Henry Venn, Henry Wright and James Johnson were at the forefront of Victorian missiology, arguing for the independent 'native

church' as a controlling objective (cf. P. Williams, 1990). So it really cannot be very surprising that such ideas, once nourished, have now spread from their colonial seedbeds and returned to their churches of origin. Moreover, Anglicanism itself can be properly said to have promoted a 'self-governing, self-supporting and self-extending' ecclesiology (Sachs, 1993, pp. 241–44).

But the focus on power also has another side to it: the efficacy and righteousness of its bearers. Reform's call for 'godly leadership' is a cipher and a trope. It is an attack on liberal Catholics in positions of authority, who betray the heritage of the church and abuse its resources: 'we believe this liberal-Catholic drift is destroying the church' (Holloway, 1993, p. 3). In this light, the unprecedented campaign against Jeffrey John should be understood as a focused attempt to draw attention to what Reform perceives as being a wider malaise, in which the appointment of Rowan Williams is also implicated. In talking to Reform members, they are unhappy with the appointment of the archbishop generally, and not simply because of his views on sexuality. It should also be said that some Reform members were not entirely happy with George Carey's tenure as archbishop either, as they felt that he made too many accommodations to Charismatic Renewal and to 'unsound' initiatives such as Alpha courses. Put more sharply, anything that takes away from the primacy of propositional faith – the revelation of God, expressed clearly and unambiguously through scripture, and most especially the Gospels – is seen to be, at best, a form of heterodoxy (cf. Jensen, 2002, pp. 257–69) and therefore dangerous.

### Reading Reform Differently

One of the advantages of studying a movement like Reform is that it is relatively easy to position within the wider Evangelical culture and, by so doing, one can gain a preliminary understanding of its controlling fundaments; the basic ethos can also be quickly grasped. However, the deeper socio-theological task will always depend on disciplines such as ethnography, and in more nuanced reflections based on the primary material that is gathered. That said, the aim of this section is to locate Reform within Evangelicalism, and then to situate it within the broader penumbra of Anglicanism.

Graham Kings' recent study of contemporary Anglican Evangelicalism maps the shape of the movement by using the metaphor of watercourses (Kings, 2003, pp. 167–84). He equates Conservative Evangelicalism with canals; moderate or open Evangelicalism is identified with broad rivers; Charismatic Evangelicalism is said to resemble rapids or waterfalls. This slightly innocent and playful set of analogies is more penetrating than it first appears. It allows Kings to sketch the strengths and weaknesses of each and, in so doing, reflect something of their truer nature:

> ...canals also have very positive aspects to them...they are the only watercourse where there can be movement uphill; they are steady and calm.... (Kings, 2003, p. 169)

Of course, canals cut through all manner of materials to maintain their course; they do not negotiate or compromise with what stands in their way, as rivers might. Another advantage of Kings' analogy is that the watercourse suggests fluidity and movement. In the case of Charismatic Evangelicals, it may be fast and frothy, and this can be usefully contrasted within the constrained, controlled and majestic movement of canals. But whether canal, river or waterfall, the clear implication of the analogy is that each movement is bound to history and therefore also to development. Kings, in summing up his analogical 'map', reminds his (Evangelical) audience that there is a commonality about Evangelicalism, just like the water of the watercourses: 'Evangelical is not a party word' (ibid., p.184).

Viewed from a slightly different perspective, David Tracy (1975) identifies five basic models of contemporary theology for engaging with modernity. They are: orthodox, liberal, neo-orthodox, radical and revisionist. Space does not permit a discussion of each of these in their own right, but Tracy's concern is to identify how the models attempt to negotiate with the complexity of the modern world. The closest 'model' to Conservative Evangelicalism that Tracy identifies is orthodox:

> In an orthodox theological model, the claims of modernity are not understood to have any inner-theological relevance.... Orthodox theologians do not seem impressed with the counter-claims of modern scientific, historical, or philosophical scholarship.... (Tracy, 1975, p. 24)

Certainly there are traces of the Conservative Evangelical approach in Tracy's other models (especially the neo-orthodox), but the orthodox is a particularly good fit for the same reasons that Kings equates the movement with canals. Tracy sees strengths in the sophisticated and single-minded approach; he understands that canals are complex to construct. But, like Kings, Tracy also sees weaknesses in the orthodox model:

> ...[the] major weakness...lies in [the] inability to make intrinsic (i.e., inner-theological) uses of other scholarly disciplines...[and the] theological inability to come to terms with the cognitive, ethical, and existential counter-claims of modernity. The weakness is directly dependent upon the presence of a relatively narrow self-referent (the explicit believer) and of an object-referent of parallel narrowness (an understanding of the beliefs and values of his own church tradition).... (Tracy, 1975, p. 25)

The outcome of this model is, in Tracy's words, a clear and 'blessed rage for order'. Writing over a decade before Hopewell, Tracy identifies the link between anger (a fury at the chaos and confusion modernity and contemporary culture allegedly wreaks upon the church and theology) and the desire to develop stability and regulation to combat this. Of course, the genius of Tracy's contribution to mapping the shape of modern theology is to see that *each* of the models is responsive and is also an attempt to reorder the tasks of theology and the nature of the church in the face of sustained challenge. The rage for order, then, is a particular feature of more conservative models of

theology that tend to resist rather than make peace with, or embrace, the forces of secularity, modernity and cultural change.

At this point in our discussion, confirmation of this emergent thesis comes from a surprising source. William Pickering's study of Anglo-Catholicism (1989) suggests that the heirs of the Tractarian movement were able to form a distinctive ecclesial culture that was able to cope with ambiguity and differences by appealing to aesthetics and the sublime. But perhaps more than this, there was some real sense in which Anglo-Catholicism actually revelled in ambiguity (for example, its stance on sexuality, its position on Rome, and so on), precisely because the unity of the movement was primarily sacramental. Through metaphor, liturgical practice, cultural bonds and appeals to the sublime, a degree of diversity came to be expected, which went hand-in-hand with hospitality towards ambiguity (Pickering, 1989, pp. 184ff).

Pickering's perceptive historical and sociological analysis identifies ambiguity as a key issue for Anglo-Catholicism:

> ...all religions contain ambiguities. Such ambiguities arise initially out of the very nature of religion itself in trying to bridge two orders of reality – that of this world and the world beyond, a transcendental world. All religions have had to come face to face with such ambiguities or ambiguities dependent on their premises. They have either to accept them fairly and squarely and perhaps say they are irresolvable, or else to attempt to deal with them in such a way as to satisfy [man's] intellect but never completely gratify it. If ambiguity is resolved, religion disappears.... (Pickering, 1989, p. 141)

The key feature of Anglo-Catholicism is that it does not resolve its inherent ambiguities at all; it defers resolution constantly and refers all deep questioning and contested issues to art, aesthetics, the sublime, mystery and the continually open texture of the sacraments. Arguably, this is why the Church of England's decision to ordain women to the priesthood presented such a deep crisis to Anglo-Catholics. A resolution had finally been reached; it was now impossible for some to rejoice in the characteristic 'unsolvedness' of Anglo-Catholic ecclesiology and identity, which had hitherto been its genius. The simple 'fact' of women priests could no longer be ignored. The sacramental understanding of the church is, generally, an adequate way of keeping a broad range of views together, since plurality of belief is always deemed to be 'under' a higher mystery. But when faced with deep divisions and hotly contested views, a sacramental understanding of the church often tends to lack the ability to create conditions under which conflicts can be successfully negotiated.

The discussion of Pickering's thesis is important here, for it helps us to understand why Reform opposes 'liberal Catholics'. As we can now see, the problem is not simply with liberalism; it also lies with the relative comfort that Anglo-Catholics have with ambiguity. Rather than valuing ambiguity, Conservative Evangelicals resist it vigorously and wish to express their Christianity through emphasizing virtues and practices associated with clarity. In contrast with the Anglo-Catholic absorption with the sensate, ethereal and

mysterious, Conservative Evangelicals wish to base their faith on a kind of scriptural rationalism. Thus, the Anglo-Catholic attachment to sacramentality, the sublime and mystery is seen by Conservative Evangelicals as heterodox: it elevates the relational and aesthetic above the propositional. It runs the risk of placing experience above revelation; of the church above the Gospel.

Correspondingly, to Conservative Evangelicals, liberal Catholics are an even more despised breed than Anglo-Catholics. Conservative Evangelicals feel that at least they could join hands with Anglo-Catholics on a 'traditionalist' platform, provided that the construction and constitution of that tradition is not scrutinized too closely. But liberal Catholics tend to be regarded as being beyond the pale, for they are deemed to have abandoned such traditionalism and embraced the many and varied forms of modernism and liberalism. To a Conservative Evangelical, that looks like nothing more than performative (but watered down) liturgy, coupled to a post-Enlightenment and modernist theology. Of course, I am aware that these remarks are, to some extent, a characterization. But they serve a purpose, namely to reveal some of the deeper, nascent reasons why the proposed appointment of Jeffrey John evoked such reaction amongst Reform members. It wasn't simply his sexuality that some found problematic; it was everything he stood for.[5]

This last remark leads us, finally in this section, to return to the question of authority. In many ways, an understanding of the sources and purposes of authority has been shown to be the key to understanding Reform. As I have noted earlier, the movement is not primarily preoccupied with money, sex and power. These issues are simply symptomatic and indicate the deeper and most contested issue: the authority of the Bible. Paula Nesbitt, in her reflections on the 1998 Lambeth Conference, shows how the Anglican communion has been unable to avoid being gradually split: caught between increasing cultural diversity, on the one hand, and the need to provide coherence and identity, on the other. She notes how successive Lambeth Conferences have moved sequentially from being grounded on traditional authority (that is, the establishment of churches and provinces during the colonial era), to rational authority (which presupposes negotiation through representative constituencies for dominance over meeting outcomes) to negotiated authority (which, however, normally lacks the power to stem the momentum of change). She notes that these kinds of authority, when pursued through the four 'instruments' of unity[6] in the Anglican Communion, are usually capable of resolving deep disputes. However, although they enable complex interaction

---

[5] Of course Canon Dr Jeffrey John was one of the key founders of Affirming Catholicism, a movement begun ten years ago to accommodate those Anglo-Catholics who supported the ordination of women and a more progressive faith. Rowan Williams was also one of the architects of the movement, and Reform's opposition to both should be understood as hostility towards the agenda of progressive liberal Catholic thinking.

[6] The four instruments of unity are the archbishop of Canterbury, the Lambeth Conference, the Anglican Consultative Council and the Meetings of the Primates. In turn, these 'instruments' generally consider how issues fall within the 'Anglican Quadrilateral': Scripture, Tradition, Reason and Culture.

and conversation, they do not lead to clear and firm resolutions. Correspondingly, Nesbitt argues that, within the Anglican Communion, a new, fourth authoritative form has emerged, which has in some senses been present from the very beginning and is now tied up with the identity of scripture. She writes of this authority:

> [It] could be used to countervail the relativism of cross-cultural alliances without affecting their strategic utility: symbolic authority. The symbol, as a locus of authority, has a tangible and timeless nature. Where the symbol is an authoritative part of the institutional milieu, either traditional or rational authority must acknowledge its legitimacy . . . scripture is an authoritative symbol . . . . (Nesbitt, 2001, p. 257)

Nesbitt points out, as I noted earlier, that the symbolic authority of sacraments may create shared bonds and enhance communal cohesion, but are normally unable to regulate or negotiate conflict. However, in contrast:

> Scripture, when canonized as complete or absolute, becomes symbolic of a particular era or set of teachings and beliefs. However, unlike sacraments, the use of scripture as symbolic authority can be constructed and constituted according to selecting those aspects or passages that address an issue at hand. Furthermore, scripture as symbolic authority can be objectified or absolutized, which transcends cultural boundaries in a way that other forms of authority can less easily do. The appeal of scriptural literalism provides an objectification of authority that is independent of the influence or control of dominant perspectives, social locations, and circumstances. As symbolic authority, it can be leveraged against cultural dominance as well as provide common ground for cross-cultural alliances . . . . (Ibid.)

In other words, with scripture raised almost to the level of apotheosis, a cross-cultural foundation for authority exists that can challenge the dominance of rational authority, which is normally associated with highly educated elite groups from the West or First World. Scripture, given symbolic authority, becomes an important tool in the hands of Southern (non-elite) Christians who are seeking to counter-legitimate more conservative perspectives. Of course, this strategy not only plays directly into the hands of groups like Reform: it can in fact be resourced by them. As Nesbitt notes, 'scriptural literalism as symbolic authority represents the easiest and most accessible form of counter-legitimation across educational or cross-cultural divides' (ibid., p. 258). And as Lambeth Conferences, like the Anglican communion itself, have become increasingly diverse in their cultural expression, symbolic authority has risen to the fore. This means that, at present, the only contender for being a focus of symbolic authority is the Bible, since cross-cultural negotiation only leads to sterile relativism – and as long as this situation continues, the dominance of Reform within the Church of England looks set to continue. We should note that the only other alternative to the Bible as symbolic authority – the Communion itself – has so far failed to attain this status, mainly because the very enabling of that possibility would require a looser, more elastic view of truth-claims and a necessary tolerance towards competing convictions.

Typically, those who press for the Anglican Communion as a natural focus for symbolic authority tend to be liberal Catholic, and, as we have already noted, the lack of clarity that this tradition embodies is largely unacceptable to Conservative Evangelicals.

## Conclusion

In a Communion that is now in a state of considerable flux, caution should be exercised in drawing firm conclusions from such a short study as this. What I have attempted to show here is that the rise of Reform in the Church of England belongs to a wider set of cultural, ecclesiological and theological trends in global Anglicanism from which Reform currently benefits. These trends include a move towards emphasizing the power and autonomy of the local church and a renewed interest in scriptural literalism as a focus for symbolic authority (cf. Ndungane in Douglas and Pui-Lan, 2001, pp. 233–46). There is also a sense, in a primarily English context, in which we are witnessing the resurgence of the cultural differences between Roundheads and Cavaliers – between the architects of a Puritan regime and a later Caroline settlement. Furthermore, the inherent 'tragic world-view' of Conservative Evangelicals seems to provide individuals and churches with a certain kind of steely resolve which makes accommodation unlikely, if not an anathema.

Having sketched the origins of Reform and attempted to suggest some of the reasons why its rise within the Church of England has been so influential, we are now in a position to hazard some guesses about the future of the movement within the church and the wider Communion. Such suggestions are, of course, contingent, but four preliminary points can be made by way of conclusion.

First, and following Nesbitt (2001), we can say that in a post-denominational age (arguably a natural development arising from postmodernity and postcolonialism), the churches that can survive as denominations will be those with a shared affinity of feeling and a shared moral consensus. This closely matches Harvey Cox's (1994) postulation that denominational labels will matter less and less in the twenty-first century and that the battle lines between liberalism and traditionalism will be redrawn. Those churches that celebrate the sensate, embodied and experiential will increasingly network together, just as those that emphasize the propositional and credal will attempt to work together. (For an alternative and theologically richer vision for the Communion, see Sagovsky, 2000.)

Second, we should note that Anglicanism, ever since the first Lambeth Conference (which was called to head off schism and therefore arguably marks the beginning of the end for the coherent 'globalization' of the Church of England), has struggled to maintain its unity amidst diversity. Indeed, Seabury's consecration as a bishop for North America by the Scottish episcopal bishops in 1784, goes hand-in-hand with the first significant blow to British imperial interests, the American War of Independence, and ably demonstrates that the Church of England could not restrain its own spread from Canterbury. It could not challenge the idea that Anglicanism was 'self-

supporting, self-governing and self-extending' (Sachs, 1993, pp. 241–44). Subsidiarity and individuation in each newly established province was then virtually inevitable. In one sense, the Anglican Communion is continually destined to play 'catch up' with an expansion and diversity that it consistently sows but cannot control (see Sachs, 1993; Douglas and Pui-Lan, 2001; Rowell, 1992).

Third, and again following Nesbitt, we note that, in the first phase of denominationalism, institutional relations can be governed through obedience, and, if necessary, punishment. However, in the second phase, interpersonal contracts emerge between congregations, regions and individuals. Here 'ecclesial citizenship' is born, and law and order develop into an agreed, rather than imposed, rule. In the third phase (postmodernity), more complex social contracts emerge between parties, which require a deeper articulation of a shared ethos and an agreement about the nature of a shared moral community. Correspondingly, any arguments about women or, more especially, 'gay issues' are far more likely to cause schism than unity in liturgy or order, since some will see this as a betrayal of the ethos. We should therefore expect arguments on key issues to increase in volume and severity. Indeed, so far, they have only been contained by an assertion of rational, traditional or negotiated authority. However, with the focus of authority posited in the Communion quickly giving way to the symbolic authority of the Bible, we should expect denominational fortunes to closely match hermeneutical coherence or fragmentation (cf. Ndungane in Douglas and Pui-Lan, 2001, pp. 233–46).

Fourth, Reform's championing of the primacy of the local congregation can be read as pro-reticulate, but as anti-denominational. It is, arguably, a postmodern movement with a premodern agenda. Reform, as an organization, seeks to renarrate denominations as shared moral communities with an explicitly harmonized ethos. This is in sharp contrast to the normative narration of Anglicanism as a civilized community of disagreement (cf. Rowell, 1992; Percy, 2000), a matrix of competing convictions and a church where its identity is ambiguous and unresolved. Here, Reform's major contribution to the future of Anglicanism is to offer clarity against ambiguity: decision instead of 'fudge', and precision and transparency in place of uncertainty and haziness. Ultimately, then, Reform represents a blessed rage for (Godly, biblical) order. It is not anger for anger's sake. It is a righteous anger, the very mirror of the fear-inspiring God that features so strongly in their core doctrine, namely that of penal substitution. The anger is directed and purposeful: it is for a new order in the Church of England, and more broadly for the nation.

Finally, the overall achievement of Reform in its first decade should not be underestimated. The movement, in concert with other initiatives and developments in the Anglican communion, has established Conservative Evangelicalism as a major force within the church. The efforts of Sydney diocese, as well as the contribution of conservative and southern bishops, have posed a serious challenge to the historic and hegemonic governance of liberal-catholic theology and its Western bishops. Moreover, it has helped to fundamentally alter the sense of balance within the Anglican churches, by

making the symbolic authority of the Bible both higher and mightier than that of the Communion itself. Reform has, like its sixteenth century precursors who pioneered the original Reformations across Europe, done no more than light the proverbial match. It still remains to be seen whether the new fire will catch and hold, but, for supporters of Reform, the signs look promising. The church looks set to be caught ablaze in new fires of passion and purgation. Such flames will test the Church of England and the Anglican Communion to its natural limits.

# Chapter 9

# Comic Turns

## Introduction

A candidate for one of the most teasing opening lines in modern English literature must be from Rose Macaulay's *The Towers of Trezibond*:

> 'Take my camel, dear', said my Aunt Dot, as she climbed down from this animal on her return from High Mass.... (Macaulay, 1956, p. 3)

*The Towers of Trezibond* is an absurd, comic and beautiful tale, which offers the inimitable Aunt Dot, her niece Laurie and Father Chantry-Pigg, and their expedition to Turkey to explore the scope for converting the Turks – not just to any old Christianity, but to Anglicanism. By establishing a High Anglican mission, the trio hope to bring salvation and civilization to the country. Aunt Dot is particularly keen on the emancipation of Turkish women – through a wider use of the bathing hat.

Despite Macaulay's comic novel, there is, ironically, a well-established Anglican presence in Turkey. But the scope of this chapter is not to take issue with parodies of Anglicanism. It is, rather, to use the work of James Hopewell once more to examine the comic and ironic identity of mainstream Anglicanism, and thereby identify those hidden aspects of its appeal that have turned a single English denomination into a worldwide presence. Globally, there are around 77 million Anglicans. They are spread over 36 self-governing churches, comprising 500 dioceses, 30 000 parishes with around 65 000 congregations, located in a total of 165 countries. Whilst not ranking amongst the largest groupings of Christians, the Anglican Church is, after the Roman Catholic Church, arguably one of the most widespread and influential denominations in the world. (Anglicanism is by no means confined to the Commonwealth, which has 53 countries – less than a third of the total in which Anglicanism is to be found.)

The study of Anglicanism (or Anglican Studies, which would be slightly different) can be undertaken in several ways. As a faith that is both widespread and concentrated, it can be scrutinized from a variety of different intellectual disciplines. Naturally, its theology can be assessed theologically. Anglicanism has a rich, distinctive and historic theological tradition, being rooted in both Catholicism and Protestantism. These theological roots condition Anglican liturgy, ecclesiology and missiology. At the same time, Anglican identity is a contested concept, and, although it has distinct instruments of unity (for example, the archbishop of Canterbury, the Anglican Consultative Council, the Lambeth Conference, and the Meetings of the Primates), its authority is

broadly dispersed (see Sykes, 1995; Avis, 2000; Sykes and Booty, 1988; Sachs, 1993). More recently Caddick and McDonald (2002) have suggested that Anglicanism is the answer to modernity. Pemberton and others (1998) have also written lucid trenchant defences of the Anglican Communion. Equally, its corporate life can be opened up to the full range of disciplines within the penumbra of social sciences. Culturally and theologically, Anglicanism tends to be a mediating and accommodating ecclesiology, rather than imposing and authoritative. Globally, each province has its own distinct history, flavour, sense of purpose and mission, yet still within the broad framework of a worldwide 'family' or Communion of churches (see Thomas, 1987). As we noted in the previous chapter, each branch or province of the Anglican family is 'self-supporting, self-extending and self-governing' (Sachs, 1993).

Yet the 'Anglican Communion' also evokes what Benedict Anderson describes as an 'imagined community' (1983, pp. 15–16). Most of its members have never met one another, and never will. Yet members will readily acknowledge a deep, horizontal comradeship of belonging. The Communion is bound together by an ethos, codes, memories and aspirations that allow it to cohere in the minds of its members, but without that coherence necessarily being practised at either a deep or extensive level. In this regard, we can regard the Anglican Communion as a kind of filial network of understanding, again like a family (see Thomas, 1987, pp. 18–143), in which certain types of belief and certain modes of behaviour are cherished. As Pascal Boyer notes:

> One thing modern humans did and still do vastly more than any other species is exchange information of all kinds and qualities, not just about what is the case but also what should be or could be; not just about their emotions and knowledge but also about their plans, memories and conjectures. The proper milieu in which humans live is that of information, especially information provided by other[s]. It is their ecological niche. (Boyer, 2002, p. 374)

There can be no question that Anglicanism and its ecological niche contains elements of coherence and a notion of a shared life and identity, bound together through a common sense of purpose, history and teleology. But what exactly are those 'things' that are particular to Anglican identity? Authors such as Sykes, Avis, Booty and Wright would be able to nominate particular theological priorities. From a sociological perspective, we can point to Pickering's work that identifies ambiguity and aesthetics as being culturally significant (Pickering, 1989), or to my own suggestion that Anglicanism is a 'sacralised system of manners' as being somehow vital to its understanding (Percy, 2000, pp. 114–25). Analogically, Boyer suggests that:

> If we consider the whole domain of information [within an organization] over time we have a gigantic 'soup' of representations and messages. The messages are constantly changing because the contexts change.... However, we also find that there are lumps in this soup of messages, that is, bits of information that seem to appear in rather similar form at different times and in different places. They are not strictly identical but we find a small number of templates that seem to organise them. Religious concepts and behaviours are like that.... (Boyer, 2002, p. 374)

In this chapter I want to suggest that the 'soup' of the Anglican Communion contains such lumps. As with the previous chapters that work with James Hopewell's interpretative methodology, I am less interested in the obvious theological priorities of the Communion, and more concerned here with the nascent cultural distinctives that shape and flavour it. In exploring and analysing these, I will seek to demonstrate that much of Anglicanism is an inherently ironic and comic type of faith which, when understood culturally, can in turn illuminate some of the current theological debates that preoccupy the church. Again, as Boyer notes:

> Religion is cultural. People get it from other people, as they get food preferences, musical tastes, politeness and dress sense. We often tend to think that if something is cultural then it is hugely variable. But it then turns out that food preferences and other such cultural things are not so variable after all. Food preferences revolve around certain recurrent flavours, musical tastes within strict constraints, and so do politeness codes and standards of elegance.... (Boyer, 2002, p. 54)

The next section will therefore look at Hopewell's 'cultural reading' of the church in order to identify and explicate these 'lumps', 'tastes' and 'preferences'. From that vantage-point, it will then be possible to explore the Anglican Communion as a cultural system (albeit strained and multi-flavoured), before moving into a brief excursion on Continuing Anglican Churches, which I hold to represent a form of non-ironic alternative comedy. A final section returns to the idea of Anglican culture, and evaluates its coherence.

## Anglicanism as Irony and Comedy

Hopewell is well aware that it is only recently that 'participant observation' has gained any credibility in academic studies of culture and that this has been driven by anthropologists and ethnographers, who have urged scholars to immerse themselves in the very field of their inquiry. However, participant observers who have studied congregations in any depth are still comparatively rare. Most studies tend to be, in Hopewell's words, 'travelogues', giving accounts of churches and congregations that are based on anecdotes and texts. In contrast, Hopewell, who in turn acknowledges his debt to the work of Melvin Williams and Samuel Heilman (Hopewell, 1987, p. 89), argue for the studies of congregations to be undertaken through the 'observing participant' – congregations themselves learning to function 'as if' they were themselves outsiders. It is through such strategies that congregations and scholars can become attuned to the myriad manners and codes that participants often take for granted. Thus, Hopewell suggests that 'sounding the depths' of a congregation must be a deeper task that pays attention to such things as:

> jokes, stories, lore...parish conversations that follow administrative meetings... sermons, classroom presentation...use of space...line of authority...use of time...conscious and unconscious symbols...conflict.... (Hopewell, 1987, p. 89)

But how could paying attention to such trivia and ephemera reveal something about the fundamental nature and identity of a church or something as complex as the Anglican Communion? To illustrate this simply, consider the following three jokes about Anglicanism:

1   **Question**: How many Anglicans does it take to change a lightbulb?
    **Answer**: Five – one to put in the new one and four to admire the old one.

2   One day, the archbishop of Canterbury is sitting alone on the beach, trying to enjoy a holiday and a retreat. It has been another hard year. He gazes out towards the horizon where the sun is still rising and sighs. Presently, his eye catches something gleaming in the sand. He brushes away the grains and pulls out a brass canister. Seeing an inscription, he spits on it and polishes it, but before he can read it, the canister explodes in a haze of blue smoke. The archbishop rubs his eyes and is surprised to find, standing before him, a large genie. 'Your Grace', says the genie, 'I will grant you one wish – whatever you want: just name it.'
    The archbishop reaches inside his cassock pocket, and pulls out a map of the Middle East. With a crayon, he draws a large red circle around the whole area. 'I'd like you to bring peace to this region', he says.
    The genie does not reply. He sits on the sand and looks at the rising sun. He says nothing for ten minutes. Then, turning again to the archbishop, he says: 'I have never said this to anyone before, but what you ask is beyond me. It is too difficult. But if you have another wish, I will grant that.'
    The archbishop pauses, and then reaches inside for another map. This is a map of the world, with 165 countries coloured in. 'This is the Anglican Communion', he explains, 'and all I ask is that you help all the many different parts to get on a little better.'
    The genie sits back down on the sand again and looks towards the sun. Again, for ten minutes, he says nothing. Then he stands up, and turns to the archbishop. 'Your Grace', he says, 'do you think I could have another look at that first map?'

3   One day, the queues of people to get into heaven are so long and thick that the angels guarding the Pearly Gates begin to panic. They fly off to see Jesus and ask for advice. Jesus suggests that potential entrants are graded. He will ask a question of everyone seeking entry and, depending on how they answer, they will either be placed in the slow track or granted immediate entry. The question Jesus proposes to use is the same question he once put to the disciples: 'Who do you say that I am?'
    The first person Jesus encounters at the gates is a Methodist minister. Jesus asks her, 'Who do you say that I am?'
    The minister hesitates and then answers 'Well, at Conference last year . . .'.
    But Jesus interrupts her immediately. 'I am sorry', he says, 'but I asked you for your opinion, and not for your denominational line. Would you mind going to the back of the queue? Thank you.'
    The next person to step forward is a Roman Catholic monk. Jesus poses

the same question, to which the monk replies, 'Well, our pope says...'.

But Jesus again interrupts and points out that he wanted the monk's opinion, not the pope's.

Third, a Baptist minister approaches. His response to Jesus' question is emphatic: 'The Bible says...'.

But Jesus again interrupts and reminds the minister that he wanted his opinion, not his knowledge. Finally, an Anglican priest approaches. Jesus regards the minister somewhat quizzically, but puts the question to him nonetheless. The Anglican replies categorically: 'You are the Christ – the Son of the living God.'

Jesus is slightly taken aback by such an ardent response from an Episcopalian, and is about to let the Anglican priest in, when he adds, 'but then again, on the other hand...'.

These jokes reveal several things about the nature of Anglicanism. First, they are jokes told by Anglicans, suggesting that they possess a capacity for gentle self-mocking comic irony. Second, the lightbulb joke makes a serious point: admiration of the past is an important feature of Anglican life – but it can get of out hand. Third, the joke about the archbishop and the genie recognizes the acute difficulties in maintaining Anglican polity. Fourth, the joke about the Anglican priest at the Pearly Gates celebrates the inherent ambivalence of Anglicanism – the way in which it glories in seeing situations from different points of view and holds a variety of viewpoints together, even though such convictions may compete with another and cause a degree of tension. Fifth, the jokes reveal a real fondness for the way Anglicanism is, including its flaws. Indeed, the flaws are being intrinsically linked to its virtues, which the jokes highlight, albeit ironically.

The careful noting of this apparently incidental material is important for any ethnography of a church, let alone an entire Communion. Paul Willis, in his *The Ethnographic Imagination* (2000) suggests that many conventional types of ethnography overlook the sensate and felt aspects of bodies, societies or situations under scrutiny. He argues that careful attention paid to artefacts, poetry, sayings, humour and sensations can provide important registers of the mood and shape of a given subject. Therefore trying to capture the visual, sensate and experienced aspects of a community can provide important indicators that conventional fieldwork might normally miss. In this respect, Willis is doing no more than building on Raymond Williams' (1976, 1986) earlier work on cultures, arguing that they are often constituted through 'structures of feeling'. Indeed, we might go further here and suggest that the Anglican Communion itself is a 'structure of feeling'; its senses its kinship, ties and shape, but hardly ever sees these fully reified.

Thus, and to return to the Anglican jokes, the mere fact that Anglicans appear to be able to tolerate (or even celebrate?) a certain amount of gentle self-mocking comic irony reveals something about the nature of the movement itself. In the previous chapter we looked in some detail at the problem of moral coherence within a post-denominational framework. Nevertheless, it still appears to be meaningful to speak of Anglicanism as a 'community of moral

discourse', despite the stresses and strains associated with particular issues (Hopewell, 1987, p. 144). But what exactly is a community of moral discourse? Hopewell suggests that it is a gathering of people that are explicitly intent on surveying and critically assessing their personal, social and moral convictions *together*, because there is already some prior nascent consensus about the loyalty that binds them together as a group. Such ties need not be explicit. Indeed, we might say that any attempt to make them so can be problematic. Part of the genius of Anglicanism arguably lies in its fundamental 'unsolvedness'. Its major problems of moral coherence only emerge when it attempts to *clarify* itself, instead of allowing competing convictions to continue to gestate within a broadly sacramental understanding of the church.

To press the discussion a little further, it is noteworthy that anthropologists such as Geertz distinguish between the ethos of a community and its world-view. The world-view is the 'ideal' shape of the world (to come?) that guides the life of community. In contrast, the ethos refers to those values and codes that the group currently maintains. The two are, of course, related and, as Hopewell points out, the bonds that link ethos and world-view are not only creeds and formal religious statements, but also whole value systems and narrative streams that may seldom be understood or explicitly revealed. In my own participant observation of Anglicanism (indeed, as an observing participant, since I am an ordained Anglican priest), I have been continually struck by the capacity of the wider Communion for what I have already described as gentle self-mocking comic irony. Could it be, in Hopewell's and Geertz's terminology, that this characteristic actually links the ethos and world-view in Anglicanism? In other words, is the cultural ecclesiology of Anglicanism mild, temperate, given to measured humour, but also anticipative of the ultimacy of a sacramental resolution to all serious forms of dispute and the threat of schism or incoherence? In order to investigate this further, it is necessary to explain Hopewell's understanding of comedy and irony in ecclesiological narrative streams and then test this 'reading' of Anglicanism against current debates.

## Anglicanism: Comic and Ironic

In David Hare's *Racing Demon* (1990), an ironic and comic play about Anglican clergy in London during the 1980s, a central feature of the plot is the division between those who think 'things will work out alright', and those for whom the church has reached breaking point. The latter position is represented by a fictitious bishop of London, who consistently narrates a 'tragic' understanding of the church and the world – a more 'catholic' version of the type discussed in the previous chapter. In Hare's play the divisions between the characters are, on the surface, theological. But Hare is able to exploit the deeper partitions that separate the characters, and these are more typically concerned with world-views and expectations. Although the play ends, to a degree, in a mire of tragedy, its overall character is ironic-comic. According to Hopewell, true comedies begin with a world in which there is misunderstanding, crisis and calamity, but end:

...in unions, pacts, embraces and marriages – that symbolize the ultimately trustworthy working of the world. Created in misinformation and convoluted by error, a comedy is resolved by the disclosure of a deeper knowledge about the harmonious way things really are.... (Hopewell, 1987, p. 58)

Hopewell sees the comic genre as one that pivots on integration. Personally, a situation of ignorance is responded to with enlightenment, with the resolution being peace. Socially, discord is met with wisdom and leads to harmony. Cosmically, illusion is addressed by process and resolved through union. The key cognitive feature of the comic world-view is wisdom, and, because of this, the minister is most commonly a 'guide', the Eucharist a 'sacrament', the church a 'pilgrimage' and the Gospel 'consciousness' (Hopewell, 1987, pp. 70–71). As with our previous studies in Chapters 4 and 5, Hopewell's descriptions must, to some extent, be understood as characterizations. But they are a reasonable 'fit' for much of the 'inner life' of Anglicanism. For example, when Canon Jeffrey John was forced to withdraw from his nomination as bishop of Reading in the diocese of Oxford in the summer of 2003, his parting shot was to write to the local paper in Reading and state that 'love, in the end, will win'. This was his response to the chaos of potential schism and disharmony: to reassert that there was bound to be a truly 'comic' ending to a tragic farce.

For many people reading Hopewell, the denominational thinking that would most closely correspond to the comic genre (or 'gnostic negotiation', as Hopewell prefers to call it) is Quakerism. This is not an unreasonable assumption, based on Hopewell's own understanding of the world-view that he articulates. Quakerism, perhaps of all the mainstream Protestantism denominations, is the one most comfortable with universalism, interreligious dialogue and religious pluralism. Quakers have been at the forefront of placing greater emphasis on the spirituality of the individual rather than on corporate credal formulae; as a religious movement it tends to eschew articles of faith in favour of a deep commitment to 'comic' inclusiveness. However, the genre also closely resonates with the kind of idealized and slightly mystical sacramentalism that characterizes much of Anglicanism's own absorption with its (imagined) Communion. Put another way, doctrinal differences or moral incoherence will ultimately 'melt away', since the Communion is gathered around one table, sharing in one common baptism, and will be unable to resist exchanging the kiss of peace. Differences over gender, sexuality and other matters will be seen in their true light – as secondary issues that do not interfere with the primacy of the sacramental nature of the Communion.

In this regard, as Hopewell correctly points out, the comic genre is 'utterly dependable': bafflement and confusion are ultimately overcome by wisdom and love; harmony replaces discord. This is, of course, a positive and optimistic ecclesiology, which assumes a kind of 'inner energy' within the ethos that drives it, teleologically, towards its world-view. Ultimately, all in the end is harvest. Not even death can stand in the way of a mystical unity, for which, at worst, a broken Communion points us towards.

The positivism of the comic genre is, of course, only one half of the equation that shapes Anglicans' self-understanding of the Communion. The other half is more contingent and is habitually posited in irony:

> Miracles do not happen; patterns lose their design; life is unjust, not justified by transcendent forces. Trapped in an ironic world, one shrugs one's shoulders about reports of divine ultimacies and intimacies. Instead of expecting such supernatural outcomes, one embraces ones brothers and sisters in camaraderie.... (Hopewell, 1987, p. 61)

Hopewell, in developing the ironic genre, tends to put a more reductionist gloss on the world-view than many would normally be prepared to own. The genre is characteristically 'liberal' in its orientation, with a strong sympathy for organic and contextual ecclesiological models. But this does not, in my view, necessarily mean that those who inhabit the ironic world-view are likely to dismiss the realm of the supernatural, which Hopewell often assumes will be the case. That said, Hopewell's characterization of ironic ecclesiology contains many features that will resonate with Anglicans. The key motif is testing; variation leads (ultimately) to conformity. At a personal level, a situation of bondage is met with honesty and resolved through love. Socially, oppression is met by justice and resolved through the establishment of community. The focus of valued behaviour is realism and integrity. Theologically, Jesus is a 'teacher', the minister an 'enabler', the church a 'fellowship' and the Gospel 'freedom' (ibid., pp. 70–71).

In discussing this outlook, Hopewell recognizes that ironic ecclesiologies and world-views are in fact best characterized as 'cosmopolitan religion'. Living with differences is a sign of integrity. Thus, and following Wade Clark Roof, Hopewell notes that those who are most attracted to 'ironic' religion may want to avoid organized religion altogether, but tend nonetheless to be faithful church members who affirm:

> (a) the centrality of ethical principles in their meaning systems; (b) a parsimony of beliefs, few attributions of numinosity; (c) breadth of perspective; (d) piety defined as a personal search for meaning; and (e) licence to doubt. (Hopewell, 1987, p. 82)

Perhaps inevitably, this draws those with primarily ironic world-views towards a theological terrain that is packed with deep ambiguity and paradox. Within Anglicanism this tradition is perhaps best exemplified by writers such as David Jenkins, John Habgood and the early work of Richard Holloway. In working with congregations and groups where the ironic world-view dominates, one can observe how paradox is not only testing, but also persuasive and nourishing. Thus, phrases that can speak of the incarnation in angular ways (for example, Launcelot Andrewes' 'the Speechless Word', or Rowan Williams' more recent notion of the 'spastic Christ-child') will invariably absorb individuals and groups in hours of patient spiritual musings. In the ironic world-view, anomaly and paradox are givens.

Given these remarks, it is perhaps reasonable to suggest that the core proponents of the Anglican Communion are, in Hopewellian terms, comic-ironic in orientation. Or, to return to Boyer, these are just two of the 'lumps' in the soup that is Anglicanism. They anticipate a form of sacramental unity that will ultimately bear its own fruit. But they are sagacious enough to know that the path to unity is littered with pitfalls and potholes that require the mind of an empiricist rather than an idealist. Again, in Hopewellian terms, the 'model' of the church that emerges from this world-view is a combination of perspectives. On the one hand, it comprises *organicist* views: 'developing towards a final integrated reality which is unapparent in its present state' (ibid., p. 200). On the other, it is both *mechanist* and *formist*, recognizing that the church is a collectivity of structures that can be regulated and adjusted. Moreover, the church is *contextualist*, shaped by the very cultural forces that it seeks to shape. For Hopewell, the analogy of the church (or Communion in this case) as a house allows an analyst to see that

> . . . as a house within the world, 'house' emphasizes its participation in the frame of all language. Human imagination as a whole provides the particular idiomatic and narrative construction of a congregation; its members communicate by a code derived from the totality of forms and stories by which societies cohere. In such a picture . . . church culture is not reduced to a series of propositions that a credal checklist adequately probes. Rather, the congregation takes part in the nuance of and narrative of full human discourse. It persists as a recognizable storied dwelling within the whole horizon of human interpretation. (Hopewell, 1987, p. 201)

The features of this 'household of faith' in relation to its problems of ordering and identity are indeed complex, and space only permits a few brief paragraphs by way of summary. So let us begin with some questions. Can Anglicanism survive the deep and divisive arguments that seem to have rocked it for more than a quarter of a century? Women priests, women bishops, liturgical reform and gay bishops have all threatened splits and schism. So what is it that holds the church together in the midst of such public disagreement? And assuming there are some virtues, instruments or habits that provide the necessary social and ecclesial glue (or lumps in soup), can such things be appealed to again in the midst of the current divisions centred on sexuality? In addition to the comments already made on irony and comedy, three further observations come to mind.

First, Anglicanism has a rich, distinctive and historic theological tradition, being rooted in both Catholicism and Protestantism. These theological roots condition its liturgy, ecclesiology and missiology. At the same time, Anglican identity is a contested concept. Classically, it is the quintessential *via media*. The genius of Anglicanism is that it has *not* resolved its identity. It is broad yet particular, synodical, yet episcopal, Protestant, but also Catholic. One might say that all the main crises in Anglican identity stem from one party or another trying to resolve its innate ambiguity.

Second, the complexity of Anglicanism is mirrored within its structures. For example it has at least four distinct instruments of unity: the archbishop of

Canterbury, the Anglican Consultative Council, the Lambeth Conference, and the regular Meetings of the Primates. But this means that authority within the Communion is broadly and peculiarly dispersed. Culturally and theologically, Anglicanism tends to be a mediating and accommodating, rather than an imposing and authoritative, ecclesiology. The archbishop of Canterbury wields no kind of putative papal power. Globally, each Anglican province has its own distinct history, flavour, sense of purpose and mission, yet still within the broad framework of a worldwide 'family' of churches.

Third, Anglicanism has tended to conduct its theological debates through a trilateral of scripture, tradition and reason – and one might add, through well-mannered and patient exchange. Indeed, the elevation of manners within Anglicanism is a significant feature of its polity. It has therefore managed, for the most part, to retain its poise within a trilateral framework which has created space for differences to emerge, but without losing sight of mutual recognition and fostering relatively peaceful coexistence. Over the past century, with the emergence of postcolonial and modern societies, the trilateral has increasingly been understood as a quadrilateral that has had to take account of context and culture. For example, the concession to 'culture' might allow some conservative Anglicans to make allowances for polygamous practices in African churches – or at least turn a blind eye. Similarly, many American Anglicans think that the concession to culture should be similarly extended theologically, and to thinking differently about gay and lesbian people.

Theoretically, this (soup) recipe ought to be good enough to guarantee continuity of identity and existence for Anglicanism. But somehow, at least at the moment, it seems strangely inadequate. Is it the case, to paraphrase Yeats, that 'things fall apart; the centre cannot hold ... the ceremony of innocence is drowned. The best lack all conviction, [and] the worst are full of passionate intensity'? To be sure, there are many reasons why the Anglican Communion (or federation?) faces so many problems at present. But one of the main ones must surely be that Anglicanism has forgotten that it was, first and foremost, a complex and well-mannered community in which differences and ambiguities remained unresolved. Indeed, these were part of its very foundations.

Yet despite, and because of, this, Anglicanism flourished. It prospered as a church because it was possible to belong to a broad community of belief in which some liberty of conscience and practice was respected, but with enough morphological similarity to foster homogeneity. It was, in short, a community of civilized disagreement. And far from hampering itself as a body, its example invited the world to take note. It embodied plurality: you can belong to one another without always seeing eye-to-eye, and you can witness like this too, because God is bigger than 'my' church.

So, and from my own Anglican perspective, the arguments that currently disturb the soul of Anglican polity somehow need to become calmer. Only when the intense heat of the argument begins to cool can Anglicanism recover its poise and start talking and listening rather than shouting. At its best, Anglicanism is, arguably, like the English weather: an essentially temperate affair. It is often cloudy, but with some sunny intervals, and the occasional outburst of rain. It is seldom born well from a climate of extremes. Given these

remarks, we now turn to the notion of the Anglican Communion as a 'house'
or 'estate'.

## Excursion: Continuing Anglican Churches as Alternative Comedy

In describing Anglican identity, I have argued elsewhere that the Anglican
Communion can analogically be visualized as a vast mansion, replete with
Evangelical and Catholic wings (Percy, 2000, pp. 114–25). It remains a large
stately home, albeit one in which the vast rooms are now being sealed off and
converted into self-contained flats. Everyone still has the same official address
and shares the imposing exterior and frontage, but different internal relations
within the 'storied dwelling' mean that the union is not as it once was. Not only
does this analogy fit the current state of Anglicanism, but it also allows us to
briefly consider the intriguing phenomenon of Continuing Anglican Churches,
whose numbers have multiplied over the last 30 years. A Continuing Anglican
Church is, strictly speaking, one that still continues to use the Anglican 'family
name', practise various kinds of Anglican liturgy and claim Anglican
identity, but has nevertheless formally removed itself from communion with
Canterbury.

Mention of 'family names' raises an important issue about ecclesial identity:
it remains the case that very few denominations choose their own names.
'Anglicanism' is a term that was popularized by James VI of Scotland and
contains a degree of mocking irony. Similarly, 'Anabaptists' had their family
name bestowed upon them by their detractors; equally, 'Methodist' can also be
read as a dubious compliment. Yet these names have been adopted and
redeemed by their respective denominational families. Even the curious double-
barrelled (and oxymoronic?) 'Roman Catholic' is, in some sense, an externally
imposed nomenclature. 'Catholic' should mean universal and comprehensive,
but 'Roman' implies imperialist centralization and hegemonic domination. No
less of an oxymoron is the triple nomenclature 'House Church Movement'.
Again, participants in the movement have not chosen this name for themselves;
it is 'given' by the wider Christian family. But the name somehow captures the
ambiguity and potentiality of the movement.

Returning to pursuing the 'family' and 'household' analogy, the phenom-
enological problem can be outlined as follows. Continuing Anglican Churches
are often very similar in style, operation, theology and 'culture' to those they
have separated from, which might raise questions about their distinctiveness.
Therefore, for Anglicans who remain in the mansion, understanding
Continuing Anglican Churches and conducting a dialogue with them is
unlikely to be part of any normal, neat, linear process of negotiation or
reception. Granted, many of the issues that created the conditions for
separatism have become secondary over time, which suggests that, in some
cases, Anglicans may be dealing with formalized estrangement rather than
trying to undo a messy divorce or, to continue the analogy, deal with groups
that have moved out of the mansion but are still living on the family estate.
Negotiating on understanding demands evidence-based research as there is no

obvious meta-ecclesiological or 'high theological ground' that can settle issues of difference or determine relations. The very existence of Continuing Anglican Churches suggests some rather more 'fuzzy borders' for Anglican identity.

Continuing Anglican Churches that still use the Anglican 'family name' are usually doing so for 'operant' rather than 'formal' religious reasons. This means that some understanding of the reasons for cession – case-by-case – is needed if the field is to be approached with any degree of care and sensitivity. Given that the nature of Continuing Anglican Churches is a contested issue and subject to some degree of flux, any debate about Continuing Anglican Churches is ultimately about the nature of Anglicanism per se. Thus, the 'subject' of Continuing Churches should therefore not be regarded as extraneous to mainstream Anglican identity.

There are about approximately 50 different types of Continuing Anglican Churches in the USA and Canada, with a combined membership of around 82000. The larger 'denominations' within the 'family' include the Anglican Province of Christ the King (founded in 1978), with a membership of around 15000 and the Reformed Episcopal Church (founded in 1873) with 12000 members. Continuing Anglican Churches in the USA/Canada can claim a total of 966 parishes or missions, 105 dioceses, 159 bishops and 1133 priests.[1] Outside the USA and Canada, Continuing Anglican Churches exist in South Africa, India, Britain and throughout the Commonwealth. Numbers are more difficult to estimate here, but it is probable that, globally, the combined membership of Continuing Anglican Churches is at least 100000. Of these, the vast majority can be found in North America, which also boasts the greatest span of variety in terms of 'denominations'.

The causes of secession – that is, no longer being in communion with Canterbury – can be reasonably traced to two areas of dispute: reactions to liturgical reform, either because of modernization or concern about 'Anglo-Catholic' or 'Protestant' tendencies being promoted or eroded; concerns about perceived theological and ecclesiological liberalism (for example, the ordination of women to the priesthood and so on). It is rare to find a Continuing Anglican Church that does not owe its *raison d'être* to one or both of these contested arenas. Thus, many Continuing Anglican Churches typically uphold the *Book of Common Prayer* and its North American variants, and do not ordain women. An exception is the International Anglican Communion (founded in 2002), which does ordain women but adheres strictly to 'traditional' worship. However, broadly speaking, Continuing Anglican Churches are evenly divided between those that seek to uphold a more obviously Protestant version of Anglicanism (a number of whom can trace their foundation to the nineteenth century) and those of a more Anglo-Catholic persuasion that have reacted to perceived 'liberal' trends within the Episcopal Church of the USA (or ECUSA) and therefore have more recent foundations. The multiplication of *types* of Continuing Anglican Churches is

---

[1] An interesting statistic in its own right, since the ratio of stipendiary priests to bishops in the Church of England is around 100:1. In Continuing Anglican Churches it is 10:1.

the result of: internal schism, leading to separation and the formation of a new 'denomination'; and 'local' theological and ecclesiological responses (for example, the Missionary Diocese of Texas).

An ethnographic sampling of statements of faith from Continuing Anglican Churches can reveal much about their self-understanding and identity:

> ...Anglicans found it no longer possible to continue being Anglican in the 'official' Anglican Church...so they decided to continue Anglicanism outside 'official' Anglican parameters....

> We simply consider ourselves to be ordinary, conventional Anglicans who have neither added anything non-Anglican or subtracted anything....

> [We were] created to preserve, to uphold, and to transmit unimpaired, the whole catholic and apostolic Christian faith and religion as received and set forth by the Church of England in the Book of Common Prayer and the Thirty-Nine Articles of religion....

> The Independent Anglican Church of Canada is not in communion with, nor part of, the 'Continuing Anglican Movement', nor with any other 'independent Anglicans'.

> [We were created] in defense of the Catholic faith....

> We enjoy intercommunion with Forward in Faith, England....

> We do what the apostles did; we don't add or take away from what the apostles did; the 1928 BCP comes closest to what the apostles did... (Interview)

> We were formed to assure the continuity of our 'low church' liturgical life....

> [We were created because of] the lack of preaching of the Bible's strong salvation message in ECUSA....

> We were created to ensure the continuation of historic Anglican Christianity in America...[preserve] traditional Episcopal liturgy and polity...intercommunion with FIF...[use] BCP 1928, American Missal, English Missal, etc...indifferent to 39 Articles....

Hearing some of the Continuing Anglican Churches speak with their own voice enables us to see that it is 'traditionalism' that tends to unite the churches across liturgical, theological and ecclesiological spectra. Moreover, these churches do not see themselves as 'schismatic', but as 'continuing', which places them outside most conventional categories and definitions in the sociology of religion, or even within ecclesiology itself.

That said, there is an immediate problem with the term 'Continuing Anglican Churches', since it lacks any agreed value amongst users or analysts. It may be fair to describe such churches as 'neo-conservative' or 'neo-traditionalist', but this does not quite capture their diversity. For example, some of the Continuing Anglican Churches are strongly flavoured by their appeal to the idea of 'returning' – either to the Roman Catholic Church, or to a

'purer' form of Evangelical faith. So far from preserving Anglican identity, certain Continuing Anglican Churches see themselves as restorationists, and therefore as progressive.

In Hopewellian terms, it is therefore possible to conceive of Continuing Anglican Churches as a form of 'alternative comedy'. However, this comedy is unlike mainstream Anglicanism, since it lacks its irony (which in turn gives 'licence to doubt'). The union Continuing Anglican Churches seek is almost wholly beyond their means, and yet many individuals and groups persist in the belief that 'we did not leave the Anglican Communion – it left us'. In this respect, a tragic world-view is being espoused, similar to that identified in the previous chapter. This notion of each specific Continuing Anglican Church being an essentialist 'faithful remnant' is vital for the maintenance of ecclesial identity, for it leaves open the possibility of a full comic reunion, in which the discord of separatism is ultimately overcome when the errant majority turn from their ways and rejoin those who, having been ostracized, are recognized as being true and faithful. Peace, wisdom and will ultimately reunite the loose threads and filial ties.


**Further Reflections**

If Continuing Anglican Churches remain related to the wider Anglican Communion by virtue of the link established through non-ironic alternative comedy, there are further issues that can be explored through Hopewellian analysis and interpretation. For example, there may be several reasons to be hesitant in adopting the term 'Continuing Anglican Churches'. First, within the 'imagined Communion' of Anglicanism, it is commonplace to suppose that there is clarity about its ordering and definition. This is, ironically, a mechanistic ideology that finds itself located within a more organic under-standing of the church. For example, is it not the case that the Methodist Church and smaller bodies, such as the Countess of Huntingdon's Connexion, technically qualify as progressive (rather than neo-conservative) Continuing Anglican Churches? Second, where does the call for a Third Province fit in with the definition of a Continuing Anglican Church? Come to that, what is one to make of the small number of churches that have moved themselves into a more semi-detached relationship with their bishop and diocese, such as St Helen's Bishopsgate in London? In both cases, there is a desire to retain the Anglican label, but not to be in communion with Canterbury – at least for the time being. Third, certain churches have actively encouraged 'church planting', sometimes collaboratively with the bishop/diocese, but this has not always been the case. Again, there seems to be some toleration for the idea that there can be an Anglican 'missionary' church within an existing parish.

Allied to these concerns, there are also some intriguing micro-capital issues to be considered. In both North America and Britain, the ownership of the church property can have a significant bearing on the nature and extent of schism or the formation of a Continuing Church. Recent cases in the dioceses of Philadelphia (USA) and Worcester (UK) come to mind. In both situations, a

priest declared himself to be no longer in communion with his bishop. In North America, because the congregation owned the church property and plant, and the bishop's powers of sequestration were therefore limited, a settlement was possible. In contrast, Charles Raven, the priest-in-charge of a potentially schismatic congregation in Kidderminster would have needed to renew his licence (and therefore reaffirm his canonical obedience) to remain in post – and the congregation did not own 'its' church buildings.

Having said this, surely the challenge of St Helen's Bishopsgate to the diocese of London, and to communion with Canterbury, should be looked at afresh? It should be obvious that, even with the economic and authority structures of the Church of England, it may be possible to operate like a Continuing Anglican Church yet remain within the fold of Anglicanism. As we began to see in the previous chapter, under the umbrella of Reform, or other comparable organizations, St Helen's Bishopsgate can operate an autonomous ministry that actively opposes the Church of England and declares itself to be out of communion with the archbishop of Canterbury. In other words, a continuing schism/church *within* a Communion is a viable option for some congregations, just as much as a schism/church *without* a Communion.

It should now be clear why a Hopewellian approach to this knotty problem is a reasonable way of exploring and assessing Continuing Anglican Churches. First, the evidence-based research relating to those churches that are happy to identify themselves as Continuing Anglican Churches suggests that the definition and category of the term is ambiguous. Second, by allowing individual Continuing Anglican Churches to speak with their own voice, we can see that, in terms of aspiration, they are more than mere sects. They are neo-conservative in character, but also 'comically restorationist' in tone and, in some respects, radical and inventive as much as they may be counted as traditionalist. Third, we can also see that beyond the penumbra of 'obvious' Continuing Anglican Churches, there are a host of situations (that is, schisms remaining *within* churches) that closely relate to the phenomenon we are exploring and assessing. In short, the study of Continuing Anglican Churches does not easily lend itself to 'pure' meta-theological assessment or to the making of 'blueprint' ecclesiological judgements. The very subject requires a combination of grounded research, interdisciplinarity and theological reflection.

So how are we to make some sense of this complex ecclesial landscape – the very *terroir*[2] of Anglicanism, where habits, customs, rubrics, liturgy, ethos and world-view can clearly survive (and flourish?) outside the 'official' Communion? James Gordon Melton's work talks of 'family types' in relation to ecclesiological categorization. A useful analogy, it permits us to recognize a morphological resemblance between churches, even where divorce or estrangement has taken place. Thus, in claiming a nomenclature – in this case,

---

[2] A Gallic word for which there is no obvious English counterpart, *terroir* refers to a combination of ethos and context. Used by sommeliers, it encompasses soil, climate, geography, tradition and human input.

'Anglican' – we can see that the label continues to be invested with appeal, signifies roots and continues to construct identity. So building on the family and mansion analogies, three points can now be made.

First, the nineteenth and twentieth centuries have seen a number of congregations abandoning their respective Evangelical or Catholic wings altogether. Some have continued to use the Anglican nomenclature, and, indeed, to replicate as much of the ecclesial *terroir* of the mansion as possible. Thus, the *Book of Common Prayer* is retained, the 39 Articles remain fundamental, and so forth. But, in every other way, the congregation has become separatist.

Second, there are congregations who wish to remain within the original mansion, family or household, but now desire to seal off the wing from contact with the centre. Separate entrances to the wing are created (for example, 'Flying Bishops',[3] alternative Episcopal oversight and so on). Continued occupancy is an uneasy truce between the centre and wing, and questions of capital, ownership and financial responsibility have yet to be tested. But the seeds of developing Continuing Anglican Churches *within* the Communion (mansion) are already present.

Third, the analogies allow us to think not only of the Anglican family and mansion, but also of the broader and more extensive 'estate' of Anglicanism, which might include the Church of South India, and perhaps even Methodism. In other words, in this third option, there is some recognition that the very boundaries of Anglicanism are not as precise as one might perhaps hope. Now this is not meant to be a (cheap) ecumenical remark, which fails to take seriously the differences between denominations. Rather, it is intended to acknowledge some part of the generative power of culture (that is, national identity, history and so on) which has some hand in shaping denominations and their interrelation. Moreover, it suggests that wherever we locate ecclesial differences – and this may be in doctrine – there are other, subtle causes of fracture and fissure that might have to be faced. This may be personality (a key factor in certain Continuing Churches that divide, then form two or three 'denominations' as the result of a single split), class (I use an elitist analogy intentionally to underline this point, to remind Anglicans of one possible contributory factor in Methodism), and gender (which may be repositioned as authority or order).

In summary, and despite the ambiguities I have highlighted, we can say that Continuing Anglican Churches are those that have consciously chosen to leave the Anglican Communion and have elected to identify their life as being separate from that of the See of Canterbury. They have taken a decision to leave, even if they deploy a reverse comic narrative: 'they left us – but we expect all true believers to eventually join us'. Those churches that continue within the

---

[3] 'Flying Bishops' – or, to give them their proper title, 'Provincial Episcopal Visitors' – are bishops set aside by the church to minister to those congregations that cannot accept the priestly ministry of women. They are formally recognized by the Church of England, and a number of Anglican provinces have now constructed informal arrangements for such congregations.

Anglican Communion, and yet wish to be hermetically separated within the tradition, can be identified as *potential* Continuing Anglican Churches, but are otherwise pursuing that honoured course within mainstream Protestant ecclesiology that is normally termed 'loyal dissent'. Inevitably, where ecclesial unity in North America is primarily achieved through *confessional* harmony and agreement, the number of Continuing Anglican Churches rises in direct proportion to the number of ecclesial spats.

In the Church of England, however, ecclesial unity is primarily maintained through *structural* and *organizational* apparatus. What makes the study of the Anglican Communion so fascinating in the light of Hopewell's work is the extent to which individual provinces throughout the world reflect this dualistic heritage. Furthermore, if individual churches in the Church of England can opt out of structural and organizational obligations and apparatus (and it appears that some are already attempting this), then it is possible to envisage the emergence of an even larger number and range of Continuing Anglican Churches that will eventually become an adjunct of the Church of England.

Given these remarks, we now turn to a brief consideration of a parallel (and unavoidable) subject that necessarily accompanies an exploration and assessment of Continuing Anglican Churches, namely the nature of Communion. Thus far, we have spoken of the Anglican Communion as though it were obvious and coherent or, at least in comic terms, as a body with a 'plot that shares a common desire for a happy and reconciled ending'. However, I wish to suggest that this is not quite the case and that an important factor in addressing Anglicanism and its offshoots lies in beginning with a more realistic understanding of the nature and reality of the Anglican Communion.

**The Cultural Nature of Anglican Communion**

'Communion' in relation to the worldwide Anglican Church is primarily a postcolonial construction of reality. That is, the present sense of 'Communion', whatever meaning is attached to it, is unquestionably a descendant of a more imperialist ecclesiology. The gradual colonization of territory in the seventeenth to nineteenth centuries often meant that it was the Church of England that was 'established' in British dominions. The emergence of the American Episcopal Church after the Revolution of 1776 was the first indication that Anglicanism could retain its shape without reference to political establishment or monarchical power. It is no accident that the first Episcopal bishop in the USA, Bishop Samuel Seabury, received his consecration through Scottish Episcopalians, who were likewise not established, although they remained loyal to the British Crown.

Ownership of the colonial past and postcolonial present is an important step in understanding the evolution of the Anglican Communion. Inevitably, in meta-ecclesiological constructions of reality, it is tempting to assume that the very idea of 'communion' was somehow the starting point for worldwide Anglicanism. True, it may be possible, using Hooker and other Anglican theologians, to construct such an argument. But rather like orthodox doctrine,

it is important to understand that such a thing normally emerges at the *end* of a series of complex negotiations and compromises, often taking account of several different understandings along the way. Orthodox doctrine does not arrive created, *ex nihilo*, as it were. It does not *commence* debates that then become more convoluted and complex as time goes on. Christian orthodoxy is the focused, end point of several types of debate, not the origin of arguments in which a pre-existent 'pure' ideology is sullied in the process of reception. Similarly, the proper way to understand the Anglican Communion is to see it as the default matrix for provincial relationality, following the collapse of the British Empire and its mutation into the British Commonwealth. Dependents became partners; colonies became member states; where there was once patronage, equivocal relationships begin to emerge.

It is important to appreciate this, since there can be a lazy assumption, sometimes made by Anglicans, that 'our' or 'the' Communion only differs from the Roman Catholic Church in terms of size and scope, whereas in reality the sources and notions of the Communion are quite different. The 'Communion' to which Anglicans belong has fuzzy edges. It embraces churches that are not Anglican (for example, those in the Porvoo Agreement), the Church of South India which is krypto-Anglican, and, at various levels, recognizes and affirms the ministry and authority of a wide variety of other churches. Allied to the 'fuzzy edges', the lines of authority are not as clear as those enjoyed by other denominations. In some provinces it is possible to be doctrinally deviant or innovative (depending on your point of view), but removal from office (say, as a priest) is only possible when canon law has been breached. Anglican ecclesiology, in both its principal monarchical and non-monarchical expressions (that is, English and American Anglicanism) protects the liberty of individual conscience to a remarkable degree. The tradition of 'loyal dissent' is tolerated and can sometimes be honoured.

This leads us to state that the idea of an Anglican Communion is not primarily about a 'static' state of being. 'Communion' is a noun, to be sure. But, in Anglicanism, the term should mainly be understood as a verb; in other words, 'in communion with' someone or something. The stress is on the 'in' and the 'with'; 'communion' is the action. It is not a description of an ideal, static state of being; rather, it describes a quality of relationship. Understood like this, we can see that there is a tension in Anglican self-understanding in relation to identity. To borrow once again a distinction from Clifford Geertz, there is a difference between *ethos* and *world-view*. An ethos is the way things are – the actual ecclesial *terroir*. A world-view, on the other hand, is what the churches could or should be. When considering the Anglican Communion, we are immediately caught between the tension of ethos and world-view, of verb and noun. To talk of the Anglican Communion is, in reality, to talk of the activity of being in communion *in* or *with*; the Communion is yet to come.

The reason that this reflection is important for the study of Anglican churches is simple enough. If the Anglican Communion is, in reality, a kind of 'serious fiction', an imagined ironic or comic community replete with 'fuzzy' edges, porous boundaries and the like, then how is it held together? Structurally, we have already pointed to the four instruments of unity, namely

the archbishop of Canterbury, the Anglican Consultative Council, the Meeting of Primates and the Lambeth Conference. But this does not suggest to us a 'Communion' in the sense that Roman Catholics might mean the term. Thus, coherence and control is not there in the same way for Anglicans as it is for Roman Catholics. For 'Communion' in Anglicanism, therefore, read 'federation'.

The use of the word 'federation' is not meant to imply that the idea of Communion has no currency for Anglicans. Clearly, it does. But federations can take many forms, and, in the case of Anglicanism, I want to suggest that the liturgical, doctrinal and ecclesial unity makes for far more than a morphological similarity across provinces. At the same time, the reality of self-determination in individual provinces and dioceses cannot be overlooked (consider Sydney and New Westminster for example). The acid test for a Communion is whether or not it would expel churches or provinces it held to be deviant. But excommunication is an uncommon phenomenon and language for Anglicans, and all the signs are that the ecclesiology is characterized by a preference for looser ties to maintain a degree of unity, rather than stricter criteria for remaining within the Communion. Put more definitively, Anglicans seem to prefer being 'in communion' with a variety of ecclesiological and theological positions than having a secure sense of belonging 'within *the* Communion' with its clear implication that there are certain lines that, when crossed, automatically render individual congregations, dioceses or provinces to be in breach of order and ecclesial polity.

Here we might ask whether this is any different from (or worse than) the Orthodox Church. Orthodoxy has similarly complex issues to negotiate. In the USA, for example, there is a range of different Orthodox traditions – Russian, Romanian, Greek, Serbian, to name but a few. But these congregations may be divided between those that still look to Europe for their priests and bishops and those that have developed along more North American lines. Thus, a recently appointed Romanian Metropolitan for North America only has authority over those congregations that continue to relate to Bucharest. His authority does not extend to Romanian Orthodox churches, which are self-governing within the USA and Canada, although relationships between the two tend to be reasonably (but not always) cordial.

The fact that the Orthodox Churches (the plural is important) can tolerate diversity and a certain degree of competition may be something that Anglicanism can learn from. After all, in speaking of an Anglican Communion, or even a federation, it must be acknowledged that one is really describing a range of Anglican Churches, with at least as much diversity as that found in Orthodoxy. Moreover, the lack of clear, central power in Orthodoxy suggests that Anglicanism may not have as much to fear as it supposes from those churches that keep the Anglican 'title', whilst at the same time trying to keep their distance. As with so many things in ecclesiology, the issue revolves around power and ownership. And it must be clear that there are many more 'Anglicans' than those who are actually in communion with Canterbury.

This last point leads us to make a number of supplementary points that relate to this discussion. First, Anglicans must be wary of being tainted by (the

fiction of) perfectionism. It is important to remember and respect the cultural forces that have both generated and shaped its polity. The activity of God – even when it can be said to be *actus purus* – is inevitably mediated through agencies that are less than perfect. Notions of 'perfected' ecclesiology are a danger to both the 'parent' denomination and to the rebelling 'child'.

Second, there is usually some scope for pastoral and ecclesial pragmatism in reception. A number of cathedrals now admit ministers from other denominations as ecumenical canons. Whilst the Anglican Church may be a very long way off from recognizing the ministry of Continuing Anglican Churches in such a way (and it must be repeated that such invitations, may, in any case, be scorned), there are nonetheless conventional modes for establishing rapport that are somewhere between the local and the diocesan.

Third, there has always been space for 'loyal dissent' within the Church of England and the wider Anglican Church. Hooker's *Laws*, the covert attacks on Anglicanism's Puritan strain and the desire for compliancy coupled to diversity all point to a church whose identity has been contested in every generation since the Reformation. Yet it is important to recognize that those traditions that press, probe and question the identity and boundaries of Anglicanism have often nourished and enriched the church at the same time. Sometimes the art of practical ecclesiology is in retaining rebellion, not in silencing it.

Fourth, there is a fundamental ecclesial reality about being 'divorced', yet 'still related'. As an analogy, it provides an important 'fit' for Anglican–Roman Catholic relations, and relations between the branches of the Orthodox Church. The recognition of this aspect in modern ecclesiology raises some teasing questions about dialogue, continuing relations and their restoration and mediation between once hostile parties.

Fifth, Anglican 'independentism' seems to be increasingly difficult to police and control. Some recognition that Anglicanism is more of a federation than a Communion may help the Anglican Church to live a little easier with its own reality and identity. Instead of feeling (almost all the time) that it is a weak Communion, it may begin to appreciate that it is, in fact, a strong federation.

Sixth, we should note that the language of 'Communion' creeps into ecumenical dialogue and thinking where it is very probably unwarranted. For example, it is common practice to refer to the 'Porvoo Communion'. Indeed, this is how those churches within are described in successive *The Church of England Yearbooks*. However, the reality of Porvoo is that it is an understanding of federalism and a mutual recognition of ministries at which a significant level of intercommunion takes place. In other words, and to repeat, a Communion is not *a* static, easily identifiable body. There is no 'a', because communion is a state of relations and being (that is, *with* or *in*). There can be *some* communion between churches or individuals, but churches that talk of being *the* or *a* Communion are expressing a world-view (that is, what could or should be); they are seldom describing their ethos (the ways things are). Thus, the 'Anglican Communion of Churches' or the 'Communion of Anglican Churches' is a far better nomenclature than 'The Anglican Communion'. Indeed, the gradual metamorphosis of Anglicanism into denominationalism seems to be almost inevitable (Swatos, 1979).

### Comic Endings: What is the Future for the Anglican Communion?

The late and lamented theologian, Robert Carroll, once described the Anglican way of doing theology as 'the Dodo's incorporative principle – a means by which everyone wins'. Anglicans, in trying to sort out doctrinal differences amongst themselves, were always arguing about the precise weight that should be given to scripture, tradition, reason and culture. The ground rules for such debates always guaranteed inclusion for participants and most reasonable points of view – even those one might passionately oppose. All sides in any debate could always claim a moral victory, since final decisions were seldom reached. It is precisely this kind of ecclesiology that has made Anglicanism – rather like a dodo – such a rare bird for several centuries. But is the rarity and novelty of Anglicanism about to slide into self-inflicted extinction?

Certainly, the archbishop of Canterbury has an unenviable task in trying to hold together some hotly held competing convictions. Liberals were calling on him to support the choice of an openly gay bishop, partly to confirm the identity of the church as being relevant and inclusive. Conservatives wanted him to offer unequivocal condemnation, claiming that a gay bishop was a departure from all scriptural and ecclesial norms. It is a no-win situation for the archbishop of Canterbury. Leading the Church of England, it is often said, is like trying to herd cats. Precocious and unbiddable creatures, they roam where they please. The job of leading the Anglican Communion is, therefore, many times more difficult. The Episcopal Church in America will go one way; Anglicans in Sydney and Nigeria will go another.

It seems unlikely, given what we have already said about Anglicanism as a denomination that expresses the comic genre that there is hope for a harmonious future in which discord is ultimately banished. But comedy needs to be rooted in reality, and, in Hopewellian terms, this is where an ecclesial synergy between irony and comedy can come into its own. The comedy can imagine a future together; irony can face the despair of separatism. In this respect, four points about the future of the Anglican Communion need to be made here.

First, it must be accepted that the worldwide Anglican Communion is really a construction of the British Empire that has evolved into a more equitable Commonwealth or federation in the postcolonial era. The Anglican Church is undoubtedly global, but it may now be too diverse to be centrally or collegially governed in a manner that guarantees unequivocal unity.

Second, 'overlapping' or 'extended' episcopal oversight must be possible in a church that has always valued a degree of pluralism. In a 'glocal' world, geographical boundaries mean less and less; congregations and churches are increasingly related by their shared affinities and agreed moral coherence. So models of episcopacy that lean on Constantine or Cyprian are less attractive today, especially in a church that is deeply infused with a democratic spirit, infected by consumerism and choice and has, in any case, always respected dissent and wallowed in differences.

Third, Anglicanism is not, and never has been, one vast 'catholic' continent. It has always been a kind of archipelago – a connection of provincial islands

that shares doctrinal, liturgical and cultural aspects. The real power of the archbishop of Canterbury and the Church of England has been waning since the American Anglicans got their own bishop (from Scotland) in the eighteenth century. But Anglicans should remember that such 'schisms' have (so far) never proved fatal.

Fourth, Anglican leaders may like to reflect on the virtues of Anglican elasticity and malleability. It is a very adaptive type of church and it ought to be able to cope with quietly dropping the chimera of 'Communion' and realizing that its identity lies in being more like a 'family' of churches. The 'Anglican family name' could, in future, be used rather like the Baptist family name. The basic essence would be shared and would continue, but the prefix ('American', 'Southern', 'Reformed', 'Strict and Particular' and so forth) would indicate the flavouring.

Whatever Anglicans decide to do, it is now clear that the worldwide Anglican Church already has too many different styles of expression and different emphases of belief to enable it to be governed centrally or collegially. But a degree of separation doesn't necessarily mean schism, let alone divorce. Indeed, a slight loosening of the ties could help the Anglican churches. Those family members that want the space 'to be themselves' should perhaps be allowed to individuate. Since 77 million members in 38 provinces all living under one roof might be a bit too stifling for the twenty-first century, it might be worthwhile exploring the possibility of developing a 'neighbourhood' or 'family' of 'semi-detached' Anglican churches instead of one single monolithic Communion. Arguably, now more than ever, Anglicans should try to be mature and realistic about the real state of the Anglican Church: instead of trying to patch things up through fear of the unknown, we should try to face the future with faith. Specifically, can Anglicans agree to live apart, but still be friends and neighbours – at least for the sake of its children? Such an ironic– comic turn should not be beyond the grasp of an Anglican Communion that combines humour, realism and hope in equal measure.

## Concluding and Unscientific Postscript: Quadripolar Anglicanism

Ultimately, Anglicanism is a faith that is formed by worship, prayer, the scriptures and an ecclesial practice that is, at once, local and catholic. It is a religiously suffused and compassionate interwovenness of faith, order, sociality and difference. It is also an extraordinarily optimistic expression of Christianity that anticipates its world-view through its ethos. Faithfully conceived, Anglicanism is a multidimensional quadripolar ecclesial system that engages its adherents in faith through a rich matrix of particularities. For example, the four instruments of unity (the Meeting of the Primates, the Anglican Consultative Council, the archbishop of Canterbury and the Lambeth Conference) link with the Lambeth quadrilateral (that is, scripture, tradition, reason and the historic episcopate).

Through using Hopewell's insights as an analytical and interpretative agent to read the Anglican Communion, we can add a third dimension to this

equation. Hopewell's four genres or world-views – ironic, comic, tragic and romantic – permit the Communion to be positioned within the wider global ecclesial milieu. Specifically, this chapter has explored Anglicanism as an ironic–comic world-view. In Chapter 8 we saw how a Conservative Evangelical form of Anglicanism can be understood as 'tragic'. And in Chapter 7 I explored the romantic culture of contemporary revivalism. This allows me to suggest that Anglicanism, faithfully conceived, is also an expression of the full Hopewellian quadripolar ecclesial system, in which the ample range and depth of world-views are allowed representation within a system of trust and hope. Indeed, using Hopewell, we can suggest that the inherent 'tensions' between the romantic, comic, tragic and ironic corners of Anglican world-views are better off when they face one another in tension (but with respect), rather than being apart in self-imposed ghettoes of certainty.

A Communion, then, is a complex body immersed in the complexity of the world, in which all seek to participate in God's purposes for a wide range of reasons. The world-views of the Hopewellian quadrilateral suggests four more corners that necessarily exert some moral force on the shaping of the ethos. How the world could or should be, to an extent, suggests how the world already is. Anglicanism is, then, a kind of practical idea that embodies how people might be together. It is not an abstract idea, and nor is it general. It is, rather, a form of knowledge that is optimistic about the future itself, precisely because it is founded on the conviction that Anglicanism is a form of faith that holds, possesses and shapes people within the dynamic life of God, but in ways that liberate rather than constrain. Part of its genius is its (ironic) attachment to paradox, especially located in ecclesiology (that is, *via media* – Catholic and Protestant) and theologically (for example, the doctrine of the incarnation – humanity and divinity).

We can also say that what singles out Anglicanism for particular attention, as a denomination, is its sheer optimism. This, as I have suggested, is primarily a 'comic' outlook, but one that is rooted in a notion of being bound up in God's future, and a particular view of reconciled humanity and sociality, rather than specific self-belief. But within Hopewellian quadripolar Anglicanism, the optimism is tempered by other particular expressions of Anglican life. For example, those of a 'tragic' hue would see sin as an inextricable (outgrown) part of human nature. But in the broader Anglican compass, the comic and ironic world still prevails strongly, at least in the northern hemisphere and developed world. Thus, 'sin' is essentially regarded as an *infection* of human nature (not as intrinsic to it) and could ultimately be banished. However, the moral optimism of Anglicanism is not habitually constituted through the moral certainty that might be anticipated in other ecclesial traditions.

Alternatively, to locate these remarks within Anglican spirituality, one could consider the synthesis of sources that Anglicans habitually draw upon to constitute and shape their inner life. The pastoral optimism of George Herbert comes to mind. Equally, the spiritual writings of Donne, Stillingfleet, Andrewes and Waterland would also serve as examples, to pick just one rich seam of Anglican expression. But even outside the main corpus of specifically Anglican writing, Julian of Norwich's theological mysticism would represent a typically

optimistic outlook that shapes many types of Anglican spirituality. 'All shall be well; and all manner of things shall be well' is an example of 'classic comedy' set within the normative Anglican cultural nexus.

Thus, the hope vested in the future by most Anglicans means that the trust placed in the present, is, perhaps, a little more conditional. The English fondness for inchoate Pelagianism, which is hardly a precise or explicit form of faith-practice, is at the same time a remarkably resilient form of modern Christian discipleship. Ultimately, it is a form of Christian faith that values deep, penetrating conversations, and is also prayerful in the midst of diverse local communities. Globally, Anglicanism is at once romantic, tragic and ironic – differently shaped in each local, regional and ecclesial context. Granted, we now know, using Hopewell, that whichever 'story' of God individuals participate in, it will most likely shape their ecclesiology and missiology. But the three-dimensional quadripolar system that is Anglicanism seems to be especially capable of holding individuals and communities in debates of considerable import and tension. United through mystical and sacramental union, Anglicanism is therefore a model of engaged polity for a complex sociality. It is a credal faith, where beliefs can be affirmed, but also doubted. But it is not a confessional church in which membership is conditional upon precise agreement with articles and statements. Despite the moral and ecclesial internal difficulties that global Anglicanism encounters, it is a faith that foresees its future optimistically. Its strength lies in its apparent weakness; its unity in its diversity; its coherence in its difference; its shape in its diffusiveness; its hope in a degree of faithful doubt; its energy in passionate coolness. It embodies 'feint conviction'; it practises 'truthful duplicity'; it is Protestant and Catholic. Like a classic Shakespearian comedy, the Anglican Communion seems to be mired within dissipation and disunity; but it ultimately anticipates resolution, reconciliation and a truer deepening of relationships. It is comic and ironic:

> We came into the world like brother and brother;
> And now let's go hand in hand, not one before the other.
> (*Comedy of Errors*, V, i)

> All yet seems well; and if it end so meet,
> The bitter part, more welcome is the sweet....
> (*All's Well That Ends Well*, V, iii)

# Conclusion

# Authentic Engagement

Part of the burden of this book has been to explore the two main faces of theological and ecclesiological engagement with contemporary culture. The first kind is constituted through an interlocking and combative encounter. Niebuhr would identify this as the 'Christ against culture' perspective, and we have explored, at the more sophisticated end of the spectrum, Radical Orthodoxy as just one example of a theology that attempts to engage with (but then overcome) culture. A second kind, normally identified as more liberal, and in Niebuhrian terms as the Christ for culture, sees the Christianity–culture debates as an interrelated binding covenant or commitment. The work of Lieven Boeve (explored in Chapter 3) was used to exemplify this position. Mediating between these two positions (extreme characterizations, granted) was David Martin's work, which along with Mudge, Healy and others, was held to be a form of sociologically informed ecclesiology that was best placed to engage with culture in a theologically discerning manner.

Within these positions, there are of course differences of emphasis. For example, there are at least two varieties of conservative engagement that vie for pre-eminence. One the one hand, a traditionalist position might make its appeal on the basis of how things used to be (or at least deemed to be). In such thinking, it is normally imagined that the culture of modernity has gone too far and that Christianity's interests would be best served by returning to a form of Christendom. Still within the conservative spectrum, another view may accept the reality of secular and modern culture, but seek to engage with it in ways that are tenacious and critical. Both positions here would be anti-liberal to some degree, but would seek to pursue the Christianity–culture debate in rather different ways. However, there is an in-built paradox with these positions. Whilst holding fast, on the one hand, to the immutability of the Christian tradition, these theological strategies also assume a degree of reflexivity in application, hermeneutics and identity. Similarly, the more 'liberal' positions that attempt to negotiate the nexus of the Christianity–culture debate show little sign of being truly anti-foundationalist. The paradox of the different types of theological and ecclesiological engagement with culture is that more unties than divides them. Each position appears to accept the need for reflexivity and foundationalism. Each, in addressing, engaging or critiquing culture, inevitably inculcates some aspect of that same culture. Furthermore, each ecclesiological or theological position that we have discussed can also, to some extent, also be understood culturally.

It is partly for this reason that the concentration of this book has rested with a focus on the concrete church. As André Dumas notes in his commentary on Bonhoeffer:

> The Church starts from what actually happens when Jesus Christ takes form as community. But the event of Jesus Christ is also the advent of a communal being and not simply an individual existential encounter. Revelation does not only come *to* the community; it takes place *within* the community. (Dumas, 1971, p. 108)

Christianity is, of course, bound to paradox; indeed, the faith revels in it. Its major doctrines (for example, the incarnation) are attempts to hold or fuse together seemingly contradictory positions, understandings or statements. Correspondingly, in its theological engagement with culture, there is something of an incarnational and sacramental paradigm which is itself rooted in the revelation of God, who is revealed both through the ordinary and the extraordinary, the natural and the supernatural, and in agents whose 'nature' (whether ordinary or transformed), are necessarily contestable. The paradoxical natures of the two main forms of theological engagement with culture are an expression of the unresolved and unsettled nature of Christianity. Thus, the church is the body of Christ in one sense, but the hope of the coming of the kingdom of God, and of the return of Christ, suggests that the church habitually lives between the tension of the present, and of the ultimacy of God's future.

When facing the paradoxes of engagement, which naturally arise from the paradoxes of the Christian tradition, I have sought to show that paying attention to the concrete church, stories and contemporary culture can result in a deeper form of theological reflection. The chapters in this book have sought to show a rich theoretical practical theology that can combine the two faces of engagement and, in so doing, restore some sense of public theology as a critical–affirming discourse that is engaged with/to contemporary culture and can also illuminate the potential for a sociologically informed ecclesiology. Indeed, the focus on culture seems to demand this, as religious expressions and institutions within contemporary society appear to be mutating at a rate that requires a significantly higher level of practical and theoretical engagement from theologians and ecclesiologists. It is partly for this reason that the sequencing of the parts and chapters in this book has been so important. Part I explored the Christianity and culture debate through various problems and theological strategies. Part II sought to narrate a vision for theology and theological education that might be more hospitable to this debate. Part III introduced the idea undertaking ecclesiology through a series of concrete studies that, each in their turn, took sociology, ethnography, anthropology and cultural studies seriously. 'Reading' religion as 'culture' can bring some advantages to theology, not least of which is 'seeing ourselves as others see us': it can help prevent (an all too common) ecclesiological self-deception.

However, I have also tried to be careful *not* to privilege social sciences or cultural studies over and against theology. The argument in this book is for fusion and dialogue, not domination. It is borne out of the recognition, ceded by Berger many years ago, that even if we begin our study of the church from an entirely human perspective, we soon run into what he calls 'signals of transcendence'. As Macquarrie points out, this is not an alien world, but

simply a deeper dimension of the one we are already immersed in; it is merely a journey from the 'natural' to the 'supernatural' (Macquarrie, 1997, p. 161). Sacramental material is ordinary material – bread, wine, oil, water (or even marriage). But in the hands of another, and in a different context, these same ordinary agents become 'doors to the sacred'. They are utterly ordinary elements and yet infused with mystery – the 'outward and visible sign of an inward grace' (Macquarrie, 1997 p. 5: cf. Martos, 1981).

That said, there is no escaping the other kinds of paradoxes we have sought to explore. Witness the gap between the ideal and real church, between the concrete church and the church triumphant, and between formal and operant religion. Increasingly, the Christianity–culture 'problem' lies in the gaps, and this can lead to a problem of authenticity and credibility for a church that is founded on being ultimate and truthful, yet is also temporal and human. As we explored in Chapter 1, such insights seem to be confirmed at grassroots level when studying almost any denomination, including Roman Catholicism. For example, an American Roman Catholic priest in an interview with *The New Yorker* magazine states that:

> People today are looking for *authenticity*, not just some kind of Catholicism where you go in on Sunday and punch your card, performing your obligation...they are looking for a framework for their lives, inspiration to go on, to be decent...to be good citizens and good people. (*The New Yorker*, 2 September 2002, p. 54)

At the same time, I have also sought to give due recognition to the fact that practices shape beliefs, and religious beliefs also shape practice. In any theology of culture, the infusion of religion within culture (and vice versa) must be given its proper due. As Tanner notes:

> ...religious beliefs are a form of culture, inextricably implicated in the material practices of daily social living on the part of those who hold them...in the concrete circumstances in which beliefs are lived...actions, attitudes, and interests are likely to be as much infiltrated and informed by the beliefs one holds as beliefs are to be influenced by actions, attitudes and interests.... (Tanner, 1992, p. 9)

But lest this sounds too arid, it is worth recalling the attention given to narrativity in Part III. As we saw here, doctrines can be 'dramatic scripts' which Christians perform and by which they are performed. Doctrines 'provide a scripted code for the motions of a Christian's life in much the same way that broader cultural codes and linguistic patterns structure the self' (Volf and Bass, 2002, p. 75). In other words, doctrines practise us; practices are not just things that Christians do in the light of doctrine: 'practices are what we become as we are set in motion in the space of doctrine' (ibid.). In this sense, we are once again close to Lindbeck's theory of theology – its performative dimension as something that is 'cultural–linguistic': it (that is, doctrine, belief and so on) 'gains power and meaning insofar as it is embodied in the total gestalt of community life and action' (Lindbeck, 1984, p. 36). But there is an irony here both for the theologian and for the church. For in gaining an understanding of

how the world beliefs and practice begin to cohere, one immediately sees that they, in fact, do not. As Tanner says:

> Christian practices do not in fact require (1) much explicit understanding of beliefs that inform and explain their performance, (2) agreement upon such matters among the participants, (3) strict delimitation of codes for action, (4) systematic consistency among beliefs or actions, or (5) attention to their significance that isolates them from a whole host of non-Christian commitments. More often than not, Christian practices are instead quite open-ended in the sense of being undefined in their exact ideational dimensions and in the sense of being always in the process of re-formation in response to new circumstances.... (Tanner, in Volf and Bass, 2002, p. 229).

So, in the light of our theological study of culture, what are Christian practices and beliefs? I take them to be 'resonances of God's engagement with the world' (Volf and Bass, 2002, p. 260). And, in this respect, we might then want to argue that theology should always be in the service of practice and belief – something to do with 'real life', the 'concrete church' and the context of 'operant' or 'vernacular' religion. It is here that the practical theologian will find individuals and communities 'working out their own salvation' (Phil. 2: 12).

It now seems appropriate to turn back to practical theology and its task. Yust reminds us that the cultivation of practical wisdom (*phronesis*) remains one of the primary tasks for the seminary and the church: 'not knowing our tradition leaves us confused; not passing it on creatively and critically transformed identifies us with the past and leaves us closed off to the present' (Yust, 2002, p. 239). So, making sense of religious life is something which practical theology can really use to help inform the church about its identity and life. Similarly, Browning calls the church and theology to account when he writes that:

> Theology can be practical if we bring practical concerns to it from the beginning. The theologian does not stand before God, Scripture and the historic witness of the church like an empty slate or Lockean tabula rasa ready to be determined, filled up, and then plugged into a concrete practical situation. A more accurate description goes like this. We come to the theological task with questions shaped by the secular and religious practices in which we are implicated – sometimes uncomfortably. These practices are meaningful or theory-laden. (Browning, 1991, p. 2)

Thus, theologians have to learn that they cannot rely on theological blueprints to determine how congregations could or should be in contemporary culture. In this respect, practical theology needs to work with fields such as Congregational Studies in helping the church to become exegetes of the text of the congregation. And, as Yust reminds us, this requires engagement with 'several social science disciplines ... [so that they can] describe congregational life in its thickness' (Yust, 2002, p. 241). The epiphany seems to lead towards what Clark Williamson describes as a 'conversational theology':

The purpose of [conversational] theology is to enter into conversation with such questions [about what we ought to do and why], to interpret the Christian faith in relation to the context in which we live, and to interpret that context in the light of the Christian faith, so that we can...have a conversation...about what God gives and calls us to be and do in this time and place.... Theology is...a practical wisdom...we are not finished with any theological point until we can talk about the difference it makes to how we see things and to what we intend to do.... (Williamson, 1999, pp. 2–8)

Quite so. And this leads us to agree with Roberts, who argues that theology itself, and most especially practical theology, is 'a practical process of discerning God's will...a community activity requiring conversation and interaction' (Roberts, 2002, p. 184). Moreover, this process is tried, tested, evaluated and put to use through the praxis of the church. Here, and in prayerful communion with the Creator and Redeemer, practical theology becomes a transforming activity for both the church and the world.

# Bibliography

Abrecht, P. (1961), *The Churches and Rapid Social Change*, London: SCM Press.

Althaus-Reid, M. (2003), *The Queer God*, London: Routledge.

Alves, C. (1972), *The Christian in Education*, London: SCM.

Ammerman, N. (1997), *Congregation and Community*, New Brunswick, NJ: Rutgers University Press.

Ammerman, N., Carroll, J., Dudley, C. and McKinney, W. (1998), *Studying Congregations*, Nashville, TN: Abingdon Press.

Anderson, B. (1983), *Imagined Communities: Reflections on the Origin and Spread of Nationalism*, London: Verso.

Archbishops' Council of the Church of England (2001), *Mind the Gap: Integrated Continuing Ministerial Education for the Church's Ministers*, London: Church House Publishing.

Astley, J. (2002), *Ordinary Theology*, Aldershot: Ashgate.

Astley, J., Francis, L.J. and Crowder, C. (eds) (1996), *Theological Perspectives on Christian Formation: A Reader on Theology and Christian Education*, Leominster: Gracewing.

Atkinson, P. (1990), *The Ethnographic Imagination: Textual Constructions of Reality*, London: Routledge.

Atoun, R. (2001), *Understanding Fundamentalism*, Lanham, MD: AltaMira Press.

Auden, W.H. (1955), *Shield of Achilles*, London: Faber.

Augustine, St (1961), *Confessions*, trans. R. Pine Coffin, Harmondsworth: Penguin.

Austin, J.L. (1962), *How to do Things with Words*, Oxford: Oxford University Press.

Avis, P. (2000), *The Anglican Understanding of the Christian Church*, London: SPCK.

Bamber, L. (1982), *Comic Women, Tragic Men*, Stanford, CA: Stanford University Press.

Barnett, R. (1990), *The Idea of Higher Education*, Buckingham: The Society for Research and Higher Education/ Open University Press.

Barnett, R. (1994), *The Limits of Competence*, Oxford: Oxford University Press.

Bauman, Z. (2000), *Liquid Modernity*, Cambridge: Polity Press.

Beaudoin, T. (2003), *Consuming Faith*, London: Sheed & Ward.

Bebbington, D. (1989), *Evangelicalism in Modern Britain: A History from the 1730s to the 1980s*, London: Unwin Hyman.

Becker, P. and Eiesland, N. (eds) (1997), *Contemporary American Religion: An Ethnographic Reader*, Lanham, MD: AltaMira Press.

Belenky, M. *et al.* (1986), *Women's Ways of Knowing*, New York: Basic Books.

Bell, C. (1996), 'Modernism and Postmodernism in the Study of Religion', *Religious Studies Review*, July pp. 197–90.

Bellah, R.N. and Hammond, P.E. (1980), *Varieties of Civil Religion*, San Franscisco: Harper & Row.

Bender, C. (2003), *Heaven's Kitchen: Living Religion at God's Love We Deliver*, Chicago: Chicago University Press.

Berger, P. (1980), *The Heretical Imperative*, New York: Harper.

Berger, P. and Luckman, T. (1971), *The Social Construction of Reality: A Treatise in the Sociology of Knowledge*, London: Penguin.

Bernstein, J. (1978), 'Christian Affection and the Catechumenate', *Worship*, **52**, pp. 194–210.

Boeve, L. (2003), *Interrupting Tradition: An Essay on Christian Faith in a Postmodern Context*, Louvain: Peeters Press.

Bourdieu, P. (1990), *In Other Words: Essays Towards a Reflexive Sociology*, trans. M. Adamson, Cambridge: Polity Press.

Boyer, P. (2002), *Religion Explained: The Human Instincts that Fashion Gods, Spirits, and Ancestors*, London: Vintage.

Bramadat, P. (2000), *The Church on the World's Turf*, New York: Oxford University Press.

Brierley, P. (1992), *Act on the Facts*, London: Marc Europe.

Brookfield, S. (1995), *Becoming a Critically Reflective Teacher*, San Francisco: Jossey-Bass.

Brown, A. (2003), 'Press Review', *Church Times*, 5 September.

Brown, C. (2000), *The Death of Christian Britain: Understanding Secularisation 1800–2000*, London: Routledge.

Brown, D. (1999), *Tradition and Imagination*, Oxford: Oxford University Press.

Brown, D. (2000), *Discipline and Imagination: Christian Tradition and Truth*, Oxford: Oxford University Press.

Brown, D., Deraney, S.G. and Tanner, K. (2001), *Converging on Culture: Theologions in Dialogue with Cultural Analysis and Criticism*, Oxford: Oxford University Press.

Browning, D. (1991), *A Fundamental Practical Theology: Descriptive and Strategic Proposals*, Minneapolis, MN: Fortress Press.

Bruce, S. (1996), *Religion in Modern Britain*, Oxford: Oxford University Press.

Buckley, F. (2000), *The Church in Dialogue: Culture and Traditions*, New York: University of America Press.

Burgess, R. (1984), *In the Field: An introduction to Field Research*, London: Routledge.

Bynum, C.W. (1982), *Jesus as Mother: Studies in the Spirituality of the High Middle Ages*, Benkeley: University of California Press.

Caddick, C. and Dormor, D. (eds) (2003), *Anglicanism: The Answer to Modernity*, London: Continuum.

Casanova, J. (1994), *Public Religions in the Modern World*, Chicago and London: University of Chicago Press.

Chevreau, G. (1994), *Catch the Fire*, London: HarperCollins.

Chittister, J. (1983), *Women, Ministry and the Church*, New York: Paulist Press.

Chopp, R. (1995), *Saving Work – Feminist Practices of Theological Education*, Louisville, KY: Westminster John Knox Press.

Clark, D. (1982), *Between Pulpit and Pew*, Cambridge: Cambridge University Press.

Clifford, J. (1986), 'Introduction: Partial Truths', in J. Clifford and G. Marcus (eds), *Writing Culture: The Poetics and Politics of Ethnography*, Berkeley, University of California Press.

Collins, S. (2000), 'Spirituality and Youth', in M. Percy [ed] *Calling Time: Religion and Change at the Turn of the Millennium*, Sheffield: Sheffield Academic Press.

Cox, H. (1994), *Fire From Heaven: Pentecostalism, Spirituality and the Re-Shaping of Religion in the 21st Century*, New York: Addison-Wesley.

Cronin, M. (2000), *Advertising and Consumer Citizenship: Gender, Images and Human Rights*, London: Routledge.

Cunningham, H. (1980), *Leisure in the Industrial Revolution*, Beckenham: Croom Helm.

Davie, G. (1994), *Religion in Britain since 1945: Believing without Belonging*, Oxford: Blackwell.

Davie, G. (2000), *Religion in Modern Europe: A Memory Mutates*, Oxford: Oxford University Press.

Davie, G. (2002), *Europe: The Exceptional Case: The Parameters of Faith in the Modern World*, London: DLT.

Davies, D. (2002), *Anthropology and Theology*, Oxford: Berg.

Davis, C. (1980), *Theology and Practical Society*, Cambridge: Cambridge University Press.

Davis, K. (1990), *Emancipation Still Comin': Explorations in Caribbean Emancipatory Theology*, New York: Orbis Books.

D'Costa, G. (ed.) (1996), *Resurrection Reconsidered*, Oxford: Oneworld.

Dean, W. (2002), *The American Spiritual Culture*, London: Continuum.

Dempsey, C. (2002), 'The Religioning of Anthropology: New Directions of the Ethnographer-Pilgrim', *Religion and Culture*, 1(2), pp. 134–52.

Dewey, J. (1966), *Democracy and Education: An Introduction to the Philosophy of Education*, New York: Free Press.

Dey, I. (1993), *Qualitative Data Analysis; A User-Friendly Guide for Social Scientists*, London: Routledge.

Docherty, D. (2000), 'Reservoir Gods' in A. Walker and M. Percy (eds), *Restoring the Image*, Sheffield: Sheffield Academic Press.

Doll, P. (1989), 'Imperial Anglicanism in North America, 1745–1795', Oxford D.Phil. thesis.

Donovan, V. (1982), *Christianity Rediscovered: An Epistle from the Masai*, London: SCM.

Dorsey, G. (1995), *Congregation: The Journey Back to Church*, New York: Viking.

Douglas, I. and Pui-Lan, K. (eds) (2001), *Beyond Colonial Anglicanism: The Anglican Communion in the Twenty-First Century*, New York: Church Publishing Inc.

Dulles, A. (1974), *Models of the Church*, New York: Doubleday. Reprinted 1987.

Dumas, A. (1971), *Dietrich Bonhoeffer: Theologian of Reality*, New York: Macmillan.

Dykstra, C. and Parks, S. (1986), *Faith development and Fowler*, Birmingham, AL: Religious Education Press.

Eagleton, T. (2000), *The Idea of Culture*, Oxford: Blackwell.

Eiesland, N. (1998), *A Particular Place*, New Brunswick, NJ: Rutgers University Press.

Eisner, E. (1979), *The Educational Imagination: On the Design and Education of School Programs*, New York: Macmillan.

Eisner, E. (1985), 'Aesthetic Modes of Knowing', in E. Eisner (ed.), *Learning and Teaching the Ways of Knowing*, Chicago: Chicago University Press.

Evans D. (1979), *Struggle and Fulfillment*, London: Collins.

Everding, E., Huffaker, L., Snelling, C. and Wilcox, M. (1998), *Perspectives of Faith and Christian Nurture*, Harrisburg, PA: Trinity Press International.

Farley, E. (1982), *Ecclesial Reflection: An Anatomy of Theological Method*, Philadelphia, PA: Fortress Press.

Farley, E. (1985), 'Can Church Education be Theological Education?', *Theology Today*, **42**(2), pp. 159–71.

Farley, E. (1987), 'Interpreting Situations: An Inquiry into the Nature of Practical Theology', in L. Mudge and J. Poling (eds), *Formation and Reflection: The Promise of Practical Theology*, Philadelphia, PA: Fortress Press.

Farley, E. (1988), *The Fragility of Knowledge: Theological Education in the Church and the University*, Philadelphia, PA: Fortress Press.

Farley, E. (2003), *Practising Gospel*, Louisville KY: WJK Press.

Ferris, R. (1990), *Renewal in Theological Education: Strategies for Change*, Wheaton, IL: Billy Graham Center.

Festinger, L. (1957), *A Theory of Cognitive Dissonance*, Stanford, CA: Stanford University Press.

Fiorenza, F. Schussler (1988), 'Thinking Theologically about Theological Education', *Theological Education*, **24**(2), pp. 98–119.

Flanagan, K. (1996), *The Enchantment of Sociology: A Study of Culture and Theology*, London: Macmillan.

Flory, R.W. and Miller, D.E. (eds) (2000), *GenX Religion*, New York: Routledge.

Forrester, D. (2000), *Truthful Action: Explorations in Practical Theology*, Edinburgh: T&T Clark.

Forbes, M. and Mahan, J. (eds) (2000), *Religion and Popular Culture in America*, Berkeley, University of California Press.

Foster, L. and Hertzog, P. (eds) (1994), *Defending Diversity: Contemporary Philosophical Perspectives on Pluralism and Multiculturalism*, Amherst, MA: University of Massachusetts Press.

Fowler, J. (1981), *Stages of Faith: the Psychology of Human Development and the Quest for Meaning*, San Francisco: Harper & Row.

Fowler, J. (1984), *Becoming Adult, Becoming Christian: Adult Development and Christian Faith*, San Francisco: Harper & Row.

France, D. (2000), *A Slippery Slope?*, Nottingham: Grove.

Francis, L. and Kay, W. (1995), *Teenage Religion and Values*, Leominster: Gracewing.

Freire, P. (1972), *Pedagogy of the Oppressed*, Harmondsworth: Penguin.

Freire, P. (1973), *Education for Critical Consciousness*, New York: Seabury Press.

Frye, N. (1957), *The Anatomy of Criticism*, Princeton, NJ: Princeton University Press.

Fuellenbach, J. (2002), *Church: Community for the Kingdom*, New York: Orbis Books.

Fuller, R. (2001), *Spiritual, But Not Religious: Understanding Unchurched America*, Oxford: Oxford University Press.

Geertz, C. (1973), *The Interpretation of Cultures*, New York: Basic Books.

Geertz, C. (1983), *Local Knowledge*, New York: Basic Books.

Giddens, A. (1991), *Modernity and Self-Identity: Self and Society in the Late Modern Age*, Cambridge: Polity Press.

Giggie, G. and Winston, D. (eds) (2002), *Faith in the Market: Religion and the Rise of Urban Commercial Culture*, New Brunswick, NJ: Rutgers University Press.

Gittins, A. (2002), *Ministry at the Margins: Strategy and Spirituality for Mission*, New York: Orbis Books.

Goldscheider, F. and Goldscheider, C. (1993), *Leaving Home Before Marriage: Ethnicity, Familism and General Relationships*, Madison, WI: University of Wisconsin Press.

Goodchild, P. (2002), *Capitalism and Religion*, London: Routledge.

Graham, E. (1996), *Transforming Practice*, London: Mowbray.

Graham, E. (2002), *Representations of the Post/Human: Monsters, Aliens, and Others in Popular Culture*, Manchester: Manchester University Press.

Graham, E. and Poling, J. (2000), 'Some Expressive Dimensions of a Liberation Practical Theology', *International Journal of Practical Theology*, **4**, pp. 163–83.

Greeley, A. (1998), *God in Popular Culture*, Chicago: Thomas More Press.

Grenz, S. and Olsen, R. (1992), *20th Century Theology: God and the World in a Transitional Age*, Carlisle: Paternoster.

Grey, M. (1989), *Redeeming the Dream: Feminism, Redemption, and the Christian Tradition*, London: SPCK.

Grigg, R. (1990), *Theology as a Way of Thinking*, Atlanta, GA: Scholars Press.

Grimes, R.L. (1990), *Ritual Criticism: Case Studies on its Practice, Essays on its Theory*, Columbia, SC: University of South Carolina Press.

Grimes, R.L. (ed.) (2003), *Disaster Ritual*, Louvain: Peeters Publishing.

Groome, T. (1980), *Christian Religious Education: Sharing our Story and Vision*, San Francisco: Harper & Row.

Guenther, M. (1992), *Holy Listening: The Art of Spiritual Direction*, London: DLT.

Hacking, P. (ed.) (1993), 'What is Reform?', at www.reform.org.uk.

Hall, J. and Neitz, M. (1993), *Culture: Sociological Perspectives*, Englewood Cliffs, NJ: Prentice Hall.

Hall, J., Neitz, M.J. and Battani, M. (2003), *Sociology on Culture*, New York: Routledge.

Hammersley, M. and Atkinson, P. (1995), *Ethnography; Principles in Practice* (2nd edn), London: Routledge.

Hardy, D. (1996), *God's Ways with the World*, Edinburgh: T & T Clark.

Hare, D. (1990), *Racing Demon*, London: Faber.

Harland, T. (1997), *Stories about Small-Group Teaching: A Problem Based Approach. Vol. 1: Lecturers' Reflections*, Sheffield: University of Sheffield Press.

Harrington Watt, D. (2002), *Bible-Carrying Christians*, New York: Oxford University Press.

Harris, H. (1998), *Fundamentalism and Evangelicals*, Oxford: Clarendon Press.

Hauerwas, S. (1996), 'The Gesture of a Truthful Story', in J. Astley and L. Francis (eds), *Christian Theology and Religious Education: Connections and Contradictions*, London: SPCK.

Hazle, D. (2003), 'Practical Theology Today and the Implications for Mission', *International Review of Mission*, **XCII**(366), July, pp. 345–66.

Healy, N. (2000), *Church, World and Christian Life: Practical–Prophetic Ecclesiology*, Cambridge: Cambridge University Press.

Heather, N. (2002), 'Modern Believing and Postmodern Reading', *Modern Believing*, **43**(1), January, pp. 28–38.

Hebblethwaite, M. (1984), *Motherhood and God*, London: Geoffrey Chapman.

Hervieu-Leger, D. (2000), *Religion as a Chain of Memory*, Cambridge: Polity Press.

Highmore, B. (ed.) (2002), *The Everyday Life Reader*, London: Routledge.

Highmore, B. (2002). *Everyday Life and Cultural Theory*, London: Routledge.

Higton, T. (ed) (1987), *Sexuality and the Church: The Way Forward*, Hockley: ABWON.

Hilborn, D. (ed.) (2001), *Toronto in Perspective*, Carlisle: Paternoster.

Hodgson, P. (1999), *God's Wisdom: Toward a Theology of Education*, Louisville, KY: Westminster John Knox Press.

Hodgson, P. and King, R. (1982), *Christian Theology: An Introduction to its Tradition and Tasks*, Philadelphia, PA: Fortress Press.

Holloway, D. (1993), 'The Background to, and the Need for, Reform' at www.reform.org.uk

Holloway, D. (n.d.), 'Finance, Centralism and the Quota' at www.reform.org.uk.

hooks, b. (1994), *Outlaw Culture: Resisting Representations*, London: Routledge.

Hoover, S. (2000), 'The Cross at Willow Creek' in M. Forbes and J. Hahan (eds), *Religion and Popular Culture in America*, Berkeley: University of California Press.

Hopewell, J. (1987), *Congregation: Stories and Structure*, Philadelphia: Fortress Press.

Horkheimer, M. and Adorno, T. (1972), *Dialectic of Enlightenment*, London: Allen Lane.

Hull, J. (1985), *What Prevents Christian Adults from Learning?*, London: SCM.

Hunt, S. (1995), 'The Toronto Blessing – A Rumour of Angels?', *Journal of Contemporary Religion*, **10**(3), pp. 257–72.

Hunt, S. (2000), *Anyone for Alpha?*, London: Darton, Longman and Todd.

Hunt, S. (2003), *The Alpha Initiative: Evangelism in a Post-Christian Age*, Aldershot: Ashgate.

Hunt, S., Hamilton, M. and Walter, T. (1997), *Charismatic Christianity: Sociological Perspectives*, London: Macmillan.

Huston Smith, J. (1990), 'Postmodernism's Impact on the Study of Religion', *Journal of the American Academy of Religion*, Winter, p. 661.

Hyman, G. (2001), *The Predicament of Postmodern Theology: Radical Orthodoxy or Nihilist Textualism?*, Louisville, KY: Westminster John Knox.

Jakobsen, J. and Pellegrini, A. (eds) (2003), *Love the Sin: Sexual Regulation and the Limits of Tolerance*, New York: New York University Press.

Jamieson, A. (2002), *A Churchless Faith: Faith Journeys Beyond the Churches*, London: SPCK.

Jenkins, D. (ed.) (1990), *The Market and Health Care*, Edinburgh: Edinburgh University Press.

Jensen, P. (2002), *The Revelation of God: Contours of Christian Theology*, Downers Grove, IL, IVP.

Jewett, R. (1988), *The American Monomyth*, Garden City, NY: Anchor/Doubleday.

Jonegeneel, J. (ed.) (1992), *Pentecost, Mission and Ecumenism: Essays on Intercultural Theology*, Frankfurt: Peter Lang.

Jones, I. (2004), *The Ordination of Women: Ten Years On*, London: CHP/LTI.

Jones, L.G. and Paulsell, S. (2002), *The Scope of Our Art: The Vocation of the Theological Teacher*, Grand Rapids, MI: Eerdmans.

Judd, S. and Cable, A. (eds) (1987), *Sydney Anglicans*, Sydney: Anglican Information Office.

Kamitsuka, D. (2002), *Theology and Contemporary Culture*, Cambridge: Cambridge University: Press.

Kelley, D. (1972), *Why Conservative Churches are Growing*, New York: HarperCollins. Reprinted 1986.

Killen, P. and de Beer, J. (1994), *The Art of Theological Reflection*, New York: Crossroad.

Kinast, R. (1996), *Let Ministry Teach: A Guide to Theological Reflection*, Collegeville, MN: Liturgical Press.

Kinast, R. (2000), *What are they Saying About theological Reflection?*, New York: Paulist Press.

King, U. (2002), *Spirituality and Postmodernism*, Oxford: Farmington Institute for Christian Studies.

Kings, G. (2003), 'Canal, River and Rapids: Contemporary Evangelicalism in the Church of England', *Anvil*, **20**(3), pp. 167–84.

Lakeland, P. (1997), *Postmodernity*, Minneapolis, Fortress Press, 1997.

Lakeland, P. (2003), *The Liberation of the Laity: In Search of an Accountable Church*, New York: Continuum.

Levine, D. (ed.) (1971), *Georg Simmel: Selected Writings on Individual and Social Forms*, Chicago: Chicago University Press.

Lindbeck, G. (1984), *The Nature of Doctrine: Religion and Theology in a Post-Liberal Age*, Philadelphia: Westminster.

Lindbeck, G. (2002), *The Church in a Post-Liberal Age*, London: SCM.

Lippy, C. (1994), *Being Religious American Style*, Westport, CT: Greenwood Press.

Lodge, D. (2002), *Thinks*, London: Penguin.

Long, R. (1978), *Theology in a New Key*, Philadelphia: Westminster Press.

Lovin, R. (1995), *Reinhold Niebuhr and Christian Realism*, Cambridge: Cambridge University Press.

Lucas, R. (1986), *Read, Mark, Learn*, London, Proclamation Trust.

Lyon, D. (2000), *Jesus in Disneyland: Religion in Post-modern Times*, Cambridge: Polity Press.

Lyotard, J.F. (1984), *The Postmodern Condition: A Report on Knowledge*, Manchester: Manchester University Press.

Macaulay, R. (1956), *The Towers of Trezibond*, London: Collins.

McCann, D. and Strain, C. (1985), *Polity and Praxis*, Chicago: Winston Press.

McCleod, H. and Ustorf, W. (2003), *The Decline of Christendom in Western Europe: 1750–2000*, Cambridge: Cambridge University Press.

McDannell, C. (1995), *Material Christianity: Religion and Culture in America*, New Haven, CT: Yale University Press.

McFague, S. (1975), *Speaking in Parables: A Study in Metaphor and Theology*, London: SCM.

Macquarrie, J. (1997), *A Guide to the Sacraments*, London: SCM.

Magdalinski, T. and Chandler, T. (eds) (2001), *With God on Their Side: Sport in the Service of Religion*, London: Routledge.

Markham, I. (2003), *A Theology of Engagement*, Oxford: Blackwell.

Markham, I. and Abu-Rabi', I. (2002), *11 September: Religious Perspectives on the Causes and Consequences*, Oxford: Oneworld.

Marling, K. (2000), *Merry Christmas!*, Cambridge, MA: Harvard University Press.

Martin, D. (1967), *A Sociology of English Religion*, London: SCM.

Martin, D. (1969), *The Religions and the Secular*, London: RKP.

Martin, D. (1978), *A General Theory of Secularization*, Oxford: Blackwell.

Martin, D. (1980), *The Breaking of the Image*, Oxford: Blackwell.

Martin, D. (1988), 'Some Sociological Perspectives' in G. Ecclestone (ed.), *The Parish Church*, London: Mowbray.

Martin, D. (1989), *Divinity in a Grain of Bread*, London: Lutterworths.

Martin, D. (1996), *Reflections on Sociology and Theology*, Oxford: Oxford University Press.

Martin, D. (2002), *Christian Language and Its Mutations*, Aldershot: Ashgate.

Martos, J. (1981), *Doors to the Sacred: A Historical Introduction to the Sacraments in the Christian Church*, London: SCM.

Maykut, P. and Morehouse, R. (1994), *Beginning Qualitative Research: A Philosophic and Practical Guide*, New York: The Falmer Press.

Mazur, E. and McCarthy, K. (eds) (2001), *God in the Details: American Religion in Popular Culture*, New York, Routledge.

Melchert, C. (1998), *Wise Teaching: Biblical Wisdom and Educational Ministry*, Harrisburg, PA: Trinity Press International.

Merton, T. (1979), *Love and Living*, ed. N. Stone and P. Hart, London: Sheldon Press.

Middleton, R. and Walsh, B. (1995), *Truth is Stranger Than It Used To Be: Biblical Faith in a Postmodern Age*, London: SPCK.

Milbank, J. (1990), *Theology and Social Theory: Beyond Secular Reason*, Oxford: Blackwell.

Milbank, J. (1991), *Religion and Social Theory: Beyond Secular Reason*, Oxford: Blackwell.

Milbank, J. (1997), *The Word made Strange: Theology, Language, Culture*, Oxford: Blackwell.

Milbank, J., Ward, G. and Pickstock, C. (1999), *Radical Orthodoxy: A New Theology*, London: Routledge.

Miller, D. (1993), *Unwrapping Christmas*, Oxford: Oxford University Press.

Miller, D. (ed.) (1995), *Acknowledging Consumption*, London: Routledge.

Miller, D. (1997), *Re-inventing American Protestantism*, Berkeley, University of California Press.

Miller, D. (1998), *A Theory of Shopping*, Cambridge: Polity.

Miller-McLemore, B. (1994), *Also a Mother: Work and Family as Theological Dilemma*, Nashville, TN: Abingdon Press.

Mishler, E. (1991), *Research Interviewing: Context and Narrative*, Cambridge, MA: Harvard University Press.

Moltmann-Wendel, E. (1982), *The Women Around Jesus*, New York: Crossroad Publishing Co.

Money, T. (1997), *Manly and Muscular Diversions: Public Schools and Nineteenth Century Sporting Revival*, London: Duckworth.

Moore, L. (1994), *Selling God: American Religion in the Marketplace of Culture*, Oxford: Oxford University Press.

Moore, M.E. (1991), *Teaching from the Heart: Theology and Educational Method*, Minneapolis: Fortress Press.

Morgan, D. (1997), *Visual Piety*, Berkeley: University of California Press.

Morgan, D. and Promey, S. (eds) (2001), *The Visual Culture of American Religions*, Berkeley: University of California Press.

Morisy, A. (1997), *Beyond the Good Samaritan: Community Ministry and Mission*, London: Mowbray.

Mudge, L. (2001), *Rethinking the Beloved Community: Ecclesiology, Hermeneutics and Social Theory*, Lanham MD: University Press of America.

Murphy, R. (1990), *The Tree of Life: An Exploration of the Biblical Wisdom Literature*, New York: Doubleday.

Murphy, N. (1996), *Beyond Liberalism and Fundamentalism: How Modern and Postmodern Philosophy Set the Theological Agenda*, Valley Forge, PA: Trinity Press International.

Nesbitt, P. (2001), *Religion and Social Policy*, Lanham, MD: AltaMira Press.

Niebuhr, H.R. (1951), *Christ and Culture*, New York: Harper & Row.

Nieman, J. (2002), 'Attending Locally: Theologies in Congregations', *International Journal of Practical Theology* 6(2), Fall, pp. 198–225.

Nieman, J. and Rogers, T. (2001), *Preaching to Every Pew: Cross-cultural Strategies*, Minneapolis, MN: Fortress Press.

Nissenbaum, S. (1996), *The Battle for Christmas*, New York: Vintage.

Norman, E. (2002), *Secularisation*, London: Continuum.

Nouwen, H. (1975), *Reaching Out: The Three Movements of Spiritual Life*, London: Collins.

Orchard, H. (2000), *Hospital Chaplaincy: Modern, Dependable?*, Sheffield: Sheffield Academic Press.

Pattyn, B. (ed.) (2000), *Media Ethics: Opening Social Dialogue*, Leuven: Peeters.

Pemberton, C. (ed.) (1998), *The Anglican Communion*, New York: Church House Publishing.

Percy, M. (1996a), *Words, Wonders and Power: Understanding Contemporary Christian Fundamentalism and Revivalism*, London: SPCK.

Percy, M. (1996b), *The Toronto Blessing*, Issue 53–54, Oxford: Latimer Studies.

Percy, M. (1997), 'Sweet Rapture: Subliminal Eroticism in Contemporary Charismatic Worship', *Journal of Theology and Sexuality*, 6, March, pp. 71–106.

Percy, M. (1998), 'The Morphology of Pilgrimage in the Toronto Blessing', *Religion*, 28(3), pp. 281–89.

Percy, M. (2000), 'Reluctant Communion', in I. Markham and J. Jobling (eds), *Theological Liberalism*, London: SPCK.

Percy, M. (2001), *The Salt of the Earth: Religious Resilience in Secular Age*, Sheffield: Sheffield Academic Press.

Percy, M. (2003), 'Reconsidering Gifts', in P. Avis (ed.), *Responding to* The Gift of Authority, London: Church House Publishing.

Percy, M. and Jones, I. (2002), *Fundamentalism, Church and Society*, London: SPCK.

Percy, M. and Walker, A. (2001), *Restoring the Image: Essays in Honour of David Martin*, Sheffield: Sheffield Academic Press.

Peterson, E. (1992), *Under the Unpredictable Plant*, Grand Rapids, MI: Eerdmans.

Phillips, T. and Ockholm, D. (1996), *The Nature of Confession: Evangelicals and Postliberals in Conversation*, Downers Grove, IL: Inter-Varsity Press.

Pickering, W. (1989), *Anglo-Catholicism: A Study in Ambiguity*, London: Routledge.

Pinsky, M. (2001), *The Gospel According to the Simpsons*, Louisville, KY: Westminster John Knox Press.

Poling, J. (ed.) (1997), *Towards Viable Theological Education: Ecumenical Imperative, Catalyst of Renewal*, Geneva: World Council of Churches.

Poling, J. and Miller, D. (1985), *Foundations for a Practical Theology of Ministry*, Nashville, TN: Abingdon Press.

Poloma, M. (1996), *A Preliminary Sociological Assessment of the Toronto Blessing*, Bradford-upon-Avon: Terra Nova.

Post, P., Grimes, R., Nugteren, A., Pettersson, P. and Zondag, H. (2003), *Disaster Ritual*, Leuven: Peeters.

Putnam, R. (2000), *Bowling Alone: The Collapse and Revival of American Community*, New York: Simon & Schuster.

Reed, B. (1978), *The Dynamics of Religion: Process and Movement in Christian Churches*, London: Darton, Longman & Todd.

'The Reform Covenant' (1993), published at www.reform.org.uk.

Rengger, N. (1995), *Political Theory, Modernity and Postmodernity*, Oxford: Blackwell.

Richard, L. (1988), *Is There a Christian Ethic?*, New York: Paulist Press.

Richter, P. and Porter, S. (eds) (1995), *The Toronto Blessing – Or Is it?*, London: DLT.

Roberts, D. (2002), 'What Does Theology Have to Do with Ministry?', *Encounter*, **63**, Spring, pp. 24–38.

Roberts, R. (2002), *Religion, Theology and the Human Sciences*, Cambridge: Cambridge University Press.

Roebben, B. and Warren, M. (eds) (2001), *Religious Education as Practical Theology*, Leuven: Peeters.

Roll, S. (1995), *Toward the Origins of Christmas*, Kampen, The Netherlands: Kok Pharos.

Roof, W.C. (1985), *Community and Commitment: Religious Plausibility in a Liberal Protestant Church*, Philadelphia: Fortress Press.

Rothman, J. (2000), *Stepping out into the Field: A Field Work Manual for Social Work Students*, Boston, MA: Allyn & Bacon.

Rowell, G. (ed.) (1992), *The English Religious Tradition and the Genius of Anglicanism*, Wantage, Oxford: Ikon Books.

Ruddick, S. (1983), 'Maternal Thinking', in J. Trebilcot (ed.), *Mothering: Essays in Feminist Theory*, Savage, MD: Rowman & Littlefield, pp. 213–30.

Rycenga, J. (2000), 'Dropping in for the Holidays: Christmas as Consumerist Ritual', in E. Mazur (ed.), *God in the Details*, New York: Routledge.

Sachs, W. (1993), *The Transformation of Anglicanism: From State Church to Global Communion*, Cambridge: Cambridge University Press.

Sagovsky, N. (2000), *Ecumenism, Christian Origins and the Practice of Communion*, Cambridge: Cambridge University Press.

Schreiter, R. (1985), *Constructing Local Theologies*, Maryknoll: Orbis.

Seymour, J. and Miller, D. (eds) (1972), *Contemporary Approaches to Christian Education*, Nashville, TN: Abingdon Press.

Sibley, D. (1995), *Geographies of Exclusion: Society and Difference in the West*, London: Routledge.

Smail, T., Walker, A. and Wright, N. (1995), *Charismatic Renewal*, London: SPCK.

Streng, F., Lloyd, C. and Allen, J. (1973), *Ways of Being Religious*, Englewood Cliffs, NJ: Prentice Hall.

Strinati, D. (1995), *An Introduction to Theories of Popular Culture*, New York: Routledge.

Swatos, W. (1979), *Into Denominationalism: The Anglican Metamorphosis*, Storrs, CT: University of Connecticut/Society of the Scientific Study of Religion.

Sykes, S. (1995), *Unashamed Anglicanism*, London: DLT.

Sykes, S. and Booty, J. (1988), *The Study of Anglicanism*, London: SCM Press.

Tamney, J. (2002), *The Resilience of Conservative Religion*, Cambridge: Cambridge University Press.

Tanner, K. (1992), *The Politics of God: Christian Theologies and Social Justice*, Minneapolis, MN: Fortress Press.

Tanner, K. (1997), *Theories of Culture: A New Agenda for Theology*, Minneapolis, MN: Fortress Press.

Tanner, K., Davaney, S. and Brown, D. (2001), *Convergence on Culture: Theologians in Dialogue with Cultural Analysis and Criticism*, New York: Oxford University Press.

Taylor, D. (1996), *The Healing Power of Stories*, New York: Doubleday.

Taylor, J. (1972), *The Go-Between God: The Holy Spirit and the Christian Mission*, London: SCM.

Thomas, P. (1987), 'A Family Affair: The Pattern of Constitutional Authority in the Anglican Communion' in S. Sykes, (ed.) *Authority in the Anglican Communion*, Toronto: Anglican Book Centre.

Thomas, T. (2001), 'Becoming a Mother', *Religious Education*, **96**(1).

Tomlinson, D. (1995), *The Post-Evangelical*, London: SPCK.

Toulmin, S. (1990), *Cosmopolis: The Hidden Agenda of Modernity*, New York: Free Press.

Towler, R. (1984), *The Need for Certainty*, London: Routledge.

Tracy, D. (1975), *Blessed Rage for Order*, New York: Seabury.

Tracy, D. (1981), 'Defending the Public Character of Theology', in J. Wall (ed.), *Theologians in Transition*, New York: Crossroad.

Tracy, D. (1983), *The Analogical Imagination*, London: SCM Press.

Van Buren, P. (1969), 'On Doing Theology', in *Talk of God*, London: Macmillan.

Van der Ven, J. (1998), *Education for Reflective Ministry*, Leuven: Peeters.

Vasey, M. (1997), *Strangers and Friends*, London: Hodders.

Veblen, T. (1953), *The Theory of the Leisure Class*, New York: Mentor Books.

Visser, M. (2001), *The Geometry of Love*, Harmondsworth, Penguin.

Visser't Hooft, A. (2000), *Teachers and the Teaching Authorities*, Geneva: WCC Publications.

Volf, M. and Bass, D. (eds) (2002), *Practicing Theology: Beliefs and Practices in Christian Life*, Grand Rapids, MI: Eerdmans.

von Balthaser, H-U. (1982), *The Glory of the Lord: A Theological Aesthetics*, Edinburgh: T & T Clark.

Vrame, A.C. (1999), *The Educating Icon: Teaching Wisdom and Holiness in the Orthodox Way*, Brookline, MA: Holy Cross Orthodox Press.

Walker, A. (1998), *Restoring the Kingdom*, Guilford: Eagle.

Ward, G. (1995), *Barth, Derrida and the Language of Theology*, Cambridge: Cambridge University Press.

Ward, G. (2000), *Cities of God*, London: Routledge.

Ward, G. (2003), *True Religion*, Oxford: Blackwell.

Ward K. (2002), *God: A Guide for the Perplexed*, Oxford: Oneworld.

Ward, P. (1997), *Growing Up Evangelical*, London: SPCK.

Ward, P. (2002), *Liquid Church*, Peabody, MA: Hendrickson.

Warren, M. (1997), *Seeing Through the Media*, Harrisburg PA: Trinity Press International.

Weber, M. (1946), 'The Social Psychology of the World Religions', in H. Gerth and C. Wright Mills (eds), *From Max Weber*, New York: Oxford University Press.

Weber, M. (1968), *Economy and Society*, ed. Guenther Roth and Claus Wittich, Vol. 1, New York: Bedminster Press. First published in German in 1925.

Whitehead, J. and Whitehead, E. (1995), *Method in Ministry: Theological Reflection on Christian Ministry*, Franklin, WI: Sheed & Ward.

Williams, M. (1974), *Community in a Black Pentecostal Church*, Pittsburgh: University of Pittsburgh Press.

Williams, P. (1990), *The Ideal of a Self-Governing Church: A Study in Victorian Missionary Strategy*, Leiden: E.J. Brill.

Williams, P. (1999), *Perspectives on American Religion and Culture*, Oxford: Blackwell.

Williams, R. (1976), *Keywords*, London: Fontana.

Williams, R. (1986), *Culture*, London: Fontana.

Williams, R. (1989), *The Making of Orthodoxy: Essays in Honour of Henry Chadwick*, Cambridge: Cambridge University Press.

Williams, R. (2000), *On Christian Theology*, Oxford: Blackwell.

Williams, A. and Davidson, J. (1996), 'Catholic Conceptions of Faith: A Generational Analysis', *Sociology of Religion*, **57**(3), pp. 273–89.

Williamson, C. (1999), *Way of Blessing, Way of Life: A Christian Theology*, St. Louis, MS: Chalice Press.

Willis, P. (2000), *The Ethnographic Imagination*, Cambridge: Polity.

Winquist, C. (1978), *Homecoming: Interpretation, Transformation and Individuation*, American Academy of Religion Studies in Religion, no. 1. 18, Atlanta: Scholars Press.

Winterson, J. (2002), *Oranges Are Not the Only Fruit*, London: Vintage.

Witzel, G. and Witzel, K. (2002), *The Sparkling Story of Coca-Cola*, Stillwater, MN: Voyageur Press.

Wollerstorff, N. (2002), *Educating for Life: Reflections on Christian Teaching and Learning*, Grand Rapids, MI: Eeerdmans.

Woodward, J. and Pattison, S. (2000), *The Blackwell Reader in Pastoral and Practical Theology*, Oxford: Blackwell.

Wright, A. (2002), *Why Bother with Theology?*, London, Darton, Longman and Todd.

Wuthnow, R. (1997), 'The Cultural Turn', in P. Becker and N. Eiesland (eds), *Contemporary American Religion: An Ethnographic Reader*, Lanham, MD: AltaMira Press.

Yust, K. (2002), 'Teaching Seminarians to be Practical Theologians', *Encounter*, **63**, p. 237.

# Index

Abu-Rabi', I., *11 September: Religious Perspectives...* 79, 82
Action for Biblical Witness to Our Nation 184
Adorno, T. 50
Advent, meaning 57
adventure motif, charismatic movement 172–4
advertising, and meaning 52–3
Alpha course 48–9, 126, 160, 186, 188, 194, 198
  and commodification of religion 50
  and contemporary culture 50
alterity, and churches 138, 139
alternative comedy, Continuing Anglican Churches as 220
*Alternative Service Book* 76
American Episcopal Church 223
Ammerman, Jack 82
Ammerman, Nancy 82
Anderson, Benedict 208
Andrewes, Launcelot 214
Anglican Communion 208, 209, 213, 215
  cultural nature of 223–6
  future 227–8
  'mansion' metaphor 217, 222
Anglican Consultative Council 207, 216, 225
Anglicanism 68
  extent 207
  identity issues 207–8
  jokes about 210–11
  name, origin 217
  nature of 208, 212, 228–9
  optimism 229–30
  perspectives 215–16
  Roman Catholicism, differences 33
  unifying instruments 201, 224–5, 228–9
  varieties 222
  *see also* Continuing Anglican Churches
Anglo-Catholicism, ambiguities 200–201
Anselm, St 115, 116

*Anvil* journal 185
apprenticeship, theological education as 150–51
Archbishop of Canterbury 207, 215–16, 221, 225, 227
ARCIC report, *The Gift of Authority*, criticisms 33–4, 35
Armitage, Karen 19
Arnott, John 158
associations, decline 4
Astley, Jeff 109, 124, 132
  *Ordinary Theology* 2
Atlanta, Georgia
  Lutheran Church 41–2
  New Covenant Church 42
atrophy, Toronto Blessing 160, 166–7, 173, 176–9
Augustine, St 114
authenticity, and authority 31–7
  tension 31–2
authority,
  and authenticity 31–7
    tension 31–2
  of Bible 39–40
  of the church 40
  and discipleship 37–40
  erosion of 30
  and knowledge 35–6
  St Paul's 32
  teaching with 29–32

Bamber, Linda 193
baptism, tattoo as 78
Barnett, R. 102
Barth, Karl 27
Battani, M. 50
Bauman, Z. 4, 8, 52
Beaudoin, Tom, *Consuming Faith* 51
Bell, Catherine 78
Bender, Courtney 163–4
Berger, Peter 60, 83, 232
  *The Heretical Imperative* 65

Bernard of Clairvaux 115
Bible
  authority of 39–40
  mothering metaphor 114–15
*bodiliness* 111
Boeve, Lieve 65, 83, 231
  theology 70–73
*Book of Common Prayer* 218, 222
*Boston Globe* 20
Bourdieu, Pierre 52, 72
Boyer, Pascal 208, 209, 215
  *Religion Explained* 46
Breen, Mike, Revd 6
*bricolage*, methodology 138, 139
Brookfield, S. 96, 109
Brown, Callum, *The Death of Christian Britain* 60
Brown, David, *Tradition and Imagination* 38
Brown, Delwin 2
Browning, Don 9, 70, 138, 234
Buckley, Francis, *The Church in Dialogue* 20, 22–4, 28
Bynum, Caroline W., *Jesus as Mother* 116

Caddick, C. 208
Canonic negotiation, James Hopewell 190–93
Carey, George 198
Carroll, Robert 227
Carter, Sidney 49, 96
Catherine of Siena 115
certainty, and doubt, relationship 119
chaplaincy services, healthcare 136–7
charismatic movement
  adventure motif 172–4
  atrophy 173
case study 157–79
Charismatic Renewal 159, 161, 167, 177, 178, 184, 186, 187, 188, 198
Chesterton, G.K. 189
Chopp, Rebecca, *Saving Work-Feminist Practices of Theological Education* 111
Christ, and culture 63
Christianity
  and consumerism 41–62
  and culture 43
    publications 2
  localization 13, 68, 194

and narrative 72, 94
  paradoxes 232
Christingle, origins 57
Christmas, transformation 54–6, 58
church attendance 47–8, 59–60
Church of England 92
  Hospital Chaplaincy 136–7
Church of South India 224
church, the
  as an interpretive community 128
  authority of 40
  'high' 126
  as a learning community 36, 128, 134
  'low' 126
  'middle' 126
  nature of 125–9
church/state ties 3
churches
  and alterity 138, 139
  and choice 48
  *see also* mega-churches
*Churchman* journal 185
civil liberties, and September 11 (2001) events 82–3
Clements, Roy, Revd 197
clergy, as professionals 144
Cobb, John 128, 145
cognitive dissonance, and Toronto Blessing 160
colleges, theological 89–90
comic genre, James Hopewell on 212–14
commodification, religion 48, 50
Congar, Yves 19
Congregational Studies 2, 25, 106, 153, 161, 165, 172, 234
  James Hopewell 189–94
congregations 152
  and narrativity 108, 190
  studies of 106–10, 161
Conservative Evangelicalism 181, 185, 187, 188, 190, 192, 196, 198, 199, 204
consumer society 50
consumerism 4
  and Christianity 41–62
  and redemption 49
Continuing Anglican Churches 217
  as alternative comedy 220
  ambiguities 221, 222–3
  membership 218
  statements of faith 219

varieties 218–19, 220
Cox, Harvey 203
cultural studies
  meaning 1
  and theology 44–6
cultural system, religion as 162–3, 233–4
culture
  and the Alpha course 50
  and Christ 63
  and Christianity 43
    publications 2
  meaning 1–2
  postmodern 6
  and Radical Orthodoxy 67–70
  and reflexive religion 78–83
  and reflexive theology 70–73
  and religion 41, 61
  theology as 2
Cupitt, Don 66

Davaney, Sheila 2
Davidson, J. 21, 22
Davie, Grace 4, 31
Davis, Charles 127
Davis, Kortright 13
de Beer, J. 96
Declaration of Independence (1776) 31
denominations, fusions 5–6
Dewey, John 141–2
discipleship, and authority 37–40
Docherty, David 56
Donovan, Vincent, *Christianity
    Rediscovered* 95
doubt, and certainty, relationship 119
Douglas, Mary 80
dress codes 104
Dulles, A. 26
Dumas, André 231–2
Dunn, James 185
Durkheim, Emile 43
Dykstra, C. 111

ecclesiology 8, 26, 27, 231
  modern, and the social sciences 69–70
  publications 2
education
  and freedom 142–3
  meaning 90
  theory, Paulo Freire 140, 142
  *see also* theological education
Eisner, Elliot 124

enculturation 22, 23, 25–6
Epiphany
  celebration 57
  meaning 56
Estonia ferry disaster, response 78, 81
ethnography 163–4
evaluation
  limits 137
  theology 136
  and transformation 136–9
  as valuing 137–8
Evans, Donald 125
Everding, E. 132

faith, development stages 99–102
Falwell, Jerry 80
Farley, Edward 12, 14, 69, 70, 119, 127–8,
    129–30, 145
  on theological education 135
feminism, and theological education
    111–13
Festinger, L. 160
Fiorenza, Francis S. 112
Flanagan, Kieran 73
Flory, R.W. 78
Ford, David 134
Forrester, Duncan 9
fortune-tellers, France 4
Foucault, Michel 164
Fowler, James 106, 109, 119, 121, 132
  *Becoming Adult, Becoming Christian* 102
  *Stages of Faith* 99, 102
Fox, Matthew 6
France, fortune-tellers 4
France, R.T., *A Slippery Slope* 196
freedom, and education 142–3
Freire, Paulo 94, 108–9
  *Pedagogy of the Oppressed* 34–5
  theory of education 140, 142
Frye, Northrop 190–92
  *The Anatomy of Criticism* 106
Fuellenbach, John, *Church: Community
    for the Kingdom* 20, 25–6, 28
Fuller, Robert 31
funeral tea, function 103–4

gay issues, Reform movement 196–7
Geertz, Clifford 44, 161, 162–3, 212, 224
  on religion 45–6
  works
    *Local Knowledge* 162

*The Interpretation of Cultures* 162
gender issues, Reform movement 196
Giddens, Anthony 72
Giggie, G. 49
Gilpin, Clark 148
Gittins, Anthony, *Ministry at the Margins* 20, 24–5, 28
Graham, Elaine 9, 139
  *Representations of the Post/Human* 43–4
  *Transforming Practice* 138
Grey, Mary 112–13
Griffiths, Paul 148
Grigg, Richard 140
Grimes, R.L. 55, 78, 80
  on ritual 80–81
Groome, Thomas 140
Guenther, Margaret 131
Gumbel, Nicky 48

Habgood, John 214
*habitus* 111–12, 130
Hall, J. 50
Hare, David, *Racing Demon* 212
Hazle, David 12, 13
Healy, Nicholas 64, 69, 83
  *Church, World and Christian Life* 2, 20, 26–8, 70
Hebblethwaite, Margaret 114, 115
Heilman, Samuel 209
Herbert, George 229
Hervieu-Leger, Danielle 60
Higton, Tony, Revd 189
  *Sexuality and the Church* 184
Hinn, Benny 158
Hodgson, Peter 141–3
  on theological education 144–5
Holloway, David 195–6
Holloway, Richard 214
hooks, bell 141
Hopewell, James 10, 99, 105, 121, 126, 152, 161, 165, 172
  Canonic negotiation 190–93
  on the comic genre 212–14
  *Congregation* 106
  Congregational Studies 189–94, 209–10
Horkheimer, M. 50
hospital chaplaincy, and theological education 137
Howard-Browne, Rodney 158
Hull, John 102

Hunt, Stephen 48, 49
Huston Smith, J. 6
Hyman, Gavin 66

Jakobsen, J. 197
James VI of Scotland 217
Jamieson, Alan 132
Jenkins, D. 149–50, 214
Jensen, Philip 186
John, Jeffrey 187, 196, 198, 201, 213
Johnson, James 197
Jones, Ian 184
Jones, L.G. 153
  *The Scope of Our Art* 148
Julian of Norwich 229–30

Keller, Rosemary S. 148
Kelsey, David 145
Killen, P. 96
King, Ursula 133–4
Kings, Graham 198–9
Kingsolver, Barbara, *The Poisonwood Bible* 194
knowledge
  and authority 35–6
  theological, non-specialist 103–4
Kung, Hans 19

Lakeland, Paul, *The Liberation of the Laity* 19–20
Lambeth Conferences 202, 203, 207, 216, 225
Latin America, liberation theology 140
Law, Bernard, Cardinal 20, 23, 29, 32–3
learning, and teaching 90
Lesbian and Gay Christian Movement 197
liberal Catholics 201
liberalism, Edward Norman on 93
liberalization 3
liberation theology 139–43
  Latin America 140
  meaning 139–40
  nature of 141
  and transformation 140–41
Lindbeck, G. 98, 122, 233
Lloyd-Jones, Martyn, Dr 184
localization, Christianity 13, 68, 194
Long, Robert 141
Loughlin, Gerard 66
Lucas, Dick, Revd 188

*Read, Mark, Learn* 182, 186
Lutheran Church, Atlanta, Georgia 41–2
Lyon, David 49
Lyotard, J.F. 6

Macaulay, Rose, *The Towers of Trebizond*
    207
McCann, D. 127
McCarthy, K. 44
McDannell, C. 51
McDonald, Jack 208
McLeod, Hugh 76
Macquarrie, J. 232–3
Markham, Ian
    *11 September: Religious Perspectives . . .*
        79, 82
    *A Theology of Engagement* 2
Martin, David 60, 66, 73, 83, 84, 100,
    231
    sociology of religion 74–7
    works
        *A Sociology of English Religion* 74
        *Christian Language and Its Mutations*
            74
Mattson, Ingrid 82
Mazur, E. 44
meaning, and advertising 52–3
mega-churches, USA 53–4
Melchert, C. 151
Melton, James Gordon 221
Melville, Herman
    *Moby Dick* 51
    *Omoo* 194
    *Tipee* 194
metamorphosis, and mothering metaphor
    121
metanarrative
    and narrative 73
    religion as 7
Milbank, John 8, 65–8, 83
    *The World Made Strange* 69
    *Theology and Social Theory* 83–4
Miller, Donald 78, 134, 135
    *Contemporary Approaches to Christian
        Education* 129
Miller-McLemore, Bonnie 117, 148
missiology 4, 19, 24–5, 28, 29, 52, 68, 123,
    195, 197, 198, 207, 215, 230
modernity
    and religious belief 4, 30
    and theology, models 199–200

Moore, Clement Cark, 'Twas the Night
    Before Christmas' 55
Moore, Laurence, *Selling God* 49–50
Moore, Mary E. 112
mothering metaphor
    Bible 114–15
    as 'cluster metaphor' 116–18
    and metamorphosis 121
    and play notion 119
    problems with 118–19
    theological education 115–18, 119–22
Mudge, Lewis, *Rethinking the Beloved
    Community* 2, 5

narrative
    and Christianity 72, 94
    and metanarrative 73
narrativity
    and congregations 108, 190
    in theological education 112, 113
Nazianzen, Gregory 149
Neitz, M.J. 50
Nesbitt, P. 202, 203
New Covenant Church, Atlanta, Georgia
    42
*New York Times* 20
*The New Yorker* 233
Newbigin, Leslie 68, 76
Nicholas, St 55
Niebuhr, R. 43, 231
    *Christ and Culture* 63
Nieman, James 104, 123
'Nine O'clock Service' 6
Nissenbaum, S. 54
Norman, Edward 37, 129
    on liberalism 93
    *Secularisation* 92
Nouwen, Henri 93, 98

Order of Mission 6
ordination, women 184, 200
'oscillation' theory, religious behaviour
    120

Packer, Jim 184, 185
parables, wisdom in 145
Parks, S. 111
Pattison, S. 9, 97, 98
Paul, St, authority 32
Paulsell, S. 148, 153
Pellegrini, A. 197

Pemberton, C. 208
Pentecostalism 126
Percy, Martyn, *Salt of the Earth* 2
Philadelphia project 6
*phronesis* concept 9, 14, 83, 138, 139, 234
Pickering, William 200, 208
Pickstock, Catherine 66
Pilgrim-Adventurer motif, Toronto
        Blessing 174–6, 178–9
play notion
    and mothering metaphor 119
    and theological education 151
pluralism
    UK 3
    US 3, 30–31
Poling, J. 134, 135
Poloma, Margaret 160
postmodernism
    concept 6–7
    and practical theology 138
    and religion 6–7
power/money issues, Reform movement
        197–8
practical theology
    meaning 7–9, 12–15
    as methodology 10–12
    nature of 96–8, 123
    need for 130
    and postmodernism 138
    tasks of 150, 234–5
    theses 14
    value 138
Putnam, Robert, *Bowling Alone* 60

Quakerism 213

Radical Orthodoxy 8, 64, 65
    basis 67–8
    criticisms of 83–5
    and culture 67–70
    purpose 66
    and September 11 (2001) events 81–2
Raven, Charles 221
redemption, and consumerism 49
Reed, Bruce 120, 121
reflexive religion, and culture 78–83
reflexive theology, and culture 70–73
reflexivity, concept 73
Reform movement 182
    authority issues 201–3
    Covenant 186, 190, 191

ethnographic study 187–9
evangelical element 185–6
gay issues 196–7
gender issues 196
issues of concern 194–8
origins 183–6
power/money issues 197–8
purpose 186–7
significance 203–5
world-view 193–4
religion
    affiliation, world-views test 106–9
    Clifford Geertz on 45–6
    commodification 48, 50
    and consumption 51–2
    as cultural system 162–3, 233–4
    and culture 41, 61
    etymology 62
    as metanarrative 7
    and postmodernism 6–7
    resurgence 66
    and society 62
    and spirituality 60–62
    theology, overlap 140–41
religious behaviour, 'oscillation' theory
        120
religious belief, and modernity 4, 30
research, meaning 92, 109
Richard, Lucien 128
Ricoeur, Paul 5, 98
ritual, R.L. Grimes on 80–81
Roberts, D. 235
Roberts, R. 67
Robertson, Pat 80
Robinson, Gene 187, 196
Rogers, T. 123
Roll, Susan, theory of time 56–7
Roman Catholic, name significance 217
Roman Catholic Adult Initiate
        Curriculum 126
Roman Catholicism
    Anglicanism, differences 33
    England, falling birthrate 21
    USA 19–29
        bishops 20–21
        post-Vatican II 21–2
        pre-Vatican II 21
        problems 29
        publications 20
        scandals 20, 32–3
Roof, W.C. 105, 165, 214

Ruddick, Sara 120, 121
Rycenga, Jennifer 54, 55

Salvation Army 40
same-sex relations 38–9
Santa Claus, origins 55
scholarship, function 10
Schreiter, R. 98, 122, 123
Seabury, Samuel, Bishop 223
secularization 4
  debates about 60
  meaning 59
September 11 (2001) events
  and civil liberties 82–3
  ordinary peoples' response 80, 81
  Radical Orthodoxy response 81–2
  theologians' response 79–80, 81–2
Seymour, Jack, *Contemporary Approaches
    to Christian Education* 129
shopping, role in contemporary life 51, 52,
    55
Simmel, Georg 173
Simonaitis, Susan 148
social sciences, and modern ecclesiology
    69–70
society, and religion 62
socio-theology 73–8
sociology of religion, David Martin 74–7
spirituality 4
  and religion 60–62
  as world-view 130–31
Stott, John 184
Sundblom, Haddon 55

Tanner, Kathryn 70, 96–7, 233, 234
  *Converging on Culture* 2
  *Theories of Culture* 2
tattoo, as baptism 78
Taylor, Daniel 94
Taylor, J.V., *The Go-Between God* 95
Taylor, Mark C. 66
teaching
  with authority 29–32
  and learning 90
  nature of 131
Teresa of Avila, St 115
theologians, response to September 11
    (2001) events 79–80, 81–2
theological education 90–91, 95–6, 98
  as apprenticeship 150–51
  congregational studies 106–10

content 153–4
criticisms of 134–5
as death/resurrection 151–2
Edward Farley on 135
and feminism 111–13
and hospital chaplaincy 137
and integrity 151
metaphors 111, 113
models 111
mothering metaphor 115–18, 119–22
narrativity in 112, 113
nature of 129–32
need for 130
Peter Hodgson on 144–5
and play notion 151
as practical wisdom 110
purpose 144
theory 99–102
tradition 129–30
and vocation 147–9
and worship 124–5
theology
  Boeve's 70–73
  critical 104
  and cultural studies 44–6
  as culture 2
  definition 104–5
  etymology 102
  evaluation, role 136
  as identity 104
  and modernity, models 199–200
  nature of 122–5, 127–8, 140
  paradigms 12
  religion, overlap 140–41
  scope 103
  Third World 13
  as world-view 104, 123
  *see also* liberation theology; practical
      theology
Third World, theology 13
Thomas, Keith 30
time
  Christian tradition 57
  theory, Roll on 56–7
Toleration Act (1689) 3
Toronto, Vineyard Christian Church 157,
    158
Toronto Airport Christian Fellowship
    157, 158
  cellular structure 175
  harvest metaphor 174

meetings 167–71
programmes 159
songs 159, 166, 167–8
Statement of Faith 166
youth work 175
Toronto Blessing 157, 166
atrophy 160, 166–7, 173, 176–9
as cognitive dissonance 160
marketing 159
Pilgrim-Adventurer motif 174–6, 178
Towler, Robert 37, 119
Tractarian movement 200
Tracy, David 65, 199
*traditio/tradita* distinction 98, 122
transformation
and evaluation 136–9
and liberation theology 140–41
Troeltsch, Ernst 63, 64
Trudelle, T. 117
Turner, Victor 80
Twitchell, James 52
Tyndale, William 89

USA
mega-churches 53–4
pluralism 30–31
Roman Catholicism 19–29

Van Buren, Paul 72
Van der Ven, J. 10, 91–2, 96, 153
Vasey, Michael, *Strangers and Friends* 197
Vatican II Council 19
Veblen, T. 50
Venn, Henry 197
Vineyard Christian Church, Toronto 157, 158
Vineyard movement 176–7
Visser't Hooft, A., *Teachers and the Teaching Authorities* 30
vocation, and theological education 147–9

Vrame, Anton, *The Educating Icon* 124

Wadell, Paul 148
Ward, Graham 51, 66, 68–9
Ward, Kevin 39
Ward, Peter, *Liquid Church* 52
Weber, Max 162
Williams, A. 21, 22
Williams, Melvin 209
Williams, Peter, Revd 185
Williams, Raymond 211
Williams, Rowan 198, 214
Willis, Paul, *The Ethnographic Imagination* 211
Wimber, John 158, 177
Winjgaards, Hans 19
Winquist, Charles 108
Winston, D. 49
Winterson, Jeanette, *Oranges are Not the Only Fruit* 99
wisdom 143–7
example 146–7
in parables 145
teaching of 145
Wolterstorff, Nicholas 147
women
idealization of 114
ordination of 184, 200
Woodward, J. 9, 97, 98
world-views test, religious affiliation 106–9
worship
performative 124–5
and theological education 124–5
Wright, Henry 197
Wuthnow, R. 163

Yust, K. 234

Ziebertz, Hans G. 10